10/89

TRIALS OF INTIMACY

Cimetière de Chailly-en-Bière,
France
Theodore Tilton
1835–1907

Greenwood Cemetery,
Brooklyn
Elizabeth Tilton
1833[?]–1897

Greenwood Cemetery,
Brooklyn
Henry Ward Beecher
1813–1887

HENRY WARD BEECHER
JUNE 24 1813. — MARCH 8 1887.
HE THINKETH NO EVIL

EUNICE WHITE BEECHER
AUGUST 26 1812. — MARCH 8 1897.

Son of famed evangelist Lyman Beecher, and brother of Harriet Beecher Stowe and Catharine Beecher, 34-year-old Henry Ward Beecher arrived in Brooklyn in 1847 and quickly established himself as a riveting preacher. Walt Whitman heard him in 1849, and recollected that "he hit me so hard, fascinated me to such a degree, that I was afterwards willing to go far out of my way to hear him talk." Ralph Waldo Emerson concurred. "A battery of strength," he called him after attending a Beecher lecture on "Patriotism" in 1855. "He is admirable for his sense, and his aims, and, not less, for his health. He has the vigor of ten men."

Theodore Tilton and Elizabeth Richards joined Beecher's
Plymouth Church as teenagers in the early 1850s, and on October 2, 1855, Theodore's twentieth birthday, Beecher officiated at
their marriage. Apparently no photograph of Elizabeth survives. Contemporary descriptions stress how youthful she appeared, and claim she was plain
looking and simply garbed. The elegant Mrs. Tilton (bottom right) is an artist's fancy.

Beecher made Plymouth Church a major cultural force during his forty-year pastorate from 1847 to 1887. In the late 1850s Beecher and his young parishioner Theodore Tilton became intimates. Their tie was personal, professional, political, and religious. It was a romantic same-sex friendship of the sort that was common among nineteenth-century men and women.

WM. LLOYD GARRISON

HENRY WARD BEECHER

WENDELL PHILLIPS

HORACE GREELEY

GERRIT SMITH

W. G. BROWNLOW

THEODORE TILTON

A DRAMATIC SCENE. THROWING THE SLAVE CHAINS TO THE FLOOR.

Beecher and Tilton were immersed in the antislavery movement before and during the Civil War. In the early 1860s they co-edited the weekly *Independent* in Manhattan, commuting to the paper's Beekman Street office on the Brooklyn Ferry.

THE PITY OF IT.

In the late 1860s, Elizabeth Tilton and Henry Ward Beecher became intimate friends, and the Tiltons wrote each other hundreds of letters trying to make sense of their lives, their marriage, and their friendships with their pastor. Henry and Elizabeth were spiritual soulmates who experienced some kind of passionate bond with each other. In 1870 Mrs. Tilton told her husband that she had gone too far in her knowing and loving of Beecher. After a harrowing series of encounters among the three of them in December, Beecher and the Tiltons agreed to try to keep stories about their private relations from reaching the public.

VICTORIA C. WOODHULL.

THE BEECHER-TILTON CASE.

Public Opinion—"GET OUT OF SIGHT AS QUICKLY AS POSSIBLE. YOU HAVE POLLUTED THE AIR LONG ENOUGH WITH YOUR PRESENCE."

In 1872, radical reformer Victoria Woodhull issued a public statement accusing Beecher of adultery with Mrs. Tilton. Her charge was assembled from conversations she had had with Theodore and other friends in the women's suffrage movement.

From 1870 through 1873, Beecher and the Tiltons made no public assertions about their intimacies. But trying to protect themselves in the event of disclosure, they spoke to selected outside parties, a course that eventually undermined the cover-up. The scandal burst forth in July 1874 when Theodore accused Henry of seducing his wife and committing adultery with her over a fifteen- or sixteen-month period between late 1868 and early 1870.

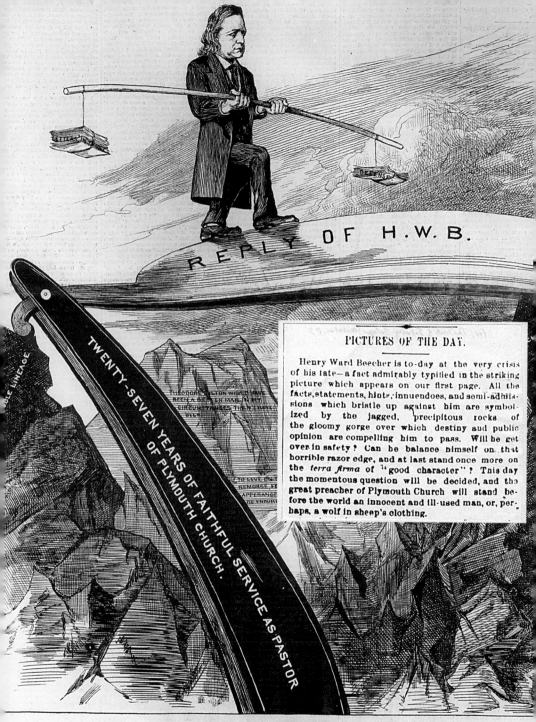

PICTURES OF THE DAY.

Henry Ward Beecher is to-day at the very crisis of his fate—a fact admirably typified in the striking picture which appears on our first page. All the facts, statements, hints, innuendoes, and semi-admissions which bristle up against him are symbolized by the jagged, precipitous rocks of the gloomy gorge over which destiny and public opinion are compelling him to pass. Will he get over in safety? Can he balance himself on that horrible razor edge, and at last stand once more on the *terra firma* of "good character"? This day the momentous question will be decided, and the great preacher of Plymouth Church will stand before the world an innocent and ill-used man, or, perhaps, a wolf in sheep's clothing.

"WILL HE DO IT?"

Beecher replied to Tilton's charge by appointing a Plymouth Church Investigating Committee, to which Henry, Elizabeth, and Theodore all testified. The Committee found Beecher innocent of wrongdoing, but the press and the public clamored for a legal proceeding equipped with subpoena powers to resolve contradictions in the testimony.

THE DEATH STRUGGLE ON THE RAGGED EDGE.

Then out spake Decius Tilton: "By all the gods of war,
One of us two must fall to-day and sink to rise no more.
And thou, Tarquinius Beecher, for that which thou hast done,
By this right hand shall die the death before the set of sun!"

Now grapple on that narrow bridge, with hell beneath their feet,
The champions of right and wrong as when two tigers meet.
God speed the right, and conquer he who knows his quarrel just;
The traitor's end of traitor friend be his who licks the dust.

THE MOST UNKINDEST CUT OF ALL.

In the fall of 1874 Tilton sued Beecher for "criminal conversation" (adultery) and "alienation of [his wife's] affections." The suit was civil, not criminal; Beecher was never in any danger of imprisonment, only of suffering a damaged reputation. The trial began in January 1875 and was concluded in July 1875, when the jury announced it could not reach a decision. The only person imprisoned in connection with the Beecher-Tilton Scandal was Victoria Woodhull, who spent time in the Ludlow Street Jail in Manhattan after Anthony Comstock had her arrested for publishing the adultery charges (she was finally acquitted on a technicality).

PICTORIAL HISTORY

OF THE

Beecher-Tilton Trial,

Containing a complete history of THE GREAT SCANDAL, and a REPORT OF THE TRIAL up to the opening for the defense, giving the evidence of mutual friend

MOULTON, MR. TILTON,

and others called by the plaintiff. Revelations by Kate Carey and Brother Richard.

THE LETTERS & STATEMENTS,

Rigid Cross-Examination and Argument between Counsel. Sketches of the Judge, Counsel, Jury, Witnesses, and all connected with the case. Illustrated with over 150 ENGRAVINGS from accurate sketches.

The following are some of the most important Engravings:

PORTRAITS

Rev. Henry Ward Beecher; Theodore Tilton; Francis D. Moulton; Mrs. Elizabeth R. Tilton; Mrs. Beecher; Judge Neilson; Ex-Judge Wm. A. Fullerton; William A. Beach, Esq.; Samuel D. Morris, Esq.; Gen. Roger A. Pryor; Hon. Wm. M. Evarts; Gen. Benj. F. Tracy; Thos. G. Shearman, Esq.; Ex Judge John K. Porter; Mrs. Victoria C. Woodhull; Miss Tennie C. Claflin; Mrs. Bradshaw, a witness; Kate Carey, a witness; the Jury, Visitors at the Court, and others.

Frank Moulton testifies from the chair, while Theodore Tilton cogitates with elbow on table (Elizabeth, head bowed, is to his left). Defense attorney William Evarts holds spectacles in his right hand and instructs plaintiff's attorney William Fullerton. At the right, Henry Ward Beecher (holding rolled-up paper in left hand) sits beside his wife Eunice.

Mr. Tilton.

Mr. Moulton.

...L OF REV. HENRY WARD BEECHER

Mr. Fullerton.   Mr. Evarts.   Mr. Shearman.   Mr. Beach.   Mr. Beecher.   Mrs. Beecher.
Mr. Pryor.

GENERAL SCENE IN THE COURT-ROOM.

This letter from Mrs. Tilton to her husband in 1871 was a centerpiece of the scandal. "I see clearly my sin," she wrote. The *New York Graphic*'s "fac-simile" publication of this and other Beecher and Tilton letters was a sensation in 1874. The principals' actual handwriting gave readers access, said the *Chicago Tribune*, to "the individuality of the writers . . . , acting out their several parts." (The text of the letter is in the Appendix.) In 1874 and 1875 Mrs. Tilton publicly ranged herself on Beecher's side by denying that her "sin" had been adultery. In 1878 she reversed herself, not for the first time, claiming that she and Beecher had committed adultery.

TRIALS OF INTIMACY

TRIALS of INTIMACY

LOVE AND LOSS

IN THE

BEECHER-TILTON

SCANDAL

RICHARD WIGHTMAN FOX

THE UNIVERSITY OF CHICAGO PRESS
Chicago and London

RICHARD WIGHTMAN FOX is professor of history at the University of Southern California. His books include *Reinhold Niebuhr: A Biography*.

The University of Chicago Press, Chicago 60637
The University of Chicago Press, Ltd., London
© 1999 by The University of Chicago
All rights reserved. Published 1999
08 07 06 05 04 03 02 01 00 99   1 2 3 4 5
ISBN: 0-226-25938-2 (cloth)

Fox, Richard Wightman, 1945–
    Trials of intimacy : love and loss in the Beecher-Tilton scandal / Richard Wightman Fox.
        p.   cm.
    Includes bibliographical references and index.
    ISBN 0-226-25938-2 (cloth : alk. paper)
    1. Beecher, Henry Ward, 1813–1887.   2. Tilton, Elizabeth M. Richards, b. [1834?].   3. Tilton, Theodore, 1835–1907.   4. Congregationalists—New York—Brooklyn Biography.   5. Brooklyn (New York, N.Y.) Biography.   I. Title.
    BX7260.B31F68   1999
    285.8'092'2—dc21
    [B]   99-22120
                                                        CIP

TO ELIZABETH
Storyteller, Believer, Mère de Famille

"It avails not, neither time or place—distance avails not."
—WALT WHITMAN, "CROSSING BROOKLYN FERRY"

Contents

Illustrations

THE MODERN LAOCOON.

Introduction

I. "No story of love was surely ever less of a 'love story,'" Henry James remarked of *The Scarlet Letter* in 1879. Many of James's readers, I suspect, thought instantly of another choice for the prize of love story with the least love in it. Every sentient American had followed the Beecher-Tilton Scandal in 1874 and 1875—thousands read the trial transcript in their daily newspaper—and the press had often compared it to *The Scarlet Letter*. There were intriguing parallels to Hawthorne's classic, already regarded as the great American novel, but two major differences. Where Hawthorne's fiction began with an admitted adultery, the tale of Beecher and the Tiltons began with a question mark. Theodore Tilton said his wife Elizabeth had confessed to adultery with his former intimate friend, pastor, and mentor, the Reverend Henry Ward Beecher, but both Beecher and Mrs. Tilton denied it. What became frustratingly clear during a full year of frenzied investigation and insinuation was that in the real-life drama, no one would ever find out what had really happened. No one would ever know if Beecher had engaged in "criminal conversation" with Mrs. Tilton, thereby, as Mr. Tilton charged in Brooklyn civil court, "alienating her affections" from him.

The second difference was that Hawthorne's novel was not much interested in the adultery itself. What intrigued Hawthorne, as James put it, was not "the passion" between the Reverend Arthur Dimmesdale and his paramour Hester Prynne, but the "moral situation" that succeeded it. And that story, James noted, "goes on for the most part between the lover [Dimmesdale] and the husband [Roger Chillingworth]." Chillingworth works a very sweet revenge by apparently befriending Dimmesdale while actually aggravating his torments; Hester is her husband's means of proving himself in an all-or-nothing male rivalry. The twisted character of Chillingworth and his ingenious payback scheme was for James the great invention of the story, the "original" element that took it beyond the familiar love-triangle plot.[1]

The story of Beecher and the Tiltons replicated *The Scarlet Letter* in offering a titanic struggle between the two men after the (alleged) adultery. But the plot of the real-life drama unfolded in the opposite direction too, looking backward from the point of imputed wrongdoing. The lawyers at Beecher's trial, like the mass newspaper readership, were interested above all in the genesis and flowering of the passion between Beecher and Mrs. Tilton. They scoured the past for any fragment of evidence that might point toward, or away from, adultery. They cared about the rivalry between husband and lover that preceded and followed the alleged adultery, but not nearly so much as they cared about Beecher's secret life with Mrs. Tilton.

Those looking for the titillation of forbidden kisses in Prospect Park were disappointed. What they got instead was a plot twist worthy of a Hawthorne. The Beecher-Tilton imbroglio was scintillating and original drama because behind all the name-calling and reputation-smashing of 1874 and 1875, there were overwhelming signs of an intense, stormy love not between clerical lover and demure mother of four but between husband and wife. Between cleric and wife, meanwhile, there was plain proof of a mysteriously romantic and spiritualized love that each of them had also shared for years with the husband. Beecher really had loved Mrs. Tilton, she had loved him, and they had both loved her husband, and he them. The Beecher-Tilton Scandal might have seemed to be a love story without much love in it, since illicit passion was impossible to certify, and since husband and wife, and husband and minister, were busy denouncing each other. But the same documents they were using to destroy one another disclosed an earlier time when love of more than one kind ran through their lives like multiple currents. Henry James's judgment was not threatened by the Beecher-Tilton Scandal: there was much more love in this love story than in *The Scarlet Letter*.

There is an urgency and bedevilment in the published commentary on the scandal that invites examination itself. There is much mockery, satire, disbelief, and anger, along with detached analysis. Commentators knew they faced an unprecedented story. Even the joke-making seems pressured, as if the comical put-downs of all the principals were a kind of defensive laughter in the face of something utterly unnerving. Beecher in 1874 was the sort of cultural icon whom late-twentieth-

century Americans might label "the most trusted man in America."
Theodore Tilton was a well-known editor and lecturer who had been
a fiery voice of the antislavery and Radical Republican movements,
and Elizabeth Tilton was to all appearances the model Christian matron. Observers had access to a long-standing "republican" and anticlerical tradition according to which saintly robes often hid despicable
acts, but very few writers employed it. They were much more interested in the dilemma they faced as interpreters. How could they be sure
Tilton was telling the truth? Why didn't his wife make a simple, direct
statement of what had transpired? What was the meaning of the celebrity status bestowed on Beecher and the Tiltons—and on such secondary players as Tilton's boyhood pal Frank Moulton, who became the
mysterious "mutual friend" to Beecher and Tilton in the 1870s, and
Victoria Woodhull, the charismatic spiritualist and reformer who first
broke the story that scandalized the nation and the world? [2]

Commentators at the time were stymied: they didn't know how to
make sense of the Brooklyn accusation or of the frantic investigation to
which they were contributing. Many of them, like E. L. Godkin of the
Nation, didn't want to add to the sensation, but did so even in registering
their objections to it. In the summer of 1874 Godkin kept hoping that
each *Nation* editorial on the scandal would be his last. "We shall now
take leave of the affair," he announced on August 27. "The case has
evidently reached a stage at which the further discussion of it will do no
good, and serve no purpose but to gratify the cravings of the actors in
it for notoriety. . . . The best thing the public can do is to let it drop."
But his lofty disdain collapsed each time a new "revelation" broke. "We
are compelled to discuss it [a public statement by Frank Moulton] in
view of what we have already said upon . . . the affair, deeply as we
regret troubling our readers with any more comment on a matter that
grows more repulsive the more it is handled." Godkin kept on scratch-
ing his head about the meaning of the scandal, and could only account
for the behavior of Beecher, the Tiltons, and their friends by likening them, in all seriousness, to "a half-civilized . . . tribe worshipping
strange gods." These aliens, remarkably, were not social outcasts, but
respected leaders of "culture," and they were, Godkin thought, sapping
the nation's vigor from within. [3]

Since middle-class Americans were zealous readers of fiction, including the fiction of Henry Ward Beecher (*Norwood*, 1868) and Theodore
Tilton (*Tempest-Tossed*, 1874), observers turned for illumination to these
and other stories that everyone knew. Elizabeth Tilton, by all accounts
an experienced reader and skilled critic of stories, had come to a new

understanding of her own role in the scandal by reading British novelist Charles Reade's 1866 bestseller *Griffith Gaunt*—the story of Catherine Gaunt's discovery that her intensely intimate (and nonadulterous) tie to Brother Leonard, her Catholic priest spiritual adviser, was morally dubious despite its technical innocence. Mrs. Tilton's eye-opening encounter with that text became part of the mythology of the case, and showed everyone that "fiction" was an essential element of "reality" for those who, like Beecher and his followers, aspired to a "higher" experience of intimate "soul-purity." Commentators ransacked the literary terrain for texts that might illuminate what had happened and was still happening in their midst, but they confessed they could not get the upper hand. The Beecher-Tilton story kept outpacing its interpreters. *Frank Leslie's Illustrated Newspaper* cited one literary parallel after another, and decided there had never been a story like this one.

> The Tilton case is more remarkable than any tale ever told in fiction—as intense as "The Scarlet Letter"—but showing a woman, whatever her sin, as devout as Catherine Gaunt, a clergyman hovering between the simplicity of Brother Leonard and the painful reserve of the unfortunate Dimmesdale, and a husband not so earnestly jealous as Griffith Gaunt but more sternly unforgiving than Roger Chillingworth.[4]

II. My historian's instinct, when I first approached the scandal, was to find out what had really happened. Who was telling the truth? At first there appeared to be two sides to the story, those who thought Beecher guilty and those who didn't. At the end of a six-month trial a jury of twelve white men divided nine for Beecher and three against, so it seemed to me the historian might go back over the evidence and do what the jury had failed to do: come up with a definitive finding. Maybe there was a smoking-gun letter or diary that no other researcher had ever found. Maybe there was a contradiction in someone's testimony that had never been noticed.

Then I realized that even if I did find new documents or cracks in the testimony, they could never close the case. Two fundamental barriers stood in the way of a retrospective verdict. First, Elizabeth Tilton switched sides three years after the trial. Having denied the charge of adultery throughout 1874 and 1875, she confessed to it in 1878. There is no way to know which story was true, or if either of them was wholly true. The reality of her relationship with Beecher may have been far too complicated for her to settle on a simple "yes" or "no" on the question of adultery. In any event, Mrs. Tilton's public change of heart undermined any effort to come to a final reading of the evidence. Perhaps she was crafty enough to have had that in mind when she reversed herself in 1878.[5]

The indeterminacy of Mrs. Tilton's position made me realize, secondly, that the whole idea of "two sides" was flawed. What confronted me as a historian was not a choice between guilt and innocence, but an interpretation of multiple competing stories, each of them, like Mrs. Tilton's, much too complex to be encompassed by the "side" metaphor. This trio of passionate and articulate Brooklynites had for years found succor in one another's presence, and when their lives crumbled and they turned against each other, they created stories to make sense of what was transpiring and to defend their reputations. Each person had a story about the other two and about himself or herself. There were, for starters, these nine different stories, overlapping in places, always evolving, drawing in some cases on the same facts but in others positing different facts. And each story mobilized rhetorical strategies designed to make the story come true for the teller as for listeners or readers. What "really happened" at the most basic level in the Beecher-Tilton Scandal is that stories were created by the principals and by the assorted friends, enemies, lawyers, and onlookers.

My goal is to listen carefully to these stories and try to hear what the tellers are saying about their selves, their relationships, their culture. I still want to determine, wherever possible, which of the stories were true and which were false. Sometimes we can be sure about discrete facts, and acts, and at other times we can infer that one of two competing stories is probably closer to the truth. And although attending to the central stories in the case will not, in my estimation, take us any closer to a final resolution of the adultery issue, it will point us toward some large truths about the lived experience of one segment of late-nineteenth-century middle-class America. Beecher and the Tiltons were paradoxically very religious and very secular northern liberal Protestants. My own story of their stories tries to do justice to their piety as well as their worldliness. Most earlier studies have done much more to emphasize the latter.

To emphasize that the Beecher-Tilton Scandal was a set of stories that were told, I depart from the historian's usual narrative strategy of chronological order. My story unfolds in a combination of forward and backward motion. It begins with the last accounts of the three principals upon their deaths, then moves to the final stories they composed about themselves and the scandal in the late 1870s and the 1880s.

Beginning with the end in this fashion helps put the process of story-creation, and story-revision, at the center of things. And it puts Elizabeth Tilton's pivotal 1878 confession—the stumbling block for any historian seeking a single true story of the scandal—where it belongs: before the public retellings that occurred in 1874 and 1875. Those retellings, in turn, give us our foundation for viewing the earlier years. Almost everything we know about the loves shared by Beecher and the Tiltons in the 1860s comes from the documents published during their public battles of the mid-1870s. Some of those texts were written in the 1870s, some in the 1860s. The earlier documents, paradoxically, were products of both decades. Sometimes they were rewritten in the 1870s, and always they were reinterpreted.

Historical documents must always be viewed contextually. They were composed or recomposed at certain times for some set of purposes. They were certainly not created with the needs of future historians (or their readers) in mind. Documents have a life of their own in some web of interests, and many of them tell stories about times already past, as people try to assert control over a pattern of events, and make their story the accepted one. This is certainly true in the Beecher-Tilton Scandal, in which documents were generated by the ream in order to prove one person's culpability or another's disinterestedness. The public retellings of 1874 and 1875 generated many such "interested" documents. It makes sense to me to tell the stories of 1874 and 1875 first, before trying to use the documents of those years to see back into the early 1870s and then the 1850s and 1860s. I know that recounting my story largely in reverse order poses problems of comprehension, but I think it saves the reader from a bigger trap—that of suspecting that there is a straightforward story to be told in the first place. To help reduce the risk of confusion about the succession of events, I have provided, in the Prologue of images that opens the book, a chronological outline of the scandal's main developments.

The public retellings of 1874 and 1875 are followed by the private retellings and initial public exposures of 1870 to 1873. Beecher and the Tiltons tried to keep their personal accounts secret during those years (although there were periodic leaks), while various acquaintances, led by Victoria Woodhull, spread their own versions of the scandal through outright publicity. Examining the storytelling of the early 1870s is the final preparatory step in approaching the private and public experiences shared by Beecher and the Tiltons in the late 1850s and the 1860s. In those years they gave a trial run to what was for them, and for their churchgoing contemporaries, a novel kind of intimacy. Long before there was any thought of a public trial, these liberal Protestants attempted to put "love" rather than "law" at the center of their daily lives. That effort amounted to a difficult trial for them well in advance of the painful probings of investigators and lawyers, and the malicious mockery of press and public, in the mid-1870s.

Many of the intimate stories of Beecher and the Tiltons are contained in the letters exchanged in the late 1860s between Elizabeth and Theodore, and chapter 8 includes a selection of thirty of those letters. I think we historians have not done enough to let our subjects speak in their own voices. We are too quick to translate their language into ours, and too hasty about locating "social" or "cultural" trends that we believe transcend merely "individual" experience. Focussing upon that experience has the virtue of unsettling premature or jerrybuilt generalizations. And if we look at our human subjects closely enough, they will help reveal the contours of the culture and society that shaped them. Sometimes they make such revelations unwittingly, and sometimes quite consciously, as they struggle to ride or resist the currents of their day. In reprinting some of the Tiltons' letters, I have tried to give them the last word—although of course I have imposed myself on them by selecting the thirty letters that seem to me most interesting among the more than two hundred (some of them very short) available to us. In the Appendix I have chosen another set of documents—letters, memos, poems, prayers, speeches—to give further voice to the scandal's principal players, word-lovers all.

My final chapter takes up the history of interpretation of the Beecher-Tilton Scandal, a stream of storytelling and legend-making that began in 1872 and continues into our own day. I have been critical of some of this earlier work, for it fails in my view to do justice to the religious and secular self-conceptions of Beecher and the Tiltons, and hence misses the full meaning of the scandal and the broader cultural drama of their times. Other studies have put more stress on literary, political, and demographic contexts than I have. I hope that future writers will find this book a useful stepping stone for further exploration of Beecher and the Tiltons in relation to those contexts and others too, such as the development of nineteenth-century language, humor, journalism, oratory, law, and theology.

III.   The irony of a largely backward-moving narrative like mine is that it is actually, much more than we realize, the way life is lived. Some hardy souls may face life pointing diligently forward, rather like George Washington, chest and chin erect, in the prow of his longboat. But many people lurch through time heads spinning, focussing backward as much as forward, bathed in memories of the pains, joys, and confusions that molded them. This sense of the past as the living atmosphere of the present may be especially potent for those who, like Beecher and the Tiltons, lived through a historical cataclysm—in their case the Civil War—which split their lives forever into a "before" and "after." The late 1860s and 1870s, for them, was a time for taking stock, adjusting to a new and very unheroic world. They kept looking back for inspiration to the era of the antislavery battle, and as their personal relations eroded, then exploded, they looked all the more intently backward in search of explanation and vindication.

Henry James's 1886 novel *The Bostonians* gives memorable expression to this dynamic in its depiction of Olive Chancellor, the postwar women's rights advocate who bemoans her distance from the valiant era of the antebellum giants. Olive's moment of reckoning, an awakening to the deluded character of her quest, provokes James's narrator to meditate on the moment that comes sooner or later to any inquiring soul, and had finally come to Olive.

> These hours of backward clearness come to all men and women, once at least, when they read the past in the light of the present, with the reasons of things, like unobserved finger-posts, protruding where they never saw them before. The journey behind them is mapped out and figured, with its false steps, its wrong observations, all its infatuated, deluded geography. They understand as Olive understood, but it is probable that they rarely suffer as she suffered. The sense of regret for her baffled calculations burned within her like a fire.

We have good reason to think that Beecher and the Tiltons suffered as Olive did, and that they suffered again and again as they reworked their pasts in successive retellings of their stories. The trial of 1875 was above all else a multilayered collision of such retellings—their own, their lawyers', those of other witnesses, even those of the wider culture, as basic northern middle-class Protestant tales were refashioned. To mention but one example: the trial was an occasion for opponents of reform, much like Basil Ransom in *The Bostonians,* to discredit what James's narrator calls "the great irregular army of nostrum-mongers, domiciled in humanitary Bohemia." [6]

Another way to put it is that while "events" (and therefore "history") unfold chronologically, people respond to events by looking back as much as they look forward. "History" needs to include that process of reflection and adaptive self-creation, along with the impersonal march of events. I hope that writing this history in a hybrid of forward and reverse motion will give extra weight to the craftedness of these lives, to the interpretive choices these people made in response to the private and public events of their time. To me the promise of history as a form of knowledge—what makes it both a factual and a moral inquiry— is its invitation to clarify our own experience by becoming better acquainted with that of earlier generations. Studying the past enlarges our present, extends it into unfamiliar realms. Often it is said that history is useful because it helps us avoid repeating the mistakes of our predecessors. Nothing is more certain than that we will repeat the mistakes of the past. The study of history, much like anthropology, gives us wider and wider contexts for understanding our mistakes, along with our dreams and our accomplishments.[7]

The public contestation of the Beecher-Tilton Scandal in the mid-1870s provoked the assembling of a documentary trail that gives us our window, imperfect as it is, on the passionate ardor of their lives together in the 1860s. That ardor expressed itself in the stories they then told each other as much as it did in whatever touching and kissing they undertook—and they acknowledged there was some of that too. We usually think of the lived experience of love as one of "feeling," but it is just as much one of "telling." Lovers whisper stories in each other's ears, write each other giddy, passionate, or tragic notes. The fullest love may be constituted by frolicking caresses, but even physical love relies on words that give bodily pleasures their meaning and much of their exhilaration—and words preserved in time give us, decades or centuries later, our partial access to that experience of love. The most basic facts of the Beecher-Tilton Scandal, and of the loving that preceded it, are not to be searched for *in* the stories. They *are* the stories.

MRS. THEODORE TILTON DEAD.

Stricken with Paralysis Last Month, from Which She Never Fully Rallied—Once Blind, but Recovered.

Paralysis, on Tuesday evening, caused the death of Mrs. Elizabeth R. Tilton at the home of her daughter, Mrs. Pelton, in Pacific Street, Brooklyn. She had a paralytic stroke in March, but partially recovered until April 7, when she was again stricken and remained unconscious until her death. Her children were at her bedside when she died.

THEODORE TILTON IS DEAD IN PARIS

Was Unconscious for Hours Before He Passed Away—Illness Very Brief.

EXILED HIMSELF IN 1883

Never Returned to This Country—Was a Friend of Beecher for Many Years Before the Suit in 1874.

Special Cablegram.
Copyright, 1907, by THE NEW YORK TIMES Co.

PARIS, May 25.—Theodore Tilton died early this afternoon. Till almost the end it was hoped that he might pull through.

SERVICES IN PLYMOUTH CHURCH, FRIDAY, MARCH 11TH.

THE DEATH AND OBSEQUIES OF HENR

ONE *Last Accounts,*
1907, 1897, 1887

I. When Theodore Tilton died in Paris in May 1907, he was 71 years old and had not set foot in America for a quarter century. He had outlived his estranged wife Elizabeth by one decade and his former intimate Henry Ward Beecher by two. He had also outlived his two sons who reached adulthood, Carroll and Ralph. Carroll, a press agent and, like his father, a stenographer, had died in 1904 at age 40. Ralph, whose paternity had been publicly questioned at the time of the scandal—his conception was perilously close to the period of alleged adultery—became an advertising man and, like his father, an editor (art editor of the *Saturday Evening Post*). He died three months before Theodore did at age 37. Tilton's estate was left to his two daughters, Florence Pelton, a music teacher, and Alice Gardin, a painter. It contained no real estate, $3,000 in personal property, and one share of stock in a New York newspaper.[1]

The Paris edition of the *New York Herald* gave his death a headline on page one, and recounted the broad outline of the trial, then more than three decades in the past. The younger generation, the story noted, had only the faintest familiarity with the events that had shaken the world of their elders. The paper had little to say about Tilton's Paris life, "in practical exile from his native land," although it did note that "he was widely known in the American colony and had many friends." When Frederick Douglass, his comrade from antislavery days, came through Paris in January 1887, the London correspondent of the *New York Times* was on hand to record that "the two heavy, large-featured, distinguished looking men, with their massive heads of white hair, attracted very general notice on the boulevards." The reporter did not speak to Tilton, but friends said he was renting "a floor in a grand old mansion . . . on the Ile de Paris, back of Notre Dame. . . . Most often he is to be met late afternoons at the Café Régence, one of the very few of the famous pre-Revolution resorts which the Haussmannization of the right bank of the Seine has left intact. Here for a century and more have the best chess players of Paris assembled." When his old friend Elizabeth Cady Stanton, the women's rights leader, visited Tilton in the spring of 1887, they "played some exciting games of chess . . . in the pleasant apartments of the late W. J. A. Fuller, Esq., and his daughter, Miss Kate Fuller." Tilton was residing with Miss Fuller at 73 Avenue Kléber at the time of his death. She took his body to Chailly-en-Bière, near Fontainebleau, where he had asked to be buried alongside the Barbizon School painters Jean-François Millet and Théodore Rousseau. Describing him in the cemetery registry as one of her "vieux amis," she bought a large plot, and in 1934 she was laid to rest beside him.[2]

In fact Tilton had published a great deal of poetry and fiction after going to France. His *Complete Poetical Works* was issued by the Clarendon Press, Oxford, in 1897. Tilton had dedicated that work to Elizabeth, who died in the year it was released. But neither his poetry (which included such well-known children's rhymes of the 1860s as "Baby Bye, There's a Fly" and "Toll, Roland, Toll," and his "Sonnets to the Memory of Frederick Douglass," published first in 1895) nor his other Paris works (*Great Tom: Or, the Curfew Bell of Oxford*, 1885; *The Chameleon's Dish*, 1893; *Heart's Ease*, 1894; *The Fading of the Mayflower*, 1906) merited any mention in the *Herald*. To the Americans in Paris Tilton was not an author of any note. "No dreams of fame or of especial achievement come now to Mr. Tilton," the *Times* correspondent heard from Tilton's friends in 1887. "The work upon which he is engaged is understood to be ephemeral in character—done as much for the sake of occupation and mental relief as anything else. His chief interest is to like his life and to keep it smooth, uneventful, restful, within the compass of simple desires and pleasant associations." Tilton kept it smooth by becoming a raconteur of the good old days—an office that made him in his own day "the most picturesque man in Paris," according to a chronicler of the American colony writing in 1912. The *Herald* said that "his work as a writer and lecturer brought him in close touch with Messrs. Bryant, Whittier, Lincoln, Emerson, Walt Whitman and many others of whom he had a fund of anecdote." But above all Tilton was noteworthy in death as a reminder of the Great Scandal of 1874–1875, an event of enormous magnitude for Americans born before and even during the Civil War.[3]

In 1907 a newspaper in Paris might take the detached long view of Tilton's significance, but feelings in Brooklyn were still taut. The *Brooklyn Eagle*, which had defended Beecher against Tilton in the 1870s, took the occasion of his death to reopen the case. Tilton had rarely discussed it in his final years, the paper reported. Yet "he did tell a friend not long ago that the charges he made against Beecher and Mrs. Tilton were absolutely true, or he would never have brought suit against the pastor of Plymouth Church." The *Eagle's* obituary writer, meanwhile, reached for a well-sharpened pencil. It could not be denied, the writer conceded, that the lanky, six-foot-four Tilton "was picturesque. His physique was commanding. His hair was kept long, for an effect which was produced. He always abjured a beard, from the time a celebrated artist requested him to pose as the type of a muscular Christ." It was also undeniable that "regardless of the quarrels and of the moral tragedy of his life," Tilton was "entitled to a favorable judgment" as an "orator, poet, and lecturer. He phrased felicitously. He imaged artistically. . . . His discourses were pungent, suggestive," even if wholly derivative. He was properly placed "in the second or third rank of the literature and of the lyceum of his time."

Yet with Tilton an "obligation to the truth" forced one to jettison the old adage that "one should speak of the dead only that which is good." For this was a man "whose life was a posture, which included imposture." Tilton, who at age 16 had sat in the front row of Beecher's Plymouth Church copying the great preacher's sermons for publication, "began as an imitator." When wealthy publisher and Plymouth parishioner Henry Bowen hired him as a cub reporter on the weekly *Independent*, he "progressed as an understudy" of Beecher, the paper's leading writer, and ultimately replaced Beecher as editor (a position Tilton held from 1863 until 1870). But his journalism, culminating in his own fly-by-night weekly *The Golden Age* (1871–1874), suffered from his injecting "the mar and jar of personality" into what should have been "impersonal comment." Tilton's "egotism" in print was "ineradicable and incurable," and presaged his irreversible decline. He "mal-developed to a rival and a hater, and he collapsed as an envious, shattered and forgotten personality, the memory of whom mankind disrelished." His moral demise was accompanied by "his abandonment by all his kindred, his desertion of his country, the despair as to him, of his former friends."

The obituary-editorial hammered home this story of a "deterioration more progressive, more palpable and more putrid" than any other known to the *Eagle* in order to quell any lingering doubts about the contrastingly elevated stature of "a brilliant and forgiving genius . . . who died in the peace of God, in the love of men, and in the certainty of an immortality of fame." Granted, Henry Ward Beecher's grave error in "discovering, befriending and promoting Tilton" was a miscalculation that would blemish his name in perpetuity. Still, Beecher was a certified "great character." This man "who largely made Tilton, . . . and whom Tilton strove to unmake," rose "superior to the moral assassination devised for him."

The obituary writer's concession of Beecher's frightful misstep in selecting Tilton as his intimate ran counter to all the drumbeating about Beecher's superiority and immortality. There was something about the miscreant Tilton that Beecher had been unable to resist, and something in Beecher therefore, from the standpoint of respectable opinion in 1907 as in 1874 and 1875, that was deeply askew. The battle between Tilton and Beecher that erupted in 1874 had been impassioned in direct proportion to the warmth the two men had once felt for each other. Now both dead, they were still entwined in a fateful embrace. Try as he might to blot out the still prevalent image of Tilton as a Romantic-if-flawed striver, the *Eagle* writer was blocked by Beecher's own inexplicable choice of Tilton. Beecher had seen something— maybe a bright youth who deserved a chance, maybe a fledgling Romantic who mirrored a remembered self of his own—that from the *Eagle*'s standpoint had disabled him. If Beecher had really been a "great character," he would have figured Tilton as a mere copyist from the start.

There was no mention of Elizabeth Tilton in the *Eagle*'s obituary of Theodore, a fitting sign that what was at stake in the Beecher-Tilton Scandal, even three decades later, was not just a three-way love relationship, and not just a rivalry between two men over her "affections," but the survival of a stable male system of "character" in which women entered hardly at all. Tilton the religious doubter and mildly freewheeling radical could stand as a graphic symbol of the menace posed to character in "his steady deterioration from faith to skepticism, from law to license, from license to licentiousness, and from that to a fellowship with lowering causes and lowering persons"—persons of the caliber of

suffragist, spiritualist, and "free lover" Victoria Woodhull, or her an-
archist friend Stephen Pearl Andrews, although the *Eagle* named no
names. For anyone with the cloudiest recollection of the 1870s it didn't
have to. Beecher's lawyers, led by former Attorney General and future
Secretary of State and U.S. Senator William Evarts, had tried to save
their client's reputation by blackening Tilton's, underlining his admitted association with Woodhull, Andrews, and others situated outside
the circle of gentility.[4]

For anyone with a moderately sharp memory of the 1870s, meanwhile, the irony in the *Eagle*'s use of Tilton as exemplar of cultural decline was that Beecher had long been employed for the same purpose.
It was he, according to one observer after another, who had imperiled
social foundations by taking the bite out of religion, eschewing hard
truths and fixed duties. He preached the "Religion of Gush," said the
New York Herald in 1874. "For many years Plymouth Church, under the
ministrations of a clergyman of incomparable eloquence, has been worshipping sentiment rather than revelation." Its faith substituted "a day's
picnic in the woods" for eternal "rewards and punishments." "Beecherism" was "the worship of phrases and personal gratification," and its
close ally was "Tiltonism," "the worship of selfishness, woman's suffrage, and gossip." The *Eagle* obituary might try to open a gulf between
Tilton and Beecher, but many commentators believed that his guilt or
innocence aside, Beecher had already, even before the scandal, done
irrevocable damage to the cause of character. He and Tilton, for all the
heat of their feud, were brothers under the skin. According to many
traditionalist critics of the day, they put individual selfhood over social
order, personal growth over communal stability. And Beecher, like
Tilton, embraced the corrosive doctrine that women deserved an equal
voice in public as well as private affairs.[5]

II. Elizabeth Tilton, a year or two older than Theo-
dore, was 62 or 63 years old when she died of a stroke in April 1897.
The very sympathetic obituary in the *Brooklyn Eagle* stayed away from
the scandal and avoided any mention of her last word on the subject—
her 1878 claim that she and Beecher had indeed, as Theodore alleged,
committed adultery. One might have thought such a confession would
qualify her, in the *Eagle*'s eyes, as a "character" assassin like her husband. But Elizabeth Tilton's statement had been doubted in 1878, just
as her various stories had been discredited when the scandal broke in
July 1874 and when the trial unfolded from January to July 1875. One

of the best-known "facts" about her from 1874 on was that she was always liable to change her mind on the adultery charge, and even to endorse documents that contradicted others she had already signed. The obituary kindly refrained from mentioning the common judgment that she was prone to confusion, and so excessively pious that she verged at times on mental disorder.[6]

Elizabeth Tilton was widely considered untrustworthy, but she was sweet, maternal, petite—not quite five feet tall—and to judge by her obituary, and much of the commentary about her in the 1870s, no peril to the culture of character. A "public woman" such as Victoria Woodhull posed a real menace (in the late nineteenth century the phrase could mean either "public figure" or "prostitute," and critics of militant women smirked at the slippage the phrase permitted). A private woman such as Elizabeth Tilton might be a sinner, but unlike her husband or Victoria Woodhull she could not materially budge the balance of forces in the cultural war for character. The obituary emphasized her attempt to rebuild her life after the trial by retiring completely from public view. "She dropped out of sight at once and avoided any action that would be likely to draw attention to herself." Already a deeply pious woman before the trial, she devoted herself completely to religion thereafter. The home she shared in Brooklyn with her widowed daughter Florence became a house of worship for the Plymouth Brethren (also called "Christian Friends") "who met there weekly or oftener in a primitive way to worship." The Brethren had no connection to Beecher's Plymouth Church, which had expelled Mrs. Tilton after her 1878 confession of adultery. The Brethren, followers of the British evangelist John Darby, found inspiration in the original Pilgrims, who had sought a purer, more direct way of worshipping God.[7]

Apparently Mrs. Tilton was a leading force in their midst, although worship was led by non-ordained male believers. "To the members of this small congregation of good people the death of Mrs. Tilton is a personal grief, as there is taken away from them a friend whose counsel and sympathy were to be had at all times, and were all the more valuable because she was one who knew the value of these intangible evidences of friendship, having herself stood in such sore need of them at one time in her life." The *Eagle* story went on at length about her courage during a period of blindness that was finally cured by an operation less than a year before her death. "A year ago hers was a familiar figure walking slowly down the street, striking the ground ahead of her with a cane, carefully feeling her way around corners, across the streets, and even down town on the trolley cars. Her sweet and at the same time strong personality impressed itself upon all with whom she came in contact."[8]

According to the *New York Tribune* story about her burial, Mrs. Tilton had protected herself after the trial not just from the scrutiny of the press, but from newspapers themselves. "It was one of the principles of Mrs. Tilton's latter-day life never to allow a newspaper to enter her secluded home. Neither she nor her daughter read newspapers." Withdrawal from the web of publicity did not mean a rejection of reading, which she had done passionately all along. It was as a reader and highly appreciated critic of his work that she first came to know Henry Ward Beecher intimately, and Theodore too claimed to value her literary judgment. Indeed, the *Tribune* suggested that even during their two decades of separation, "Mrs. Tilton always took great pride in her husband's literary ability. She was fond of reading his writings." She had always wished her childhood friend Theodore to become a minister, but if he was not called to serve God in the clergy, she wished him to write. Perhaps she even saw a copy of his *Complete Poetical Works*, published in London the year of her death, or at least found out he was dedicating it to her. Theodore's sister Annie (Leslie) was at the funeral, and may have brought Elizabeth news of her husband during the month-long illness that preceded her death.

The ban on news extended to her illness and death. "To such an extent has Mrs. Tilton and her family avoided publicity," wrote the *Eagle*, "that at the present time there is no crape on the door to tell passers by that death has visited the household. The blinds are not drawn down and there is an absence of the gloom which sometimes surrounds the house in which one of the inmates has died." Several of her children were gathered around her bedside as she died. This image of Mrs. Tilton in her sickbed may have evoked memories of the scandal for older readers, since Mrs. Tilton was in her bed—recovering from an illness that followed a miscarriage—during the single most notorious event described in the scandal documents of 1874 and 1875.[9]

The transcript of the 1875 trial, which ran to 2,700 large pages of tiny print, was a catalogue of the most basic cultural practices, and this was one of them. Women in their sickrooms did not rest in seclusion; not only their children but their husbands and friends and visitors streamed by their beds and camped out there to get comfort or transact business. Elizabeth Tilton was always surrounded, even when very ill,

and her illnesses were multiple and prolonged. Often they were associated with childbirth. Her famous miscarriage was followed by the most
acutely serious of her illnesses, but she suffered from various ailments
after most and perhaps all of her six live births. Three days after her
death she was buried in Brooklyn's vast, hilly Greenwood Cemetery
alongside her two children, Mattie and Paul, who had died in infancy.
Only the month before, Henry Ward Beecher's widow Eunice had
been buried there too. She had died on March 8, a decade to the day
after the passing of her husband.

III. There was another likely source for the Tilton
household's aversion to crepe besides a dislike of publicity. It was one
of Henry Ward Beecher's cardinal doctrines that death was not to be
mourned; it was a quick and painless passage to a bright life in eternity,
and those left behind should smile. When he died at age 73 in 1887, a
decade before Elizabeth Tilton and Eunice Beecher, two long white
satin ribbons hung on his door. "For Mr. Beecher had a horror of the
dismal emblems of mourning, and especially of crape," wrote *Frank Leslie's Illustrated Weekly*. "Throughout all the succeeding funeral ceremo-
nies, flowers, green leaves and light colors were employed in place of
the conventional black."

Beecher too was surrounded in death. His long-suffering wife, four
of whose nine babies had survived, was holding his hand as he expired.
She had never appreciated his boyish pranks, his friendship with the
Tiltons (Elizabeth had been a schoolmate of their daughter Hattie), or
even his close ties to some of his distinguished siblings. But she had
stood by him during the scandal. She had always, through a long marriage, put the interests of the family first, seen herself as the vigilant
party reining in Henry's enthusiasms. Around the bed were three of
the four children, their spouses, and all of his grandchildren, as well as
several friends. That night the embalmer and two sculptors arrived,
and the latter pair "succeeded in taking an excellent plaster cast of the
face." The next day his body was placed in an open coffin, and for two
days the family kept him to themselves. After a private funeral service
in the parlor, the "Thirteenth Regiment," of which Beecher had been
the chaplain, moved him to Plymouth Church for the public viewing
and then funeral. At the same hour as the Plymouth burial service,
memorial gatherings were held at four other Brooklyn churches. Flags
stood at half-mast, and crowds spilled through the streets of Brooklyn
Heights.

The account of the service in *Frank Leslie's* said nothing about the rite itself or the sermon preached by Beecher's friend the Reverend Charles Hall, Rector of Holy Trinity Episcopal Church (they had agreed that whoever lived longer would officiate at the other's funeral). But it gave an elaborate inventory of all the greenery and floral arrangements that blanketed the church. The organ loft was "hidden by palms, callas, azaleas, Easter lilies and roses. . . . A design of ferns, smilax, and roses covered the pulpit, and three doves crowned it. Mr. Beecher's olive-wood chair was concealed by immortelles, carnations and ferns. A cross of roses and carnations from the regiment bore the words 'Our Chaplain' in purple immortelles. . . . Laurel wreaths were hung beside the coffin, while upon it were maidenhair fern, lilies-of-the-valley and roses. . . . The decorations extended around the front of the gallery and along the top of the side walls, ropes of holly, laurel and ivy being gracefully festooned." [10]

A century later this detailed catalogue may seem bizarrely disproportionate, but the middle class of Victorian America was mad about flowers. Beecher, like Theodore Tilton, was a flower lover and authority. He had an elaborate greenhouse at his summer residence in Peekskill, New York, and published a book in 1859 called *Plain and Pleasant Talk about Fruits, Flowers, and Farming* (it was reprinted in 1874 with eighty additional pages). The zeal Henry and Theodore shared for everything that blossomed was a sign of their over-the-top Romantic worship of the natural world. But in their floral infatuation they were also mainstream men of their times: flowers were less a hobby for the late-nineteenth-century bourgeoisie than an entire language. This was a culture in which one did not straightaway reveal what was on one's mind, especially in the realm of the heart. Instead one read poetry aloud, or gathered around the piano for song, or gave flowers, each of which expressed a particular message, according to a complex (and codified) calculus of meanings. [11]

At the 1875 trial, for instance, Tilton expressed disbelief that someone might not know what orange blossoms signified. "I think the meaning must be very apparent," he said. "Orange blossoms are the symbol of marriage. A bride wears orange buds in her hair. To ask a lady if she will accept an orange bud is the oriental way of proffering marriage." Tilton and Beecher had given each other flowers as signs of affection many times in the 1850s and 1860s. And flowers came between them, in the 1870s, when everything else did. "During my absence on lecturing tours," Tilton said publicly in 1874, "he kept [Elizabeth] constantly supplied with flowers. To these he added some flower-vases to hold them, of various patterns." At the trial Tilton's lawyers repeated that

Beecher had given Mrs. Tilton far too many flowers. The defense countered by admitting that Beecher had showered her with flowers, but pointed out that he had given everyone else mountains of flowers too. Under re-cross-examination Tilton conceded that his house was always aglow in botanical arrangements and that Beecher's "occasional" floral gifts had not been concealed from him.[12]

Frank Leslie's story about Beecher took an equal interest in one other subject: his net worth. It estimated his wealth at between $100,000 and $200,000. His total career income might have come to a million dollars, *Leslie's* added, but the events of the 1870s had cost him dearly. He had been forced to mortgage his residence at 124 Columbia Heights, and his astronomical salary, raised by the Plymouth Church board to $100,000 in 1875, was eaten up by legal bills. In earlier years he had spent money with relish, not only on his own travel, engravings, paintings, and gems, but on gifts for his friends. He and the Tiltons exchanged presents all the time in the 1850s and 1860s. During the period of their three-way friendship, Theodore copied Henry's lavish spending habits. He put down $500 on a portrait of Beecher (it required thirty hours of sitting on Beecher's part, a generous outlay for a man of his responsibilities), which he hung in his home at 174 Livingston Street, a mile from Beecher's house. When Elizabeth and Henry developed their special attachment in the late 1860s, he gave her many gifts (books especially) which Theodore claimed during the trial to have discovered, to his dismay, in a closet. Tilton's lawyers elicited the information that Mrs. Tilton had kept multiple pictures of Beecher in the same closet. The defense countered that the closet was home to similar mass-produced pictures of many other male public figures, also in multiple copies. She had collected them.[13]

In the wake of Beecher's death, articles and books poured off the presses. The obituary in the monthly *Andover Review* ran to well over ten thousand words. It never mentioned the Tiltons or the scandal, alluding only, toward the end, to "defects of character" and "teaching" that biographers would later, properly, bring to light. Beecher had offered the same sympathetic, slightly mixed judgment, the writer noted, in his own eulogy of Ulysses S. Grant in 1885: "Men without faults are liable to be men without force. The faults of great and generous natures are often the shadows which their virtues cast." But even without mentioning the Tiltons the editorial went far toward accounting for the initial bond that formed between Theodore and Henry: their common devotion to the oratory of great men.[14]

It is nearly impossible for us to comprehend the degree to which nineteenth-century Americans appreciated great speechmaking. We must try to imagine a culture without television, without radio, without film, without microphones, but with a love of the written and spoken word—secular as well as religious. The culture of Victorian Americans was in this way closer to that of the classical world than to our own. They venerated great speakers, measured them by models going back to the ancients, mobilized well-developed criteria for judging them. Audiences sat for hours at a time being instructed, inspired, and entertained. We need to think of these audiences as fundamentally different from twentieth-century ones: they were informed critics of rhetoric, gesture, and voice, and they held speakers to high standards. Whole vocabularies were available to describe the "timbre" and "register" and "method" of orators whose words could not be mechanically recorded. When *Frank Leslie's* provided a brief sketch of Theodore Tilton at the start of the trial, it described his appearance, his hobbies, and his "oratorical method": "declamatory, antithetic, and with a tendency towards epigram." [15]

Protestants North and South held great preaching and great lyceum lecturing in equally high esteem, and when a figure like Beecher emerged, who had a commanding presence in both domains, audiences were enthralled to the point of dizziness. Beecher, the *Andover Review* said, was "our Demosthenes," "the greatest preacher of the English-speaking race," "the foremost private citizen of the Republic." He had no peer in his capacity to light up all the forums of public speech: the sermon, the lecture circuit, the political rally, the after-dinner talk. He did not have a commanding physical stature like Tilton. Beecher had a huge head, and a "most compact, sinewy and stalwart make," but he was only five foot nine. It was his quickness of mind, his phenomenal repertoire of allusions religious and secular, his effortless tonal shifts from humor to pathos to detachment to prayerfulness, his robust baritone voice, his attitude of thoroughly enjoying himself while transmitting an utterly serious message, that made him one-of-a-kind, a culture hero whose like we have not seen since. That is partly because of his unique gifts of speech and sensibility, but it is even more because our culture is no longer doubly hinged on Biblical and secular exposition of the sort that Beecher had mastered. [16]

In the late nineteenth century, liberal Protestantism was the established religion of a nation without an officially established religion. Beecher's force derived from his command of a religious tradition that was rapidly secularizing itself thanks in no small measure to his own work—and his work had influence in part on account of his pedigree as the son of Lyman Beecher, himself a modernizer if not quite a secularizer of Protestant evangelicalism (he put more emphasis on moral purity than he did on doctrinal exactitude). It is customary to make too much of Beecher's secularism, however. He could cultivate a Romantic identity and a secular style because he was so firmly rooted in Christian language and symbolism. Nineteenth-century accounts are rhapsodic about his prayers as well as his sermons. Every sermon he preached was preceded and followed by an elaborate prayer, in which (said the *Andover Review*) "confession and petition were ample," but in which "there was much more of thanksgiving, of aspiration, and communion. . . . many amongst his parishioners valued his ministry of prayer more than the message of the sermon. In our personal experience we never heard but one man besides Mr. Beecher—the English Unitarian, James Martineau—who seemed actually *communing* with God face to face. . . . every suppliant seemed to feel, '*That* is *my* prayer, that is for *me*.'" [17]

A remarkable ten-page section of Lyman Abbott's 1903 biography of Beecher (Abbott was Beecher's friend and successor at Plymouth Church) compares him to nine other great orators Abbott had heard, including Daniel Webster, Wendell Phillips, Charles Sumner, Charles Grandison Finney, and Phillips Brooks. Less significant than Abbott's specific judgments are his categories and criteria. He deployed elements of a whole critical apparatus that has disappeared. In his summary he used "charm" and "power" to demarcate Beecher from the rest:

> in particular elements of charm or power he was surpassed by some of them; in combination of charm and power by none; but his power was greater than his charm, and his charm was subsidiary to power, and its instrument. If the test of the oration is its perfection, whether of structure or of expression, other orators have surpassed Mr. Beecher; if the test of oratory is the power of the speaker to impart to his audience his life, to impress on them his conviction, animate them with his purpose . . . then Mr. Beecher was the greatest orator I have ever heard. [18]

Beecher has been roundly criticized from his day to ours for putting too much weight on feeling. His motto, the *Chicago Tribune* editorialized in 1874, was "feel good" instead of "be good." But his nineteenth-century critics had themselves to blame, in part, for what even his defenders granted was an excessive endorsement of the imagination at the expense of the mind. Many of his opponents, cool to the emotional outbursts of the Second Great Awakening of the 1830s, were so one-sidedly antagonistic to "feelings" that they made the unnuanced embrace of them by Beecher and his ilk inevitable. The rationalists had themselves forgotten the balance between reason and passion, intellect and affect, that Jonathan Edwards had insisted upon in his *Treatise Concerning Religious Affections* (1746).[19]

Beecher was popularizing the wave of Romantic thought in Europe and America that expressed a profound and widespread fear: human vitality was drying up as industrial society became ever more rationalized and standardized. According to Abbott, Beecher realized by the end of his career that he needed to redress the balance and model for his congregation a Christian life that tempered effusive piety with disciplined theological inquiry. In fact it was the scandal itself that forced him to reposition himself, to develop the "orthodox" side of his teaching. In the 1860s, when he came to know and love the Tiltons, he was still in flight from Calvinist rigidity of doctrine and behavior, and still troubled by the spreading routinization of urban life. The Gospel he preached then, while centered on Christian truths and rooted in Christian language, was a call to emotional release and passionate aspiration.

There is no telling how either Theodore or Elizabeth Tilton reacted to the death of Beecher. Maybe with sorrow, scorn, emptiness, perhaps a combination of those things, and perhaps some gratitude. Beecher's 1927 biographer Paxton Hibben, who spoke with the Tiltons' daughter Alice Gardin while preparing his book, claimed to know that Theodore got the news as he sat in the Café de la Régence in Paris playing chess. Hibben also claimed to know exactly what Theodore said and did, although his report has the quality of legend—perhaps family legend, perhaps authorial invention—about it: "For a long time [he] sat staring out of the window. . . . [He] turned back at last and bowed to his adversary with that formal, old-world courtesy that had always been his. 'I beg your pardon, Sir,' he said. 'Is it my move?'" [20]

Whatever the Tiltons felt—even if they felt nothing—their reactions were a product of the powerful bonds forged between them and Beecher from the time they were teenagers. They had been drawn to him because he made them feel the living presence of God, and because he could help them establish themselves as successful middle-class Christian adults. In his sermons and prayers he told them the Gospel-based stories, week after week, that allowed them to make sense of and try to deepen their affection for one another. What Theodore later called their "confessed love" (informal betrothal) had just begun when he commenced sitting at Beecher's feet each Sunday, copying his sermons by Pitman's method of "phonography." Four years later, on October 2, 1855, Theodore's twentieth birthday, Beecher married them. Elizabeth was 20 or 21, and Beecher was 42 years old—perhaps a father figure for Elizabeth, whose father had died when she was a small child, and certainly for Theodore a vital mentor, a potent embodiment of the man of streaming words he wished to become.

Henry James remarks of Hawthorne's *Scarlet Letter* that its power derives not from its allegorical pretensions but from its mythic simplicity. The story gives us characters who invite profound reflection because their meaning is so unfixed, so mysterious. Hawthorne imagined and depicted them "large," yet without turning them into chiseled archetypes. We enter their world and feel their utter distinctiveness as well as their brimming significance. The text is a template: readers feel it as an eerily apt representation of the apparently straightforward but actually weird world they themselves inhabit. The power of the Beecher-Tilton Scandal for late-nineteenth-century Americans flowed from a similar source. Beecher and the Tiltons, storytellers all, created a drama to which people were irresistibly drawn. It was a drama of such amplitude and instability that people could hang their own confusions, disappointments, and dreams on it. It did not just mirror some larger social reality, it was not just a disclosure of some social or cultural trend, although it did mirror and disclose. It was above all a story of awesome scope and tingling particularity. It couldn't have happened, but it did. Americans rubbed their eyes in shock, but sensed the story was somehow "right." It was big enough to stand for the swirling and surreal moral atmosphere of their time.

The Beecher-Tilton Scandal featured the horrifying dissolution of a family (the Tiltons), a spectacle all the more dreaded because the husband broke all respectable precedent by not trying to stop his wife from leaving him. He claimed she was a free agent. The scandal showcased the widely perceived moral incompetence, if not also the adultery, of the nation's most famous preacher. It encompassed the central but murkily understood participation of several leaders of the growing but widely calumniated women's rights movement—Victoria Woodhull, Elizabeth Cady Stanton, Isabella Beecher Hooker (Henry's half sister) and Susan B. Anthony (whose refusal to "talk" was maddening to the press, and to her colleague Mrs. Stanton). And it bred (and was bred by) a newspaper feeding frenzy that drew upon and helped deepen Americans' growing infatuation with celebrity. Anyone concerned about men's and women's increasingly fluid social roles, about the fate of the family and of religion, about the gap between vaunted cultural ideals and sordid social realities—in other words, everyone— fixed on the scandal as a confirmation of some ominous or hopeful development. Beecher and the Tiltons had involuntarily given their lives to the cultural work of mythic representation. A new system of exposure and publicity tied them inexorably to a vast process of social reconfiguring. My guess is that upon Beecher's death in 1887 Elizabeth and Theodore Tilton may have felt, more than anything else, that the story was finally over.

ISSUED BY THE NATIONAL COMMITTEE OF REPUBLICANS AND INDEPENDENTS.
No. 35 NASSAU STREET, NEW YORK.

GEO. WALTON GREEN, *Secretary*.　　　GEO. WM. CURTIS, *President*.

ADDRESS OF HENRY WARD BEECHER

AT THE BROOKLYN RINK, OCTOBER 22, 1884.

I confess, at the risk of the imputation of some immodesty, that my appearance here to-night to antagonize the organized action of the Republican party, is itself a fact of the most significant character. Before many of you were born I was rocking the cradle of the Republican party. [Applause.] I fought its early battles when it was in an apparently hopeless minority. I advocated its cause—speaking day and night, at the risk of my health and of my life itself—which I counted as nothing compared with the interests of my country [applause] when Fremont was our first notable candidate. When Mr. Lincoln [cheers] became our candidate I gave all I had of time, strength, influence, and persuasion, and when his election was ascertained and efforts were made to intimidate the North and to prevent his being chaired, I went up and down through this country stiffening the backs of willow-backed patriots. [Applause and laughter.] I faced mobs. I preached day and night in my own church to hold the North up to its own rights and interests. When the war broke out I sent to it the only boy I had big enough to hold a musket [applause], and it greatly grieved my oldest child, a daughter, that she was not a boy. [Laughter and applause.] And as the war went on my contribution could not be much, but such as it was I gave it—I gave it as a mother gives her breast to her child. [Renewed applause.]

And when seeking some rest from exhausting cares and labors, I went abroad, I did not suffer the grass to grow under my feet, but in the face of royalty and aristocracy and of great wealth in England I upheld the justice and the rectitude of the cause for which we were all striving. [Great applause.] And at every canvass from that day to this I have not held back health, strength or influence. Why, then, is it that I am now opposed to the organized movement of the Republican party ? That is a significant question. For, gentlemen, I have never fed on official pap. [Laughter and applause.] I have never asked a favor for myself, nor could one be given me. I would not take a seat in the Senate of the United States, even if I could get it, and I fear that I am too good a man to get it. [Great laughter.] Pardon me some little vanity when I say that I regard the platform of Plymouth Church as unspeakably higher than the presidency of these United States—for me, not for others. [Renewed laughter and applause.]

I am now opposing the party whose cradle I rocked, because I do not mean to be a pall-bearer to carry the coffin of that party to the grave. [Applause.] Gentlemen, the Republican party is on its way to destruction, unless you turn the switch and run it on a side track. [Laughter.] And by all my love of my country—and it is next to my love of my God—by all my pride in the past—I feel bound to do whatever God will inspire me to do to stop the ruinous progress of the Republican party and to save it. [Applause.]

It behooves you, therefore, not to make mere amusement of the work of this evening. I speak to you as to a jury. The case before you is not that of some trembling culprit, or some wronged citizen seeking redress. It is your whole country that is before you to-night, whose cause I am to plead—to plead as if life or death hung on the issues. [Applause.] I am in dead earnest. It is very natural that men working through a political party should by and by come to look upon all events in the community in their relation to party welfare and party success. But I, who have had nothing to do with parties, except as moral instruments, naturally look upon their movements and purposes from the moral standpoint. What are they attempting to do for this great people ? What does their success mean ? How does it stand alongside the intelligence, the morality, the true religion of this people, alongside that patriotism which rests its feet on morality, but whose head stands in the

---

VOL. XXVII. NO. 8297.

MRS. TILTON PLEADS GUILTY

HER ADULTERY WITH MR. BEECHER ADMITTED.

A WRITTEN CONFESSION MADE PUBLIC THROUGH MRS. TILTON'S LAWYER—SHE SOLEMNLY AFFIRMS THAT SHE COMMITTED ADULTERY WITH HENRY WARD BEECHER — AN EMPHATIC DENIAL OF GUILT BY MR. BEECHER—OPINIONS OF VARIOUS PERSONS CONNECTED WITH THE GREAT TRIAL.

The following letter was furnished to THE TIMES yesterday for publication by Mr. Ira B. Wheeler, Mrs. Elizabeth R. Tilton's counsel :

Mr. Ira B. Wheeler :

MY DEAR SIR : A few weeks since, after long months of mental anguish, I told, as you know, a few friends, whom I had bitterly deceived, that the charge brought by my husband, of adultery between myself and the Rev. Henry Ward Beecher, was true, and that the lie I had lived so well the last four years had become intolerable to me.

That statement I now solemnly reaffirm, and leave the truth with God, to whom also I commit myself, my children, and all who must suffer.

I know full well the explanations that will be sought by many for this acknowledgment ; a desire to return to my husband, insanity, malice, everything save the true and only one—my quickened conscience, and the sense of what is due to the cause of truth and justice. During all the complications of these years you have been my confidential friend, and therefore I address this letter to you, authorizing and requesting you to secure its publication.

ELIZABETH R. TILTON.

BROOKLYN, April 13, 1878.

Mr. Wheeler has long been not only Mrs. Tilton's legal counsel, but her friend and advisor. In presenting the letter in THE TIMES office he said that Mrs. Tilton carried the manuscript of the letter to his office personally yesterday morning, and put it in his hands, greatly to his surprise. She requested that Mr. Wheeler would furnish the newspapers with copies of the letter, that it might be made public at as early a date as possible. Mr. Wheeler accordingly had the letter put in type, and slips of it were given to the newspapers late yesterday afternoon. Mr. Wheeler is an attorney and counselor at law at No. 239 Broadway, Room No. 19. Besides this gentleman's statement of the origin of the letter, inquiries made by TIMES reporters of nearly all the persons interested and informed in the Beecher-Tilton scandal, place the authenticity of the document beyond a doubt.

Mr. Theodore Tilton, according to the landlady of the house in which he lodged, in Second-avenue, kept possession of his room until yesterday, and said that he would not again occupy it, as he intended to go into the country. There is at least a striking coincidence in the fact that Mr. Tilton's proprietorship in the lodgings ceased on the same day on which his wife's confession appeared, particularly in view of the recent rumors of a reconciliation between them ; and Mr. Tilton's statement that he intended to go into the country, as it was in the country, as rumor had it, that he was to rejoin his wife.

There seems to be little doubt that the latter

---

prise of my counsel and of all her friends, she rose in the court and demanded of the Judge that she be permitted to testify to her innocence. She was examined repeatedly by my counsel, and plied with the most searching questions, and by her consistent and explicit testimony satisfied them all of her innocence and won their esteem. When the council of 1876 was called, several interviews were arranged between her and eminent gentlemen, both of the clergy and of the law. In every case she satisfied them of her absolute innocence. Subsequently to that, at an interview arranged for the purpose of giving prominence to her declarations and form to her testimony, which was taken down by a short-hand writer, and which I believe to be still in existence, although I have never seen it, she elaborately and in detail reaffirmed her innocence and mine. These are the most prominent instances of her uniform testimony. It should be borne in mind that she first charged me with this offense to her husband. Upon my visiting her she withdrew it in writing. She subsequently renewed the charge. She then again and indignantly denied it, and left her husband's house, and for four years has continued, in every conceivable form and under the most solemn circumstances, to deny it, until now, when once again, for the third time, she renews it. Against this long and tortuous career, I oppose my uniform and unimpeachable truthfulness.

In addition to the above the following dispatch has been received from Mr. Beecher :

To the Editor of the New-York Times :

I confront Mrs. Tilton's confession with explicit and absolute denial. The testimony to her own innocence and to mine which, for four years, she has made to hundreds, in private and in public, before the court, in writing and orally, I declare to be true. And the allegations now made in contradiction of her uniform, solemn, and unvarying statements hitherto made I utterly deny.

I declare her to be innocent of the great transgression. HENRY WARD BEECHER.

WAVERLY, N. Y., Monday evening, April 15.

THE CONFESSION CONFIRMED.

In conversation with a lady friend of the family, Mrs. Tilton said she had written the confession which was sent to the papers for publication, adding, with firmness, that every word of it was true. The friend reproached her bitterly, and asked how she could have remained under the crime of perjury so long, but was answered that Mrs. Tilton did not know, but that she had so remained nevertheless. She said her daughters were aware of the truth before they went to Europe. Mrs. Tilton was very firm in defending the justice of her present course toward Mr. Beecher, although evidently in a high state of nervous excitement. Mrs. Morse was present at the interview, and added to the information given by Mrs. Tilton that Mr. Tilton was absent on a lecturing tour, at a great distance ; that he provided for his children everything that could contribute to their comfort, and that he had seen Mrs. Tilton recently. Mrs. Morse further informed her visitor that she had sent for Mr. Tilton herself ; that the house at present occupied by them was to be re-

TWO *Final Stories,*
1876, 1878, 1884

I. The interminable civil trial of 1875 ended with the whimper of a hung jury. Amidst the general frustration of the press at so inconclusive a dénouement, and a few hardy calls for a new trial (Henry would sue Theodore for libel, and Elizabeth would testify at last), Beecher and the Tiltons looked to their own storytelling resources for a deliverance the legal proceeding had denied them. They tried to formulate final stories with which to justify or purify or promote themselves. These were actually revisions of tales they had begun fashioning at least by 1870 — accounts they could use to make sense of what had befallen them and to secure a path into the future.

They each faced a formidable uphill campaign. No story could clear away all of the public doubts the trial had raised about them. They were now famous above all for their flawed characters. None of them could expect to reverse that cultural judgment. But for Henry and Theodore there was a second problem as they tried to reconstruct their public careers in the wake of devastating publicity. The very language each of them spoke was the product of another era. The Christian sentimentalizing that had held them aloft in their quests for justice and intimacy and transcendence during the 1850s and 1860s was rapidly losing credibility in post-Reconstruction America. Beecher had himself been a vaunted innovator in the realm of cultural styles — he had been "naturalizing" the spiritual, and vindicating the worldly, for decades — but intellectual innovation was outrunning him. He tried to keep pace by reading up on "evolution," but it was too late for him to retool as a scientific or even empirical thinker. Tilton was doubly stranded, intellectually and politically. His sentimentalism, like Beecher's, was offkey in an era of emerging "realism," and his principled republican-ism (which Beecher had jettisoned right after the Civil War) was widely viewed as a relic.

In the 1850s and 1860s Abraham Lincoln, Henry David Thoreau, Walt Whitman, and many other Americans and Europeans had made the pilgrimage to Plymouth Church to absorb Beecher's "personal" performance of intimacy. Whitman, for one, was deeply affected by it. But by the late 1870s Beecher's style had lost its edge. The trial, meanwhile, had forced him to salvage his Christian credentials by emphasizing his orthodox roots. In his last decade he was treading water as a religious leader while young ministers like Washington Gladden—who followed Tilton as editor of the *Independent* in 1871 — were moving toward the Social Gospel. Beecher was still a mass hero-celebrity (and pitchman for Pears' Soap and other products). But the cultural vanguard among secular and religious liberals was hitching moral endeavor to the "scientific" investigation of social problems. By the 1880s, in the wake of the economic depression that provoked the Great Railroad Strike of 1877, American intellectuals were turning away from "individualism" as bedrock doctrine. The liberalism of the untrammeled self and unregulated marketplace had gotten out of hand, they felt, and justice required the spread of "social control" administered, in the German manner, by trained profes-sionals.[1]

Neither Beecher nor Tilton, both of whom in their youth had fled what to them were the harsh constraints of Calvinism, could imagine any alternative to the Romantic striving they had embraced before the Civil War. For all their criticism of old-fashioned mores—from crepe-shrouded mourning rituals to women's exclusion from the vote—they still endorsed the system of individual character-building (reaccented to stress "growth" in "personality") in which they had recently been judged, during the trial, so lamentably wanting. It appeared at the time that the free-flowing Beecher and Tilton were at the opposite end of the cultural spectrum from the upright E. L. Godkin and other stout traditionalists. In fact Godkin, Beecher, and Tilton all jousted in an arena that was slowly crumbling. They all thought "liberty" was the issue. Whether they harped on free markets, free labor, free soil, or free love, they were bent on liberating the self from arbitrary and oppressive shackles. The next generation tended to think "society" was the primary issue—how to grasp it, rebuild it, fold the self into it. After their trial of 1875, Beecher the preacher and Tilton the lecturer

faced a dire problem of vocabulary and thought-pattern: how to succeed in a shifting mental climate, how, indeed, to make sense of the
crisscrossing and colliding elements in their own linguistic and intellectual makeup.[2]

Theodore was part dreamy idealist and part schematic fact-gatherer.
It may have been the futility of his impassioned fact-arranging on the
adultery charge that thrust him backwards in time to the heroic, clas-
sically inspired verse that he composed in Paris into the early twentieth century. Henry spoke simultaneously on "spiritual" and "natural"
planes, often claiming there was no substantive difference between the
two. The trial's caricaturing of Plymouth Church as a free-love out-
post would have forced him to move back toward traditionalism in doctrine even if he had not decided, on the basis of his own experience
with the Tiltons, that he needed to restore "sin" and "judgment" to his
preaching on "love." But it was too late, in the last decade of his life, to
throw his intellectual engines into full reverse. He took refuge in the
richly figurative and symbolic language he had learned from his father
Lyman Beecher's preaching. Elizabeth found it hard even to approxi-
mate in language the religious feelings that overwhelmed her, so she
relied, not wholly intentionally, on parable, indirection, and appeals to
God for an understanding that she knew eluded her and other mere
mortals like her. Her favorite metaphors for "knowing" were "listening" and "reading."

II. Theodore Tilton lay low in the final weeks of the
trial and after the nonverdict was announced. But during the lecture
season that ran from the fall of 1875 to the spring of 1876, he appeared
twice at the Academy of Music in Brooklyn, to speak on "The Human Mind" and "The Problem of Life." Theodore had come to public
prominence in the 1860s as a leading light in Brooklyn's well-developed
lyceum culture. Brooklyn had been touting itself since the 1830s as the
"city of churches"—it far outdistanced Manhattan in per capita numbers of churches and church members, and continued to do so into the
twentieth century—but it was equally famous as a center of oratory.
The Brooklyn Institute was a center of educational endeavor by the
1850s, and the Brooklyn Academy of Music was added in 1859. The
avid pursuit of both religious piety and secular enlightenment was a
sign of the cultural dominance in Brooklyn from the 1830s to the 1870s
of middle-class Yankee Protestants. Walt Whitman observed in the
Brooklyn Times in 1858 that "men of moderate means" could buy houses

in Brooklyn "at a moderate cost." This "middle class," he believed, was "the most valuable class in any community." Many of them were New England evangelicals such as Henry Ward and Eunice Beecher, who arrived, after a missionary stint in Indiana, in 1847. The New Englanders settled especially in Brooklyn Heights, which took on the atmosphere of a Yankee village. "It seems almost," wrote one chronicler of Brooklyn's past in the early twentieth century, "as if a New England town had been transplanted bodily to the western end of Long Island, there to maintain the culture and sedate atmosphere of the old Bay State in the very heart of the greatest financial and commercial center of the world."[3]

Irish immigrants had arrived in Brooklyn in large numbers in the same mid-century years as the main rush of Yankee Protestants. The population swelled: 36,000 in 1840, 97,000 in 1850, 200,000 in 1855, 266,000 in 1860. Gaslights arrived in 1848, horse cars in 1854, and a new water system in the mid-1850s. A steam railroad was extended to Coney Island in the 1860s. There was no bridge yet—it opened in 1884—but ferries had been plying the East River since Robert Fulton's steam ferryboat made the first run in 1814. Theodore Tilton was a leading customer, visiting Elizabeth Richards at her mother's boarding house before he moved to Brooklyn, then commuting back to Manhattan to work at the *Independent* on Beekman Street after they got married and moved in with Mrs. Morse.

Brooklyn was an independent city until its merger with New York in 1898, and by 1855 it was already the nation's third largest, after New York and Philadelphia. In that year it was also 47 percent foreign-born, and just over one-fourth Irish. The crush of Irish Catholics in the teeming quarters just below the Heights, along the wharves of Red Hook and the Navy Yard, put the native-stock Protestants in a culture-building frame of mind. The liberal Protestants of Brooklyn Heights' Plymouth Church resisted the antiforeign nativism that frequently erupted in Brooklyn and the rest of the country in the antebellum years, but they were nonetheless eager to model habits of temperance and decorum for the (in their view) besotted, ignorant, and reproductively undisciplined working-class Catholics—whose women passed in a steady stream through their homes as servants. Even middling Protestant couples like the Tiltons had three or four Irish servants at a time.

The Tiltons were not New Englanders—his family was from New Jersey, and hers from Manhattan—but they were converts to the Yankee-style Congregationalism that the New England migrants had carried with them into the Presbyterian fortress of the mid-Atlantic states. The Tiltons' rise into the respectable middle class of Brooklyn started with serious schooling: Theodore attended the Free Academy (later City College) in Manhattan, and Elizabeth went to Brooklyn's Packer Collegiate Institute while living at her widowed mother's boarding house at 48 Livingston Street. After their marriage in 1855, the couple lived with Elizabeth's mother off and on for the next decade (for a time they rented a place of their own on Oxford Street). In 1866 they scraped the funds together for a down payment on their own house at 174 Livingston Street—a mixed commercial and residential district a few blocks east of Brooklyn Heights. Homeownership was one sign of their having made it; leadership positions in the Plymouth congregation was another (he ran the Sunday School in the 1850s, she taught one of its sections, the Bethel School for working-class women, in the 1860s); Theodore's success as a wordsmith, in journalism and lyceum lecturing, was a third.

At Tilton's first 1875–1876 lecture at the Academy of Music, "the building was crowded from orchestra to amphitheatre," according to a Brooklyn newspaper report. "The audience was an enthusiastic one. There were very many ladies in the throng." Three of Tilton's lawyers from the trial had prominent seats in the parquet. When he walked onto the stage, the applause was deafening. "He advanced toward the front of the platform and was about to speak, when the applause was renewed. Men stamped and cheered and ladies waved their handkerchiefs. Mr. Tilton was visibly affected." When quiet had been restored, he said, "It is written: 'Out of the abundance of the heart the mouth speaketh.' [Applause.] Ah! But it might be written: 'Out of the abundance of the heart the mouth is dumb.' [Applause.] I have no words for that which is beyond the power of words. All I can say to you is, thanks—many, many thanks. [Loud applause.]"

Tilton's talk was a treasury of other people's sayings about the human mind, delivered with élan and humor and deft references to contemporary politics. To judge by the constant clamor, the audience loved it. The human mind had not been developed to its fullest potential, he said, because people had stressed book learning to the exclusion of cultivating the whole self (an old Emersonian theme). The human body had been developed further than the mind. Take gymnastic skill.

I have seen a copper wire stretched as it might be from the rim of this platform to the rim of that gallery, and a man step upon it with a balancing pole in his hand, and hold himself in delicate precision, like an anxious Presidential candidate between the second and third term. (This hit [noted the reporter] was received with a tempest of applause, during which a boy who had been waiting in the orchestra for an opportunity to deliver a huge basket of flowers to the lecturer, placed the basket upon the stage and retired. Mr. Tilton looked at the flowers a moment and then continued.) These are the tube roses which they scatter over graves. Let it be the monument and the sweet memorial of the death and burial forever of the un-American idea of any third term. [Tremendous applause.] Now, ladies and gentlemen, do not tempt me to turn this into a political meeting [laughter], for you know I am always on the wrong side in politics [laughter].

This was a very clever gibe at Henry Ward Beecher, artfully couched in self-deprecation. Tilton was on the wrong side in politics only in the sense that he was on the other side from Beecher. Since 1872 Tilton had ranged himself with the "liberal" Republicans, those upset about the "corruption" of President Grant and the local Republican machine in Brooklyn. Beecher was a "regular" Republican who supported Grant in 1868 and 1872 and found the antimachine views of the liberals unduly fastidious. The audience did not have to turn the gathering into a political meeting. Judging by the their reactions, they were mostly liberal anti-Grant Republicans drawn to Tilton's talk out of prior political affinity. They were probably also drawn from the ranks of those locals who believed Beecher guilty of adultery with Mrs. Tilton. The warmth of this audience's welcome for Theodore was not a sign of general enthusiasm for his message among the lyceum-goers of the North and "west" (the Midwest and plains states).

Theodore was not going to refer directly to the trial or to Henry, but he was going to rival him by showing that he, Tilton, was religious to the core. From the opening Biblical invocation about the abundance of the heart, he made sure everyone knew he was a believer and a Bible reader. True, anyone who had followed the trial knew he had stopped going to church long ago, and denied the divinity of Christ. But he had no doubts about the sovereignty of God. "Now what is the mind?" he asked.

Well, no man knows. Being a part of God himself, lodged in human nature, it is, like God, past finding out. The most that the wisest man could say, I think, would be this: That the Author of time and eternity has spread the earth under our feet, has lodged the Heavens over our head, and then has put between these twain this cunning instrument called the human brain, whose stupendous function it is to clasp these two worlds and hold them, I might say one in either hand, for three score years and ten, until at last we drop the one, flinging it behind us as a school boy his idle toy, that we may seize hold of the Heavens for our immortal prey. Why, what a cabinet of curiosities is a human brain. What a treasure of remembered sights and sounds. What a cunning loom, weaving perpetual fancies. What a rose garden, planted with thick blossoming affections. Aye, what a cathedral, enshrining devoted aspirations and—where? Within the globe of a human skull, which you and I may well nigh span with meeting thumb and forefinger. . . . 'Great and marvelous are Thy works, O Lord, God Almighty, and in wisdom hast Thou created them all.' And among all the miracles of His handiwork, His masterpiece is the human mind.[4]

During the lecture season of 1 875 –1 876 Theodore Tilton was working the cultural Center. He would indeed stay away from politics, and from cultural critique, focussing instead on the eternal, unchanging "thick blossoming affections" of the mind. And he would project the aura of one who had come through the trial with aplomb. His lawyers had claimed the trial vindicated him, for a jury in Brooklyn—Beecher territory—had failed to exonerate the Plymouth pastor. Tilton would not appeal for anyone's sympathy, would not advert to any suffering he had undergone, perhaps in part to quell any suspicion that he had not come out on top.

Yet for his talk on "The Problem of Life" later in the season, Tilton ordered the Academy to "remove all reporters' tables, and not to give them any facilities for reporting his remarks." He had adopted a non-cooperation policy after the lambasting he had received from much of the press after the trial. The one thing he and his wife and Beecher had in common after 1875 was their antipathy toward the newspapers. Henry could have been speaking for all of them when he cried out in February 1876 to a group of sympathetic churchmen, "I have not been hunted as an eagle is hunted; I have not been pursued as a lion is pursued; I have not been pursued even as wolves and foxes. I have been pursued as if I were a maggot in a rotten corpse." Beecher and the Tiltons were not complaining about being misquoted or misinterpreted; they were upset about being turned into hunted animals, and hunted animals, in Henry's apt metaphor, that were denied either heroic stature or a chance to run.[5]

Tilton's return performance was chatty, funny, and stuffed with choice lines from classical, Biblical, and modern authorities. The audience laughed and clapped all evening long. His serious point was a conventional and sentimental one—he spoke of sacred altars, undisturbed cradles, tranquil graves—but in the immediate wake of the trial it provoked an impassioned response. By "life," Tilton said, he meant "this everyday life of ours, whose burdens we bear, whose prizes we seek, whose vicissitudes are such a mystery and whose functions are so little understood."

> For I suppose that every man who has had some fair share of human experience, who has gone far enough into life to feel the burden and heat of the day, who has stood at the altar of his marriage, who has looked into the cradle of his children, who has laid away his dead in precious and holy graves, every man who has come to what Wordsworth calls 'the years that bring the philosophic mind,' every such man is often brought to a standstill in the midst of this hurly burly that we call the world, to ask himself the question . . . , what is the problem of life?

Before he offered the answer, Tilton ruled some possibilities out. The problem of life was "certainly not the acquisition of wealth, nor of fame, nor of power, nor of learning, nor even of happiness." Each of these was eliminated in its turn with a winning lightness of touch. Learning was not it. "How many of you are learned? . . . How many of you could give me the entire chain, no link unbroken, of the Presidents of the United States? [Laughter.]" Nor was happiness. "How many of you are happy? Now there is a great deal of happiness in the world. Indeed, Carlyle says, 'Happiness is cheap if only you apply to the right merchant for it.' Still with all that, I don't think the market is glutted with it. We all remember the immortal incident [of] a king whose misery could be only cured by wearing the shirt of a happy man, and when the man was found it was found he had no shirt. [Laughter.]"

The problem of life, he finally concluded, to the surprise of no one, was "the development of a man's character. How could it be anything else?" How indeed? Tilton had come a long way from his speeches of the 1850s and 1860s, when he had preached on-the-edge doctrines, from radical antislavery and female equality to systematic divorce reform. Tilton, it turned out, had something else in common with Beecher in 1876 besides an aversion to the press. In the wake of the trial they each chose to tighten, conventionalize their messages, lead the cheering for mainstream values—values that each man's own lawyers conceded he had helped undermine. "When I say character," Theodore intoned, "I don't mean reputation [Applause.] . . . A man's character is what he is; a man's reputation is what other people may imagine him to be. [Applause.] And oftentimes even the great world thinks well of bad men, thinks ill of good men, in either case the character is the same, it is the reputation only that differs." Since Jesus himself, "the greatest character in all history[,] was a man of no reputation," one would have to look elsewhere than public acclaim for evidence of a person's worth. This was self-exculpation, a plea that his own true character be allowed to emerge from the shadow of his tarnished reputation, but it was a broad-minded formulation. It applied equally to himself, to his wife, and to Beecher. None of them could be judged by what had been said about them. Tilton's final story may have been self-justifying, but he had the grace, at the end, to refrain from blaming the others.[6]

Coming out for "character" in the 1870s was the rough equivalent of coming out for "family" in the 1970s. The only danger in that course was the risk of embarrassment at the distance one had traveled, tail between legs, in response to social pressure. But Theodore had laid out a story he hoped would secure his career as a lecturer: he was a religious man, a defender of cultural proprieties, and, having always told the truth, he had no need of sympathy from anyone. According to his friendly biographer of the 1920s, Paxton Hibben, Tilton stoically kept up his oratorical pilgrimage into the 1880s. But Plymouth Church had turned its cannons on him: "Beecher's partisans among the clergy everywhere [were enlisted] to prevent Tilton from earning his living by lecturing." After several summertime visits to France after the trial, Theodore settled into his new life of coffee and chess at the Café de la Régence in Paris.[7]

Hibben supplied no evidence that the Plymouth brass had managed to blackball Theodore with the national lecture bureaus or the liberal churches of the heartland. Surely they tried to torpedo him. But a *New York Times* report of Tilton's 1878 lecture on "Heart's-Ease" suggests that audiences may have lost interest without any prompting from anti-Tilton malefactors. "Chickering Hall was not by any means crowded with persons who desired to hear Mr. Theodore Tilton last night," the paper said. Theodore spoke for two hours about the "hard times" the country was suffering, and about various proposals to alleviate mass poverty and unemployment in the wake of "the holocaust of Pitts-burgh" (the shooting of twenty workers by the state militia during the Great Railroad Strike of 1877). None of the proposals—"the equal distribution of property, the exclusion of Chinese cheap labor, the benefits of co-operation, . . . the plan of inflation"—made sense to him. Since "this mournful state of affairs could not immediately be remedied," it would have to be "manfully endured." The path forward was to take refuge in the "heart's ease": "home comforts, the unselfish love found in families, and the blessings of religion."[8]

This sentimental resolution must have seemed archaic to many of those perplexed about class conflict and prolonged economic depression. And by the 1880s many would have found Tilton's classicism as antiquated as his sentimentalism. He was still ruminating about the un-changing features of the problem of life when vanguard thinkers like the young John Dewey were moving toward a historical conception of selfhood and society. Tilton still wished to see the mind as a "cathe-dral, enshrining devoted aspirations," at a time when young Harvard professor of psychology William James—only seven years Tilton's ju-nior—was lecturing about the physiological roots of the ever-adaptive human psyche. For Theodore exile in Paris in 1883 may have been an escape from persecution, as Hibben supposed, but it may also have been an attractive intellectual alternative to the dawning scientism and historicism of American thought. France offered him a still-vital legacy of republican ardor that was richly classical in inspiration. Across the sea, "liberty" was still defending itself against monarchical habits of mind. In that battle against lingering autocracy Tilton was very much at home.

III.   As Theodore Tilton was distinguishing "reputa-tion" from "character" at the Academy of Music, Beecher was cleaning house at Plymouth Church. Two publicly renowned members who had come to believe him an adulterer were excommunicated: Emma Moul-ton, his former intimate friend (like her husband Frank), and Henry Bowen, founding member of Plymouth, long-time Beecher benefactor, and the publisher of the *Independent* who had hired Beecher as writer and editor, and Tilton as office boy and ultimately editor in his turn. Bowen, himself editor as well as publisher of the *Independent* since Wash-ington Gladden's resignation in 1873, went down swinging. He devoted most of the February 10, 1876, issue of the *Independent* to the case, and concluded, "calmly, without malice," that "the Rev. Henry Ward Beecher, without even the shadow of doubt in my mind, is guilty of the awful crimes of adultery, perjury, and hypocrisy."[9]

Five days later Beecher convened two hundred Congregationalist churchmen to help legitimize the proceedings against Bowen and Moulton, and, addressing the gathering, he reflected at length upon his recent experience as "the focal point on which journalism was expending itself."

> For so many years I have read of myself and heard of myself, that I have ceased in some moods to have any actual self, and am projected as an idea before my own mind. . . . I have often read as if I were reading in a novel about the bad hero, and waked up from the dream and grimly laughed as I asked myself: "Is it me that they mean? Is it possible for a man to live as long as I have, and as openly, and to have acted upon so large a theatre, and been agitated by such world-shaking events, and be so utterly misconceived?" . . . I have no love of being a hero, and I have still less of being such a hero as I have been made to be.

He spoke implicitly for Theodore and Elizabeth Tilton too when he decried the peculiar celebrity status they now all enjoyed: stars of the private life, experts on feeling, emotion, sentiment. Beecher and the Tiltons were public dramatists of innermost desire. It was part of their office to have something in reserve still to reveal. They must be withholding some conversation or yearning, some actual touch or glance. Probably something rotten lay beneath all their sweet talk. "I am questioned, and questioned," Beecher declared, "on the supposition that the truth has not been got out. And I suppose it will be so to the end of my life. . . . I expect to walk with a clouded head, not understood, until I go to heaven."

Already for a century at least many Americans had equated "democracy" with the "exposure" of hidden realities—the corruption of colonial or federal officials, the conspiracies of smug elites, even the peccadilloes of amorous holy men—but this army of reporters drumming up or inventing "discoveries" of private relations was something new. It must have been especially titillating, because frightening, for newspaper readers in a militantly bourgeois culture—one that took middle-class domestic "purity" so seriously—to be handed a clerical hero whose alleged transgression was not just any old sexual escapade, but the undoing of a young couple he himself had blessed and bound together.

Beecher himself had true insight into the dawning culture of exposure, which fed on ever more sensational allegations of private wrongdoing. As long as he was hiding *something*—and there was no doubt he, like everyone, was hiding something—he would remain a target of suspicion. "Nothing that I say is taken to be true, and I am put upon a perpetual trial of my veracity. . . . Tomorrow morning it will be said in the local journals: 'Well, Mr. Beecher—how rhetorically he managed the matter!' And it will be put in the religious papers: 'Oh! yes; that was a very plausible statement at the time, but—but—' And I am in judgment between two devils, 'But' and 'If.'" No amount of confession, he realized, would ever be enough, unless he confessed to having lied. Then he would be forgotten, if not forgiven, and attention would turn to some other prospective wrongdoer who could be made to sweat and confess.[10]

What Beecher could not or chose not to see was his own contribution to the culture he now bewailed. By resituating the religious experience in heightened feelings and intimate sentiments, removing it from the realm of duty, doctrine, or convention, he helped ensure that a "modern" culture would center its attention on the charged and evanescent "truths" of each person's private life. Truth was either outside individual experience—firm and unbending—or it was inside individual experience. If it was outside, then human beings at their best would strive to reach the truth, fall short, but be taken as heroes if their quest was valiant. If truth was inside, celebrity spokesmen for the moral life would have to prepare themselves for a new kind of scrutiny. They would be expected not to reach for the truth, but to embody it. Other people would construe them not as truth-seekers, but as truth-bearers. Any inkling of a fall from that vaunted station would spark an investigation, and a greedy hunt for some new icon of simon-pure stature.

Beecher's final story about himself concerned victimization and persecution, but he made a second claim as well: that with a nature like his he could not stop loving. "You may rebuke me for loving where I should not love," but only if you also "rebuke the twining morning-glory," which "holds on to that which is next to it." He was blameless for having loved first Theodore, then Elizabeth, because he could not help it. But his floral analogy was faulty, for in the case of Theodore and Elizabeth he had not held on to what was next to him. He and

Theodore had warmed each other's hearts in the late 1850s and early 1860s, as he and Elizabeth had in the late 1860s. It was in Beecher's nature to love, perhaps, but unlike the twining morning glory, it was also in his nature to stop loving.[11]

IV. Elizabeth Tilton had nothing to say publicly after the trial ended in 1875. But in 1878 she brought the Great Scandal back to page one around the country by issuing one more confession—her last. In a letter addressed to her lawyer, and published with her approval in papers all over the country on April 16, she wrote that

> a few weeks since, after long months of mental anguish, I told, as you know, a few friends, whom I had bitterly deceived, that the charge brought by my husband, of adultery between myself and the Rev. Henry Ward Beecher, was true, and that the lie I had lived so well the last four years had become intolerable to me. That statement I now solemnly reaffirm, and leave the truth with God, to whom also I commit myself, my children, and all who must suffer. I know full well the explanations that will be sought by many for this acknowledgement: desire to return to my husband, insanity, malice—everything save the true and only one—my quickened conscience, and the sense of what is due to the cause of truth and justice.

It was also widely reported (the *New York Times* called it a rumor, the *Chicago Tribune* judged it a fact) that Mrs. Tilton had told friends her conscience had been quickened in particular by a recent Beecher sermon. Beecher had preached it, according to the *New York Times,* on the occasion of "the downfall of his relative, William C. Gilman," and he had insisted on "the duty of those who have committed any sin or crime, however great or small, to confess."[12]

Beecher's Friday evening lecture about William Gilman—the husband of his sister Mary Perkins's daughter Katherine—took place on October 12, 1877. Gilman had just been convicted of a series of major forgeries, and Beecher observed, in the paraphrase of the *New York Times* reporter, that "since the war, men have had little discretion concerning the nature of wrong-doing and sin." Gilman, he believed, had become addicted to wrongdoing. "When Gilman committed his first forgeries he had no doubt he could make it all right, but he found that he had so blunted his moral sense that he found no difficulty in pursuing his sinful career. . . . [Beecher] closed with a sobbing voice, saying he could not trust himself to speak further. He would ask them to remember the old English adage—'He who would sup with Satan must have a long spoon.'" The *Chicago Tribune* called Mrs. Tilton's claim about being influenced by Beecher's performance "ingenious and sentimental," but did not think it dispelled the "mystery" around her "motive" for confessing.[13]

No contemporary newspaper took Elizabeth Tilton's confession seriously. Even those like the *New York Times* that had judged Beecher guilty of adultery in 1875 thought her confession irrelevant as evidence of what had really happened. She had already demonstrated, to the satisfaction of nearly all her contemporaries, that her word was not to be trusted. "This weak and erring woman," said the *Times*, "has so hopelessly forsworn herself as to forfeit all claim to attention or credence." Beecher remained, in the *Times*'s estimation, what he had been before, "the impure and perjured man which any rational construction of his own letters proved him to be." The newspapers had a feast placing Elizabeth Tilton's confession next to quotations from her earlier, diametrically opposed, public statements, such as her claim in 1874 that it was Theodore, not she, who had defiled their home by laying "the cornerstone of free love" in it and "desecrat[ing] its altars up to the time of my departure, so that the atmosphere was not only godless but impure for my children."[14]

Editorial analysis settled not on the consequences of her action—there would be none, the press thought, aside from the general nausea of the entire populace—but on its causes. Many observers figured she was crazy, others that she was again under the mind-control of her husband, as she had said (at the time of the scandal) she had often been during their marriage. According to press reports, Theodore had seen her at least twice in the recent past, and had repeatedly communicated with her through their teenaged son Carroll. She and Theodore each denied the reconciliation story, and our hindsight knowledge that they did remain separated gives us every reason to believe them. But as the *Chicago Tribune* noted, if the confession was not motivated by a reconciliation, and if she was not insane (the reporters who talked to her or to her friends did not think she was), there was no logical way to account for it.[15]

Henry Ward Beecher opted for the "crazy" explanation, and tried to laugh off the renewed press scrutiny by washing his hands of his former bosom friend. "'Poor woman!'" the *Times* quoted him as saying (based on an interview with a *Rochester Express* reporter). "She is the strangest combination I ever knew. You see her one time and you would think her a saint on earth; at another time she is a weak, irresponsible being and anything but a saint." Beecher, who like most of his cohort of white Americans found black accents and black ignorance especially funny, "said the confession reminded him of a story of a Negro waiter who was asked by a guest if it was the second bell for breakfast that had rung. 'No, Sah; it's not the second bell, it's de second ringin' ob de fust bell.'" In this maliciously chosen analogy, Elizabeth Tilton had no speech at all; her bell just kept ringing.[16]

She had enough speech, however, to reiterate her confession two months later to Plymouth Church's Examining Committee, appointed to decide whether to bar her from further fellowship. "I now repeat and reaffirm," she wrote on June 10, "that the acknowledgement of adultery with the Reverend Henry Ward Beecher, Pastor of Plymouth Church, was the truth and nothing but the truth, and that having previously published a false statement denying the charge, I desired to make the truth as world-wide as the lie had been." The two hundred members of the church who showed up for a special meeting on Friday, June 21, voted unanimously to accept the Committee's recommendation that she be excommunicated.[17]

In the wake of her confession the press pursued Mrs. Tilton for interviews, without success. A *Chicago Tribune* reporter surprised her at 278 Madison Street in Brooklyn, her mother Mrs. Morse's residence. "Mrs. Tilton answered the bell in person, and the reporter was quite astonished at the change in her appearance."

> Instead of the slight, delicate woman in unrelieved black whose haggard, pale face was frequently seen in Judge Neilson's courtroom during the progress of her husband's suit, there came to the door a plump, pretty little woman with rosy cheeks and bright eyes, a quick strong step and erect carriage. The morning gown had given place to a stylish, close-fitting dress of dark goods, plentifully ornamented with blue ribbons. There seemed to be a much greater proportion of gray in her naturally black hair than there was two years ago.

The reporter tried to engage her in conversation, but she "flushed violently and cast down her eyes." She confirmed that she had written the "card" herself before giving it to her lawyer, then asked "that the interview might not be continued."[18]

If we assume that in writing the confession Elizabeth Tilton was in her right mind and doing not Theodore's bidding but her own, how can we account for it? The biggest hurdle to explaining it is the effect an admission of adultery was liable to have on her children for the rest of their lives. They had to survive in a culture that cared a great deal whether one's mother was an adulteress. If she was guilty of the sin, and conscience-stricken, as she claimed, about withholding the truth, she nevertheless had a substantial stake in protecting her children. The *Chicago Tribune* reported that one of her friends, "a lady member of Plymouth Church," had barged into her house upon hearing of the confession and demanded that she explain herself. One of the friend's first questions concerned the children: had she told the oldest children, Florence and Alice (now about 21 and 19), before their recent departure for Europe? Yes, said Elizabeth, who was now "almost broken down . . . in a state of nervous excitement." Meanwhile, the *Tribune* printed a story from the Western Associated Press claiming that a Plymouth lady friend had received a letter in which Mrs. Tilton said "she did not think she should disclose [the confession] to Carroll [now 14 or 15] until he was a man." If she truly thought she could conceal the news from her teenaged son, even after a public confession, then she certainly would have thought she could keep it from her still younger son Ralph, who was eight. To judge from the press reports, therefore, Elizabeth thought her daughters could stand the news, perhaps in part because they were studying in Stuttgart, Germany, where (according to Theodore) they were to remain for the next three years. And she thought her sons could be kept in the dark.[19]

If Elizabeth and Henry did commit adultery, her confession is easy to explain: she was overcome with guilt and could not conceal the truth any longer. During the scandal she would have lied about the facts both to protect her family and to protect the cause of religion, which she identified with Beecher's continued success as a preacher. It would certainly make sense if Henry and Elizabeth, who were in a state of rapturous excitement in the late 1860s at their discovery of each other, had sexual intercourse. It would be surprising, under the circumstances, if they had not wanted to. But her confession can't be taken as hard evidence that they did have sexual relations, given her earlier changes of mind on the question. And there is another plausible way to explain her final story. By confessing to adultery she may, ironically, have been *better* able to protect the children than she had been between 1875 and 1878. Despite the hung jury at Beecher's trial, despite the technical finding of "not proven guilty" for Henry (and hence herself) on the adultery charge, their wrongdoing was still widely assumed. She had discovered in 1874 and 1875 that there was no shielding her children from the prying and hounding of the press and public, and the divided verdict had done nothing to stop the abuse. Her confession states that to God she commits herself, her children, and "all who must suffer," suggesting that her children and she were among those who must suffer—and they had already been suffering, well before this final confession.

Far better then to admit to adultery, if that would clear her conscience, since the confession would imply to those familiar with the scandal that she had acceded to sexual intimacy only when overwhelmed by Beecher's earnest entreaties (as she had at one time, according to Theodore, confessed to him). Her confession does not actually assert that she was victimized by Beecher, but she may well have sensed—given her earlier well-known account of being bossed around by Beecher as well as her husband—that the public would draw that inference. To confess to adultery with Beecher was in effect to deny once again and for all time her own responsibility, and therefore to invite the public to go easier on her children and perhaps herself.

There is every reason to take Elizabeth Tilton at her word when she said in her confession that she had suffered "long months of mental anguish" because of "the lie I had lived so well these last four years." What may have wracked her spirit was the half-conscious realization that the "truth" was much more complicated than any either-or statement on the adultery charge could possibly convey. There was a "lie" in every position she might adopt. She had loved Beecher, by her own admission—not just in the friendly way that she "loved" many men and women, but in the special way that one loves a person whom one knows uniquely and by whom one is uniquely known. She had delighted in his company, yearned to sit with him as he read to her and then listened avidly to *her* ideas. He appreciated her, she said in 1874, in a way that Theodore did not. She felt herself a different, and better, person with Henry. But all that and a good deal more can be true and she may still never actually have slept with him. She may have felt justified, therefore, in denying the adultery charge in 1874 and 1875 — and at that time she believed such a denial was essential for her family's well-being, and for Beecher's reputation.

Yet having publicly taken one side of the either-or position, she may have been tormented by the ensuing "lie," the burial of the truth that she had really loved her pastor, perhaps really desired him, perhaps actually touched him, or been touched by him, in some sexual manner that stopped short of intercourse, perhaps even been penetrated by Henry in some fashion in a murky scramble amidst the trousers and petticoats or bed linens, perhaps engaged with him in some mutually sought and pleasurable lovemaking. Had she simply been overwhelmed or coerced by him to the point of sexual intimacy, she might not have been so stricken in memory. The intensity of her anguish suggests that whatever actually happened between her and her pastor, a part of her had wished something to happen that counted, in her book, as a sin. A Christian as zealous as Elizabeth Tilton would have been devastated by an adultery even of the heart, and would have felt an intense compulsion to confess her sin.

The words of her confession may lend support to the idea that the truth, in her view, transcended any one answer to the adultery question. She said that in undoing the lie she had lived for four years, she would "leave the truth with God." Maybe she meant only that God would know she was telling the truth, and his opinion was all that mattered to her. But maybe she wished her phrase to mean that the truth in this instance was of a magnitude and complexity that only God *could* understand. Only his perspective was large enough, dispassionate and magnanimous enough, to encompass all the wrinkles of all the stories—stories more or less true, stories partially true, stories with slivers of truth in them—that had been and were still being told by herself and the two men she had loved.

Did it occur to her that since her life had been absurdly shaped by the reductive simplifications of the legal system, and the frenzied machinations of the "news" industry, the best way to do justice to the intricacy of her relationship with Beecher was to add a "yes" to her earlier "no" on the adultery charge—to leave her human judges at a loss, unable ever to solve the mystery of the scandal? Probably not. She was more worried about daily survival for herself and her children than she was about the interpretive quandaries of her detractors. But having decisively added a "yes" in 1878 to the "no" of 1874 and 1875, she had nothing further to say. She settled into what the *Brooklyn Eagle* obituary writer later called her "ceaseless activity in her small circle of acquaintances, which obviously was composed of those who would value her for her actual worth." [20]

In December 1878, six months after Elizabeth Tilton's excommunication from Plymouth Church, Henry Ward Beecher was riding in a train in New Hampshire when he noticed, two seats in front of him, the famously wavy locks of Frank Moulton. Moulton had been catapulted to national celebrity by the 1875 trial: everyone knew he had been a close friend of Theodore Tilton's from boyhood, and an intimate of Henry's in the early 1870s, when he and the Tiltons were attempting to keep a lid on compromising news about their private lives. During the trial he had been one of three key witnesses against Beecher, the other two being his wife Emma and Theodore. In April 1878, Moulton had been widely sought after by the press since he was the one well-known person (apart from Theodore) who believed Elizabeth Tilton was now telling the truth. In a *New York Times* paraphrase, he had said that

> for some time she was helpless under Mr. Beecher's influence, but the truth was in her, and she would have told it before if she had been free to do it. She is a religious fanatic, and so long as she believed she was protecting a saint she could say things that were not true. She is unlike Mr. Beecher in this respect. She believes in God and the angels, and when she speaks she feels that God is looking right at her. Mr. Beecher will swear by God and the angels, but he knows that God and the angels won't touch him.

Mrs. Tilton might lie for a time, in other words, but God's penetrating eye would eventually overcome even her devotion to a venerated saint like her pastor. Beecher, on the other hand, put himself on a godly pedestal where he was subject to no judgment but his own.

Half a year later, when Beecher caught his glimpse of Moulton on the train, he wrote a jocular but caustic note to his wife about the incident.

> Right before me, only an empty seat between, sits Frank Moulton, of radiant hair. . . . I am permitted to gaze upon his hyacinthine locks, his promontorial nose, his eyes, that glow like springs deep set in rocky nooks. How can I be enough grateful? . . . Could I be happier? Oh yes, if another were only here. If only my T. T. could complete this Trinity! It was a comfort to me to see on Moulton's wrists a pair of noble jasper medallion sleeve buttons which I gave him. It shows how tenderly he cherishes my memory, although circumstances [have] been somewhat against an open friendship.

Beecher's reference to the erstwhile "trinity" of male comrades would have called to his wife's mind—as it would to the mind of anyone who had followed the scandal—another threesome besides Beecher, Tilton, and Moulton. The other one—Beecher and the Tiltons—would also have made Henry wince in late 1878, only a few months after Mrs. Tilton's confession of adultery. From his standpoint in that year, he had

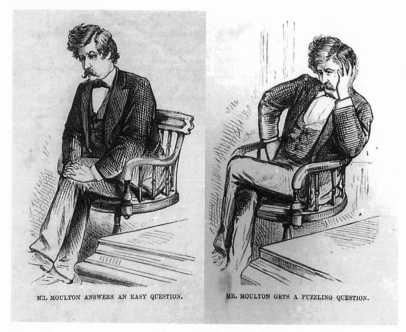

MR. MOULTON ANSWERS AN EASY QUESTION.   MR. MOULTON GETS A PUZZLING QUESTION.

Frank Moulton depicted by a Brooklyn courtroom artist in 1875.

been sucked into a destructive spiral a decade earlier when he became close to Theodore and Elizabeth. Skewering the idea of trinity in his bantering note to his wife was a way of reassuring her that he grasped the foolishness of both earlier adventures in triune friendship.[21]

V. In the summer of 1884, the Democratic Party nominated "reformer" Grover Cleveland, the Governor of New York, for the Presidency. Cleveland was widely heralded as spotless in all his political dealings, a marked contrast to the Republicans' nominee James G. Blaine, known for his active foreign policy as Secretary of State but also suspected of shady dealings with railroads. When Cleveland's nomination was announced, the good-government Republican "Mugwumps" ("big chiefs" in Algonquin) bolted to the Democrats. Henry Ward Beecher, to the dismay of many Plymouth Church Republicans, who associated the Democracy with Irish Catholic ward bosses, was among them.

Beecher may not have known, as Cleveland told Mrs. Beecher in a letter of sympathy upon her husband's death three years later, that as a young man in the 1850s, Cleveland had often heard him preach. Two years younger than Theodore Tilton, Cleveland was part of the stream of young Protestant migrants to the big city who found Beecher's church a haven of recognizable symbols. These were symbols, of course, made freshly palatable: Beecher's preaching, Cleveland said, "relieved the precepts of Christianity from gloom and cheerlessness." [22]

His sermons were also a catalogue of inspired advice. Invited to a memorial service for Beecher in 1903, the sixteenth anniversary of his death, Cleveland brought tears to the entire Academy of Music throng when he broke down recalling a Beecher sermon that had guided him throughout his life. Beecher had told a parable of two young men entering the world, one with "avaricious plans and sordid expectations," the other with "a light step and cheerful determination." Beecher's dichotomizing may seem simplistic and sentimental to a later generation, but the aging Cleveland's weeping remembrance of it in a public meeting in 1903 tells us a great deal about Beecher's hold on Cleveland's (and the Tiltons') generation—and about the severe character of the adjustment that generation had to make to a rapidly secularizing as well as industrializing society. Beecher's preaching challenged young men to keep an even keel in turbulent waters, and supplied indispensable comfort for their emotionally taxing voyage.[23]

Cleveland had another good reason to recall Beecher with favor. No sooner had the Mugwumps jumped ship to support him in 1884 than the press jumped on reports that Cleveland—the virtuous Christian from the provinces—had fathered a child out of wedlock and kept a succession of hired women in convenient proximity to the Governor's mansion in Albany. Cleveland immediately admitted he had an illegitimate son, but denied the rest of the allegations. Beecher at first let on that it might now be difficult to support the Governor, but an investigation by another minister set his mind at rest. Various advisers still cautioned him to stay well clear of Cleveland, but Beecher threw himself into the campaign with exuberant abandon. Maybe his support mattered: Cleveland won the election by winning New York, and he carried New York by 1149 votes.[24]

The investigation of Cleveland's personal life by the Rev. Kinsley Twining (a writer for the *Independent*) concluded that there had indeed been an "illicit connection" in Cleveland's bachelor days, the product of "a culpable irregularity of life . . . for which it was proper and is proper that he should suffer." On the other hand, there had been "no seduction, no adultery, no breach of promise, no obligation of marriage. . . . After the primary offense . . . his conduct was singularly honorable, showing no attempt to evade responsibility, and doing all he could to meet the duties involved, of which marriage was certainly not one." Cleveland's backers happily quipped that it was far better to elect a man who was pure in public and sullied in private than to choose a man like Blaine who was blemished in public and spotless in private. The latter sort should be returned to the private life in which he so obviously excelled.[25]

Beecher's response to Cleveland's scandal in 1884 was historically significant in helping him get elected, but it also tells us something about how the 71-year-old Plymouth pastor viewed his own scandal, a decade after the fact. In his political speeches for Cleveland, Beecher did not hesitate to cultivate sympathy for himself while seeking it for the governor. It is plain that he was still hurting from the trial and its persistent ripples of public mockery, doubt, and dismissal. His "Brooklyn Rink" speech on October 22 was a gifted stump performance, a bitter and satiric blast at Blaine and the Republicans. As he approached his conclusion, Beecher gave a dramatic reading of Cleveland's recent letter to his wife, in which the candidate owned up to his one youthful escapade but rejected charges of general carousing. "I am at a loss to know how it is that such terrible, wicked, and utterly baseless lies can be invented," wrote Cleveland. "The contemptible creatures who coin and pass these things appear to think that the affair which I have not denied makes me defenseless against any and all slanderers." Beecher ended by drawing the obvious parallel to his own passage through the fire of publicity.

> When in the gloomy night of my own suffering, I sounded every depth of sorrow, I vowed that if God would bring the day star of hope, I would never suffer brother, friend or neighbor, to go unfriended, should a like serpent seek to crush him. . . . I will stand against infamous lies that seek to sting to death an upright man and magistrate. Men counsel me to prudence lest I stir again my own griefs. No! I will not be prudent. If I refuse to interpose a shield of well-placed confidence between Governor Cleveland and the swarm of liars that nuzzle in the mud, or sling arrows from ambush, may my tongue cleave to the roof of my mouth, and my right hand forget its cunning. I will imitate the noble example set me by Plymouth Church in the day of my calamity. They were not ashamed of my bonds. They stood by me

with God-sent loyalty. It was a heroic deed. They have set my duty before me, and I will imitate their example.[26]

Beecher's 1927 biographer Paxton Hibben, whose book is an aggressive brief for Theodore Tilton, considers the Brooklyn Rink speech a confession by Beecher of his own adultery: "he could hardly have confessed his own transgression . . . in plainer words." Milton Rugoff's 1981 biography of the Beecher family suggests that Beecher may have sensed, on the contrary, that coming to Cleveland's aid would vindicate him retrospectively, for "how could anyone believe that he would dare to bring up the whole wretched affair again if he had been guilty?" Clifford Clark's 1978 biography argues that the speech "proved to himself and to the public that the scandal that had plagued his own name was dead and that his reputation had survived intact."[27]

It makes more sense, however, to see the speech, and Beecher's vigorous support for Cleveland, not as an implicit confession or denial of the charges in his own scandal, and not as proof the scandal was finally over, but as evidence of how deeply it was still eating away at him and of why it was still doing so. Cleveland's situation may have been irresistible to him not because of the ways his own case resembled it, but because of the ways it did not. Cleveland's case was much simpler: a young man's "indiscretion," an allegedly conscientious effort to provide for a child he was not even sure was his own, an apparent concern for a very troubled, alcoholic woman who ended up (at his urging) in an asylum and who, unlike the uncontrollable Elizabeth Tilton, did not keep changing her story. Even more importantly, as soon as his impropriety was made public, Cleveland owned up to it, whereas Beecher, along with the Tiltons, did not know what to say. It had been difficult for them even to decide what was improper about their relations, and how much of that—whatever it was—they could get away with keeping private, for the sake of the four Tilton children as well as themselves. Their multiple story lines were so hard to keep straight that they kept rewriting them to make them yield to understanding.

The most reasonable way to take Beecher's Brooklyn Rink speech in 1884 may be as a final attempt to simplify his own scandal, to make it, like Cleveland's, a straightforward case of serpents and liars nuzzling in the mud or slinging arrows from ambush. Maybe some of Cleveland's own present equanimity—his ability to put the "culpable irregularity" of his life in the past, where it belonged—would rub off on the still contorted Beecher. His plunge into the Cleveland campaign suggests that in the last years of his life he was tormented by the story in which he was the leading protagonist, a story that would not submit to the manipulative stratagems of any single storyteller. He was more innocent than Adam, who chose sin and was punished by expulsion from the garden. In Beecher's story the multiple serpents, lying in the mud and lying about the truth, simply attacked without reason. He was Adam, therefore, fused with Hamlet, driven to the edge by the realization that fortune had dealt him an unplayable hand. His "slings and arrows" were as undeserved as the Dane's. Like Hamlet, he felt powerless to avenge himself. What he could do, a decade after his own scandal, was help avenge Governor Cleveland, and vindicate himself, however partially, in retrospect.

In the face of modern journalistic assassination, Beecher realized, an individual was helpless. Only his "noble" congregation, unashamed of his "bonds" (his attachments, his chains, his position of impotence imposed by the conditions of modern celebrity?), had kept him from giving way, and only a similar shielding by loyal friends would preserve Governor Cleveland. He grasped his age as one of strangely dissolving selfhood: "I have ceased in some moods to have any actual self," he told his Congregational Council in 1876, "and am projected as an idea before my own mind." The attenuated heroism of such an age allowed only for banding together with fellow sufferers to withstand the unmerited attacks. His evocative imagery of swarming liars and concealed assailants, straight out of his father Lyman's antebellum vocabulary of moral emergency, did a good job of diverting attention from the exact provenance of the attacks. Which liars did he have in mind? Not just the press, surely, but his former intimates, the Tiltons and Moultons. Elizabeth Tilton had joined the enemy camp with a flourish in 1878. One wonders if he ever thought of her as a human temptress, one embodiment of the groveling serpent. In 1878 he called her "weak and irresponsible," "anything-but-saintly." Did she ever strike him, in his frequently fevered moments, as a weak and irresponsible Ophelia, or an anything-but-saintly Eve, who deserved the full blast of his scorn for seducing him with the fruit of the knowledge of her heart, then ambushing him to relieve her conscience? If he did, he never said so. Beecher said he was caught in a web of malicious publicity, not trapped by illusory, enticing promises. He would keep loving, since that was in his nature, even if it meant exposing himself to attack by cowardly evildoers.[28]

Theodore saw himself in his final story as a truth-teller who had been misunderstood, and he chose the path of exile. He abstained from blaming others. Henry took himself in his final story as an aggrieved innocent, barely hanging on to a stable sense of self. It had to be some- one else's fault. If Elizabeth heard about his Brooklyn Rink speech—she probably didn't read it, having sworn off newspapers years before—she quite likely prayed for Henry to cease looking for justification from men. Her final story was about leaving the truth to God.

DISCORD AMONGST THE ANGELS.

T——n.—"I say you did it!"　　　B——r.—"I say I didn't—now what are you going to do about it?"
Old Plymouth Lady.—"Drat it! these stains appear to be indelible."

"I see Tilton is out with a new 'Statement' which heaven forbid that I shd. read. Between the supposition of a villainy more fiendish than that of Iago & Richard III rolled into one on the part of Moultan [sic], or of a cheek and brazen genius for hypocrisy on Beecher's part almost as incredible, it seems hard to choose. Either horn of the dilemma is an improbability." William James, 1874.

THREE

Public Retellings,
1874

I. In 1874 Theodore Tilton decided he had had
enough—enough covering up the "criminal intimacy" (his phrase) between Beecher and his wife, enough turning the other cheek when he
was assailed for spreading rumors about it. In March, Yale's Dr. Leonard Bacon, an old evangelical ally of Lyman Beecher's, had taken part
in a Congregationalist assembly called to look into the state of affairs at
Plymouth Church—which had just formally dropped Tilton from its
rolls after one church member had charged him with slandering the
pastor. Henry had tried to stop the gathering wave of publicity before
it was too late: he told his congregation that he had no complaint to
utter about Theodore. But in a New Haven speech in April, Bacon
decided he had had enough of the behind-the-scenes warfare between
Tilton and Plymouth Church. To force matters into the open he insinuated that Tilton was a "knave" and a "dog." That horrific one-two
combination was too much for Theodore—or else he used the pretext
that it was too grave an insult for a man to take lying down. He demanded that Henry clear his name once and for all. When Beecher did
nothing, Tilton issued a lengthy document in June that threw down the
gauntlet.

> The common impression that I have circulated and promoted scan-
> dals against Mr. Beecher is not true. I doubt if any other man in
> Brooklyn, during the whole extent of the last four years, has spoken to
> so few persons on this subject as I have done. A mere handful of my
> intimate friends—who had a right to understand the case—are the
> only persons to whom I have ever communicated the facts.

Theodore's 1874 story about himself featured a discriminating story-teller—fully factual, and selective about his hearers. Tilton's June statement forced Beecher to act. He appointed a six-man Plymouth Church Investigating Committee to look into those "facts." The creation of the Committee compelled Elizabeth to choose sides. She chose Beecher.[1]

When Henry's handpicked body of Plymouth dignitaries exonerated him of any serious wrongdoing, the press clamored for an impartial judicial inquiry to weigh "all" the evidence. The result was the civil trial of 1875. Most of what we know about the experience of intimacy among Beecher and the Tiltons in the 1860s comes from the transcripts created in 1874 and 1875 by these two bodies, one private and one public, and from the ancillary interviews and statements and analyses published in response to them. Even the 1860s marital correspondence of the Tiltons was edited by Theodore in 1874 before publication. All of the principals struggled to remember, and to remold. Memory is always active, even when reputations are not on the line. In the Beecher-Tilton Scandal, memory was white-hot. Honor, and livelihoods, were at stake.

As we peel back the layers of documentary evidence in search of the early experience of intimacy, we get few hard facts and a lot of conflicting stories. But even an actual event, one that we know took place, can be very indeterminate, subject to slippage even at the moment it "happened." Consider the kiss that took place one evening in the late 1860s between Henry and Theodore. What kind of kiss was it? Their later testimony agreed that a kiss took place, but they did not concur about where it was planted. Theodore said Henry kissed him on the forehead. Not a chance, said Henry, it was on the lips. Our confusion about what this kiss meant may mirror their original experience of it. From the start it was an open field of interpretation. Meanings multiplied and shifted from the instant the kiss occurred, and they kept evolving later. By the mid-1870s they were probably both sure the other was wrong about the location of the kiss. The history of intimacy among Beecher and the Tiltons is the whole spread of these meanings and remembrances. The stories themselves, in all their contradictory splendor, are facts worth having. They speak volumes about these individuals and the cultural worlds they inhabited and incensed.[2]

At a personal level the chaotic charges and countercharges of 1874 amounted to a double battle: Theodore vs. Henry and Theodore vs. Elizabeth. And in the latter squaring-off Elizabeth defended herself tooth and nail. The spectacle of this spiritually vaunted Christian matron going for her husband's jugular, and of him striking back, was utterly unprecedented for Victorian audiences. The struggle between Beecher and Tilton was eye-opening and scandalous enough. The exchange of venom between husband and wife was benumbing—and irresistible. It was an event of cultural as well as personal import because it gave concrete narrative shape to a widely suspected upheaval in middle-class life. By erupting in public, dragging domestic secrets into the papers, the Tiltons exposed fissures that many observers considered a threat to the bedrock of bourgeois marriage. Theodore quoted liberally from Elizabeth's letters to him and wrote of "the weakness of her character." She lived at times "in a sort of vaporous-like cloud," and altogether lacked "a will that guides and restrains." Elizabeth countered that she "had been treated by my husband as a nonentity from the beginning, a plaything, to be used or let alone at will." "Surely," wrote E. L. Godkin in the *Nation*, "no scene in the amphitheatre was ever more shocking than the assault on each other in which Tilton and his wife have been engaged."

> His production of her letters, written in moments of happy and confiding if somewhat effusive tenderness, to justify his desperate attack on her reputation, and her bitter and incoherent imputation to him of all base and malignant passions, of meanness, falsehood, treachery, of envy, hatred, and malice—and all this under the eyes of millions of spectators, to whom the mutual rage and destruction of this unhappy couple gave but a keener relish for their breakfasts—what is there so horrible as this in the *spectacula* or the bull-fights? Is it not somewhat disgraceful to our civilization that such quarrels should have to be fought out in this way, that we should have to protect domestic happiness and purity by inviting the whole world to see the Furies tearing a household to pieces?[3]

A few weeks after the story broke, the press started protesting the very "trial by newspaper" that had sold so many copies of their product. For Beecher and the Tiltons were using the papers to air their captious denunciations and denials, and the papers naturally felt they were being used. A never-ending series of "statements," they realized, was a dead-end. Readers wanted to know which, if any, were true. So the newspapers appealed for a legal inquiry. A trial was necessary not for its verdict but for its powers of subpoena and cross-examination: a court could get more facts and dispose of more rumors. The ultimate verdict would still be rendered by "the community," as Godkin noted, not by the jurors. "When the community exalts a man as it has exalted Mr. Beecher, it insists on deciding in the last resort whether its confidence has been misplaced." The community as jury-of-the-whole would in effect use the trial as its own star witness, collect whatever additional testimony the newspapers could pick up through interviews or inquiries, then deliver the final judgment on Beecher's character.[4]

The trial happened because Theodore filed a lawsuit in a Brooklyn court, but the causation is more complex. Some wider entity, some amorphous but very real social body—"public opinion," informed "society," Godkin's undefined "community"—"wanted" and "needed" a trial, and this need was broader than the newspapers' craving for sales (the *New York Graphic* sold as many as 400,000 copies of key printings, and other papers realized similar bonanzas). Theodore did the culture's as well as his own work, though he was probably conscious only of defending his honor against his two attackers. From Godkin's standpoint, Theodore and Elizabeth were of no interest. Giving them ink was a deplorable diversion from the vital issue: determining the fate of the sole figure of "influence and celebrity." "We now beg to remind the editors of the daily papers," he wrote,

> that their sole justification for serving us up every day such a quantity of unwholesome gossip and speculation lies in the fact that the person whose reputation is assailed in it is a man of great prominence and respectability. . . . The public is not sufficiently interested in Mr. Tilton, and he does not occupy, and never has occupied, a sufficiently prominent place in the community, to entitle him to this species of notoriety. His domestic history is not a public concern. . . . It can serve no purpose beyond deepening the flood of indecency which is already flowing over the country. . . . [The community] cares nothing and wants to know nothing about Tilton's morals or religious opinions, or about his relations with "advanced thinkers" of the female sex.[5]

Godkin knew very well what "the public" was "interested in"— shocking and entertaining revelations of family disintegration and clerical shenanigans. He was urging the public to come to *its* senses and leave the private realm (as well as "advanced" ideas about gender relations) alone. But he missed the point that Beecher's whole public career had been devoted to dissolving the line between the private and the public, so as to revitalize the same culture of "character" that Godkin championed. It was Beecher's intersecting private and public life that mattered to *him*, that constituted the terrain of growth, in his view, for "personality" and "character." For Beecher (and his disciples Theodore and Elizabeth) "love" could not be divorced from "duty." Love was the highest duty. Bonds between individuals must be intensely felt as well as socially correct; a morally stable society needed citizens who were passionate as well as obedient. The wide public educated by Beecher since the 1840s could not be faulted for caring deeply about his private relations with the Tiltons, for wondering who the Tiltons really were and what his life with them had really been like. Why had he cared so fiercely about this young couple, not to mention becoming intimate with the far murkier Frank Moulton, an unchurched man of the world? There was moral and religious meaning to be found there, not just a titillating bath in Godkin's "flood of indecency."

II. On Sunday morning, June 7—seven weeks before Theodore formally charged Henry with debauching his wife—the *Chicago Tribune*'s New York correspondent (the anonymous "Most") made his "annual pilgrimage" to Plymouth Church. He found the place unchanged. "The same simple reading-stand, made of wood brought from sacred lands; the same beautiful basket or pyramid of flowers rising at one side of the platform, with a fragrant bouquet standing on the desk; the same soft hat thrown carelessly beside the chair." The only change was in the chair's occupant. The "scandal" provoked by Victoria Woodhull's accusation of adultery in 1872 had given Beecher "bitter days and nights" and aged him considerably. "His hair is grayer—so much so that it startles one who has not seen him for an interval." But more striking for "Most" was how Henry hadn't changed.

> He takes up the little Bible—he never uses one of the huge gilt affairs—and reads, in a low, far-reaching voice, a selection of Scripture. The charm of that sweet, impressive, simple utterance, once heard, can never be lost. . . . There is no affectation or display in his reading. It is done in the most familiar and unpretentious way, but there is in his simplicity more power and feeling than in the forced and ambitious elocution of the most famous readers. His prayers are offered in the same reverent, modulated tone. . . . They are always supremely sympathetic. They seem so in harmony with the day and the hour, so fraught with the essence of praise, so warmed by the sunlight and perfumed with the flowers, that women weep tears of pure joy.[6]

On the sermon itself "Most" made the by-then-formulaic observations that Beecher ranged wondrously through humor, pathos, condemnation, and celebration, put parables into scintillatingly conversational form (and flawlessly acted out the various characters in them), drew on a rich diction that included "many old and quaint words . . . which are probably derived from his reading in the early divines, of whom he is said to be a close student." But "Most" noted that Beecher had mastered technical, commercial language too.

> Whether speaking gravely, or jocosely, or vehemently, one thing is apparent which will explain to you one great secret of his power, and that is his practical knowledge. He [has] stored his mind with the details of men's trades and businesses, the technical terms of the mechanic arts. . . . In the sermon I heard he used as illustrations the sailing of a ship, the plowing of a farm, and the cutting of a diamond. . . . The man who comes fresh from his shop or office, and hears this student using the terms of his daily work with as much apparent familiarity as if he worked side by side with him, admires him and is drawn to him.

Beecher was avid about life, a sponge for new experience, and serious about work. His Romantic sentiment and oratorical prowess explain only part of the stir he caused among his hearers. There was also his very concrete enthusiasm about their workaday lives. "He once said," observed "Most," "that he never met a man from whom he could not learn something." Henry's "sympathy" was a kind of knowledge as well as feeling. His desire for intimacy was joined to a craving for information and a veneration of skill. We are so used to seeing Beecher as the advocate of leisure, who advised workaholic parishioners to smell the flowers or spend a day in the woods, that we are liable to miss his embrace of production and expertise. And we are so accustomed to viewing him as a sentimental "feminizer" of religion that we are apt to miss his "masculinizing": his self-conscious effort to bring men into the church by addressing their work lives and by speaking to their deeply felt (and in the 1870s very male) dilemma, that of reconciling their desire for virtue with their drive for worldly success.[7]

It was Beecher's quest for knowledge as well as intimacy that drew Theodore and Elizabeth to him at the start. He singled the two of them out, in succession, for special attention. He appears to have recognized in each an ardor that resembled his own. Theodore was his precocious apprentice at the *Independent* in the late 1850s, and director of the Plymouth Church Sunday School. "His mind was opening freshly," Henry recalled, "and with enthusiasm upon all questions. I used to pour out my ideas of civil affairs, public policy, religion, and philanthropy." Elizabeth was his appreciative but forthright critic in the late 1860s as he read her his manuscript pages from *The Life of Christ* and *Norwood*. Whatever else may have happened when they were together, they also worked. Theodore confirmed that Elizabeth's reading sessions with Henry were a joint labor of production. "She was one of the best of critics," he said. "She never praised an article because it was . . . his, but only when she liked it." With Theodore and then with Elizabeth, the gift of intense knowing and feeling was reciprocal. Each friend saw his or her own best self—they called it their "highest" or "purest" self—reflected in the other.[8]

III. Mrs. Tilton was the most articulate of them all about this deliverance, perhaps because her voyage of self-discovery was the longest, and the most treacherous. She testified at great length to the Plymouth Church Investigating Committee on July 31—after she and Theodore had spoken privately to the Committee (she on July 8 and he on July 10), after she had finally separated from him (on July 11), after his published attack on Henry and her as adulterers (on July 21), and after Henry's and her initial responses to that attack (on July 22 and 23, respectively). Her oral remarks on July 31 contain an eloquent testament to the power of friendship to reawaken selfhood. She called that power "love" and "friendship" interchangeably, as she did in her public "card" of July 23, which spoke of "my love to my friend and pastor."[9]

The immediate context for her reflections about Henry was the Committee's concern about the "*Griffith Gaunt*" letter she had written her husband from Schoharie, New York, in 1871, in which she confessed that she had sinned in her knowing of Beecher. It was a potential bombshell because unlike the other most incriminating letters, this one was written with no coaching or coercion from Theodore. The letter was now a public item, since Theodore had reproduced it in his statement of July 21. It was "perfidy," "sacrilege," to try "to make my own words condemn me," Elizabeth had said publicly two days later of his publishing excerpts from eleven of her letters to him. She had seen nothing yet: in August he would publish an entire treasury of two hundred of their love letters in the *Chicago Tribune*. The "*Griffith Gaunt*" letter began as follows:

> Today, through the ministry of Catharine Gaunt, a character of fiction, my eyes have been opened for the first time in my experience, so that I see clearly my sin. It was when I knew that I was loved, to suffer it to grow to a passion. A virtuous woman should check instantly an absorbing love. But it appeared to me in such false light. That the love I felt and received could harm no one, not even you, I have believed

unfalteringly until four o'clock this afternoon, when the heavenly vision dawned upon me.[10]

"Had you at that time any reference to adultery, or thought of it?" queried a committeeman. "No, sir," Elizabeth said. "What did you refer to?" "I will try to answer that question." She answered with a side-stepping reflection. "The one absorbing feeling of my whole life has been Theodore Tilton; neither Mr. Beecher, I assure you, nor any human being, has ever taken away from that one fact, my love for him." It was essential groundwork for the emerging legal case (and for her own well-being) to establish that her love for Henry had never rivaled her love for her husband. It was also important for her to go on record as having had many other "friends," male and female. "I felt very great helpfulness in my own soul from having had the friendship of Mr. Beecher, and also of other people, as many women as men." These opening remarks were not just about laying legal foundations. If the Committee wished to understand her tie to Henry or anyone else, they had to reckon with the complex love she felt for and shared with her husband.

The gentlemen steered her back to the question at hand. "In your Schoharie letter you spoke of your 'sin.' What did you mean by that?" "Theodore's nature being a proud one," she said, "I felt, on reading that book [Griffith Gaunt], that I had done him wrong, that I had harmed him in taking anyone else in any way, although, on looking it over, I do not think but that I should do it again, because it has been so much to my soul." Her roundabout response was bewildering to the Committee, which kept trying to get a direct answer. "Taking any one else in what respect?" wondered a committeeman. "I do not think if I had known as much as I do now of [Mr.] Tilton that I should ever have encouraged Mr. Beecher's acquaintance; I think I did wrong in doing it, inasmuch as it hurt Theodore." The committeeman must have scratched his head, musing on the wandering female or mystical mind. But Elizabeth was only warming up for her hymn to friendship with Henry—who was not just one friend among many, after all:

I do not know as I can make myself understood; but do you know what I mean when I say that I was aroused in myself—that I had a self-assertion which I never knew before with Theodore; there was always a damper between me and Theodore, but there never was between me and Mr. Beecher; with Mr. Beecher I had a sort of consciousness of being more; he appreciated me as Theodore did not; I felt myself another woman; I felt that he respected me; I think Theodore never saw in me what Mr. Beecher did.

Liking what he heard, a committeeman gave her a supportive prompt: "Do you mean to say that Theodore put down self-respect in you while Mr. Beecher lifted it up?" "Yes," she replied, "I never felt a bit of embarrassment with Mr. Beecher, but to this day I never could sit down with Theodore without being self-conscious and feeling his sense of my inequality with him."

The Committee tried again for a pithy answer: "Will you state, in a few words, what was that sin which you spoke of in that letter?" Again she gave them a both-and response. "I do not think that I felt that it was anything more than giving to another what was due to my husband—that which he did not bring out, however." Another committeeman: "Do you mean that you thought you let your affections, or your regard, or your respect, go out for Mr. Beecher unduly, and so censured yourself?" "No, sir," she answered. "I do not think I ever felt that, because I did not think I harmed Theodore in that; I harmed him in his pride by allowing any one else to enter into my life at all; I think that was sin." Her sin, she thought, lay not in *undue* affection—not in some excess of passion or attachment—but in the initial reception, the first opening of the gate to her heart. That act of welcome had disrupted the surrender of her self to Theodore, a surrender required not by law or custom or morality, in her view, but by his "pride."

In her testimony Elizabeth refused to limit herself to the narrow issue of sex, or to the narrow logic of either-or, sin or not-sin. Perhaps she was simply confused. Perhaps she was thrown by the fact that she had indeed had sex with Beecher and couldn't speak of it. Perhaps she was blocked by the knowledge that she and Henry had done something physical together that wasn't quite sex but wasn't quite not-sex either. Perhaps she had an insight into the tragic tangle of love and friendship in which she or her husband—or both—had been destined to suffer. What she voiced was clear enough, but it was a paradox: her sin resided in her assertion of self in the first place, and yet this assertion of self might not be a sin at all. It depended on how one held her action up to the light. If it were a sin, she believed she would quite likely sin all over again, however much she might wish not to hurt her husband.

The Committee's abortive quest for a straight answer provoked Mrs. Tilton to make another claim about herself and her husband, one that helps us see the full sweep of her attachment to Henry. "When you speak of your sin," a committeeman asked, "you do not mean to be understood as going further than that ['than allowing any one else to enter into my life at all']?" "No," she replied. "Let me tell you a little more."

Theodore, up to that time, in his accusations, would often talk to me by the hour to show me the effect that he said he knew I carried about my personal presence with gentlemen, and I would become nearly crazy in my conscience; he would say that he knew there was no one who carried such an influence as I did; I would say, 'Theodore, I do not think that is a fact; if I did, I would never speak to another man in all my life.'

"Did he define that influence?" wondered a member of the Committee. "He said I had a sensual influence," she answered. "I used to become impregnated with this idea of his myself while under his influence, and I wondered if it was so, and would think it over and over; he would often talk to me in that way by the hour, and try to persuade me that it was true; and then, when I used to get out from under his influence, I was perfectly sure that no man ever felt that way toward me." Theodore's own fears about her person—that her vivacity was a come-on to other men—sent her reeling into self-doubt. That spinning state made the deliverance announced by friendship with Beecher all the more urgently attractive. He could free her, she imagined, from the ordeal of "influence" altogether—from her husband's constraining power and from the spectre of her own sensual allure. She would be free of arbitrary human controls, subject to God's scrutiny alone.

A final set-up question by the Committee: "Was there in the sin which you referred to anything that was unjust, or that was giving to Mr. Beecher any affection that belonged to your husband?" "No, sir; I think that the wifely feeling which I gave to my husband was [as] pure as anything that I could give him; there was nothing more than confidence and respect which I gave to Mr. Beecher, and I teach my daughters that if they give to their husbands what I have given to mine they will do enough." The committeemen must have squirmed, for it did Beecher's cause no good for her to imply that she had given Theodore only some grudging minimum of devotion. They let her continue, and their patience was rewarded as she returned to Theodore's fears and their crushing impact upon her.

"I would like to have you, gentlemen, realize how very severe that was to me, because it has been day after day and week after week—the hearing that that was the effect of my presence upon persons; it made me sick and caused me to distress myself; it kept me in embarrassment; it was a hard thing to live under." Theodore's criticism of her sensual presence extended to her body itself. When they were entertaining at home, or out together at public events, "I was so insignificant that he was ashamed of me; and I remember perfectly in two or three instances of going to hotels, where my being short of stature was a dreadful trial to him. . . . I would have cut off my right arm to have been five inches taller; he seemed to be unwilling that I should be as the Lord made me." [11]

Elizabeth's love for Theodore, by her 1874 account, was interwoven with a longing to escape his judgment and the "impregnating" of that judgment within her. She had been turning against herself, making his viewpoint her own, forcing her very real love for him into the warped channel of assuaging him, and protecting them both from what she considered the sinful assertion of her self. After Henry took an interest in her, friendship with him promised release from the downward spiral of self-vilification and love-as-appeasement. With an assist from Henry, she thought, self-creation could replace the self-erasure with which she placated Theodore. Henry had the power to make her believe that her sin was no sin at all. If Elizabeth was making an accurate assessment of the psychic forces at play, Theodore would have taken Henry as a mortal threat. For Henry would have been doing much more than "alienating affections." He would have been tampering with an intricate system of love and loathing, in which Elizabeth loved Theodore and loathed herself.

Mrs. Tilton was a double-edged sword for the Investigating Committee and its creator Henry Ward Beecher. They had to use her to slice up her husband, but they had to shield Henry from accidental slashing. Elizabeth alone could destroy Theodore's credibility. Yet she was a confessed liar: under his "mesmeric" influence, she claimed, she would say or write anything. How could the Committee guard against the quite logical deduction that under Beecher's influence or the Committee's she might also be lying? First, by drawing her out on the horrible evil (and absolute uniqueness) of Theodore's mind-control over her, and second, by encouraging her to get away from him. If Theodore had had hypnotic power over her, as she alleged—and as the Committee's "medical testimony" attested was "not infrequent" and "consistent with an honest mind"—then her testimony, given two weeks after she escaped his irresistible authority, could be trusted. On the same day (July 11) that Beecher had announced the creation of the Investigating Committee, Elizabeth had awakened Theodore to tell him she was moving out. "I rose quietly," she wrote in her public card of July 23, "and having dressed, roused him only to say: 'Theodore, I

will never take another step by your side. The end has indeed come!'"
She went to stay with Maria and Edward Ovington, Plymouth Church
stalwarts, and never lived with Theodore again.[12]

In the fall the *Boston Journal* reported that Mrs. Tilton had become a
recluse. Even before leaving her husband in July she had abandoned
her weekly Sunday afternoon song-leading at the "Christian Association rooms" and given up her "general Christian work." She was still
at 143 Hicks Street, the Ovingtons' home, and her children were staying in New Jersey with her mother. Hicks Street was six substantial
blocks west, toward the East River, from the Tiltons' Livingston Street
home. She was now in the heart of Brooklyn Heights, with its brick
Greek Revival homes from the 1820s and 1830s, and its quiet gaslit
streets. Yet even there she was pursued and "greatly annoyed by the curious who crowded on her privacy. She went from place to place, and
was even called by another name to escape attention. But all in vain."
The press joined the gawkers in invading her privacy. Rebuffed in their
attempts to get an interview, the papers focussed on locating a picture. "The greatest effort has been made to get a correct likeness of
Mrs. Tilton. One house offered $1,000 for a photograph. There are but
two known ones in existence. One of these Mr. Tilton has, and keeps on
his parlor mantel. When anyone speaks of his wife, he takes it down
and shows it. The other is held by a distinguished New York photog-
rapher. He has resisted the glittering offer for the picture. He regards
the disposal of it as a breach of faith that would hurt his business."

But what *does* she look like, *Boston Journal* readers still wished to know.
"Nothing that has appeared gives the slightest idea of this now famous
woman," wrote the reporter. "She is a small, fragile woman, dark com-
plexion, low in stature, girlish in look, her hair parted in the centre and
falling in ringlets behind—looking more like a school-girl of 18 than a
matron of 40." Beecher made an identical assessment in his testimony
to the Investigating Committee, but he saw character reflected in physique. "Childish in appearance, she was childlike in nature." Her spiritual purity emanated from this youthful innocence. He should be forgiven, he thought, for failing to notice the gradual transformation of
her interest in him from "due" to "undue" attachment. "I would as
soon have misconceived the confidence of her little girls as the unstud-
ied affection she showed me." For Beecher there was nothing wrong
with the original attachment that had suddenly struck Elizabeth, on the
afternoon of June 29, 1871, as sinful. Her complex and still evolving
story concerned a sin that paradoxically bestowed new life. Guilt and

innocence, remorse and renewal, were mysteriously but undeniably entwined. His simpler story was about a spontaneous affection that she allowed, gradually and tragically, to spin out of control. Like Theodore's, Henry's 1874 story about himself was a tale of faultlessness.[13]

IV.   Publishing Elizabeth's private letters may have been perfidious and sacrilegious, as she asserted, but the excerpts Theodore included did suggest he was not just the manipulative ogre that she (with the Committee's encouragement) had depicted. When he published excerpts of 201 of their letters in the August 13 issue of the *Chicago Tribune,* it became even clearer that Elizabeth's testimony was at the very least one-sided. Her cross-examination emphasized her self-loathing, and Theodore's failures as husband, father, friend, and journalist. It omitted her eager devotion to him and his charisma, generosity, stamina, and inventiveness—all amply documented in the letters. His excerpting of the letters was of course one-sided too, even if he did include much evidence of his mental fragility, a condition that made Elizabeth cleave to him all the more. But their love, at least in the late 1860s, and at least during the long separations that produced the amorous letter exchanges, had been much more passionate and enthralling to Elizabeth than she could concede, or remember, in the summer of 1874.

In her cross-examination there was a single glimmer of the ease and humor of the good times. "Literary people came to the house," she said. "They would sometimes call in his absence, and when he came home I would laughingly tell him so and so had been there during the day, and he would ask, 'What did you have to say?' I would reply, 'Well I am a first-rate listener if they are good talkers; if not, I am a good chatterer myself.'" The Committee quickly steered her back to deprecating Theodore. "Did you understand that he said that as an expression of doubt as to your ability to entertain people?" "Yes, sir; there is not a shadow of doubt of it; I have lived under that always; he was very critical about my language; when under Theodore's influence I do not think I ever said anything freely or naturally." But her comment to him about listening and chattering was itself utterly natural. And it was no more a direct answer to his question than her responses to the Committee were. Her mind ran on a different track. She answered not the literal question that was asked, but the much more capacious question that would have been asked had the inquirer wished to know what she thought was most significant about the matter at hand.[14]

Theodore's extravagantly detailed public statements of July 21 and September 18 (the former his written offering to the Committee, the latter a forty-thousand-word response to Beecher's own lengthy document of August 13) assembled documents and arguments like infantry on a battlefield. "There is one thing that I was born for," he told the Committee, "and that is war." His texts and oral comments were blistering on Beecher. "This desperate man must hold himself only, and not me, accountable for the wretchedness which these disclosures will carry to his own home and hearth as they have already brought to mine." Theodore did volunteer to the Investigating Committee that in his early life "I loved that man as well as I ever loved a woman." But that sentiment was swamped by a torrent of antipathy. Beecher was "damnable": "he ought to spend the rest of his life in penitence and anguish." Henry's worst crime, of course, was the alleged adultery. But in September 1874, Tilton was even more incensed by the abuse to which he believed Beecher had just subjected Elizabeth.

> I know no words of measured moderation in which to characterize fitly Mr. Beecher's recent treatment of this broken-hearted lady, whom he has flung against the wall of Plymouth Church and dashed to pieces. First, he instituted a public committee to inquire into her adultery with him, whereas he ought to have protected her against this exposure; then he beckoned her away from her husband's house, making her very flight bear witness to her guilt; then he suborned her to give false testimony against her husband, with a view to destroy him before the world; then, with unparalleled baseness, he turned upon the companion of his crime and accused her of having been the tempter rather than the tempted—declaring that she had "thrust her affections upon him unsought." . . . All this base and brutal conduct by Mr. Beecher towards Mrs. Tilton prompts me to speak of him in fierce and burning words. But I forbear. "Vengeance is mine, I will repay, saith the Lord." I have become so used to sorrows in my own life that I cannot wish for their infliction upon another man, not even on my worst enemy. I will not ask the public to visit upon Mr. Beecher any greater condemnation for the desolation which he has brought upon those who loved, trusted, and served him, than I have in past times seen him suffer from his own self-inflicted tortures in contemplation of the very crime for which he has now been exposed to the scorn and pity of the world. I know well enough how his own thoughts have bowed him in agony to the dust; and this is enough. Wherefore, in contemplating my empty house, my scattered children, and my bro-

ken home, I thank Heaven that my heart is spared the pang of this man's remorse for having wrought a ruin which not even Almighty God can repair.[15]

Theodore was still, in his own mind, his wife's designated protector.

I shall believe to the end of my life that Elizabeth Tilton is a woman of pure heart and mind, sinned against rather than sinning, yielding only to a strong man's triumph over her conscience and will, and through no wantonness or forwardness of her own. I have been told that I endanger my success in the battle which I am now fighting, by making this concession to my wife's goodness of motive. But I am determined in all this controversy to speak the exact truth in all points; and I know that no indelicacy in Mrs. Tilton's behavior ever proceeded from her own voluntary impulse or suggestion; but that, on the contrary, her highly emotional religious nature was made by her pastor the means whereby he accomplished the ruin of his confiding victim.[16]

In his own eyes Theodore was so devoted to the exact truth in all points that he forthrightly exposed to the Investigating Committee his own intricate way of proceeding as a truth-teller. It was perfectly all right, he told them, to convey the exact opposite of the truth as long as your words, technically considered, did not lie. A committeeman had asked how Tilton could reconcile all his professions of his wife's "purity" with his accusation that she had committed adultery. "I have always had a strange technical use of words," he replied. He gave an example. If someone asked him directly if Elizabeth was "pure" (asked, that is, if she had committed adultery), he might say to them, "Go and ask Mr. Beecher himself and he will say that she is as pure as gold"— leaving his auditor persuaded that Theodore thought so too, when in fact he did not. If his listener made an incorrect inference, it would be his own fault for not being as technical in receiving information as Tilton was in transmitting it.

At least one committeeman still didn't grasp the point. "Did you not say that she was pure?" "No," said Theodore. (He had only said she had a pure heart, not that she "was" pure.) Again the committeeman: "Did you not use expressions which you intended to be understood as meaning the purity of the woman?" "I did, exactly. There are many ways in which you can produce such impressions, and I have written this document [the sworn statement he had just read to them] to produce the same impression." Of course by pulling back the curtain to

67

reveal his stratagem, he was tossing Elizabeth to the lions—letting everyone know she wasn't pure after all. But he would not actually say, even now, that she was impure. He would only take the slowest committeeman by the hand so that he could infer it. His technical truth-telling remained intact even as he unveiled its workings.[17]

Tilton went on to tell the Committee that his six-hundred-page novel *Tempest-Tossed*, published in early 1874, was another self-conscious effort at managing the public's view of Elizabeth. He had created a character, Mary Vail, to stand (in "veiled" form) for his wife. To make the match as perfect as possible, he attributed to Mary actual passages from letters Elizabeth had written to him. Art would not imitate life, but partake freely of it.

"I had this feeling," he said to the Committee, "that if in this novel I could . . . paint that character, and have it go quietly, in an under-handed way, forth, that that was Elizabeth (for I think I drew it faith-fully) it would be a very thorough answer, as coming from me, to the scandals in the community, and that people would say, 'Theodore respects his wife,' as I do today." Written during calendar 1873 (after Victoria Woodhull's published accusation of November 1872), *Tempest-Tossed* was supposed to convey the impression that Elizabeth was pure since Mary was, and to demonstrate that Theodore, author of the glowing portrait, held his wife in high esteem. He would not have to lie to whiten Elizabeth's public image; Mary Vail would do the whitewashing for him. Fiction was a perfect instrument for the indirections of Tilton's technical truth-telling. He followed the "veiled" springtime publication of phrases from Elizabeth's letters in *Tempest-Tossed* with the summer-time unveiling of major excerpts in the *Chicago Tribune*.[18]

The same sense of honor that compelled Tilton never to lie also forced him to take the battle to the enemy's home ground: Henry's relationship with his wife Eunice. In an "ordinary controversy," attacking one's antagonist's wife would be out of bounds, Theodore thought, but "the truth constrains me to do so now." For Henry had said in his August statement that his home, unlike Tilton's, had been, "in times of adversity, a refuge from the storm and a tower of defense." On the contrary, Theodore contended, Beecher's house "was more often the storm itself, from which he sought refuge in mine." Henry had "a wife who was not a mate."

> He often pictured to Mrs. Tilton the hungry needs of his heart, which he said Mrs. Beecher did not supply. . . . He used to pour in my ears unending complaints against his wife. . . . He said to me one day,

'O Theodore, God might strip all other gifts from me if he would only give me a wife like Elizabeth and a home like yours.' . . . Many of his relatives stand in fear of this woman, and some of them have not entered her house for years—as one of Mr. Beecher's brothers lately testified in a public print. I have seen from one of his sisters a private letter concerning the marital relations of Mr. and Mrs. Beecher which it would be scandalous to reproduce here. . . . I know that my allusion to Mr. Beecher's home-life is rough and harsh, but I know also that it is true.[19]

Tilton's assault on Eunice—complete with a proclamation of adherence to high standards of propriety, which prevented him from saying more about the alleged letter on the Beechers' marital relations, but did not prevent him from mentioning it—reminds us that there was one truly silent party in the Beecher-Tilton scandal of 1874–1875. Elizabeth was barred from speaking in court, but Eunice was silent throughout. Her avoidance of the press was not from lack of interest or involvement. In August 1874 she was holding down the fort, "keeping watch and ward," as she wrote to her daughter Hattie, "that no one gets access to father or *interviews* anyone." Henry took off for their Peekskill, New York, "farm" on the weekend of August 9–10, 1874, leaving Eunice to fend off newsmen and hunt among his papers for documents he would need. She was also fending off her sister-in-law Harriet Beecher Stowe, who had arrived to lend a hand. She "makes my work much harder," Eunice wrote. "She can't understand that till father has a chance to be heard we allow no talk to anyone that comes inside our door. . . . 'Oh let me go, I'll soon settle it,' she exclaims, when she hears me badgered by reporters as I stand in the door preventing their entrance."

Mrs. Beecher had been struggling to keep Mrs. Stowe quiet and laboring to open her husband's eyes to the "naked depravity" of "both Tilton and Moulton." "It has been hard work," she wrote to her daughter, "to convince the dear guileless simple-hearted man that such baseness and treachery could exist save in the most sensational novels. . . . after one or two days of sharpest agony—equal to that which a young maiden ever felt when her idol lay shattered before her—the noble old *Lion* roused himself. He now shakes his mane *and paws*." Eunice was Henry's strident defender, but her letter also discloses some of the hurt she felt at being further from the center of action than Frank Moulton, the "mutual friend" who had collected the key Tilton and Beecher letters for safekeeping. "*Safekeeping!! Safekeeping*," she wrote, "as if he, the infernal villain, would be a safer repository than I, father's wife."[20]

Taking the gloves off with Eunice can hardly have helped Tilton in the court of public opinion, but he was certainly right about the distance between her and her husband. Henry had kept her in the dark about the gravity of his situation, including money problems stemming from aid he was dispensing to the Tiltons. For some time he had been telling her to reduce expenses, she told her daughter, but she had only recently discovered why. "Now is explained his stern appeals to me to . . . economize. He was on the verge of financial ruin and he was just finding out that his sympathies had carried him too far and well nigh brought his family to poverty." In his own published cross-examination Beecher confirmed that for years he couldn't speak to her about the scandal. Trying to account for the near-suicidal despair expressed in one of his 1872 letters, he explained that the one person on earth to whom he could talk about the whole affair, Frank Moulton, seemed at that moment to be rebuffing him. In the best of times being found "irksome" by anybody was "enough to kill me," Henry said. But "to be treated so by him at that time made it seem to me as though the end of the world had come. . . . I was shut up to every human being. I could not go to my wife, I could not go to my children, I could not go to my brothers and sisters, I could not go to my church." Theodore was correct about the gap between Henry and Eunice. Maybe that split was one cause of Henry's interest in Elizabeth. But there was no reason to doubt that the Beecher brownstone—with a vigilant Eunice slapping him into consciousness of dire threats—was "a tower of defense." Eunice appears to have had something in common with Theodore: she was "born for war" herself.[21]

Tilton, by his own account, was fully aware of what a fierce antagonist Mrs. Beecher could be. His attack on her may have been "constrained" by his loyalty to the truth, but it was also payback for what he considered her long-standing "conspiracy" against him. Theodore believed that after confessing her adultery to him, Elizabeth confessed it also to her mother, Mrs. Morse. In Theodore's scenario, Mrs. Morse, concerned above all to protect Elizabeth from exposure, forged an alliance with Mrs. Beecher to try to discredit him—so that any charge he might make against Elizabeth (and therefore against Henry) would fall on disbelieving ears. The two conspirators went beyond speaking ill of him, according to Theodore. When Elizabeth left him briefly in 1870 and took refuge at her mother's, Eunice appeared on the scene to recommend (with Henry's accord) that Elizabeth seek a legal separation.[22]

Whatever truth there may have been in Tilton's theory of a Mrs. Beecher–Mrs. Morse conspiracy against him (Henry's 1875 story about the recommended separation contradicted Theodore's), there was no doubt about Eunice's feelings towards him. She detested Theodore and wouldn't allow him in her house. It was more than dislike: she considered him a threat to Beecher's and therefore to her own and her family's well-being (she must have thought the same of Mrs. Tilton). Maybe the day finally came when Henry granted that his wife was the prescient one, and that he had put her in jeopardy. One of the prime ironies in the showdown between Theodore and Henry is that they were cut in so many ways from the same cloth. Each, for example, had a boyish faith in his own potent charm. Neither could credit his own wife's discomfort and trepidation. Elizabeth and Eunice often seemed to their husbands to be hectoring worrywarts. Each man spun silky webs of endearment with male and female friends alike, oblivious to the risks. The Beecher-Tilton Scandal was not only a calamity for the three principals and for the silent but very active fourth party. It was also a "tragedy," in the classical sense, since they were all brought down, in part, by this fatal flaw in the two Romantic male strivers. Henry and Theodore, blinded by excessive confidence in their own likability, never quite knew what hit them.

The big difference between them was that Henry did have a refuge in the storm, a tower of defense, that Theodore lacked. It was not Henry's home, but his faith in Jesus. Indeed, it was in part Theodore's loss of belief in the incarnate God in the late 1860s that provoked the whole chain of events in the first place, since it sent Elizabeth to Beecher for advice and solace, which aggravated Theodore's suspicions of Henry. Theodore was poignantly aware of the magnitude of his loss of Beecher's love, if not of God's. But the two losses were so intermingled that he may have sensed they reinforced one another. He began his July statement to the Investigating Committee by noting that for a period of fifteen years "an intimate friendship existed" between him and Henry, "which friendship was cemented to such a degree that in consequence thereof the subsequent dishonoring by Mr. Beecher of his friend's wife was a crime of uncommon wrongfulness and perfidy."

This adultery was worse than the usual infidelity because it shattered a preexisting love between him and his best friend. He was *my* friend first. At the start of his September statement he made the same point even more movingly, by quoting from Beecher's already famous letter written to him from England in 1863. (Harriet Beecher Stowe had printed it in a biographical essay on Henry.) Friends frequently sent if-I-should-die letters to their intimates before taking ocean voyages. Tilton quoted only a part of one sentence of Beecher's note: "Should I die on sea or land, I wanted to say to *you who have been so near and dear* to me . . ." Then he voiced his great pain at the loss of his friend.

> The single phrase which I have italicised is sufficient to show that Mr. Beecher, while travelling in a foreign land, having left behind him a greater multitude of friends than most men could have claimed, and seeking to choose from all these one to be the custodian of his special and secret thoughts, chose *me*. And his affectionate reason for so doing is stated by himself to be that I was "*near and dear to him.*"[23]

Theodore had been Jonathan to Henry's David.

By the summer of 1874 all Theodore had left was his faith in the truth and a house stuffed with documents and emptied of people. He hunkered down with his bits of paper and generated more. He got his aged parents Eusebia and Silas, in retirement in rural New Jersey, to certify in writing that "we never heard of any ill-feeling between our son Theodore and his wife, nor any complaint of ill-treatment by him towards her, until we lately heard of it for the first time in Elizabeth's published testimony, which we believe to be untrue." His "venerated mother," he reported, "who recently made a journey from her country home to visit me in Brooklyn, did me the sweet honor to declare that both she and my father, in lately looking back over my nearly forty years of life, were unable to recollect that I ever spoke to either of my parents a single harsh word, whether as child, youth, or man." Other family members could witness as well. "My own children could testify that never one of them has received from me a solitary stroke from whip or rod, nor ever once a blow of the hand in corporal punishment." Elizabeth had not claimed actual physical abuse, but had asserted that he once "threatened to strike me." This charge cut Theodore to the quick. "Many of the former inmates of my house, including relatives, friends, and domestics, stand ready to testify to my uniform gentleness towards Mrs. Tilton and towards all other persons in my home. As God is my witness, I solemnly aver that I never laid my hand on my wife save in the way of caress, nor did I ever threaten her with violence, nor subject her to privation [as Elizabeth's statement to the committee also alleged]."[24]

The *Chicago Tribune* took Tilton's side in the summer of 1874, and its star reporter George Alfred Townsend, author of a well-known book on John Wilkes Booth, became his chosen confidant among the reporters gathered around him. It was logical for Tilton to give his wife's letters to the *Tribune,* since the New York press mostly reviled him. In one of his lengthy interviews with Townsend—who signed his stories "Gath," an ironic Biblical reference ("Tell it not in Gath")—Theodore spoke protectively of his departed wife, whose whereabouts "I cannot learn." "Mrs. Tilton was jealously hidden away, as Tilton said, because the Beecherites thought she might fall into his hands sooner or later. 'It may be many years,' he said. 'She will confess the whole truth. Confession, with her, is absolutely necessary for the repose of her soul. Poor child, they will not let her cleanse her soul by speaking.'" Tilton was an excellent prognosticator, since Elizabeth confessed to adultery four years later. Whether her 1878 confession was "the whole truth" is another matter.[25]

V. In his August statement and "cross-examination" before his own Committee, Beecher lit into Tilton. "I had loved him much, and at one time he had seemed like a son to me," he wrote. Henry still believed, he told his friends, that "Mr. Tilton has a great deal in his upper nature. If he could be cut into, and his lower nature could be separated from the upper, there is a great deal in his upper nature that is capable of great sweetness and beauty." But Theodore's "insatiable egotism," combined with "a fatal facility in blundering (for which he had a genius)," laid him low. "Mr. Tilton is a man that starves for want of flattery; and no power on God's earth can ever make him happy when he is not receiving some incense." The incense had stopped billowing, according to Henry, when Theodore "became the associate and representative of Victoria Woodhull and the priest of her strange cause. By his follies he was bankrupt in reputation, in occupation, and in resources." Henry could not heap enough scorn on "the disreputable people and doctrines," the "wild views and associates," the "loose notions of marriage and divorce," that had supposedly bedazzled Theodore. Beecher did not hesitate to roll out the heavy artillery: Tilton's ideas had undergone "constant change in the direction of free love."[26]

We can be sure the bogey of free love carried colossal clout in 1874, since Beecher, the Tiltons, and their many enemies all made such lavish use of it. Elizabeth repeatedly called Theodore a free lover in her statement and testimony, and Tilton called Beecher the same thing in his. Mrs. Tilton escaped the label only because Theodore thought she floated in a "vaporous-like cloud," which ruled out settled convictions on any subject. She still felt compelled to defend herself against the noncharge (or else Beecher's committeemen were laying foundations for

THEODORE TILTON'S TWO NATURES.

MR. BEECHER HAS DISCOVERED THAT "TILTON HAS TWO NATURES, AN UPPER AND A LOWER NATURE."

the trial to come). She maligned Theodore for himself breaking their marriage vows—laying "the corner stone of Free Love" in their household by having sex with numerous women, including, she alleged, their middle-aged servant Ellen Dennis—and then gratuitously dissociated herself from the free-love ideas that no one accused her of holding: "I would fain lift my daughters and all womanhood from the insidious and diabolical teachings of these latter days." Theodore contended, meanwhile, that Beecher had studied "free love philosophy" his whole life— Tilton had that information on the authority, he said, of Henry's half sister Isabella Hooker (another friend of Victoria Woodhull's)—and secretly practiced it at the Tilton residence as well as at his own.[27]

Theodore and Henry could deny the free-love designation as much as they pleased, but it kept sticking to them—partly because of their own repeated recourse to it. In his cross-examination the Committee tossed Beecher a fat pitch on the subject. "An anonymous letter to the committee, from a free lover" had warned them that Beecher could truthfully deny wrongdoing in his relations with Mrs. Tilton because he believed having sexual relations with her was right. What did Beecher think of that? "I am not versed in the philosophy and casuistry of free love," Beecher replied. "I stand on the New England doctrine, in which I was brought up, that it is best for a man to have one wife, and that he stay by her, and that he do not meddle with his neighbors' wives. I abhor every manifestation of the free love doctrine that I have seen in theory, and I abhor every advocate of the free love doctrine that I have known." Henry's declared distaste did nothing to stop the rumors and insinuations that he was himself "loose" on marriage and divorce. Conservatives who disliked the "religion of gush" at Plymouth Church used "free love" as a handy and very effective weapon. Cultural traditionalists who feared family dissolution brandished the same club: they went after anyone who appeared to put love and feeling on a par with duty and restraint. By passing the hot potato of free love back and forth between them, Beecher and Tilton unwittingly collaborated with all the conservatives who saw liberal religion as a slippery slope toward cultural disintegration. For each of them was a famous liberal Protestant, and each of them, according to the other, had slipped over the moral precipice into debauchery.[28]

The conservatives may have been guilty of faulty logic—liberalism was no more proven to be the cause of cultural disarray than rigid adherence to old-fashioned norms—but they still had a plausible point about Beecher and Tilton. These two might be innocent on the narrow charge of embracing "free love"—if that variable term meant either promiscuity or an end to state-regulated marriage—yet guilty of loosening up the marriage pact. Beecher and both Tiltons subscribed to the view that intimate friendships with married people of the opposite sex were perfectly appropriate, even when one's spouse found those friendships disconcerting. Commentators at the time chastised Elizabeth Tilton for pursuing a private "non-pastoral" tie to Beecher after Theodore had expressed misgivings about it (well before the alleged adultery). What few realized was that Theodore, for all his jealousy, believed any spouse, including his own, should freely pursue cross-gender friendships—as he had long done himself.[29]

Theodore was on weaker intellectual ground than Henry in resisting the free-love epithet, because unlike Beecher he was on record with his belief in one key doctrine dear to free-love advocates: individual autonomy within marriage. His behavior on July 11, 1874, caused many jaws to drop: when Elizabeth announced she was leaving him forever, he let her go without protest. At the trial in 1875 his own lawyer William Fullerton tried to establish that Mrs. Tilton had left without his "consent," and Theodore abruptly denied Fullerton's premise. "She did not leave against my will, Sir. No, Sir, because she was a free, sovereign actor in the business." Her action did cause him "great surprise and grief," but it was irrelevant to speak of consent. "She never did anything against my will. She had a will of her own and acted according to it. . . . I never applied any coercion to her in any way."

Beecher's lawyer William Evarts immediately objected to the last sentence about never applying "any coercion to her," but he must have been thrilled at Tilton's gratuitous endorsement of a common free-love plank. Traditionalists such as Evarts contended that sovereign independence for individuals was poor doctrine for bolstering familial bonds. Theodore kept quiet about "individual sovereignty" during the summer of 1874. Neither Tilton nor Beecher said anything publicly about their actual practice of marital opening. Their silence made it much easier for their opponents to argue that liberal experimentalism was propelling the culture to destruction. Of course in such a charged ideological climate they could not defend their behavior without serious cost to their reputations. What they acknowledged doing with women not their wives would have qualified in most minds, wrongly, as an endorsement of free love. Even a shrewd observer like the *New York Graphic*'s anonymous "Inquirer," who understood early on that Theodore approved of his wife's "freedom," assumed that he therefore believed Elizabeth "had a right to do as she pleased with Beecher or any other man." To the "Inquirer," freedom for a spouse could only mean free love, pure and simple.[30]

Henry may have been on stronger ground resisting the free-love epithet than Theodore was, but he was plainly worried about escaping the adultery charge. He felt compelled to bare some exceedingly private details about his emotional life. The story he told about Mrs. Tilton in his statements to his Plymouth Committee in 1874 is folded into an account of his own moral and psychological crisis in the early 1870s. Elizabeth underwent a "strange change" in 1870, he said. "Nothing had seemed to me more certain during all my acquaintance with her, than that she was singularly simple, truthful, and honorable. Deceit seemed absolutely foreign to her nature, and yet she had stated to her husband those strange and awful falsehoods [about having committed some kind of sin with regard to Beecher]; she had not when daily I called and prayed with her given me the slightest hint, I will not say of such accusations, but even that there was any serious family difficulty." The dramatic transformation in her undid him. "My distress was boundless," he contended. "I had a profound feeling that I would bear any blame, and take any punishment if that poor child could only emerge from this cloud and be put back into the happiness from which I had been, as I thought, if not the cause, yet the occasion of withdrawing her." She was not to be blamed, yet his mind was swimming and he couldn't help blaming her: "I both blamed and defended Mrs. Tilton in one breath." As he put it to the Committee, he had a "divided consciousness" about her: "she was a saint and chief of sinners."[31]

Henry believed Elizabeth "had been overborne by sickness and shattered in mind until she scarcely knew what she did, and was no longer responsible for her acts." His statement pleads for everyone to see him in the same light. He was so distraught by the "strange change" in his friend, and by the cascading fears that soon engulfed him—what would become of his church, his writing, his family, "the name which I had hoped might live after me"?—that he unveiled a genius for blundering that matched or exceeded Theodore's. He tried, pell-mell, to patch things up with Tilton, and he surrendered his autonomy to Frank Moulton, who stepped forward to mastermind the cover-up. "I felt that my mind was in danger of giving way," Henry said. Moulton was a prince of reassurance, and his wife Emma a fountain of comforting words and kisses. Beecher's psychic distress was magnified, he said, by his inherited "hypochondria," but also by severe (unspecified) medical symptoms that began in 1856 and seemed to presage paralysis or worse. "Very often I came near falling in the streets. During the last 15 years I have gone into the pulpit I suppose one hundred times with a very strong impression that I should never come out of it alive."[32]

In his 1874 story about himself Beecher had been such a physical and emotional mess in the early 1870s that he had had no alternative but to let Moulton make decisions for him. And Moulton, he claimed, was unfortunately enamored of secrecy and manipulation. As Henry told the Committee, "Moulton is a man that loves intrigue in such a way that, as Lady Montagu said of somebody, 'He would not carve a cabbage unless he could steal on it from behind and do it by a device.'" By handing the affair over to Moulton, whom he then scarcely knew, Beecher guaranteed that any later exposure would exact a heavy price. At a minimum his own mental distress—which many would judge a failure of character—would be disclosed in his initial lurching for Moulton's lapels and in the doom-and-gloom letters he subsequently wrote to him. Beecher's urge to find Mrs. Tilton blameless for awful acts committed while "overborne by sickness and shattered in mind" was self-exculpating: he wanted the same merciful judgment applied to himself. "That I have grievously erred in judgment with this perplexed case, no one is more conscious than I am. I chose the wrong path and accepted a disastrous guidance in the beginning." His medical and psychological circumstances explained his lapse. The peace of mind Moulton bestowed from 1871 to 1873 had been bought at the cost, in 1874, of the "sad exposure of my weakness, grief and despondency."[33]

There is a subplot in Beecher's overall story of illness-unto-exculpation. The subplot concerns a morally aware agent in a real-life tragedy. In this story he was not barred by depression or disease from acting responsibly. There was simply no morally safe course open to him. Every available option inflicted serious injury upon someone. This conviction that all choices were tainted helped deepen the depression he voiced in his letters to Moulton. But at times he escaped the blackness and went back over the spectrum of possibilities. "The case, as it then appeared to my eyes, was strongly against me."

> My old fellow-worker [Theodore] had been dispossessed of his eminent place and influence [at the *Independent*], and I had counselled it. His family had well nigh been broken up, and I had advised it; his wife had been long sick and broken in health and body, and I, as I fully believed it, had been the cause of all this wreck, by continuing that blind heedlessness and friendship which had beguiled her heart and had roused her husband into a fury of jealousy, although not caused by any intentional act of mine.

At this point he still saw choices, not just impasse and surrender to Frank Moulton's ploys. "Should I coldly defend myself? Should I pour indignation upon this lady? Should I hold her up to contempt as having thrust her affection upon me unsought? Should I tread upon the man [Tilton] and his household in their great adversity?" Beecher may be faulted for not enumerating other choices, such as admitting his own affection for Mrs. Tilton, which complemented and deepened her ongoing longing for him. But a forthright acknowledgment of their mutual enthrallment would have humiliated his wife while further sullying Elizabeth's reputation. Her love for her pastor would then have been an elective passion rather than the mystical derangement that Henry and Theodore both depicted in their stories about her. Protecting Elizabeth and Eunice prevented Beecher from taking the soul-baring option that he occasionally told the Moultons he was considering. Pursuing Moulton's managed silence would not necessarily protect them either, but even after the fall of 1872, when Victoria Woodhull published the skewed account she had in hand, the principals still thought the cover-up might work. Concealment was not a good solution, Henry thought, but it was plausibly the least damaging one.[34]

Near the end of his cross-examination Beecher told the Committee that "in the retrospect of all this trouble, I can say truly that I am better capable of interpreting the comfort of the Word of God to the sorrowing heart than ever I should have been if I had not passed through this discipline. I have lost children; I have lost brothers; I have had many friends who have died, and some who would not die, and yet under all this I have never been more sustained than I have in this." After half choosing and half falling into the cover-up, he perceived his dependence on God in a new way. Before his travail God was an ever-flowing fountain of grace, a warm bath of approval and sustenance; afterwards God was an inscrutable judge as well as a sweet savior. God had his own logic of punishment and forgiveness. The rain would fall alike on the just and the unjust.

There is no reason to doubt Beecher's conclusion that, like Arthur Dimmesdale in *The Scarlet Letter,* he was better able to interpret the word of God after his experience of suffering. But one of his critics, his half sister Isabella Beecher Hooker, believed he would have risen even further into what he called the "higher regions of Christian life" if in the summer of 1874 he had chosen the path of confession. Admitting his sin—at the very least admitting he had thrust himself on Elizabeth as much as she had thrust herself on him—would have entailed surrendering his reputation and his influence. It would have meant throwing himself on God's mercy rather than trying to win the battle for public opinion.

> I feel so intensely for my brother I cannot give him up and yet my soul revolts at his conduct beyond the power of words to describe. Why did he not listen to me and close the revelation of the worst by confessing deep guilt and humbly taking his place among the chief of sinners—oh God why not—I say continually and there is no answer as yet and the future is fearful to look upon.[35]

Theodore, having lost the conviction of God's judgment and reassurance, could not imagine such an option. All he had was the conviction of his own rectitude. Henry had the chance to choose God's painful love as his sole foundation (though Isabella failed to consider the impact a confession of guilt would have on Elizabeth and Eunice). In the end, when Henry and Theodore composed their final stories in the late 1870s and 1880s, it was Tilton, not Beecher, who rose to a higher humility, refusing to blame the others for what had befallen him. In his secular frame of mind and his foreign exile he came much closer to Isabella Hooker's model of the Christian martyr. In 1874 both Henry and Theodore repeatedly cast the first stone at the other. Each was tired of suffering, and each craved the comfort of human commendation. Beecher picked up the gauntlet thrown down by his "old fellow-worker" Theodore Tilton and chose warfare, to be followed, he prayed, by vindication in a court of law.

VI. Elizabeth Tilton, according to both Henry and Theodore, placed her faith in God alone. She knew that human judgment was fickle and put her trust in the Lord. "She ought to be an intense Roman Catholic," Tilton told the Investigating Committee, "like Mme. Guion—a mystic." A few months after she first intimated to Theodore (in July 1870, according to his 1874 story) that she had somehow "sinned" in knowing Henry, she wrote her husband to caution him not to "think or say any more that my ill-health is on account of my sin and its discovery [disclosure]. It is not true, indeed. My sins and my life's record I have carried to my Saviour, and his delicacy and tenderness towards me passeth even a mother's love or 'the love of woman.' *I rest in him, I trust in him,* and though the way is darker than death, I do hear 'the still small voice' which brings to me a peace life's experience has never before brought me." As she wrote this letter Elizabeth was pregnant with his baby, a child she would lose to miscarriage in late December. Her savior's delicacy and tenderness had produced new life within her, and she could rest in the knowledge that God forgave her even if men did not.

Yet Elizabeth—who believed in God the way her pastor did, but knew him far better, Henry said, than he did—apparently chose warfare over martyrdom too. She turned on Theodore with the same bellicosity that Henry worked up. Why would a woman as God-fearing as Mrs. Tilton have embarked upon the same course of vilification, and the same search for human vindication, that Henry and Theodore embraced? There is a portion of her letter to Theodore that provides a clue. She was protesting her husband's rumormongering about Henry and her: "Do you not know, also, that when in any circle you blacken Mr. B.'s name—and soon after couple mine with it—you blacken mine as well?" But she was worried about Beecher's reputation apart from its consequences for her. "Would *you* suffer were I to cast a shadow on any lady whom you love? Certainly, if you have any manliness you would. Even so every word, look, or intimation against Mr. B., though I be in nowise brought in, is an agony beyond the piercing of myself a hundred times. His position and his good name are dear to me." [36]

Her pastor's influence in the world mattered to her in its own right. Theodore, testifying to the Committee, said that Elizabeth had always seen her friendship with Beecher as a means of furthering "the cause of religion." The Tiltons' letters show that they believed in the 1860s that Henry was in danger of squandering his promise as a spiritual leader by lounging with fawning admirers, in particular with "adoring ladies." According to Theodore, she consecrated herself to keeping her pastor on task. "She had been much distressed with rumors against his moral purity," Tilton wrote in his July statement, "and wished to convince him that she could receive his kindness, and yet resist his solicitations; and that she could inspire in him, by her purity and fidelity, an increased respect for the chaste dignity of womanhood." Her interest in him was moral and religious. No doubt it was more than that too, and neither Theodore nor Elizabeth wished in the 1860s to delve too deeply into that emotional tinderbox. Depicting her tie to Henry as a missionary one was a good way to justify it in her own eyes and her husband's. [37]

Elizabeth, like Eunice, understood Henry to be a religious leader, not a saint. They both believed in his work, and in 1874 they would make sacrifices to further it. Eunice would keep quiet, while attacking Theodore privately. Elizabeth would attack her husband publicly. Would she lie for Beecher, if she thought it would help keep him in his pulpit at Plymouth Church and in the nation as a whole? We will never know. Suppose she was unwilling to lie herself. She may nevertheless have been willing to tolerate Henry's lying about never having sought her affection. Tacitly endorsing that aspect of the Beecher defense (which she knew to be false), while vigorously attacking her husband's falsehoods, may have been her contribution in 1874 and 1875 to the continuation of Henry's work, and the Lord's. Her silence would have been a form of Theodore's technical truth-telling. And it would have been a small martyrdom, since she cared little about human judgment herself. Yet if she did make this calculated assessment of the religious stakes—of the greater spiritual good to be served by falsely endorsing Beecher's one-sided story of her undue affection for him—that compromise with the truth may have eaten away at her as time passed and helped spawn the guilt that provoked her confession of 1878. Of course if they did commit adultery of the flesh as well as of the heart, there was a good deal more than technical truth-telling eating away

THE BROOKLYN BATTLE—BLOWS TO BE GIVEN AS WELL AS TAKEN.

Having dispatched Theodore Tilton and Frank Moulton, Beecher, in pilgrim shoes, turns to Mrs. Tilton.

at her. It stands to reason that Theodore, between 1874 and 1878, did everything he could to nudge her guilt along toward the confession that he predicted would come sooner or later, though it might take "many years."

VII. Theodore Tilton's *Tempest-Tossed: A Romance* appeared in early 1874, and sold well enough during the spring and summer to permit him to refuse the dozens of speaking offers—some allegedly at $500 per lecture—that followed his accusations of July. He thought it immoral, he told reporters, to profit from his family's calvary. Certainly, in spite of his scruples, the sales of his book—about a family set adrift in the Atlantic for fifteen years by a terrible storm—boomed on account of the Tiltons' notoriety. Press reports in the fall claimed that four presses had been kept running all summer at Sheldon and Company to keep up with demand for the book. In his testimony to the Plymouth Investigating Committee he stressed that the character of Mary Vail was meant to tell the world that Elizabeth was pure. In fact, ever since 1866 he had been talking about writing a novel with a character based on his wife. One of his 1866 letters to her published in the *Chicago Tribune* in August 1874 said that "I have never met a character in any romance equal to one which, if I were a romancist, I could draw from a certain woman I know." But that December 7, 1866, letter also suggests that a larger purpose animated *Tempest-Tossed*. It would go beyond showing the purity of any one character—and if it showed Elizabeth was pure, it showed Theodore was too, since his evident stand-in Rodney Vail matched Mary sentiment for sentiment as an unblemished striver for higher things. It would portray the purity of love itself, "the love that dwells in the soul rather than the heart." The flaw in Charles Reade's huge hit *Griffith Gaunt,* which prompted this letter to Elizabeth, was its depiction of "love as a passion, as a jealousy, as a madness, as an intense adoration for the time being." A "true and perfect love," by contrast, was centered in "honor, fidelity, constancy, self-abnegation—not the clasp of the hand, nor the kiss of the lips, nor the ecstasy of fondness."[38]

Indeed, the perfection of love as a union of souls was most perfectly expressed in physical separation, and in the acts of writing that bridged the distance. "To bear each other in memory, in daily and hourly pictures of the fancy, in constant mutual communings of soul without contact of the flesh, in perpetual nearness notwithstanding miles of distance, in an abiding reverence, unfeigned, lofty, and ennobling—this is the great prerogative of true love." Or as Philip Chantilly, Mary and Rodney Vail's future son-in-law, put it in describing his love for their daughter Barbara,

> By absence this good means I gain,
> That I can catch her
> Where none can watch her—
> In some close corner of my brain:
> There I embrace and kiss her,
> And so I both enjoy and miss her.

Theodore drew these lines from John Donne's "Present in Absence," in which Donne had imagined that "hearts of truest mettle" could find "Affection's ground / Beyond time, place, and all mortality." But that ground in absence depended for Donne upon prior presence. Tilton pushed Donne's conviction to its ethereal and sentimental limit: Philip fell in love with someone he had never seen. His love for Barbara, who was born at sea during a raging hurricane, grew to perfection because of a photograph of her mother Mary. That photo had been taken when Mary was 17; it had been sent to Philip's mother, and he had acquired it upon her death. He venerated the photograph like a saint's relic, placing it in a locket, always "waiting for an opportunity to be alone that he might open it, gaze at it, and imagine from it the unknown face of the tempest-tossed waif Barbara." Fetishizing a photo of her mother taken before the storm permitted him to create a fantasy of himself and Barbara in a life together after the storm. As Theodore sat at his desk writing this scene of ecstatic union-in-separation, he had his actual photo of his own "pre-storm" Elizabeth by his elbow. Philip, for his part, was "captivated" by the "imaginary angel that he has beckoned into his heart; for as the most beautiful faces are those that are never seen, but only dreamed of, or sighed for, so [Barbara], dwelling at a blue and purple distance from the common sphere of mortals, became suddenly to [Philip] what an ideal virgin in heaven becomes to an adoring aspirant on earth." The fertile ground of union between Barbara and Philip was their perfect isolation from one another, which lasted for fifteen years—an isolation overcome by the higher love of the soul, kept alive by the changelessly pure image of her mother as young woman.[39]

Writing, in Theodore's view, was the highest ground of true love because, undertaken in solitude, it permitted the most profound honesty. Speech was too attuned to a listener's immediate reaction. In another December 1866 letter home, Theodore contrasted "the prayer-mongers at Friday-night meetings, . . . who indulge in religious cant" (i.e., Henry) to the letter-writers who try "never to admit an untrue word—never a conventional for a direct expression—never any of the little lies of polite usage." Writing let one chip away at the calcifications of social deceit and convey "our secretest and deepest hidden thoughts, without disguise and without misrepresentation." And among the forms of writing, letters were the most "personal." "A letter is mutually enkindling—it puts both writer and reader in a glow of love and goodwill toward the other." *Tempest-Tossed* is naturally full of letters and diary entries, a sign of the characters' utter truthfulness. There is of course much sincere speech in the book too, and the family's long removal from society—from corrupting prayermongers, among other contaminants—keeps their speech from veering off into dramatization or obfuscation. Theodore was a gifted orator, but a part of him was suspicious of the public renown that had come to him—as to Beecher—from his speaking. Letter-writing, fiction-writing, and no-holds-barred, fully "personal" journalism (taking on opponents by name) were his antidotes to the spurious acclaim inevitably generated, he thought, by oral performance.[40]

Ascribing the peak of virtue to the solitary, truthful activity of the writer, who created union with another by etching it in pure language, had decided advantages for a soul, like Theodore, who seems to have been most at home in his own reveries. In 1874 his most able defender in the press, George Alfred Townsend, noted a vast difference in the temperaments of Tilton and Beecher, and in the way that the "hundred and twenty reporters on the New York press" approached them.

> This man Theodore is a strange fellow—familiar yet unfamiliar; companionable, yet distant; lovable, yet austere. We all call him "Theodore" familiarly, yet not one of us would dare make a vulgar remark in his presence, nor tell a story such as ladies might not hear, nor in anywise offend the most scrupulous taste in thought or word. On the other hand, although none of us would think of saluting Mr. Beecher as "Henry," yet we could all go to him with the last new story, certain that, though broader than the "Broad Church," he would be sure to give it a welcome, for the great pastor's genius is after all of the earth earthy, and so are his tastes.

Townsend visited Tilton at his home after his final summer statement—the pamphlet-size treatise on Henry's and Elizabeth's sins—and found "a man who expects a long fight, and who means to endure to the end of it." Tilton was unperturbed, nearly without affect, "wast[ing] none of his nerve in useless excitements." As always, he was "a self-contained man. . . . He rises at six, goes down to his dining room, meets his aged housekeeper 'Katy,' receives from her an egg and a cup of coffee, thanks her as if he were her bishop absolving her sins, goes to his writing desk, and works steadily until noon."

> The only trace of emotion visible in his manner is when someone makes an allusion to Elizabeth. He speaks of her invariably in private in the same terms of respect and good-will which gave such a singular gilding to his examination before the committee, and to his two

published statements. Her portrait by Page hangs on the wall of his study, and his favorite photograph of her, taken years ago, before the troubles came, stands at his elbow, as if to lead him back from the woman who betrayed him to the wife of his youth. When his children come to see him—as they frequently do, from the country where they are staying—he makes no allusion to the existing sadness, but speaks of their mother as if she were merely away on a visit to some friend. The kindly opinion which this man entertains of his wife has not been obliterated either by her original crime or subsequent falsehoods against him. "Human nature is weak," he says, "even in the strongest, and Elizabeth, after all, is above the average. She is better than most of her critics. As her great fault is known to the world, so I feel bound to add to this disclosure my constant testimony to her great merits. 'Even her failings lean to virtue's side.'" [41]

Rodney Vail, the engineer-physician hero of *Tempest-Tossed,* who drifted with Mary and Barbara for a decade and a half (fortunately their ship was carrying a cargo of food preserved in tins, enough to keep them going, he calculated, for twenty-eight years), was himself a model of unwasted "nerve." He faced "a long fight" for survival and expected "to endure to the end of it." But once in a while the fictional character let down his emotional guard.

> A painful sense passed through him of his long exile, which had already lasted through weary years, and which, for aught that he could foresee, might last through still wearier years to come—indeed, possibly through all the years of man's mortal span. "Am I to live all my life on this ship," he exclaimed, "and never again behold the shore? Is my little family never to join the fellowship of mankind? Am I to waste here to old age, and die, and be left to fall to dust in this drifting bark, till she herself moulders, drops to pieces, and goes down?"

At least, like Philip Chantilly, Theodore had a photograph of "an imaginary angel" to cheer him as he withstood his isolation. But unlike Philip, Theodore had written aids to the contemplation of his idealized lover: the letters he and Elizabeth had exchanged in the 1860s. He had them in Elizabeth's hand and, for good measure, he had them now in Mary's. "Today a new mysterious feeling came over me which I never before detected—a kind of awe, or waiting, or listening to learn what God will do for me—and an agony of fear lest, by reason of my unworthiness, I should fail to receive His blessing." So wrote Mary to her fictional diary in 1854, and so, almost word for word, wrote Elizabeth to her traveling husband in 1869. But Mary, unlike Elizabeth, never really doubted her own purity—she chose the word "unworthiness" to replace Elizabeth's word "sin." And Mary never had the slightest misgiving about her husband Rodney's virtue. Readers of the *Chicago Tribune* version of the marital letters in August 1874 knew full well that Elizabeth (like Theodore himself) was stricken with doubt about Theodore's. As he sat in his silent house in the summer and fall of 1874 and beheld an eternally pure Elizabeth fixed in photographic form, he could find sustenance in Mary Vail's diary entry of 1853: "How beautiful is Rodney's nature! How grand his resources! If he were among men he might prove his genius and power; but how could the world, even if he were in it, ever know his purity and tenderness? These are known only to God—and to me. 'My beloved is mine, and I am his.'"[42]

FRANK LESLIE'S
ILLUSTRATED
NEWSPAPER

Entered according to the Act of Congress, in the year 1875, by FRANK LESLIE, in the Office of the Librarian of Congress, at Washington.

No. 1,009—Vol. XXXIX.]   NEW YORK, JANUARY 30, 1875.   [PRICE 10 CENTS. $4 00 YEARLY. 13 Weeks, $1 00.

Rev. D. C. Talmage.   Mrs. Ovington.   Mrs. Tilton.   Mrs. Beecher.   Mr. Beecher.   Mr. Morse.   Young Beecher.   Mr. Shearman.

MR. BEECHER, WITH MRS. BEECHER, GREETING MRS. TILTON IN THE COURT-ROOM, AFTER A DAY'S SESSION.

FOUR

Public Retellings,
1875

I. The adultery trial began in Brooklyn in early January, and the jury returned its divided verdict in early July. City Court Chamber II was packed solid at the start, and whenever a star witness was due. There was seating for three hundred, but standing room was available all the way around the forty- by fifty-foot room, and the crowd often exceeded five hundred. Several thousand spectators were turned away as the trial opened, according to the *New York Tribune* reporter who doubled as official court stenographer. Invited dignitaries—local politicians, leading citizens, officials from out-of-town and overseas—sat up on the bench alongside Judge Neilson. The jury of twelve white males occupied the box to his right, just beyond the witness stand, and observers from the legal profession were placed at the large table to his left.

Fanning out in front of the bench were the plaintiff Theodore Tilton and his five lawyers, and defendant Henry Ward Beecher, his wife Eunice, his son Colonel Henry Beecher, and his six lawyers. The sixty-or-so newsmen from around the country were scattered about the floor at eight small tables, always in close proximity to the judge, the jury, or the principals and their attorneys. Elizabeth Tilton, always accompanied by a female companion (usually Mrs. Anna Field, a friend she knew from the suffrage movement in the 1860s), was positioned beside one of the press tables. The Beecher party was about fifteen feet to her left. Whenever she looked at the judge or the witness chair, Theodore's lanky frame rose up in her line of vision, no more than ten feet away.

Those armed with tickets often had to wait for hours to get in, since the tickets were unreserved and could be used on any date. Once inside, they either squeezed into the courtroom proper, sitting or standing amidst the main players, or crowded into the bleacher-style benches in the gallery upstairs. The gallery group was on the plebian side, to judge by the *Tribune* reporter's complaints about its behavior. Brooklyn's working-class as well as middle-class population growth had been brisk before and after the Civil War (there was an overall increase of 43 percent between 1870 and 1880, to 567,000), and in 1875 many workers had time on their hands due to the severe depression that followed the Panic of 1873. One-third of all laborers in New York City were unemployed during the winter of 1875, when the trial began. By midday the floor of the gallery was littered with refuse, and the laughter and applause that often greeted the testimony came mostly from the masses in the loft. But even the well-heeled and elegant sometimes broke into raillery—encouraged by the judge, who vacillated between reprimanding the audience for its odious manners and launching humorous quips of his own that brought down the house.

The fashionable spectators, like the popular forces in the gallery, brought lunches from home or bought ham sandwiches and mince pies from the courthouse's elderly pieman. He sold his offerings seat-to-seat during the lunch break from 1 P.M. to 2 P.M., since the spectators feared losing their places if they got up. The reporter expressed his amazement at two ladies in the gallery who put up with the "crunched peanuts" covering the floor—and the "coarse language" of the "red shirted men who expectorated tobacco juice"—without once leaving their seats between the opening of court at 11 A.M. and adjournment at 4 P.M.

Class relationships and tensions were dramatized in this sort of commentary, as they were in the spatial separation between main floor and gallery. But they were also signaled in the testimony. The attorneys made frequent sport of working-class, black, and immigrant accents, word choices, and behavior. Beecher's chief counsel William Evarts was unrelenting in his mockery of former Tilton servant Kate Carey's drinking habits. Of course he was trying to discredit her recollection of Henry and Elizabeth embracing in a secluded corner of the Tilton dining room. But he relied on the stereotype of Irish tipsiness to do much of the work for him, and a good part of the audience snickered on cue. When she mispronounced "bronchitis," Evarts said back to her, "bronchitis or 'brownkeetoes,' as you call it." The court reporter duly spelled her original word "brownkeetoes." When James Woodley, a "colored" witness who had been a servant of Victoria Woodhull, testified about her relations with Theodore, the judge collaborated with the spectators in using the occasion for light relief. The court permitted the black man, uniquely, to perform as a standup comic. When one of Tilton's attorneys attempted to establish Woodley's general ignorance by driving home that he had no idea what a "proof sheet" was, Woodley smiled and answered, "Well, I think we have taken up enough time on that matter." The lawyer promptly objected to Judge Neilson, who laughingly praised the witness for sharing the court's concern about the wasting of time.[1]

Of course the crowd, gallery and main floor alike, was entranced by the spectacle of Beecher and Tilton crossing swords: maybe one of them would break down on the stand and confess to the real truth. But the audience was also drawn by the renowned lawyers' speeches. Writing of ex-Judge Samuel Morris's opening for the plaintiff, the *Tribune* reporter supplied a lengthy critical analysis for a nation of oratorical devotees. Morris's "movements are easy and graceful," he began, "his manner is cool and deliberate, and his gestures are strong and full of force, being made with the full arm in long curves. His delivery is rather monotonous, for there are no changes in tone to vibrate through an audience. In the upper register his voice has a metallic ring, and is surcharged with force and earnestness."[2]

The air in the courtroom was foul from the overcrowding, but also fragrant with the floral tributes lavished on the three principals. "The violet vied with the lily," wrote the reporter, "and the chaste camellia was in contrast with the petals of the 'red red rose.'" Beecher's and his wife's places were decorated with bouquets of violets, and Mrs. Tilton held "a delicate cluster of violets and white rose-buds," whose "significance" lay in its "intimation that she was still kindly remembered in Plymouth Church." On the plaintiff's side, a "magnificent" bouquet of roses, violets, lilies, and arbutus was brought to Mr. Tilton, who "blushed like an innocent school-boy as he detached the card . . . and read the inscription, 'To Theodore Tilton, with the compliments of his friends.'" Two more bouquets for Mr. Tilton followed, adding to his "embarrassment."[3]

Amidst all the blossoming hoopla, the *Tribune* reporter left no doubt which individual was the most captivating to courtroom observers, and to his own readers. He described Mrs. Tilton's arrival on the second day of the trial as the crowning moment of the day. Beecher and Mr. Tilton had "scarcely taken their seats before a loud buzz ran around the courtroom. Mr. Tilton cast a quick, nervous glance toward the door," and saw his wife. "Mrs. Tilton was attired in a black silk dress and dark velvet cloak, with a black velvet hat ornamented by an ostrich feather. She removed her vail, and glanced for a moment at her husband. Mr. Tilton returned the look, and then whispered softly to [his] lawyers, [who] simply smiled, and made no answer." At the end of the day Eunice Beecher made a point of walking over to Elizabeth Tilton, smiling, shaking her hand, and whispering in conversation with her for five minutes. That scene was repeated on other occasions, perhaps to show the jury and the newspapermen that the wife had no misgivings about the alleged paramour. "Taking his wife gently by the arm," the reporter wrote the next day, Beecher "led her over to Mrs. Tilton," who "warmly pressed" her hand. "The two held a short, subdued conversation, Mr. Beecher joining in it only once, with a remark that brought a smile to the faces of the ladies."[4]

The male reporters who covered the trial were fascinated by Mrs. Tilton, but also by the entire sprinkling of women who appeared in the "public" arena of the courtroom. The women's presence was not quite shocking in 1875, but it was unsettling enough to merit much bemused, censorious, or derisive notice. Of the *San Francisco Chronicle*'s decision to send a female correspondent to New York, a leading weekly quipped dismissively: the *Chronicle* "has a lady reporter, not beautiful but good, at the Tilton–Beecher trial. That's enterprise for you." But the attendance of women spectators brought more serious and widespread complaint. "Fourteen ladies infused the amiabilities of their sex into the choking assembly," said a *Chicago Tribune* dispatch. Mrs. Morse, Elizabeth Tilton's mother, drew this writer's special interest. She bore "an excellent likeness of Mrs. Tilton, with a bolder front and snowy hair," but she represented a contrary, and much more alarming, female type: "in the ratio of Mrs. Tilton's meekness and dejection are Mrs. Morse's audacity and fire."

> Her chevelure is a wonderful confection of white puffs and frizzes, which resembles as closely as may be the icing on a wedding cake. They tempt you to break off a puff or two to see whether they are sweet. Her nose is a trifle aquiline; her mouth small and cruel and her eyes as keen as a pair of daggers. Fortunately for the weal of man, those eyes are usually sheathed by black-rimmed eyeglasses.

Yet Mrs. Morse's diffident daughter elicited his disapproval too. "Someone once said that Mrs. Tilton would attract anybody in search of advice touching the cut of a nightshirt, but hardly the devotion of a great mind. I must confess that, after a continuous view of her red shawl, her hideous black velvet hat, and her fluffy hair, I must doubt her taste even as regards nightshirts."[5]

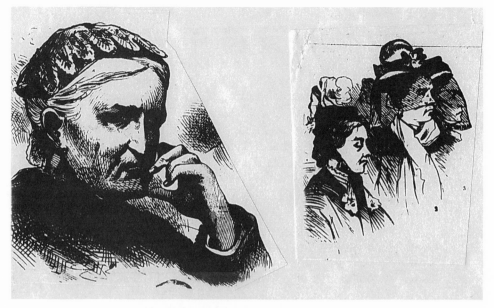

Mrs. Beecher and the *San Francisco Chronicle* reporter (center of trio) drawn by a Brooklyn courtroom artist in 1875.

Mrs. Tilton's "meekness" was often set off in press reports against Mrs. Beecher's "confident air." "Mrs. Tilton is *petite* and shy. She is the yielding, compliant helpmeet." Mrs. Beecher's "clear-cut, classic face is full of character. . . . There is apparently no simulation in the contemptuous smile with which she receives her share of the strokes that fall upon her husband. . . . She always appears the embodiment of earnestness and . . . if there lingers in her breast the faintest doubt of her husband's final vindication, it is never once reflected in her face."

> What the spectator sees as he catches his first glimpse of Mrs. Beecher is a narrow ribbon of perfectly white hair which the deep black of her bonnet allows to border her forehead. The effect of this is singularly heightened by the appearance of her eyes. Her head is held down, and as she looks steadily at Mr. Tilton's face from under her deeply lined brows, they, too, show more of white than of color. It is a remarkable face.

Mrs. Beecher's strength of character resided, for this reporter, in her chiseled, expressionless visage: no feeling or emotion could be registered there. For the most part, Mrs. Tilton had also "schooled her emotions so that they do not reach her face"—which showed "only calmness and resignation, emphasized by the sadness revealed in her eyes. Her veil is never lifted. It does not hide her pale, girlish features." Yet her self-control wavered. She was frequently caught weeping, and was once observed sobbing convulsively. Even in her moments of calm, journalists claimed access to her thoughts. She "occasionally leans forward and looks for moments at a time at her husband as he sits at his counsel's table or in the witness chair, and the observer imagines he sees a remembrance of the old affection in her eyes. There is a something in the expression of her face that hints at a desire to rejoin her husband if the restraint that keeps her from him were for an instant removed."[6]

The same reporters who endlessly described the women in the courtroom—their clothes, their body language, their emotions—lamented their presence in the ranks of the spectators. Some, like George Alfred Townsend, objected even to Mrs. Beecher's and Mrs. Tilton's daily attendance. It was indecent, he thought, to expose Mrs. Beecher, a completely innocent party, to "publicity." Mrs. Tilton's presence, meanwhile, was "a gross violation of good taste. . . . she has added to the probability of her unworthiness by this bold display." The resistance to the general admission of women stemmed from two concerns. First, the women's moral purity would be assaulted by exposure to certain stories or language (the words "sexual intercourse" were spoken from time to time). Second, the women undermined the proper atmosphere of solemnity in the courtroom. Even when they were perfectly quiet and decorous, their intent was to revel in "scandal," not to savor the august deliberations of the men of the bar, the bench, and the press. The *Mobile* (Alabama) *Register's* correspondent summed up the objection, frequently voiced by Northern writers too:

> A full dozen of women were present the other day, listening eagerly to words that no woman should hear without a blush, and every day since the trial got fairly under way from half a dozen to a dozen scandal-loving matrons have occupied good places in the court. They are mostly partisans of the defendant, and get in through favor of Mr. Beecher's lawyers. These women are very respectable, of course, otherwise Plymouth Church would not be sponsor for them in court, but their presence is in no way necessary, is the reverse of creditable to female modesty, and is frequently commented on as improper in every way.[7]

Judge Neilson had sought to keep women out altogether, but Beecher's defense team wanted them there—to accommodate the heavily female membership of Plymouth Church. Thirty women seems to have been the peak number at any one time in the ranks of what the *Chicago Tribune* reporter termed "the Amazonian squad." "Unquestionably," a *New York Graphic* writer asserted, "if Judge Neilson should relax his stringent rule, the seats would be filled with early-coming ladies, to the exclusion of the less curious sex." The judge did not relax his rule, and sometimes he tightened it. During Beecher's testimony in April, when the crush of spectators was at its height, he ended the proceedings one Monday afternoon with the words, "I ought to say to the ladies who are now present, and who are not immediately connected with the suit or the parties, that it would be well not to attend tomorrow morning."

> Friday morning and this morning I refused admission to a great number of ladies with regret. I think in some of the weeks to come there may be an opportunity, but just at present I think the ladies who are here, and who for one day have seen the place, might as well be content. Members of the Bar complain that they cannot get in.[8]

The irony of the female presence in court is that an occasional witness could command, on account of her sex, a degree of respect from the assorted male observers that they denied to the women spectators (and to the few working-class women who testified, mostly Mrs. Tilton's former servants). When Emma Moulton, Plymouth Church member and once a Beecher intimate, testified against him, the press found her especially praiseworthy because of the kind of woman she was. Not only was she "a lady of high position and unspotted character," as the *Chicago Tribune* put it. Even more telling was the evidence of her demure behavior throughout the scandal. "She has modestly kept herself secluded, while almost every one else has sedulously sought public notoriety." Judge Neilson went out of his way to emphasize her "honesty." In his final instructions to the jurymen he said that "her manner on the stand, and the opinion which the defendant himself had of her moral character and worth, as stated in his letters, commend her to your respect."[9]

Ultimately, the force of Mrs. Moulton's testimony against Beecher—she claimed that he and Mrs. Tilton had each independently confessed the adultery to her—was muted by two perceptions. First, she was the wife of Frank Moulton—now Henry's antagonist and Theodore's ally—and hence could not be taken as a free agent. Her testi-

Emma Moulton, encircled by male observers, on the witness stand.

mony might be unconsciously bent by the duty she owed her husband. Indeed, she was so loyal to her husband that she admitted under
cross-examination to having once called Theodore Tilton "treacherous" for whispering to friends about the scandal while her husband was
trying to help cover it up. Tilton's lawyers gasped: they had put her on
the stand to discredit Beecher alone, not plaintiff and defendant alike.
Second, it seemed implausible to some that such a high-class matron

of old-stock roots, and the caring mother of a young boy, would have agreed to converse with her pastor about adultery even if he had brought it up. Paradoxically, the very modesty that commended her to the press and the bench as a truth-teller undermined her testimony: a woman as respectable as she could not have had the tête-à-têtes she claimed to have had.[10]

Like Mrs. Tilton, Mrs. Moulton was for the press of 1875 a contradiction in terms. The Beecher-Tilton trial exposed to urgent view a perplexing turn in nineteenth-century American bourgeois life. To traditionalist observers the situation seemed surreal. One religious woman claimed she had repeatedly sat in her parlor with her minister discussing his adultery. Another said she had sinned in knowing him and might sin all over again, so enlivening had been their intimacy. Marriage was being eroded not just by the spread of divorce but by a bizarre erosion of solemnity and sentiment within the marriage bond. As Henry James put it in *The Bostonians,* his 1886 novel about what he termed "the decline of the sentiment of sex" in the 1870s, it was an era in which a beautiful young woman (the charismatic if shallow Verena Tarrant) could talk "of the marriage tie as she would have talked of the last novel—as if she had heard it frequently discussed."[11]

Tilton's chief attorney William Beach traced the marital crisis to 1848, when "the vandalism of modern legislation" permitted "the wife . . . to sue the husband." Now the wife "may go out into the world and barter and trade and tussle with the energies of commercial and business life. . . . She is ushered into the busy scenes of life and becomes an active and independent actor in all struggles." It was too late, said Beach, for the defense to argue that the trial was about protecting the "sacredness" of "the marriage relation, that idea of the confluence of two souls mingling all their affections and sympathies and interests in one, and hand in hand meeting the contingencies and adversities of life with mutual encouragement and love." Thanks to the so-called "progress of civilization . . . that idea has been mangled and torn asunder." The defense scripted a sentimental drama of marital sanctity, the plaintiff presented a realist story of marital degeneration, and the trial introduced a mass audience to the tantalizing spectacle of a middle-class life, and the interpretation of it, in fundamental disarray.[12]

II. The reporters' persistent infatuation with Mrs. Tilton mirrored the nation's. She was the chief player about whom the least was known. What was known was disconcerting. Everyone understood she had made contradictory statements about her relationship with Beecher. Worse, she made contradictory statements in rapid succession. On the single night of December 30, 1870, as the whole country had learned in 1874, she first (under pressure from Beecher) recanted in writing a confession of improper relations with him (a confession earlier made to Theodore), then a few hours later (under pressure from her husband) retracted the recantation, again in writing. Since 1874 commentators had been blasting her for these unconscionable, damnable reversals. But some sympathized with her too, since she had also reported that Theodore was an abusive husband. By 1875 she was regarded in contradictory fashion as a hopeless liar and as the one person who could clear up the mystery. Either Beecher or Mr. Tilton was a bald-faced liar, and she alone could disclose which one it was.

As the trial crept along through the winter and into the spring, she kept her own counsel, siding with Beecher but issuing no statements of her own. Then, on May 3, as the seventy-seventh day of the trial began, Mrs. Tilton stood up and addressed the judge. She rose "like an apparition," in the *Tribune* reporter's words, and "cried out in her low voice, a little tremulous from embarrassment, 'Judge Neilson.'" "Your Honor," she said, "I have a communication which I hope your Honor will read aloud." She passed a note up to him, he read it to himself, but he declined to read it out loud. Mrs. Tilton took her seat again, as spectators exchanged disbelieving glances.[13]

For the journalists following the case, Mrs. Tilton's rising to speak was a sensational moment. The trial had begun on January 4, she had attended almost every day, every twitch of her head had been probed for meaning (why, when her husband testified, did she hand "little white sheets of paper" to William Evarts? and why, when one of her erstwhile servants took the stand, did she put on her "gold eyeglasses"?), but this was the first breach of her silence. The papers had tried without success to interview her, and were clamoring for her to testify. If she were compelled to answer questions under oath, as the *New York Graphic* expressed it, "the truth would appear all the clearer . . . , as gold shines the brighter the more it is rubbed." A New York statute of 1867 did rule a wife to be "incompetent" as a witness for or against her husband, but Theodore loudly waived that legal protection. "Mrs. Tilton has been silenced by others, not by me," he told Charles Dana's *New York Sun*, one of the few New York–area papers to support him in his battle with Beecher. He would never resort to "the legal craft or moral littleness of forbidding my wife to testify in her own behalf."[14]

Beecher's lawyers, who intimated at the start that they would put her on the stand, eventually thought better of it. Her earlier changes of mind would look ridiculous. Facing Theodore in the courtroom, she might waver in her support of Beecher. Far better the spectacle of a demure mother pleading (unsuccessfully) for the right to speak, a gesture that might convey to the jury an aura of innocence on the adultery charge. If innocence could be associated with Mrs. Tilton, it might cling to Beecher too. The newspapers, meanwhile, joined their zeal to get to the bottom of things with a lively interest in more revelations that would sell. They responded to her request for a hearing with a wave of concern for her plight. There was no relief "from the terrible load under which she staggers," said the *Chicago Tribune,* "and which she must bear alone to the last." The legal system was standing in the way of truth as well as justice. "The most valuable testimony in the case has not been heard," intoned the *Tribune.* "The facts are not all in, and never will be until Mrs. Tilton testifies." [15]

On May 4 Mrs. Tilton did the next best thing: she released her statement to the press:

> I ask the privilege from you for a few words in my own behalf. I feel very deeply the injustice of my position in the law and before the Court now sitting. . . . I have been so sensible of the power of my enemies that my soul cries out before you and the gentlemen of the jury that they beware how, by a divided verdict, they consign to my children a false and irrevocable stain upon their mother. For five years past I have been the victim of circumstances most cruel and unfortunate, struggling from time to time only for a place to live honorably and truthfully. Released for some months from the will [Theodore's] by whose power, unconsciously, I criminated myself again and again, I declare solemnly before you, without fear of man and with faith in God, that I am innocent of the crime charged against me. I would like to tell my whole sad story truthfully, to acknowledge the frequent falsehoods wrung from me through compulsion, though, at the same time, unwilling to reveal the secret of my married life, which only the vital importance of my position makes necessary. I assume the entire responsibility of this request, unknown to friend or counsel of either side, and await your Honor's honorable decision. With great respect.
>
> (Signed) Elizabeth R. Tilton." [16]

Before seeing her statement some newspapers supposed she had written and released it on her own. Once they read it they agreed that such an ingenious piece of legal strategizing could only have been planned by Beecher's defense team. Generating sympathy for Mrs. Tilton would take some of the heat off them: they, of course, were the ones capable of putting her on the stand if they really cared so much about letting her speak. The reference to the damage a "divided verdict" would do to the Tilton children was especially shrewd. Beecher's lawyers were already fearing the tepid victory of a hung jury—no finding of guilt, but no ringing declaration of innocence either. Planting that concern in her statement could help spread the view that the expected hung jury *was* an injustice, most obviously to the suffering innocents, Mrs. Tilton's children, but also, by extension, to Beecher.

The heavy imprint of Beecher's lawyers on her statement does not mean that it fails to express her perspective. This document is no different from any other public statement issued by her or by Theodore or Henry in 1874 and 1875: all of their remarks were pored over by lawyers before release. Even if her statement was entirely penned by a lawyer, it might still reveal something important about her consciousness. It will if we have other evidence of her thinking, like her testimony the previous summer to the Plymouth Church Investigating Committee. Her 1875 statement repeats that testimony: she has been delivered, she says, from a psychic enslavement to Theodore. Now she can apprehend the truth, confess to falsehoods spoken in the past. Declaring her independence from Theodore's tyranny, she can defend her honor against the "enemies" conspiring to besmirch her name. This is a story about attaining moral maturity, becoming both an autonomous individual and a mother better able to protect her offspring. Of course we know that three years later she told a very different tale when she confessed to adultery with Beecher, but her change of story in 1878 does not belie what may have been a real shift in her moral compass in 1874 and 1875. She may have started thinking things through for herself, apart from Theodore's wishes, even if her actions were still substantially controlled by others (Beecher's lawyers) and even if she shifted her account as time went on. That new process of self-reflection may have been responsible for her final "confession" in 1878, a statement designed not to persuade her detractors (they were unpersuadable), but to clear her conscience.

Her "enemies" at the time of her statement in May 1875 included her husband. Yet even if she were to testify, she notes, she would not divulge "the secret of my married life," a refusal she ties to "the vital importance" of her (undefined) "position." She seems to be saying that she won't talk about her relationship with Theodore—however "necessary" such disclosures might be to Beecher's defense. There is a limit to what she will do to save herself and her children: that limit is the sanctity and privacy of the family, intermingled perhaps with some persistent bondedness with or indebtedness to or love for Theodore. Whatever the nature of the limit, it suggests that despite the "injustice" of her "position in the law," Elizabeth cringed at the prospect of cross-examination—which might force her to expose the familial sanctum. It was much safer to make a vehement published statement of her innocence, followed by a hoped-for tide of sympathy over the dastardly gagging imposed on her by a cruel legal system. This sincerely sentimental defense of the domestic sphere against the prying scrutiny of the world was a way of sneaking her own (much disputed) moral purity into her statement, but it also bespoke a genuine commitment to shielding her family.

There is no evidence from Elizabeth or Theodore that she was still in love with him in 1875, but some observers thought she was. One of Beecher's attorneys, ex-Judge John Porter, claimed in his closing oration for the defense that she still, inexplicably, loved her husband.

> It is one of the things which seems to me marvelous in the sight of man, and only explainable when we shall be able to look at it with the light which comes from Omniscience. That woman, loathing this man as she does to this hour, loves him as I have never seen woman love man. It is the strangest anomaly that I have ever witnessed in the whole course of events. The most idolatrous, and, if I might so use the term, abject love; but it is no longer that love which is absolutely blind. Then it was love idolatrous and blind, but now it is love idolatrous but blasted. She can see it; she knows to whom she pledged her prostrate and abject soul.

Why would Porter make such a point of her still being in love with Theodore? Perhaps to help justify the defense's decision not to put her on the stand. But there was a deeper reason. The defense strategy of saving Beecher by blackening Tilton's character had been complicated by the plaintiff's introduction of many of the intimate letters Elizabeth and Theodore had exchanged during his lecture tours of the late 1860s, the letters he had edited and released to the press in 1874. If he was as lovable as those excerpted letters made him seem, the jury might lean toward finding him credible as well as sweet. So Porter set about defining her love, yesterday and today, as deranged. She might now have escaped Theodore's psychic mind control—"she can see it"—but her emotions were still inexplicably bound to him. It would of course be pointless to put such a woman on the stand, since her love, however objectively "blasted," was still subjectively "idolatrous."

Tilton's lawyer William Beach answered Porter in the plaintiff's summation: he was mystified by Porter's claim that Mrs. Tilton loved as well as loathed her husband. For it was obvious she hated him, and it was self-evident that one could not love and hate at the same time. A woman who left "the sanctity and protection of a husband's love and a husband's home, to appear as an open accuser of that husband, and as the defender and vindicator of her seducer," was *ipso facto* a loather. The plaintiff's side needed to establish that she had earlier loved Theodore—because he had merited it, not because he was a manipulator—and that she had been led, by Beecher's wanton seduction, to renounce him. Tilton was still lovable (and credible), yet Mrs. Tilton had fallen, via Beecher's vile endearments, into a state of enmity.[17]

The actual Elizabeth meanwhile, was quite likely divided and distraught. She had known Theodore since he was 10 and she was 11 or 12. In the 1840s they had lived in the same New York City square, and played together along with her younger brother (and Theodore's schoolmate) Joseph. They had been married for almost twenty years. Powerful sentiments of attraction or responsibility must have mingled with spasms of disgust. Her feelings of anger and abhorrence had peaked the year before when Theodore released her letters, spreading her innermost feelings across the world for public rummaging and titillation. That act was to her an unspeakable violation, and in the spring of 1875 she may still have felt much more loathing than love. But she may still have feared the consequences, for herself, the children, and even Theodore, of following his example by opening their family life to the public's smirking delectation.

Seven weeks after rising like an apparition in the courtroom, Mrs. Tilton spoke out again, this time surely under Beecher's lawyers' tutelage. It was to be her last public statement on the case before her final "confession" almost three years later. Testimony in the trial had come to a halt in early May, but new "evidence" kept emerging in the newspapers, a sign of their unwillingness to let the story die, and evidence too of the public's own hankering for more of their favorite serial drama. Two Brooklyn upholsterers made the most serious of the new allegations: they said they had seen Beecher with Mrs. Tilton in her house in October 1869. Henry, according to one of their affidavits, "put his arm around [her] waist and drew her to him, partly lifting up her

body, at the same time kissing her on the cheek and she kissing him."
A few minutes later, one workman alleged, he saw "Mrs. Tilton re-
clining on a lounge" in the parlor, "with her clothes up above her
knees," and "Beecher in the act of rising from the said lounge." The
prosecution tried to reopen the case on the basis of this racy report, but
the Judge dismissed the motion after Elizabeth Tilton signed a detailed
denial of all of the upholsterers' charges. Her statement, along with the
workmen's, appeared in the papers a week later, while the jury was
embroiled in its week-long deliberations.

Given Elizabeth's expressed dread of "revealing the secret" of her
married life, she must have winced hard at the Beecher team's need for
a quick rebuttal of the story. She would have foreseen that her affidavit
to the court, like most documents in the case, would be featured in the
press. And the lawyers required a document that put the interior of her
Livingston Street home on public display. Her lengthy denial insisted
that even if the workmen, of whom she had no recollection, had been
to her house, the events they described could not have happened. For
there *was* no privacy in the front parlor, the alleged site of the lounge
incident. Anyone could see into the parlor at any time from the hallway
and from the porch (the "piazza"). The blinds on the windows were
always open in October, so anyone, including the children who were
always playing unsupervised on the piazza, could have easily looked in
the windows. *All* the children ran around the porch *all* the time — except, she added with bitter sarcasm, the infant. "The front parlor was
therefore a place in which no secrecy was possible." The upholsterers,
some avid readers must have felt, had not paid close enough attention
to earlier revelations about the Tilton residence: secrecy *was* possible
upstairs, as earlier testimony had revealed. Her rebuttal built its own
credibility upon the public knowledge of that fact. The upholsterers
were untrustworthy because they were innocent of the true blueprint of
privacy at the Tilton home.[18]

Mrs. Tilton's affidavit undid the upholsterers but it went further, gratuitously, to reaffirm her general denial of wrongdoing with Beecher.
Her (or the lawyers') choice of words suggests they may have been worried the judge would reopen the case. "There never was any act of
familiarity or mark of friendship or affection," she said, "either on the
part of Mr. Beecher or myself, in the absence of my husband, of greater
degree or different kind from what took place habitually between us in
the presence of my husband. Nor was there ever as great familiarity
between Mr. Beecher and myself as there was between me and my step-

RESIDENCE OF THEODORE TILTON.

father or brother, nor did any act or word ever pass between Mr. Beecher and myself which could not with equal propriety have passed between a father and daughter."

Putting her affection for Beecher and her male relatives on a balance
scale, and asserting there was more of the latter, may have been another savvy legal move. Etymologically speaking, there *had* to be more
"familiarity" among "family" members. Perhaps this argument influenced the judge's decision not to reopen the trial. Yet everyone who
had read her letters to Theodore from the late 1860s knew that the love
she had acknowledged between herself and Beecher was *sui generis*. It
had sparked a life-altering emotional and intellectual growth. Apart
from the legal maneuvering, the use of the father-daughter analogy
suggests that Elizabeth may have found it helpful generally in grasp-

ing or shaping her tie to Beecher. Perhaps it offered a way to sort out the passionate feelings she had felt for her pastor. Choosing the father-daughter story may have been a means of self-definition, even self-correction. For in 1874 Elizabeth had gone much further than the father-daughter image. Then she had described Beecher as a precious soulmate.[19]

III. It was clear to the entire country in May 1875 that Elizabeth Tilton had been silenced in the courtroom. It was equally obvious to the whole nation that Theodore Tilton and Henry Ward Beecher had spoken profusely: Tilton was on the stand for fourteen days—nine of them under cross-examination and redirect, and two in rebuttal—and Beecher for fifteen, six of them under cross-examination and redirect. Tilton's and Beecher's testimony each took up over three hundred micro-font pages of the published transcript. Many newspapers reprinted column after column of their exact words.

But appearances were somewhat deceiving. Theodore and Henry had been partially silenced too. The lawyers kept interrupting them, and stopped them from being their usual expansive selves. Tilton and Beecher had taken the oath to tell the "whole truth," but the rules of evidence blocked testimony about what third parties had said (witnesses could only divulge what they themselves had seen or heard), and prevented disclosure of any confidential communications between Theodore and Elizabeth (society had an overriding interest in protecting the marital bond, the judge noted, even if injustice to some person should result). The Anglo-American adversarial system was based on the paradox that the "whole truth" was most likely to emerge if each side's lawyers patrolled the testimony and stopped individual witnesses from trying to speak the whole truth on their own. The very accomplished attorneys in this case usually kept the principal witnesses on a short leash. Henry and Theodore tried to rebel by giving their opinions and conclusions, by protesting against the demand for simple "yes" or "no" answers, or by being witty, but there was no outwitting either the lawyers or the rules of evidence. Neither of them could gather oratorical momentum. The lawyers made a special point of preventing Beecher or Tilton from reciting any Biblical passages, even when those passages appeared admissible under the rules of evidence.[20]

Nevertheless, when it served the lawyers' purposes they let the witnesses speak, and over a total of twenty-nine days of testifying, Tilton and Beecher said a great deal. One of the main ironies of their testimony is that they both owned up to having a terrible memory for conversations, yet each of them confidently dismissed most of the other's recollections. Beecher was especially forthright about the constructed character of his own testimony: "Allow me to say that in every interview that I shall narrate I profess to give only the substance, and if there be an exception, I will mention it." He proceeded to put the "substance" of conversations in dialogue form, thus creating a fictional account in order to convey his "true" version of each encounter. It was paradoxically by inventing dialogue that Beecher demonstrated his fidelity to the rules of evidence, which on a strict construction limited witnesses to what they had actually seen or heard. The rules thus encouraged witnesses to "recollect" exact words if they wished to slip their opinions and conclusions into the record. The whole system was based on the elaborate fiction that witnesses had in fact said or heard all the things they claimed to have said or heard, as opposed to merely thinking them at the time or inferring them later.

Beecher assured the court that he remembered the substance of conversations by acting them out as he repeated them. In 1870 Theodore had torn up a vital document while accusing him of wrecking the Tilton family, so Beecher, relating the story, tore up a piece of paper and let the confetti drift to the floor at the feet of the jury foreman. Elizabeth had been sick in bed on the night in 1870 when he got his recantation memo from her, so in his narration of the event, as the *Tribune* reporter put it, "his voice changed to the appealing tones of a weak and almost dying woman. He even threw back his head, closed his eyes, and folded his hands over his breast, as he described the position occupied by Mrs. Tilton." Tilton refrained from acting out his testimony, but made almost the same concession about language. He was much better, he told the court, at remembering visual images; he had "no special gift at recalling words," though he did think he was better at dredging up those of other people—like Beecher—than he was at summoning his own.[21]

Of course the testimony they gave on the tie between Henry and Elizabeth was contradictory on the adultery charge—Theodore (and the Moultons) claimed that Beecher had confessed it, while Henry (and Elizabeth in the ongoing "trial by newspaper") denied any such thing. But testimony from Beecher as well as Tilton pointed to a deep emotional and spiritual attachment between Henry and Elizabeth. Indeed, the supreme irony of the trial is that while it was convened to determine whether Beecher had "alienated the affections" of Mrs. Tilton from her husband, Beecher, in order to exculpate himself, conceded he had unintentionally done just that. He admitted his moral fault to establish his legal innocence. Too much evidence of Henry's and Elizabeth's intimacy had come out in 1874 to allow the defense to deny a transfer of her passionate feelings from husband to pastor. But Theodore could collect no damages, the defense argued, since Henry had not *sought* to alienate Elizabeth's affections. Henry's story about himself stressed his head-in-the-clouds insouciance, and his moral culpability in the aftermath. Given his age and experience, he said on the stand, he should have noticed that Elizabeth was falling in love with him. He should not have "wrought in that quiet little woman a smoldering fire that . . . burned unknown to me within her, and finally broke out with such infinite mischief." In 1874 he had seen himself as faultless in relation to Elizabeth. In 1875, he conceded a serious moral failing. In 1876, for his final story, he went back to the stance of innocence and victimization.[22]

A successful defense required that Beecher account satisfactorily for the many letters of the early 1870s in which he expressed overwhelming remorse for his role in what had happened to the Tilton family. The stance of moral guilt for unwittingly alienating Elizabeth's affections fit the bill perfectly. Beecher could deny he had ever slept with Mrs. Tilton or even made "improper advances" or "solicitations." He could admit to moral sleepwalking and claim to have been heartbroken when he woke up and realized what awful damage he had done. The plantiff's attorneys might wave the letters of contrition in the faces of the jury and claim that only adultery could explain the urgency of Beecher's self-laceration. Beecher could answer that as a Christian his having done even unknowing harm to the Tiltons was enough to send him over the "ragged edge" of despair. "There was enough, to *my* thought, in hurting a friend, in destroying a household, in being unfaithful to the highest honor of obligations—there was enough in that to torment *me* with the torments of the damned." For good measure he repeated his 1874 story about the Beecher family's history of "hypochondria," a term that signified "the most profound depression," the kind he had suffered as a boy. "I think as I have grown older and tougher that it stops in . . . profound sadness rather than in the more developed form of hypochondria, which my father had and my ancestors." There was no need to posit sexual wrongdoing to explain his apparently suicidal thoughts of the early 1870s.[23]

It was perhaps foreordained that the trial would end in a hung jury, since the principal witnesses were more or less credible and they presented contradictory accounts of dozens of events. After the jury had cogitated for a week the foreman told the judge that "it is a question of fact, a question of the veracity of witnesses on which we do not agree, your Honor." There was no way to tell whether Beecher or Tilton was lying (or supremely forgetful) on a whole string of issues. Take the question of Ralph Tilton's paternity. Theodore said he had summoned Henry to his house one morning in the second week of February 1871, taken him upstairs to his study, and asked him, on his word of honor, whether he had started sleeping with Elizabeth when Elizabeth (he claimed) said he did—October 10, 1868. If her date was right, Theodore was sure Ralph, born June 21, 1869, was his own son. "And he told me, on his word of honor, as before God, that the date which Mrs. Tilton had assigned was the correct date. At that moment Mrs. Tilton herself, who had followed me upstairs, came into the room, and when I stated to her the point of conversation, she burst into tears, and asseverated, as she had once or twice done before, that the date which she had given was correct." When Beecher got on the stand his attorney asked him if "any such conversation . . . [or] topic of conversation was ever raised between you and Mr. Tilton," and Henry answered that no "such conversation, or anything out of which such a conversation could be made or imagined, took place. It is a monstrous and an absolute falsehood." Even if the conversation never occurred, Theodore's recollection or invention of it is very revealing about his sense of honor among men—indeed, even among thieves. He believed he could count on the truthfulness even of a man he accused of stealing his wife's affections. All he needed was Henry's "word of honor." [24]

IV. In 1875 Henry and Theodore were at each other's throats, so it is remarkable to find them insisting over and over during the trial on the depth and duration of their original love for one another. When Theodore first got to know Henry intimately, he told the court, Beecher was "a man of large fame and had a great church and was in the exercise of very manly and illustrious powers," but "I always regarded him as a big boy rather than a man at all. . . . His manner was large, and hearty, and gay, and companionable, and winning. . . . He was very . . . hail-fellow-well-met, fond of a joke and a frolic, fond of the things which boys liked. That made him very companionable to us, for I was very little more than a boy myself. . . . I thought he was the most charming man I ever saw. . . . Mr. Beecher was my man of all men. . . . I loved him, Sir, next to my father." [25]

Beecher, in turn, had an almost identical recollection when he took the stand weeks later. He told the court it felt to him as if he had known Tilton ever since coming to Brooklyn in 1847 (Theodore had joined

Plymouth Church in 1853, two years after Elizabeth did). "He was youthful, very youthful, and of an engaging manner, and a very comely appearance. . . . [He] won my sympathy from the first. . . . [He] was witty and amusing in conversation." As their bond deepened through "common employments" on the *Independent,* which brought them together "almost every day" by the early 1860s, the relationship became "downright loving on my part." They would visit the libraries and "picture shops," "walk the street," as Theodore had put it, and go "everywhere around the town" together. Tilton was always "doing me little kindnesses that were very agreeable," and they were always exchanging presents and giving one another testimonials. They had some disagreements, even in public, but nothing got in the way of their friendship: one of their serious disputes in the 1860s, in Beecher's recollection, was only a "lover's quarrel."[26]

Each side in the legal battle was of course trying to depict its man as the amiable one with nothing but love in his heart for the other until he discovered the other's true self—Beecher the hypocritical seducer, Tilton the wooden idealist and mercurial blabbermouth. But each man's testimony was so full of compliments for the other, so lavish in portraying an idyllic early friendship, that one cannot miss their genuine loss at its ending. Tilton wept on the stand when his lawyer read from one of Beecher's testimonials to him. True, he and Beecher were renowned "theatrical" spirits (a word Beecher's attorneys loved to hang on Theodore), hence it is possible that Tilton was playacting. But the *Tribune* reporter, a tough-minded skeptic on such matters, did not think so. "Mr. Fullerton [Tilton's lawyer] read effectively the article of Mr. Beecher . . . in which Mr. Tilton was referred to as a brilliant young writer and orator. The reading of the note seemed to affect Mr. Tilton, for he closed his eyes and the tears rolled down his cheeks."[27]

One of the first points Beecher's lawyer William Evarts established in cross-examining Theodore was that Henry had first come to know Elizabeth well because Theodore wished him to. It was a natural consequence of the prior affection between Theodore and his older bosom buddy. Elizabeth was already in awe of her pastor: she "loved him dearly," Theodore said, despite being "a little afraid of him." He wanted Henry to come around more often so as to pay her the same "respect" Henry already paid him, and to grant the Tilton household the same favor he showed other parishioners. Beecher did not need much persuading. He adored going there. "It was very simple," he recalled in his direct examination, "and without the slightest formality; they kept an open, hospitable house, and left all their friends the utmost personal freedom; there was great propriety, with as little convention-ality as I ever saw in a family; and therefore I felt perfectly free to go in and out as I chose, almost." [28]

If Theodore wasn't home, Henry and Elizabeth would talk about "the interests of the church . . . the reformatory movements of the time, in which we are all engaged, of books, of literature, and, above all, of Theodore Tilton" (this last quip unleashed a torrent of laughter in the courtroom). The plaintiff's attorney wondered in the cross-examination if that was really all they talked about. Beecher added that he would also tell Elizabeth of his "great pleasure in the way of her household, and what a place of peace it was, and how I was glad to resort to it, and that it was where people could not find me; I was not run down by people that were at my door all the time. . . . I spoke to her in great admiration of some of her letters which she showed me, of her own, which she had written, one in particular; and a variety of such things; it was entering into her life, and in some sense giving her an insight into mine." The Tiltons' eager welcome allowed him to live "in their household a life of intimate friendship for many years." [29]

There is every reason to believe Beecher's claim that the Tilton house at 174 Livingston Street, a mile away from his own at 124 Co-lumbia Heights, was a refuge—if not from Eunice's persistent scowling, as Theodore alleged, then at least from the crush of his daily demands. The first-floor parlor of Beecher's three-story brownstone overlooking the East River was a hectic business office. Until the scandal broke, he held open house in the parlor from October to June every weekday afternoon from two to four, apparently seeing everyone who called. A reporter who visited in 1874 said the parlor was "an apartment which has no counterpart as to odd variety of contents."

> It is long and wide, and old-style in finish. The walls are divided into panels by projecting posts and by a wooden ledge that runs entirely around the room about four feet from the floor. Bunches and festoons of autumn leaves are hung plentifully about, and there are enough pictures, from oil paintings to cheap ferrotypes, to leave but little of the walls uncovered. The furniture is a chaos of styles. A sofa is high-backed and mushy-bottomed, merging into the softness of second childhood. A concert grand piano is new and shiny. A nondescript cabinet, huge and time-worn, is in a corner. A contrasting new book-case is full of fresh gilt-backed volumes. Two yellowed geographical globes, on high pedestals, stand like sentinels at the corners of the fireplace. A table is covered with a brown woollen spread. Every-

thing is littered with big and little ornamental articles. . . . Handsome bronzes, plaster figures, china articles, countless things impossible to describe as to material or intent, are on the mantel, on the table, on the cabinet, and on carved brackets. Lacking any semblance of method or taste in its furniture, the apartment gains in an air of careless comfort.

By repairing to the Tiltons, Beecher found a "careless comfort" that surpassed his own. The Tiltons' spirit of welcome was the main attraction. But the warm atmosphere was embodied materially in their spacious two-story house, a dwelling set in a busy crossroads a block south of the Fulton Street shops and two blocks east of Court Street, the north-south thoroughfare that split off the elegant "village" of the Heights from the workaday flatlands to the east. "There is comfort and ease in everything," wrote a reporter in 1874 of his visit to the Tiltons' home. "The chairs and lounges are tempting, and seem to have been well used." Another observer stressed the lush casualness of the decor. There were rich carpets, and hanging baskets of flowers changed every day. "Sofas and ottomans were strewn about the rooms in luxurious carelessness." The Tiltons' home had Gothic allure as well as Oriental cushiness, for there were "full-winding passages and mysterious stairways—late at night, if you should be alone in it, it would impress you as a place very likely to be haunted." But the place was safely pious too. Not only were there (in the parlor and adjoining library) "many beautiful pictures in oil and steel engravings, among them the famous painting of Shakespeare, showing the scar over the left eye, by the artist William Page. . . . There also was the celebrated painting of Christ, made by Page, from sittings of Tilton, his friend, whom the painter thinks resembles the great Advocate of Mankind." And a glass dome over one stairway was inscribed with the words "Mine eyes are unto thee, O God."

Whatever the enticing comforts, intriguing quirks, and familiar pieties of the Tilton residence, it would scarcely have attracted Beecher apart from the joy he and his young friends found in each other. His personal significance in their home was signaled by the William Page painting of him that hung in the parlor—along with Shakespeare, Wendell Phillips, De Witt Talmage, and Horace Greeley, *New York Tribune* editor and another frequent guest of the Tiltons in the late 1860s. "Whoever in those years had the pleasing fortune to accept the hospitality of this brilliant man and of his beautiful wife," said one Prof. V. B. Denslow (who apparently knew "the parties intimately"), "must have

retained forever the delightful image of that home. All that could con-
duce to make home lovely was there." [30]

It did not require many visits to Livingston Street for Beecher to
conclude that Mrs. Tilton had an appealing character. "At first," he
said, "I thought she was a woman of great simplicity and purity, and of
fair intelligence." After a while he saw much more.

> As I became better acquainted with her I admired her domestic traits,
> and . . . after some considerable acquaintance [what] I found out was
> a very deep and unusually religious nature, developing itself so differ-
> ently from what we see ordinarily, that it struck me very much. . . .
> Some religious characters develop themselves in ethical strength and
> conscientiousness in all duties; some persons develop themselves in
> their religious nature more largely in social enthusiasm and generosi-
> ties; and some persons develop themselves in veneration and awe.
> Now, in her case it was a very unusual sight for me to see a person
> whose religious character developed itself in the [last] two forms, of
> ecstatic devotion, serenity, peace and trust in God, and . . . generous
> social sympathy and excitement.

Mrs. Tilton was "incessantly" engaged in social service, always telling him "about some case that she had in hand, some poor man, or
some family." Her sense of responsibility for the poor combined with
a mystical sensibility to produce a virtual saint—even if (by Beecher's
telltale omission) she was not so highly developed in the first of the
three religious orientations: "ethical strength and conscientiousness in
all duties." [31]

In the face of all the disagreements between Henry and Theodore
documented in the trial proceedings, it is stunning to find them in absolute accord on one subject: the sainthood of Elizabeth Tilton. She
was a heavenly presence, untainted by sin, responsible for no wrongdoing. She was "beloved of God," in Beecher's phrase, and in Theodore's "as pure as the driven snow, as pure as an angel." Their joint
conviction on this point is so relentless that it prompts us to ask why
a blameless Elizabeth was so indispensable to them both. In part, of
course, they found her radiant because they were smitten by her and
blinded to her imperfections. Love made her glow. But their common
image of a hallowed saint was also indispensable as a legal strategy for
winning the trial, as an emotional strategy for surviving the tensions of
their personal relations, as a spiritual strategy for cultivating the love
that tied them ultimately to their creator. [32]

Dwelling on Elizabeth's sanctity, outdoing one another in their pious worship of her, was a way for both men to divert attention—their own and everyone else's—from less palatable or comprehensible aspects of their ties to her. It was also a way for them to cope with and play out—aggressively and competitively, but under the veil of selfless, irreproachable, religious fervor—the loss of love for each other that they experienced soon after the Civil War. The erosion of their camaraderie did not mean they ceased to have anything in common or that they stopped being friends. They continued to cultivate friendly relations into the early 1870s—after Theodore had accused Henry, at the very least, of improper advances toward Elizabeth. (Theodore claimed on the stand that he had accused him, in December 1870, of adultery; Henry testified he had had no knowledge of such a charge until 1874.) Their shared project of glorifying Elizabeth was a bond between them that persisted even into the ritualized conflict of the "criminal conversation" and "alienation of affections" suit in 1875.

Of course in the weird alchemy of triangular (not to mention binary) love, putting someone on a pedestal does not protect that person from surreptitious assault by the worshipper. Theodore and Henry spoke repeatedly at the trial of their limitless regard for Elizabeth, and meanwhile each tried to save his reputation by divulging sadly that the saint was also disturbed. Her gifts were so pronounced that she was incompetent in such everyday human activities as truth-telling or the calm containment of passion. The saint, in the end, was a temptress. Both men had been fooled, they confessed, by the bright illumination of Elizabeth's ardor for the Lord. Her genuine religious genius had prevented them from recognizing her disorder.

Theodore could not, any more than Henry, speak too highly of Elizabeth's piety and purity. William Evarts skillfully drew Tilton out, during the cross-examination, on the sanctity of Elizabeth's religious character and the passion of her charitable endeavor. She was the organizer and teacher in Plymouth Church's "Bethel" school for married women from Brooklyn's poorer neighborhoods. "Her whole heart was on her duty. She made little notes and sketches in advance of the lessons which she was going to teach them; occasionally some of the women of her class would call and see her." She was not only selfless, but "a perfect lady." What about her views on "feminine chastity?" Evarts wondered. "I think my wife loves everything good and hates everything bad; and I believe today she is a good woman—" Evarts cut him off there, having sprung the trap around him: "Well," Evarts interjected, "we do not differ from you." Theodore was reduced to pleading, "I was going to say that I have never blamed her for the blame which belongs, not to her, but to her betrayer." Evarts was not through. Two days later he made Tilton repeat himself. "I think she is a pure woman," Theodore said. "I hold, with Mr. Beecher, that she is guiltless." [33]

When his own lawyer got him back on the stand under redirect, he tried to get Tilton out of the jam: if she had committed adultery, as Theodore asserted, how could she still be "a good woman"? Tilton's carefully plotted answer first implied he might have been wrong to consider her blameless—perhaps his own judgment had been blinded by his long acquaintance with and veneration of her—but then he abruptly reasserted her total innocence. She was so religious that a spiritual teacher such as Beecher could get her to do anything he wished, as long as he told her it was "pure."

> You must remember, Sir, that I knew Elizabeth when I was ten years old; that I became her confessed lover [i.e., he proclaimed his love for her] at sixteen; that I was married to her at twenty; and that, for fifteen years of her married life, I held her in my reverence perhaps almost to the point of making her an idol of my worship; and when she came to her downfall, it was the necessity of my own heart—I must find some excuse for her; other people might blame, but I must pardon her. I found that excuse in the fact that she had been wrapped up in her religious teacher and guide; she had surrendered her convictions to him; she followed his beck and lead trustingly; she would go after him like one blinded; I think she sinned her sin as one in a trance; I don't think she was a free agent. I think she would have done his bidding if, like the heathen priest in the Hindoo-land, he had bade her fling her child into the Ganges or cast herself under the Juggernaut. That was my excuse for Elizabeth. [34]

Theodore had needed his wife to be a guiltless saint in the past, he was saying, and while he could grasp the justice of the opposing view— that of those "other people" who "might blame"—he couldn't let go of his conviction. He would grant she had sinned but would relieve her of responsibility. His legal suit was menaced by this interpretive balancing act. Was it really plausible to see her as no more than an automaton responding to Beecher's despicable commands? If she was not a free agent, if she was dazed by God and living in a trance, perhaps her affections had been alienated from the start—by God—and Beecher was just caught in her crosshairs, the unwitting target of her unwilled fixation. Tilton was caught himself, for his suit was also threatened if he conceded his wife was morally blemished. Then he could not explain why he had continued living with her peacefully for four years after her original confession to him in 1870 (he said in 1874 she had admitted adultery in that confession; she said in 1874 she had admitted to an unspecified "sin"). To have forgiven her for a morally culpable adultery would have seemed so unmanly to so many responsible gentlemen that the jury might well conclude the adultery story was a concoction to punish Beecher for other transgressions—wrongs that Theodore claimed were multiple.

Theodore's case teetered no matter which way he went on the issue of Elizabeth's "whiteness." And since he had other reasons for asserting her saintliness, it was natural for him to choose purity as his legal strategy. Holding her faultless was a means of magnifying Beecher's wrongdoing, etching a diabolical image of an outside invader bent on destroying the Tilton hearth. Theodore saw himself first and last as Elizabeth's protector. Even in December 1870, when he summoned Beecher to his dressing-down for improper advances (Beecher's version of the charge) or adultery (Tilton's version), his goal was not at all, he said, to threaten or harm Beecher. "The object of that interview was to protect Elizabeth." He obtained a written confession from her as the "basis on which I, as an honorable man, maintaining my self-respect," could hold the interview designed to defend her. Given his all-consuming adoration of his wife, it was impossible for him to believe he acted in a manner contrary to her well-being. She had to be guiltless to be worthy of that boundless devotion, just as some outsider had to be resoundingly guilty.[35]

A "spiritual" theory for Theodore's rigid adherence to Elizabeth's purity overlaps with this psychological one. It had already become clear from the testimony of 1874 that after the Civil War Theodore felt religiously adrift. As he put it on the stand in 1875, "When slavery was abolished, and the war was over, and my occupation, in a certain sense, was gone, . . . I turned to examine the theology in which I had been trained from childhood, and it gradually faded away before my inquisition." He gave up on the divinity of Christ, left Plymouth Church (both to Elizabeth's extreme distress), and looked for other causes and friends to spark his enthusiasm. The liberalization of divorce and the women's suffrage movement came the closest to meeting his needs. Meanwhile he watched Elizabeth turn to Henry for a spiritual bond like the one she had formerly had with Theodore. Henry welcomed her emotional and religious overture, launching Theodore on a dual path: unspoken withdrawal from Henry—although, as a convinced cultural liberal, he did not prohibit his wife's friendly relations with him, and indeed continued to be amicable himself—and competitive veneration of Elizabeth. In the late 1860s, as he was off for months at a time lecturing as far west as Kansas, she became, in the absence of church or divine savior or all-absorbing social cause, his own personal religion. With God's love now reduced in his mind from saving grace to mythic symbol, Theodore embraced a compensatory faith in spousal blessedness.[36]

Beecher's reasons for finding Elizabeth blameless and saintly were different. For his legal defense he needed her to be pure, of course, so that she could not possibly have committed adultery with anyone, much less him. Marital infidelity had to be a concept of which she could not even conceive. When William Evarts asked him if he had "directly or indirectly solicited improper favors" from Mrs. Tilton, Beecher answered, according to the transcript, "[Emphatically] Never!" When Evarts asked next if he had ever "received improper favors from her," he said, more expansively, "[With great emphasis] It was a thing impossible to her—Never! [Applause.]" One of Beecher's defenses against the charge that he had confessed to sexual improprieties was that he himself could not possibly have used the language that was attributed to him by Tilton and the Moultons. He could of course never have spoken of such things with Emma Moulton, he said, since until she joined what he called the "conspiracy" against him he had considered her "a lady" as well as a "sister": "she was more to me than a bank of Spring flowers." But he was incapable even with a man of discussing what his lawyer termed "sexual intercourse," for that was (in Henry's words) "loathsome and odious stuff, that I don't talk about. . . . Such language is simply impossible to me." Since he himself allegedly never talked about such things, Elizabeth Tilton, on his account, was not likely to pay them any mind.[37]

Beecher had his own psychological and spiritual reasons for elevating Elizabeth to the apex of religious perfection. It was essential for his own well-being that he judge his relationship with Elizabeth to be sacred, not profane. He had to believe, as he put it on the stand, that he had come to have "affection and respect for her as a Christian woman, and a mother, and a wife, surrounded by a lovely family," but not, in his lawyer's phrase, any "affection or love toward her, as a woman, otherwise than in these connections." He had known her since girlhood, had performed her marriage, and considered her religiously one-of-a-kind. "I loved her as one would his own child," he said in a prepared statement issued in 1874, and read into the trial record. "She had grown up under my teachings. She had never known any other religious teacher, and she had associated with my name, and illumined it by her imagination, whatever was worthy of affection and trust."

> Leaving to others the unwelcome task of refined moral criticism upon this gentle and pure-minded woman, it is for me explicitly to defend her from any charge of criminality of conduct, and to dissipate even the shadow of a reproach upon her untempted honor, and to join with her husband, who has again and again, with loyal affection and with justice, defended the personal purity of his wife.[38]

Like Theodore, Henry didn't mind suggesting that "other people might blame" her with some justice. But he would not. He had been shaped by her spiritual greatness. He had come to depend on her for the validation of his own spiritual power: her piety, learned in part from him, was one visible sign of his own chosenness. Moreover, his very theology depended upon the model piety of inspired women like Elizabeth. He had long since thrown over the guilt-inducing irascible Father and embraced a faith heavy on the divinity of a tender Jesus, the fecundity of nature, and the passionate spotlessness of women. Elizabeth was one of the foundational beams of his theology, as she was proof of his pastoral competence. There was no place in his Romantic, liberal vision for the orthodox Reformation viewpoint in which one's best efforts to do good inevitably contained, under the heavy drapery of good intentions, a thick mesh of sinful acts and dismal consequences. Elizabeth's purity protected both of the men she loved from undue assaults on their preferred self-conceptions. It offered each of them critical support as they worked out and sustained their religious beliefs. "She had a genius of religious sentiment," Beecher said in the 1874 statement. "Had she lived in other days, and in the Catholic Church, she has always seemed to me to be one of those who would have inspirations and ecstatic visions."[39]

V.   Henry still had a problem in the legal case even if he and Elizabeth had been irreproachably proper. Theodore's lawyers wished to know how Beecher could then account for all the kissing that went on, by his own admission, between himself and Elizabeth. Henry's defense team came up with an effective counterattack. They had Beecher respond that he and Theodore kissed as much or more than he and Elizabeth did, and had him assert — often with very winning, self-deprecating humor — that the kissing was just a jolly touch of bohemianism in the unconventional but thoroughly respectable Tilton household. Then the lawyers deftly reminded the jury of rumors that Theodore was the one who had long engaged in actually illicit kissing. Aside from the legal strategizing, Henry's testimony on the kissing at 174 Livingston Street, combined with Theodore's, revealed another tie that bound them in spite of their bitter conflict. They both felt superior to all the sanctimonious New Yorkers and Brooklynites who blushed at hearty bodily contact. Far from being a taint on anyone's honor, it was a healthy frolic, an instance of natural piety.

Tilton family friend Sarah Putnam said on the stand that the Tiltons "always were very cordial and warm, and always greeting with a kiss and . . . always calling each other by their first names, after the style of the Friends." Theodore told her that kissing people was "Scriptural; that the Bible said: 'Greet one another with a holy kiss,' and he thought he liked the Oriental style of kissing; he liked to see gentlemen kiss." According to Theodore's testimony, he and Henry kissed occasionally, not frequently. They agreed on the propriety of friendly kissing, even if they had divergent recollections of particular kisses—such as the one Theodore remembered Henry planting on his forehead. That positioning of the kiss was off "by about four inches," Henry claimed. "I kissed him on his mouth." Beecher enjoyed himself on the stand talking about the kissing, and about sitting periodically on Theodore's lap, for he generally got a good laugh, even from the judge. He left everyone in stitches when he said that after a momentous "interview" with the two Tiltons in early 1871, in which they all agreed to be friends despite Theodore's having charged him (in Beecher's version) with improper overtures, they sealed their euphoric resolution with a round of kisses. "When we arose," Beecher said, "I kissed him and he kissed me, and I kissed his wife and she kissed me, and I believe they kissed each other. [Laughter.]"[40]

But under cross-examination Beecher faltered once on the subject of kissing, and left an opening for Tilton's side. Plaintiff's attorney William Fullerton worked his way up to the kissing by reopening the subject of Beecher's "buggy" rides with Mrs. Tilton. Under direct examination Henry had spoken of two such rides in early 1870, one of them at Theodore's urging. Fullerton wished to know if there were any other rides. Beecher replied, "I think that before these I had taken some rides, but I have no recollection of them definitely." Fullerton asked if those past rides might have taken place in a "close[d] carriage," and Beecher said, "I have no recollection whatever, Sir, of it." Nor did he recall when the earlier rides occurred, how long they lasted, whether he and Mrs. Tilton ever alighted from their vehicle(s), where he got the vehicle(s) and who drove them, whether they ever went to Greenwood Cemetery (where two of her babies were buried in the Tilton plot), or whether anyone else ever accompanied them.[41]

As he often did during his testimony, Beecher was here applying a very strict standard to the notion of "recall": if he didn't recall an event perfectly, he didn't recall it at all. There was some amorphous mass of prior rides in his memory, but since he could not distinguish them with absolute clarity from one another, he had nothing further to offer about them. Theodore had applied exactly the same high standard of recall when he was on the stand weeks earlier. And they both used that rigid standard in responding to lawyers' questions about conversations others had testified to having had with them. If there was anything in the alleged conversation that was not exactly accurate, then the entire recollection was, in Beecher's or Tilton's view, a "pure fiction." Since each of them in his testimony invented dialogue to convey "substance," the other, when asked about it, could readily dismiss it as fiction, which it literally was.

Having established that Beecher, at the very least, was reticent about discussing his buggy rides, Fullerton moved on to kissing.

"Were you in the habit of kissing her?" he asked.

"I was when I had been absent any considerable time."

"And how frequently did that occur?"

"Very much; I kissed her as I would any of my own family."

"I beg your pardon. I don't want you to tell me you kissed her as you did anybody else. I want to know if you kissed her."

"I did kiss her."

"Were you in the habit of kissing her when you went to her house in the absence of her husband?"

"Sometimes I did, and sometimes I did not."

"Well, what prevented you upon the occasions when you did not?"

"It may be that the children were there then; it might be that she did not seem in the——to greet me in that way."

"Well, do you mean by that that you didn't kiss her when the children were present?"

"I sometimes did, and sometimes did not."

"Did you kiss her in the presence of the servants?"

"Not that I ever recollect."

"Was it not true that you did not kiss her in the presence of the children or the servants, but did kiss her when she was not in their presence?"

"No, Sir, it is not true in any——as I understand your question."

"I don't know how you understand the question; it is about as plain as I can make it. Did you not purposely omit to kiss her in the presence of the children and the servants?"

"No, Sir, I did not; in the presence of the children, certainly not."

That clarification muddied the waters by suggesting he might have purposely omitted to kiss her in the presence of the servants. That implied admission raised the question why, if the kissing was so familial, he would have hesitated to do it in their presence. Beecher was at the very least unsettled, and perhaps, as with the buggy rides, unwilling to divulge or confront some truth about his tie to Mrs. Tilton. His hemming and hawing proved nothing damaging in itself. But it showed, in conjunction with other halting or evasive responses, that something had gone on between him and Elizabeth that he was very uncomfortable talking about. Perhaps it was some act or touch he was hiding, perhaps it was something he could not admit or even articulate to himself. There is no reason to conclude it was sexual, although it may well have been. There is every reason to conclude there was an intense, emotional, spiritual connection between him and Elizabeth that prompted them to imagine a still closer, physical bond.[42]

The closest the plaintiff's side came to producing a smoking gun was the "clandestine letters," as they came to be known, that Beecher wrote to Mrs. Tilton in the early 1870s. Together with the awkward performance on his kissing habits and several other subjects, these letters showed that Henry and Elizabeth had had some kind of secret relationship—a relationship hidden at least partially from other people. The plaintiff hoped that proving a secret connection would persuade the jury that sexual intercourse had occurred. Otherwise, why would Henry and Elizabeth have needed secrecy?

On January 20, 1872, Beecher wrote to Mrs. Tilton that "I shall be in New Haven next week, to begin my course of lectures . . . on preaching. My wife takes boat for Havana and Florida on Thursday." Elizabeth would have understood that Eunice was going away for the winter, on her annual sojourn to warmer climes. In March of 1871 or 1872 Henry wrote Elizabeth a note that became known as the "true inwardness" letter, which said, in part, that "no one can ever know—none but God—through what a dreary wilderness I have wandered!"

> There was Mount Sinai, there was the barren sand, there was the alternation of hope and despair that marked the pilgrimage of old. If only it might lead to the Promised Land!—or, like Moses, shall I die on the border? Your hope and courage are like medicine. Should God

inspire you to restore and rebuild at home, and while doing it to cheer and sustain outside of it another who sorely needs help in heart and spirit, it will prove a life so noble as few are able to live! And, in another world, the emancipated soul may utter thanks!

If it would be a comfort to *you*, now and then, to send me a letter of true *inwardness*—the outcome of your inner life—it *would* be safe, for I am now at home here with my sister; and it is *permitted to you*, and it will be an exceeding refreshment to me, for your heart experiences are often like bread from heaven to the hungry. God has enriched your moral nature. May not others partake? [43]

During the direct examination, William Evarts took the letter up part by part, but he elided the phrases "it would be safe, for I am now at home with my sister," and "it would be permitted to you." He let Beecher claim that "safe" and "permitted" meant the same thing. They signified, according to Henry, that "when a woman is invited to pour out her innermost thoughts on religious subjects, it is——she has a right to the knowledge that it shall not be shown; it was to be one of those letters that I would not take to [Frank] Moulton"—who, by agreement with Henry and Theodore, was safeguarding all the documents related to their delicate situation. A letter of "true inwardness," touching only upon Elizabeth's interior spiritual life, would be for Henry's eyes only—not Frank's, perhaps not Theodore's either. Hence such a letter, despite the agreement, was "permitted" to her. There was no other sense, Beecher repeated, in which he had meant "it would be safe." [44]

On cross-examination William Fullerton zeroed in on "safe." "Why did you say that it would be safe for her to do it?" he asked. Beecher tried again to elide "safe" and "permitted," but Fullerton pressed him further.

"Your wife was away, was she not?"

"She was."

"And that [Eunice being at home] would not have been so safe, would it?"

"It would have been safe, perfectly safe for her [Elizabeth], but if she [Eunice] was gone [temporarily] and my sister was not there, the letters were liable, therefore, to be misled or lost, or might fall into hands that ought not to have them."

"Who opened your letters in the absence of yourself and your wife?"

"I opened them."

"In the absence of yourself and your wife?"

"Oh, I think they were not opened, Sir; they were taken by the servants, and, or ought always to be, put where they would be safe, but were not always."

"Well, your servants had no authority to open letters?"

"No, Sir; but they had a habit of misplacing a good many papers."[45]

Fullerton had fallen well short of demonstrating adultery, but he had nicely established Beecher's desire for secret communication with a woman who was balm for his soul. The only logical explanation for "safe" was that Eunice wouldn't see the letter. If "safe" meant what he now said it did—that the servants wouldn't fumble with it—then it was *never* safe for Elizabeth to send a letter: both he and his sister might be out, and it might fall into the inept hands of the hired help. Fullerton had shown how edgy Henry was with the whole subject. Maybe he was tense because he had been cornered and forced to lie to protect himself, his family, and Elizabeth Tilton and her family. Maybe he was uneasy because he could not confront—at the very least publicly, and perhaps even consciously—the magnitude of his emotional and spiritual bond with Mrs. Tilton.

There was no need to assume adultery, Henry had avowed earlier, to explain the pit of psychic angst unveiled in his "ragged edge" letter to Frank Moulton in 1872. Likewise there was no need to posit adultery to account for the secrecy and yearning revealed in the "true inwardness" letter—although a befuddled Beecher was not about to perceive the parallel. The plaintiff, compelled by the judicial rules to prove sexual intercourse, had to pray that the jury would infer physical love from evidence of concealed communication in the March letter and the merest hint of planning a rendezvous in the January letter (as in, Eunice leaves Thursday, I'll be in New Haven next week, so how about Friday or Saturday?). Theodore was in the ironic position of hoping the jurymen would misconstrue the Romantic Christianity he had long shared with Beecher, would miss its quest for the bliss of profound religious union, would reduce it to a hunt for sexual gratification.

VI.   Beecher's lawyers conducted a two-front war, defending Beecher and attacking Tilton. If the jury could be persuaded that Theodore had alienated Elizabeth's affections all by himself, there would be no affections left for Henry to have alienated. Beecher might have mistakenly believed he had alienated them, and felt horrible as a result, but it would have been Theodore who had destroyed his own marriage. The defense matched many of the charges made against

Henry with equivalent countercharges against Theodore. If Henry was accused of sleeping with Elizabeth, then they would smear Theodore with stories of him sleeping with several women, including Victoria Woodhull and young Bessie Turner, a servant in his own house, whom he not only regularly "kissed" and "caressed," according to Beecher's report of her story to him, but twice carried off to bed. If Theodore accused Henry of having told Elizabeth that sexual intercourse outside of marriage was just fine as long as it was spiritually motivated, then Henry's team would accuse Theodore of using identical language to seduce Bessie Turner.[46]

Meanwhile, if the plaintiff wished to call Beecher the preacher of a feel-good religion of love and gush, then Tilton was a wayward disciple who went beyond the pale into "free love" (after all, he supported freer divorce), "spiritualism" (he approved of Woodhull, who was a medium and a clairvoyant), and "Communism" (he marched in support of the French Commune in 1871). If Beecher went out on buggy rides with Elizabeth, then Tilton rode off with Woodhull to Coney Island and quite possibly went "bathing" with her (Theodore heatedly denied the bathing part). Theodore's memory was just like Henry's: he could only definitely remember two Coney Island outings with Woodhull, but had to grant there might easily have been more—about which he could "recall" nothing. Moreover, if Beecher's exact whereabouts on October 10 or 17, 1868, were in doubt—on both of those Saturdays, with Theodore in New England lecturing, Henry was (he conceded) in Brooklyn with nothing particular on the agenda—then what was Theodore doing spending an entire night at Woodhull's place in September 1871? Writing her "biography," Theodore responded (part of the plan to buy her silence, he claimed), then catching some winks on the couch.

Beecher's lawyers were merciless in their ridicule of Tilton, going far beyond Henry himself in holding Theodore up to scorn. They no more proved him immoral than the plaintiff proved Beecher an adulterer, but each side showed that the other's client had his head floating frequently in the clouds. Henry said he went for years without registering Elizabeth's womanly affection for him. Theodore said, to take one example, that he'd had no idea a poem he'd published could possibly have been interpreted as being about his wife. Six months after Victoria Woodhull's first public charge that a well-known public figure had debauched the wife of another well-known public figure, Theodore published "Sir Marmaduke's Musings." The poem included these two stanzas:

> I gained what men call friends
> But now their love is hate
> And I have learned too late
> How mated minds unmate
> And friendship ends.
>
> I clasped a woman's breast
> As if her heart I knew
> Or fancied would be true
> Who proved—alas! she too
> False like the rest.

Referring to the last stanza, William Evarts wondered why, "after there had been in circulation enough of imputations upon your wife to have reached Mrs. Woodhull," Tilton did not think publishing the poem under his own name and in his own paper *The Golden Age* might pose a risk to his wife and family. "I will answer you, Mr. Evarts," Theodore replied. "If I had stopped to reflect that the publication of that little poem which I wrote one day on a railway train, would have led any human being to have supposed that I meant Elizabeth, I would have cut off my right hand rather than have printed it." [47]

Tilton was remarkably unruffled by the cross-examination. The closest he came to losing his cool was during the direct examination by his own lawyer William Fullerton. He turned and pleaded directly to the jury on the thorny subject of Mrs. Woodhull. Evarts, always quick to object, let Theodore go ahead and erupt. "I wish to say distinctly to the jury that my relationship to Mrs. Woodhull was a foolish one and a wrong one, as the event has justified, and I do not ask any man to defend me for it, but to blame me for it. But I say here before God that Mr. Beecher is as much responsible for my connection with Mrs. Woodhull as I am myself." Theodore's befriending of Victoria, he said, was part of an unsuccessful plan, approved by Beecher, to keep her from tattling on them all. Tilton's plea suggested he knew he was in danger of sinking on the Woodhull connection. All he could do was grope for the nearest lifeboat: contend that he was no worse than Henry, who was in on the whole deal from the start. (In his later testimony, Henry said he was always dubious about the Woodhull plan, and always, unlike Theodore, disapproving of her.) The parallels to Beecher's testimony continued: Henry tried to save himself by depicting Elizabeth as "bereft of reason," Theodore by proclaiming Victoria treacherous. Each man sought readmission to the culture of character by confessing to having acted foolishly, having been burned, but having learned his lesson: you can't be too careful with spirited women liable, despite their charms or virtues, to take you down.[48]

The defense strategy of smudging Tilton's name may have sparked some sympathy for him, since he bore the brunt of the attacks with grace and even, at times, with self-critical humor. He laughed with the audience when Evarts made fun of his faulty French in a published poem that repeated, as a chorus line, "Aimer, aimer, c'est à vivre." He halfheartedly countered that it was a misprint—it should have been "Aimer, aimer, ah! c'est vivre"—but admitted to a faulty command of the French language. Theodore was at times eloquent, and always articulate, if sometimes too long-winded for the taste of the pro-Beecher *Tribune* (and official court) stenographer. Unlike the clipped and efficient Frank Moulton, whose testimony began the plaintiff's case, Tilton spoke "with almost aggravating deliberation. . . . His answers sometimes were long to the point of wearisomeness." Yet his patient, cooperative attitude even under cross-examination won him many supporters at the time, as well as a majority of twentieth-century writers on the scandal, who have regarded his often voiced interest in exposing the entire truth as evidence that what he exposed was the truth. Tilton has frequently stood in the historical literature as the herald of twentieth-century openness in a Victorian world of dark secrets.

His self-conscious posture of methodical truth-telling was much less persuasive to contemporaries. Many of them saw him as a moody, unpredictable squealer who proclaimed his desire to safeguard his family from scandalous charges, then bruited them recklessly about. Evarts got Tilton to admit that he shared his wife's alleged adultery confession with a whole series of individuals. Evarts also showed that the only plausible source of some of Victoria Woodhull's spicy information about the case was Tilton himself. Tilton's acknowledged strategy of talking about adultery between 1870 and 1873 was widely taken in 1874 and 1875 as a sign of his desperation. On the one hand, he wanted to protect Elizabeth, so he had to keep stories about her and Beecher quiet. But protecting Elizabeth also meant having a job, and Beecher was conspiring with *Independent* publisher Henry Bowen, he thought, to get him fired. Beecher had to be pressured to desist, and the only available pressure was the threat to expose his relation to Elizabeth. Theodore was reduced to lurching back and forth between silence and disclosure: affirming his wife's purity, then telling a few friends she had confessed. Those friends would tell their friends, and Beecher would feel the heat. Theodore was indeed in a fix, and his

understandable zeal to save his family by protecting his livelihood—
and that meant safeguarding the reputation upon which his livelihood
as a writer and lecturer depended—may have left him no other course
than the extremely risky path he chose: tacking back and forth between
secrecy and exposure.

In the legal struggle and the battle of public images, Tilton probably
stood no chance of overcoming the biggest strikes against him: he forgave his wife for the alleged adultery and then, a few years later, pinned
a scarlet letter on her chest. Many people, unable to imagine his initial
forgiveness, concluded he had made up the adultery story. Those who
could imagine it condemned him for not keeping his silence once he
had forgiven her. But there were also points in the testimony that were
damaging to Beecher, and they may have given Tilton some faint hope
of a surprise victory. The clandestine letters weakened Beecher's case
considerably, but they did not in themselves generate as much sympathy for Theodore as a single admission made by Beecher on the
stand—an admission that gave some substance to the charge that he
had willfully, not inadvertently, wrecked Theodore's home.[49]

On December 14, 1870, according to his recollection, Beecher had
a visit from Bessie Turner, who summoned him to Mrs. Morse's. Elizabeth had left her husband, Turner told him, and was staying at her
mother's. Beecher was astonished, and Bessie told him Mrs. Tilton
"was justified in taking some such step" because "Mr. Tilton had
abused her," treated her "with great rudeness and cruelty." When Beecher arrived at Mrs. Morse's, Elizabeth sat quietly by and her mother
did the talking. Beecher recalled her saying that "her daughter had
lived a life of great unhappiness, that she was subject to great cruelty,
and to deprivation, and that her life . . . had become intolerable to her,"
and that she had decided to separate from Theodore. On the stand all
Beecher remembered asking Elizabeth herself was "how is it that I have
been so long with you and you never alluded before to me about distress in your household?" She answered that "she sought to conceal, in
the hope that the difficulty would pass away."

Beecher counseled "patience" and "forbearance," and said he would
return the following day with his wife, "a much better adviser about
domestic affairs than I was." The next day Eunice talked briefly with
Elizabeth, then went alone upstairs with Mrs. Morse. Henry could not
recall whether he and Elizabeth spoke when left by themselves. When
Eunice returned with Mrs. Morse (had they talked about how best
to join forces against Theodore, as Tilton claimed in 1874?), they all
prayed together and the Beechers said they would go home, think

things over, and return the following day with a recommendation. Thinking it over at home with his wife, Henry told her "it was not best to break up the family relation," while Eunice thought "Mrs. Tilton ought not to continue living with her husband." Their deliberation was cut short by the arrival of company, so Eunice never told her husband what Mrs. Morse or Mrs. Tilton had revealed to her. Yet as Eunice went out the door to go back to Mrs. Morse's, Henry scrawled a note, writing, "I incline to think that your view is right, and that a separation and settlement of support will be wisest." That was the course Eunice recommended.[50]

The Tiltons' separation lasted only a short time—between a few days and a couple of weeks. But Beecher's behavior allowed the plaintiff to divert attention from Theodore's performance as husband and mark Henry as a home-wrecker. Why, having counseled patience and forbearance, and having never had an inkling of any marital trouble in a household he had known intimately, did Beecher not seek information from Tilton, whom he conceded he still at this time considered a friend? (Beecher admitted he made no effort to contact him.) Why concur so readily with Eunice's judgment when he had initially opposed it, and had not heard what Mrs. Tilton and Mrs. Morse had said to her? These questions about Beecher's actions did not point to adultery any more than his clandestine letters or his despairing letters of apology did. But a mass readership sensed a curious lapse in Henry's performance as a pastoral adviser and friend. In Theodore's wider war of reputations with Henry, this was a rare moment of victory for Tilton.

VII. On June 25 the jury was still deliberating, and the newsstands were featuring Elizabeth Tilton's defense against the upholsterers' charges. That evening Henry Ward Beecher addressed an overflow crowd in Plymouth Church's lecture room. He did not refer to the Tiltons by name, but he told a story about them, wrapped in a meandering story about himself. "Things are judged by the way in which they stand tests," he began. To test a thoroughbred horse you ride him across a plowed field, for "a level turnpike does not show his wind or bottom like a ride over plowed ground." A bridge can't be rated by its elegance, but by how it handles "a train of cars" passing over it. The Seventh Regiment can't be judged by how it looks in its "parade on Broadway," but only by "its performance when it is sent to march with Sherman to the sea."

This stream of images prepared the way for a general meditation on the moral development of a young man and woman. Like the two young men in the parable Grover Cleveland remembered hearing in the 1850s, this pair was going to encounter tough times. Beecher let everyone know whom he was talking about by dropping the otherwise extraneous detail that the young woman "when about 22 gets married." Children arrive, the trials of life follow. The husband "goes through the fluctuations that come with experience." Like the Tiltons, they suffer financial reverses, and "various dissenting elements come between her and her husband." At this point, without explanation, the young man drops out of the story. "Now the test comes of her religion. Did it enable her to bear burdens herself that others might go free? Did it fortify her in the practice of patience? This is the test of religion."

Beecher said no more about her. He left the audience to decide whether Elizabeth Tilton had passed the test. The parable was unfinished, the jury still out on her moral development. She had performed well of late, patiently bearing her burdens. But Beecher had been rocked before by her changes of story and he was going to reserve judgment. The husband, meanwhile, did not fail the test, since he had never shown up for the examination. Like Theodore, he had strayed from the religion of his early adulthood that might have equipped him to face the reverses of life. Beecher banished him from the terrain of legitimate moral struggle.

As his tale proceeded Beecher glided imperceptibly from Elizabeth's test into his own. "Does [religion] take away the snarls and troubles of life, and enable a person to bear up under the insults of men? It is the tested men who show what religion is."

> I have gone through as many troubles in the last five years as ordinarily fall to the lot of any one man. . . . Without the resources of religion I would have been overwhelmed and smothered by them. . . .
> I have gone through great trials, and I must have the opportunity to say to you, as I would like to say privately and confidentially, that God has tried me sorely. And although I have gone under the wave and have been almost overcome, God has sustained me. . . . My heart is not embittered against any living person, nor is it soured in any way nor turned against anyone. Nor is there a person in the world the latchets of whose shoes I would not rejoice to unloose in the way of my duty. [Applause.]

Responding to the many critics who had dubbed his religion a mere marketing of good feeling, Beecher offered "a word more" by stressing the stringency of his Christian doctrine, which mirrored St. Paul's.

I have gone through these trials and have come out with forgiveness in my heart, and whether I go up or down, I am victorious, for God is my power, my strong fortress, and He cares more than man can care for me. I have, therefore, the right to say that it is not in vain to follow Christ, and that religion is more than a sentiment or a rhapsody—that it is good to live by, to die by, and to live hereafter by. . . . For whether I live or whether I die, I am the Lord's first and men's afterward.

Beecher closed by lashing out at the press for its vicious sarcasm, especially its glee at reporting his frequent tearful displays in private and in public. The papers had mocked Theodore as unmanly for the same reason. "I would ask," Henry concluded, "that what I have said should not be reported. But the very things that ought not to be reported— that hurt somebody, but benefit no one—are the things that are reported, and it is our misfortune to live, as it were, out of doors. We cannot cry or wipe our eyes but it is known and commented on."[51]

On July 12, in the aftermath of the divided verdict that came down on July 2, Beecher repeated these themes to a crowd at his summer home. "The people and temporary residents of Peekskill, N.Y. and that neighborhood, preceded by a band of music and a company of militia, marched to Rest Hill" and "serenaded" him. After "Judge Wells" expressed the crowd's "confidence in him as a man and a Christian minister of the Gospel, Mr. Beecher spoke for nearly an hour." What he added now, with the trial finished, was a veiled comment about himself in relation to Theodore Tilton. "I have no new course to take. I am too old to change my position. I shall go on trusting men. I have pursued that doctrine all my life and only once in forty years have I made a mistake. I shall love men; I shall not stop to think of their faults before I love them."[52]

VIII. Mrs. Tilton, after her denial of the upholsterers' charges in June, slipped off the historical stage, to return only briefly three years later for her last confession. The *Chicago Tribune* reported in May that she was still living at the home of Plymouth Church friends Edward and Maria Ovington, who had taken her in when she left Theodore the previous July. (They considered her a saint too: she had visited them daily in the late 1860s when Edward was chronically ill.) "Letters of sympathy and offers of assistance have been received by her from different parts of the country. . . . She receives very few visitors, and passes her time between reading and writing. She is reported as being about to keep a boarding-house, through the summer, up the Hudson." Elizabeth had kept boarders on Livingston Street to help pay the bills, and had lived for years, both as a child and with Theodore after their marriage, in the Brooklyn boarding house her mother ran after the death of Elizabeth's father. Elizabeth was allegedly busy writing more than letters. "It is said Mrs. Tilton is engaged in the composition of a novel founded on the incidents of her life." If she did write a novel, there has never been any trace of it. If she didn't, the story that she was writing one was a fitting concoction. She loved fiction. She made sense of her life by reading novels and letting their characters inform and illuminate her view of herself.[53]

Critics at the time, and later historians, have had much fun with her for her alleged inability to distinguish reality from art (supposedly a part of her general problem with telling the "truth"), or for infusing her life with the frothy sentimentalism of her favorite books. But these critiques miss the central point. She turned to fiction not to escape from life but to get help in grasping the strange forces and desires that made up her everyday world. Her own story made more sense when she saw it in relation to other tales of men and women struggling to love, work, build families, obey God. Whether those tales were merely written or also lived, they had the same power to convey wisdom. Her reading of Charles Reade's *Griffith Gaunt* in 1871 may have begun as restful diversion, but the book opened a dam in her self-understanding. Her insight that she, like Catherine Gaunt, had sinned in loving her spiritual adviser was anything but an evasion of reality. It marked her refusal to give way to sentiment or fantasy. It was a decision to face the truth about herself, come what may.

As she sat silently in court for almost six months in 1875, however, she occupied a cultural position that had little to do with her own story. She had come to stand for a particularly female changeability and unreliability, but she was a unique case too. Mystery hung about her like a shroud. She could not be lodged in a stable story, a precondition for passing judgment upon her. Most Americans felt it was easy to laugh off Victoria Woodhull and the other "public" women who campaigned in the 1870s for revolution in the relations between the sexes. They were ridiculous on the face of it, with their short hair, their brazen performances on lecture platforms, their shameless assault on the sanctity of marriage. It was harder to know what to do with a Christian mother of four whose famous pastor regarded *her* as a spiritual mentor. Here was a shy and prayerful woman who considered her impassioned knowing of Beecher a sin, yet who considered the sin a path to personal awakening. With him she had finally felt known and loved. Some, like Catharine Beecher, thought she was intermittently insane. Others believed she had succumbed to the destabilizing women's rights clamor. Still others suspected she had gravitated into the netherworld of spiritualist "mediumship." Henry and Theodore considered her a mystic, and in many ways a saint. Whatever they thought of her, a mass of Americans felt her as a marker for strange unsettlings in the deepest regions of middle-class life.[54]

Victoria Woodhull, Elizabeth Cady Stanton, Susan B. Anthony.

Mrs. Woodhull and Her Critics.
To the Editor of the New-York Times:

Because I am a woman, and because I conscientiously hold opinions somewhat different from the self-elected orthodoxy which men find their profit in supporting; and because I think it my bounden duty and my absolute right to put forward my opinions and to advocate them with my whole strength, self-elected orthodoxy assails me, villifies me, and endeavors to cover my life with ridicule and dishonor. This has been particularly the case in reference to certain law proceedings into which I was recently drawn by the weakness of one very near relative and the profligate selfishness of other relatives.

One of the charges made against me is that I lived in the same house with my former husband, Dr. WOODHULL, and my present husband, Col. BLOOD. The fact is a fact. Dr. WOODHULL being sick, ailing and incapable of self-support, I felt it my duty to myself and to human nature that he should be cared for, although his incapacity was in no wise attributable to me. My present husband, Col. BLOOD, not only approves of this charity, but co-operates in it. I esteem it one of the most virtuous acts of my life. But various editors have stigmatized me as a living example of immorality and unchastity.

My opinions and principles are subjects of just criticism. I put myself before the public voluntarily. I know full well that the public will criticise me and my motives and actions, in their own way and at their own time. I accept the position. I except to no fair analysis and examination, even if the scalpel be a little merciless.

But let him who is without sin cast his stone. I do not intend to be made the scape-goat of sacrifice, to be offered up as a victim to society by those who cover over the foulness of their lives and the feculence of their thoughts with hypocritical mouth of fair professions, and by diverting public attention from their own iniquity and pointing the finger at me. I know that many of my self-appointed judges and critics are deeply tainted with the vices they condemn. I live in one house with one who was my husband; I live as the wife with one who is my husband. I believe in Spiritualism; I advocate free love in the highest, purest sense, as the only cure for the immorality, the deep damnation by which men corrupt and disfigure God's most holy institution of sexual relations. My judges preach against "free love" openly, practice it secretly. Their outward seeming is fair; inwardly they are full of "dead men's bones and all manner of uncleanness." For example, I know of one man, a public teacher of eminence, who lives in concubinage with the wife of another public teacher of almost equal eminence. All three concur in denouncing offenses against morality. "Hypocrisy is the tribute paid by vice to virtue." So be it. But I decline to stand up as "the frightful example." I shall make it my business to analyze some of these lines, and will take my chances in the master of libel suits.

I have faith in critics, but I believe in public justice.   VICTORIA C. WOODHULL.

NEW-YORK, Saturday, May 20, 1871.

For $72 per line, we will insert an advertisement ONE MONTH in 229 first-class New-York newspapers, including twenty-two dailies. We refer to the publisher of this paper.

FIVE *Private Retellings, Public Exposures, 1870–1873*

I.   For more than three years Beecher and the Tiltons kept a lid on their secret, whatever it was. They were not all hiding the same thing, and they were not keeping quiet to the same degree. Henry was the mutest, concealing his love for Elizabeth as well as his emotional meltdown. Elizabeth was covering up her love for Henry and her habit of signing contradictory documents dictated by others. Off and on she was telling her mother and various friends, including suffrage leader Susan B. Anthony, that her husband mistreated her, and that she had been overly involved with Henry. Theodore was keeping officially quiet about the love between his wife and her pastor, thus cloaking what he believed was his own cuckolding. Meanwhile, although technically protecting his wife's purity, he was telling a lot of people (at least twelve, by his later grudging admission to William Evarts) some kind of story about Beecher debauching her. The one thing all three principals shared was an acute sense of danger: the rumors circulating about Henry and Elizabeth's connection could do them all immense damage.

We naturally think of the "cover-up" as a plot to prevent the public from knowing the "truth." But the deeper meaning of the cover-up is that for three years it permitted the three main players to suspend their own efforts to figure out what was true. In effect they agreed to disagree about what had happened among them. The pressing need was to dispel the ugly stories, not to settle on a single story, whatever that might have been. They could formally forgive and forget, and sometimes feel a rekindling of the close bonds they had known in the 1860s. They could concentrate on how to stop the rampant rumors from dripping

like acid through the outer crust of their reputations. Of course in retrospect we can see that the cover-up was doomed by the double games
all of them were playing. Theodore kept spreading the very rumors
they were ostensibly trying to contain; Elizabeth continued to dispar-
age Theodore to family and friends; Henry went on communicating
secretly with Elizabeth, and she with him. The latter two generated
new secrets while Theodore heightened demand on the outside for exposing the whole festering pool of them. The public call for "truth"
gathered in waves beginning in 1871 and pounded through the dike
in 1874.

But as Beecher and the Tiltons actually lived through the cover-up,
they may have felt as much hope as foreboding. There are signs that
between 1871 and 1873 they viewed the horrible flare-up of December 30, 1870, as an aberration. That was the evening when Theodore
accused Henry of either improper advances or adultery, and they each
in turn—first Henry, then Theodore—roused Elizabeth from her sick-
bed to take back, in writing, what she had told the other. Aberration or
not, the night was a catharsis. Henry and Theodore, each armed with
a note from Elizabeth offering insurance against assault by the other,
declared an *entente cordiale.* They appointed Frank Moulton their "mutual friend," and soon thereafter found Victoria Woodhull lying in wait
as their common enemy. Resisting Woodhull gave them shared purpose, as embracing Moulton gave them shared support. Moulton kept
promising the cover-up would succeed. The blowup of December 30
would recede into memory as they put their friendship on a higher
foundation of truly spiritual union. This time Beecher and the Tiltons would really form a trinity, not the binary bonds—first Henry-
Theodore, then Henry-Elizabeth—they had formed in the 1860s.

Only a few weeks after the fracas of December 30, Beecher and the
Tiltons affirmed their three-way compact. In mid-February 1871, as
Henry recalled in his courtroom testimony four years later, the three of
them sat in the Tiltons' parlor for a session of "amnesty and amity."
Theodore vowed to recover his editorial career and said that he and
Elizabeth might find a "nobler affection" at the end of "this very trial."

By and by their love and their household state might be better for the
trial—words to that effect; and then he said to his wife that he had
had a conversation with me upstairs that was satisfactory, and that he
was bound to say that Mr. Beecher had taken on himself very honor-
ably the blame of the trouble that had befallen his family, and exon-

erated his wife; and then he said to me: "I feel also bound to say that Elizabeth exonerates you and takes the blame to herself," and other remarks of that kind, intended to be cordial all around; and when the interview terminated, when we arose, I kissed him and he kissed me, and I kissed his wife and she kissed me, and I believe they kissed each other. [Laughter.] [1]

Recounting the scene for laughs in 1875, Beecher may have downplayed the Christian intensity of the moment. By consecrating themselves to love and forgiveness, he and the Tiltons sought to rise above the pursuit of individual interest, to resist not just their enemies but their own selfish impulses. The two orthodox Christians, Henry and Elizabeth, had already discovered that their yearnings could not easily be circumscribed, and had reaped a harvest of divine judgment and self-recrimination along with the hope of ultimate forgiveness. The self-described "Unitarian" Theodore no longer submitted himself to God's judgment or mercy, but he did strive for self-development and broadmindedness, and had the ability to bestow a certain kind of forgiveness. He was intensely aware of his own shortcomings—his "unworthiness" was a constant theme of his letters to his wife in the 1860s—and he appears in early 1871 to have shared with Elizabeth and Henry a new solidarity of earnest aspiration.

II. Beecher and the Tiltons could focus on Christian love and forgiveness because they had handed over to the worldly and unchurched Frank Moulton the responsibility for managing the actual crisis. He set about tracing rumors to their sources, and arranging the most efficient damage control. He also set about monitoring the contact between Beecher and both Tiltons. These Romantic Christians might be full of good intentions, but they were not to be trusted with their own reputations. In his eyes Theodore, his friend and classmate from childhood, and Henry, his very devoted booster from 1871 to 1874, were big kids, disarmingly effervescent but hopelessly unprepared for the roll-up-your-sleeves job of character maintenance. Moulton refused to permit them, or Henry and Elizabeth, to communicate or see one another without his prior approval, and, according to his recollection in 1874, Henry and Theodore consented to the "interdiction." [2]

Beecher's assent may have been technical, for he sent Mrs. Tilton letters that Moulton claimed in 1874 not to have known about at the time. One of those was the "true inwardness" letter, in which he told her that spiritual messages to him were "permitted to her," that is (as he explained at the trial in 1875), not covered by the prohibition. But Elizabeth had apparently already figured this out for herself, since she had written Henry an unsigned letter dated only "Wednesday," which he then marked "received March 8, 1871" (a Wednesday). "My Dear Friend: Does your heart bound *toward all* as it used?" she wrote.

> So does mine! I am myself again. I did not dare to tell you till I was sure; but the bird has sung in my heart these *four* weeks, and he has covenanted with me never again to leave. "Spring has come." Because I thought it would gladden you to know this, and not to trouble or embarrass you in *any way*, I now write. Of course I should like to share with you my joy; but can wait for the Beyond! When dear Frank says I may once again go to old Plymouth, I will thank the dear Father.[3]

Beecher's "true inwardness" letter seems to have followed hers later that day, since it was sent on a March 8 and since it opens with an apparent reference to her "Spring has come." "The blessing of God rest upon you," Beecher began. "Every spark of light and warmth in your own house will be a star and a sun in my dwelling. Your note broke like Spring upon Winter, and gave me an inward rebound to life." The fact that it was unsigned and "undirected" (there was no "My Dear Mrs. Tilton," his usual salutation) may not imply hanky-panky, as the plaintiff alleged at the trial, but it does suggest haste. If indeed it was written in 1871—Henry said at the trial he thought it was sent a year later—he had wasted no time letting her know that writing him intimate messages about her "inner life" was not only "permitted" to her, but "safe, for I am now at home here with my sister." Moulton the permission-giver would not be allowed to intrude upon either the soulful sharing or the practical planning about how to remain in touch. Whether the letter was composed in 1871 or 1872, the central point remains: Henry and Elizabeth had reestablished their intimacy, at least to the extent that they could write one another. Beecher was once again, as in the late 1860s, eagerly soliciting the "exceeding refreshment" of Elizabeth's "heart experiences," "like bread from heaven to the hungry." The trinity of friendship may still have been a serious goal, but it was vying against Beecher's and Mrs. Tilton's persistent acts of pairing.[4]

Elizabeth's "Wednesday" letter, and another secret note she sent Henry on May 3, 1871, disclose a good deal about her particular way of feeling and expressing her intimacy with Henry. Her May note reads as follows:

Mr. Beecher: My future either for life or death would be happier could I but feel that you *forgave* while you forget me. In all the sad complications of the past year my endeavor was to entirely keep from *you* all suffering; to bear myself alone, leaving you forever ignorant of it. My weapons were love, a larger [large?] untiring generosity, and *nest-hiding*! That I failed utterly we both know. But now I ask forgiveness.

Of course we first notice her contrition: she feels herself judged harshly, and Henry's repeated role was to deliver her from debilitating blame. Their love was squarely based on his power to forgive, a role he played for untold thousands of Mrs. Tilton's contemporaries, weary migrants from the Calvinist strictures of their parents' piety. Elizabeth had ironically migrated into a religiously "liberal" marriage in which she still felt blamed, but the deeper point is that she felt judged even in her love with Henry. Try as she might to love him, she caused him "suffering." Her love for him was laced with guilt—not just her guilt about wronging Theodore, but her guilt about wronging Henry. His place in her life was a potent compound: she loved him for his own power, and for the higher power he represented and conveyed, that of God's forgiveness; and she loved him because he found similar power in her. She was closer to God than he was, he always said. With her he could forget the power everyone told him he possessed and admit to being weak, needy for her tenderness and for the divine mercy she channeled.

But much more is happening in her very self-consciously crafted note, a note designed, like all her writing, to please its writer and recipient as an aesthetic production (the alliterative rhythm of "forgave while you forget," the repetitive, cumulative accenting of "to entirely keep from you . . . to bear myself alone"). The phrase "nest-hiding" supplied a ton of grist for the plaintiff's mill at the trial. Tilton's lawyer William Fullerton ground it up over and over again, hoping the jury would retain its unsavory aroma. It didn't prove adultery, he conceded in the plaintiff's summary, but it did prove concealment of love. How did he know what it meant? Cross-textual analysis. Beecher's 1868 novel *Norwood* was the interpretive key to "nest-hiding" and to several phrases in the "Wednesday" note. Beecher had read the book to her in draft in 1867, and she had now "shared" her "joy" by sending him back his own published words. Perhaps she was telling him that four years later their connection still ran deep, whatever the messy circumstances of their lives. Certainly she was reminding him of their first intimate meetings, when he read to her from his novel. Two months after her

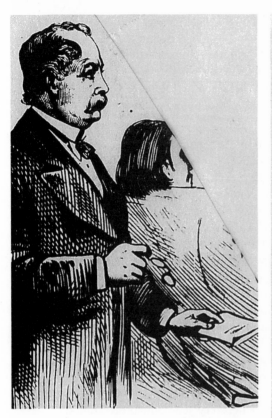

Fig. 74. WILLIAM M. EVARTS.
Continuity large; U. S. Senator, great-grandson of Roger Sherman. Head very long from opening of the ear forward and upward; a clear, far-reaching intellect; fine language, excellent moral development, and keen wit.

William Fullerton portrayed by a Brooklyn court-room artist in 1875 (left); William Evarts analyzed in a phrenology manual in 1888.

May 3 note, reading *Griffith Gaunt* gave her the character, Catherine Gaunt, who showed her in what sense her love for Henry was sinful. But on that spring day, *Norwood* gave her the character, the Romantic heroine Rose Wentworth, who let Elizabeth signal her fondness for Henry and her renewed delight in life.[5]

The plaintiff's cross-examination of Beecher on the two letters from Elizabeth was a tour de force of textual research and forensic strategy. William Evarts, knowing his client was vulnerable on the subject, had asked him in the direct examination if "nest-hiding" was "a word of any use by you, or with which you are conversant," and Beecher had replied, "No, Sir; it is not my word in any sense or way." "Had it been a word used between you and Mrs. Tilton in any way before this let-

ter?" "Not that I remembered—it was certainly not a common word."
William Fullerton, in the cross-examination, refreshed Henry's memory by reading several passages of *Norwood* into the record. Reflecting
upon the undemonstrative love Rachel Wentworth (Rose's mother) had
for her husband, Beecher had written that "it would seem as if, while
her whole life centered upon his love, she would hide the precious
secret . . . , as a bird hides its nest under tufts of grass, and behind leaves
and vines, as a fence against prying eyes." Beecher said he had no recollection of having written that sentence.

Fullerton interposed an apparently irrelevant question. "Did you,
among other things, present Mrs. Tilton with a picture called 'The
Trailing Arbutus'?" Beecher did recall doing that. Did he give it to her
after reading *Norwood* to her? Yes. Did he remember writing in *Norwood*
that the flower of the trailing arbutus was like "the breath of love"? No.
Fullerton read the rest of the passage. "The pure white and pink blossoms, in sweet clusters, lie hidden under leaves or grass, and often
under untimely snows. Blessings on thee! Thou art the fairest, most
modest, and sweetest-breathed of all our flowers!" So, Fullerton wondered, was he right in concluding that Beecher gave Mrs. Tilton a picture of the trailing arbutus after reading that passage to her? "Yes; not
immediately," answered Henry.[6]

Fullerton was not finished. He inquired whether in *Norwood* Beecher
had written of "the impression which a flower makes upon a sensitive
mind." Henry couldn't recall. Fullerton helped him: "The image which
a flower casts upon a sensitive plate is simply its own self-form; but cast
upon a more sensitive human soul, it leaves there not mere form, but
feeling, excitement, suggestion." Fullerton also wished to know if in
Norwood Henry had linked "the song of a bird with a 'love-call,' as it is
termed." Beecher didn't know. Fullerton read the text. "A robin flew
into one of the trees in the meadow, and began singing that plaintive
call for its mate. . . . Rose had always associated this evening robin song
with the idea of a love-call to one absent. Tonight it seemed more
yearning and passionate than usual. . . . It seemed to Rose to say: 'The
night is coming on. Where is my love?'" Fullerton asked if the passage
might shed some light on Elizabeth's "the bird has sung in my heart
these four weeks" in the "Wednesday" note. Beecher didn't think it did,
since in his view she was expressing joy about having been reconciled
with Theodore, not longing for "one absent." "Spring has come," Fullerton noted in conclusion, a phrase Elizabeth had put in quotation
marks, was also a citation from *Norwood*.

Fullerton had demonstrated two things beyond any doubt. First, assuming Henry was telling the truth, he had a faulty memory in 1875 for something he had written in 1867—something he surely knew would come up during cross-examination as it had in the direct. Second, Elizabeth had intended in 1871 to give special weight to her letters by couching them in phrases from the tenderest time of their early joining. If Beecher hadn't suspected what she was doing in her "unapproved" 1871 letters, he was not only a forgetful author, he was a dense companion. If he hadn't understood what he was doing in the late 1860s by giving her the picture of the trailing arbutus—soliciting her affection—he was delinquent as well as dense, for he was toying with her emotions. It seems much more likely that Beecher knew what he was signifying to her, knew what she was signifying to him, and also knew both things when he was on the stand in 1875. Whatever Beecher knew or didn't know, Fullerton's textual analysis shed much light on Elizabeth's style of feeling and loving. She knit Henry and herself together in her very choice of words.[7]

III. Frank Moulton told the Investigating Committee in 1874 that he considered Elizabeth's "Wednesday" note (which Beecher had duly handed over to him) "a breach of good faith. But desirous to have the peace kept, and hoping, if unanswered, it might not be repeated, I did not show it to Tilton, or inform him of its existence." Likewise her May 3 letter. Beecher surrendered it, promised not to "answer" it (although technically speaking, perhaps, not all "replies" were "answers"), and Moulton said nothing of it to Theodore. The impartial umpire had been drawn into making as well as managing secrets. Only two months (by his count) after taking charge of their personal relations, Moulton was hiding vital information from his old friend Theodore. No doubt he hid things from the other two as well. He was in the very awkward position of trying to be tough with close friends. Keeping up the friendships warred with his diplomatic duties. To have made a stink about Elizabeth writing Henry would have jeopardized his warm ties to the Great Man, who was showering him with the same high-beam affection he had lavished on Theodore and Elizabeth in the 1860s. Beecher was baring his soul to Moulton, complete with maybe-I'll-kill-myself musings. Frank must have been mesmerized by the attention, and by the privilege of becoming, at 35 years of age, behind-the-scenes Father Confessor to America's greatest preacher.[8]

During the cover-up Henry established ties with Frank and Emma Moulton that mirrored those he had formed with the Tiltons: spirited camaraderie with the husband, soulful intimacy with the wife (Emma, unlike her atheist husband, was a member of Plymouth Church), and emotional stroking from both of them. Into 1874 Beecher repeatedly stressed his undying love for husband as well as wife. Emma especially brought out the worshipful side of him. She "has been to me one of God's comforters," he wrote to Frank in 1873. "It is such as she that renews a waning faith in womanhood." Even at the trial in 1875, when she was a key witness against him, he still spoke of her with gushing enthusiasm. He was welcomed at the Moultons, Beecher told the court, "as if I had been a connection or relation in the household."

> While I was shown usually in the parlor, after a time I went right up into her chamber, which was in the second story front room, most of the time, and she received me, in the absence of her husband, with that strict propriety which you might expect of a lady. But, after a year or two—after a year perhaps, I cannot be sure of the time—she not infrequently kissed me, when I met her, in the presence of her husband—never but once except in his presence; and she used to say very kind and cordial things of me to him.[9]

Emma, like Elizabeth, was "a very patient listener, and she was very quick, apprehensive [apprehending], but she did not generally talk one word to my twenty." Yet the trait he most appreciated in her was one she did not share with Elizabeth: Emma "was very sympathetic," he told the court, "without being sentimental." She gave him what no one else dared to give him: a no-nonsense rebuff whenever he got down on himself. "In my moods of outpouring I oftentimes offended her taste, and she oftentimes made one of those remarks which a woman knows how to make, and which, it is said, 'lets the wind out of that bladder.' [Laughter.] . . . I was groaning and saying it did not seem to me that I could live, and I didn't want to live," and she retorted with "Hmmm . . . you come [in] and you are going to die, [but] I notice you . . . like to live well enough." Emma knew how to puncture self-indulgent whining and she knew how to comfort physically too: she would lie Henry down on a sofa and rub his feet. And once she planted what Beecher called "a holy kiss" on his forehead. He wanted to kiss her back, but feared, as he told the very amused courtroom of hundreds of men and a handful of women, "that if I had returned the kiss, I might have returned it with an enthusiasm that would have offended her delicacy; it was not best, under the circumstances, that she and I should kiss."

Emma Moulton provided friendship, comfort, and something else

Henry, and Elizabeth, needed: a conduit for communication. His own lawyer William Evarts asked him if he "sent any messages of any kind by Mrs. Moulton to Mrs. Tilton." Beecher answered, "I have no——I don't single out any special instances; I did send words of encouragement to her, exhorting her to build her house again and to renew the love of her youth; not to be discouraged; that God would take care of her and of the children, and such counsels as a pastor and a friend might send to a woman betided with such trouble." Elizabeth picked up his words of encouragement to her by stopping regularly at the Moultons' house. The Beechers, the Moultons, and the Tiltons all lived within a mile of each other. They were always running into each other on the streets, the horse cars, the ferries, and even the out-of-town trains. (Beecher ran into Walt Whitman on the ferry too.) Henry told the court of accidentally meeting Elizabeth on the street at least twice during the cover-up. It was easy for them to establish a line of communication through a friend like Emma Moulton. Not to mention a line of credit. Henry and Emma feared that Elizabeth, for want of funds, might go back to her mother's to live, provoking a crisis that would wreck the *entente cordiale.* Beecher offered to "deposit funds" with Emma "to be expended by her, when she saw any such wants as a woman's eye would know." [10]

If Emma "to me was like a sister," as Beecher testified in 1875, then it was to be expected that he would "love [Frank] like a brother." He was "a splendid specimen of a man," with "qualities so utterly different from mine, and in which I thought that he surpassed; that, by the principle of counterparts, I suppose, I took to him very strongly. He did seem to me to have given a new meaning to friendship—and I think so still. [Laughter.]" During the cover-up Beecher was positively giddy about Frank's gifts. Tilton's lawyer William Beach read a litany of Henry's most fulsome endorsements of Moulton into the record. "During all this time," he wrote in February 1872, "you are literally all my stay and comfort. I should have fallen on the way but for the courage you inspired, and the hope which you breathed." "Should any incident befall," he said in February 1873, "remember how deeply I feel your fidelity and friendship, your long-continued kindness and your affection. I confide everything to your wisdom, as I always have, with such success hitherto, that I fully trust for the future." [11]

Contemporaries were dumbstruck by Beecher's letters to Moulton. They were not prepared for existential writhing of the sort that Henry unloaded on his young friend. Some took the letters as *ipso facto* evidence of adultery, since they thought only the most cardinal of sins

FRANK MOULTON.

could account for such fierce self-whipping. As E. L. Godkin put it in his comment on the trial verdict in 1875, the letters "would probably, in the case of any other man living, have been accepted as of themselves proving his guilt. Their language points, according to all the moral and social experience of this country and of England, to one particular offence and to no other. We believe there is no case on record where a man has used similar language about anything else." And virtually everyone was perturbed about a leading moral teacher venting such sentiments to a near-stranger, or even feeling them in the first place.[12]

There is a consensus in the press commentary on Beecher that self-condemnation of his emotionally unctuous sort was out of the ordinary and embarrassing. Protestant American culture had become so liberal, so secular, thanks in part to Beecher's own work, that apparently no one (except him) saw his suffering as a spiritual struggle, as wrestling with real demons. Beecher's own well-publicized words, written to the secular nonbeliever Frank Moulton, did little to help them understand. Rather than portray his predicament as a religious crisis, he told Moulton that no one on "the outside" could possibly grasp the "wearing and grinding" of all his troubles on his "nervous system." [13]

When Moulton published these most private thoughts of Beecher in 1874 — thus doing to him, also out of "self-defense," what Theodore did simultaneously to Elizabeth — Beecher's "ragged edge" and "day of judgment" letters of 1872 and 1873 became famous. The phrase "ragged edge," one newspaper claimed in 1875, had already passed into popular speech. This 1872 letter, roughly a thousand words in length, was very cogent about the touchy position he found himself in as pastor of a great church. Faced with outraged parishioners seeking to launch a take-no-prisoners crusade to vindicate him, he had "to stop them without seeming to do it." Their "ruinous defense of me" would target Theodore and provoke him to retaliate. Henry had "to keep serene, as if I was not alarmed or disturbed; to be cheerful at home and among friends, when I was suffering the torments of the damned; to pass sleepless nights often, and yet to come up fresh and full for Sunday." The theatrical existence was killing him.

Theodore was apparently turning on him, Henry wrote Moulton. Elizabeth had just sent him that news in yet another "unapproved" note. Tilton blamed him for not doing enough to help revive his sagging journalistic standing. But the problem was "chronic," Henry said, and could not be met by any mere public statement of support, however rousing. He ended his letter to Moulton with an ominous series of reflections:

> Chronic evil requires *chronic remedies*. If my destruction would place him all right, that shall not stand in the way. I am willing to step down, and out. No one can offer more than that. That I do offer. Sacrifice me without hesitation if you can clearly see your way to his safety and happiness thereby. I do not think that anything would be gained by it. I should be destroyed, but he would not be saved. E. and the children would have their future clouded. In one point of view I could desire the sacrifice on my part. Nothing can possibly be so bad as the horror of great darkness in which I spend much of my time. I look upon death as sweeter-faced than any friend I have in the world. Life would be pleasant if I could see that rebuilt which is shattered; but to live on the

sharp and ragged edge of anxiety, remorse, fear, despair, and yet to put on all the appearance of serenity and happiness, cannot be endured much longer. I am well-nigh discouraged. If you, too, cease to trust me—to love me—I am alone. I have not another person in the world to whom I could go. Well—to God I commit all—whatever it may be here, it shall be well there. With sincere gratitude for your heroic friendship, and with sincere affection, even though you love me not, I am yours (though unknown to you), H. W. B.

The "ragged edge" letter ended with these two successive points—the beleaguered promise to step aside and the distraught plea for Moulton's affection—but they were intertwined. In both cases Beecher was acknowledging Moulton's preeminent authority, throwing himself at his feet. Speak but the word and I will sacrifice myself; please love me. Henry feared that Frank's love was destined only for Theodore. Earlier in the letter he fretted that "T. is dearer to you than *I can* be." [14]

Beecher's five-hundred-word "day of judgment" letter sixteen months later showed a marked change of spirit even though it too spoke of approaching death. "The whole earth is tranquil," he began, "and the heaven is serene, as befits one who has about finished his world-life. . . . I have determined to make no more resistance. Theodore's temperament is such that the future, even if temporarily earned, would be absolutely worthless, filled with abrupt charges, and rendering me liable, at any hour or day, to be obliged to stultify all the devices by which we have saved ourselves. . . . My mind is clear. I am not in haste. I shall write for the public a statement that will bear the light of the judgment day." After delivering himself of a bitter character assessment of Theodore, he concluded with a flurry of gratitude and another menacing warning. "I have a strong feeling upon me, and it brings great peace with it, that I am spending my *last Sunday* and preaching my last sermon. Dear, good God, I thank thee I am indeed beginning to see rest and triumph. The pain of life is but a moment; the glory of everlasting emancipation is wordless, inconceivable, full of beckoning glory. Oh, my beloved Frank, I shall know you there, and forever hold fellowship with you, and look back and smile at the past. Your loving H. W. B." [15]

If Emma Moulton saw this letter when her husband received it, she must have said, "the pastor talks about his last Sunday, but I notice he likes to preach well enough." And by his own 1875 account (of course he may have been lying or forgetting), he was not truly suicidal when he wrote it. The "day of judgment" letter worked on two levels at once:

he voiced genuine peace at having transcended mundane cares, and he begged for Moulton's support by adverting to killing himself. His craving for Moulton's favor does not mean he was not truly suffering, spiritually and psychologically. It does mean that his Christian commitment to putting the love of others over the love of self had run up against a severe obstacle: his overweening need for the affection of others.

Defenders of theological orthodoxy and social tradition had long criticized Beecher for putting love first, judgment second, in his preaching of the gospel. E. L. Godkin made a fresh statement of this view when he argued in 1874 that Beecher's "God is wholly love," so that "attempts to imitate Him result simply in the deliberate and systematic suppression of all discrimination touching character and conduct, and the cultivation of a purely emotional theology, made up, not of opinions, but of sighs and tears and aspirations and unlimited good-nature." Beecher failed to judge harshly, in Godkin's view, because he feared harsh judgment.[16]

But events since 1870 had brought Henry back to a clear-eyed sense of God's judgment, a notion he had always preached abstractly but rarely since his youth allowed to penetrate the armor of his self-assurance. Perhaps he was so stricken by this new awareness of God's wrath that it exacerbated his dependency on Frank Moulton, and led him—in cringing self-surrender—to confess repeatedly, in Frank's and Emma's hearing, to awful, vague crimes against Elizabeth and Theodore Tilton. His language may have had only one possible meaning, as far as the Moultons could tell: adultery. When Frank and Emma testified to that effect at the trial, they may well have been telling the "truth," while perhaps exaggerating the explicitness with which he had identified his wrongdoing. They, like Godkin, may have believed that language of the sort he chose pointed to one sin only. Whatever he told them—and of course he may have told them that he and Elizabeth had had sexual intercourse, even if those vile words (as he said at the trial) were unutterable by him—we can be sure it was uttered in doomsday rhetoric of self-denunciation. Like Elizabeth's love for Theodore, Henry's love for Frank was heavily veined with scourging of the self and placation of the other.

IV. When Beecher tried, in 1874 and 1875, to account for the vehemence of his self-flagellation during the cover-up, he pointed to a series of transgressions he had committed against Theodore. The major one, of course, was letting Mrs. Tilton develop her undue affection for him in the late 1860s. Another was his joining

Eunice in recommending (in December 1870) that Elizabeth separate from her husband. If he had understood that Elizabeth's passionate feelings were turning toward him, he claimed, he would not have counseled that she move out. The third transgression was supporting publisher Henry Bowen's decision (also in December 1870) to terminate Theodore as editor of the *Independent*. Bowen had told Beecher that he had it on good authority that Theodore was an adulterer, so he could not be kept on as editor of a Christian journal. Beecher agreed that Tilton had to go, only to learn shortly thereafter, he said, that the accounts of Theodore's adultery were untrue. "I am informed," he wrote to Bowen in January 1871, "by one on whose judgment and integrity I greatly rely, and who has the means of forming an opinion better than any of us, that he knows the whole matter about Mrs. ——, and that the stories are not true, and that the same is the case with other stories." Henry said his remorse over hurting Theodore at home and at work explained the sickness-unto-death that permeated his letters to Moulton.[17]

Beecher was taking a calculated risk in bringing up his relations with Henry Bowen. He needed to mention the Bowen connection in order to account for his depressed state, which many people thought only guilt over adultery could have provoked. But Bowen had been spreading stories about Beecher too: Theodore claimed in 1874 that Bowen had told him in the early 1860s that Beecher was an adulterer. This prominent publisher and Plymouth Church founder had been whispering for years that Beecher had in fact debauched Bowen's own deceased wife Lucy, who supposedly revealed her pastor's wrongdoing on her deathbed. The fact that few believed Bowen's stories—if they were true, why would he keep renting his Plymouth pew year after year, and taking communion from Beecher's hand?—helped reduce the danger. Yet Bowen was still a threat. If he went public with his claims (a course that would certainly destroy Bowen's own reputation), it would be very difficult for Henry to win the battle for public opinion. The defense at the 1875 trial did not call Bowen, and when the plaintiff finally did call him as a rebuttal witness, his testimony was kept within narrow bounds.[18]

Henry and Theodore were entangled with Bowen in a Byzantine web of personal, journalistic, ecclesiastical, and political disputes, and Bowen was exploiting all of them, as best he could, for his own advantage. He was a regular Republican and a liberal Christian sliding back toward religious traditionalism. Tilton's radical religious and political views were increasingly disturbing to him. Beecher's at least passive support for President Grant and the Brooklyn Republican machine put him and Bowen on common ground, but the Plymouth pastor was also close to a Bowen competitor in Republican circles—Plymouth stalwart Benjamin Tracy (later one of Beecher's attorneys at the civil trial)— and to various Democratic members of his church.

Bowen was a religious builder, a Congregationalist from Connecticut who wished to spread the true religion of the Puritans in heavily Presbyterian New York. He was an excellent judge of ministerial talent: it was he who brought Beecher to Brooklyn from Indianapolis in 1847. He gave large sums to conservative Congregationalist churches as well as liberal ones like Plymouth. The efflorescence of Protestant piety in mid-nineteenth-century America owed much to the efforts of savvy evangelical businessmen such as Henry Bowen, who erected religious edifices along with commercial ones. First Bowen sold marble, then he sold the written word—the *Independent* and a newspaper, the *Brooklyn Union*, which Tilton began editing, in addition to his ongoing *Independent* duties, in early 1870. Tilton was a snappy writer, with a good nose for the controversial issues that snagged an audience. As long as Tilton's writing garnered a readership, Bowen overlooked their deepening ideological divergence.

But in late 1870 Bowen decided to fire Tilton from the newspaper as well as the magazine. Tilton had put the paper, contrary to Bowen's explicit wishes, behind the liberal (anti-Grant) Republican candidate for Congress, and the publisher was incensed. Beecher, meanwhile, had frowned on the uncompromising militance of Tilton's Radical Republicanism since the end of the Civil War, so it was natural for him to echo Bowen's political displeasure. The stories about Tilton's alleged adulteries—already in the air, perhaps true, but whether true or false spread as a matter of course by his political and religious detractors— were convenient tools for expediting his firing. The accord between Beecher and Bowen on Theodore's leaving the *Independent* was ironic, since the two Henrys had actually parted ways professionally in 1866 when Beecher resigned his *Independent* position after Theodore attacked his moderate views on Southern Reconstruction. Bowen backed Tilton then, since radical sentiment was strong in the magazine's readership, as it was even at Plymouth Church. A chagrined Beecher stopped writing columns for the *Independent* and began planning the *Christian Union* as a competitor—it emerged in January 1870 with the financial backing of yet another Plymouth Church founder (and a Democrat), John Howard. At the very time, therefore, when Beecher was competing with Theodore for Elizabeth's affection—between 1866 and 1870—

he was also her husband's (and Bowen's) competitor in the arena of religious journalism.

By 1870, Theodore's increasingly radical cultural views—especially on divorce and women's rights—were generating vigorous complaints among *Independent* readers. By November, Bowen had had enough of Tilton politically at the *Brooklyn Union* and culturally at the *Independent,* and he secured Beecher's support for an ouster from both organs. Theodore, petrified about his professional viability, cried conspiracy, and struck back as hard as he could. Having learned from Bowen years before about Beecher's alleged adulteries, he tried to form his own alliance with Bowen by telling him about Elizabeth's "confession" of the previous July. Theodore's report of his wife's alleged admission of adultery was a last-ditch effort to save his livelihood by putting a wedge between Bowen and Beecher. But the plan blew up in his face. According to Tilton's account, Bowen managed to get him to write a threatening letter to Henry ordering him to resign from Plymouth Church and immediately "quit the city of Brooklyn." Instead of insisting that Bowen sign the letter too, Tilton foolishly believed a story Bowen told him about "honor": while he could no longer, as a gentleman, charge Beecher with adultery himself (having already pardoned his pastor at his request), he would nevertheless support Tilton's driving Beecher out of Brooklyn. In fact Bowen did nothing of the kind: he showed Beecher the letter, but failed to endorse it. If Theodore's story was accurate, Bowen was only using the letter to drive Tilton and Beecher further apart. For good measure, Tilton was now faced with an angry and shattered Elizabeth, whose worst nightmares—that her relations with Henry would be publicized and that her pastor's career would crumble because of her love for him—were coming true.[19]

As with the triangle of Beecher and the Tiltons, the three-sided relationship between Bowen, Beecher, and Tilton defies our best efforts to ferret out the truth. The only way to be sure that Bowen even *believed* Beecher was an adulterer—much less to conclude that he was in fact an adulterer—is to arbitrarily accept his (or Tilton's) story as true. But Bowen (and Tilton) had plenty of pressing motive, individually and jointly, to do whatever they could to tarnish Beecher's reputation. If Tilton's story about Bowen's double-crossing him was true, then the publisher was more than unscrupulous enough to make up a story about Beecher, about Tilton, or anyone else. But he didn't need to make up stories about Beecher being an adulterer. Earlier enemies had been circulating those stories as well.[20]

Victorian Brooklyn was a bubbling cauldron of personal, political, and religious animosities. It was also a culture that rigidly tied status and power to "character." It was therefore a rumor mill full of tales about moral transgression, as competitors tried to undermine one another's prestige. What Theodore Tilton learned from years of association with Bowen was not that Beecher had in fact committed adultery with anyone, but that some leverage over Beecher might be gotten by charging that he had. The plausibility of the accusations against Henry, like those against Theodore himself, did depend upon a prior public perception of loose behavior with female friends. But the prevalence of the stories—given their utility for other purposes—does nothing to establish that adultery actually took place.

Of course Beecher may indeed have slept with the young and (by all accounts) attractive Lucy Tappan Bowen, the daughter of the famous antislavery merchant Arthur Tappan, and with other admiring followers too, in Indiana and in Brooklyn. The trouble with concluding too quickly that he did—as many writers have done—is that it blocks an understanding of the regime of reputation in which heated moral accusation was a central pillar. But whatever the truth of Henry Bowen's charge against Beecher, it seems likely that he did hear something from his wife Lucy, as she lay dying, about her pastor, something that colored Bowen's subsequent feelings about him. Beecher himself spoke openly in 1874 and 1875 about the "very intimate" tie he had shared for years with the Bowens, who lived a block away. On her deathbed Lucy may well have expressed guilt about having been too close to her minister. Even if Bowen made up the adultery part, he would not have had to make up the pique and bitterness about what he considered Henry's undue intimacy with his wife.[21]

Henry Bowen was the *éminence grise* behind the Beecher-Tilton Scandal, and he remains a figure of mystery for us as he was for his contemporaries. They regarded him as completely incomprehensible. Indeed, his very existence contributed to what some observers took as the surreal moral atmosphere of the times. "Mr. Bowen is looked upon as a Phenomenon," said the *New York Graphic*. "In this terrible drama he appears on the stage in all characters and under all costumes. . . . This is not two-facedness but twenty-facedness, and the more the Phenomenon is studied the more phenomenal he appears." Frank Moulton was already confusing enough: a young man of superior education and bearing and a partner in the dry goods (and informal banking) firm of Woodruff and Robinson, he thought being a gentleman compatible with lying to suppress what he believed was a famous minister's adultery. Moulton's behavior, seconded by his eminently respectable wife, drove E. L. Godkin to distraction. "That an English-speaking Protestant married couple in easy circumstances, and of fair education, and belonging to a religious circle, should not only be aware that their pastor was a libertine and should be keeping it a secret for him, but should make his adulteries the subject of conversation with him in the family circle, is hardly capable of explanation by reference to any known and acknowledged tendency of our society."[22]

But Moulton, for all his friendships with religious men, was a declared atheist. Defenders of social foundations could take his moral turpitude as a product of his alienness. Bowen, by contrast, was an enigma of staggering proportions. Here was a major Christian philanthropist, an apparently exemplary bourgeois pillar, who claimed his minister was an adulterer yet kept right on renting his front-row pew. Bowen spent his life and his fortune promoting the Christian religion and then mocked the faith by upholding the stature of a man he accused of the most heinous crime. The *New York Graphic* pointed out that a Catholic might tolerate a wayward priest by distinguishing between the pastor's office and his person: a sinner could still exercise a sacramental calling. But this dialectical solution was not available to a Protestant activist like Bowen, or to the Protestant observers who tried to understand him. For them the personal and the religious were necessarily wedded. And Bowen did much more, publicly, than merely tolerate Beecher.[23]

Deprived of the Catholic option, many Protestants were further blocked from making sense of Bowen by their tacit utilitarianism: sane people pursued their rational self-interests. Bowen was wrecking his own investment as a major bondholder in Plymouth Church by surreptitiously branding Beecher a wicked reprobate. Perhaps contemporary commentators were buffaloed by Bowen because they lacked ready access to a view of selfhood that would allow him to be a walking contradiction: to wish simultaneously that Beecher would thrive and go to hell. It may be a sign of the cultural supremacy of the liberal Protestant assumptions shared by Beecher, Bowen, and Tilton that the ancient Christian paradox of St. Paul—there is a law in one's members that wars against the law in one's mind—did not come immediately to analysts' minds. Bowen was divided against himself, and hence a puzzle defying solution.

V. The Beecher-Tilton-Bowen triangle bore a strong formal resemblance to the Beecher-Tilton-Tilton triangle. The triangles actually touched during the incendiary events of December

1870. In the wake of his firing by Bowen, Theodore took aim at Henry, and to strengthen his hand he got Elizabeth to sign an accusation of improper advances by Beecher. Each triangle had its subsequent reaffirmation of friendship. Once Theodore got a job editing a new weekly, *The Golden Age* (bankrolled in large measure, at Moulton's insistence, by Beecher—a fact they hid from Theodore, who said he would not have accepted money from that source), the Beecher-Tilton-Bowen threesome signed their secret "tripartite covenant" in April 1872. In that document they proclaimed their hearty good feelings and promised not to spread nasty stories about one another. Despite the agreements effected within each triangle, Tilton kept spreading stories about Beecher, as Bowen did about Beecher and Tilton.

Each triangle, moreover, had its moment of "truth." The tripartite agreement was anonymously published in May 1873 by a business associate of Beecher's, Samuel Wilkeson, who had had enough of Bowen's continued rumormongering. Beecher claimed the exposure was a surprise to him, but by mid-1873 he may have been ready to have someone force a public confrontation with Bowen, and even with Tilton. His "day of judgment" letter on June 1 shows that he felt a good deal of relief shortly after the exposure. Even if Victoria Woodhull had never made her public accusation in November 1872 about the Beecher-Tilton-Tilton tangle, the exposure the following spring of the Beecher-Tilton-Bowen pact would probably have put an end to the wider cover-up. The "public" would have demanded to know how much truth there was in the accusations of adultery Bowen had apparently been making against Beecher for more than a decade—accusations (it was now revealed) that Tilton had known about for a very long time.

Theodore's *Golden Age* was a tragicomic creation of the cover-up. It never established itself with readers and limped along until 1874. Theodore was reduced to pleading for subscriptions on the inside cover of each issue. He had no galvanizing issue such as antislavery or national reunion to hang his editorial hat on. Where a fellow crusader such as Wendell Phillips had turned his energies after the Civil War to the labor movement (not a path to respectability either, but a sure home for a talented orator), Tilton had gravitated to divorce reform, a cause increasingly equated with the free-love virus. He cared about women's suffrage, but the suffrage movement was already served by the new *Woman's Journal* in Boston, the moderate organ of Lucy Stone and her husband Henry Blackwell. The more militant *Revolution*, run by the Tiltons' friends Susan B. Anthony and Elizabeth Cady Stanton in New York, had just folded in 1870 for want of readers. The demise of *Revolution* showed there was no market for a reform sheet that called for suffrage as one part of women's overall liberation from social oppression. Yet in 1871 Theodore went right ahead and printed a cheery thirty-three-page tribute to Victoria Woodhull, whose attack on bourgeois marriage went far beyond Stanton's, and Elizabeth Stanton was much more radical on this issue than Susan Anthony. If that decision was a calculated effort, as he later claimed, to purchase Woodhull's silence, it was also journalistic suicide. His breathless "biography" of "the Woodhull," as opponents dubbed her, had the effect of identifying Tilton not only with "free love," enough to kill any magazine after the Civil War, but with the almost equally tarnished mystery-world of "spiritualism."

By 1871 the few readers who could still fathom or tolerate the dialectics of free love, which had been widely debated in the 1850s, were not likely to give a hearing to the notion of listening to spirits. Tilton gave subscribers a glib and glowing account of both in his essay on Woodhull. "The essence of her system," he wrote, is that "marriage is of the heart and not of the law, that when love ends marriage should end with it, being dissolved by nature, and that no civil statute should outwardly bind two hearts which have been inwardly sundered." As for her religious accomplishments, she was controlled by spirits (Demosthenes was her chief guide) and claimed the power to heal the sick and raise the dead. In Indiana alone, "she straightened the feet of the lame; she opened the ears of the deaf; she detected the robbers of a bank; she brought to light hidden crimes; she solved physiological problems; she unveiled business secrets; she prophecied future events." The often facetious Tilton played it straight. He trotted out all her self-promoting claims and concluded with a rousing, if roundabout, endorsement.

> Known only as a rash iconoclast, and ranked even with the most uncouth of those noise-makers who are waking a sleepy world before its time, she beats her daily gong of business and reform with notes not musical but strong, yet mellows the outward rudeness of the rhythm by the inward and devout song of one of the sincerest, most reverent, and divinely-gifted of human souls.[24]

There is no doubt that Victoria Woodhull was charismatic. She took suffrage reform circles by storm in 1871. She set off a wave of "radical chic"—lionization by middle-class reformers—because she was an uneducated working-class beauty from Ohio who could overpower audiences with logical argument and rhetorical flair. She was magic: spirit-possession or not, her new friends thought it *was* a miracle that a certified commoner (who dressed to high-bourgeois perfection) could articulate complex ideas with such aplomb. Reports of ongoing legal conflict with her scruffy white-trash relatives only enhanced her allure. Well-bred admirers shook their heads in disbelief at how flawlessly she wheedled men and women alike, and then they got in line to be wheedled in turn. Tilton may have waltzed up to her only to keep her from talking, as he claimed. But his closest friend among the women's rights workers, Elizabeth Cady Stanton, was herself badly smitten, so it makes sense to suppose that he was too. By his own account he spent a great deal of time with her in 1870 and 1871, although there is no reason to admit Victoria's claim that Theodore was her "devoted lover for more than half a year, and . . . during that time he was my accepted lover." As her defenders acknowledged, she was an unrestrained storyteller.[25]

Woodhull earned her very temporary stature among the militant New York suffragists because she was dazzling and because they initially suspected she might help broaden the movement at a time when the moderate suffragists in Boston appeared to have the upper hand. Anthony seems to have cooled on Woodhull first, believing she was using the suffrage movement for her own aggrandizement. The remarkable thing is that the hard-nosed Anthony was so taken by her in the first place. It was one thing for the hyper-Romantic idealist Theodore Tilton to be swept away. It was another thing for the realistic, politically astute Anthony to find Woodhull so appealing and, like Tilton, to be untroubled by her spiritualism. In the 1870s respectable American opinion was rapidly moving to banish spiritualism from the approved spectrum of middle-class beliefs, but Tilton's and Anthony's toleration for it shows that in the early 1870s it was still alive as an option for serious people. A few years later it was not.

At the trial in 1875 the lawyers and the audience (notably unpoliced in this instance by Judge Neilson) made merciless sport of spiritualist witnesses, thus signaling the judgment of well-heeled America that communing with spirits and with the dead was now beyond the pale. Tilton's attorney William Beach had much fun cross-examining the spiritualist medium and clairvoyant Elizabeth Palmer, who obliged by revealing she could not only read minds and interact with good and evil spirits, but that as a matter of fact she observed one such spirit standing beside Beach at that very moment. "Well, is that one of the good or bad ones?" asked Beach, "I would like to know. [Laughter.]" Not about to be silenced by the dismissive raillery, Palmer replied matter-of-factly, "I cannot tell you, only I should think it was a daughter, a young lady." Beach had to admit to having "one of that kind." [26]

Victoria Woodhull made her public charges against Beecher in the fall of 1872 because, as she claimed, she wished to force middle-class culture to own up to its hypocrisy, but also because she felt cornered. Her spiritualism was being savaged, her standing with the militant suffragists was waning, and Henry Ward Beecher's older sisters Catharine and Harriet (Beecher Stowe) were ridiculing her—Stowe by sending her up as "Virginia Dangereyes" in the novel *My Wife and I*, which satirized her and Stanton alike. She had given fair warning of her intent to expose Beecher and the Tiltons by publishing a "card" in the *New York Times* and *New York World* in May 1871. She knew of one man, she wrote, "a public teacher of eminence, who lives in concubinage with the wife of another public teacher of almost equal eminence. All three concur in denouncing offences against morality. . . . I shall make it my business to analyze some of these lives." Woodhull turned up in *The Golden Age* office the next day to be sure Theodore hadn't missed it, and he then promptly convened with Henry at Moulton's house. Beecher heard from her directly in November 1871. "Two of your sisters have gone out of their way to assail my character and purposes," she wrote, "both by the means of the public press and by numerous private letters written to various persons with whom they seek to injure me and thus to defeat the political ends at which I aim. You doubtless know that it is in my power to strike back, and in ways more disastrous than anything that can come to me. . . ." [27]

Tilton's befriending of Woodhull, whether based on infatuation, calculation, or both, was having no effect—unless it was to make her insist on his loyalty all the more as her other supporters faded away. By the spring of 1872 she was desperate, as financial reverses forced her to vacate her apartment. Suddenly no respectable hotel would lodge her, her husband Colonel James Blood, and her former husband Dr. Canning Woodhull—all of whom lived together in a ménage à trois the love and naturalness of which Tilton had especially praised in his so-called biography of her. In June she wrote again to Beecher that "the social fight against me being now waged in this city is becoming rather hotter than I can well endure longer. . . . I have been shut out of hotel after hotel, and am now, after having obtained a place in one, hunted down by a set of males and females, who are determined that I shall not be permitted to live even, if they can prevent it." She demanded his "assistance" in being "sustained in my position in the Gilsey House, from which I am ordered out . . . simply because I am Victoria C. Woodhull, the advocate of social freedom." Beecher dashed off a note to Moulton telling him he would do nothing, and Moulton sent Woodhull no reply.[28]

The last straw for Victoria was her pal Theodore's active role in Horace Greeley's hapless 1872 Liberal Republican and Democratic Presidential campaign—Theodore was angling, Woodhull insinuated, for the aging Greeley's editorial chair at the *New York Tribune*. She reproached Tilton for not supporting her substantially more hapless candidacy for President, sponsored by her on-paper-only Equal Rights Party. Anthony and Stanton had dropped her too, not for Greeley, a committed antisuffragist, but for Grant and the regular Republicans, who had made a modest gesture (short of a platform plank) in the direction of women's rights. When Woodhull arrived in Boston in September for the ninth annual meeting of the American Association of Spiritualists, she was ready to strike. On the evening of September 10 she mounted the platform of John A. Andrew Hall in Boston and delivered a barn-burning, featured speech which, in the words of the *Boston Herald* reporter, "for bold and unwarranted statements, and vile vituperation, as we believe, [has] never been equaled, even by herself."

> She attacked her accusers in the most passionate manner, calling them liars, villains, cowards and many other opprobrious epithets, and startled her hearers into numb amazement by saying, "Go to your houses of ill fame, and there you will find the most responsible and aristocratic of your citizens, revelling in debauchery and licentiousness." She claimed that she had had for years numerous secret spies all over the country, investigating the character of public men and women and reporting privately to her. According to her reports there seemed to be a skeleton in every house, and if her words were considered to be of the least weight, the most eminent teachers of morality in the land must be classed as the most arrant hypocrites and the deepest dyed villains. She declared her intention of having revenge upon those who had, as she claimed, vilified her, by publishing to the world the stories of their shame, and opened her tirade by an attack upon Rev. Henry Ward Beecher, whom she openly declared had been living in illicit

intercourse with the wife of Theodore Tilton, that he was the father of some of her children, and that this criminal intercourse was still continued. [29]

There is no telling how many readers of the report gave her sensational remarks "the least weight," but she accorded them and everyone else another chance by publishing her own lengthy account in late October. The "November 2" issue of the recently dormant *Woodhull and Claflin's Weekly* fired the same magazine of charges at Beecher, while earning some money to pay the rent. This version included juicy stories that she omitted from her speech or the *Herald* man left out of his report—details salacious enough to ensure increased sales and close scrutiny by defenders of purity. (For example, there had been "terrible orgies" between Henry and Elizabeth in front of the Tilton children, Victoria alleged.) "Secret agent of the Post Office" Anthony Comstock, whose command of publicity and headlines was as wily as Woodhull's, got her written up on obscenity and slander charges; she spent time in the Ludlow Street jail off and on for the next six months. [30]

Claiming the mantle of William Lloyd Garrison, who "not only denounced slavery in the abstract, but . . . in the concrete," she told the world that Henry Ward Beecher had committed adultery with Elizabeth Tilton, as (she alleged) Theodore Tilton and suffragists Paulina Wright Davis and Elizabeth Cady Stanton had all informed her. "The fault I find with Mr. Beecher," she added, "is . . . the exact opposite to that for which the world will condemn him." She upbraided him because "he entertains, on conviction, substantially the same views which I entertain on the social question," yet "in seeming and pretension he is the upholder of the old social slavery, and, therefore, does what he can to crush out and oppose me . . . in forwarding the great social revolution." Woodhull thus coyly claimed Beecher's mantle as well as Garrison's. The great preacher was not up to leading his own privately championed cause. He was being theatrical rather than true: playing the part of the upstanding man of virtue, denying the integrity of his own advanced vision of selfhood. [31]

VI. Theodore was certainly the ultimate source of Victoria's information, whether he told her himself or only told Stanton, who then (as she admitted later) spilled at least some of what she knew to Woodhull. We can only wonder what Tilton's exact words were to either of them. Knowing from Theodore's 1874 testimony about his technical approach to the truth, we can suspect he used language that suggested adultery (in order to keep the pressure on Beecher) and that also suggested his wife's purity (to protect her and the children). At the 1875 trial William Evarts showed that no surviving documents backed up Theodore's recollection that he had charged Henry with adultery before 1874. From 1871 to 1873, according to available sources, he used vague phrases like "improper solicitations." He may have wavered until 1874 not only on the question of whether the news about adultery should be broadcast but on the issue of whether adultery had actually occurred. Victoria Woodhull may have "known" it was adultery before he did, even though she got the story, directly or indirectly, from him.[32]

Of course Theodore claimed in 1874 to have heard Elizabeth confess to adultery in July 1870. But suppose he did. He might still not have known what to think. He could not have been satisfied by whatever Elizabeth told him in 1870, or anytime thereafter. He believed his wife weak enough—especially in states of spiritual excitement—to say or do anything, so it was impossible for him ever to be sure, on her account alone, of what she had in fact said or done. He would have demanded ever fuller confessions from his wife, in an endless quest to pin down the sin. Not trusting Elizabeth's stories, he would have sought confirmation from Beecher. That is precisely what he did, according to his recollection (denied by Beecher), when he asked Henry in early 1871 to corroborate Elizabeth's "dating" of their first sexual encounter, and thereby to confirm little Ralph Tilton's legitimacy.

Confirmation from Henry may also have been part of what he wanted on December 30, 1870, when he confronted Beecher at Frank Moulton's house. On that evening, according to Tilton's 1874 account (again denied by Beecher), Theodore accused Henry of "criminal intimacy." Then and there, Tilton claimed, Beecher confessed. But what exactly, by Theodore's own testimony, did Henry say to him? "He received my accusation without denial, and confessed it by his assenting manner and grief." In other words, Henry said nothing at all. Theodore "knew" the silence was a confession of adultery because of Beecher's general tenor and overwhelming remorse. But it seems plausible that Tilton actually "knew" it only years later, when the accusation entered the documentary record. Perhaps the three years of the cover-up were the time during which Theodore came to believe Victoria was right: Henry's disabling remorse, added to Elizabeth's periodic admissions of "sin," equaled "criminal intimacy." But even that phrase, as William Evarts took pains to point out at the trial, had no clear meaning, and certainly no legal standing. It could be taken to imply adultery (as the technical Tilton surely intended), but it was vague enough to cover a wide spectrum of possible misbehavior, from improper advances to sexual intercourse.[33]

In the aftermath of Victoria Woodhull's charges, Beecher and Mrs. Tilton issued full denials. Paulina Wright Davis and Elizabeth Cady Stanton also denied telling Woodhull anything (Stanton soon admitted she had spoken to Woodhull, but claimed Victoria had engaged in unspecified exaggerations). Theodore let Elizabeth do the talking for the Tiltons until late December 1872, when he published a card in the *Brooklyn Eagle* in response to a letter he said he had received from "a complaining friend" (the letter and the friend were inventions). The "friend" advised him to "give the lie to the wicked story, and thus end it forever!" "But stop and consider," replied Theodore. "The [Woodhull] story is a whole library of statements—a hundred or more—and it would be strange if some of them were not correct, though I doubt if any are."

> So extensive a libel requires, if answered at all, a special denial of its several parts; and . . . not only a denial of things misstated, but a truthful explanation of the things that remain unstated and in mystery. . . . but when the truth is a sword, God's mercy sometimes commands it sheathed. If you think I do not burn to defend my wife and little ones, you know not the fiery spirit within me. *But my wife's heart is more a fountain of charity, and quenches all resentments.* . . . I shall try with patience to keep my answer within my own breast, lest it shoot forth like a thunderbolt through other hearts.

This masterfully double-edged statement made Elizabeth apoplectic, and announced a bitter and corrosive turn in their marriage, which had been more or less on the mend since January 1871. Supposedly burning to defend her, he had divulged that there was another whole story waiting to be told—and a number of hearts waiting to be pierced—whenever the public got around to demanding it. Of course the hearts prospectively menaced by his thunderbolt could not possibly include his wife's, since he was driven solely by the desire to protect her. Elizabeth saw it differently. "Your note in the *Eagle* of last night was so heartless," she wrote to him the next day (even though they were apparently both at home). The next sentence breaks off nonsensically, perhaps indicating how upset she was. "You should have sheltered me (a noble man would) *all the more* because the truth. *Innocence demanded nothing from you.*

To you I owe this great injustice of exposure, such as has never before befallen a woman. Blow after blow, ceaseless and unrelenting these three years! O cruel spirit born of the devil of anger and revenge! *You know what I am.* Yet now that exposure has come, my whole nature revolts to join with you or standing [*sic*] with you." [34]

One might expect that this kind of breakdown between Theodore and Elizabeth would lead her to seek Henry's comfort, but there is no evidence that they saw each other privately after the Woodhull thunderbolt. He may have taken steps to distance himself, given the growing likelihood that he and Theodore were headed for public blows. But he did write. His undated letter to her in the spring of 1873 was perhaps evidence—with its preacherly formulas—of a new distance between them, or of a determination on his part to add to a documentary trail of narrowly "pastoral" advice. Yet in her state of affliction religious reassurance may have been what she most craved, and Beecher's grasping her need for a message about ultimate things may be a sign of how well he knew her. Here was a case in which the clergyman performed an office that transcended his own personal troubles or motives. "I pray daily for you 'that your faith fail not,'" he wrote.

> You yourself know the way and the power of prayer. God has been your refuge in many sorrows before. He will now hide you in his pavilion until the storm be overpast. The rain that beats down the flower to the earth will pass at length, and the stem, bent but not broken, will rise again and blossom as before. . . . I have not spoken of myself. No word could express the sharpness and depth of my sorrow in your behalf, my dear and honored friend. God walks in the fire by the side of those He loves and, in heaven, neither you nor Theodore, nor I, shall regret the discipline, how hard soever it may seem now. . . . I commend you to my mother's God, my dear friend! May His smile bring light in darkness, and His love be a perpetual Summer to you! [35]

After reading Theodore's "letter to a complaining friend" in the *Brooklyn Eagle* Elizabeth had been livid. True, as she had written in her public denial in November, it was Victoria Woodhull who had "broadcast to all the world" the "preposterous and wicked slander." But it was Theodore who had subjected her to "blow after blow, ceaseless and unrelenting, these three years!" Looking forward, we can see that her fury set the stage for her final departure from their conjugal life in 1874. Looking backward, we can see that it clouded her memory of the three years of 1870, 1871, and 1872, a period in which she and Theodore frequently fought, but in which she often expressed grand hopes for rebuilding her life with him. Indeed, her confession in July 1870 of "adultery" (Theodore's story) or of some kind of "sin" regarding Beecher (her story), and her confession a year later of a particular "sin" with Beecher (allowing an "absorbing love" to become a "passion"), were aspects of the reconciliation, not of an impending breakup. In each of those summers she was trying to effect a *mutual* confession and forgiveness. She was trying to get them both to bury their less-than-faithful pasts.[36]

Theodore said in 1874 that after July 1870 his wife's tone changed completely, and he attributed the change to guilt over adultery with Beecher. He was right that a big change took place. She was no longer the sweet, self-abnegating wife of their correspondence from the late 1860s. But the voice in her letters after July 1870 contained much more than guilt. She blamed herself, as she always had, but now she was forthright in her blame for others—especially her husband, but also Beecher and the women's rights leaders Susan B. Anthony and Elizabeth Cady Stanton. Her new vehemence seems to have flowed in part from the discovery that she and her husband were both sinners, not in the abstract (she had always known that), but in their daily relations with others. Conceding their weaknesses to one another, they could start over. Elizabeth was striving to return their marriage to a religious base. They would confess to God as well as each other, ask his forgiveness as well as their own. Her overtures were bound to fail. He did not speak her God-centered language of love, confession, and sin, but a human-centered language of love, confession, and personal growth. At times their languages did overlap. She would speak of her growth in self-confidence (through knowing Beecher), he would point to God's wondrous creation and the eternal life of the soul. But they had no shelter of common conviction when external events overcame them in 1870 (Bowen's firing of Theodore) and 1871–1872 (Woodhull's accusations).

The letter Elizabeth sent to her husband from Marietta, Ohio, in November 1870 is striking evidence of how she had changed since the previous summer. He said (in 1874) that the shift occurred on July 3, when she confessed to adultery. She said (also in 1874) that there was no confession of adultery, and no single discussion of significance, but a whole summer's worth of conversations. By her account, each of them was then accusing the other of infidelity, at least of the heart. One apparent effect of these summertime deliberations was that Elizabeth renounced her own ties to the suffragists, with whom she had worked, alongside Theodore, in the late 1860s. Susan Anthony had been her particular friend. Maybe it was Theodore's acceptance of the titular Presidency of the New York–based National Woman Suffrage Association—a job she said would pull him away from the family—that caused Mrs. Tilton to turn against Anthony, Stanton, and the entire movement. Maybe it was Theodore's intimate friendship with Laura Curtis Bullard, one of the *Revolution* editors.[37]

And it may have been a particular evening's altercation at the Tilton residence, one that involved Anthony, Stanton, and Bullard as well as Theodore and Elizabeth. It is impossible to date that evening with precision. We know it happened in the spring or fall of 1870, and Elizabeth's angry departure for Marietta, Ohio, in late September or early October to stay with her old friend Sarah Putnam (who later testified at the trial about the quirky kissing customs of liberal Brooklyn) suggests it may have been the fall. If the evening of arguments did happen in the fall, we can only commiserate with Theodore and Elizabeth about the staggering events that bombarded them in the last several months of 1870. "I went [to Marietta] to get rested from Theodore's constant talkings," Elizabeth told the church committee in 1874. "I was worn out by them." What she didn't say was that she had left because of a disagreement with her husband, and that she was determined not to go back to Brooklyn until he had changed. Nor did she say that she had just gotten pregnant, with the baby she would lose to miscarriage in December. Frank Moulton insinuated in 1874 that the baby might have been Beecher's, since Henry came down from Peekskill in August to see her, at her request. But in this case Theodore had no doubt about whose baby it was. Elizabeth, for her part, used the prospective new arrival as part of her appeal to Theodore for a renewed relationship, without which she would not go home. Being pregnant with Theodore's baby was the one bright spot for her in a season of calamities, and losing the child in December was the worst of them, the ultimate sign of how bad things could get.

As with the stormy evening of December 30, 1870, when Theodore summoned Henry to his dressing-down and Elizabeth on her sickbed delivered documents of each man's begetting, the conflagration at the Tiltons earlier in 1870 is beyond our power to reconstitute. We have two contradictory versions of what happened, one from Elizabeth Tilton and one from Elizabeth Cady Stanton. Both of them are recollections published in 1874. What we do know is that Susan Anthony had some kind of battle with Theodore, that she then spent much of the night with Elizabeth talking about the latter's relationship with Henry, and that within a few months Victoria Woodhull had heard some of that scuttlebutt from the lips of Anthony's collaborator Mrs. Stanton. And we know that Elizabeth, despite being re-elected in May 1870 as corresponding secretary of the Brooklyn Equal Rights Association, decided by fall to have nothing further to do with Anthony or the women's movement. And she tried her best to get Theodore to withdraw too.

On July 27, 1874, a reporter from the *Brooklyn Argus* knocked on Stanton's door in Tenafly, New Jersey, and asked if he could interview her about the "affair" between Henry Ward Beecher and Theodore Tilton. She eagerly agreed, and he asked her when she had first heard of it. She then told him the story of an afternoon and evening in 1870:

> Susan B. Anthony, Mr. and Mrs. Tilton, Mrs. Bullard, and myself were in Brooklyn together. It was afternoon, and after calling at the office of the *Revolution* Mr. Tilton and myself accompanied Mrs. Bullard to her residence and remained to dinner. Through some misunderstanding, Miss Anthony went with Mrs. Tilton and dined with her instead of us. There was some feeling on the part of Mrs. Tilton in regard to this, although it was quite unintentional on my part. Well, at the table no one was present but Mrs. Bullard, Mr. Tilton, and myself. Theodore told the whole story of his wife's faithlessness. As I before observed, he did not go into details; but the sum and substance of the whole matter he released in the hearing of Mrs. Bullard and myself. We were reformers. He gave us the story as a phase of social life.

Stanton did not see Anthony the next day. But she heard from someone that Susan "was a little piqued at me for leaving her on the day before." For some reason she and Anthony did not rendezvous in Brooklyn to find out what had happened and set things right between themselves. Instead Stanton returned to New Jersey, and to her surprise found Susan waiting there for her. That evening Stanton divulged the "very strange story" Theodore had related to her and Bullard. Anthony "listened attentively to the end," then said, according to Stanton's recollection, "I have heard the same story from Mrs. Tilton." "We compared notes," Stanton told the reporter, "and found that by both man and wife the same story had indeed been told." She then related what Anthony had said to her about her evening at the Tiltons.

When Mr. Tilton returned home that evening some angry words growing out of the separation in the afternoon passed between him and his wife. Both became intensely excited. In the heat of passion, and in the presence of Miss Anthony, each confessed to the other of having broken the marriage vow. In the midst of these startling disclosures, Miss Anthony withdrew to her room. Shortly after, she heard Mrs. Tilton come dashing upstairs, and Mr. Tilton following close after. She flung open her bedroom door, and Elizabeth rushed in. The door was then closed and bolted. Theodore pounded on the outside, and demanded admittance, but Miss Anthony refused to turn the key. So intense was his passion at that moment that she feared he might kill his wife if he gained access to the room. Several times he returned to the door and angrily demanded that it be opened. "No woman shall stand between me and my wife," he said. But Susan, who is as courageous as she is noble, answered him with the words: "If you enter this room it will be over my dead body," and so the infuriated man ceased his demands and withdrew. Mrs. Tilton remained with Susan throughout the night. In the excitement of the hour, amid sobs and tears, she told all to Miss Anthony. The whole story of her own faithlessness, of Mr. Beecher's course, of her deception, and of her anguish, fell upon the ears of Susan B. Anthony, and were spoken by the lips of Mrs. Tilton.[38]

Stanton's interview was page-one news all over the country on July 28. Her attention to Theodore Tilton's rage actually obscures the main import of her remarks in 1874: she was chastising Theodore but also defending him, while attacking Henry Ward Beecher and Elizabeth Tilton, whose statement denying adultery with Beecher had appeared in the *Brooklyn Eagle* on July 23 and in papers all over the country on July 24. When Mrs. Tilton appeared before the Plymouth Church Investigating Committee on July 31, she responded to Mrs. Stanton's interview with a story of her own about the evening at home with Theodore and Susan B. Anthony. She prefaced her account by noting that "Miss Anthony and another lady [Stanton] have both reported that I made confidants of them, and it came in this way; I have, full of anguish of soul, many times talked freely to them; and on one occasion Susan Anthony stayed all night, and I talked with her."

She came with Mrs. Stanton one afternoon to our house, and they proposed going to Mrs. [Bullard]'s to dinner. Mrs. Stanton and my husband went first, early in the afternoon, and we understood that

Theodore was coming back to bring Susan and myself there. I was not going, however. The evening came, and Miss Anthony was very much annoyed to think that Theodore didn't come, and she filled my mind all that evening with stories about Theodore's infidelities. He came home about 11 o'clock; Mrs. Stanton remained at Mrs. [Bullard]'s all night. When Theodore came in, Susan began in a very angry way to chide him for not coming after her, and charged him with what she had been telling me about ladies; and he grew very angry at Susan—so much so that she ran upstairs and locked herself up in the front room; I followed, and he said to me, "You have done this thing; you have been talking and putting it into her mind"; "No," I said. I never was the one to talk against Theodore in that manner; he was so angry that I feared he would be really crazy; for the first time he threatened to strike me; he went in to his own room, and was so much excited that I was alarmed; I thought I would sleep with him and apply water to his head and feet, but Susan would not let me; she said it was not safe and that I should not stay with him; so I went into her room and went to bed with her; but during the night I went frequently to see how he was; he did not sleep, he was restless; that night I told Susan of my alarm for Theodore; I told her I never saw his brother in a state when it seemed to me that he was more crazy than Theodore then was [Theodore's brother had apparently died in a mental institution], and I went on further to tell her how he was, she having seen this exhibition of his, of his being angry, and of his striking; I told her, also, in the conversation that he had charged me with infidelity with one and another, and with Mr. Beecher particularly, and that, when he sat at his table, many times, he had said that he did not know whom his children belonged to.[39]

There are many obvious differences between Mrs. Stanton's and Mrs. Tilton's stories, and intriguing discrepancies within each story. In Stanton's it is Mrs. Tilton who is miffed at Theodore's failure to pick her and Anthony up for dinner and who argues with him upon his return and then dashes upstairs. In Mrs. Tilton's story it is Anthony who is miffed, who argues with Theodore, and who dashes upstairs. In Stanton's account Anthony valiantly defends Mrs. Tilton from her husband's wrath and forces Theodore to back down, accede to her authority, and do without his wife's presence for the night. In Mrs. Tilton's account Anthony does protect her, but she also bars her from helping or sleeping with her husband. In her own account Elizabeth quietly rebels against Anthony's control by repeatedly slipping out of Susan's bed during the night to minister to Theodore.

Mrs. Stanton's version, meanwhile, has Mr. and Mrs. Tilton telling "the same story" to their separate audiences—"the whole story" of her "faithlessness." Yet they were not the same story after all: the tale she heard from Theodore at Mrs. Bullard's had no "details," while the account Susan got from Elizabeth included Beecher's "course" and Elizabeth's "anguish" and "deception" (was it Elizabeth's deception "by" or "of" someone else?). And Theodore's revelations to Stanton, in her recollection, concerned only his wife's indiscretions, while Elizabeth's disclosures to Anthony, according to Stanton, spoke of broken marriage vows by both of them. For her part, Mrs. Tilton made no mention of any misdeeds of her own, although she told the Plymouth Investigating Committee that she spoke to Anthony at length of the *allegations* spread by her husband that she had sinned with Beecher. The Committee asked her pointedly if in Anthony's company she had explicitly denied Theodore's charges. "No," she replied, "it never occurred to me to do it. I took them to be reasonable persons, and I never thought of their even wondering if it was so." [40]

There is no way to decide which of the stories, Mrs. Stanton's or Mrs. Tilton's, is true, or if either of them is. But these dueling accounts share some ground, and point therefore to some likely truths. They both assert a split between Elizabeth and Theodore, of course, and they both establish a gap between Anthony and Stanton, one that Stanton was perhaps still trying to bridge in giving her interview in 1874, where she went out of her way to put in the present tense that Susan "is as courageous as she is noble." Stanton apparently did not want Anthony and/or Mrs. Tilton at the dinner with Mrs. Bullard. She knew they expected to be picked up, and she did not insist that Theodore go and get them. It appears that the "misunderstanding" Stanton alludes to was between her and Susan, and it may have been operating on several levels at once.

Perhaps this is what happened: We know from other sources that Anthony was fonder of Elizabeth, while Stanton was fonder of Theodore. Each may have wished to spend the afternoon with her favorite Tilton. As the day progressed and the Tiltons began baring their souls—or at least telling the stories they wished the suffrage leaders to take out into the world—Mrs. Stanton decided not to break the revelatory momentum by reminding Theodore to fetch Susan and Elizabeth. Maybe she thought that Anthony would concur in that judgment: each of them was helping one young Tilton ride out a difficult moment in their marriage. Yet Anthony may have felt that Stanton was exacerbating the Tiltons' problems by drawing Theodore into Bullard's orbit for the evening. Stanton may have sensed this, for she knew Mrs. Tilton had "some feeling" about the dinner at Mrs. Bullard's, and appears in the interview to be saying that someone (probably Susan) blamed her for the misunderstanding (which "was quite unintentional on my part").

The tension between Stanton and Anthony regarding the Tiltons was still apparent in 1875. Stanton was giving interviews to all comers, trying to protect her own credibility and to defend the women's movement at a time of great danger. The Beecher-Tilton Scandal, by adding force to the traditionalist cultural wave of the mid-1870s, and by giving gifted wordsmiths such as Evarts a daily opportunity at the trial to mock women reformers, was threatening to undo all of their efforts for the equality of the sexes. Anthony, for her part, kept silent, and seems to have augmented her cultural stature in a conservative hour by staying above the battle. She was on her path toward putting suffrage for women above all other reform goals, a course Stanton regarded as narrow and capitulatory. While Stanton kept attacking Beecher, claiming he was surrounded by cronies like her (estranged) brother-in-law Samuel Wilkeson—who worried only, in her view, about their material investments in his church and publications—Anthony said nothing about her knowledge of the facts. She did not hesitate, however, to rebuke Stanton in public. Reporters pursued her up and down the lecture circuit trying to get a confirmation or denial of the tale Stanton had attributed to her, a story Anthony's brother in Kansas was also reported to have heard from her. "If I did say it," Anthony quipped, "it was very ungracious of them to repeat it; if I did not, it was worse of them to make it up."[41]

There is some evidence that privately Anthony disagreed with Stanton's firm conviction of Beecher's and Elizabeth Tilton's guilt on the adultery charge. A letter Anthony wrote in 1872 to Beecher's half-sister Isabella Hooker has been taken by several historians, as it was by Theodore Tilton and Frank Moulton in 1874, as proof that Susan believed Henry guilty, and that (given her credibility) he was in fact guilty. Anthony wrote that "I feel the deepest sympathy with all the parties involved, but most of all for poor, dear, trembling Mrs. Tilton."

> My heart bleeds for her every hour. I would fain take her in my arms, with her precious comforts—all she has on earth—her children—and hide her away from the wicked gaze of men. . . . For a cultivated

man [Beecher], at whose feet the whole world of men as well as of women sits in love and reverence, whose moral, intellectual, social resources are without limit—for such a man, so blest, so overflowing with *soul food*—for him to ask or accept the *body* of one or a dozen of his reverent and revering devotees, I tell you *he is the sinner—if it be a sin—and who shall say it is not?*

"If it be a sin." Anthony is either saying that adultery is not always a sin, an unlikely assertion for a woman with her very traditional moral views, or she is saying that Beecher may not be a sinner. Even if she considered his guilt likely, her letter is a diplomatic document designed to hedge her bets. It shows that her guarded view of Beecher's wrong-doing diverged considerably from Stanton's eager certainty about it.[42]

On one thing Stanton and Anthony must have agreed: Susan had shown courage and nobility in standing up to an enraged Theodore during the tense evening of revelations in 1870. A late-twentieth-century reader confronted with Stanton's account of Anthony's barri-cading the door against a flailing maniac is liable to adopt their position too. Susan was shielding a woman in danger of being struck by her husband, and Elizabeth must have been grateful for this display of a strength that in Stanton's account Mrs. Tilton herself lacked. But con-sider another possibility. Even if we assume that Elizabeth lacked the courage to stand up to Theodore's threats, she may have been intimi-dated by Susan as well as by Theodore. The evening's events may have been humiliating to her because Susan presumed to dictate where the lady of the house could sleep and when she could go to her husband.

For some reason or combination of them, in the summer or fall of 1870, Elizabeth Tilton renounced all her ties to the women's move-ment. Perhaps she abandoned it because Theodore had gotten too close to Laura Bullard, or because he was playing too much chess with the anticlerical Mrs. Stanton. Elizabeth would show Theodore that the well-being of their family demanded a new course, centered on Plym-outh Church, not secular politics. But perhaps she pulled out too be-cause Susan Anthony, who loved Elizabeth in a commanding, motherly fashion, had gone too far in arrogating the management of Tilton fam-ily affairs. What looked to Anthony and Stanton like valiant and loving protection bestowed upon a helpless friend may have looked to Eliza-beth like an unconscionable invasion of her sphere.

VII. Theodore published his wife's Marietta letter of November 1870 in his lengthy "final statement" in the summer of 1874 because, in his view, it was "as plain a confession of Mrs. Tilton's intimacy with Mr. Beecher as language can express." One section of the letter does refer to a sudden awful revelation she had made to her mother, a comment overheard by her 13-year-old daughter Florence.

> When, by your threats, my mother cried out in agony to me, "Why what have *you* done, Elizabeth, my child?" her worst suspicions were aroused, and I laid bare my heart then—that from *my* lips and not yours she might receive the dagger into her heart! Did not my dear child learn enough by insinuations, that her sweet, pure soul agonized in secret, till she broke out with the *dreadful question?* I know not but it hath been her death blow!

That was certainly a "confession" of some wrongdoing, but it was scarcely "plain" regarding the nature of the act or its relation to Beecher. If Theodore truly considered this published passage to be an unambiguous confession of adultery, one wonders what other sort of foggy statement Elizabeth might have made in the summer of 1870 that would also have struck him as a straight admission of it. Elizabeth claimed her mother and daughter had gotten wind merely of her confession of "sin" with her pastor. The dagger to her mother was not an admission of adultery, but of disordered passions and loyalties. The death blow to her daughter was not a piece of knowledge she received, but a question she had been led to formulate. Of course Elizabeth may have been lying: the dagger and death blow may have been some silent acknowledgment, some nondenial on her part, of physical love with her pastor.

The rest of the lengthy Marietta letter would not have helped Theodore's cause in 1874. He must have figured he had to publish the whole thing if he was going to print any of it. Whatever its practical effect in that year, it exhibited an unexpectedly assertive Elizabeth ordering him to change his ways, and accusing him of—and forgiving him for—multiple sins. "Theodore, *your* past is safe with me," she wrote, "rolled up, put away never to be opened—though it is big with stains of various hue—unless you force me for the sake of my children and friends to discover [disclose] it, in self-defence or their defence. . . . Once again I implore you for your children's sake, to whom you have a duty in this matter, that *my Past* be buried—left with me and my God. He is merciful. Will you, his son, be like him?"

Another part of the letter pleaded with him to return to God as well as his family, and tied his rebirth to the new life of their expected baby.

Allow me to advise with you now, my dearly beloved, for surely I am your best friend, and for the sake of our precious born and unborn. I tell you that since I have *been conscious* of wronging you I needed only to *know* that, and always in everything I utterly forsake the wrong, repent before God alone, and strive to bring forth fruit worthy of repentance. Will you for the added reason of your soul's sake *do the same?*

I feel that you are not in the condition of mind to lead the "woman's suffrage" movement, and I implore you to break away from it and from your friends Susan [Anthony], Mrs. Stanton, and every one and everything that helps to make a conflict with your responsibilities as husband and father. My life is still spared; my heart never yearned over you more in sorrowing love than now. But there must be a turning to God that will lead you to forsake forbidden ways, so that the sources and springs of your life be renewed, ere I shall feel it my duty to return.

I have gained a little, and with this small addition of strength my first impulse is to fly to you and comfort you in these new distractions which come to you through your business and its threatening changes. I have long felt, dear husband, you did not fill up your responsibilities toward the *Independent* as its religious chief and head. Oh, that you could be made to see and feel the amount of good you might do for Christ from that pulpit! Oh, my babe would leap in my womb for joy did your soul but awake to love God, and serve him with the fervor of the early days.[43]

Mrs. Tilton did return home in December, only to greet a succession of disasters: the urgent meetings with Mr. and Mrs. Beecher at Mrs. Morse's on the subject of separation from Theodore, her husband's firing by Bowen, her miscarriage and subsequent illness, and finally the infamous Friday night of December 30, an evening that became, four years later, the centerpiece of the Great Scandal. It also became the night for which Elizabeth Tilton was most remembered—as a tragi-comically vacillating liar, or as a thoroughly abject woman brutally bossed by both of the men she loved.

December 30 was a stormy, snowy evening in Brooklyn, dark and swirling with foreboding, as Beecher, Moulton, and other witnesses— with sure command of melodramatic convention—testified in 1874 and 1875. "The winds were out and whistling through the leafless trees," Beecher told the Plymouth Church Committee, "but all this was peace compared to my mood within." Elizabeth lay sick in her bed, recovering from the physical and emotional pain, and resulting infection, of her miscarriage suffered the day before Christmas. (Since the fetus was three months old, it was a miscarriage that felt like real labor.) On Thursday, five days after the loss, Theodore had asked her to put in writing what he claimed she had told him six months earlier, that Henry had made "improper solicitations" of her. After being assured by her husband that the document was essential for protecting the family's livelihood, and after extracting from Theodore the promise that he would never use the memo to harm Beecher, she signed it.

The next day, the 30th, Theodore took this document to Moulton's house at 143 Clinton Street, had Frank summon Henry away from his Friday evening prayer meeting, and confronted Henry with the charge. Henry was thunderstruck, and according to Theodore's testimony (denied by Beecher) said that he felt he had been thrown into Dante's inferno, and that the charge would ruin him. Theodore did not show Henry the memo signed by Elizabeth; indeed, according to Henry's testimony, Theodore tore it into small pieces as he delivered an endless monologue of accusation. Instead, Tilton suggested to Beecher that he go by himself to see Elizabeth in her sickroom and have her verify the charge verbally. It was then sometime after nine o'clock, and Henry trooped three blocks through the tempest to 174 Livingston Street. The housekeeper appeared to be expecting him, and told him to go right upstairs and wake Mrs. Tilton up.

"The bed was dressed in pure white," Beecher said in his direct testimony in 1875, in a graphic story that had the rhythm and polish of his published writing. "Mrs. Tilton was dressed in pure white, and her face as white as the bed, lying a little above a level, reclined on pillows, her hands in that form on her breast [the witness here placed his hands palm to palm], in a very natural way. I drew a chair, or there was a chair by the bedside. I sat down in it. . . . Her eyes were closed. . . . She was as one dead, and yet she was living." Beecher shed tears on the stand as he recounted (i.e., recreated) the exact dialogue that followed. "I said to her: 'He says that you have charged me, Elizabeth, with making improper advances. Have you stated all these things . . . ?' And she opened her eyes and said: 'My friend, I could not help it.' 'Could not help it, Elizabeth! Why could not you help it? You know that these things are not true.' 'Oh, Mr. Beecher,' said she, 'I was wearied out. I have been—I have been wearied with his importunities,' or something to that effect. 'He made me think that if I would confess love to you it my desire. Mr. Moulton's company was always agreeable enough, but it was not at my request or desire.

Q. Didn't you think it somewhat strange that he should propose to accompany you? A. I thought it as out of politeness.

Q. Nothing more? A. I do not recollect that I did.

Q. Well, he went to the house with you, did he? A. He did, Sir.

Q. He did not enter it, I believe? A. I believe not, Sir; I will not be sure.

THE INTERVIEW IN MRS. TILTON'S SICK-ROOM.

Q. Well, you went up stairs and found Mrs. Tilton in bed, I think? A. I did.

Q. In what room was it, Mr. Beecher? A. The left hand room, front, as you go up, and turn toward the street.

Q. As I understand you, you then informed her of the charges which her husband had made against you? That was the result of our interview.

Q. Had Mrs. Tilton retired for the night? A. I am sure I do not know, Sir; she was in bed.

Q. Well? A. Your question implies the act of going to bed.

Q. Yes, sir. A. I know nothing about that.

Q. Was she dressed in the ordinary costume of a lady who had retired for the night? A. She was dressed in white; whether it was the dressing gown of a sick-room or a night-gown, I do not recollect that that occurred to my mind.

Q. What time in the evening was it? A. I should say not far from 9 o'clock, or in that neighborhood.

Q. She was ill, was she not? A. She was ill; yes.

Q. Well, didn't you suppose that she had retired for the night? my impression was that she had been in bed all day, being ill.

Q. In your direct examination you emphasized the fact that "she was dressed in pure white; her face was as white as the bed?" A. I did.

Q. Were you surprised to find her dressed in pure white under those circumstances? A. No, Sir, I was not surprised.

Q. What did you first say to her, Mr. Beecher, after arriving in the room? A. I can say what I did, except to ask her good evening.

Q. And what was her reply? A. Nothing.

Q. What next did you say? A. I will not be positive as to the order of the opening remarks, but in general I said that I had just come from an interview with her husband, and that he had been making a good many serious charges against me. I think I introduced it in that way.

Q. State all that you said before she made any answer? A. I can't.

Q. All that you recollect? A. I can't divide it in that

way. I think that it was not until I had begun to say to her, "He charges me with improper—with having withdrawn your affections from him," or something to that effect. I think it was only then that she began to show responsiveness.

Q. And how did she show responsiveness? A. By the tears falling down her cheek, and by a little motion of her hands.

Q. Did she make no other motion? A. Not that I recall, Sir.

Q. Didn't she bow her head in acquiescence to something that you said? A. Later she did.

Q. Well, Mr. Beecher, I want you to give us the whole of that interview, as you now recollect it.

[Mr. Fullerton here paused, and asked to have better ventilation in the room.]

Q. Now, Mr. Beecher, will you give us the interview between yourself and Mrs. Tilton as it occurred on that occasion? A. I will give it to you in substance as near as I can recollect; when I went in, and after a salutation, I sat down by her side and said to her: "Elizabeth, I have just come from an interview with your husband, and he has been making very serious charges against me;" I do not now remember distinctly whether I alluded in detail to business charges, but I said: "He has charged me with having withdrawn your affections from him, and with inducing great distress and discord in his family," or words to that effect, "and he—is this so?" she made no response to it; I said to her in substance: "Elizabeth, he says that you have told him that I had won your affections from him, and that you had transferred your wifely affection to me," and at that, I think it was (though I will not be certain about that matter), the tears ran down her cheek, and she made still no response; I went on and said to her: "Elizabeth, Mr. Tilton says that you have declared to him that I have made improper advances toward you;" and she was very much agitated. Said I: "Elizabeth, have you ever said that to your husband?" and she bowed her head, and then it was that I spoke to her with more emphasis than I had (for she was a sick woman), and said to her, "Elizabeth, what could have tempted you to do such a thing as that? Wherein have I acted wrongly toward you?" I said—I expostulated with her on the subject, and said to her: "You know that it is not true that I have intentionally drawn you away from him, or that I have ever made—been guilty of impropriety, intentionally." She then began slowly to speak, or at about that time; she was feeble, and her conversation was somewhat hesitating. I plied her still—she seemed reluctant and grief-ful, and I still dwelt upon those charges, and my astonishment at her making such charges, and—"How could you have done such a thing?" She, in a slow, and in a sad voice, said, "I could not help it; I was tired out with his persistence; he pursued me, and importuned me;" and then I think she alluded to an interview of the Sum-

mer before about which I was not—I yet had not any clear or distinct idea, but I think it was in connection with that interview that she said that he had told her that if she would confess to him her strong and undue affection for me, it would be easier for him to confess his alien loves, and that they should, standing together again for a reformed and a better life, go on more happily than they had, or words to that effect, which, according to my recollection, referred to the interview of July which he said that he had had with her; I plied her in respect to that—that is, in respect to the course of conduct that she had pursued toward me, and she said, "Well, what can I do?" I don't know but that was in response to some saying of mine that she ought to retract and to do me justice; I know that that occurred somewhere in the conversation, but I cannot say in that order; but at any rate, the question came up, "What can I do?" and I said, "You ought to make a written retraction, as you have made written charges." She made some reply in respect to that, that it would be an injury, if I should have such a paper, toward her husband; and my general reply was that I intended it not for an offensive document at all; that I wanted it for my own justification; that if matters should ever, by rumor or otherwise, come to the knowledge of friends, or of the church, I ought to have something which should be a clearance of me from her; or words to that effect. She said if I would not use it to the injury of her husband, she would be willing to give me such a statement, and I told her I should not, certainly; that that was not my object, but simply self-defense.

THE WRITING OF THE RETRACTION.

I went, by her direction, to the little private writing desk which she had in the other room, which was open, and took out the note paper and the pen and the ink, and brought them to her. She had meanwhile sat up in the bed, upheld by pillows behind her, and she took the paper and wrote it on her wrapper, upon her knee, and, reading it over, she held out her hand for some ink (I held the inkstand,) and added something which—another sentence—and then signed it with her full name. Some further, but not very much pertaining to that; conversation took place, and I told her that I thought she had only acted justly and rightly toward me, and I then expressed solicitude for fear the excitement of this interview might be of injury to her in her sickness, and I took my leave.

Q. You state in your direct examination that as she lay upon the bed "she appeared as one dead;" do you remember that? A. When I first entered the room, yes, Sir.

Q. She rose up in bed without your assistance, did she not, to write that paper? A. Yes, Sir.

Q. Who placed the pillows behind her when she wrote it? A. I don't know, Sir; I did not.

Q. Did she do it herself? A. I don't know, Sir.

A portion of Beecher's 1875 trial testimony about the evening of December 30, 1870.

would help him to confess to me his alien affections,' or words to that effect."

"I spoke some—I am afraid with severity sometimes," Beecher added, though none of the recreated dialogue he offered in court was especially severe. He commanded her to retract the charges in writing. She agreed to do so "if it could be done without injury to her husband"—a condition, he testified, "which I did not at all understand." Beecher denied giving her any instruction about what to write, except for telling her that he needed a "recall" general enough to cover all of the charges, which included "corrupting" her "simplicity" and "truthfulness," and "alienating" her "affections" as well as "attempting improprieties." Elizabeth obliged by writing that "Mr. Beecher has never offered any improper solicitation, but has always treated me in a manner becoming a Christian and a gentleman." Armed with the denial, Henry left her. "And when I went away, I felt very sorrowful [about having been so tough on her]. . . . I said to her that I hoped my visit would be for peace, and that it would not be the means of throwing her back in her sickness. . . ." "Did she reply to that?" wondered William Evarts. "I don't know, Sir," Beecher replied. By prearrangement with Moulton, Beecher stopped back momentarily at Frank's house, perhaps to signal that he had left the Tilton residence. He then went home, without telling Theodore or Frank that he had obtained his own document from Elizabeth.[44]

The evening was over for Henry, but not for Elizabeth. Around midnight Theodore returned home, woke Elizabeth again, and found out that she had recanted the confession. He was furious (according to the nurse who had been in bed with Elizabeth), and had her write him a note nullifying Beecher's. In it she wrote that "he (H. W. B.) dictated a letter, which I copied as my own, to be used by him as against any other accuser except my husband. . . . I was ready to give him this letter because he said with pain that my letter in your hands addressed to him, dated December 29, 'had struck him dead, and ended his usefulness.'" (The Dec. 29 "letter" was the confession she had written.) Each man now had what he needed to sleep on. And contrary to what one might expect, this evening of dueling documents did not provoke all-out war between Theodore and Henry. Each man seems to have felt relieved and protected—maybe, despite the nocturnal agony, Elizabeth did too, because she had given to both the men she loved what they wanted. That night marked the beginning of three years of relative peace among Beecher and the Tiltons, and two years of marital rebuilding for Theodore and Elizabeth.[45]

In the 1870s, observers of the evening's stormy events were liable to conclude that Elizabeth Tilton was an inveterate and pathetic liar. A century and a quarter later, they are apt to judge that she was a wretchedly abused woman. Both perspectives miss a crucial fact. She was responsible for setting the evening's events in motion. Theodore and Frank Moulton both testified in 1874 and 1875 that Beecher was summoned to Moulton's house at her urgent request. She was terrified that her husband's dispute with Bowen might explode into a public airing of her relations with her pastor. Her husband, she feared, might try to save his livelihood (and thus, he thought, his family) by striking blindly at Beecher, a course that would inadvertently take them all down. To forestall such a debacle, she insisted on a face-to-face encounter between Henry and Theodore.[46]

Elizabeth had never yet told Henry about her "confession" of sin to her husband of the previous summer. Maybe she intended to when she called on Henry to come down from Peekskill to visit her in August, but she didn't. As the events of December piled crazily one on top of the other, Theodore may well have made a deal with her: he would agree to meet with Beecher (reassuring her), if she, on the same evening, would agree to tell Henry she had confessed (reassuring her husband). She was certainly expecting him to come by, since the housekeeper had been prepared for his arrival. But under her pastor's severe reprimand she surrendered more than Theodore had expected: the whole confession of adultery or improper solicitations. When Theodore commanded her to confess again, she had no choice but to buy whatever peace she could by flatly contradicting herself—for the second time in three hours. That was a double self-incrimination for which, beginning in July 1874, she would be subjected to merciless ridicule by her contemporaries and by later writers.

Within two weeks she, like Henry and Theodore, was feeling much better. In a letter to a "female friend" (probably Laura Bullard) on January 13, 1871, she wrote sadly of her husband's firing by Bowen, which she attributed to the latter's erroneous belief in "Theodore's infidelity" (with none other, ironically, than Bullard herself). Her husband's "dismission" caused the "anxiety night and day [that] brought on my miscarriage: a disappointment I have never before known—a *love babe* it promised, you know." Theodore had fanatical enemies, she noted, including her own mother Mrs. Morse, "but with a faithfulness renewed and strengthened by experience *we* will, by silence, time, and patience, be victorious over them all. . . . We have weathered the storm, and, I believe, without harm to our *Best*." Elizabeth wished she could visit her friend, a writer: "I would help you in the care of your loved ones, for *that* I can do. 'My heart bounds towards all.' Then your spirit would be free to write and think." The letter grew ever more cheerful as she described her own children. "I am glad you love Alice. I have kissed her for you many times. I will teach all my darlings to love you and welcome your home-coming [her friend was in the South seeking sunshine]. Ralph is a fine, beautiful boy, and to be our only baby— very precious therefore."[47]

VIII. Theodore was spending much time with Victoria Woodhull in the spring of 1871, and Elizabeth was reestablishing secret contact with Henry. The rebirth of her marriage was part of a wider pattern of affections. Both Tiltons seem to have thought these outside friendships were fully compatible with their conjugal bond, however much each spouse distrusted or (in Elizabeth's case) despised the outside party of the opposite sex. Mrs. Tilton told the Plymouth Church Committee in 1874 that she could always find some good in anyone, but she found none in Woodhull. Victoria returned the sentiment. "The moment they saw each other," according to Theodore, "their eyes flashed fire." Henry may never have praised Eunice's foresight in discountenancing the Tiltons, but Theodore repeatedly celebrated Elizabeth's in distrusting Woodhull. She "had a violent feeling against her," he told the Investigating Committee, "a woman's instinct that Mrs. Woodhull was not safe. . . . Mrs. Tilton said she thought I would rue the day [that he wrote the whitewashing biography of her]. She was far wiser than I was."[48]

Maybe it was Theodore's spirited attachment to Woodhull that led Elizabeth to her sudden insight of June 29. She picked up Charles Reade's *Griffith Gaunt,* the trans-Atlantic best-seller published in 1866, and, reflecting on Catherine Gaunt's excessive devotion to her priest-friend Brother Leonard, decided she had been wrong about intimate friendships outside of marriage—including her own with Henry. She was instantly flooded with the gravity of her sin. Catherine had led her to grasp a fine distinction in the art of loving. A love that was glorious in itself might not be for the best, because of the pain it caused elsewhere. Before reading the book, Elizabeth assumed that all loves were harmonious. They all combined to create one large mushrooming love. That was Henry Ward Beecher's doctrine: divine love and human love magnified one another, true love could hurt no one; open your spirits to God's bounty. The goal was to be able to say, in Elizabeth's favorite line from Hannah More, "My heart abounds towards all." Catherine Gaunt's "ministry" had taught her that love was not open-endedly expansive, like some gaseous entity. Contrary to her expectation, and to Beecher's teaching, it was limited in its reach, contained in and by concrete acts of fidelity to particular persons.

In 1871 Theodore apparently did not get Elizabeth's point about Catherine Gaunt. He conceded to William Evarts that in that year he had perhaps believed that the sin of Catherine's to which Elizabeth referred was adultery with Brother Leonard. (He could not remember on the stand in 1875 if he had actually read the book. In fact he had, shortly after its publication, and immediately urged his wife to read it.) His assumption that Catherine had confessed to adultery might have led him to infer that Elizabeth's confession of sin—which she likened to Catherine's—was an admission of adultery. From start to finish the scandal was full of comparisons between the experiences of the real players and their many fictional analogues. It is fitting that one of the most pivotal misunderstandings of the entire Beecher-Tilton imbroglio may have been the result of a botched reading or misrecollection by Theodore of one of the key novels in the case.[49]

Catherine Gaunt may have caught Elizabeth's fancy for an additional reason. Charles Reade's heroine was a strikingly independent woman who made strong judgments about the men she loved. On July 4, 1871, Elizabeth wrote her husband a letter that showed she had found a new position of judgment too, a position from which both Henry and Theodore could be found wanting. As for her husband, he was enthralled, she hinted, by someone else, in all likelihood Laura Bullard. Elizabeth had not given up hoping that she and Theodore would find common ground. But she seemed prepared to leave that to God.

> I had expected you all day yesterday and today, but now your letter was put into my hand instead. I feel the bitterest disappointment, but we are both in God's hands, and while I now hear him say, by my heart's intense yearnings, 'Return to the love of your youth,' oh, my dear husband, may you not need the further discipline [of] being misled by a good woman as I have been by a good man. I rejoice in your happy face and peaceful mind, though I am not in any wise the cause. It will be God's gift alone if ever your face illumines or heart throbs with thoughts of me. As for me, I will wait on the Lord. I thank you for the sufferings of the past year. You have been my deliverer.[50]

Elizabeth Tilton had laid the foundation, in the early 1870s, for the post-trial and post-Plymouth Church years in which she would consecrate herself to prayer and to the community of the Plymouth Brethren. She met the vilification to which she was subjected after 1874 with silence, apart from her parting "confession" of 1878. One suspects that like Henry and Theodore, she had many difficult moments after the trial, but one can't assume that her avoidance of publicity, and her consequent absence from the historical record, means that she had lost heart. She had a gift of faith, she had her children, and she may still have had a fond memory of the two intimate loves she had shared with her husband and pastor. Perhaps, looking back, she felt from time to time what she had expressed in January 1871, when she wrote to her friend and sister, "You, like me, have loved and been loved, and can say with Mrs. Browning,"

> Well enough I think we've fared,
> My heart and I.[51]

THE TILTONS IN THE COUNTRY.

MR. AND MRS. THEODORE TILTON, NEAR THEIR SUMMER BOARDING-HOUSE ON THE SHORT-CUT RAILROAD, NEAR NEWBURG, N. Y., IN AUGUST, 1870.
SKETCHED BY JAY CHARLTON.

SIX *Early Stories,* 1855–1866

I. A compendium of the leading "men of our day" published in 1868 starred Henry Ward Beecher, of course, but it also featured Theodore Tilton, the "still youthful" editor of the *Independent* who "looked at least six years younger" than his 33 years. No current journalist in the country had "risen earlier or more rapidly, or given indications in early manhood of greater genius and intellectual grasp" than this "tall and commanding" writer and poet. Some of his editorials "have hardly been surpassed, in the way of newspaper writing, during the present century." His oratory sparkled as well. "He is today perhaps foremost in reputation among the younger class of speakers. His electric energy, playful fancy, ready wit, and fiery eloquence, make him very popular with audiences everywhere."

The book noted Beecher's long-standing influence on this veritable Wunderkind. He had gotten him true editorial responsibility at the *Independent* when he was only 26, and modeled how to "control and magnetize an audience." "Without the slightest wish or attempt on [Tilton's] part to imitate Mr. Beecher, there is a very considerable similarity" in their oratorical methods. Both men alternated "the humor which provokes a smile" with "the pathos which causes the tears to moisten the eyes." Both of them "draw their illustrations mainly from nature." And both "possess that power of word-painting which enables them to make their hearers see what they describe." The compiler then let Theodore do the talking: the last three pages of the six-page entry were excerpts from his December 1865 "toast" at the "New England Society dinner" (probably in Brooklyn). That speech, the compiler believed, "will give a very good idea of his humor, the delicacy of his conceits, and his descriptive power."[1]

Theodore's toast to the all-male assembly also gives a very good idea of the kind of success Tilton had achieved by the age of 30, and how different it was from the kind he would aspire to in the late 1860s. At the end of 1865 Theodore was a man among men, rising quickly as a backslapping fellow in a culture that still commonly split male and female social worlds. He was already a young master of a sharp and witty repartee that might be "delicate" in its "conceits" but was, like Beecher's, fully masculine. There was no better way to demonstrate his manliness than to offer his lighthearted but deeply sincere disquisition on the assigned topic of the toast: "woman—the strong staff and beautiful rod which sustained and comforted our forefathers during every step of the Pilgrims' Progress." The assembled gentlemen loosened their belts, leaned back into the cigar smoke, and heartily applauded this earnest young champion of the Pilgrim foremothers—and of the bourgeois male culture of the 1860s.

In a year or two Theodore would begin spending more and more time with foremothers of a different era: Susan Anthony, Elizabeth Cady Stanton, and other women's rights activists. His preferred arena of imagined success switched to an androgynous realm of "purity," one in which the proverbial "long-haired men and short-haired women" (Tilton and Stanton were poster-persons for that stereotype of radical activists) gathered together for a re-gendering of equality. His letters to his wife in the late 1860s are full of dismay at the old success ideals that had tempted him, ideals that put worldly positions and rewards ahead of moral perfection.

In the years before the end of the war Theodore could still join Henry in celebrating the male sphere of achievement. There was an actual war to fight from 1861 to 1865, and an ideological campaign against slavery before and during the military battle. The 28-year-old Tilton was in fact drafted in 1863, but when he "furnished for a substitute a Prussian sergeant," as he reported to Henry, only the "Copperheads" and other critics of abolitionism, such as Thurlow Weed, challenged his manhood. "The editor of the *Independent*," wrote Weed, "whose zeal for the draft led him to rail at all who questioned its wisdom, when drafted himself, ingloriously shirks from taking *his* share of duty and danger! *Shame on such a sneak!* . . . Mr. Tilton must be craven in spirit, without patriotism, pride or manhood, to skulk a draft himself, while he is merciless in regard to the mechanic and laborer who is compelled to leave his wife and children." Republicans with credentials more radical than Weed's, meanwhile, knew they needed Theodore in the manly endeavor of editorial work, where (as he told Henry) "my chief aim, just now, is to keep the moral sentiment of the people brought up to the point of *no compromise* [on conditions for readmitting Southern states and on the timetable for emancipating the slaves]."[2]

But for Beecher and Tilton and many other men of mid-nineteenth-century America, the male realm was not only one of battle and debate, work and camaraderie. It was one of intimate friendship and what they never tired of calling "love." Henry and Theodore were far from unique, although they may have pushed sentimental profusions of affection beyond the norm of the Northern Protestant men of their day. One of Beecher's chief achievements in the 1850s was to create at Plymouth Church a social world that not only mixed the sexes, but blended gender ideals by inviting men and women to widen their emotional and imaginative repertoire. Christianity always had the potential to undermine cultural distinctions between the sexes, since the paradoxical spiritual quest it envisioned—dying to self, losing one's life so as to find it—could be understood as identical for women and men, whatever the culturally gendered forms the life of faith inevitably took. Rather than see Beecher as a "feminizer" of religion (because he threw off the tough-minded Calvinism of his youth and had a congregation that was 60 percent female), we should see his work as a Romantic protest against the nineteenth-century bourgeoisie's further domestication of a religion that had been "feminized," if that word applies at all, ever since Jesus taught men and women to turn the other cheek. Beecher did habitually use feminine imagery to represent the divine, but the deeper point is that his ministry offered resistance to the middle-class relocation of "virtue" (from the Latin root "vir," "man") to woman's tranquil domestic domain. Virtue, in his eyes, was found in the passionate embrace of love and the natural world, and in cheerful devotion to one's work. He personally modeled a new ideal for men and women alike, robustly worldly yet alive to tender feeling, casting off Calvinist constrictions and opening oneself to novel experiences of self-giving. He did it in his preaching and he did it, with Theodore, in his living.[3]

Tilton and Beecher "loved" one another in the early 1860s. Their attachment was intense, emotional, and exhilarating. It was a closer bond than either of them had with the other men whom they also said they "loved" in those years. The term "love" could be applied to a whole range of relationships within and across gender lines, from the general charitable feeling Christians had for one another (and for strangers) to the exclusive soul-mating between God and believer, married spouses, declared lovers (future spouses), or same-sex friends. Theodore and

Henry considered one another the closest of soul-lovers. A sermon Beecher delivered in 1866 lays out the meaning of the "soul-affinity" that bound them together.

> In society, men are related by blood and legal propinquity; but in the greater invisible society, with all those who have a higher life than that of the body, relationship takes place, not by blood, but by the spiritual law. Not those who have your blood in their veins, but those who have your disposition in their soul, are your true kindred. Many and many a one is born sister to you, and is not sister; is born brother, and is no kindred of yours. And many, whose father and mother you never know, are own brothers to you by soul-affinity. Saul was not David's father, yet David and Jonathan were more brothers than if the same loins had begotten both, the same cradle rocked them, and the same mother nourished.

Soul-mating took place, according to Beecher, not just among one's intimate friends, but among all true lovers of humanity, whatever their nationality, and whatever their geographic distance from one another. All true patriots, for example, were tied indissolubly to the republican heroes Giuseppe Mazzini, Lajos Kossuth, and Victor Hugo.

> As men grow toward love, finer and finer are those interpreting sympathies by which they select out of the masses of men, and out of their seeming antagonists, those that by elective affinity are theirs by purity, by capacity, by self-denial; theirs by the power of humiliation; theirs because they can bear as Christ bore, and Godlike as he was, through suffering. And so the generous, the truly Christian, the inspired heart, seeks its brotherhood, not in sects, not in near affiliations of interest, but everywhere through the round world. Wherever men have achieved, done, there it claims them for its own, and they seem to appear in the present.[4]

Henry and Theodore thrilled each other, bounded down the street arm in arm. In a jaunty "Letter to the Office Editors" published in the *Independent* in 1859, Beecher joshed the office staff for being stuck at their desks in Manhattan while he, on a trip west, was sauntering in the luscious open air of spring. His choice of adjectives to describe Theodore bespoke the special intensity of his feeling for him. "And thou younger, God-given, ply thy tasks, nor think of birds, flowers, streams, budding birch, and fragrant spice-bush, but only of copy, items, and proof-reading. Meanwhile, farewell." The spring of affection between them does not imply that their relationship was what the twentieth century would come to call "homosexual." It was "homosocial," perhaps, in the sense that it grew out their common grounding in a male social world. That world existed apart from, while also crisscrossing, their family ties to wives and children and their spiritual fellowship at Plymouth Church. The friendship-love between Theodore and Henry was of course shaped by the Christian community at Plymouth, but it drew much of its emotional force from an independent culture of male companionship.[5]

Beecher's six-month absence in Europe in 1863 produced a letter exchange that points to the lift and joy of their male affection. His mentor's "private" letters, Theodore said in August, had "been like so many kisses and handshakes. Send some more! My love multiplies for you every day." "When you come home," he added on September 18, "I will put my arms around your neck and kiss you on both cheeks!" "I toss to you a bushel of flowers," he closed, "and a mouthful of kisses." Theodore was joking when he wrote to Henry in July that "I am in constant bereavement at your absence, and think of taking to drink, and to reading the Bible," but the ironic rollicking was part of the closeness. "My Dear Bishop," the letter began. "My Venerable Bishop," the September letter started. There was still plenty of room amidst all the jesting for sincere affirmations of love. "There is no man in America whom I love as much as one man out of it," Theodore said in ending the July note. "I have just come into the house from watering my Wax Plant," he wrote in June, "which has been set in the garden since you saw it. I poured a cool drink over its leaves, and the leaf on which you scratched your initials held itself up to me as green as the memory in which I hold your Lordship."[6]

Tilton's 1863 letters to the traveling Beecher make passing mention of Elizabeth's fondness for him, and always put that affection for her pastor in the context of the intimate bond shared by Henry and Theodore. In June he wrote that "my wife, who sits at the other end of my table (still waiting for her coming baby [Carroll]) sends this message: 'Tell him (that is, *you*, not the baby) I love him dearly.' So does her husband—now, henceforth, and forever. Amen." Two weeks later he closed his letter with "my wife, who has no baby yet, sends her love to you, and so does Theodore Tilton." After Carroll's birth on August 6, Beecher sent a "kind remembrance" that according to her husband "overwhelmed" Elizabeth, "the little lady," who after the birth had suffered "a long sickness, with her old trouble of milk legs." The baby himself "does not call you by name but hears of you every day. Florence, the oldest daughter, holds you in great reverence, taught of her mother. I never knew how much I loved you till your long absence. I am hungry to look into your eyes."[7]

Theodore said a decade later in one of his published outcries that Henry's "dishonouring" of Elizabeth in the late 1860s was "a crime of uncommon wrongfulness and perfidy" because it put an end to his own fifteen-year "intimate friendship" with him. He was exaggerating the length of the connection, but not its character. When they were the closest, in the early 1860s, they were blissful partners, each magnifying and renewing the other. From England in 1863 Henry sent workaday letters full of instructions about the conduct of the *Independent,* but he also sent sentiments of tender effusion. Before embarking on his ship back to America, he told Theodore he "wanted somebody to know the secret of my life."

> I am in a noisy spectacle, and seem to thousands, as one employing merely worldly implements, and acting under secular motives. But should I die, on sea or land, I wanted to say to you, who have been so near and dear to me, that in God's own very truth, *"the life that I have lived in the flesh, I have lived by faith of the Son of God."* I wanted to leave it with someone to say for me, that it was not in natural gifts, nor in great opportunities, nor in personal ambition, that I have been able to endure and labour. But that the secret spring of my outward life has been an inward, complete, and all-possessing faith of God's truth, and God's own self, *"working, in me to will and to do, of His own good pleasure."*

There is a special intimacy in Henry's selecting Theodore to speak for him in case of his death. Theodore was to be the guardian of his life's intended meaning, the carrier of his deepest truth. Beecher was honoring Theodore with a quasi-official responsibility. Asking him to perform a public duty of this magnitude was the sign of an uncommon private bond. At age 27 Theodore was his spiritual executor.[8]

The letter also suggests that Henry was relying on Theodore for the kind of reassurance that Theodore would seek from Elizabeth in the late 1860s during his own lecture trips. Beecher had gone to the continent in June on an extended vacation, and expected to continue to rest in England during the summer. Instead he was roped into making speeches in defense of the Union, a task he quickly warmed to when he heard pro-Southern sympathizers were mobilizing to hoot him down. When his addresses were reported in New York, much of the press declared him a hero for intrepidly facing down John Bull. Even if his contribution to winning the war for British public opinion was vastly exaggerated by many of his followers—and anti-Beecher biographer Paxton Hibben, writing in the 1920s, insisted that it was—the pro-Union meetings had a huge impact at home and increased Beecher's political visibility immeasurably.[9]

As he prepared for the talks, he was nervous. And after giving several he doubted his voice could hold out. "After resting 20 weeks," he fretted to Theodore, "to begin so suddenly such a tremendous strain upon my voice has very much affected it. Today I am somewhat fearful that I shall be unable to speak tomorrow night in Exeter Hall. I want to speak there. If the Lord will only let me, I shall be willing to give up all the other openings in the Kingdom." To judge by his own report three days later, he need not have worried. The audience at Exeter Hall was "more . . . than hearty, than even eager, it was almost wild and fanatical." After the speech he might have been "killed with people pressing to shake my hand, men, women and children. . . . I was shook, pinched, squeezed and tormented in every way an affectionate enthusiasm could devise." The letter reports Henry's campaign to spread the news of his exploit in England itself, and it instructs Theodore about publicizing it in the *Independent*. "Do not say too much eulogistically of *me*—or let it appear that the Independent is gone into enthusiasm. The *Cause* should be kept uppermost—and as the great end and object of these movements in England. It is fine, it is modest, so to do, and will lead many to rejoice in it. . . ." Theodore was his sympathetic ear on the one hand, his publicity man on the other.[10]

Tilton touted Henry in the pages of the *Independent*, and Henry proclaimed Theodore's stature from the rostrum in Britain. To a volatile audience in Liverpool he let on that Tilton—a name the crowd recognized—was the source of some direct intelligence from Abraham Lincoln. Lincoln was a minority President, and he needed all the support the evangelical Republican *Independent*, critical of his desultory churchgoing and his go-slow approach to abolition, was willing to give him. Hence his intermittent cultivation of the young Tilton, along with other antislavery publicists, including Beecher. "I will read you a word from President Lincoln," Beecher bellowed. The crowd responded with a "renewed uproar," according to the published report.

> It is a letter from Theodore Tilton. [Hisses and cheers.] Won't you hear what President Lincoln thinks? ["No, no."] Well, you can hear it or not. It will be printed whether you hear it or hear it not ["hear," and cries of "Read, Read"]. Yes, I will read. "A talk with President Lincoln revealed to me a great growth of wisdom. For instance, he

said he was not going to press the colonization idea any longer, nor the gradual scheme of emancipation, expressing himself sorry that the Missourians had postponed emancipation for seven years. He said, 'Tell your anti-slavery friends that I am coming out all right.' He is desirous that the Border States shall form free constitutions, recognizing the proclamation, and thinks this will be made feasible by calling on loyal men." [A voice: "What date is that letter?" and interruption.] Ladies and Gentlemen, I have finished the exposition of this troubled subject.[11]

The difference between the love-friendship Henry had with Theodore in the early 1860s and the one he had with Elizabeth in the late 1860s may be less than we imagine. Of course there was a passion between Henry and Elizabeth that grew out of sexual difference, and it was a passion of mutually dazzling spiritual force however circumscribed its physical expression. Beecher's most disarming love was going to be with a woman like Elizabeth, who could offer maternal sympathy and mystical inspiration along with whatever bodily intimacy he and she may have permitted themselves. But with Theodore too there was the experience of an identity, of two souls united in a battle against slavery and in a common quest for God's love and nature's bounty. In both cases the two people in love felt a transformative rush as they were elevated to new heights of sensibility and faith. The greatest difference between the two friendships may be that with Theodore Henry could afford to be much more forthright in the public expression of his sentiments.

When Theodore wrote in 1874 of his pain at losing Henry's fifteen-year intimacy, he was probably feeling that it was only the first of two such cataclysmic losses. Fifteen years vastly overestimated the period of peak fondness with Henry—while showing in the very exaggeration how hurt he was and how he treasured the memory of the friendship. But fifteen years was precisely the length of time he had been in relatively untroubled intimacy with Elizabeth, from the "confessed love" of 1851 (when, as teenagers, they were betrothed in some fashion) until roughly 1866. He called his long tie to Henry a "cemented" friendship. "Cemented" means set and firm, but it also means unperturbed and uniform, intermingled and joined. Theodore's love with Elizabeth may have been comparably calm and assured in the early days of their marriage, but it was not tranquil after the mid-1860s. In 1874 he told himself the story of overlapping fifteen-year loves, both of them lost forever, the one with Henry perhaps more fully "cemented" at its peak than the one with Elizabeth.[12]

There were many reasons for the gathering stress between Theodore and his wife, including his religious drift and Elizabeth's jealousy of her husband's female friends (in her own 1874 statement she said that the first sign of discord between them was her own "jealous[y] of his attention to the ladies"). But the deepest rift may have been caused by Henry's appearance at Livingston Street. Theodore would later declare, and surely believe, that Beecher was the outside agitator who shattered the Tilton household. But one wonders if he sensed that Elizabeth was responsible too—not for the breakup of his family, but for the loss of his preexisting friendship with Henry. If that thought occurred to him, he would not have blamed her outright. Theodore believed she could control the "sensual influence" that he claimed (according to her) she exerted over other men. But she could not hide her mystical magnetism. She had a spiritual gift, and all three of them knew it. Theodore must have mused in the mid-1860s that it was just a matter of time before his wife and his pastor recognized that they were what Elizabeth called "counterparts."[13]

II. The friendship-loves Beecher had with each Tilton resembled one another in their general emotional intensity, but also in a very particular structural fact. He was old enough to be either one's father: twenty-two years older than Theodore, about twenty years older than Elizabeth. He frequently portrayed his relationship to Elizabeth as that of a father to a daughter, and his portrait of *Norwood*'s mystically gifted Rose Wentworth may have drawn on paternally inspired feelings or fantasies generated by his encounter with Elizabeth. Between him and Theodore there was also an elemental parent-child tie, and it was doubled by another traditional male bond, that of master and apprentice.

As a teenager Theodore was already sitting at Beecher's feet, recording his sermons by Pitman's "phonographic" method. Writing down Beecher's exact words was one means of learning to speak with his master's voice. A surviving letter from the young stenographer to his soon-to-be mentor exhibits the seriousness with which Tilton pursued his labors. "Mr. Beecher," Theodore wrote.

> You drew a comparison of a man going down into a dungeon and coming up again, which you doubtless will be able to recall. I broke

down while you were in that flight, and if I were to write out, in my report, all that I caught of that part of your sermon, you would be disgusted with the figure. I therefore overleap the whole of it, and leave a blank of a complete paragraph. This is a sin of *omission* for which I am as sorry as you will be. Yours, Theodore Tilton" [14]

Whatever his mistakes, Theodore's work must have pleased Beecher, for in the spring of 1856 the newly married, 20-year-old Tilton actually became his apprentice. He was hired by Henry Bowen to join the editorial staff of the *Independent,* for which Beecher was the leading writer. Founded in 1848, the *Independent* had become the leading evangelical weekly, with a circulation of about seventy thousand in the 1860s. Henry may also have had a role in the hiring of Theodore's new brother-in-law (and childhood playmate) Joseph Richards, who soon joined the paper as publisher. In December 1861 Beecher took over as editor on the condition that the 26-year-old Tilton be appointed managing editor. Sharing the editorial duties of a major magazine during the Civil War was the day-to-day foundation for their intimate friendship. [15]

Beecher and Tilton made an excellent editorial combination. Henry handled the "religious" side by supplying his weekly sermon (an uncorrected transcription of his actual spoken words) and often his Friday evening Plymouth "talk," also usually on a spiritual topic. Tilton built up the "secular" poetry and fiction offerings, many of which were so steeped in the sentimental striving of liberal Protestant culture that it was hard to distinguish them from Beecher's religious contributions. And some poetry was purely religious. One such poem, entitled "Dying Deaths Daily," was prominently printed on page one in 1865. It was authored by "E. T.," in all likelihood Elizabeth Tilton. Theodore's and Elizabeth's favorite poet was Elizabeth Barrett Browning, a frequent contributor. When she died in 1861 Theodore authored a lengthy front-page obituary, later expanded into a "memorial" preface to her *Last Poems.* "Not a finer genius ever came into the world, or went out of it," he wrote. "Not a nobler heart ever beat in a human bosom; not a more Christian life was ever lived; not a more beautiful memory ever followed the name of man or woman after death." [16]

Meanwhile, both Henry and Theodore burned white-hot on wartime politics and military strategy, and the editorial page drew the fire of some churchmen for veering too far into the secular. When Tilton was sacked by Bowen in 1870 it was partly on the grounds that he had forgotten the paper's evangelical mission and had turned it into the polemical mouthpiece of his Radical Republicanism. There was nothing new about that complaint: critics were raising their eyebrows over Tilton's iconoclasm and personal style of attack as early as 1859. "Tilton is his name and tilting his profession," wrote *Vanity Fair*. The *Round Table* said of the *Independent* (with hefty exaggeration) that "a religious article in its columns is an accident." Yet Theodore's diatribes and the paper's attention to worldly affairs may have been one major reason for the *Independent*'s growing circulation in the early 1860s. "During 1862 and 1863," Bowen later wrote with pride, "it was placed on a paying basis." Tilton's scorching rhetoric suited Bowen fine as long as it pleased the paper's antislavery and Republican Christian readership.[17]

Beecher shepherded Theodore as a writer at the *Independent* and as an orator at Plymouth Church. Lyman Abbott, who joined the church in 1854 and went on to succeed Beecher as pastor (and to write a still useful biography of him), noted that Plymouth, in the old Congregational style, was a "meeting house" as well as a house of worship. It was a center of "literary, political, and moral reform lectures" as well as "religious instruction." The new church building completed on Orange Street in 1850 was unmatched for gatherings of up to three thousand listeners. (The interior of today's Plymouth Church of the Pilgrims has been refitted for a smaller congregation.)

> Standing upon the platform, which serves as a pulpit, the speaker is seen by every person in the house—there are no great pillars to obstruct the view—and heard by every auditor in the house—there is no vaulted roof in which the voice is lost, no angles to catch and to deflect it. A voice of very ordinary carrying power can be heard in a conversational tone throughout the edifice, and a voice like Mr. Beecher's, of extraordinary carrying power, can be heard in tones scarcely raised above a whisper.

The church was "a pure democracy," said Abbott, since Beecher preferred to leave policy decisions to a vote, and his voice was no weightier in the tally than anyone else's. Abbott granted that Beecher had substantial informal power, but the pastor preferred to leave formal decisions to the collective body.[18]

Beecher's approach to leadership encouraged vigorous discussion, and dissension, on many issues within the congregation. In January 1860, for example, Plymouth debated whether to stop funding the American Board of Commissioners for Foreign Missions. For five successive nights a packed house listened to speakers on both sides. Beecher led off for those who supported continued funding in spite of the

Board's checkered record on slavery: its missions in the west still tolerated church membership by slaveholding Cherokee Indians. On the fourth night Theodore delivered a blazing assault on Henry's position, using Beecher's own earlier antislavery speeches against him. There could be no compromising with the Slave Power. If the American Board was not completely pure on the slavery question, it was complicit with evil and should get no money.

The speech was a virtuoso performance for a 24-year-old. Theodore had learned from Henry about humor: his talk was filled with clever gibes at Beecher and other backsliders from timeless principle. Missionaries with slaveholders in their flocks? Theodore was mortified. "I have heard of a woman who was asked what she thought of the doctrine of total depravity, and who replied that it was 'a very good doctrine if people would only *live up to it*' (laughter)." The American Board "of course instruct their missionaries to preach the doctrine of total depravity; the missionaries preach it, and are in that respect very orthodox and sound; but, in justice to them, it must be also said that they not only preach, but practice it (laughter)."

Tilton had also learned from Beecher about props. Not only did he unfurl a large map of Indian territory and point to it like a geography professor. He reached for a green sack and pulled out a rifle, one of the famous Sharpe's rifles that Plymouth Church had sent to Kansas in 1856 to help defend antislavery settlers against armed slavery-supporting interlopers from Missouri. "Is it loaded?" yelled a parishioner, unleashing a wave of laughter. "Only with an argument," Theodore flashed back, to more laughter. A church that had risen to the moral occasion in 1856 with firearms must now send "the testimony of a strong word" by switching its funds to the resolutely antislavery American Missionary Association. To judge by the printed text of his speech, Tilton must have held the audience for two hours or more. Yet Beecher's side had the votes, and Henry could afford to be paternally congratulatory after Theodore's barn-burning speech. At the trial in 1875 Tilton went out of his way to commend Beecher for that show of support in 1860. "He met me just before I went into the pulpit that night to make my speech, patted me on the shoulder, and said, 'Theodore, go and do as well as you can'; and the next day, after the discussion was over, he came around to see me, and said, 'Theodore, I am proud of you.'" [19]

At the trial William Evarts kept trying to make Theodore say that the speech marked the beginning of a split between him and Henry. But in response Tilton kept repeating the same thing he had said fifteen years before in the speech itself: Beecher was his generous mentor and benefactor. "He always encouraged the utmost latitude of discussion," he told the court. "There never was a more friendly discussion than the one between Mr. Beecher and myself concerning those missionary funds." Sharp difference of opinion, Beecher had taught him, was perfectly consistent with love as well as friendship. At the start of the speech in 1860 Theodore noted that in Beecher's opening address he had spoken fondly of "some of the young men of this Church, who, growing up for years under his teachings, had at last found themselves differing in certain points from their teacher." Tilton then praised his pastor's "large-heartedness" and "warmth of nature."

> I remember reading of a nobleman of the Court of Queen Elizabeth, who thought it a sufficient honor to himself to be called "the friend of Sir Philip Sidney." On very many occasions, both in private and in public, I have been received into new circles of society as the friend of the pastor of this Church; and I am sure that never in my life have I been more proud of any introduction! When Louis Kossuth called Walter Savage Landor his friend, the old poet lifted up his hands and exclaimed, "Henceforth, no man can honor me!" I need not say to any member of this Church that I love its minister, almost as I love no other man! Nor need I say that when I come tonight to speak in opposition to his views, it is from no lack of good-fellowship or good feeling towards him; for, standing in this pulpit, in the presence of this Church which has grown up under his labors and his prayers, I humbly now invoke upon him the blessing of God, and pray that he may be sustained with unabated strength in his noble and successful service in this Church of Jesus Christ, until, after many years, he shall be as old and white-haired as that venerable man, his father, who now, past four-score, has travelled up so near to the summit of the Mount of Vision that his head is already among its snows, waiting to break through into the glory beyond! [20]

The invocation of Henry's father Lyman, now residing in his dotage with his third wife in Brooklyn, was a fitting gesture in view of Theodore's son-like relation to Henry. In the early 1860s there must have been times when Theodore struck him as the ideal son, a far cry from his own eldest boy. Harry Beecher had enlisted in the army when war broke out in 1861. According to a story that has all the earmarks of embellished legend, he committed some serious moral infraction while encamped with the Army of the Potomac, and was dismissed in disgrace. His father, who had preached a sermon early in the mobilization on "The Camp, Its Dangers and Duties," was naturally heartbroken. He shared his grief with Theodore, who took immediate action to fix the problem. An unidentified letter writer to the *Pittsburgh Commercial* in 1874 told what allegedly happened next.

> Tilton asked Beecher for his (Beecher's) pocketbook, and took from it fifty dollars. He took the first train for Washington, and on reaching there, went direct to the house of Secretary of War Cameron. Mr. Cameron was dressing preparatory to entertaining a breakfast party of Governors of States. Tilton ascertained this fact from the servant, and, of course, announced himself as a Governor. He met Cameron, challenged his admiration, enlivened the table, and when the guests had departed, importuned for a commission for young Beecher in the regular army. Tilton would not be satisfied with a promise, and after an interview with President Lincoln, secured the desired commission. . . . He returned by the next train, handed Mr. Beecher the commission, at which his friend and patron fell on his breast and wept tears of gratitude. Theirs was no ordinary friendship, seemingly. Beecher's light reflected on Tilton, and he was happy.[21]

Whatever the accuracy of the details—one wonders if Cameron was quite so gullible and Lincoln quite so accessible—there is no doubt that Theodore went to Washington and somehow wangled a commission for Harry as a lieutenant in the artillery. At the trial in 1875 Beecher was still expressing his gratitude for Tilton's act, and Theodore was denying he deserved special praise. "He told me that I had saved one of the members of his family from destruction; I didn't see the imminent destruction." Yet he had gladly done what it took to help his bosom friend. "My purpose was not only friendly, but it was affectionate and loyal." Beecher remarked on the stand that Tilton "was always doing me little kindnesses that were very agreeable; but there was one that stood out beyond all others and was very specially valuable to me." Evarts: "And that was in reference to your son?" Beecher: "Yes, Sir." Evarts: "It has been sufficiently referred to. Did you feel it very much?" Beecher: "I did, and I do."[22]

In 1874 Theodore looked back and grieved over the loss of a roughly fifteen-year intimacy with Henry—he must have been counting from the time of his baptism (1853) or marriage (1855) at Plymouth until the end of the 1860s. Henry looked back and mourned the loss of a three- or four-year intimacy with Theodore: 1861 to 1863 or 1864 inclusive. Henry's dates are closer to the mark. The two of them were arm-in-arm pals from the time they took over the *Independent* in 1861 until at least Beecher's return from England in the fall of 1863. The special bond may have continued into 1864, when Theodore was running the magazine by himself, with Henry's name still on the masthead.

A letter Theodore wrote Henry in November 1865 appears to show that Tilton had never been fonder of him.

> The more I think back upon this friendship, the more am I convinced that not your public position, not your fame, not your genius, but just your affection has been the secret of the bond between us. For, whether you had been high or low, great or common, I believe that my heart, knowing its mate, would have loved you exactly the same. . . . Moreover, if I should die leaving you alive, I ask you to love my children for their father's sake, who has taught them to reverence you and to regard you as the man of men.

This effusive document may be a true statement of Theodore's feelings in late 1865. But he wrote it after consulting with Henry about the best way to snuff out rumors that there was ill will between them. Henry had just confronted him with the charge that he had been spreading rumors about Beecher being engaged in "loose conduct with women" (Beecher's phrase). Charles Judson, a friend of both men, had come to Beecher's house and reported that Tilton, over lunch at Delmonico's, had uttered the disparaging remarks. Judson had observed to Theodore at lunch that charges of immorality were fogging the Brooklyn air, and expressed his satisfaction that Beecher for one was pure. To which Theodore responded, several times according to Judson, "I have lost my faith in man." Perhaps Judson misunderstood, or perhaps Tilton was already engaged in technical truth-telling and Judson got his point perfectly: Beecher was not pure, even though Tilton had not said so directly. Henry took Judson's interpretation straight to Theodore, who denied it. They agreed to write each other loving notes that could be shown to "either's friends." Here at the end of 1865 was an eerie adumbration of the impression management that would mark the scandal cover-up five years later.[23]

Was something already being covered up in 1865, and perhaps earlier? Something was surely being buried, but there is no way to tell whether it was actual wrongdoing or simply rumors of wrongdoing. What we do know is that Elizabeth wrote to her husband in 1866 that the previous three years had been "dreadful" because her and Theodore's "confidence" in Beecher had been "shaken." She was therefore referring to something—an event or an allegation—that had come to light in 1863. That was the year when Henry Bowen apparently wrote to Theodore that on her deathbed Lucy Bowen had confessed to adultery with Beecher. Tilton said in 1871 that he had a letter from Bowen dated June 16, 1863—several weeks after Beecher's departure on his extended holiday to Europe—that read as follows:

> I sometimes feel that I must break silence, that I must no longer suffer as a dumb man, and be made to bear a load of grief most unjustly. One word from me would make a revolution throughout Christendom, I had almost said—and you know it. . . . You have just a little of the evidence from the great volume in my possession. . . . I am not pursuing a phantom, but solemnly brooding over an awful reality.

Theodore added (also in 1871) that Bowen had even before this— "during the early part of the rebellion (if I recollect aright)"—"intimated to me that the Rev. Henry Ward Beecher had committed acts of adultery for which, if you [Bowen] should expose him, he would be driven from his pulpit. From that time onward your references to this subject were frequent, and always accompanied with the exhibition of a deep-seated injury to your heart." [24]

Theodore had therefore heard rumors about Henry beginning in 1861 or 1862—during or just before the peak period of their own intimacy. We have no idea if he discussed Bowen's repeated accusations with Beecher, if Bowen ever made the charges directly to their pastor, or if Beecher's departure for Europe was related to them. Theodore said that Bowen had told the same story to other people, so it stands to reason that the six-month vacation to Europe was connected to the circulating news, whatever its accuracy. We do know that Bowen's allegations did not prevent Theodore from pursing his intimate friendship with Henry. All of his warm letters to Henry in England in the summer and fall of 1863 came after the June 16, 1863, letter from Bowen. In fact, Theodore's letter of June 17 appears to refer directly to Bowen's epistle of the previous day, and mentions no charge of any wrongdoing. "I have just received from him a letter in which he writes like a conquered man, whose sorrows have crushed him into the dust. He says that the world-life-fortune-ambition—all are almost as nothing to him, and he has never before felt so willing to die." Theodore did repeatedly express to Henry the hope that being abroad would restore his vital forces—and he relayed with approval a friend's prayer that Henry would return in the fall "with strength to be true to himself"— but he never implied to Henry that there had been any accusation from Bowen or anyone else. Nor did Bowen's allegations stop Elizabeth from pursuing her close bond with Henry starting around 1865. Indeed the

stories about Beecher's wrongdoing seem if anything to have deepened her interest in befriending her pastor. She claimed, according to
Theodore's later testimony, that she wished to rescue him from the attentions of conniving ladies who did not have his true spiritual interests
at heart.[25]

One wonders if Beecher and Tilton's joyous intimacy of the early
1860s survived Henry's encounter with Charles Judson, or the calculated composition of loving letters for the eyes of doubting friends.
Beecher claimed at the trial that it did. "We had some conversation
afterward . . . it was a very cordial meeting to me and a very satisfying
one." Writing the letters to each other put an end to a "kind of lovers'
quarrel." But a severe political difference emerged between them in
1866, and it built upon whatever personal doubts either of them may
have felt toward the other. They each emphasized in 1875 that their
parting of the ways politically did not end their friendship, but they
conceded that it changed the tone. It certainly ended the breathless
ardor of the early 1860s—unless it had already been ended by Judson's report, Bowen's rumors, or Mrs. Tilton's growing attachment to
her pastor.[26]

III. Theodore Tilton learned a militant antislavery doctrine when he was a mere lad, and much of it he learned from Henry
Ward Beecher. Theodore joined Plymouth Church in 1853, when he
was 17 or 18, but he had been taking down Beecher's sermons before
that, and probably reading his contributions to the *Independent*. Henry's
editorial "Shall We Compromise?" in 1850, for example, was a strident
dismissal of Henry Clay's (and Daniel Webster's) proposal to split the
difference between North and South—give the North the free state of
California and a prohibition on the slave trade in Washington, D.C.,
give the South no restriction on slavery in the western territories won
from Mexico and no abolition of it in Washington, D.C. The South
also got the promise of stronger efforts to return fugitive slaves to their
masters. Beecher threw down the gauntlet at the slaveholders and "every party that secretly or openly connives" with them. "The spirit of
Bondage and the spirit of Liberty . . . cannot dwell together. Moses'
rod must swallow the chanter's, or the magician's rod must swallow
the prophet's." One of the two irreconcilable principles must give way
in the end, and slavery would do all the bending. He did not care if
the Constitution appeared to countenance the coexistence of the two
principles. He maintained that the Constitution did no such thing, at
least not for the long term, and even if it did, there was a higher truth

than the Constitution. "I put Constitution against Constitution—God's against man's. Where they agree, they are doubly sacred; where they differ, my reply to all questioners, but especially to all timid Christian scruples, is in the language of Peter: *'Whether it be right in the sight of God to hearken unto you more than unto God, judge ye.'*" [27]

The Compromise had other heinous features, but its fugitive-slave provision made Beecher seethe. He called on Christians to disobey it, drawing a distinction between laws which disadvantage a person and those that force a person to harm someone else. "Every citizen must obey a law which inflicts injury upon his person, estate, and civil privilege, until legally redressed; but no citizen is bound to obey a law which commands *him* to *inflict* injury upon another. We must *endure* but never *commit* wrong. We must be patient when sinned against, but must never sin against others. The law may heap injustice upon me, but no law can authorize me to pour injustice upon another." When Stephen Douglas proposed the Kansas-Nebraska bill in January 1854, Beecher immediately joined the opposition. Repealing the Missouri Compromise of 1820, permitting new states to decide by popular ballot whether to permit slavery, was a direct assault on Liberty. The bill was "the death-struggle of slavery for expansion, seeing that she must have more room to breathe or suffocate. . . . The mask is off, and all disguises are thrown to the winds, and the slave power stands out in its true character, making its last and most infamous demands upon the North. All we have to do is to say No." When the Kansas-Nebraska bill became law in May 1854, Beecher was on his path to the purchase of twenty-five Sharpe's rifles for the free-soilers in Kansas. Defending the provision of firearms for the defenders of freedom, Beecher remarked that rifles were of more utility than Bibles in arguments with wolves. It was not long before Sharpe's rifles were known nationwide as "Beecher's Bibles." [28]

As a teenager gobbling up his pastor's words in the early 1850s, Tilton must have detested the Southern conspirators against freedom. Even before following young Elizabeth Richards to the Sunday services at Plymouth Church (which she had joined in 1851), he had been charged by the antislavery preaching of Dr. George B. Cheever at Manhattan's Church of the Puritans. By 1860, when he gave his address at Plymouth on the funding of missionaries, it was plain he would have no truck with temporizers. His speech was an announcement to Beecher that he would not permit his pastor to back off from the dramatic doctrine he had taught in the 1850s: war-to-the-death against the enemies of Liberty. Theodore had become, according to his own

1875 recollection, "an extreme Abolitionist." Since Henry, for all his antislavery zeal, was opposed to "immediatism"—insistence upon the immediate "abolition" of slavery—there may have been significant political tension between him and Tilton from 1860 on. But if there was, they submerged it during the war as they haunted the picture galleries of Manhattan and attacked Lincoln in the *Independent* as insufficiently godly and woefully indecisive. They thought John C. Frémont ought to take Lincoln's place as the Republican candidate in 1864.[29]

With the end of the war and Lincoln's assassination, Beecher's gradualist antislavery doctrine (firmly resist all expansion of slavery but don't insist on immediate emancipation) turned into a moderate Reconstruction line: guarantee the property rights of black men, but don't insist they be given the vote. His accommodating stance came into full public view on October 22, 1865, when he endorsed Andrew Johnson's conciliatory Southern policy. Theodore told Elizabeth that Henry's evening sermon that day was "aimed at the *Independent*. I have a reply in this week's paper. Mr. Bowen heartily sustains me in my course. I have not seen Mr. Beecher, and I suppose his difference is a difference only of opinion, and not of good will. But I am right, and won't be shaken from the rock under my feet." The following Sunday evening Henry returned Tilton's fire when he addressed his congregation on "Conditions of a Restored Union." "The South should be restored at the earliest practicable moment to a participation in our common government." The principle of universal suffrage was correct—and it was a right, not a privilege—but it was futile to hold out for enfranchising black men if it would "excite the animosity" of whites. As a temporary measure the vote could properly be restricted to those black men who had taken up arms for the Union. Theodore and Henry were launched on divergent political paths, but they persisted in calling each other friends. It is at this point that they wrote letters of friendship and love to be shown to anyone who doubted their mutual affection. The letters were designed to prevent a private dispute over Judson's charges and a public one over Reconstruction from damaging their reputations or hurting the *Independent*.[30]

But the gap between their political viewpoints continued to widen as Tilton beat the drums for Radical Reconstruction and Beecher kept calling for harmony between the sections. Radical sentiment was strengthening among Northern Republicans, including most of those at Plymouth Church, yet in his famous "Cleveland" letter Beecher made what was widely taken as an overture to the Democrats. He wrote to the pro–Andrew Johnson Convention of Sailors and Soldiers convening in Cleveland, declining their invitation to serve as chaplain, but praising the efforts of "what party soever . . . whose object is the restoration of all the States late in rebellion." Beecher was calling for immediate, unconditional readmission on the grounds that it was the only way to avoid military governments imposed by the North. Such governments would amount to "a course of instruction, preparing our Government to be despotic, and familiarizing the people to a stretch of authority which can never be other than dangerous to liberty." Granted, the withdrawal of Northern troops might be tough on the emancipated slaves. But "unless we turn the Government into a vast military machine there cannot be armies enough to protect the freedman while Southern society remains insurrectionary."

> Civilization is growth. None can escape that forty years in the wilderness who travel from the Egypt of ignorance to the promised land of civilization. The freedmen must take their march. I have full faith in the results. If they have the stamina to undergo the hardships which every uncivilized people has undergone in their upward progress, they will in due time take their place among us. That place cannot be bought, nor bequeathed, nor gained by sleight-of-hand. It will come to sobriety, virtue, industry and frugality.

Henry believed love across sectional lines was more fruitful than abstract invocations of justice. Cultivating bonds of affection between North and South would encourage "the wise and good citizens of the South," as he had put it at Plymouth the year before, in their own "kindness" toward the former slaves.[31]

Now Theodore was incensed. He reprinted Beecher's letter in the *Independent* and attached a blistering editorial on "Mr. Beecher." "We know and love him well," Theodore wrote. "No man's motives are purer; no man more affectionately reveres his native land. But, under the spell of an unhappy blindness which has rested on his eyes for a year past, he has done more injury to the American Republic than has been done by any other citizen except Andrew Johnson." Beecher was a "deserter" from the Republican cause, a tacit endorser of "Copperhead politics." He "has entered into league and covenant with the Johnson party, a party whose only hope of victory is by a league of traitors against loyal men." The Republican Party, as Theodore put it in his 1875 testimony, wished to impose stringent terms on the Southern states before allowing them back into the Union—including repudiation of the rebel debt, acquiescence in Constitutional amendments abolishing slavery, and securing "to the Negro the elective franchise." Yet Henry was saying "No, return to Congress first and then settle the conditions afterwards."[32]

For Theodore there could be no lasting love in the social arena that was not premised upon immediate justice for all. He agreed with Henry, as he made plain in a speech on "The Negro" to the American Antislavery Society in 1863, that "slavery has reduced the blacks to the lowest point of ignorance and humiliation of which humanity . . . is capable." But once again Tilton used Beecher's own teaching against his master by arguing that one cannot "rank men only by a superiority of intellectual faculties. God has given to man a higher dignity than the reason. It is the moral nature. . . . In all those intellectual activities which take their strange quickening from the moral faculties—processes which we call instincts, or intuitions—the negro is superior to the white man—equal to the white woman. The negro race is the feminine race of the world." And the most religious. "Is not the religious nature the highest part of human nature? Strike out the negro then, and you destroy the highest development of the highest part of human nature." Blacks could gain in rational attainments while whites gained in religious ones, and voting could be race-blind all the while.[33]

Beecher was stung by Tilton's assault on his Cleveland letter. He felt, as he put it on the stand in 1875, that "a paper that I had helped fashion from its birth was now being used to destroy me, and that I could not, with self-respect, maintain my connection with it." He had left the editorship in 1864, but had continued writing occasional columns and furnishing his weekly sermon. Now he terminated all his ties to the *Independent*. Both Henry and Theodore claimed in 1875 that while Beecher was, in Tilton's words, "very sore" about the *Independent*'s comment on the Cleveland letter, "still it did not break our friendship." But the tone changed decisively. When Henry wrote Theodore a letter of advice in June 1867 regarding his religious quandaries, a new formality and distance was evident. Theodore could at least take heart from Henry's parting comment that he had decided against starting another religious paper. "I am sure that I could not bear the strain and yet carry on my church." Two and a half years later Beecher would change his position: in January 1870 he became editor of the *Christian Union*, the direct competitor of Tilton's and Bowen's *Independent*. Less than a year after that, Bowen had fired Tilton, the charge of adultery or improper advances had been hurled, and the scandal cover-up had begun.[34]

Theodore and Henry were probably still amicable until 1870, as they both later said, but their friendship in the late 1860s was based upon generous toleration of difference, not giddy celebration of affinity.

Perhaps something they called "friendship" survived their animated disagreement about the most urgent public issue of the day, but the intimate bond they had built in the early 1860s did not. In 1866 Theodore stopped attending Plymouth Church and stopped thinking of Beecher as his hero. As he explained at the trial, "I ceased, as I grew older, to look upon Mr. Beecher as a leader, either in politics, or art, or religion; not that I dethroned him in my respect, but that he was less to me, as I grew older, a leader than he had been originally." William Evarts: "Do you ascribe that change to him, or to yourself?" "Well, Sir, I think quite likely it was due to my own growth to a certain degree. I think if any other man had occupied the same position in my heart's affection in my youth, I should probably have thought less of him, or at least less of his great superiority over other men, as time progressed, but I was not responsible for Mr. Beecher's betrayal of the Republican Party in 1865." Theodore drifted away from Plymouth and from religion, and Elizabeth joined Henry in lamenting her husband's departure from their spiritual universe. Now the Beecher-Tilton bond switched to the Henry-Elizabeth axis, and Theodore would gradually come to see that intense pairing, in its exclusion of his prior bond to Beecher, as the second of Henry's betrayals, the first being his abandonment of the Republican Party.[35]

In the late 1860s, as sole editor of the *Independent*, Theodore insisted all the more strenuously on loyalty to principle over flabby compromise. Marriage must be pure—if it wasn't built on perfect love it was already "divorce"—and the Republican Party must be pure, protected against spoilsmen and backroom deals. He attacked the enemies of love and the practitioners of graft until the end of his editorship in 1870. One of his chief enemies, of course, was Andrew Johnson, and his editorials were especially fiery during the impeachment crisis. One of his most scathing pieces of "personal" journalism, on May 7, 1868, was directed at one of the lawyers who had just agreed to defend President Johnson: none other than William Evarts. "Mr. Evarts, counsel for the President, has pawned his honor for a lawyer's fee," Tilton wrote. "The charge is grave, but true."

A conspicuous actor in Republican conventions, a trusted adviser in Republican councils, an ambitious orator before Republican assemblages, a once beaten but still aspiring candidate for the United States Senatorship, a leading Republican member of the recent New York State Constitutional Convention, Mr. Evarts was summoned to the President's defense, not because he was a shining light in the legal profession, but because he was an influential leader of the Republican Party. The President did not look to the bar of New York to hire its most skillful advocate, but to buy its most serviceable Republican. . . . But Mr. Evarts has thus made traffic of what among honest men is too precious to be an article of merchandise, and which no man can ever sell except by throwing his honor into the bargain."

When Johnson rewarded Evarts's successful defense strategy by making him Attorney General in July 1868, Tilton lowered the boom on him again. "Mr. Johnson had no money, but could pay his lawyer with an office; and his lawyer not needing the money accepted the office." The "ghostly little attorney" might be the grandson of a signer of the Declaration of Independence, but he had "hired himself for lucre . . . put his little measure of Roger Sherman's blood to an unwonted blush by bartering for a price the safety of the Republic. Sing to him Robert Browning's song:

> Just for a handful of silver he left us;
> Just for a ribbon to stick in his coat.[36]

In 1875 Evarts would eagerly accept another office without concern for remuneration: chief counsel for Beecher's defense team and chief disemboweler of Theodore Tilton. In that capacity he exacted some sweet revenge. The criminal conversation proceeding was called to judge whether Henry Ward Beecher had alienated Elizabeth Tilton's affections, but Evarts hammered away at the character of her husband—a character so apt, in Evarts's version, to alienate his wife that there could have been no affections left for her pastor to steal. Yet the animosity between Evarts and Tilton was not only personal. Evarts was a mainstay of the Conservative Republican contingent that by the early 1870s was putting the Radicals—Theodore Tilton among them—to rout. Evarts went on to serve as President Rutherford B. Hayes's Secretary of State in the late 1870s, and as a Senator from New York in the 1880s. Tilton would try in the late 1870s to move to the cultural Center by preaching the stabilizing benefits of "character" and religion, but he could not shed the image Evarts had painted: wooden fanatic, subversive radical. On the lecture circuit he would prove unable to fight the traditionalist swing in cultural temper—a swing exacerbated by the scandal—or to transcend the anachronistically sentimental idealism of his own speechifying.

In 1867, just after his severe political breach with Theodore and the start of his new affective bond with Elizabeth, Beecher sat down to draw the characters of the young protagonists Barton Cathcart and Rose Wentworth in his novel *Norwood*. Rose was a saint, Barton was not. And in her infinite sensitivity (and wisdom in heeding the advice of her physician father, the town sage) she knew even as a teenager that Barton's potential for greatness was jeopardized by his tendency to "fanaticism."

> He has the heroic element, because he is strong, patient, capable of suffering without complaint, and because on occasion he would give every thing in the world, his life itself, for that which he loved or for whatever he considered just and right. As to fanaticism, father says that it is the fermentation of strong natures, who, not having outlet for their feelings, grow inwardly, until they mistake their own feelings and thoughts for outward realities. I can easily imagine circumstances in which Barton would see the whole world in the color of his own heart.

Rose, as it turned out, need not have worried about her future husband Barton, who matured into a valiant Civil War general. But her creator may well have worried in the late 1860s about his former intimate friend Theodore. Tilton was worried too, as he wrote many times to his wife in the late 1860s, about growing excessively inward, cut off from easy interchange with the world. But whatever Theodore's actual "fanatical" proclivities may have been, William Evarts would do everything he could in 1875 to mark Tilton for the rest of his days as a lunatic who had misjudged the state of the world and lost his moral compass.[37]

IV. While Theodore was learning from Henry in the late 1850s and early 1860s about editing, oratory, and saving the Union, Elizabeth was having babies, overseeing servants, and reading some poetry and fiction. Florence was born in August 1857, Alice came about two years later, and Carroll followed in August 1863. Mattie was born sometime before or during the war and died in infancy. Elizabeth was shattered by her death, according to the published recollection of "Mrs. X" in 1875. The child died in Newburgh, New York. Passing through Newburgh in 1866 reminded Theodore that "I never see that city in the night, with its bank of light, but I think of our dear child who rose from it at midday into Heaven. I thought anew of all our moon-light sail down the river that night, carrying that precious corpse in the bow of the steamboat, while the moonbeams silvered the box in which our jewel was locked."[38]

A fourth "child" arrived in 1864: 13-year-old Bessie Turner. Bessie entered the household as servant and ward, and remained with the

Tiltons until the familial meltdown of 1870—when she was sent to boarding school in Ohio (bills paid by the exceedingly repentant Henry Ward Beecher). Elizabeth took her on initially, it appears, for two reasons: to have some help taking care of baby Carroll, and to give a Christian home to Bessie, who had wandered from family to family since arriving from the South at age four or five. The Tiltons were just getting established as a middle-class family, and Bessie was a double sign of their emergent social stature. Although they were boarders with Elizabeth's mother, Mrs. Morse, at 48 Livingston Street—they would not move into their own comfortable house up the street at number 174 until 1866—they now had live-in help and a protégée to shepherd toward bourgeois values.[39]

In the standard middle-class division of labor, Theodore battled for his family's position in the world while Elizabeth took charge of the kids, the servant, and the general polish of the hearthstone. Bessie herself claimed in 1875 that Theodore vigorously upheld a principled separation of public and private spheres. "He said to her [Elizabeth] that she must not come to him with her household matters; that it was none of his business; he attended to his business and she must attend to hers, and he didn't wish to be bothered with the servants." But in Bessie's view that was all talk. "I think he generally had matters his own way with regard to the house." Whatever his power at home, there is no doubt that Mrs. Tilton devoted herself to Bessie's formation as she did to her own children's. For Elizabeth, Bessie was not only a chance to do her Christian duty to the poor, but an active spiritual testing ground. Her letters to her husband are full of her torment at trying to make Bessie over without losing her own center. While he was writing his wife about being tempted by other women, she was writing him about being tempted to throttle Bessie Turner.[40]

By the late 1860s the Tiltons employed as many as five servants at a time, not counting Bessie (who frequently went off for weeks or months at a time to work for Tilton relatives or friends). Testimony at the trial in 1875 gave the names of at least ten women, nearly all of them Irish, who passed through the household in those years as cook, nurse, housekeeper, wet nurse, "waiter girl," or "upstairs girl." According to one source, Elizabeth was an inefficient manager of all this domestic labor—which may explain Theodore's at least covert intervention. An acquaintance (and supporter of Theodore at the time) told a newspaper in 1875 that Mrs. Tilton was "an utterly incompetent housekeeper, without either administrative or executive power." The servants "ran over her, wore her dresses, stole her underclothing." And they got into fights. The one servant who testified in support of Theodore's case in 1875 had been discharged by Elizabeth for having fought back when hit with a hair brush by Bessie Turner (herself a witness for the defense, and hence for Elizabeth as well as Henry). Elizabeth thought there were problems with the help, but didn't think the fault lay in her management skills: "they were very poor servants," she told the Plymouth Investigating Committee in 1874.[41]

Rather than run a tight ship, Elizabeth shepherded her children. She let the servants do the cooking and cleaning, reformer Lucy Stone observed in the *Woman's Journal,* but she never let them near the kids. "She said to me," Stone wrote, "'I hire service for other things, but I want to take care of my children myself, so I make their clothes and teach them their lessons, and am never happier than when, surrounded by them here, I watch their opening intellect.'" She took their religious training very seriously: no toys or games on Sunday, so they would learn it was not a day like any other. Every day she taught them to pray, Bessie Turner remembered. But there were also plenty of games, along with piano playing (Florence became a music teacher) and singing, sewing, and artwork (Alice became a painter, exhibiting in Manhattan into the 1930s, and Ralph the art editor at the *Saturday Evening Post*). On Saturday, January 12, 1867, Elizabeth had planned to spend the day making dolls with 9-year-old Florence and 6- or 7-year-old Alice (who named one of hers "Rose Wentworth"). Instead Henry showed up, and after playing with the children for an hour, he took Elizabeth out on his parish calls and then to "the toy stores" in search of a "grown-up" doll for his granddaughter Hattie.[42]

Bessie, for her part, took pride in being treated just like one of the children. "Mrs. Tilton was a mother to me always," she told the court in 1875. A letter Bessie wrote her in 1869 (when she was 18) was entered into the record. "I have thought of you every moment since I left you, and thought how little I appreciated all the long years you bore so patiently with my sullen nature; and now that I am thrown among strangers and dependent upon myself is the time that I have felt the need of such a friend as you were to me, but as you have often told me there is still a dearer friend who would be a father to the fatherless, and if I ever find Him I should be very happy." There is no doubt about how much the young-adult Bessie Turner cherished the mothering of Elizabeth Tilton. But the irony of Bessie's conviction that she owed everything to Mrs. Tilton is that, according to Turner's trial testimony, Elizabeth taught her not just about God and overcoming sullenness, but how to sign false documents out of love and loyalty. Asked in court

why she had signed a statement denying Theodore's alleged mistreat-
ment of her, a statement she believed was untrue, she replied: "Because
I loved Mrs. Tilton, I wanted to do it because she said if I would put
my name to that paper, it would get Mr. Tilton out of all difficulties
with Henry C. Bowen . . . and that all was needed was my signature
and my retraction of that. That is why I signed it."[43]

One might have thought that Bessie Turner's loyalty to Mrs. Tilton
would be very bad news for the plaintiff. All of her testimony was designed to cast discredit upon Theodore, whom she depicted as often on
the verge of madness (in the night he would rise to rearrange the paint-
ings on the walls, or would order Elizabeth to move from bedroom to
bedroom with him until he found a bed that felt comfortable) or moles-
tation (when she was a teenager he would carry her from bed to bed
while she was asleep). But press commentary, and that of the official
court stenographer, suggest that Bessie Turner, the working-class waif
made over, Pygmalion-fashion, by the Tiltons, was not taken seriously
as a witness. "Tragedy and comedy jostle one another in the Brooklyn
trial as closely as they do in the Shakespearian drama," said the *New
York Graphic*, which put Turner with James Woodley, the hilarious black
witness, and Elizabeth Palmer, the spiritualist, as the comic players of
the spectacle.[44]

Yet observers took Bessie Turner very seriously as a symbol of a
larger prevarication—class deception—compared to which her signing of false documents was a minor matter. All of the participants in the
trial (with the partial exception of Emma Moulton, routinely praised
for her natural grace and aplomb) were seen as players of parts, but
Turner was the quintessential actor, posing as what she was not. Indeed, she was so chameleon-like that she was apt to be misread not just
as middle class, but as upper class. "She is a slender, well-shaped girl,
about 5 feet 4 inches tall, and about 18 years old [she was actually 24],"
wrote the *New York Sun*, which like other papers was fascinated by all
the details of her "appearance" in relation to her essence.

> Her face is bright and intelligent in expression, but not beyond pret-
> tiness in the direction of beauty. Her features are such as, if she were
> of titled parentage, noodles would deem aristocratic. That is to say,
> they have the daintiness of outline and the lack of obtrusiveness which
> the cheap novelists give to high-born heroines. Her complexion is re-
> markably light and clear, her eyes are blue, with long lashes, her hair
> is auburn, and her teeth are very white. Her apparel yesterday was
> inexpensive, but tasteful. The dress was black merino, trimmed with

Bessie Turner, sketched by a Brooklyn courtroom artist in 1875.

the same material. The hat was black velvet with a feather and a wing
of the same color, and was worn with a forward tilt over the forehead.
Her hair was frizzed below the rim of the hat in front, and brought
into a knot behind, with two curls hanging below. Her hands were
gloved with brown kid, and on her feet were low-heeled, buttoned

gaiters. A white lace scarf and a gold chain were around her neck, and white linen cuffs, with initial sleeve-buttons in them, showed at her wrists. There were no rings in her ears, which are small and pretty. A black fan and a beaded belt were the rest of the visible outfit. Her face was entirely free of rouge or powder.

In this report as in others, Bessie Turner was an embellished posturer, whose true identity might be difficult to probe. She was a Barnumesque "humbug." The challenge confronting the observer was to outsmart the hoaxer by exposing the authentic core beneath the shimmering veneer, a difficult assignment in this case since an unblemished face "entirely free of rouge or powder," and a mouth full of healthy white teeth, announced that her act might prove unusually natural. Yet when she reached the witness box—after taking a "devious route" equal to twice the width of the courtroom, during which pilgrimage "she was watched with unpitying curiosity"—she was so nervous that she let her guard down. "She tapped nervously with her fan, and shifted her position with a quick, jerky movement in the brief interval between the oath and the first question." This giveaway body language revealed her as a low-grade and hence comic figure, readjusting all her accoutrements before getting on with the show. This was no Emma Moulton, whose sincerity was embodied in a flawlessly graceful physical carriage. If Mrs. Moulton or Mrs. Tilton were lying, it was out of their otherwise proper subordination to a man, not out of pretending to be something they were not. They might be marionettes, but they were not posers. Bessie Turner was pure pretense.[45]

V.   Theodore and Elizabeth Tilton were deeply in love in the 1850s and early 1860s. The "friend" who disparaged Mrs. Tilton's household management described the first night she met the young couple in 1858. "Mrs. Tilton at this time was 24 or 25 years old, having a year or two the advantage of her husband in age."

> She was not charming, or graceful, or pretty, as either men or women count prettiness; but her eyes were pleasant, her teeth white, and her manner caressing. That night I saw in her great capacity for devotion and entire absorption in those she loved. She lost herself in her husband and child [Florence]. . . . I marvelled afterwards that two such impractical people could manage a house at all; but the married lovers were very happy. Their admiration for each other was boundless, and on that first night she said in answer to this sally of mine, "What if you should find a clay foot on your gold idol?" "That is impossible!"

Theodore gave appropriate form to this joint passion on August 21, 1865, when he wrote from his parents' home in Keyport, New Jersey, and quoted Elizabeth back to herself. "Today's letter [from you] brought me *this* sweetness: 'Oh, when I *do* see your face again, you shall have a taste for a few minutes of a woman's pure love, if I know how to express it.' My darling, I wish you were here at this moment! I fancy what I would do if you were to ring the door-bell *just* now." [46]

A little over a month later, on October 2, the Tiltons celebrated their "tin" wedding anniversary (and Theodore's thirtieth birthday). A "festival" was held on Livingston Street, according to a compiler of Beecher-Tilton Scandal documents a decade later. It was "attended by a crowd of Brooklyn's best known citizens, including the clergy, the press, the bar, the mercantile class, the politicians, and everybody." Various dignitaries sent good wishes. Chief Justice of the Supreme Court Salmon P. Chase hoped "your tin may brighten into silver, and your silver into gold, and your gold into diamonds, and your diamonds into the everlasting crown." Lydia Maria Child, the famed antislavery writer, concurred—"May your tin become silver, and your silver gold!"—but cautioned that "spiritual" silver and gold were more to be hoped for than "material" metals. George William Curtis, associate editor of the *New York Tribune,* joined "all other friends" in wishing "with all our hearts, that the tin may refine to silver, and the silver to gold." Abolitionist stalwart Gerrit Smith "and Wife" sent a poem that made up in sincerity for what it lacked in finish.

> We thank you for your pretty card;
> We value highly your regard.
> My wife and I who are but tin,
> A golden wedding hope to win.
> And hence to us it seems a sin
> That you, who're gold, should sink to tin.
> A silver wedding God grant you;
> Aye, and a golden wedding, too.
> And then a wedding in the skies,
> Where neither partner ever dies.

The "central figure" at the Livingston Street festival, according to one witness, was Henry Ward Beecher, "acting the part not only of the pastor, but I might almost say, the father of the family." [47]

In retrospect Beecher and the Tiltons may have seen that summer of 1865 as a moment of emotional equipoise, before their loves turned tragic. Theodore was climbing the ladder of achievement, delivering deft orations like his toast at the New England Society, feasting on his favored status as Henry's bright young man. In the spring he had accompanied Beecher, William Lloyd Garrison, and other civilian and military notables from New York to South Carolina, where Henry gave the featured address at the official Fort Sumter flag-raising ceremony on Good Friday, April 14—the day, it turned out, of Lincoln's assassination. "Finally, Mr. Beecher arose," Theodore wrote of Henry's performance, "and set his strong voice into a struggle against a sea-breeze that kept whisking his locks and flapping his manuscripts, and threatened at first to wrestle him down, but the man who conquered a Liverpool mob was not to surrender to an east wind. Manly, wise, rich, and eloquent was the speech . . . but no speech could rise to the height of that occasion: what could" [except the flag]?

On Sunday, April 16, Beecher preached to a congregation of four thousand blacks at Zion Church in Charleston, and Tilton spoke to the Sunday School. The *Independent*'s correspondent wrote that "when the preacher rose to his climax, and smiting on his breast, said, 'Now you can say, every one of you, "I have a freeman's heart to give to Christ,"' the scene was one chaos of tears and clamorous joy." Beecher requested that "the negroes close the exercises with some of their own peculiar religious choruses." They were sung in a "dialect a dozen glossaries could not disentangle," but in a "rhythm Haydn and Mozart would hardly criticize." Of Tilton's afternoon speech to the assembled children, the correspondent exulted that "Mr. Tilton, among other manifest destinies, was predestinated from all eternity to talk to little ears, and to fill them with music." When the troop of Northerners walked to the dock the next day for their return voyage home, the "streets were full of colored people," Beecher reported. "When we reached the wharf it was black; and yet it glowed like a garden. They had but little to bring as testimonials of their remembrance and gratitude; but what they had they brought. One had a little bunch of roses. Another had a bunch of jessamines and honeysuckles. Others had bunches of various kinds of flowers. I saw Mr. Tilton loaded down with these treasures that had been showered upon him, and struggling beneath his burden as he came on board." [48]

In mid-1865 Henry and Theodore were smothered in blossoms as heroes of union and emancipation. They had not yet become public antagonists over Reconstruction, and had not yet begun composing warm letters for the sake of managing impressions. Theodore and Elizabeth thrilled to each other's touch, and savored a spiritual accord.

Elizabeth and Henry were just embarking on their friendship-love. Theodore had not yet begun to feel Henry as a threat to his family. On the contrary, he was begging him to come around more often, reminding him what a rare sweet wife he had, inviting him—as the witness to the summer "festival" put it—to become a kind of father to the whole family. In January 1865 Henry came by Mrs. Morse's boarding house to visit Elizabeth. "I am glad Mr. Beecher called on you," wrote Theodore afterwards. "I will write to thank him for it." In August 1865 Beecher came by the *Independent* to see Theodore when Elizabeth was vacationing at Monticello, New York. "Mr. Beecher has been in this morning, inquiring after you and the chicks, and leaving his love for all." [49]

Love for all. A simple enough sentiment, perhaps, but there was a social basis for its expression and reception. Theodore was now an accomplished editor, and owed it all to Henry. Elizabeth was enthralled by her husband and her three children, four counting Bessie, five counting the departed Mattie (asked at the trial how many children they had, Henry and Theodore included their dead babies: four with me and five waiting for me, said Henry; four living and two lost, said Theodore). The Tiltons knew they were moving up in the world, but that gladdened them only because they were also moving up in the spirit of Christ, giving and receiving love. Henry gave them love, received it from them, and tendered the whole religious framework that gave it meaning. In their eyes the family's rise in both world and spirit was heavily Henry's doing. Whatever the nature of the doubts they had had about him since 1863, nothing dimmed their eagerness for his companionship. Henry, meanwhile, found in the young couple the same thing that Susan Anthony, Horace Greeley, and their other close older friends did—rejuvenation—but he also found religious refreshment. After the Tiltons moved into their own house in the summer of 1866, Henry became one of the regulars, "perfectly free," as he put it at the trial, "to go in and out as I chose, almost." [50]

"Love for all" remained the unifying sentiment of choice, but its strength was slowly sapped when Elizabeth and Henry turned toward one another for solace and renewal as Theodore left their spiritual orbit. Beecher got a big laugh at the trial when asked what he and Elizabeth talked about in their meetings at her house: above all, he said, "Theodore Tilton." As he launched that quip from the stand, Henry was slicing to the heart of the matter. Sometime in the late 1860s Theodore became the preoccupying subject of an irresistible, impassioned, two-way conversation. Whether that conversation was "criminal" or not, it made the honorary "father of the family" into an ally of the wife and thus a competitive "father" of a more literal sort. That imbalance set off the chain reaction that metamorphosed Beecher's and the Tiltons' "love for all" into an exploding mass of suspicions, allegations, rationalizations, and self-defenses.

THE HALLWAY OF MR. THEODORE TILTON'S RESIDENCE, NO. 174 LIVINGSTON STREET, BROOKLYN.

SEVEN *Early Stories,*
1867–1869

I. In the early 1870s Elizabeth Tilton tried to revitalize her marriage on the basis of mutual forgiveness for past sins. Maybe those past sins included adultery by Theodore, by her, or by both of them. In 1874 they each claimed vociferously that the other had been an adulterer. But adultery or not, Elizabeth made an effort with her summertime "confessions" of 1870 and 1871 to provoke a reciprocal plea for forgiveness by Theodore. A dynamic of mutual submission would fortify their love by putting it on Christian bedrock. The effort failed, defeated by circumstances and by the unbridgeable gap between their outlooks. She saw herself as an inveterate sinner judged by God and begging for mercy. He saw himself as a reformer pushing honesty in private and public and as a mental sufferer battling foul moods. His ethical and psychological strivings displayed much religious intensity and rhetoric, but for him "sinfulness" was a state of gloom to be climbed out of. It was this deeply felt "unworthiness" that his fictional Mary Vail, in her journal derived from Elizabeth's letters, substituted for the letters' original term "sin"—in Elizabeth's eyes a repeated failure to obey the commandments to love God and neighbor.

Mrs. Tilton's aim to revivify her marriage after the blowup of December 1870 provides an important clue to the kind of love she and Theodore shared during the late 1860s. Long before there was any allegation of adultery with Beecher, Theodore and Elizabeth were struggling to put their marriage on a firmer basis, to make it resemble their years of passionate union, the late 1850s and early 1860s. Their correspondence after the Civil War is full of the pattern of joint abasement that Elizabeth tried to reinvoke in the early 1870s. Shared self-disparagement had become a basic element of their love. They considered their love strongest, "purest" (their favorite term for it), when it combined a rush of pleasure at each other's bodies and spirits with reciprocal testimony to their multiple flaws.

Like Beecher, these liberal Christians had chosen to abandon the stern Judge-God of their childhoods, but that God was not so easily waved aside. Middle-class consciousness was in part a continuous process of internalizing the social controls that earlier societies had lodged in explicit communal commands. Liberal Christian middle-class consciousness in the nineteenth century was often, in addition, a process of internalizing the severe judgment earlier exercised, in thunderbolt fashion, by God. Some evidence suggests that after the trial Theodore reached a final standpoint beyond judgment, beyond blaming himself or anyone else. But in the late 1860s he was writhing in the same kind of agony that haunted Henry into the 1880s and Elizabeth at least through her confession of 1878. The intimate lines the Tiltons wrote to each other when they were in their thirties—the time when Henry and Elizabeth were pairing off emotionally and spiritually—were heavily composed of self-castigation.[1]

When Elizabeth testified to the Plymouth Church Investigating Committee in 1874, she spoke poignantly of her submission to Theodore's imperial judgment. Her depiction of herself as the docile victim of a brutal spouse may have described an actual element of their marriage during the early 1870s or even before. But the notorious letter excerpts from the late 1860s, broadcast by Theodore, show both spouses striving to deepen their love by self-criticism and submission to the other. In her church testimony Elizabeth either chose to give a very partial picture of their earlier years together or could not remember them as she had lived them. That original lived experience was always made up of mental judgments as well as feelings, emotions, and sensations. Their loving was not sensate first, interpreted second. Their acts of intimate speech, even acts of bodily contact, were always laden from the start with prescriptions, conventions, memories, expectations— about which they were more or less conscious. The period of the cover-up between 1870 and 1873 was so difficult for them both because it amounted to a prolonged search for a new interpretive structure for experience, or more precisely, *of* experience. By 1874 they had given up seeking union on the basis of joint confession and submission. Theodore had his story of Henry's assault on him and his family, and Elizabeth had her story of Theodore's assault upon her.[2]

Theodore's abridgements of their letters were designed to show that

Elizabeth's church testimony regarding his abusive treatment of her was a malicious fiction. And indeed the letters as he edited them are full of professions of love from both of them. We will never know if Tilton threw out letters that did not fit the pattern of mutual longing and admiration. The letters that survive give us an Elizabeth repeatedly apologizing for her treatment of him, but no indication that Theodore was ever ungenerous to her. The fleshed-out versions of the letters presented by the attorneys at the trial sometimes put Theodore in a less favorable light than his own editions do, but they don't make him abusive. They reveal more details about a marriage already well documented in his own chosen passages—a marriage in which deep attachment mingled inexplicably with debilitating conflict. Each spouse reflected frequently on the paradox that they seemed to love one another better during his long winter lecture tours to the "west" (the middle west, with brief forays into Iowa, Missouri, Kansas) than they did when they were together. As the months of separation lengthened, each writer voiced the thrill of anticipated reunion, when their bodies and spirits would join in a prolonged embrace. "Shall we ever be done with our caressing," Elizabeth wrote in January 1867, "when this long waiting is ended?" When the long waiting was over, they began the usual slow descent into fatigue and quarrelling relieved only by the next separation.[3]

Letters written from a distance gave Elizabeth and Theodore the leisure to delineate their failings while being assured of a sympathetic response. Theodore's very affectionate letter in March 1867 to "a woman whom I sometimes vex but whom I always revere," was typical of their repeated breast-beatings. He was doing his best to work on his deficiencies, he said, but he was troubled by oscillating moods. During the winter's trip he had felt nothing but joy, yet having returned home the week before (and gone off again for a talk in upstate New York), he had been overtaken by "despondency" and "bad blood." His letter was full of Biblical references—a sure point of contact with Elizabeth—but it spoke of improving himself, not of confessing his sins.

> I think my two or three recent days of darkness have been, on the whole, a moral benefit, in that they have revealed to my mind its most easily temptable points. It was good for the Pilgrim to go into the Valley of the Shadow of Death. 'No chastening for *the present* is joyous, but grievous; nevertheless, afterward it worketh out the peaceable fruits of righteousness.' . . . O, happy misfortune! that carried a man first into miserable wretchedness in order that it may then carry him,

like the prodigal, back to his Father's house. As Luther thanked God for his sins, so I, too, can thank Him for my sorrowful glooms. Be assured that whatever happens, whether cloudy or clear skies, I love you boundlessly and forever.[4]

In January 1868, as he set off on his lecture trip, he was in a much sunnier frame of mind. The Tiltons' son Paul had just been born, and the spouses had spent his final night at home in a "long interview" of "mutual confessions." It was an occasion of penitence and purity of the sort they had rarely if ever experienced before in person, and they celebrated it repeatedly in their letters during the weeks that followed. "I am by nature so frank," he wrote, "that the attempt to hide my feelings, to cloak my short-comings, to deny utterance to my inward sorrows, had lately driven me almost to despair." The evening of openness, during which he exposed himself to his wife as "a hypocrite, a deceiver, a whited sepulchre filled with a dead man's bones," had turned him around. Now he could say that "life never seemed to me to be more full of objects and ends worth living for."

Elizabeth's best friend Mattie Bradshaw had accompanied him to the train depot when he left town, and she and Elizabeth glowed in his mind with perfect radiance. Elizabeth herself had "never seemed so noble to me as during last evening and this day." Mattie "is the personification of moral uprightness. You and she were formed by nature for mates. If women could marry women, you ought to marry each other." He presented Mattie with a bottle of wine at the station, "that you and she together might drink it when you meet, and particularly that you might drink it to my health and happiness." Two weeks later he was still agog about the big night. "I regard my last evening spent with you at home as the most memorable point in my whole life. You opened for me, that night, the gate of Heaven, which had so long seemed shut."[5]

Elizabeth's letters mirrored her husband's in their stringent self-examination and in the expressions of elation that followed such purging. The previous winter she had asked him to forgive her "cruelties" (her frequent outbursts of temper). "I will never forget them," she promised, "and, with God's help, will try to never repeat them. It makes me very happy to have you say you need me, while I wonder that I have any power to comfort; still, no music is sweeter than those dear words." The evening of joint confession in January 1868 again gave her the deliverance of catharsis, but it also bestowed a fresh supply of faults to apologize for. "I carry in my soul this burden black of sin, yet appear to my children and friends calm and happy. 'Woe unto you, whited sepulcher,' I hear perpetually. I will carry these agonies gladly, for I know a life of happiness awaits *you*." She was blaming herself for provoking the failures Theodore had confessed to. "Oh, Theodore, darling, I am haunted night and day by the remorse of knowing that because of my harshness and indifference to you you were driven to despair—perhaps sin, and these last years of unhappiness. I sometimes feel it to be the unpardonable sin. God cannot forgive me. But if you only may be restored to your former loveliness, I shall be content to live my life in penance, yea, in disgrace. I am the chief of sinners!!"

"Perhaps sin," she wrote, in reference to Theodore's unidentified disclosures. Her husband had not confessed to the actual sin of adultery, then, but to something else, probably to temptation, perhaps to adultery of the heart. The reference was surely to bodily temptation, since later in the same letter Elizabeth reiterated her view of the "ideal marriage": "to you and you only a wife—but contact of the body with no other—while then a pure friendship with *many* may be enjoyed, ennobling us. Let us have not even a shadow of doubt of each other— tho' all the world are weak yet will *we* be strong." [6]

Other letters from Elizabeth also seem to indicate that Theodore's late-night soul-baring in January 1868 had touched on his relations with female friends. In her February 3 letter, for example, she first chastised herself for having held back in telling him or showing him how much she loved him. "I have lived under the fatal mistake that I would make you selfish; but, oh, what it has cost me to learn that a large, generous love cannot, in its very nature, minister but to our best and holy states!" She held herself responsible for the look of suffering that now hung perpetually about his face. It would be her job "to restore, if possible, the beautiful image I have marred." The next paragraph of her letter initiated the restoration campaign by speaking of his influence over women bedazzled by his oratory and fame.

> I have been thinking, my darling, that knowing as you do your immense power over an audience to move them at your will, that same power you have with all public men over any woman whom you may love. To love is praiseworthy, but to abuse your gift of influence is a sin. Therefore I would fain help restore to you that which I broke down—SELF-RESPECT. Your manhood and its purity and dignity if you feel it is stronger than even love itself. I know this because here I am strong. No demonstrations or fascinations could cause me to yield my womanhood.

Theodore must have told her he had been tempted to abuse his gift of influence, to invite a female admirer to yield her womanhood. His dwindling self-respect, for which she accepted the blame, explained his wayward heart. If he could regain that self-possessed dignity of manhood, he could discipline and purify the love he rightly felt, in Elizabeth's view, for other women as well as men.

Between the lines of her testimonial to Theodore's renaissance, Elizabeth was clearing the ground for a renewal of her own. Here in February 1868 she was embracing the idea that "a large, generous love" naturally "ministered to our best and holy states." She and Theodore had probably agreed upon this view during their magical evening of disclosures in January. It was a fundamental Beecherism, this doctrine of proliferating loves, each magnifying the others. Soulful love exchanged with more and more companions was a sign and means of divine grace. Love was not a zero-sum endeavor but a cumulative growth. This vision of limitless expansion in heart and soul was the very tenet of Henry's teaching that she would reject after reading *Griffith Gaunt* in 1871. In early 1868 she could endorse the notion of spiraling love and friendship because she was so sure of the strength of her "womanhood." Theodore's view of her as a saintly mystic must have encouraged this sense of herself as "strong," impervious to male "demonstrations" and "fascinations." By 1871 she had learned something herself about the power of temptation to disorder one's life. But as they imagined their love in the late 1860s, it appeared to them as a widely cast net of (nonphysical) friendships supporting the central marital passion. The purity of the entire web was secured by the regular practice of spousal confession—Theodore's to extramarital temptations, Elizabeth's to shortness of temper and spousal neglect.[7]

The single most dominant theme of the entire (surviving) correspondence is Elizabeth's zeal to serve Theodore in his reformation, in her view the key to their marital and familial strength. On February 18, for instance, she wrote that "the idea of a faithful, true marriage will be lost out of the world—certainly out of the literary and refined world—unless we renew it." As usual, she accused herself of causing Theodore's unhappiness, and then felt buoyed up. "I yearn to caress and tenderly care for you, read, sing, and gladden those dear eyes once again. I feel as never before, how dreadful a thing it is to wound or stab any human heart by sharp, stinging words. Perhaps the dear Father has given me another lease of life, that I may learn this lesson. I praise him for his goodness." Elizabeth's devotion to Theodore's reconstruction allowed her to take her overwhelming sense of sinfulness and convert it into a passionate love for her husband.[8]

Theodore and Elizabeth were both attuned to the pleasures of the flesh, as the trial versions of their letters make clear (even Theodore's *Chicago Tribune* excerpts contain many hints of their passion). We can be very sure they hungered for one another's touch. When Elizabeth criticized herself in January 1868 for having been "indifferent" to him, she may have meant sexually indifferent, as one recent writer assumes, but if she did it was not because she was indifferent to sex. She frequently expressed her joy at their physical relationship, and her regret at the gap between their bodily élan and their emotional and spiritual separation.[9]

It was Theodore, not Elizabeth, who solemnly declared on one occasion that spiritual love was decidedly superior to physical love. He was heading west by train through northern Indiana on December 7, 1866, and he was reading *Griffith Gaunt*. As soon as he finished it he wrote to his wife that Charles Reade's novel put too much weight on the "passion" and "madness" of the "natural instinct for loving." "The noblest part of love is honor, fidelity, constancy, self-abnegation—not the clasp of the hand, nor the kiss of the lips, nor the ecstasy of fondness. Sometimes that which most delights the heart most cheats the soul. It is for this reason that lovers ought sometimes to be separated." But when he delivered himself of these lofty principles he was trudging westward pining for his wife. At a time like that he would naturally have tried to persuade himself of the glories of nonphysical love. It was a way to protect himself from the temptations of the road about which he had confessed in January 1868.[10]

No doubt Elizabeth agreed with him that the purest love was nonphysical. Like most of their middle-class contemporaries they thought passional love could easily get out of hand. It was the dissolute upper and lower classes, in the sober estimation of middle-class Americans like the Tiltons, who mistakenly gave the passions free play. Bodily pleasure was a wondrous force, but it needed the disciplining scrutiny of the spirit if it was not to degenerate into mere indulgence. But the Tiltons' safety-net dichotomizing of soul and body did nothing to quell the delight they expressed about one another's bodies. Three weeks after putting "honor" and the other virtues above "the kiss of the lips" and other sexual feelings, Theodore told her he wanted to "hang" on her lips. A month after that Elizabeth was writing that she had "an irresistible desire to penetrate somewhere that I may once again look upon your dear face and kiss your sweet lips." "My lips hunger to kiss you," she said again several weeks later. "Pray take care of your precious body, for tho' I am your soul lover still we manage very poorly in this world without the body." There was even a physical ecstasy for these two lovers when they held the letters that celebrated their love. Theodore reported the pleasure it gave him to touch them as well as read them. He adored the ink on the page. Elizabeth wrote in February 1868 of her ritual of reading his letters. "I read every word eagerly; drop instantly whatever I am doing when the postman comes, and give myself up utterly, body and soul, locking the doors to prevent intruders, just as we are wont to do after an absence." [11]

II. There is no doubt that Theodore and Elizabeth had a passionate relationship, and no doubt that their passion was intensified by the emergence in the late 1860s of a special friendship between Elizabeth and Henry Ward Beecher. Elizabeth was very explicit about this. "My beloved," she wrote on December 28, 1866, "I have been thinking of my love for Mr. B[eecher] considerably of late."

> I remember Hannah Moore [More] says: "My heart in its new sympathy for one abounds towards all." Now, I think I have lived a richer, happier life since I have known him. And have you not loved me more ardently since you saw another high nature appreciated me? Certain it is that I never in all my life had such rapture of enthusiasm in my love for you—something akin to the birth of another babe—a new fountain was opened, enriching all—especially toward you, the one being supreme in my soul.

One might expect Theodore to have been troubled by his wife's "new sympathy" for her pastor, and Elizabeth reported that he was periodically insistent about getting full accounts of Henry's visits to 174 Livingston Street. But in the winter of 1866–1867, he expressed equanimity about them—at least he did in the letters he selected for publication. He could even joke about Henry's calling on his wife and about her "cleaving" to the man who married them rather than to her husband. Trying to persuade her to meet him in Chicago between lectures (she decided not to go), he quipped that "you can afford to come to *me* . . . now that the *other* man has gone off lecturing (as your letter mentions)."

> You ought to be enjoying what I am enjoying on this magnificent trip—for instance, this afternoon, a dinner party. Leave home, chil-

dren, kith and kin, and cleave unto him to whom you originally promised to cleave. You promised the *other* man to cleave to *me*, and yet you
leave *me all alone* and cleave to *him*. "O, frailty! Thy name is woman."
If you can get anybody to pour tea for you, and to take sauce from the
servants, and to receive pastoral visits, I shall expect to meet you under the roof of Robert Hatfield. Yours eternally, Theodore.

Of course his joking about his wife's attachment to Henry does not
mean he was unconcerned about it. It does mean he thought it was
illegitimate at this point to upbraid her for it. In February 1867 he
added that in view of Henry's "kind attentions to you this winter, all
my old love for him has revived, and my heart would once more greet
him as of old. I sometimes quarrel with my friends on the surface, but
never at the bottom. With yourself, oh! friend above all friends! I am in
perpetual love." [12]

As the editor of this correspondence in 1874, Theodore had an interest in selecting excerpts that pointed to a loving relationship between
himself and Elizabeth (and to a renewed friendship between himself
and Henry) prior to the alleged adultery, which he claimed began in
October 1868. At that time Henry was supposed to have invaded his
home and alienated his wife's previously fulsome affections. Yet even
the selected pre-1868 letters, as edited by Tilton, sometimes insinuate
home-wrecking behavior on Beecher's part. "Mr. B[eecher] called Saturday," Elizabeth had written on January 28, 1867. "He came tired
and gloomy, but he said I had the most calming and peaceful influence
over him, more so than anyone he ever knew. I believe he loves you.
We talked of you. He brought me two pretty flowers in pots, and said
as he went out, 'What a pretty house this is; I wish I lived here.'"

Theodore ended the *Chicago Tribune* excerpt with that phrase, which
implied that Henry was seeking to displace him from the hearth. Yet
Elizabeth's next sentence (put into evidence by William Evarts at the
trial) left a very different impression: "It would make me very happy if
you could look in upon us without his knowing it." So did her next two
sentences: "Deacon Freeland called in today. He wanted to know if I
was good enough to live in so pretty and tasteful a home." Beecher's
comment, in Elizabeth's rendering, was a commonplace about the nice
decor, not part of a campaign for another man's homestead and its
female occupant. Of course Elizabeth may have composed the letter
itself so as to mute the effect of Henry's remark. For him to say "I wish
I lived here," even if the context was interior decorating, was to signify
strong, if unfocused, desire. The indeterminacy of Henry's comment

may well have been intentional in the original utterance. He may have been unsure of his own intentions, but as he went out one door he was seeking to open another. And Elizabeth was trying to cushion the statement for Theodore's benefit and perhaps her own. Wishing that her husband might watch them, unobserved by Beecher, may have been a way of telling him she needed watching or Henry needed restraining. Theodore's editing, meanwhile, suggests that he was working at cross purposes with himself, trying on the one hand to document a pre-1868 familial harmony, and on the other to expose Henry as perpetual rapscallion.[13]

Another example of Theodore's editorial legerdemain was more egregious. His *Chicago Tribune* version of Elizabeth's January 25, 1867, letter said that "I do love him [Beecher] very dearly, and I do love you supremely, utterly—believe it. Perhaps, if I, by God's grace, keep myself white, I may bless you both. I am striving. God bless this trinity! I can nor will no denial take. . . . Hereafter I guard my temper. You shall have a true, pure wife by and by." Elizabeth's prayer to keep herself "white" and "pure" refers obliquely to her immersion in the "trinity," and to her link to Beecher. But Theodore had excised two vital sentences. The trial version of the letter restored them: "I can nor will no denial take. I will be more patient and forbearing toward Libby [Bessie Turner] from henceforth. I pen you my vow. Hereafter I guard my temper. You shall have a soul-pure wife by and by." (Between "true, pure" and "soul-pure," both of them stenographers' copyings from the original letter, there is no way to choose.) In this letter Elizabeth feared that her irascibility, not some romantic or sexual impropriety, would get in the way of the trinity. Maybe Theodore had reason to believe, from some other comment Elizabeth had made to him, that she was troubled about another kind of threat to whiteness. Maybe he thought doctoring this letter was a way of communicating that larger truth. But his editing practices, casual at best, greatly hurt his credibility when Beecher's defense revealed them in 1875.[14]

Perhaps Theodore resorted to this cutting-and-pasting of the references to Beecher in the pre–October 1868 letters for the reason that there was nothing in the correspondence during the period of the alleged adultery (October 1868 to January or February 1870) that suggested adultery. Indeed, Theodore published only one letter from the last three months of 1868, a period in which he was away each week lecturing. (Given their usual practice, the Tiltons would both have written frequent letters during that period. But the sudden death from illness of their infant Paul in August 1868 may have silenced them, or the letters that they did write may have been lost.) And the 1869 letters have remarkably little to say about Beecher, much less than the earlier ones do. On February 4, 1869, Elizabeth told Theodore that because of a heavy work schedule "Mr. B[eecher] does not come as often as in the fall," so perhaps there was just less news to report.[15]

Of course if something sexual or romantic was going on between Henry and Elizabeth, she would scarcely have mentioned it in her letters. What she did report to her husband after October 1868 was the same thing she told him before October 1868: she loved Henry's calls, as Theodore would have if he had been at home. "I shall have much to tell you of our dear friend, Mr. B[eecher]," she wrote on February 18, 1868. "He has opened his heart, as you would love and admire him. To believe in one human being strengthens one's faith in God." And on February 10, 1869, she told of Henry's reading her the opening chapter of his *Life of Christ*. "I liked it, and you will, I think. . . . His visit was refreshing and comforting to me."[16]

To judge from the correspondence, the only change that took place between 1866 and 1869 in the Tiltons' connection to Beecher was that Theodore became more jealous beginning in 1868. The letters disclose a surge in Theodore's suspicions without showing any change in Beecher's or Elizabeth's behavior or sentiment. "About eleven o'clock today, Mr. B[eecher] called," she wrote on February 1, 1868. "Now, beloved, let not even the shadow of a *shadow* fall on your dear heart because of this, now, henceforth or forever. He cannot by *any possibility* be much to me, since I have known you. I implore you to believe it and look at me as in the Day of Judgment I shall be revealed to you. Do not think it audacious in me to say I am to him a good deal, a rest, and can you understand it I appear even cheerful and helpful to him."[17]

Henry's presence in Elizabeth's life was romantic, as far as the letters go, only in the sense that it spurred her to new heights of religious Romanticism. "I am ashamed that I am so often unattractive to the Great Lover of my soul," she wrote on January 25, 1867. "I am striving to make myself beautiful that He may admire me! You know full well how far short I come, but this is my aim. If He can only say my life is blameless, you and I will then be satisfied." A year later she identified "three jets to the fountain of my soul": "the Great Lover and yourself, to whom as *one* I am eternally wedded; my children; and the dear friends who trust and love me." There was no doubt that in the latter group Henry Ward Beecher was *primus inter pares,* and that she longed to bring Henry and Theodore together into the trinity of pure souls. But in her letters to the increasingly wary Theodore, Elizabeth went out of her way to stress the primacy of her love for her husband. "Don't you know," she wrote him on January 28, 1868,

> the peculiar phase [phrase?] of Christ's character as a *lover* is so precious to me because of my consecration and devotion to you? I learn to love you from my love to Him. I have learned to love Him from loving you! I couple you with Him, nor do I consider it one whit irreverent as a *man, bowed with grief for my sins.* And as every day I adorn myself consciously as a bride to meet her bridegroom so in like manner I lift imploring hands that my *soul's love* may be prepared.[18]

III. Perhaps Theodore's jealousy mounted in response to actions of Elizabeth or Henry that went unmentioned in the letters published in the *Chicago Tribune.* But he must also have become more jealous because as his own religious faith waned, he watched Henry and Elizabeth become ever closer as spiritual confidants. Elizabeth might try to reassure her husband that he was her soul's model as she adorned herself for her Great Lover, but Theodore was rapidly losing touch with this kind of aspiration. Her very effort to quell his fears may have aggravated them, since it was so plain that she was now speaking Henry's language, not his. For Theodore there seems to have been a tragic inevitability about this development. Being honest with himself meant giving up the faith that still animated Henry and Elizabeth. Giving it up meant giving her up, spiritually if not sexually, to his rival. Theodore was above all else a man of ideas, constitutionally unable to bend on a matter of principle. On religion Elizabeth saw no room to bend either. She begged him to return to the faith, a course that to him was no longer even a live option, much less an appealing prospect.

Theodore's religious evolution was a major topic at the civil trial in 1875 and at the Plymouth Church investigation in 1874. His opponents on both occasions painted him as a Christian dropout, a renegade free lover with unseemly interest in Victoria Woodhull and her coterie of Communists and spiritualists. He did his best to retort that he was a committed Christian of the Unitarian sort, but William Evarts had little trouble making him look like a heretic. Theodore's correspondence with Elizabeth in the late 1860s gives us a much better angle on his religious shift than the public inquiries of the 1870s, which focussed on the abstract question of which doctrines he accepted and which he renounced. His letters of the late 1860s show us the struggle he lived through as he tried to redefine his outlook.

It amounted to a two-step and very painful separation from Elizabeth's world. First he gave up the main orthodox beliefs they had shared since joining Plymouth Church in the early 1850s: the divinity of Christ, the miracles, the atonement, the Fall. As he shed those doctrines he embraced a compensatory faith in self-improvement, taking Elizabeth herself as his model of Christian perfection. Just as she imagined Jesus in the form of her bridegroom, he took Elizabeth the female saint as his icon. Each of them viewed the divine from a decisively gendered standpoint: access to the holy came through an experience of gendered otherness. The main difference between them was that for Elizabeth (as for Henry) God transcended the symbolic imagery through which she approached him. Theodore's God was mythic, not an active agent in his life. Elizabeth felt God as transcendent but also immanent—an immediate presence with an agenda of his own, a daily comfort but also a *provocateur*.

Over the course of the late 1860s Elizabeth lost some of the aureole of sanctity she had always had for Theodore. It appears to have faded step-by-step as she gravitated toward Beecher. In public, during all the investigations of the 1870s, Tilton would still voice his old view of her saintliness. Probably he continued to believe it privately much of the time. But a turning point came around the time of Paul's death from "childhood choler" [*sic*] in August, 1868. Theodore, away on tour during the winter and into the spring, had only just started to get to know him. Henry had seen more of the infant in the early months of his life than his father had. Beecher came down from Peekskill to officiate at the funeral service, and gave a dazed Elizabeth the comfort she needed. Susan B. Anthony was present, and described in her diary (according to one of her biographer's paraphrases) "the departure from the usual customs [no doubt a ban on black crepe], the house filled with sunshine, the mother dressed in white, and the inspired words of Mr. Beecher." Theodore just felt empty. Lacking any spiritual framework for understanding their loss, he probably could not help magnifying his jealousy of Elizabeth's pastor. It may have been an overwhelming triple jealousy: jealousy of Henry's connection to his wife (whom he loved, and feared losing), of his wife's tie to Henry (whom he had loved and had lost as intimate friend), and of Henry's longer connection to the departed Paul (whom Theodore had lost before getting to know). Or else it was a quadruple jealousy: Henry and Elizabeth still loved the God whom Theodore had lost or left behind.[19]

Theodore's retrospective story in 1874–1875 about his loss of orthodox faith linked it to the end of his abolitionist career. As he told the court in his redirect testimony (his lawyer William Fullerton was trying to salvage Tilton's Christian credentials), he had never had the "leisure" during the war "to examine the foundations of those religious opinions in which I had been brought up from childhood." He had the time after the war, he said, to turn from "public questions" to religious ones, and to decide that his "extreme, severe, overpowering Calvinistic views" ought to give way to "a more genial view of God and of His kindly disposition towards man."

> I think I removed from my mind the apprehensions of future judg-
> ment, the wrath to come. I suppose the one great point, that on which
> my chief struggle took place, was as to what theologians call the Deity
> of Jesus Christ. I had been brought up to recognize Jesus of Nazareth
> as the Lord Jehovah, and I passed from that to the Unitarian view,
> which recognizes Him as the Master and Teacher of us all, still [but]
> less in degree than God the Father.

Fullerton then asked him a series of setup questions: "You believe in the existence of God?" "Yes, Sir; very profoundly." "In his omniscience and omnipresence?" "Yes, Sir." "Do you believe in the immortality of the soul?" "I do, Sir." "And in a future accountability?" "I do, Sir."[20]

But Theodore's letters to Elizabeth in the late 1860s show that his religious doubts emerged while his immersion in the "public" questions of the Reconstruction period was at its most intense. "I am lecturing in dead earnest," he told his wife on December 12, 1866. "I have a message to deliver. I could not endure to speak night after night on any merely literary or entertaining theme. I believe I love my country purely and passionately, and seek her honor and integrity. I must work while yet the strength and life last." The letters also show that he was not coming to doubt "extreme" Calvinism, as he would claim at the trial. He had long since, under Beecher's tutelage, disposed of that kill-joy childhood regime, ingrained in him by "Dr. Alexander," his old-school Presbyterian minister in Manhattan. What he was starting to doubt, as he informed Elizabeth on December 18, 1866, was "every-thing but the Christian character."

> The more I think of the whole subject of religion, of theology, of the
> church, of doctrines, of creeds, I am inclined to undervalue, or rather
> see the little value, of everything but the Christian character. All my
> life long I have [been familiar with] religious creeds, exercises, and
> worship; and still, after all, I am yet to lay a first foundation of a true
> Christian character. . . . The words that keep ringing in my ears are
> "Be ye therefore perfect, as your Father in heaven is perfect." Our

lives are to be not merely good, but the best; our thoughts not merely high, but the highest; our purposes not only noble, but the noblest.

In 1874 Theodore was not the temple-destroying free lover depicted by Evarts, but he was also not the avidly theological Unitarian believer conjured up by Fullerton's friendly questions. He was the same relentlessly ethical individualist in search of personal perfection that he had been in 1866, but he had dispensed, once and for all, with "creeds, exercises, and worship." [21]

By 1874 his quest had led him into the exclusively secular course of "honesty" and "truth-telling." In the late 1860s he was on a secularizing but still religious path, modeling himself after an ethically absolutist Jesus of Nazareth and after his own saintly wife. "Your letters are a well of living water from which I drink daily, quenching my soul's thirst," he wrote her on January 3, 1867. "They are a Newer Testament than the New. I think, on the whole, you do me as much good as St. Paul, who hadn't a very great opinion of women! But if he were alive now, and were acquainted with you and your loving ways, what an Epistle he could write!" "Not a day passes," he added on January 21, "but I have some rare, and high, and beautiful transfiguration of yourself before my soul; by this I see an image that fills me with love, reverence, and humility." A year later he told her that "I wish to walk in the way in which *you* are going. . . . Aid me to advance my soul." [22]

Theodore grasped the paradox that while he was praising his wife's spiritual perfection he was renouncing her actual religion. "Sometimes I think I have advanced to a higher plane than before," he wrote on February 1, 1867, "then I am filled with doubt, and sometimes I am in the very dust. But at least one thing is certain: I hold myself to a higher ideal, and judge myself by a severer criticism than in the olden days. And yet I am conscious of departing more and more from the peculiar religious and theological views which you regard as sacred. Perhaps this statement may give you trouble, but certainly this fact has given me peace." [23]

Elizabeth also knew what was happening. She endorsed the idea that she had special spiritual gifts, and accepted the consequent responsibility of drawing her husband, and her pastor, closer to God. "I realize," as she put it on December 28, 1866, that "what attracts you both to me is a supposed purity of soul you find in me. Therefore it is that never before have I had such wrestlings with God, that He would reveal Himself to me, and ever in my ears I hear 'the pure in heart shall see God.'" Both Tiltons had the Sermon on the Mount ringing in their ears. Theodore took "Be ye therefore perfect" as a command that launched him on a lonely pilgrimage beyond the imperfect creeds and churches. Elizabeth's text was from the Beatitudes. Matthew 5:8 was a hope, a prediction, not a command like his Matthew 5:48. Her Sermon-on-the-Mount instruction led her ever more deeply into the church, where she could take her ever sinful self and petition God to infuse her soul with his spirit.[24]

She would model Christ's love for husband and pastor, but she would not endorse Theodore's splitting off of her inspirational power from her actual religious practice. She pleaded with Theodore to return to Plymouth. "The church tonight was filled with medical students," she told him on February 3, 1867, "Mr. B[eecher] preaching before their Christian Union."

> He certainly is greatly roused this winter, and works most earnestly. Will you not on your return throw in your inspiration and join me in fulfilling our vows as members of this Christian church? Your beautiful spirit would help many there, as it does everywhere. And to me there is no spot so sacred in all this earth as Plymouth Church. Full of delicious memories. If we now, with all its members, bring into it our various rich and growing experiences, its later days would gloriously fulfill the enthusiasms of its beginning.

She was still pleading for his return to her faith two years later. Their baby Ralph, born in June 1869, was "growing finely" in August, yet as she vacationed in Monticello, New York, and tried to regain the weight she had lost after childbirth, she was afflicted by the thought that she and her husband diverged in their faith. "Oh, dear Theodore," she wrote on August 3, "may I not persuade you to love the Lord Jesus Christ?"

> Do not let this entreaty estrange us more, for my pillow *oft* is wet with tears and prayers that we may come into sympathy in our religious natures. Do have patience with me, for, as the time remains to us, I feel as though my heart would break if I did not speak to you—not that I am right in any sense, and you are wrong; God forbid! But we are not one in feeling, and it is *impossible* for me to be indifferent, especially while God blesses us with dear children. I once again ask forgiveness if I have offended you by showing my heart. [Last sentence not in the *Chicago Tribune* version of the letter.][25]

Theodore could not accede to Elizabeth's entreaty. He was now, in the summer of 1869, a secular striver, unchurched even if still praising a distant God who upheld an ethical ideal. In response to her latest plea for a religious accord, he voiced the sinking realization that his spiritual touchstone—his wife's sanctity—was fading. "I have discovered, by searching the depths of my soul," he wrote on August 28, *"that I love you more than any human ought to love another."* He "trembled at the thought that you are almost as much to me as God Himself." He still considered her "the only human being who touches my highest nature." He was not "worthy of your goodness, your self-denial, and your singleness of heart. Occasionally, in some supreme hour, I am your fit mate; but, at all other hours, you are high above me." But he had caught a glimpse of the gap between Elizabeth and God, and of his own idolatry in putting her on a heavenly pedestal. That double insight came to him when he realized she could not lead him to purity. She could not do that, he thought, because she could not stand hearing about his loss of faith. Worse: there was a wickedness in him, he believed, that he could not speak of in her presence. "I am filled with distress to think that I must keep you uninformed, for the sake of your own tranquility, of many of my thoughts, and of some of my conduct [the last six words were deleted in the *Tribune* version]." [26]

Theodore implied that the wicked conduct in question related to women he had seen in his wife's absence. But his problem ran deeper, as he had said in his despairing letter of November 3, 1868, a few months after their baby Paul's death. He had been wracked by their multiple "sorrows," and could not talk to Elizabeth about any of them, "not even Paul, our chief [sorrow]." His "religious doubts and difficulties have been, and are, and I fear must be, shut within myself, because I cannot open my mouth to you concerning them without giving you a wound. You are the finest fibered soul that ever was put into a body; you jar at my touch and I am apt to touch you too rudely." [27]

A correspondence that for years had accommodated an open exchange of confessions and reveled in references to their joy in touching each other, had come to this: my feelings are "shut within myself," "you jar at my touch." There was no reference to Beecher in any of Theodore's sad musings of 1868 or 1869, no evidence of alienated affections, apart from Theodore's vague allusions (in his August 28, 1869, letter) to other women alienating some of his own. The religious split between the Tiltons had solidified by the time of Paul's death, and by the summer of 1869, an emotional expanse seems to have opened between them. In the summer of 1870, after further conversations with his wife, Theodore would come to believe that Beecher's invasion of his home had been the root cause of their estrangement.

There is no direct evidence of Elizabeth's feelings about Theodore or Henry or her baby Paul in the summer or fall of 1868. In the winter of 1869, once again pregnant (with Ralph), she was writing her husband warm, newsy, affectionate letters. (The published correspondence peters out after March 1869, with only a handful of letters in the summer of 1869 and another few in the winter of 1870.) As always, she apologized for her temper and other flaws. "I cannot understand," she said on January 26, 1869, "why the demons weariness, fault-finding, ungenerous selfishness, and many hateful little spirits, perpetually hang about me when you are with me, to modify and lessen our possible enjoyment." "If we could only run to each other in our best moments," she mused on February 5, "and flee away when they do, would it not be delicious?" [28]

Her 1869 letters have little to say about Henry (who "does not come as often as in the fall," as she reported on February 4) or about Paul. It is Theodore, to judge by the letters, who was incapacitated by Paul's death. "I am well-nigh sick with very grief," he wrote on January 15. "My eyes are red and full of pain. I have been saying, 'Little Paul, come and help your father.'" Becoming pregnant with Ralph the previous September or October—a month or two after Paul's death—seems to have delivered her, at least by January, from the debilitating grief of his passing. "I talk not so much of him," she wrote on February 7. "Yet this new mysterious feeling *I know*, which I never before have uttered—a kind of awe, or waiting, listening to learn what he will do for me, and an agony of fear at times, lest I should fail by reason of sin—what he could bring. Already, in many things, I am a *changed woman*, through his precious ministrations. Yet fearing such a statement may be too positive, let me modify it by a *woman changing*." Her erstwhile friend Mrs. X said in 1875 that Elizabeth had been transported after Paul's death. "I expected to find her overwhelmed with grief, as, when her little daughter [Mattie] died, she was inconsolable for months; but, instead, she was lifted up into a rapt, spiritual state of communion with the invisible world. Like St. Dorothea, she heard spiritual voices and saw visions which consoled her." Had she been born a century earlier, she "would have been canonized as St. Elizabeth the Second." [29]

IV. Mrs. X stepped forward anonymously in 1875 in order to help Theodore in his struggle with Henry and Elizabeth. She wished the public to know that hearing "spiritual voices" and seeing "visions" was a sign of readiness to sleep with one's pastor, as long as he was shrewd enough to push the right religious buttons. Mrs. X also pointed out that mystical Mrs. Tilton had a secular side: in the late 1860s she was active in the suffrage movement. "She had become much interested in woman's suffrage, and gave her whole soul to working for it. She mentioned with great exultation that after much entreating and many months of labor on her part, she had conquered Theodore's indifference and persuaded him to join her in forwarding the cause." Mrs. X gave her interview during the last stages of the civil trial, and she was trying to support Theodore's case by de-radicalizing his image. Going to work for women's rights in the 1860s was so mainstream, Mrs. X was saying, that even a middle-class Christian matron like Elizabeth Tilton was for it. When Theodore was on the stand, he attributed his initial interest in the women's movement to Henry as well as Elizabeth. When William Evarts asked him "how early" he had taken part in women's rights organizing, Theodore said that "shortly after Mr. Beecher made a speech in Cooper Institute [in 1860], declaring for women's rights, Mrs. Tilton said that I ought to join in that enterprise, that it was right and proper, and I entered in it." Theodore wanted the world to know that if supporting the cause of women's emancipation was now suspect, Beecher and Mrs. Tilton were just as tainted as he was.[30]

Elizabeth's involvement in the women's movement was always minimal, although surely wholehearted. She was never anything like "the leading woman-suffragist in Brooklyn," as Theodore's lawyer "Judge" Morris stated in 1874. Morris's goal was to discredit her recent Plymouth Church testimony, in which she had expressed strong antipathy to Susan B. Anthony, Elizabeth Cady Stanton, and other leading suffragists. Mrs. Tilton's words were plainly composed by Beecher's henchmen, Morris alleged, since in 1869 and 1870 she was one of Anthony's and Stanton's lieutenants: corresponding secretary of the Brooklyn Equal Rights Association, and organizer of suffrage meetings at the Brooklyn Academy of Music, for which her daughters had taken tickets at the door. Morris could also have pointed out that she had been "poetry editor" of Anthony and Stanton's *Revolution,* in which capacity she had gotten the magazine several poems written by her husband. But all of those activities, which she suddenly abandoned in the summer or fall of 1870, still did not qualify her as a "leader," much less "the leading woman-suffragist in Brooklyn." Nor did they undermine her Plymouth testimony, since she had indeed turned against Anthony and Stanton in 1870, and could be expected to speak ill of them in

1874. But Morris, like Mrs. X, was right on one point: as a booster of women's rights, Theodore was no more radical, and no more to be vilified for that reason, than his wife was.[31]

Even if Elizabeth did get Theodore interested in women's issues in the first place, his commitment to them after the Civil War dwarfed hers. The suffrage movement, and the related cause of divorce reform, were Theodore's choices in the late 1860s as the movements most likely to rekindle his public life. Elizabeth's participation in suffrage organizing was perhaps one small way for the Tiltons to express common purpose as their religious beliefs diverged. On March 13, 1869, she wrote to Theodore that she had gone to the Executive Committee meeting of the Equal Rights Association at the *Revolution* office. "You will be amused to know that Susan [B. Anthony] made me Chair*woman*, and said afterwards that 'I did as well as Theodore himself.' I always want to represent you well." But to judge by her letters, the significance in her own eyes of this secular work paled beside her leadership of the Bethel group of working-class women at Plymouth Church.[32]

The Tiltons' common suffrage work was already threatened well before 1870, when Elizabeth turned against Anthony and Stanton, and stories surfaced of Theodore's liaison with Laura Bullard. For in the late 1860s he was turning more and more toward divorce reform as the critical issue of the postwar period. In that preoccupation he shared much more ground with Stanton than he did with Anthony or his wife. The strongly anticlerical (and anti–Henry Ward Beecher) Stanton was a chess companion of Theodore's, and loved his sentimental, lyrical poetry. They sometimes differed on political strategy—as in 1866, when Tilton sided with Wendell Phillips, Frederick Douglass, and other former abolitionists in arguing that the rights of black men must be secured before those of women. But Stanton and Tilton were kindred spirits in their firm commitment to the principle of individual sovereignty for all. They encouraged one another to put divorce reform at the center of debate. Anthony, not an intellectual and not interested in revolutionizing marital structures, took an intense liking to Elizabeth Tilton, for whom she felt a quasi-maternal concern—as she did for another young reformer, Anna Dickinson, also a friend of the Tiltons.

In gravitating toward one or the other Tilton, Stanton and Anthony were giving implicit voice to an ideological gap between them, and Elizabeth and Theodore were doing the same in moving toward Stanton or Anthony. Their earlier common suffrage commitment dissolved just as their religious accord had. Theodore's loss of his religious faith made him turn all the more toward political republicanism as his intellectual raison d'être. That shift made Elizabeth all the more wary of the women's rights leaders. We naturally concentrate on Mrs. Tilton's worries about Victoria Woodhull and Laura Bullard, to both of whom her husband may have been romantically attracted, and neglect Elizabeth's concern about Mrs. Stanton, who was old enough to be Theodore's mother. But it was Stanton's militant advocacy of individual liberty, and her distaste for the churches (and Beechers), that was helping Theodore erect a secular alternative to the Christian belief without which, in his wife's estimation, her family was endangered.

Henry Ward Beecher, meanwhile, after coming out for women's right to vote in 1860, had made it clear that his suffragism was conservative: give women the franchise, but do not begin revolutionizing social institutions such as marriage. Theodore's increasing radicalism on divorce (extend the liberal Indiana statute to New York, he argued, where adultery was still the sole grounds for divorce) widened the ideological gap between him and Henry: it was now a split over social as well as religious and political ideas. The irony is that it was Henry, not Theodore, whom the national press took to task in 1869 for undermining the sanctity of the marriage bond. On November 30 Beecher agreed on very short notice to perform an unusual marriage ceremony at Astor House in Manhattan. The bride was actress Abby Sage McFarland, and the groom, lying on his deathbed, was her lover Albert Richardson, a *New York Tribune* journalist. He had been shot at close range in the *Tribune* office by Abby's estranged husband Daniel McFarland, from whom she had obtained an "Indiana" divorce, the validity of which was questionable in New York. Beecher apparently acted spontaneously, in response to urgent requests from *Tribune* personnel, and without inquiring too closely into Abby Sage's marital status. It was enough for him that she claimed to have suffered repeated abuse from McFarland, and that well-placed advocates at the *Tribune* vouched for her. At the end of Beecher's big-selling novel *Norwood*, published the previous year, there was a deathbed scene of momentous, soul-purifying transparency. The heroine Rose Wentworth declares her everlasting love for her childhood friend Barton Cathcart, wounded at Gettysburg and hanging to life by a thread. Throughout the book the hour of death is the hour of spiritual revelation and resurrected life. Once Henry heard that the expiring Albert Richardson and the soon-to-be-mourning Abby Sage had declared their love for one another, he was not going to refuse to marry them.

No sooner had Beecher performed the marriage than he was pilloried in much of the press for blithely tearing down the temple of the

American family. The Astor House ceremony, wrote the *New York Sun* on December 2, "seems to us to set at defiance all those sentiments respecting the relation of marriage which regard it as anything intrinsically superior to prostitution."

> The high priest of this occasion was Henry Ward Beecher. . . . Consider, married men of New York! Husbands and fathers! By what frail and brittle tenure your homes are yours. If you fail in business—and it is said that ninety-five out of one hundred business men fail [as Daniel McFarland had]—then your neighbor may charm away your wife, and the Rev. Henry Ward Beecher stands ready to marry her to the first libertine who will pay—not in affection, but in gold and greenbacks—the price of her frail charms.[33]

Unprepared for all the vituperation, Beecher backed down even as he defended his action. At the moment of decision, he said, he had believed that the McFarlands were "legally and morally divorced," although he conceded "it would be difficult to tell exactly on what grounds" he had formed that opinion.

> The question for me to answer was, ought this dying man to extend some protection to the woman who has been joined with him in this miserable tragedy? Ought this woman to be left by him without name or support? Whether correctly or not, I believe that she was legally and morally free from her husband on the grounds of the strictest construction of Christianity. . . . No man can act upon any after knowledge, and must depend upon the light which he has at the time.

Beecher concluded equivocally that "this marriage was at once an act of justice and of mercy," but that he might on further investigation be shown to have been wrong. If it turned out that he "had formed a judgment injurious to McFarland," he would "accept the truth and make such reparation to McFarland as I can."[34]

Theodore Tilton, like Elizabeth Cady Stanton, took the McFarland-Richardson case as proof that New York's divorce law needed an overhaul. Stanton addressed a rally in May 1870 organized to protest McFarland's acquittal on homicide charges (he had been temporarily insane, the jury ruled), and declared that "divorce at the will of the parties is not only right but . . . it is a sin against nature, the family, the state for a man or woman to live together in the marriage relation in continual antagonism, indifference, disgust. A physical union should in all cases be the outgrowth of a spiritual and intellectual sympathy and anything short of this is lust and not love." Theodore concurred, and transformed Henry's unreflective act of justice and mercy into doctrinal principle. He took off from the same Gospel text he had singled out to Elizabeth in 1866: "Be ye therefore perfect, even as your Father in heaven is perfect." According to Jesus, Theodore wrote in 1870, anything short of full spiritual union in marriage was already "nothing but divorce." The "essence of Christ's idea" was that "marriage without love is a sin against God."

> The greatest question which has been propounded to modern society is: What is to be the legal status and what the social fate of persons who find themselves married, but not mated? The common and pusillanimous answer is: To remain in a bondage which it is ostracism to break. But a just moral sense, piercing a sham morality, which is only another name for custom, asks, What excuse can be given to God and to virtue for keeping two human beings in an enforced union which each knows to be degrading to both their souls? . . . No matter with what solemn ceremony the twain may have been made one, yet, when love departs, then marriage ceases, and divorce begins.

Tilton knew his position would be labeled "free love" by his antagonists, so he stressed that the *Independent*, "with its liberal views on divorce, remains an austere moralist on marriage. It utterly spurns, rejects and repudiates the doctrine of free love." [35]

But in a reply the following year to a critic who called him a free lover, he made a limited concession.

> In justice to a number of noble reformers (to whom more honor will be rendered in the next generation than they can look for in this), I ought to say that this term [free love] is used by them in a technical sense, as meaning "love, free from the civil law"; or, in other words, that marriage and divorce should be (at least to a great extent) removed from the realm of legislation and left (as religion is left in free countries) to be governed by its own higher law. If this definition shall be popularly and permanently attached to the term "free love," then, as I thoroughly believe in this idea, I shall cheerfully accept this designation. [36]

To hold that when marriage fell short of full spiritual union it was already divorce, and that marriage should be civilly disestablished ("at least to a great extent"), was to endorse a profound revolution in American social life. And it was calculated to throw Elizabeth Tilton into a spin, since she well knew how far short of full spiritual union her own marriage fell. As his ideas moved toward at least "technical" free love, Theodore could justify his own marital tie to Elizabeth in only one of two ways: either it was a full spiritual union, meriting preservation, or it was an imperfect union in need of dissolution. But a third option saved him from the rigors of his logical dichotomy: Theodore arrived at the conviction that Henry Ward Beecher had stolen his wife's affections. Now all of the tensions documented in his letters of 1868 through 1870 could be reinterpreted as shocks administered by the seductive pastor, not as manifestations of the widening split between him and Elizabeth. As she moved after 1870 to a story about sinning with her pastor, her husband told a tale in which she was more sinned against than sinning. Beecher was such an artful seducer that he had enlisted her spirituality as part of his treacherous campaign. "They were years," in Tilton's memorable phrase, "courting each other by mutual piety." It may have been mutual courting, but in Theodore's eyes it was a one-sided culmination, as Henry beguiled Elizabeth into sexual surrender. Starting in 1870, Tilton gathered his evidence and created a new story, which he related to a few select listeners until, in 1874, he told the world.[37]

V. As the Tiltons were conducting their intimate correspondence in the late 1860s, Beecher was writing more than one new story. His novel *Norwood* was published in 1868 (after running serially in Robert Bonner's hugely popular *New York Ledger*, circulation roughly four hundred thousand), and the first volume of *The Life of Jesus, the Christ* came out in 1871 (the second volume, a casualty of the scandal, was never completed, although the unfinished manuscript was released in 1891, four years posthumously). Elizabeth had a role in the creation of both books. The role we know about is that of sympathetic critic: Henry read chapters of each manuscript to her. The role we can only guess at is that of muse, spark, generative presence. None of the published letters between Theodore and Elizabeth refer to her listening to *Norwood* in manuscript. We know he read sections of it to her because at the civil trial in 1875 he said that he had gone "down to Mrs. Tilton once or twice in the opening chapters and read them to her, to see what impression they would produce. She was good enough to speak very enthusiastically of them."[38]

We know that both Tiltons liked the book. "Mr. Beecher gave us a pleasant episode yesterday—a visit of more than an hour," Elizabeth wrote to Theodore on March 8, 1868. "He said, with great earnestness, you never could know the gratification your letter appreciating 'Norwood' gave him. He meant to give you the American edition and me the English, or vice versa, so that we may have one each." In Theodore's copy Henry wrote, "To Theodore Tilton—who greatly encouraged the author to begin and persevere—with the affectionate regards of Henry Ward Beecher. March 18, 1868." In the frenzy of 1874 Theodore still recalled "the good cheer with which he said I inspired him during the composition of that book." [39]

One of Elizabeth's letters to her husband does mention Henry's reading *The Life of Jesus, the Christ* to her. It was the opening chapter, she told Theodore on February 10, 1869. "I liked it," she said, "and you will, I think. It is fresh and interesting." Henry's visit was "refreshing and comforting to me," she added, and we can imagine it was restful and inspiring for him. After listening to his text, Elizabeth, visibly pregnant with Ralph, "ran upstairs" to get the written outline of her Bethel lesson on "Mary, the Mother of Jesus," and proceeded to read it to Henry. Two creators exchanging their work: occasions of this sort were the substance of their friendship and love in the late 1860s. This visit amounted to a joint study session on the Holy Mother, since Beecher's chapter 1 spoke of her too. He called on Protestants to join Catholics in cherishing "this sweet and noble woman." Mary, he wrote, "may be accepted as the type of Christian motherhood." [40]

It would be tempting to see much of *Norwood* as a gloss on Beecher's relationship with Theodore and Elizabeth, since Rose Wentworth is the perfect Christian woman and Barton Cathcart and Tom Heywood, her two primary suitors, bear striking resemblances, respectively, to aspects of Theodore's and Henry's personalities. "Heywood's face was genial, and when excited radiant. His whole soul shone through it. Excitement shot fire through every feature of Cathcart's face; but everyone felt that more lay behind than was expressed. There was a sense of repressed feeling and reserved enthusiasm." These "contrasting elements" were apparent in "mental qualities" too. Barton's mind was "reflective," Tom's "perceptive." "Both were reasoners; but Heywood loved physical facts, and reasoned upon them. . . . Heywood loved to reason upon the actions of men, the events of society. Cathcart inclined to the study of the causes of events, the nature of the mind, and the structure of society." Cathcart's impulse, like Theodore's, was to abstract from primary experiences; Heywood's, like Henry's, was to linger in them, save them from the corrosive grip of logic and theorizing. The danger in Cathcart's makeup was that he could as easily become a "fanatic" as a "hero." Fanatics were so rigidly single-minded that they mistook "their own feelings and thoughts for outward realities." In the end the down-to-earth Virginian Heywood, a broad-minded champion of harmony between the warring sections (like Beecher after the war), dies at Gettysburg, while Cathcart, now a Northern general, is wounded in the same battle but survives to marry Rose.[41]

But if Beecher intended *Norwood's* characters to offer actual parallels to him and his friends, and he never said he did, it makes more sense to see Henry in the character of Rose's father, Dr. Reuben Wentworth. And of course in 1874 and 1875 Beecher explicitly likened his relationship with Elizabeth Tilton to that of a father with a daughter. If *Norwood* was meant as a reflection of his own life, it lay in the depiction of a father-daughter tie that is intimate to the point of identity. Each sees the other as a spiritual partner. They enjoy an effortless kinship of perception, aspiration, and endeavor. In the real-life version of soul-sharing, Henry saw Elizabeth's "true inwardness" as a gift of which he wished to "partake." In the fictional version, Reuben cultivates his bright flower from her birth, in a careful nurture that was Christian and natural in equal measure. Rose escapes the repressions of Calvinist duty and middle-class domesticity alike. Raised by Reuben as an androgynous spirit-child at home with bugs, streams, and men and women of all classes and types (although curiously unconnected to her mother), she loves God, humanity, and nature, and undergoes no anxious spiritual crisis of the sort that afflicted Theodore Tilton in the 1860s or Henry Ward Beecher in the 1820s. Like Elizabeth Tilton, Rose Wentworth was, as Henry described his real-life friend, "a genius of religious sentiment." The bond Beecher craved with Elizabeth was the bond he effected between Reuben and Rose: "so perfectly were father and daughter in sympathy, that it hardly needed words to interpret between them. They seemed like one soul in two bodies." [42]

Yet in the end it is a mistake to probe *Norwood* for evidence that its author was dropping hints about real-life relationships. It is more fruitful to examine the novel, and his 1871 treatise on the life of Jesus, for the light they shed on Beecher's ideas and feelings about love—ideas and feelings that he brought to his encounter with the Tiltons, and that were reshaped in part by that encounter. Henry's relationship with the Tiltons was fundamental to his life in the late 1860s, but it was not the only force operating on him, just as he was not the only force influencing them. Even if one chooses to believe that the books he wrote in those years flowed directly out of his tie to the Tiltons, one cannot assume that they were depictions of it. They could just as well be escapes from it, alternative imaginings, sublimations that addressed it by changing the subject in essential ways. He may have been rewriting his story rather than telling it.

Critics mostly panned *Norwood* at the time and they have faulted it as a piece of fiction ever since. But as William McLoughlin showed a generation ago in *The Meaning of Henry Ward Beecher*, the novel is a pivotal document of a major change in northern Protestant middle-class life. It marks the final dismantling of Calvinist America. In *Norwood* the early nineteenth-century Unitarian and Transcendentalist rejection of orthodox belief was made readily digestible to the Protestant masses. The same migrants from small-town, old-school values who flocked to Beecher's sermons found in *Norwood* a new set of marching orders. It showed them how to adjust their sights to a post–Civil War world in which the "world" was not a temptation and a snare but a promising terrain of opportunity and fulfillment. Beecher's buoyancy even helped Northerners get over the carnage of the war (the main characters all turn up at Gettysburg during or after the battle) at the same time that they got over Calvinist proddings and prohibitions. McLoughlin knew that *Norwood* was not the cause of so momentous a cultural change, but he also knew that the book was one real contributor to that change. It captured the broad currents of its time and retransmitted them, adding to their force.[43]

Norwood was a disquisition on love, and love was the liberal Protestant's all-purpose answer to Calvinism. "Love over law" was their motto. The more rationalistically inclined (like Theodore Tilton after the 1860s) stressed ethical obligation as the alternative to such Calvinist doctrines as human depravity, substitutionary atonement, and infant damnation—doctrines that more and more middle-class Northerners thought irredeemably pessimistic, legalistic, and unjust. The more Romantically inclined, like Beecher in the late 1860s, saw the natural world as God's second gift to humanity (Jesus was the first). *Norwood* is a paean to trees and flowers and birds as salvific forces. The entire created world is supernatural as well as natural. Human and natural spheres are shot through with divine spirit; they pulsate with God's presence. Theodore's ethical absolutism was liberal in its preoccupation with individual growth toward purity and righteousness. Henry's naturalist supernaturalism was liberal in its fixation on individual growth toward ever fuller sensate experience and human sympathy.

Both of these liberal positions envisaged a future world without conflict, but they differed on how to attain it. Theodore's utopian vision was still a militant quest for truth and justice as well as a plea for love; Henry's was a call to love and let live. Theodore sought out discrete evils to confront, in himself and in the world. Henry looked to harmonize differences, overcome them with good will. At the end of *Norwood* his mouthpiece Dr. Wentworth finds an adult soulmate to take the place of Rose, who will soon be departing as Barton Cathcart's wife. Reuben's new friend is the Quaker farmer Paul Hetherington, who had tended to Barton's Gettysburg wounds. Hetherington was "sympathetic and hospitable to others' thoughts, loving rather to think with and compare thoughts than to dispute; capable of seeing things from other people's grounds; . . . carrying an undisclosed life of meditation concerning the whole mystery of human life, and the hope of the life to come; heartily in sympathy with his own sect, yet not believing it to be more than a sect; . . . and, above all, believing in God, and therefore not accepting the golden dust-specks of the sects as the whole mine." [44]

It would be easy to misconstrue Beecher's Romantic Christianity as a pantheistic nature religion. But his God of 1868 is still very transcendent, just not distant, angry, or judgmental. McLoughlin was right that Beecher spoke to and for a mass of Protestant Americans who had had it with an angry God sentencing sinners to hell. But by halting his analysis in 1870, McLoughlin left the impression that Beecher was giving up on the utter sovereignty of God. *The Life of Jesus, the Christ* of 1871 makes it plain that he was not. Unlike the modernist naturalists of the next generation of liberal Protestants, Beecher still believed in the New Testament miracles. He was in some ways a great secularizer of American Protestantism, urging his fellow believers to immerse themselves in the world and enjoy it, but his happy eclecticism kept a prime place for unexpected divine action. In his estimation there were miracles aplenty in the ordinary processes of nature, and believers could find God performing wonders every day in the woods of Peekskill or the flower stalls of Brooklyn. But God was not limited by the workings of the natural order he had set in motion. "That nature is but an organized outworking of the divine will, that God is not limited to ordinary law in the production of results, that he can, and that he does, produce events by the direct force of his will without the ordinary instruments of nature, is the very spirit of the whole Bible. . . . The gospels should be taken or rejected unmutilated." [45]

For Beecher there was no division between the natural and the supernatural. God preserved his independence and freedom of action, but there was no essential difference between divine and human "natures." "Man's nature and God's nature do not differ in kind," he contended in *The Life of Jesus, the Christ,* "but in degree of the same attributes. Love in God is love in man." In *Norwood* Rose Wentworth is the model human being because she effortlessly embodies the "disinterested benevolence" that Jesus identified in the Beatitudes as the heart of divine and human love. She knew from the start what other characters in the story learned only at length, if at all: "a deep and true love is full of humility and gratitude." It was inevitable that Beecher's ideal fictional character would be a woman, just as his real-life saintly models were—his mother Roxana Foote Beecher, who died when he was three but remained his lifelong lodestar, and his own mystical Madame Guyon, Elizabeth Tilton. Rose Wentworth is compelling for Henry because like Roxana and Elizabeth she is a nurturant female who embodies a vibrant humanity. As a young girl she was "buoyant, joyous, free-moving, and artless," a convention-stretching natural soul. "Perfect physical health produced an even flow of spirits, and an exhilaration of manner, such as leads lambs to skip, and kittens to frolic; and this, in Rose, prevented any of that little-girl saintship of manner which many are fond of depicting" (as in his sister Harriet's famous portrayal of Little Eva in *Uncle Tom's Cabin*).[46]

As she reached maturity, Rose's independence from bourgeois prescription was evident in the realm of love. Thanks to her father's careful "rose-culture," she had never been "a sentimental girl." As a product of a natural culture (the oxymoron that seemed commonsensical to Beecher), she could never "fall in love" in the usual grand swoon. She would evolve into love in a "gradual unfolding." Men would systematically mistake her ease of "friendliness" as an indicator of love, which she would instinctively reserve for her one true mate. Friendliness in her case was but the "outer court," not a sign of admission to the "holy of holies," which only "the ordained of God" would enter."[47]

While the Tiltons were scrambling in their letters to demarcate the real-life boundaries between love and friendship—in part to cope with Henry's potent presence in their intimate lives—Henry was laying down those boundaries in the calm deliberations that occurred under Reuben Wentworth's elm tree. Here, in his thinking on love and friendship, is where his novel intersects most visibly with his life, and with that of the Tiltons. There may be no fence between divine and human love for Beecher, but there is a minefield between love and friendship. The moral greatness of Rose Wentworth lies in her instinctive awareness of that no-man's-land, and her practical wisdom in staying clear of it. She will know which suitor is finally to have access to her innermost life. The men in the story are too ardent, too bewildered to read the signs. Reflecting on Barton Cathcart's confused feelings about Rose, the narrator feels for him: "Could he have said that Rose was to him only like a sister? Yes, he could have *said* it sincerely. But is every sincere saying of course true? Do we know all that we think we do? Are there not, below what we *do* know, great depths of truth not yet made plain to us? In things of the heart our knowledge is as a little child lying in a skiff upon the ocean, seeing only the sides of the pretty boat but nothing of the great underlying sea that heaves it!" Theodore Tilton (at least in the letters he published) relied on his wife's help for guidance in navigating the treacherous path between friendship and love for other women. One wonders if Beecher relied on her to decide where the proper limits lay for their own friendship and love. Perhaps he shared Barton Cathcart's self-assessment: too impulsive, too addled to trust his own judgment.[48]

Rose does not so much know as feel the moment when friendship has turned to love. Her intuitive reckoning can be trusted since her "character" is strong, all her faculties in alignment. "Every part of her nature was in sympathetic relation to every other part. There were no repulsions or discrepancies between her mental powers." Hence when she hears a robin's love call, and her mind turns involuntarily to Barton, she has begun to invite him from the outer court to the inner sanctum. This particular robin's "plaintive call for its mate," "more yearning and passionate than usual," was cited at the trial in 1875 as evidence for Beecher's liaison with Mrs. Tilton. Was Henry thinking of her when he wrote this passage? Quite possibly. Just as he may have been thinking of her when he composed the chapter on Rose's birth, in which her father tramps through the woods to find some trailing arbutus to bestow upon her as she greets the world. The thought of Elizabeth, along with the memory of his mother, probably summoned in Henry the passionate cravings that he voiced in both passages. But that does not make the passages "about" him and Elizabeth. And if they were, consider the possibility that he was not simply modeling Rose on Elizabeth, but offering Elizabeth, in his portrayal of Miss Wentworth, the gift of a high ideal to pursue. Elizabeth had much in common with Rose, but she surely needed, as she said repeatedly in her letters, to work on putting "every part of her nature" into "sympathetic relation to every other part."[49]

Norwood suggests that what Henry yearned for most deeply was the perfect soulmate whose judgment could be trusted as implicitly as Rose's could—in matters of the heart and in matters of the spirit. Elizabeth was more reliable in the latter domain than in the former. He must have felt that he fell as far short of Reuben Wentworth's perfectly balanced character as Elizabeth did of Rose's. Like Barton Cathcart and Tom Heywood, he needed direction as well as stimulation from a woman wiser than he. In the imaginative terrain of *Norwood,* he produced the kind of woman who could cradle him to tranquility even as she modeled the higher life of natural and divine aspiration. To create the character of Rose was to come as close as he could to resurrecting his mother or joining himself to an emotionally integrated Elizabeth Tilton. Henry may never have effected a "nest-hiding" relationship with Elizabeth, however hard Theodore's lawyers tried to prove one from the text of *Norwood*. But he built one for himself in fantasy with Rose Wentworth.[50]

Rose could only be the completely nurturing and enlivening woman Beecher needed by rising above the gendered conventions of the day—as other fictional heroines like Catherine Gaunt did before her, establishing literary conventions that challenged lived ones. Part of *Norwood*'s popular appeal in the late 1860s derived from its deft handling of fading Calvinist belief, but another part lay in its imaginative play with cultural gender drift. The Northern Protestant middle class was perplexed about what was "feminine" and what was "masculine," and *Norwood* dramatized the confusion while promising a safe resolution. Women could be manly: Rose was never "sentimental," always robust and physical in her woodsy independence, always "real" as well as "ideal." "While ideality gave to every one of her faculties the quality of aspiration, this tendency was never followed by discontent. Her ideal life was not an escape from an uncomfortable reality. Her real life was full and joyous, and ideality was employed only to deepen and refine it."

Men, meanwhile, could be womanly: Barton discovered through the contemplation of a brilliant sunset that he has "awaked all my mother in me!" "What?" Rose asks. "My mother has the sense of infiniteness and mysteriousness more than any that I have ever known," Barton responds. "Something of her spirit I have inherited." "I know what you mean," Rose replies. In *Norwood* the most honored image of the sanctified life is that of a person (Rose) transcending gender in spirit and body: imitating Christ by grasping love as disinterested benevolence, cultivating a healthy body as a foundation for harmonized faculties. *Norwood* is a treatise on health as well as love. Thanks to its "reputation" for "health and beautiful scenery," the town was a "place of favorite resort, through the summer, of artists, of languid scholars, and of persons of quiet tastes." For spiritual illumination they would have congregated not in the uninspiring Rev. Jedediah Buell's Congregational Church, but under Dr. Reuben Wentworth's capacious elm. Beecher was not reducing salvation to therapy when he located religious wisdom in the doctor rather than the minister, for Wentworth is a teacher as well as a physical healer. Beecher was removing the Bible from the incompetent hands of a superannuated Calvinist and putting it in the grip of an authentic evangelizer, for whom "all the world has become my Bible. My Savior is everywhere—in the book and out of the book. I see Him in Nature, in human life, in my own experience as well as in the recorded fragments of His own history. I live in a Bible. But it is an unbound book!" Like his daughter, Reuben joined divine and natural inspiration as he celebrated the wonders of soul and body.[51]

Beecher was roundly attacked in his own day, as he has been in ours, for making Christianity a therapeutic feel-good faith. He is supposed to have sentimentalized and feminized religion, with the active support of the adoring ladies who flocked to his side. Ironically, Elizabeth Tilton herself offered a version of this critique: she told Theodore that she wished to protect Henry from the fawning admiration of frivolous women who were diverting him from his religious mission. She believed that at his best her pastor was an androgynizer, not a feminizer. In Christ there was neither Greek nor Jew, male nor female. And yet given the preexisting gender differences within middle-class Protestant culture, Beecher's preaching—itself heavily gendered insofar as his own path *to* Christ required female modeling—may have had divergent effects on men and women. Perhaps the women were more likely than the men to hear his words as a call to independence, to the development of individual selfhood. That is the message Elizabeth Tilton said she heard from him: she was "roused in herself," she told the Plymouth Church Investigating Committee in 1874, she was conscious of being something "more." Perhaps the men were more likely than the women to hear Beecher's message as a call to broaden and invigorate the independence they already thought they had by experiencing nature and by opening themselves to tender feeling. There was one spiritual end in view for men and women alike: dying to the old self, submitting to God's love command. Beecher's insight was to propel Victorian Christians toward that spiritual end by scrambling some of their gendered expectations.[52]

The charge that Beecher unduly sentimentalized Christianity has often been joined, in his day and ours, to the view that he ministered to the Gilded Age business elite, reassured them of their goodness as they cut their greedy swath through the consolidating industrial marketplace. Beecher supposedly made everyone feel good about themselves, flighty ladies and corrupt financiers alike, reducing the gospel to commerce as well as sentiment. As "an old-fashioned Christian" complained in 1874, Plymouth Church was "conducting itself generally on the basis of speculation and the principles of the Stock Exchange, and proclaiming as the last gospel the right of every man to make his own religion and his own morals." In fact Beecher did play a key role in accommodating Christianity to liberal capitalism, but his influence was much broader than the common image of the glad-handing friend of rich businessmen, or the money changer in the temple, allows. As the "free" marketplace of liberal dreams spread through northern culture in the mid–nineteenth century, men of evangelical backgrounds such as Beecher were faced with a quandary. How could they devote themselves to their self-interest, as liberal doctrine recommended, when cherished notions of stewardship told them to put the community—including the well-being of the poor—first? In *Norwood* Dr. Wentworth asserts explicitly that this is a false dichotomy. He lectures at tedious length to one Mr. Brett, an "eccentric merchant and manufacturer," who remains troubled about spending money on himself and his family when there are so many others in need. Wentworth marshals wave after wave of argument to show that the full development of self—opening male and female selves to new experiences of nature, beauty, health, and sympathy—is itself the finest, and most urgently needed, service to the community. Renewed selves will undergird a higher civilization, in which justice will finally be merged with beauty. Pursuing one's self-interest, properly conceived as a higher and higher striving for beauty and goodness, did not mean one was turning one's back on either the commonweal or religious inheritance.[53]

With the eruption of class conflict in the late 1870s and 1880s, this hopeful synthesis would come to seem banefully anachronistic to leading intellectuals and ministers alike, and Beecher would be criticized for his social complacency as well as his commercialism and sentimentalism. Yet his sermons are full of warnings against unbridled selfishness. Of course his well-off listeners and readers (not many of whom were his parishioners at Plymouth Church, which remained a very middling congregation) may have disregarded those warnings. And Beecher made it easy to ignore them. His Romantic individualism, forged during the antebellum breakaway from Calvinist communalism, had no place for the "social control" of wealth that figured prominently in traditional Christianity, as it also would in the next generation of liberal Protestantism. During the depression that followed the Panic of 1873, Beecher had nothing to offer underfed workers but the reassertion of individual striving. In the 1880s, Washington Gladden (who had moved from the *Independent*'s editorial chair to a pastorate in Columbus, Ohio) preached on "social salvation," but Beecher stood pat. He did not see that his liberal individualism would be seized by laissez-faire opponents of state regulation. He stuck to the old middle-class doctrine of mid-century: autonomy in the marketplace for every sober white male. Rather than revise that doctrine he worked its fringes: renewal in nature and in love for men and women alike.[54]

Theodore Tilton's letters to Elizabeth in the late 1860s are full of his anguish as he tried to subordinate selfishness—his own and his society's—to the common good. Theodore's objection to liberal marketplace values had a double genesis: evangelical in its attention to the ethical idealism of Jesus, republican in its vision of selfless citizens battling for the public weal. For Theodore, the merely private lacked honor, and the commercial world betrayed itself in banishing higher ends. Even in pressing his lawsuit against Beecher he emphasized his rejection of a commercial standard of honor: should he win the case, he would not accept a penny of the prescribed $100,000 in damages. Of course he also rejected the older regime of honor that "criminal conversation" suits had been invented to replace: the chivalrous code of the duel. But his rejection of the commercial standard was only partial. The trial was not about immediate financial gain, but it was about protecting his viability in the marketplace as a lecturer and writer. Ironically, a financially successful future depended upon a well-publicized rejection of financial gain at the trial. It also depended upon a methodical and "manly" campaign of vengeance, against his wife and her pastor, that had much more in common with dueling than first met the eye. "If there is anything I was born for," Theodore told the Plymouth Investigating Committee, "it is war."

Beecher could not endorse Theodore's dichotomizing of private and public, selfish and heroic. For Henry there was one world only, infused with God's spirit. There were opportunities everywhere for witnessing God's miracles and embracing his love. Beecher honed this reassuring message over decades of advice-giving to religious youths troubled by the conflict between gospel prescriptions of selflessness and liberal injunctions to self-assertion. Theodore Tilton was one of these tense young evangelicals, one of Beecher's favorite pupils, a disciple who proved in the end resistant to a liberalism so friendly to the things of this world in general, and to commercial enterprise in particular. But Tilton's unbending republicanism was losing force in 1870s America. Theodore would either have to move toward the working-class movement himself, as his old abolitionist colleague Wendell Phillips had done, or find another place where the republican battle against monarchical and aristocratic ideals was still viable. With the added push of a destroyed career, he chose France.

VI. The Tiltons' tin anniversary festival in 1865, just as they entered their thirties, was their peak moment in private harmony and public estimation. Brooklyn's finest flocked to Livingston Street to celebrate their promise. A year later Theodore could still feel that "God has been exceedingly kind to you and to me. Our love and marriage, our children, our friends, our good repute among people whose good opinion is golden, our daily comforts—all make me thankful for my lot as it is, rather than restless after what it is not." A decade later their marriage was over, their means of support uncertain, their good names in tatters. In the eyes of the press the civil trial rendered a mixed verdict on Beecher, but a very clear one on the Tiltons. Most papers judged Elizabeth a pathetic liar at best, a rank betrayer of womanhood at worst. Theodore was a misguided idealist at best, and at worst a conniving conspirator against religion and decency.[55]

It had all happened very quickly, and to a very young couple. Henry was already 61 when the scandal broke in 1874, and could estimate the number of working years he had left. "I propose to work fifteen years yet," he told his Plymouth Investigating Committee. He was off by two years. He worked thirteen more, and upon his death in 1887 was heralded as a community hero. A monumental statue of him went up in 1891 in front of Brooklyn's Borough Hall. It showed him as a fearless antislavery advocate: a female slave clung to one side of the pedestal, imploring him to help her gain her freedom. Theodore and Elizabeth, however, had most of their adulthoods ahead of them. Theodore, at 38, had little idea what shape his future work might take. He was unlikely to get an editorial post. The Brooklyn City Directory began listing him as a "lecturer," but he could scarcely count on an audience. He did know one thing: before long Elizabeth would make a public confession of adultery with her pastor. In 1874 the roughly 40-year-old Elizabeth may not have thought much about her future course, since she still had 11- and 5-year-old sons to care for, along with her nearly grown teenaged daughters. She went into seclusion in 1875, and emerged from it only once, for her last words in 1878.[56]

But we cannot assume that retirement from the light of publicity meant resignation. We know that she turned to a vibrant community of "primitive" believers—the Plymouth Brethren—for spiritual sustenance. Doubtless she spent some time thinking about the past, and its narrowing impact on the present. She had written to Theodore about that in 1868: "If the past were not ever present, I believe I might yet bless you." Perhaps she tried to counteract an impulse to regret the past by meditating on the printed text of Henry Ward Beecher's "Prayer before the Sermon" preached on August 30, 1874, at the height of the scandal:

> May whatever is good in us ripen. May whatever is evil in us be more and more overruled. May we not refuse to go forward by sitting down in sinfulness and remorse, and forever looking backward and bemoaning our mistakes, or our want of improvement of privileges, or our sorrows in bereavement. May we forget what is behind. We are children not of the past, but of the future. We live by faith, and are filled with hope.

Given what Beecher told us about her piety, she may have smiled at Henry's urge to escape sinfulness by moving forward, forgetting "what is behind." For Elizabeth faith and hope were free of time, God was ever present and ever transcendent. She longed for her heavenly lover in a place apart that was always in her midst. "Therefore it is," as she had written Theodore in 1866, "that never before have I had such wrestlings with God, that He would reveal Himself to me, and ever in my ears I hear 'the pure in heart shall see God.'" [57]

Perhaps one day in the 1880s or 1890s her daughter Florence, with whom Elizabeth lived out her final years in Brooklyn, asked her mother what had really happened between her and Theodore and Henry in the 1860s, when Florence was a little girl. Jagged fragments of tearful encounters among them would have lodged permanently in her memory. I imagine Elizabeth's voice in elusive reply: "God's love is pure. All of us are sinners. He moved through us in spite of our sin. I loved your father and I loved Mr. Beecher, and they both loved me, and that was God's way with me, drawing me closer to Him in suffering. Mr. Beecher and I knew each other in knowledge unbidden, and neither could dismiss it. Your father saw it arriving, a flight of the dove, and waved it away. Mr. Beecher whispered it was the rush of angel's wings. The fine repose of love was in words read on winter afternoons, so easily we forgot the time. Was there sin within spirits rising in God's love? It was sinful to burden your father's heart. I know God loves me and tries me and never refuses to forgive. We sin in our loving and our loving brings faith and hope for the higher love that is soul-pure."

Whatever she may have told her daughter, Elizabeth, like Theodore and Henry, told herself and others some deeply felt stories about love and loss. We are rather like the adult Florence, who (assuming she was interested at all, and had not chosen Beecher's path of forgetting what is behind) had to try to reconstruct what really happened. All she could remember were bits of muffled conversations and angry exchanges, and they shifted in memory as she aged. What really happened, Florence knew better than anyone else, was that confusing, devastating, and heartening tales were told by her mother, her father, her grandmother Morse, her pastor, and assorted friends and enemies. Those stories took possession of a vast public in the 1870s, and have remained in circulation, remodulated by other storytellers, to our own day. The editorial writer for the *New York Graphic*, perhaps editor-in-chief David Goodman Croly, understood the drama's scope:

> And it is because we are human beings ourselves, and dealing with the same elements and passions and perplexities, and weaving the same strange web of experience, and working our own figures into the changeless fabric after one fashion or another, that we are rivetted to the loom where other human beings have so terribly tangled their skeins and tied their heart threads together.[58]

THE TILTON LETTERS.

From the New York Tribune.

Mr. Theodore Tilton's counsel furnished, and THE CHICAGO TRIBUNE has published thirty-two columns of the letters passing between Mr. and Mrs. Theodore Tilton, chiefly during the years of Mr. Tilton's editorship of the *Independent*, and down to a few months prior to the alleged confession of his wife. Those to Mrs. Tilton had been left among her other private papers when she fled from her house to Mr. Ovington's. Mr. Tilton seems to have sought them there for them, and collated them for the public. The letters are very monotonous reading, being nearly all written, on both sides, in the most strained style of sentimental and transcendental gush. The ostensible object of their publication is to show that Mr. Tilton was an exceedingly devoted husband,—and the letters certainly show it in the matter of correspondence, since he seems frequently to have written every day during his absence,—and that Mrs. Tilton professed ardently to reciprocate his love up till a very short period before the breach.

THE TILTON LETTERS

The Marital Correspondence of Mr. and Mrs. Tilton.

Extending Over a Term of Years to Within Three Months of the Confession.

A Series of Remarkable Tributes of Love and Confidence.

The Unconscious Testimony of a Kind and Beloved Husband.

Picture of a Man's Heart and a Woman's Power.

The "Pastor" Figures Prominently Throughout the Letters.

Constant Efforts of Mrs. Tilton to Allay Her Husband's Suspicion.

Mr. Tilton's Jealousy Occasionally Seeks Expression.

Marius and Cosette of "Les Miserables" Over Again.

The Passion of Youth in Middle Age and Matrimony.

Excitement in New York and Brooklyn Over "The Tribune's" Revelations.

"Gath's" Dispatch Is Generally Circulated in Extras in Both Cities.

Mr. Beecher's Organ Admits that It Changes the Whole Situation.

It Is Said to Have Broken Up the Proposed Compromise.

AN IDEAL HOME.

THE CHICAGO TRIBUNE'S ENTERPRISE.

"THE VERY BEST PAPER IN THE UNITED STATES."

From the Terre Haute (Ind.) Gazette.

THE CHICAGO TRIBUNE, through the agency of its incomparable correspondent, George Alfred Townsend ("Gath"), has secured, and published yesterday, six pages of correspondence between Tilton and his wife, written during the several years last past. It is, looked at from a journalistic standpoint, a splendid stroke of enterprise upon the part of THE TRIBUNE, which thus again has given evidence that is not only the very best paper in the West, but the very best in the United States.

"BEATEN ALL THE NEW YORK AND BROOKLYN PAPERS."

From the Dubuque Telegraph.

THE CHICAGO TRIBUNE has beaten all the New York and Brooklyn papers in bringing to light and giving to the voracious public correspondence on the Beecher scandal. THE TRIBUNE was obliged to issue a supplement on Thursday to accommodate the voluminousness of this correspondence.

"WALKED AWAY WITH THE PALM FOR ENTERPRISE."

From the Rock Island (Ill.) Argus.

THE CHICAGO TRIBUNE of Thursday, contained copies of the much-sought-for Tilton letters,—the letters of love and confidence which passed between Tilton and his wife for some years past and nearly down to the time she made a confession of guilt. They fill thirty-six columns of fine type in THE TRIBUNE, and have produced a decided sensation throughout the country, East as well as West. THE CHICAGO TRIBUNE has walked away with the palm for enterprise in this respect, and obtained and published these remarkable letters before any other paper in the United States.

"AN ADMIRABLE STROKE OF ENTERPRISE."

From the Indianapolis Journal.

It has been reserved for a Western newspaper to contribute one of the most interesting and startling pages of the Beecher-Tilton scandal. While the Plymouth Church Committee has been expending its energies in covering up the facts, and the press of New York has been engaged in misleading and deceiving the public by suppressions of the truth and suggestions of falsehoods as best suited their purpose, THE CHICAGO TRIBUNE has made a bold dash at the heart of the matter, and by an admirable stroke of enterprise has brought out a series of facts little less than stunning in their character. Having commissioned a special correspondent to go to Brooklyn and get all the information he possibly could about Moulton's suppressed statement, and the case generally, it has the satisfaction of first publishing a series of facts and of letters which cannot fail to have a marked influence on public opinion. On Tuesday THE TRIBUNE published an outline of Moulton's first statement, in which he made positive charges of guilty conduct against Mr. Beecher, and supported them by remarkably circumstantial statements. THE TRIBUNE of yesterday contains a second installment of startling information, embracing the private correspondence between Mr. and Mrs. Tilton during the last eight years. The letters fill about thirty-five columns of THE TRIBUNE. . . . No such letters have been published in modern times. We entirely agree with THE TRIBUNE in its statement that, "as literary productions, the correspondence between this now unfortunate couple will rank among the celebrated love-letters of the world."

"THE MASS OF LETTERS."

From the Indianapolis Sentinel.

The Sentinel of this morning contains a selection from the correspondence of Theodore Tilton and his wife. The reader will say that the selection is a pretty extensive one, and yet it forms but a part of the mass of letters printed in yesterday's CHICAGO TRIBUNE.

EIGHT *The Tilton Letters,*
December 1866 *to*
August 1869

The Tiltons exchanged hundreds of letters between 1864 and 1870. Theodore published parts of 201 letters (89 from his wife, 112 from him) in the August 13, 1874, issue of the *Chicago Tribune,* which devoted 32 columns to them. Elizabeth's letters begin in 1866, and the correspondence is densest from the end of that year through the summer of 1869. At the Brooklyn civil trial in 1875, plaintiff's and defense attorneys entered many of the *Tribune* letters into the record, often providing the entire text of documents that Theodore had edited. A few of the letters introduced at the trial had not appeared in the *Tribune.* In all, the defense entered 40 letters into the trial transcript (21 from ET, 19 from TT), the plaintiff's side 16 (10 from ET, 6 from TT). In the following selection of 30 letters (16 from ET, 14 from TT), the texts combine the entirety of Theodore's *Tribune* excerpts with all of the lawyers' additions at the trial (the latter in bold type). Any remaining ellipses are in the original documents. Minor discrepancies between *Tribune* and trial versions (stenographers were working quickly in both 1874 and 1875, and inevitably made mistakes in copying) have been resolved wherever possible according to the context of the letter.

Introducing the *Tribune* collection on page one, the paper's star reporter "Gath" (George Alfred Townsend) wrote that "more remarkable letters we have never seen between husband and wife—particularly to be written, not in the heyday of youth and courtship, but in the sober years of middle life, and after ten or fifteen years of marriage."

These letters are the testimony which Mrs. Tilton gives to the character of her home before she had any occasion to submit such testimony to the manipulation of lawyers bent on crushing her husband for the sake of saving Mr. Beecher. Her statements in these letters are utterly irreconcilable with her recent criticism on her husband's treatment of her. [Theodore's lawyer] Judge Morris has been for several days past solicitous to publish these letters in the Brooklyn press, but Mr. Tilton has withheld his permission on the ground, first, that such a publication seemed a violation of good taste, and that no such testimony was needed in his behalf in the community in which he lived. But Judge Morris says that Mrs. Elizabeth Tilton's published testimony has been shaped with a deliberate purpose to affect public opinion by creating a false issue against the husband, and he (Judge M.) therefore insisted on giving Mrs. Tilton's true testimony, in her letters, to counteract her manufactured testimony before the [Plymouth Church] Committee.

"Gath" claimed to have been allowed "to make extracts of such passages as he pleased," but it seems far more likely that Tilton and Morris made a prior selection of publishable passages, then told "Gath" to print as much of them as he wished. The *Tribune,* eager to establish its national clout by scooping the New York press, would in all likelihood have published every word it was permitted to print.

The letters were ballyhooed nationwide. Newspaper editorialists became literary critics. The *New York Graphic,* edited by David Croly (father of Herbert, then five years old), called them "a rich addition to the love-literature of the world. . . . No one can read them without a feeling of admiration for a pair who preserved such idyllic affection in such a rude, matter-of-fact, chilling world as ours" (Aug. 17, 1874, p. 324). The *New York Tribune* disagreed: "The letters are very monotonous reading, being nearly all written, on both sides, in the most strained style of sentimental and transcendental gush" (quoted in *Chicago Tribune,* Aug. 19, 1874, p. 1). The *Chicago Tribune* editorialist, with one eye on the market for his paper, naturally shared the *Graphic's* view. "As literary productions, the correspondence between this now unfortunate couple will rank among the celebrated love-letters of the world. They are fit to be classed with those of Marius and Cosette in Victor Hugo's *Les Miserables,* with those of Petrarch and Laura, or with the immortal effusions of two other most unfortunate hearts, Heloise and Abelard" (Aug. 13, 1874, p. 6). "Nor," the paper added on September 20 (p. 8), "can we overlook the fact disclosed by this correspondence that Mrs. Tilton is a woman of more than ordinary intellectual gifts. Though her moral nature has been so undermined and eaten away that nobody can believe anything she says, the public cannot have failed to notice in her letters the evidences of a mind well worthy to be mated to Tilton's brilliant parts."

The *Brooklyn Eagle* ("Elizabeth Tilton—La Nouvelle Heloise," Aug. 15, 1874, p. 2) found the "progressive Christianity in these letters perfectly overwhelming," and judged Theodore (but not the newspapers) irredeemably base for "making merchandise out of the confidences given by the cradle and in the bridal chamber." The *Eagle* concurred with the *Chicago Tribune* that "these letters do indeed prove that Mrs. Tilton wrote to her husband in a vein very different from that in which a woman would write, were her statement of his cruelties, made to the [Plymouth Church Investigating] Committee, true." But the *Eagle* nevertheless considered the letters bad news for Theodore. "Unfortunately for the fellow [Theodore] they over prove. They prove that all through he knew that woman's love for Mr. Beecher, and that he knowingly, and for years, left her within the danger of it; and they prove either that he wanted Beecher to yield to the temptation, or that he thought Beecher's honor beyond all reach of temptation." The *Eagle* mocked the letters' heartfelt yearnings by printing a column of spoofs. "You are my own hunkidory darling," ran one. "I am as weary as a crab with one claw, without you. As the cucumber vine clings to the sea-girt rock, so my affection sticks to you." ("Theodore's Love Letters—An Important Supplement to the Portion Published," Aug. 19, 1874, p. 2).

In fact the Tiltons were devotees of Robert and (especially) Elizabeth Barrett Browning—"I love you as Mrs. Browning loved," Elizabeth wrote to her husband on January 25, 1867. They did try to express their feelings in a poetic idiom that joined perfect sincerity and high aspiration—a style already by the mid-1870s drawing the snickers of "realists." The Tiltons' literary sentimentalism was a commitment to the spiritual power of writing and reading: words uttered honestly, polished and then savored on the page, fortified a couple's face-to-face connection. Their letters disclose a fervent, Romanticized, middle-class faith: middle-class because it emphasized individual autonomy; Romantic because it located autonomy in growth toward ever more fulsome expressiveness—an expressivity modeled by their favorite novelists and poets. Middle-class because it stressed internalized self-control (Theodore would rein in his passionate interest in other women, Elizabeth would check her passionate temper); Romantic because it imagined that individual independence, control, and expression were fully compatible with, and indeed undergirded by, wider webs of organic solidarity, beginning with the soul union of two lovers. Middle-class Romantics like the Tiltons saw in acts of perfect intimacy (the secret reading of a love-letter, the reading to oneself or the reading aloud of a novel, both of them texts that evoked soul-interiors) the seeding of virtue in the broader social world.

Henry Ward Beecher, meanwhile, having been born into the strict controls and lofty expectations of middle-class propriety, had an easier time than the Tiltons calling for release from arbitrary constraints upon the emotions. He had no need to prove his own respectability, which came to him (for all his genuine psychic turmoil) by inheritance. He could finesse the problem of control by handing ultimate authority to God while giving ever wider license to humanity. Indeed, his originality lay in seeing God's authorizing love as a continuous releasing of human beings from tight, anachronistic limits. The Tiltons had to struggle to reconcile a Romantic interest in novel experience with a vigilant middle-class campaign of self-improvement. A tiny instance illustrates their conundrum: Theodore wrote Elizabeth on December 6, 1866, to say she must read Charles Reade's best-seller *Griffith Gaunt,* which he had been devouring on the train. The next day he wrote (in the December 7 letter marked "on the cars") to say he didn't care if she read it after all. The novel experience it promised was vitiated by the sensuous passion it highlighted. His change of heart on *Griffith Gaunt* is a nice example of the delicate oscillation in middle-class culture between respectability and renewal—and of the ever-constant devotion in that class to words written, words read, and words spoken in full sincerity.

> TT to ET, Sunday Night, Akron, Ohio, Dec. 2, 1866
> My Darling:
> I have just been moved to write a long letter to Mrs. [Mattie] Bradshaw [Elizabeth's best friend] about [her daughter] May. It is chiefly about having a purpose in life, and how to carry it out. Of late, I have been thinking much of my own life.
>
> You know that I don't attach as much importance as many do to certain churchly ideas of the Christian life. It seems to me that the truest method, and the surest, of developing a Christian character, is never to swerve from one's own inward ideal of right, whether or not this ideal be in conformity with the prevailing conventional notions of good men, or of the best of men.

I have been looking back upon my ten years of public life, and judging of its motives. Looking back thus, I can see that I have been always earnest and straightforward, but always too much in the interest of myself, and too little willing to be counted as nothing in comparison with the work which I have been set, as an instrument, **to perform.**

Lately I have been endeavoring to ascertain what are my earthly ambitions; to struggle with them and conquer them. I have no ambition to be rich—and never had; none to be in political office; none for social or fashionable pre-eminence; none, that I can detect, for oratorical distinction; and not a great deal for a literary reputation. My public notoriety occasionally flushes me with pleasure. But on the whole, I believe I can truthfully say that I have in great measure put aside the idols which I used to worship.

I once believed, judging by my personal experience, that public life—particularly such a life as that of a young man prematurely famous—was bad for the character; crippling to the soul. I used to feel this at times in many keen self-reproaches.

But when one has at first tasted the sweets of reputation, and at last of their insipidity, I think he gets a more sober, philosophical and just view of what is valuable, and what is valueless in life, than in almost any other way.

As a consequence, many of the men of great fame whom I intimately know, make no such ruling impression on my mind as many of my private friends do.

But if I had no reputation myself, I should still be dazzled with theirs, as I was once dazzled years ago. For instance, I like Mr. Beecher in many respects as well as I ever did. But he has ceased to be my soul's prop—ceased to inspire me to my best life. I believe he is not as morally great as he once was. I do not now refer at all to his political views. His political views have made no change in my feelings toward him as a friend. But there was an older virtue which has since gone out of him—an influence which used to brighten my life when I came under its ray; an influence, however, which became gradually quenched like a vanishing sunbeam.

Henceforth I take no patterns after public men—great men—famous men. They are not so good as my wife and children. Half an hour's talk with Mrs. Bradshaw makes me a better man than a half dozen sermons could do. I have had a sweet Sabbath day—one that has baptized my soul.

I spoke to a thousand children this afternoon, and I have been in a glow ever since. This will account for the fact that I have written two such sermonic letters. But now I send, goodnight.

Forever yours,

Theodore

Chicago Tribune, Aug. 13, 1874, p. 3, col. 4; *TT v. HWB,* 1 : 503

Six weeks' worth of Elizabeth's letters from November and December 1866 disappeared when Theodore lost the packet he had placed them in for special safekeeping. "The sacred archives . . . of those delightful manuscripts now belong to the lost literature of the world," he wrote to her on Jan. 30, 1867 (*Chicago Tribune,* p. 4, col. 5; *TT v. HWB,* 1 : 496).

TT to ET, Laporte, Indiana, Dec. 6, 1866

My Darling:

I have ridden all day long, and am just arrived at dark, about an hour before my lecture. I am so excited in mind by a sense of my being imprisoned away from home, barred out by impassable walls, hindered from seeing you by cruel obstacles, that I can do nothing at this moment but make an outburst of feelings.

I ought now to be composing myself for my task, but I feel more like taking flight eastward in the next train.

All day long I have been reading "Griffith Gaunt." Go to the bookstore, buy a copy, and read it—that is, if you would like to be doing the same thing with myself. I am not yet far enough in the story to know the moral meaning, but it has excited me considerably. It turns on jealousy. I am not jealous. Nor do I know the feeling. I think any man is a fool who is jealous. If he is jealous without cause, he is foolish; if with cause, more foolish.

But I am somewhat disturbed, and have been for a long while past, at the diminishing faith which I entertain for human nature. Human characters do not seem so lovely to me as they once did. Perhaps this view is temporary—the result of a passing shadow. Or, rather, perhaps it is because I do not entertain so fond an opinion of my own character—its moral strength and unbending rectitude—as I once supposed I could justly entertain.

During my travels I have had profound reflections on my life. I am a weak man supposed to be strong; a selfish man, supposed to be the world's lover and helper; an earthly-minded man, supposed to be more Christian than my fellows. I cannot endure the mockery—it breeds agony in me.

At this moment I am completely wretched, yet expect in ten minutes to step forth to a public welcome! The outside life is one thing; the inside, another. I dare not show the inside to the world. And yet I must show it perpetually to God.

I am endeavoring to live a manly life—not what the over-generous world shall so esteem, but what, in my inmost conscience, I shall know to be such. I have had many wrestlings of my soul with Heaven of late. I feel myself scarred, spotted, miserable, and unworthy. From this feeling during the day I have taken refuge in my lecture at night—sometimes turning it almost into a sermon. I have come to feel exactly as the Prodigal felt. An inward revelation of a man's self to himself is an awful thing. It lifts one's face to the Eternal World. Henceforth my prayer is, that God may keep me nearer to Himself. My life is so unprofitable that I sometimes dare not turn round and look upon it.

You cannot guess for what one thing I most yearn to see you. It is to kneel by your side at our familiar evening-prayer. My prayers of late have seemed all spiritless without you. I am never so true a man as in my prayers—when I have prayed with my arm around your neck. It seems to me now that I cannot live this winter without at least seeing you once or twice—if for no other moments than first these greatest of all moments.

I see, with agony in the retrospect, how my life has been marred by social influences coming from your mother—how they disastrously have affected us both. If you should ever appear to me anything less than the ideal woman, the Christian saint that I know you to be, I shall not care to live a day longer. I cannot write further. I must stop to go to my audience. It is dreadful to be so full of feeling as I am at this moment.

God bless you!

Theodore

Chicago Tribune, p. 3, col. 4; *TT v. HWB*, 1: 494–95

TT to ET, On the Cars, Northern Indiana, Dec. 7, 1866
My Darling:

This rattling train shakes my pencil, but I must endeavor to write to say that I have just finished "Griffith Gaunt."

It is a powerful and interesting story—well constructed, though not remarkably well written. I don't care particularly whether you read it or not. It has not baptized and anointed me like our mutual reading of [George Eliot's] "Felix Holt" [published 1866]. Do you not often recall that sweet evening in Twelfth Street, when, late at night, we finished that heroic story?

I can see you at this moment lying propped on the sofa, your red shawl around your shoulders, and your water-proof cloak over your feet. That night, and the day that followed it, filled me as full of human happiness as my heart could hold.

"Griffith Gaunt" ends in a far sweeter and more agreeable manner than one expects when he is in the midst of its pages. But I have never met a character in any romance equal to one which, if I were a romancist, I could draw from a certain woman I know.

The novels turn too much on a love as a passion, as a jealousy, as a madness, as an intense adoration for the time being; and it is only here and there that one sees in a novel the true and perfect love of a true and perfect woman—the love that dwells in the soul rather than in the heart.

Men and women who have the mere natural instinct for loving, love with the heart, but they who have a true genius for loving, love with the soul.

The noblest part of love is honor, fidelity, constancy, self-abnegation—not the clasp of the hand, nor the kiss of the lips, nor the ecstasy of fondness. Sometimes that which most delights the heart most cheats the soul. It is for this reason that lovers ought sometimes to be separated.

Now, to bear each other in memory, in daily and hourly pictures of the fancy, in constant mutual communings of soul without contact of the flesh, in perpetual nearness notwithstanding miles of distance, in an abiding reverence, unfeigned, lofty, and ennobling—this is the great prerogative of true love.

No man loves a woman as a woman loves a man, until he has attained to such an experience as this of the union of two souls by their noblest possible interchange. But, in some lives, this comes not at all; and, in the best lives, it comes only at the crowning moments. O that we were heroic enough to seek always to live our best possible life! I am trying more than ever. God help us both. Thine immortally,

Theodore

Chicago Tribune, p. 3, col. 5; *TT v. HWB*, 1 : 495

TT to ET, Aurora, Illinois, Dec. 7, 1866

My Delicious Darling:

It is a comfort to get out of the cars, and sit down to pen and ink, and send you my love.

. . . A good landlord and a contented hostler make a good inn.

. . . The chief burden of my reflections has been, how shall I henceforth keep myself nobler in spirit, more patient under crosses, more heroic to attain a true manhood, more consonant with God's will? My life seems to have been thus far a folly. I am ashamed of it. I have been winning what the world prizes—honor, reputation, influence—but all these, to the possessor, are like the golden apple of the fable; they fall to ashes in his grasp.

Seated by the car-window, gazing on the prairies, thinking of God's blessing in allowing my selfish heart to beat against your unselfish one—a wife of whom I am unworthy—I see how clearly you have outstripped me in what, after all, constitutes true Christian character, true nobility, and the true object of human life.

A thousand miles are this moment between us, but you seem to be near me and around me, like a guardian angel. O my sweet wife! If sometimes I am undemonstrative, and carry my love unexpressed, yet at other times it glows and burns within me like a holy fire!

I see in myself so many points of weakness wherever you stand against me as my prop, that I am convinced, in my reflective moods, that I owe my good name and fame in the world more to your influence on my character than to my inherent character itself.

You charged me, when I came away, to write my secretest thoughts, and not to chronicle external events. I love the people among whom I am here thrown. These Westerners are a noble race. They grip my hand with a splendid welcome. But, after all, in all their thrift, their activity, their prosperity, there is something in nearly every man whom I meet that savors too much of this world. I see in you, and in a few women, more greatness, such as Christ would have called great, than in all the motley, rushing company of brave and hardy men whom I encounter day by day.

And I too am no better than they. But you, and Mrs. [Bradshaw?] and the Saints, are far ahead of us all in the pilgrimage toward Zion.

I have thoroughly tested the vanity of all that part of this life which most people think best worth the living. Henceforth I wish to join you, and the company of the good, the pure, the prayerful, the self-denying, the Christ-loving.

Indeed, my sweet pet, the other world seems not far off even when this world seems most near. Let us be wedded anew—with love inseparable and everlasting.

Theodore

Chicago Tribune, p. 3, cols. 4–5

TT to ET, Alton, Ill., Dec. 22, 1866

My Dear Pet:

. . . I sat down with the idea of writing for the *Independent*. But, apparently finding nothing in my brain worth saying to my public readers, I have switched off from the main track, and am here scribbling another of my daily nothings to the one dear creature who thinks that my chaff is always wheat. What is it that you find in my letters to excite your praises?

I am sure that, after I have written, and turn around to read them, they appear to be poor and meagre enough. Now and then I come upon some womanly, Christian, profound sentence or expression in your letters, that proves (what I knew before) that the art of writing beautiful letters does not belong to literary men and women more than to other men and women. As in a mirror one shows his face to himself, so in a letter one shows his heart to his friend. The writing may be poor, and yet the letter good. But, in a perfect sentence, which is made to fit like a glove around the modeled shape of some worthy thought, there is something in the mere expression, independent of the thought, that sometimes has a charm indescribable.

Some of the finest literature in the world is contained in wise and rich letters—many of them never destined to be read by more than one reader. The most interesting books are biographies, mainly on account of their personality. But letters are still more personal. A letter is mutually enkindling—it puts both writer and reader in a glow of love and good-will toward the other. Letters, like prayers, ought never to admit an untrue word—never a conventional for a direct expression— never any of the little lies of polite usage.

For instance, I don't like a letter to end with, "I am your obedient servant." No form of expression, however customary, ought to be used which is not strictly honest. Accordingly, to a man whom I did not like, I would never say, "My Dear Sir," but simply, "Sir." The more I see of the little fibs current in society, the more I despise them. Let us teach our children to speak the truth; and, to this end, let us speak it ourselves. I have long thought that the habit of communicating to each other, as husbands and wives, as friends and friends, our secretest and deepest hidden thoughts, without disguise and without misrepresentation, would finally breed a greater reverence for honesty and truthfulness than now prevails.

If a man willfully misstates an outward fact, it is a lie, and he sins against society. But if he willfully deceives by representing his thoughts to be better than they are, which is usually the case with men who indulge in religious cant, and are the prayer-mongers at Friday-night meetings, then such a man equally is guilty of lying, although his sin of falsehood is not so much against society as against himself. I believe that, of all the virtues, the greatest is to speak the truth. With which moral, as Robert Browning says, "I drop my theorbo."

This is enough sermonizing for Saturday night. O, my little, black-eyed pet. I love you better than my life itself.

Theodore

Chicago Tribune, p. 4, cols. 1–2

ET to TT, Friday Night, Dec. 28, 1866
My Own True Mate:
One of the most severe days we have had. Have not been out, except to call on Mr. [Edward] Ovington. A consultation was held upon his case today, resulting in assuring his wife that with *great* care, he might recover. I seem to have some power to cheer him, wherefore I give about an hour a day to him. I was obliged to call in Dr. Barker, for Flory [Florence, their daughter] was sick this afternoon, and already his remedies have helped her. She had anticipated much during the holidays—a visit to Jo's [Mrs. Tilton's brother], and other places have been given up—but she bears it well.

Annie [Theodore's sister] **had a fine time at Emma Beach's party last night—it was a grand affair. She will not go back to Nyack—stay with me awhile, and I hope you will decide to send her to Lexington, tho' perhaps rest from study this winter would be best. She seems very happy with me, and while you are away I am glad of her company—since she has learned to be agreeable, and is far more helpful than of old. Burrows's wife has a son two weeks old. I have not been there.**

My beloved, I have been thinking of my love for Mr. B[eecher] considerably of late, and those thoughts you shall have. I remember Hannah Moore [More] says: "My heart in its new sympathy for one abounds towards all." Now, I think I have lived a richer, happier life since I have known him. And have you not loved me more ardently since you saw another high nature appreciated me? Certain it is that I never in all my life had such rapture of enthusiasm in my love

for you—something akin to the birth of another babe—a new fountain was opened, enriching all—especially toward you, the one being supreme in my soul. "I love thee with the breath, smiles, tears, of
all my life!—and if God choose I shall but love thee better after
death."

It is not possible for any human creature to supersede you in my
heart. Above all else you rise grand, highest, best. I praise God that He
is teaching me of His great mercy and love, shown by His gift of so
great a heart as your own, to be mine. For many years I did not realize
the blessing. What remorse it brings to me! Memories bitter, awful! But
to return to Mr. B[eecher]. He has been the guide of our youth, and
until the three last dreadful years, when our confidence was shaken in
him—we trusted him as no other human being. During these early
years, the mention of his name, to meet him, or, better still, a visit from
him, my cheek would flush with pleasure—an experience common to
all his parishioners of both sexes. It is not strange, then, darling, that on
a more intimate acquaintance my delight and pleasure should increase.
Of course I realize what attracts you both to me is a supposed purity of
soul you find in me. Therefore it is that never before have I had such
wrestlings with God, that He would reveal Himself to me, and ever in
my ears I hear "The pure in heart shall see God."

Oh, fulfill this promise unto me, my Lord and my God! Darling
husband, I have endeavored to express to you, without cant or any
such thing—my true feelings, as they appear to me. **It is true that I
live in an agony of soul daily; nevertheless I am profoundly
happy in my privileges, opportunities and blessings.**

**God is with us. We have had great experiences this winter.
He will keep us, I am sure—our trust is in Him.**

**Let us pour out our souls in prayer that we may never
sin as before, when we meet again. Will it be possible that
I shall ever again cause you a pang? God in great mercy
forbid!!**

Good night.

**Oh, for one embrace. My whole being goes out toward you.
I believe it does. May I not hope now that between us there is
a true union of souls? Holy Spirit, searcher of all hearts, incline us wholly toward one another!**

Yours,

Elizabeth

Chicago Tribune, p. 1, col. 4; *TT v. HWB*, 1: 493

TT to ET, Waterloo, Ia., New Year's Night, 1867
My Darling:

I wish you a Happy New Year. I wonder how you have spent the day. I spent it mainly in a wagon-ride of 30 miles over the prairies from Vinton to Waterloo—starting at 9 in the morning, and arriving at 3 in the afternoon. Bitter cold the day has been, and yet I enjoyed my ride as almost a luxury. There is something wonderfully invigorating in this Iowa atmosphere. Wrapped securely against the cold, one makes his journey with perpetual refreshment of soul. During all my ride I was thinking of what good resolution would be most profitable for me to make, with the least fatality of breaking it as soon as made. At last I determined that to resolve that I would be a better man would simply be vague and intangible; to resolve that I would be more unselfish, or more self-denying or more prayerful would be simply to repeat old good intents which I had grown into a habit, long ago, of non-fulfilling; and accordingly I resolved that, instead of attempting to attain some improved inward state, I would chain my mind to the daily perfor-mance of some outward act which would react upon my mind and heart within. Finally I fixed my resolution at this: "Resolved, That I will henceforth make it my bounden duty to perform each day some act of kindness, however small, to some fellow-creature." I shall try this plan of improving my character; and I think it will work out a better result than much of my religious, and perhaps somewhat morbid, med-itations, reveries, and longings. Will you join me in the resolution? Let us carry it out hand in hand.

. . . Oh, how my heart bounds at the sight of your handwriting! I never have loved you half as well as during my winter's separation. Day by day, and hour after hour, I think of you, live in you, cast my honors at your feet, invoke Heaven's blessing on your life, and place you before me as my pattern of saintship in this world. You are a darling! Your sweet letters make my blood dance with joy. I pour out my soul upon you tonight. May the New Year bring you a horn of plenty, full of bene-dictions, and empty them all into your lap! You are the best, the truest, the purest, and the wifeliest of women! I kiss you goodnight.

Theodore

Chicago Tribune, p. 4, col. 3

ET to TT, At Your Desk, Monday, Jan. 7, 1867
My Precious Husband:

I find our language very poor in superlatives when I attempt to de-scribe my soul's love. What a delicious way you have of rebuking and

teaching me! **I will never again forget to date my letters, be
sure, yet as I have written daily to you I supposed you would
receive them in regular succession, and it did not occur to me
that the date was always necessary.**

And then, my sweet, will you talk to me as you write? Pretending always that you think I am the loveliest and best of little wives.

My bump of approbativeness is so thoroughly satisfied when you
praise me—tho' it be true or not, I am content. I go singing and lighthearted about my work, every difficulty is straightened, and life is
sweet.

**Yes, darling, I will join you in your New Year resolution, as
far as possible. I will go hand and hand with you, yet you
know your strides will far outreach mine.**

. . . What a blessing you are to me in every way. **Mrs. Belcher
[*sic;* not Beecher] made a long call on me today, and sent
much love to you. Mattie and Katy Bradshaw also called.
Please mention Mr. Ovington in some of your letters, it
would so gratify him that you remembered him. I bless God
for your continued good health. Do not go to places off the
railroad, where you must expose yourself by long rides. You
cannot afford to risk your precious life thus. The little girls
I'm afraid are going to have their wish by having the whooping cough; they cough dreadfully. Goodnight, love. Shall we
ever be done with our caressing when this long waiting is
ended?**

Yours entirely,

Elizabeth

Chicago Tribune, p. 1, col. 4; *TT v. HWB,* 1: 448

ET to TT, Friday Evening, Jan. 11, 1867

My Sweet:

. . . You write today of the love of two interlocked souls remaining
wedded for immortality, and ask whether such love is not more tenderly
beautiful than those same souls can possibly feel toward God. Darling,
I live in profound wonder and hushed solemnity at this great mystery
of soul-loving to which I have wakened the past year. Am I your soul's
mate? How few find this pearl of great price in this life! I cannot make
myself believe I have capacity to meet your soul's want, though you
entirely fill mine. When I look at you, I say: "Yes, my soul is satisfied—
our union is perfect." But when I turn and look at myself as supplying

your need, I bow my head and pray God to add the needed grace. . . .
As to my love toward God, I understand it only as I know my love to
you: it is one and inseparable. I learned of God, the Father, as I know
my children. I learn of Jesus as lover of my soul—as I know *thee*, my
lover, husband, friend. Oh, God, lead us! "Thou art the way, the Truth,
and the Life."

<blockquote>
"Forgive us if too close we lean
Our human hearts on Thee."
Goodnight.
</blockquote>

Yours

Chicago Tribune, p. 1, col. 4

ET to TT, Sunday Evening, Jan. 13, 1867

My Dearest:

. . . Pardon me if so many of my letters are filled with accounts of
the pastor's visits. It is because I would have you know all that fills my
thoughts that I write so frequently of him.

Yesterday he made us very happy. It was Saturday. He came in
about 11:30 A.M., bringing flowers, as usual. After visiting with me
twenty minutes he said, "I am hungry to see your children." "Are you,
really?" said I; "then come up directly and see them." I had set apart
this day for doll-dressing, as I had not time before Christmas. So he
followed me upstairs, where, for one full hour, he chatted and played
with them delightfully. . . . After this he invited me to accompany him
to Mr. Ovington's, which call he had intended to make for some time.
He said he had planned going there with his wife, and then to say to
her, "Come, mother, Mrs. Tilton lives right up here, let's call on her;
she is all alone this winter." "She might or she mightn't."

Whether he will follow up this plan, I know not.

We had a very pleasant call there, cheering the sick man. We
stopped a moment at Moulton's and then I brought him to A's. He had
never called on her. There, too, his presence was a blessing. Having
been inspired by our dolls, he then wished me to go with him to the toy
stores and advise him in selecting a doll for [his daughter-in-law] Hattie
B[enedict Beecher]'s little girl. "It must be as large as my Carroll [the
Tilton's son]." But we were not successful, as such grown-up dollies do
not live in Brooklyn. By this time it was my dinner hour, and I jumped
into a car and rode home. This is the only time I have *been out* with
him since your absence. Thus ended an interview of real pleasure to us
both. You, too, would have enjoyed it. I wish you would write him. He

has real, high, true status of mind. Oh, if you two dear men were once more reunited in perfect sympathy. . . . As I look at you from this distance, how grand, great, pure, and satisfying you are. . . . Goodnight.

Your Dear Wife

Chicago Tribune, p. 1, cols. 4–5

ET to TT, Friday Eve., Jan. 25, 1867

My Own Dear Husband:

Four letters from you reached me today, including one to Mrs. Desmond and Oliver [Johnson]'s letter to you. I did not go to Mrs. D's wedding as it was celebrated at Mrs. M's in Springfield. Mother went on and has not yet returned. I will forward your letter though not the kiss.

I think, in reference to Oliver's opinion of Mr. B[eecher]—as his remarks were made to Mr. Bowen, and *they* are embittered toward one another—that what Mr. B[eecher] said of you may appear very different through the coloring that Mr. Bowen may give it. Oh, how my soul yearns over you two dear men! You, my beloved, are higher up than he; this I believe. Will you not join me in prayer that God would keep *him* as he is keeping *us?* Oh, let us pray for him. You are not willing to leave him to the evil influences which surround him. He is in a delusion with regard to himself, and pitifully mistaken in his opinion of you. I can never rest satisfied until you both see eye to eye, and love one another as you once did. This will not come to pass as quickly by estrangement. But, with all the earnestness of my being, I commit you both to God's love. He has signally blessed you both, and He will keep His own beloved. Why I was so mysteriously brought in as actor in this friendship, I know not, yet no experience of all my life has made my soul ache so keenly as the apparent lack of Christian manliness in this beloved man. Mattie [Bradshaw] feels as I do. I saw her today. She said she received two letters from you today. I do love him very dearly, and I do love you supremely, utterly—believe it. Perhaps, if I, by God's grace, keep myself white, I may bless you both. I am striving. God bless this trinity! I can nor will no denial take.

I will be more patient and forbearing toward Libby [Bessie Turner, the Tilton's teenaged ward and servant] **from henceforth. I pen you my vow.** Hereafter I guard my temper.

You shall have a soul-pure wife by and by.

I am ashamed that I am so often unattractive to the Great Lover of my soul. I am striving to make myself beautiful that He may admire me! You know full well how far short I come, but this is my aim. If He can only say my life is blameless, you and I will then be satisfied. Cheer up, my darling, the work is mighty to which you are called, and you are doing it nobly. I love you as Mrs. Browning loved. Don't you know it? Pray for me always. I pray for you, though I have such assurances of God's love and care for you, that you seem high up and safe.

If I could sit in your lap, and look into your dear eyes now, I'm afraid 'twould be more than I could bear. At any rate I should have a good cry—*that* I am now going to have without you. It always baptizes me—to use your word. **Carroll is with me in bed. Annie is at mother's. I have had only two or three guests with me all night since you've been gone.** Angels guard us *all*.

Goodnight.

Your Own Wife

Chicago Tribune, p. 1, col. 5; *TT v. HWB,* 1: 499

ET to TT, Monday, Jan. 28, 1867

My Beloved [Husband]:

I am very sorry my letters are lost, they contained so much that stranger eyes should never see.

I was obliged to omit my Saturday and Sunday letter as usual.

Mr. Haskell came over Sunday afternoon. We went to hear Mr. Beecher, who preached an uncommonly fine sermon on the divinity of man, from the text "Ye are Gods." **In the morning Dr. [Richard] Storrs preached for us. A collection was taken up for our city missions, amounting to nearly $6,000.**

Mr. B[eecher] called Saturday. He came tired and gloomy, but he said I had the most calming and peaceful influence over him, more so than any one he ever knew. I believe he loves you. We talked of you. He brought me two pretty flowers in pots, and said as he went out, "What a pretty house this is; I wish I lived here." **It would make me very happy if you could look in upon us without his knowing it.**

Deacon Freeland called in today. He wanted to know if I was good enough to live in so pretty and tasteful a home.

. . . The picture which came from Springfield has just reached me. I do not like it. It is old, thin and cold looking.

Nevertheless I talk to it, love and caress it. It would please you to know how much Carroll talks of you—often cries to see you.

The children are passing through the stages of the whooping cough very comfortably—thanks to homeopathy. It is nearly 12 o'clock and I must say goodnight, adding with it my very best love. Soon I shall look again upon your dear face and be satisfied. But if I was traveling about with you I know my body is not in the condition to bear journeying without great fatigue, and though I might look upon your face, yet absent from these children in winter, I could not say I am satisfied, but when you are in your own home once again I shall then be perfectly at rest. "Oh, hasten 'round ye wheels of time!"

God keep us both.

Your Darling

Chicago Tribune, p. 1, col. 5; *TT v. HWB,* 1: 488

> TT to ET, On the Cars, Chicago to Milwaukee, Feb. 12, 1867

My Darling:

Once again on the cars, and once again confronting a lecture-appointment, I feel that I am once again at work, after my two days of pleasant rest.

And I confess that rest is sweet. I do not mean rest for wearied limbs, though that, too, is sweet; but rest for one's spirit; rest in the midst of a circle of kind and loving friends; rest to one's own vagrant, untamed and unconquerable homesickness; rest in the tranquillity of spiritual peace.

I have been enjoying two days of such rest. The spell is still on me this morning. I rode five hours to Princeton yesterday afternoon, and five hours back, after midnight, on purpose to spend a long and delicious evening with the Lovejoy family. This family and its influences have helped to make me a better man. The very roof seems to spread over me a benediction. I am grateful for the Providence that ordered my steps last December to the threshold of this cottage. Tarrying with these dear people has been a new experience in friendship—a new delight of life.

The whole subject of friendship has been much in my mind this winter.

I am satisfied that whoso makes no intimate or confidential friends, both among men and among women, friends with whom he girdles himself round about as with a halo—friends who are props to keep him lifted perpetually toward his highest life—friends whose friendship is a kind of sacred wedding that knows no sex—such a man neglects one of the greatest **of human** opportunities for intellectual, moral and spiritual growth.

I have had abundant occasion this winter to test the impressions which different kinds of new friends make upon my mind and heart. "Ye have not many fathers in Israel," said Paul; in addition to which I have also found that one has not many mothers, or sisters, or brothers, or friends. The number of people who mate each other—who fit one another exactly—who are (to use your word) "counterparts," is very small. A man must see in his friend something that supplements himself. That for which we hunger in another is that which is needed to keep us from being incomplete ourselves. The best type of friendship, therefore, is that which excites the souls of true friends to their highest spiritual states. My friends are legion, and yet only here and there one affects me powerfully in my moral nature. By most of my friends I am influenced (so far as I can see) for neither better nor worse; but by a few whose names are precious, I am purified and ennobled. Their society is like a ministry of angels. To talk with them, to live among them, to be near them, or simply to be thinking of them is a blessedness.

I have lately realized this in an exquisite and delightful degree.

And this fact reveals the one prolonged mistake of my past life—my association with your mother. I can now plainly see what I might have been if, for instance, I could have lived under such a roof as sheltered me in Princeton, instead of breathing, during all these years, the atmosphere of Livingston Street. If my mother-in-law had been such a woman as Mrs. Lovejoy, and the influences of Brooklyn had been like the influences of Princeton, I believe that I might have grown by this time as unselfish as a good woman. How much more I would then have been to yourself and the children! How many pangs you might have been saved! How many unknown joys you might have experienced! I have not been a wise man or I would not have consented, eleven years ago, to pitch my tent in a bank of fog. Moreover, let us beware of the tragic and dreadful mistake of teaching to our children that when they shall be married their first and chief allegiance will still be to their parents as heretofore, and that only a secondary fealty is sufficient between husband and wife. I have never seen so plainly as I have seen this winter what Livingston-Street mildew I have been carrying on my garments for eleven years. Six months ago I was accustomed to say to myself in my secret hours, "Theodore Tilton, it is time for you to die; your soul grows not whiter but darker: die soon and save yourself from total destruction." But I believe that if I shall return to Brooklyn at all, I shall return a different man. God grant it! I know that I have tried to wash myself clean at the fountain of a better life.

The old religious teachings, the Orthodox view, the dread of punishment, the Atonement, have less and less power over my mind. Of course you will mourn over this. But I must be an honest man. I don't believe in Orthodoxy, and therefore I will not pretend to do so. From you, as from God, I have no secrets; so I tell you day by day my thoughts. And these are my thoughts this morning. But the car is now growing crowded; a man has taken a seat at my elbow, and I must stop writing. Blessings on your saintly head!

Ever yours,

Theodore

Chicago Tribune, p. 4, col. 6; *TT v. HWB*, 1: 496–97

TT to ET, Monongahela House, Pittsburgh, Jan. 30, 1868

My Darling:

I am here in one of my old, familiar, and favorite hotels. A good welcome has always awaited me in this smoky, Presbyterian city. From the beginning, my audiences here have been large; none ever larger than tonight's, which filled every tier of the Academy of Music. I had full liberty of utterance, and spoke as well as I usually succeed in doing, when I do my best.

Perhaps your loving letter, which awaited my arrival, and greeted me as with a kiss, had something to do with my good spirits and my evening's success.

All the colored men in this hotel know me and are full of

attentions. My face gets shaved with unusual care, my boots get blacked to an unwonted polish, and my hot-bath is arranged with noticeable nicety.

I am now well established in my new housekeeping. My plan of traveling with a trunk, instead of a mere carpet-bag, is a great addition to my comfort; in fact, it is a positive luxury. My little reticule has become quite a curiosity shop. It contains my New Testament; the North American Review; a new English tooth-brush; a long, patent-pointed lead-pencil; a little portfolio for writing in the cars; a comb and a brush; a wisp-broom; a railroad map; a roll of letter stamps and a wad of ice-cream candy.

My trunk is carefully set right once a day, but gets dreadfully topsy-turvied in the baggage-man's hands. In opening it, I always find the stockings sticking among the shirt-bosoms, and the handkerchiefs scattered about among the legs of my flannel-drawers. It is lucky that I carry no bottles of wine, for they would be broken a dozen times a day, and my shirts made of the color of robin redbreast's bib.

A gentleman tonight said that the Pittsburgh papers had lately quoted your remark about your four children; and he wondered whether or no so young a looking man as I could lawfully have so many!

All this day, while riding thither in the cars from Cleveland (for I had to go all the way to Cleveland to get here in time for my lecture tonight), I spent in writing an article to *The Independent,* entitled "The Tongue of Fire; or Extemporaneous Preaching."

I inclose a hundred dollar bill. Perhaps it is risky to send money by the mail, in large amounts, but I must leave too early in the morning to get a draft at the bank. Use it according to your discretion in paying the debts. I hope I do not frighten you with the long list of them which I sent in my last letter. I simply made that exact statement in order to appoint you my cashier and business agent.

It is now about midnight and I ought to be snug in my bed, for I have had a hard day's and also a hard night's work. But your letter of this afternoon was so full of affection and so beautiful in the manner of its expression that I must do something for the sake of expressing my heart's feelings. I have never loved you more than now, nor have I ever had

a more serene, cheerful, hopeful and patient spirit than at this very time. Our memorable interview on the evening before I left you lingers with me like a sunset in the sky; it makes all my thoughts rosy and all my feelings pure. I seem, all of a sudden, to have grown ten years younger in hope and ten years older in strength. The knowledge of your love, your confidence, your respect, your satisfaction in me, this is more than all that the rest of the world can give, and far more than I can ever deserve.

My mind of late, or rather my heart, has gone out very tenderly toward the children. I am made more proud to be loved and yearned after by them than to be the President of the United States. But, most of all, my strongest passion in this life is to be greatly loved by their mother. Oh! my sweet wife, I have a great heart when its fountains are stirred and loose, have I not?

Affectionately thine,

Theodore

Chicago Tribune, p. 9, col. 2; *TT v. HWB*, 1: 618, 627

ET to TT, Friday, Jan. 31, 1868, 11 o'clock P.M.

My Dear Husband:

I have just returned from Mattie's, and saw your bust [sculpted by Mack Bradshaw]; loved it, and could not bear to leave that precious head behind me. **I felt a sense of cruelty. Oh, Theodore, darling, I am haunted night and day by the remorse of knowing that because of my harshness and indifference to you you were driven to despair—perhaps sin, and these last years of unhappiness. I sometimes feel it to be the unpardonable sin. God cannot forgive me. But if you only may be restored to your former loveliness, I shall be content to live my life in penance, yea, in disgrace. I am the chief of sinners!! I understand perfectly how you have felt. I carry in my soul this burden black of sin, yet appear to my children and friends calm and happy. "Woe unto you, whited sepulcher," I hear perpetually. I will carry these agonies gladly, for I know a life of happiness awaits *you*.**

To return to the bust. The spirit of your face is caught in its earnestness; the eyes do not quite suit me, but this must ever be the fault of statues. I received this morning your letter from Syracuse inclosing check for $100. It makes me

very happy that you give me an exact statement of your affairs. I appreciate the confidence, after all you have suffered through me, to the depths of my soul, and shall try to follow your wish *in every particular,* and tho' I'm a poor housekeeper and provider, I never felt so great an impulse to use my judgment and all my abilities to help you. If the past were not ever present, I believe I might yet bless you. You are the only human being I have harmed! Oh! wretched woman that I am!

I learned from Mattie that Mrs. Gibson was left entirely destitute, Mr. G. having even sold his life insurance a few weeks before his death. Mrs. Gibson and all the family are visiting at the Beechers' since the funeral. I have not seen him since you left, nor do not wish to unless he believes in and loves you perfectly.

Darling, we must both cultivate our self-respect by being what we seem—then will be fulfilled my ideal marriage—to you and you only a wife—but contact of the body with no other—while then a pure friendship with *many* may be enjoyed, ennobling us. Let us have not even a shadow of doubt of each other—tho' all the world are weak yet will *we* be strong.

God accept and bless us *both.*

Now we are *one.*

By bye, Faithfully yours,

Be not offended that I iterate and reiterate my love. I *must,* but destroy all my letters.

Chicago Tribune, p. 1, cols. 6–7; *TT v. HWB,* 1: 503

ET to TT, Saturday Evening, Feb. 1, 1868

My Beloved:

The last day of the week I have been accustomed to look for your home-coming, so that today and this evening I am peculiarly lonely. Your precious letter from Pittsburgh came in your stead, which I have read four times already. *Blessings on you,* **dearest, they have the last winter's ring in them. I did not dare expect you would remember your aforetime punctuality. Your closing lines are, "have I not a great heart when all its foundations** ["fountains" in TT's letter] **are stirred?" Yes, most truly. Beloved, generous, noble, pure, I do thoroughly feel beyond all other men. Forgive me for tell-**

ing you when forbidden. By so much as you are *great.* I too
stretch out to reach you and *thus* we do lift up each other.
God forbid I may never more drag you down!! Oh, well *I
know* as far as I am capable *I love you.* Now, to keep this
fire high and generous is the ideal before me. I am glad you
carried a trunk, and are comfortable. I realize with mingled
pain and pleasure, how much more satisfactory your physical life is away from home, and maybe an ideal wife and
children are in fact more helpful to you even as the memory of my Father has been more of an inspiration to me than
his presence would have been. In this, separations become
blessings; yet, with myself, darling, in my present growing
passion and admiration and sympathy, I am only *perfectly
contented* and restful when you are with me. These latter
months, I have thought, looked and yearned for the hour
when you would be home with longings unutterable; surely
you must have *felt* the joy in my eye. *I know* that now mother,
children or friend have no longer possession of my heart: the supreme
place is yours forever; are you really glad to hear this, my sweet? When
you speak your love for me it is delicious harmony to my soul.

The flowers you ordered came today; I kissed every one.
Then I gave them over to Flory to arrange, as she desired
to. I gave a few to gladden Carroll, and as I read the line
to him in your letter where you say you were "more proud
to be loved by your little children than to be the President
of the United States," large tears filled his eyes, and he said,
"I *do* love my Papa." We do not at all realize the blessings
we have in our children! I have filled my sheet with the tale
of my love—so old but *ever* fresh and gushing in me. I will
now tell you of the guests I have had since I wrote to you
yesterday.

Susan Anthony came to tea last night, and went away after breakfast. I learned nothing particular from her; was entertained with her talk; and regarded your wish by curbing
my enthusiasm for you, while I must impress unmistakably
the minds of all I meet the single end and aim of my life—to
be faithful in so far as *I know* to the great privilege whereto I
am called. "Elizabeth, thou art highly favored, chosen among
women," are words ever sounding in my ears.

About eleven o'clock today, Mr. B[eecher] called. Now, beloved, let not even the shadow of a *shadow* fall on your dear heart because of this, now, henceforth or forever. He cannot by *any possibility* be much to me, since I have known you. I implore you to believe it and look at me as in the Day of Judgment I shall be revealed to you. Do not think it audacious in me to say I am to him a good deal, a rest, and can you understand it I appear even cheerful and helpful to him. **He told me in confidence that Mrs. [Gibson] and his family were at his house; that Mr. G. had sold most of his insurance policies; what remained was not equal in amount to what Mrs. G. had been accustomed for pin money—that on Monday she with her three younger children would return to their place in the country, while he, Mr. B[eecher] kept the three older sons at his house, for they could not even pay the cheapest board, and on a personal matter he intended to get employment for them—they having been with their father in business only. He said his sympathies had gone out for them more than if they were his own—they all as a family seemed so unfitted for poverty.**

After seeing the children, I asked him if he would go with me to Mattie's and see the bust—without any hesitation he said he would. I immediately got ready, and I took my first walk to the Court St. cars [two blocks from their house], without much difficulty, so that I feel free again and will walk out every pleasant day. [She had recently given birth to their son Paul.] **We found neither Mattie nor Mack at home to my great disappointment,** seeing **only Laura Bradshaw and Gip—and** your dear head, darling, which on second seeing is more than ever to me. Mr. B[eecher] expressed great satisfaction with it, feeling it was far better than he expected to find it, and he believed as correct a likeness as you could have. He is very desirous for Mack to try him. We came directly home, nothing noteworthy occurring, save that he left at the door with the remark that "he had had a very pleasant morning."

You once told me you did not believe that I gave you a correct account of his visits, and you always felt that I repressed much. Sweet, do you still believe this? I strive in my poor word-painting to give you the *spirit* and impression which I give him, and he to me. It would be my supreme wish and delight to have you *always with me*. This trinity of friendship I pray for always. **I gave Miss —— her money. She desired me to thank you sincerely for your generosity. Carroll will come down for dinner tomorrow.**

I will try to have a letter awaiting you at every appointment. Now, darling, *goodnight.* I hope to dream of you, love.

Tell me frankly what I can *be* or *do* for you, because I am altogether

Your Own

Chicago Tribune, p. 1, col. 7; *TT v. HWB*, 1: 489–90

ET to TT, Monday, Feb. 3, 1868, 9 o'clock (I think it is) A.M.

What may I bring to my beloved this bright morning? A large throbbing heart, full of love, single in its aim and purpose to bless and cheer him. Is it acceptable, sweet one? As my body gains daily in strength, my enthusiasm bubbles up perpetually, so that I even felt I saw you reflected in my eyes this morning when my thoughts of you so literally filled me as to gush out of my face. Most truly do I love, and I am resolved never more to repress the expression of it. I have lived under the fatal mistake that I would make you selfish; but, oh, what it has cost me to learn that a large, generous love cannot, in its very nature, minister but to our best and holy states!

The picture of your dear face, most constantly with me, is one glowing with love, but *always* bearing the look of one that has suffered. Can I, who am the cause thereof, ever again be indifferent? Nay, the little life which remaineth is consecrated to restore, if possible, the beautiful image I have marred. There is no sacrifice too great that I would not enthusiastically make to this end. **If God will only consider me worthy to work with him.**

I have been thinking, my darling, that knowing as you do your immense power over an audience to move them at your will, that same power you have with all public men over any woman whom you may love. To love is praiseworthy, but to abuse your gift of influence is a sin. Therefore I would fain help restore to you that which I broke down—SELF-RESPECT. Your manhood and its purity and dignity if you feel it is stronger than even love itself. I know this because here I am strong. No demonstrations or fascinations could cause me to yield my womanhood.

You have not yet replied to my inquiry whether the giving you my whole heart in my letters offends you. I was with you all day yesterday, Sunday. What holy associations cluster around that day in our own experiences. The morning hours suggesting Mattie's death, and who can tell what that

**hath done for us, and now the evening memorable forever of
confessions, with repentings, cleansing and sacred vows!! I
wanted to write to you, but could not. I went to church in
the morning, was blessed, spoke with Mr. Bowen, who was
cordial, and Professor Raymond. He commences another
course of readings at the Packer tonight with Henry the
8th—$5 a course. Were you out. . . .** [Beecher's defense attorney
said that the rest of the letter was missing.]

Chicago Tribune, p. 1, col. 7; *TT v. HWB*, 1: 487–88

TT to ET, Crawfordsville, Ind., Sunday, Feb. 9, 1868
My Dear Angel:

I dreamed of you all last night, and awoke thinking of you this morning. How much I want to see you! How I yearn after you! How my soul
blesses you day by day! I can never describe how precious your love of
your husband has appeared to him during these few weeks past. Your
singleness, your fervor, your purity, your devotion—they fill my mind
and heart with reverence, adoration and humility.

I regard my last evening spent with you at home as the most memorable point in my whole life. You opened for me, that night, the gate of
Heaven, which had so long seemed shut.

Ever since, I have had nothing but glory, thanksgiving, and praise.
If ever a man was made a new creature, that man was I—no more
despondency—no more repining—no more vain regrets—no more
loss of self-respect—no more groveling in the dust. On the contrary, I
am once again a man among men, and a Christian among Christians.
Now, this transformation I owe to yourself, to your irrepressible love
and devotion, to your ceaseless prayers, and to your victorious faith.

You always have it in your power either to crown or dethrone me.
You have the chief ruling influence of my life. Your words, your wishes,
your looks, your thoughts, act on me like magic. When I am doing you
an injury, or slight, or hardness, I am made so miserable that I do not
wish to live. When I am making you happy, I walk like a Prince newly
come into his kingdom.

Your letters, since I have been from home this last time, have been
the dearest you have ever penned. They are royal in their love. Each
one fills me with renewed pride and joy in my wife. O, my darling, in
comparison with such love as you express, how poor is the friendship
of all other friends! I have never seen any one who loves as you do. You
have the richest of all human hearts. I am pledged to you forever. My
vows I shall keep and not break. With God's help and with yours I shall

be the faithfulest man in the world. Blessings on your soul this Sabbath day.

Ever yours,

Theodore

Chicago Tribune, p. 9, col. 2; *TT v. HWB*, 1 : 451

ET to TT, Friday Evening, Feb. 14, 1868

My ——:

Supply, to gratify your own heart most perfectly, some endearing epithet. I sent you my valentine this morning, and because I have laid out work for the morrow, with the little girls, I come again to you tonight that you may not miss my Saturday letter.

Blessings on you! Blessings on you, beloved! Yours from Crawfordsville (I shall evermore remember that place with gladness) came today. To hear that you are happy, cheerful, and love me, is more than even my faith could hope. I wept over it, I laughed over it, I prayed over it, and in the midst of my exultation, Mattie called in; and though I was under vows not to read your letters, I did the next best thing, which was to get the bottle of wine you sent me the night you left, and drank to your bodily and spiritual health. **While we were doing so, Mrs. Rooker called, and I got her a glass that she might mingle her blessing with ours upon you; I am sure they will follow you.**

Mattie is hungry to hear from you. I think she feels a little care that Mr. B[eecher] visits here. See how great a power he and your dear self have over the heart. She said: "Lib, I heard through Mrs. Morrill that Mr. B[eecher] called on you Wednesday. I believe he likes you ever so much." Now, my darling, I have often urged him to visit Mattie, believing he would find her more comforting and restful than I can be. *She* would be refreshed and cheered—while, as for me, I who am rich in the fullness of your delicious love, have no need. Save for his sake I am gratified if I may minister, and thank God the while.

Oh, dear Theodore, husband, how much I rejoice in your love— am kept in perfect humiliation that he who knows me so well should love so grandly. This is the theme of all my thoughts. No other sentiment or creature hath power to move me.

The chords of my heart are set to the harmony of love *for you*. Now, how I may be able to express this to you when you return, I know not. That the flame will always burn, I know—but that, by reason of infirmities, it shall glow upon the cheek and through the eye, I know not. In God only is my trust. He knows my heart's desire. I implore you to live "by faith, and not by sight," with regard to your dear little wife. Now to Him who is able to keep both soul and body, I commit you this night. Farewell.

Yours devotedly,

Elizabeth

Chicago Tribune, p. 2, col. 1; *TT v. HWB*, 1: 450

ET to TT, Monday Morning, Feb. 24, 1868

My Darling of Darlings:

I am most happy to sit down in writing talk with you. This is my first break in my daily correspondence. Saturday to Monday, owing to Sis and Eddie, Joe and Fanny coming up on Saturday to spend Sunday with me, and Sunday, when I yearned to write to you after church, was prevented by calls from Mr. Ovington and friend, Mr. Augustus Storrs, Mr. Freeland, and the Rev. Mr. Adams, which occupied the whole afternoon. Then I gave an hour to my children, to our mutual delight, and the evening passed with Joseph and Fanny, until weary. I was forced to go to bed without giving you my Sabbath love. Today I thank you; I thank you for a look into your heart—for, with one or two exceptions, you have not shown it to me since you went away. Your work and fatigue is the cause, I know.

Oh! my beloved, I feel unutterable love and sympathy for you in your anguish and "heartbreak," as you say. It is too true you have given largely, grandly, and bountifully of your best love to friends, aye even to your wife, while in return you have received most often indifference, and at best, love not deserving the name, in comparison with thine own.

Do you wonder that I couple your love, your presence, and relation to me, with the Saviour's? I lift you up sacredly and keep you in that exalted and holy place, where I reverence, respect—and love with the fervency of my whole being. Whatever capacity I have, I offer it you. The closing lines of your letter are these words: "I shall hardly venture again upon a great friendship. Your love shall be *enough* for the remaining days."

That word *enough* seems a stoicism in which you have resolved to live your life. But I pray God He will supply you with friendships [the trial version has "friendship"], pure and wifely love, which your great heart demands, withholding not Himself as the chief love, which consumeth not tho' it burn, and whose effects are always perfect rest and peace.

Again, in one of your letters you close with "faithfully yours—that world 'faithful' means a great deal." Yes, darling, I believe it, trust it, and give you the same surety with regard to myself. *I am faithful to you, have been always, and shall forever be, world without end.*

Call not this assurance impious. There are some things we *know*. Blessed be God.

I sorrow more than you can, for your lost friendship—as my soul stings with remorse that I was the cause—and yet for all this, you love me. Henceforth let no one point the finger at your Christianity. The love which is in Christ Jesus abounds in your soul. **Flory is persistent in her wish to unite with the church. Shall she do so when you return, at the May communion—that—**. . . [Beecher's defense attorney said that the rest of the letter was missing.]

Chicago Tribune, p. 2, cols. 1–2; *TT v. HWB*, 1 : 494

TT to ET, At the *[Independent]* Office, Nov. 3, 1868
My Deary:

Your kind and loving note falls so pleasantly on my spirits that I would immediately go home this afternoon were it not that I have engaged to go out this evening. There is so much sunshine pouring into my little office at this moment that I think I never knew a brighter day in my life; and I hope that some of the light and warmth will steal into and remain within my cold and cruel heart.

It is the greatest regret of my life that I do not seem constituted so as to make you as happy as you deserve to be; but I have the best of intentions—and the worst of success.

The cause of so much trouble at home is my general anxiety about everything. Latterly I worry more or less concerning every matter which I touch. I have hardly ten minutes a day of uninterrupted freedom from care. This may seem an exaggerated statement; but it is the painful truth. I feel as if I were growing old before my time. Lights that used to burn within me have been quenched. Hopes are faded; ambition is killed; life seems a failure.

As I cannot bear to see any expression of pain, or sorrow, or regret, on your face, I cannot bring myself to speak to you familiarly on any subject connected with any of our sorrows—not even Paul, our chief. I am literally *tormented* at having no grave for his crumbling clay. Every allusion to the subject has been a pang through my heart.

Then, too, all my religious doubts and difficulties have been, and are, and I fear must be, shut within myself, because I cannot open my mouth to you concerning them without giving you a wound. You are the finest fibered soul that ever was put into a body; you jar at my touch, and I am apt to touch you too rudely.

As for my own character, I saw, at the time of Paul's death, what it was to be a man, and how far short of it I am myself; and I have ever since been utterly overwhelmed with my own worthlessness, selfishness, degradation and wickedness. At some time I expect to recover from this slough of despond, but not now; I must remain longer in suffering before I can emerge into peace. I have been overthrown, and, before I rise, I must be made to feel like Antaeus that strength comes from touching the ground.

But the chief of all my mistakes is this: that I impart them to others. Let me say, with the utmost fervor of protestation, that neither you, nor the children, nor the house, nor the servant, nor anything that is within our gates—not one alone—nor all combined—no, none of these persons or things *has the slightest originating share in my troubles.* Those troubles (such as they are) are of my own making. Would to God they were also of my own enduring! But they have to be inflicted upon others—upon yourself and the children. It is this fact that doubles my affliction.

But your kind and tender words, penciled in the studio [William Page's studio, where she was sitting for her portrait] this morning, were very precious to me—sweeter than honey in the honeycomb. I write this letter on purpose to thank you for them. God bless you evermore.

Lovingly yours,

Theodore

Chicago Tribune, p. 9, cols. 4–5; *TT v. HWB*, 1 : 500

TT to ET, Akron, O., Jan. 15, 1869
My Dear Wife:

Ever since last October I have been lecturing every week—sometimes every night, and the proceeds have all been swallowed up in my extravagant debts. If this spendthrift tendency of mine is ever to be curbed it must be by your helpful criticism of it—not by a parallel liberality of outlay by yourself. I am putting myself daily to as much fatigue as human nature can endure, in order, if possible, to clear off my obligations to my creditors, and to keep afterwards abreast with the world. Your letter, a few days ago, stating that you could not live on your salary, made me sick at heart, and temporarily I felt like giving up my journey and going home. Today you send me a bill of $58 for Cad's [Carroll's] clothes—an amount which I regard as so great for a family of our moderate resources as to be almost as wicked as my own outlays for pictures. In all the three weeks of my last absence I have not made, above expenses, $400. Not one penny of all my lecture earnings for years has ever yet gone into a bank. I look upon our money-spending tendencies as cruelly wrong. At this moment I am well-nigh broken down in voice, and know not how I shall get through with tonight's lecture. Am I wrong when I say that I cannot look with equanimity on squandering so much money in fine dresses for the children? My heart suffers a pang in saying this, but I cannot help saying it. We must either sell our establishment in Brooklyn or else manage it on a less expensive scale. I have made a vow to buy not another picture, and not another unnecessary article, during the present year. It is with something like a shudder that I look forward to the prolonged slavery of public lecturing every winter; and, if the proceeds are to be freely thrown away by both of us, I may as well stop it now. I have suffered for ten days past an agony of remorse at the fruitless exertions I have made by three years of speaking—fruitless because their harvest has been unprofitably spent. Judging by all the families I visit, *I know that we are literally throwing away our inheritance.* At last I am aroused; and I appeal to you to put a peremptory check upon any and every unnecessary expenditure which *you see me make.* Dress the children in calico for a year, and let me get out of my misery. Yours in dust and ashes,

Theodore Tilton

Chicago Tribune, p. 9, col. 5; *TT v. HWB,* 1: 502–3

TT to ET, Empire House, Akron, O., Jan. 15, 1869
My Dear Wife:

I am in a heartbreak—yes, I have been on my knees in this chamber, crying more bitterly than any child. Two years ago, in this same spot, I had a terrible wrestling with my soul. The moment I entered the room today, the old experience was revived. Since that occasion—which I can never lose out of my memory—I seem to have suffered much and profited little. My life looks very much like a waste—a blank—a plight. Of all the past, I thought today that I had saved nothing but Paul—and him too I have lost. The little key in my pocket seems not to bring him nearer, but to keep him farther away. All the afternoon I have been weeping, trembling, and agonizing. I am well-nigh sick with very grief. My eyes are red and full of pain. I have been saying, "Little Paul, come and help your father." My life seems utterly wretched and unworthy. I cannot bear to look in upon myself. I wrote to you about our failure to live within our means; but this shortcoming is nothing to what I feel in myself of moral truthlessness. It seems to me as if I were a spiritual castaway. I ought not to trouble you with these disclosures; but, if I do not utter them to you, they must go unuttered. Your own confessions seem to indicate that you are in a perpetual trouble. Ah! the morning of life is rosy, but the noon is sometimes leaden and gray.

I make a great many re-beginnings, but do not get along far before I lose the little that I have gained. Your ask for "glimpses in my heart." It is a dark place to look into. God help your sorrowful and groaning husband!

Yours affectionately,

Theodore

Chicago Tribune, p. 9, cols. 5 – 6

TT to ET, Friday, Midnight, Akron, O., Jan. 15, 1869
My Dear Wife:

I will add a few words more before going to bed—I mean, add them to the letter[s] which I have written to you today.

My whole frame seemed weak this evening on the platform. My eyes were very sore, and kept stinging round the edges. But I was in a very calm mood. My spirit was at rest. The great agony of this afternoon has lifted me to a higher level. For a few minutes I never suffered more in all my life than when my heart this afternoon went to pieces once again over Paul's key, and death, and presence in my room. I now feel perfectly tranquil. You are probably fast asleep at this hour. I can almost peep into your bedroom—I see the picture so vividly before me. I give you my blessing. Now, I wonder if it be worth anything? Not much. It is the prayer of the righteous, and not of the wicked, that avails with God.

Tell the children that I have been thinking of them very tenderly tonight.

Yours fondly,

Theodore

Chicago Tribune, p. 9, col. 6

Twelve letters from Elizabeth dated between January 22, 1869, and February 28, 1869, were excerpted in the *Tribune;* no letters from Theodore were printed for that period. But in hers of January 27, beginning "My Dear Beloved," she sends him her "grateful love for your tender words written at Ann Arbor," words that were "as healing balm to my aching heart" (*Chicago Tribune,* p. 2, col. 3).

ET to TT, Brooklyn, Thursday, Feb. 4, 1869

My Dearly Beloved Husband:

. . . My darling, I must believe that this beautiful home which you have made for us must have given you a greater amount of satisfaction than we generally secure from earthly labors. . . . I was glad to hear from you in the *Independent* this week. Oliver [Johnson] told me of Mr. Bowen's desire to publish *his* reply last week to the Methodist assailant. This led to the object of his visit to me, which was to inquire of me the origin of the story told him by a lady from Brooklyn, whose letter you saw before going west. I then told him at length—how that he knew himself how I felt years ago regarding him, for I had sought an interview along with him at the *Standard* office, and all that had passed there, I had told Mattie B[radshaw], but at present my feelings toward him had changed entirely, because my husband was no longer young, and that very few, indeed, I could not name *one* whom I thought possible to influence him for harm. Besides, I had learned to trust in the friendship of my husband. I realized how sincere his attachment was for you, and I believed in it. But I had felt a growing indifference for some time past between him, Oliver, and myself, and therefore I had been always more glad to welcome Mary Ann than himself to my house. We had a very frank, conscientious talk, ending by my telling him that I desired with all my soul to feel no ill thought or suspicion toward any human being, and I only wished to live to attain to this. I felt very much better in spirit after it, and think that *here* now we are again in sympathy.

The reception to Lucretia Mott has fallen through, because of that dear old lady's unwillingness to be lionized. . . . Mr. B[eecher] does not come as often as in the fall. His labors are heavy, and he too *feels* just like work, more than for several years past. . . .

Farewell, Your Darling,

Elizabeth, Wife

Chicago Tribune, p. 2, col. 3

ET to TT, Sunday, Feb. 7, 1869

My Beloved:

I have just finished reading to Emma Lowell's "Extreme Unction," and the chapter in "Norwood" of Parson Buell's grief in the death of his wife. It is very touching, and I realized for a moment what that agony must be, the parting at the river between a husband and wife who have truly loved—how inevitable it is! God only can sustain the one who remains, while He enables the one who departs to say, "I shall be satisfied!"

Allow me to say, without cant, that God has given me a blessing today. He has enabled me to do something for Him, and that conscious privilege overflows my heart utterly. At home he helped me to be patient, willing, yea, glad, to spend myself for others; and in the Bethel— my little room was crowded—the interest increases in my class. They all love me. I *feel* it, because I too love every one. I do indeed feel grateful for the encouragement they give me in these new labors. I tell you rather more at length than usual of my work here, because I earnestly wish your sympathy and to feel free to *talk with* you of everything in which I am interested, as in "Auld Lang Syne." Howe'er imperfect we may appear to each other, yet the dear Lord does not hesitate to use us. Now, tonight, I give myself to you—my *best*, my worst, "just as I am," take me once again into your confidence; bear with my follies as in early days. I consecrate myself to you so long as I shall live, before God this night as a fitting close of this Sabbath day. Forgive all my infirmities and help me to overcome to final victory. Wilt thou? So will I you, if you permit. The freedom with which you write of Paul gives me great pleasure. Then the fountains are unsealed and we flow together. I talk not so much of him—yet this new mysterious feeling *I know*, which I never before have uttered—a kind of awe, or waiting, listening to learn what he will do for me—and an agony of fear at times lest I should fail by reason of sin what he could bring. Already in many things I am a *changed woman* through his precious ministrations; yet, fearing such a statement may be too positive, let me modify it by a *woman changing.*

Your change of route upsets my reckoning, and I am not able to place you tonight, which I regret because, as I told you before, I have known not only what place you are each night, but also which letter of mine you will find there. After Friday I shall be all right again; meanwhile I hope you will enjoy to the utmost your recreation with dear friends.

I have no items of news today. I am trying to be a *cheerful, good* woman—that's good news.

Goodnight. If I might only write an easy, flowing, beautiful letter to my Beloved!

Elizabeth, Wife

P.S. Lizzie Wood sent her love to you today, which I forgot, and Frank Moulton called to say that he had spoken to the prisoners at the

Penitentiary and would write you about it. Mattie mailed you a letter for Danville.

All these things I forgot earlier in my letter.

Your Own

Chicago Tribune, p. 2, cols. 3–4; *TT v. HWB,* 1: 491–92

ET to TT, Wednesday Night, Feb. 10, 1869

My Dearly-Loved Husband:

I will take up my home-story from where I left off yesterday morning; mailing the financial letter to Des Moines. About an hour later Mr. B[eecher] came in, bringing the manuscript sheets of his first chapter in the "Life of Christ" to read to me. He had read them to no one else, and wanted to know how his opening chapter would sound. I liked it, and you will, I think. It is fresh and interesting. After he had finished reading, I ran upstairs and brought a little sketch of one of my Bethel lessons on "Mary, the Mother of Jesus," as an example of woman's faith, which I read to him. His visit was refreshing and comforting to me. . . .

But I am too tired to think or write more. How blessed to know that these bodies are not always to clog and hinder us. Accept and welcome my spirit of love, which is as fresh and ardent as ever, faithful, and ever devoted to you. Blessings on you, my dearly beloved.

Elizabeth, Wife

Chicago Tribune, p. 2, col. 4

ET to TT, Thursday, Feb. 11, 1869

My Darling:

. . . You will find a worn and weary woman thoroughly satisfied when once again she may rest in your bosom. I cannot sleep until I have returned thanks for the letter of good cheer reaching me today, written on the cars to Chicago. I had been waiting all the week for a word, and had fallen in spirits, but, as the hymn says, "What a change a word can make." I took my letter in the room and by the spot where the Heaven *[sic]* opened once for little Paul to enter, I knelt down and gave thanks for your life, for your love, and again (as in many, many times) *there* the heavens have opened and brought peace to my soul. If tears could atone for sin, my soul would be clean therefrom, for alone and often I cry unto God to "create in me a clean heart." . . . Joseph is with mother, having that long-expected settlement. Father [her stepfather Judge Nathaneal Morse] is firmly set upon a separation [from her mother]. I would be happier were she to seek an asylum for a season before that step be taken. Oh, my beloved, may you never suffer as I have over a mother turned to an enemy. . . . I rejoice in the spirit of your editorial; it has the good old ring in it. Now may not home influences dull the strain! Elizabeth, behold what you do, or undo! So I keep in mind. Goodnight, my sweet.

Yours always,

Wife Elizabeth

Chicago Tribune, p. 2, col. 4

ET to TT, Sunday Evening, Feb. 28, 1869
My Beloved:

"This is the last day of winter," little Carroll said as he got into bed tonight. "Papa will soon be here." "Yes," I replied, "spring will certainly come, and I hope in three Sundays more Papa will come as surely."

We had a delightful "sing" after tea—read in turns two chapters in the Bible, then followed our little prayer meeting. I felt it was good and acceptable. You were not forgotten, be assured. Blessings must follow the prayers of little children for their parents.

My Bethel meeting today was *good*. I am sure no one of the little band went away uncheered. How munificently God rewards the faintest, feeblest efforts we make for the good of others.

I will go back a little, and tell you yesterday's story, a day so full as to crowd out entirely my writing you. First of all, then, my heart overflowed toward you, because of your generous kind letter concerning mother. She was quite touched by it, and desired me to give you her thanks for your sympathy, **saying again as she has often said before, "Because I made an idol of *you*, Elizabeth, is why Theodore has made me so wretched. I have felt he did not appreciate you, and often neglected you, but I want to forgive all the agony he has caused me."**

This was the first time your name has been mentioned since her stay with me. Forgive the indelicacy of quoting her remark; it seemed to me a concession on her part toward you; the least sign I must welcome as a promise of the fulfillment of my life-long prayers—my married life, I mean. . . .

My head and heart have been so full of divorce cases since you left—this difficulty of mother's [her separation from her husband] following on the heels of Mrs. M——k has been a kind of experience of which I have had quite enough. Were I a lawyer I would certainly change my profession or beg, rather than investigate such miseries. . . .

Now, my sweet, after so long a tale let me for our mutual refreshment turn to our own sweet love. I bless God that it abideth! Among the terrible changes of many hearths [the trial version has "hearts"], God has kept us steadfast, with a growing love, admiration and respect for each other. Oh, let us praise His name forever! All the differences, misunderstandings, we have had are as Whittier says "like mountain ranges overpast."

"If God be for us, who can be against us?"

Give me your patience while I spread out before you the fruitage of your beautiful love, like the rare-cut flowers of a bouquet. They are the closing words of your letters—select and precious, reminding me of the soul-stirring benedictions of the Apostles' epistles.

Fruit No. 1—"But among all my losses, I have lost no jot or tittle of my ever-increasing love for the sweetest of wives, and the fairest of children." "My heart longs for you today."

"Grace, mercy and peace. Ever thine."

"You and the chicks, and the house, and all, are in my thoughts every day and hour."

"Good bye, and all hail! Ever yours."

"*With overflowing love* I am now and ever, yours devotedly."

"I send you now, as ever, the fervid love of yours devotedly."

"I think you and I are yet to walk in Paradise together."

"I would rather have my wife and children at this moment than all the honors under the sun."

"Every day of my life I love you more and more, and shall unto the end."

"With my whole soul I am yours faithfully."

"If now I had a little personal comforting and petting from the little lady at No. 136, I would be perfectly satisfied." ["136" may have been an earlier number for the house at 174 Livingston Street.]

"But Paul and I keep our companionship. To you, his mother, be God's peace."

"I love you fervently and entirely. Blessings with you always."

Then, fearing that these extreme delights "would make a woman mad outright," you have six epistles ending: "Yours in dust and ashes."

"Yours doggedly." "God help your sorrowful and groaning husband."
"Yours achingly," &c.

How like you the receiving a letter from yourself? I keep a list of
these delicious tit-bits. Most tenderly believe it. Thou knowest that I
love thee.

Good night.

Wife Elizabeth

**P.S. A little home news. Went with Mattie to the organ con-
cert. I send the inclosed programme. . . . Do you remember
when you returned last year Mr. Mitchell brought little Paul
down in the parlor to see you, and the smile of welcome he
gave? I wish so it might be that the dear little expected might
be brought to you in like manner. You would then avoid my
suffering, and all would then be happiness. Flory says: "Oh,
Mamma, if you were not obliged to suffer and be sick, how
happy we all should be."**

**I have a great unwillingness that those who love me should
suffer for me.**

Once more, goodnight.

Your Dear Wife

Chicago Tribune, p. 2, col. 4; *TT v. HWB*, 1 : 492–93

TT to ET, Saturday Night, Brooklyn, Aug. 28, 1869
My Dear Wife:

**I find myself alone, but hardly lonesome, wearier but not
sleepy, restless but not without peace of soul tonight; and so
I turn my thought to you and the children in your mountain
nest** [at Dr. McCabe's in Monticello, New York, where she had gone
to recuperate and gain weight after the birth of Ralph in June].

**My letters of late have been so hurried and barren that I
have sometimes wished I had not sent such and such a one.
I know your sensitiveness to my words, and I have been
chiding myself for allowing you to see by pen and ink that
I have been greatly driven day and night, for two or three
weeks past, to the apparent neglect of you and your cares.
But tonight, although my table lies covered with unfinished
work, I end it with abruptness for the sake of expressing
to you some thoughts which have lately been occupying my
mind, or rather some feelings which have been stirring my
heart, in reference to our married life.**

I will confess frankly that I have passed the most wretched summer of my life, and no one knows it but myself; indeed, no one who has been with me has seen me other than outwardly gay and cheerful. All the exhibitions which I have made of myself to my friends have been of unusual hilarity. This has been the utmost shallowness of superficiality. *One* thing I *have* enjoyed; that is, my work. It has been unusually heavy, and therefore unusually beneficent. But, leaving my work aside, all my other pleasures have been pains. For two or three weeks I resolutely repressed all allusions to my feelings, when writing to you, not wishing to mar your vacation. But, as the time of your home-coming cannot be very far off, I open the flood-gates tonight. I will, therefore, say that I have missed you for the past month with something of the same awfulness and heartbreak as if I had lost you forever by death. **The idea has haunted me that perhaps I should never see you again, and this has prostrated my spirit to an agonizing humility, and led me into ten thousand self-reproaches for the past. Of course I do not lay any stress on any superstition. I expect to see you again, and hope to do so as soon as you think advisable for the children to return.** But I have discovered, by searching the depths of my soul, *that I love you more than any human ought to love another.* I have seen some noble women this summer, whom I admire, and whom, in a certain way, I love. All my life I have known something of the nature and experience of true friendship.

From my early years I have loved, and loved *you*. But all the past experiences of my heart's affections have been as nothing compared with the unusual and solemn sense which I have had, during all the hilarities of this Newport [Rhode Island] week, that the only human being who touches my highest nature is yourself. This being the case, I am filled with distress to think that I must keep you uninformed, for the sake of your own tranquility, of many of my thoughts, **and of some of my conduct.**

I would to God I were a man worthy of your goodness, your self-denial, and your singleness of heart. Occasionally, in some supreme hour, I am your fit mate; but, at all other hours, you are high above me. But, if you could know the inward reverence which I have borne toward you for many days past, even while appearing to be absorbed in the companionship of other ladies, and particularly at Newport, I am sure you would almost dread to be so much loved by any human (and therefore infirm and wayward) creature like myself.

I have several times tried to keep myself from writing you any such letter as this, because it is unlike most of my past correspondence. It is my request that no other eye shall ever see it except your own. Indeed, after this letter is in the mail, I shall probably grieve to think I wrote it. But, on the other hand, I shall never feel content until I have in some measure confessed to you that all summer long, I have trembled at the thought that you are almost as much to me as God Himself, and yet that I am constantly treating *you* as ungratefully as I treat *Him*.

One thing more, but I do not urge it, or even request it. I only state it. If you could come here and stay with me two or three days in this house, with no other person to intrude upon our communion, I would bless you for it as long as I live. I want to show you my heart, and its too great load.

Yours in frankness,

Theodore

Chicago Tribune, p. 9, col. 6; *TT v. HWB*, 1 : 504

"THE MINISTER'S VIGIL."

THE REV. ARTHUR DIMMESDALE, THE SEDUCER OF HESTER PRYNNE, HEROINE OF HAWTHORNE'S STORY OF "THE SCARLET LETTER," STANDING AT MIDNIGHT ON THE PUBLIC SCAFFOLD OF BOSTON, IN VAIN EXPIATION OF HIS CRIME.—DRAWN BY J. N. HYDE.—SEE EDITORIAL PAGE.

NINE *Legends, Histories,*
1999–1872

I.   "Future history will attach as little emphasis to this episode in the life of Mr. Beecher as history now attaches to analogous imputations, with far more to give them color, brought against John Wesley in his lifetime." So wrote Beecher biographer Lyman Abbott in 1903 of the Beecher-Tilton Scandal, well remembered by all of his readers over the age of 50. Many must have smiled at his Pollyannish prediction. The scandal had been a momentous event in their own lives, and they knew it would endure as a pivotal chapter of Beecher's story. What they could not have imagined was that the charge of adultery against the Plymouth pastor would evolve from a much-disputed allegation in the late nineteenth century to a settled fact in the twentieth. A *New York Times* op-ed writer in 1997 voiced the long-standing consensus: at his trial Beecher was "found not guilty of an adultery he had in fact clearly committed." The writer's error on Beecher's legal fate—he was not judged "not guilty," for the jury could not reach a decision—reveals the firmness of the retrospective verdict. Twentieth-century observers know he was guilty even though his contemporaries were not sure. "They" were tricked by Beecher's glossy showmanship; "we" are worldly-wise and see through his cover-up. Americans have not lost their appetite for tales of corrupt Victorian playacting, and Beecher is still one of the leading suppliers.[1]

For the last three-quarters of a century he has starred in accounts of the Gilded Age as sentimental fool, long-winded buffoon, hypocritical stuffed shirt—and the scandal has been the moment of his richly deserved unveiling, one of the pivotal scenes in the modern era's own sentimental fiction of deliverance from the unserious, feminized culture of Victorianism. From Paxton Hibben's muckraking biography of

Beecher in the 1920s to Ann Douglas's skewering of Protestant senti-mentalism in the 1970s to Barbara Goldsmith's aggressive redemption of Victoria Woodhull (and savaging of Beecher) in the 1990s, he has been pronounced guilty not only of seducing Elizabeth Tilton, but of embodying a culture whose ultimate sin was to have hid its sordid truths behind a decorous facade. Woodhull set the standard for expo-sure in 1872, and shows us that the assault on Victorian pieties was launched by the Victorians themselves. She was compelled, she said, to "ventilate" what she knew. If she did not, she would be "conniving at a putrid mass of seething falsehood and hypocrisy." It was her "duty" and "mission" to "destroy the heap of rottenness which, in the name of religion, marital sanctity, and social purity, now passes as the social system." Woodhull did not get the acclaim she felt she deserved as "prophetess," "evangel," and "Saviour," but her "bomb-shell" laid the groundwork for the polemical "exposés" to come.[2]

Beecher's and the Tiltons' strenuous efforts to shield their private relations from the public eye drew the outright scorn of many early-twentieth-century writers, for whom it was a telling instance of the ne-farious Victorian culture of concealment. Rheta Dorr's 1928 biography of Susan B. Anthony was typically disgusted in describing the Beecher-Tilton campaign to keep their problems private. "For nearly four years," she wrote, "the nauseating [secret] had rotted and crawled be-neath the surface of the hymn-singing, tear-shedding, sermon-shouting smug religiosity which gave Brooklyn its proud title of the City of Churches." Attacking the ideas and behavior of Beecher and his Plym-outh Church followers has been one favored means of stripping the velvet curtain from the Gilded Age bourgeoisie and erecting an alter-native, "modern" culture of tough-minded realism, a culture suppos-edly free from illusions about human nature and society.[3]

Woodhull's early version of this cult of exposure was marred, in the opinion of twentieth-century writers, by the superstitious, premodern accretion of her spiritualism. They chuckled at Woodhull for consort-ing with spirits while they blasted Beecher for hiding his sins. Woodhull seriously thought the entire Beecher-Tilton "embroglio" was governed by "the higher powers" of the "spirit world," which "has always exerted a great and diversified influence over this [world], while it is not till quite recently that the spiritual development of this world has made it possible for the other to maintain real and continuous relations with it." Woodhull's first public recitation of "the whole history of the Bee-cher and Tilton Scandal," at a national convention of spiritualists in

September 1872 was not an intentional act: it took place only because she was "taken out of myself . . . by some power stronger than I."[4]

In the 1870s it may have required someone prone to "overwhelming gusts of inspiration," to speaking not in her own voice but in that of spirits over whom she had no control, to utter the kind of beyond-the-pale denunciations of bourgeois love and marriage in which Woodhull engaged. In the 1850s "free love" had been seriously examined by respectable idealists such as Henry James, Sr. But even before the outbreak of the Civil War, the sectional crisis was shoving such merely cultural issues off the intellectuals' agenda, and the war itself put an end to organized experimentation with middle-class family norms, even if holdovers like Mormon polygamy or Oneida "complex marriage" survived briefly into the postwar era. Those norms solidified further in response to Woodhull's "mission" and to the scandal she unleashed. Free love was now a useful epithet for assailing one's foes, not an idea in which there might be merit as well as menace. In this climate Woodhull's national career depended upon her spiritualism: the spirit world was the only place for so radical a woman to root her social critique, and to find comfort and support when she was reviled and blackballed. Twentieth-century writers would dispense with the otherworldly baggage not because they were sharper critics than Woodhull—in the 1870s her insights were often probing and her polemical talents were stunning—but because the aid of spiritual string-pullers was no longer needed. But to Woodhull goes the prize for inaugurating the attack on Beecher as the "representative" "moral coward" of an "effete" Victorianism—an attack the next generation of critics methodically streamlined.[5]

The novel departure in Barbara Goldsmith's recent retrieval of Woodhull is her effort to salvage Woodhull's spiritualism from the condescending dismissal of earlier twentieth-century observers while keeping up their fusillade against Beecher. Her sympathy for Woodhull's perspective—indeed, her actual belief in Woodhull's real powers as a "magnetic" healer, including precognition and psychokinesis—permitted a real advance in understanding late-nineteenth-century culture. Spiritualism, Goldsmith showed, did not have to be taken as merely ridiculous, as one more Victorian evasion of reality. But that step forward was matched by a step backward. In order to ground her attack on Beecher (and on Theodore Tilton after 1872, when he began lambasting Victoria), she arbitrarily assumed the literal truth of many of Woodhull's claims. Yet her own careful attention to Victoria's intercourse with spirits had already showed that Woodhull was often not speaking even her own thoughts, much less the literal truth.[6]

Goldsmith's sympathetic approach to Victoria Woodhull can and should be extended to the rest of Woodhull's contemporaries, including Beecher and the Tiltons. Sympathy need not mean exculpation or whitewashing. It need only mean letting them all live and breathe in their historical moment, and respecting our restricted access to their thoughts and acts—access limited by the quirky character of the available documents, which usually give us stories about facts, not facts themselves. Sympathy for past people's struggles *can* be "critical" in the sense of judgmental—we may, for example, want to judge Beecher and Woodhull harshly for their treatment of Elizabeth Tilton—but historical sympathy *must* be "critical" in the sense of methodologically skeptical. Historical documents of the sort produced by Beecher and the Tiltons and Woodhull do not often deliver hard nuggets of information. They offer a web of contradictory stories. But those stories, with all their contradictions, are very instructive about Victorian culture. Historians now have a golden chance to let the Victorians enter the deep past, where they can be apprehended as alien to us—still "useful," but useful in disclosing other ways of being human, not in legitimizing our own.

Historians are prone to thinking that in America the late nineteenth century was in its cultural essentials (scientific, technological, and industrial progress, moneygrubbing and other forms of this-worldly satisfaction) more or less like the twentieth. Even if this picture is correct in the main, we must attend all the more diligently to the differences of outlook and habit that separate us from those born, like Beecher and the Tiltons, 160 or 180 years ago. We must restrain ourselves from plundering nineteenth-century documents for those forms or expressions or meanings that seem most familiar and take the documents instead as clues to a world beyond memory and resistant to easy reckoning.

In the case of Beecher and the Tiltons, there are abundant truths about Victorian culture to be learned from them once we give up the quest to vindicate "our" probing exposure over "their" secretive circumlocution. They speak a language strangely different from our own, and from some of their contemporaries. Both the spoken and written word meant something different to them than they do to us. They sat for hours listening to earnest oratory. They produced immeasurable quantities of verbiage. The amount of printed material devoted to the Beecher-Tilton Scandal is stupefying—proof that the scandal was a sensation, and evidence that many Victorians, in the working class as well as the bourgeoisie, were indefatigable readers. In addition, the

novels, poems, letters, memos, interviews, and official testimony produced by Beecher and the Tiltons—not to mention the vast literature
authored by their friends, enemies, lawyers, witnesses, and other observers—were often embedded in now archaic discourses of power and
persuasion, truth-telling and truth-shielding. To Victoria Woodhull,
Beecher's and the Tiltons' intricate game of "character" defense—in-
volving secrecy, gift-bearing (Tilton's thirty-page "biography" of Woodhull), and elaborate threats—was already anachronistic. She refused to
play. And so, sometimes, did Theodore.

Not only was there more than one Victorian language, as scientific or empirical modes of thought emerged to challenge and entwine
themselves with religious or sentimental ones. There was more than
one Victorian language in the Beecher-Tilton trio, and in each of the
members of it. Henry, Elizabeth, and Theodore were all speaking
multiple tongues. Theodore's heroic poetry, filled with archaic classical motifs, ran head-on into the hyperrationalistic schematizing and
"fact" gathering that marked his public statements on the alleged adultery. Elizabeth's letters reveal a conflict of their own: between the cultural boundedness of the language available to her and her culture-
transcending aspiration for a mystical encounter with the divine. Her
solution was to stress the limitations of "writing" or "thinking" in comparison to "listening" or "feeling," and to situate the divine encounter,
incarnationally, in everyday acts of attentiveness to her children,
friends, servants, the working-class women in her Bethel group, and the
characters in her favorite novels—above all, Catherine Gaunt. Henry's
whole career can be seen as an embroidering of languages by an undoubted master of English oratorical expression and a diversified crafts-
man of the written word. His pulpit and lecture performances astonished even antagonistic listeners because they swung so rapidly and
evocatively from one form of speech and thought, one posture of personality and impersonality, to another. He was poet, theologian, and
sociologist; teacher, actor, and exhorter; above all he was a preacher
of Christian doctrine who embodied sentimentalism by becoming, on
stage, a personal confidant, intimate and emotional in revealing his apparently innermost feelings. That ritual performance of intimacy may
well have spurred him to seek a more authentic experience of soul-pure
transparency in his private encounters with Elizabeth Tilton.

These Brooklyn Victorians can seem immediately recognizable.
But just when we get lulled into believing they were rather like us, except for their bizarre prudery and quaint turns of phrase, we are liable
to receive a shock. We discover, for example, that they were wont to

engage in delicate negotiations about honor, reputation, and publicity, in which they would write, sign, and hand over to friends, enemies, or third parties intricate memos attesting to complicated facts, intentions, and states of mind; that they regularly expressed emotions we have tended to suppress, such as remorse, shame, or guilt; that respected men could still drape themselves in one another's arms and speak sentimentally of their eternal love for one another, often on that account bursting into tears in public; that it was still at least borderline-acceptable to believe that departed spirits could communicate with the living through (usually female) mediums; that blasphemy, like slander, still carried profound cultural weight even if they were no longer to die for; and that the idea of "scandal" itself conveyed not only the secular meanings it has retained ("a grossly discreditable circumstance," "offence to moral feeling"), but the original religious meaning dating from the thirteenth century: "discredit to religion occasioned by the conduct of a religious person," "perplexity of conscience occasioned by the conduct of one who is looked up to as an example." [7]

We will never know whether Elizabeth Tilton and Henry Ward Beecher slept together. What we do know gives us plenty to think about. Beecher and the Tiltons did far-reaching cultural work in their three-way campaign to cultivate new forms of intimacy while remaining faithful to their moral and religious inheritance—an inheritance that evolved dramatically because people like them stretched it nearly beyond recognition and became, in part intentionally and in part against their wills, potent public symbols of the transformation. They promoted a new world in which, to put it schematically, the private infiltrated and colonized the public, and the personal tended to displace the impersonal.

At the simplest level, this meant that public discourse—as many commentators noted at the time of the trial in 1875—became increasingly dominated by sensational disclosures or inventions about private life. At a deeper level, it meant that a Romantic craving for intense feeling tended to squeeze out the old republican search for sober, self-denying citizenship. Finding and experiencing intimacy tended to become the preeminent virtue in life, not cultivating a calling or undertaking civil service. Perhaps the very anachronism of these ideals in a market-driven world helped propel private life to the forefront of public debate. In an era of mass-circulation newspapers, revelations about private goings-on could substitute for earlier forms of civil discussion. Or perhaps the lingering authority of the older values paradoxically promoted the new exposure. All the succulent revelations of private misdemeanors could be justified as a vital form of housecleaning, as a reconsecration of the public domain to the cause of selfless endeavor.

Beecher's religion was such a powerful instrument of the privatization of the public because he joined his Romantic quest for fulfillment through intimacy to the already traditional and very mainstream ritual practice of communal revivalism: dynamic emotion and intense feeling elevated over adherence to formal doctrine or impersonal norms. When traditionalists branded Beecher, the Tiltons, Woodhull, and many of their friends and associates as "free lovers," they had a point: Beecher and the others wanted to free all human experience, including love, from the hidebound conventions of the past. Woodhull had a point too: Beecher was a cultural radical in religious shepherd's garb. But she missed Beecher's dialectic. He believed that his campaign to broaden gendered identities—in the case of men, to get them to cultivate the breadth of sensibility that women, in his view, more frequently achieved and modeled—was the best way to preserve a stable world of leadership by publicly spirited citizens. His gender-bending revivalism was, as he called it, "spiritual engineering," designed to shore up the solid bourgeois regime of property and propriety. Beecher was as worried about social fragmentation as William Evarts. But he thought the best defense against the dissolution of bourgeois "character" was a broad-based infusion of "personality" into the "vast multitudes." And personal growth for the "great mass" meant the liberation of spiritual energies hitherto restrained.[8]

Most male leaders of the day were not pleased with Beecher's program. Part of the cultural importance of the adultery trial was that while it formally let Beecher off the hook, it actually disciplined him, the Tiltons, and Woodhull for untethering identity from conventionally gendered fixtures. It also took them to task for encouraging multiple cross-gendered friendship-loves among adults already married. Hitting Beecher for getting too close to Mrs. Tilton was a way of striking at a wider cultural erosion that traditionalists believed was undermining public spirit by weakening stable families. William Evarts, put on the defense team for a fierce dissecting of Theodore Tilton, actually chastised his own client along with Theodore and Theodore's erstwhile pal Victoria.

Evarts did the job subtly and with flair. Plaintiff's attorney William Fullerton matched him in reasoning skill, as he showed in his literary-forensic reading of *Norwood*. But Evarts was an American Victorian orator with few peers in his mastery of a classical rhetorical argumentation that destroyed entire ramparts in waves of satirical fulmination building in patient crescendo. In his trial summation he let Beecher have it in a masterpiece of indirection. He put the story of *Griffith Gaunt* into the record to show that the "sin" to which Elizabeth confessed was not adultery, but the one to which Catherine Gaunt had admitted: too much affection for her spiritual shepherd, an emotional bond that upset relations with her husband. Elizabeth and Henry were mirrors of Catherine Gaunt and Brother Leonard: no sex, just "confusion of affections," a "division and disturbance of allegiance" between her and her husband. But that was plenty bad enough. Like Leonard—a "man of genius, and of fire and of rapt devotion"—Beecher had joined a woman in the "mischief" of interfering in "things secular" between her and her husband. Beecher's innocence on the adultery charge did not exculpate him for tampering with the marital bond, in Evarts's view the sine qua non of social tranquility.[9]

We need to see Evarts and the other lawyers on both sides as literal "*public* defenders" who tried, through ridicule as much as argument, to excise what they considered a cancer on the body politic: the elevation by Beecher, the Tiltons, and the others, of the personal and the unstable over the impersonal and stable. Private life for the traditionalists needed elaborate safeguards, especially the fixed proprieties of the family relation. For the plaintiff's attorneys Beecher was the primary threat; for the defense it was Theodore Tilton and Victoria Woodhull. Protected by well-cemented institutions, personal life, even a life of temperate feeling and appropriate passion, could blossom; without such protection by the impersonal agency of public authority and communal tradition, personal life would careen and spin out of control. Beecher's practice was as destabilizing as that of the more outlandish Woodhull, who yelled her scorn for established conventions from rooftops. Evarts did try to mock the paranoid few who thought virtuous pastors like Beecher might slip into their homes in broad daylight and debauch their wives. If that were true, said Evarts, "we shall have to have a Wife Deposit Company, where we can leave our wives during the day, and . . . some patent contrivance of paramour-proof alarms by which we can be called to the rescue." But his analysis of *Griffith Gaunt* showed there was already good reason to fear for the future of marriage and the family when even the most virtuous, armed with their poetic and Romantic religion of intimacy, were out and about breathing "fire and rapt devotion."[10]

Evarts and his fellows lawyers in 1875 were already reworking the tradition of interpretation of the scandal that began with Victoria

Woodhull's 1872 allegations: Beecher was a "poltroon, a coward, and a sneak," she had said, for practicing free love but not preaching it. One of her main points was quite correct. Beecher and the Tiltons were doing something—experimenting with inherited codes—that they did not wish to speak about publicly. Woodhull found such inconsistency unconscionable. For the immediate future, according to her, the path of virtue lay in completely erasing the line between public and private. In the good society to come, by contrast, there would be perfect privacy and no exposure. "The true sense of honor in the future will be, *not to know even* what relations our lovers have with any and all other persons than ourselves—as true courtesy never seeks to spy over or to pry into other people's private affairs." For Beecher, for Elizabeth Tilton, and even for the far more perfectionist Theodore Tilton, talk of future utopia was chimerical. Virtue depended upon the messy, daily patrolling of the boundary between public and private: injecting private issues into public discourse, but concealing many private imbroglios—tensions, compromises, contradictions—from public view. In their eyes Woodhull's appeal for a pure correspondence between private behavior and public expression was a prescription for cruelty—cruelty above all to Elizabeth Tilton and her children.[11]

Evarts's defense of Beecher against Woodhull's and Tilton's adultery charge was "successful" in 1875—the jury did not convict—but judging by the current consensus on Beecher's guilt, Woodhull and Tilton have had the last laugh. Woodhull may be laughing louder than Tilton, because the charges against Beecher have recently been extended beyond adultery: Henry, we have now been informed, was the father of a "love babe" that Elizabeth lost either to miscarriage or to an abortion urged upon her by Theodore. William Evarts may have believed what he telegrammed to Beecher in July 1875 after the jury announced it was deadlocked: "regard the result as a complete triumph of truth. A few days will show the dissent is but the emphasis of the real verdict. . . . my hearty congratulations to you." But his exquisitely Ciceronian trial summation did not arrest the Woodhullian quest to expose the "heap of rottenness" at Plymouth Church. That quest gathers steam in our own day.[12]

II. The respected authors Millicent Bell and Francine du Plessix Gray, writing in 1998 in the *New York Review of Books* and the *New Yorker*, respectively, reported that Henry got Elizabeth pregnant. In the 1870s not even Victoria Woodhull or Frank Moulton, both of whom publicly broached that idea, dared assert in print that Mrs. Tilton had conceived a child by Beecher. Nor did Paxton Hibben, the irately anti-Beecher biographer of the 1920s. How could authors so accomplished as Bell and Gray have made such a statement themselves? They made it because the book they were reviewing featured it, and perhaps because, given the conventional wisdom on Beecher, they found no reason to doubt it.

It is worth examining this story about Beecher impregnating Mrs. Tilton, and about the possible abortion, since it illuminates the ongoing process of mythmaking about the scandal that began with Woodhull's scattershot allegations in 1872. One author after another draws on and extends the already inventive work of earlier writers, adding to Beecher's reputation as, in Gray's words, a "corrupt," "skillfully devious," "consummate showman," "with his unctuous smile, his tousled matinée-idol hair." In a regress of unreliability, writers use earlier books on the scandal as if they were original sources. Factual errors and dubious interpretations pile up helter-skelter as they are passed on. It is probably too late to put balance back into Beecher's reputation, already well shredded by Hibben's colorful diatribe a half-century ago. It may even be too late to save Elizabeth Tilton from having carried (and miscarried) his baby. Perhaps it is not too late to save her and her husband from the latest rumor-about-to-be-fact: that she didn't miscarry but aborted Beecher's baby on Theodore's malicious instructions. But for the record: the allegations about Beecher fathering her child, about Theodore urging an abortion, and about Elizabeth having one are, as Beecher and Tilton said of one another's trial testimony, pure fiction. It is true that the stories are pure fiction based on gossip that was already circulating in their own day. But century-and-a-quarter-old gossip is no closer to the truth than yesterday's gossip.[13]

Bell and Gray were each reviewing Barbara Goldsmith's *Other Powers*, which besides resurrecting Victoria Woodhull offered a detailed and freewheeling account of the Beecher-Tilton Scandal—an account perhaps unintentionally modeled, in its sheer inventiveness, on Woodhull's own 1872 accusation. The reviews show how facts get distorted as they are reported. Just as Goldsmith went beyond all earlier interpreters, from Woodhull on, in asserting that Henry got Elizabeth pregnant, Bell and Gray went beyond Goldsmith in stating that Elizabeth confessed this to Theodore. In Gray's words, "Lib soon became pregnant by her pastor and, racked by guilt when her husband came home, she told him everything." In Bell's words, "in July, 1870, Lib admitted to Tilton that she had conceived a 'love babe' while he had been away on a speaking tour." In fact Goldsmith wrote that when Elizabeth spoke to him in July

1870 (after she, not Theodore, came home), she "did not mention . . . that she was pregnant again," since "her husband would realize that this time the child could not be his." Nor did Mrs. Tilton make any such admission in October, when according to Goldsmith her husband confronted her with his belief that the father was Beecher. Goldsmith writes that at that point Mrs. Tilton "trembled but did not reply"—a scene of silent shaking for which Goldsmith supplied no evidence.[14]

As far as we know Elizabeth never told anyone she was pregnant by Beecher, and never nodded her head in silent assent when anyone else said so. Is there any reason, then, to believe that Henry got her pregnant? Or to believe that Elizabeth was even pregnant at all in July 1870? Neither item comes from anything Elizabeth ever said or wrote. Goldsmith claimed the information was to be found somewhere in Theodore's 1874 statements and 1875 testimony, but he never said either of those things in any of his statements or testimony. Goldsmith's revelations appear to have been based on one very rickety source, Woodhull's bombshell, which includes a report of what reformers Paulina Wright Davis and Elizabeth Cady Stanton allegedly told her they had heard, respectively, from Elizabeth and Theodore. But the course of verbal transmission from Elizabeth and Theodore to Davis and Stanton and then on to Woodhull was crooked indeed.

We know how crooked it was because of something Woodhull said about the alleged adultery between Henry and Elizabeth—something Goldsmith did not pass along to her readers. Goldsmith took as actual speech by Theodore the words Woodhull attributed to him, words that came from Woodhull's recasting of Stanton's retelling of Tilton's original comments. But Goldsmith left out a critical phrase. Here is her version of Theodore's remark about the adultery itself: "Oh, that the damned lecherous scoundrel should have defiled my bed and at the same time professed to be my best friend." Here is Woodhull's version of the same sentence: " 'Oh!' said he, 'that that damned lecherous scoundrel should have defiled my bed for ten years, and at the same time have professed to be my best friend!' "

To leave out the pivotal words "for ten years" not only changes the meaning of the sentence, it changes the legitimacy of the sentence. The phrase "for ten years" proves that either Tilton or Stanton or Woodhull was grandly exaggerating or making the story up. We know this because in his 1874 statements and his 1875 testimony he accused Beecher of sleeping with his wife over a fifteen- or sixteen-month period. But if Woodhull's account is so glaringly wrong about Theodore's sense of the duration of the adultery, it may also be wrong about his thinking

Elizabeth was pregnant by Beecher, and wrong about Elizabeth even being pregnant in July 1870. Woodhull's bombshell cannot be used as a reliable source of information about what really happened or what was really said by anyone. It was a marvelously written polemical document, not a catalogue of facts. She did exactly what Beecher and Tilton did in parts of their trial testimony: she put stories she had heard or imagined into quotation marks and attributed them to people.[15]

The story about Beecher fathering the baby comes from the following words that Woodhull put in Theodore's mouth: "I felt sure that the child would not be my child." Theodore probably did intend at some moments to accuse Henry of impregnating Mrs. Tilton. Elizabeth Tilton, in her 1874 statement to the Church Committee, claimed that Theodore often ranted about her sleeping not only with Beecher but "with one and another," so that "when he sat at his table, many times, he had said that he did not know whom his children belonged to." If Elizabeth is to be believed, Theodore got into frenzied moods in which he moaned about a variety of men getting her pregnant. Even if we concede to Woodhull (and Goldsmith) that he was thinking of Beecher when he said "the child would not be my child," we have to give at least as much credence to Mrs. Tilton's testimony as we do to Woodhull's. Theodore's statement to Stanton, reported by her to Woodhull, may have been one of those frantic exaggerations that his wife said were common. In any event, Woodhull herself, on the evidence of a reported conversation, concluded only that Theodore considered it a "great probability" that Elizabeth "was enceinte by Mr. Beecher instead of himself."[16]

As it happens, Beecher cannot have been the father of the "love babe" that Elizabeth lost to miscarriage on December 24, 1870. At least he cannot have been the father if we are to believe Theodore Tilton—and Goldsmith joins Woodhull in advising us to rely ultimately upon his word. Theodore claimed in 1874 and 1875 that the adultery began on October 10, 1868, and lasted fifteen or sixteen months. That takes the allegedly sexual relationship up to February 10, 1870, at the latest. No fetus lost on December 24, 1870, can have been conceived before February 10. In fact there is no reason to believe Elizabeth was even pregnant at all on July 3, when according to Theodore she confessed her sin to him, and when according to Goldsmith she concealed her pregnancy from him.[17]

If there is no reason to believe that Elizabeth confessed to being pregnant by Beecher, no reason to believe Beecher ever got her pregnant, and no reason to believe that Elizabeth was pregnant by anyone in July, 1870, is there any reason to believe that Elizabeth aborted the "love babe" (her 1871 term for the child lost to miscarriage in December 1870), or that Theodore (in Goldsmith's words) "wanted her to abort Beecher's baby"? Goldsmith cited an undated "later account" in the *New York Sun,* alleging that Beecher had provided the funds and that Elizabeth was seen, with her mother and Bessie Turner, arriving and departing from the abortionist Madame Restell's Fifth Avenue office. There is nothing in the *Sun* piece, as reported by Goldsmith, that refers to Theodore urging an abortion on her. And even if we grant that the threesome seen on the sidewalk was correctly identified and was on the way to an abortion—and a knowledge of Elizabeth Tilton's religious beliefs makes us skeptical in the extreme—nothing in Goldsmith's account of the story gives us the least reason to think Mrs. Tilton was Mme. Restell's client. It could equally well have been Bessie Turner.[18]

Goldsmith's fictionalized storytelling, and Gray's and Bell's endorsement of it, suggest that in one respect we have not traveled very far from the 1870s, when Woodhull, the Tiltons, the Beechers, and many others exchanged their accusations of adultery, free love, prostitution, insanity, graft, skullduggery, blackmail, and (with good reason) slander. Woodhull's well-known capacity for truth-decorating was certainly matched by Beecher's and the Tiltons', but the avid fictionalizing of the entire group forces us to take many of their assertions as self-interested fables. Their storytelling is fascinating in its own right as evidence of an intense Victorian preoccupation with a person's position on the ladder of reputation. Goldsmith provides an amply embellished instance of this cultural fixation when she relates a story about Beecher's half sister Isabella Hooker. "Belle" had threatened to go on record in support of the adultery charge. Whereupon, according to Goldsmith, Tilton went to see her and said he would accuse *her* of adultery with a Washington senator. That threat, along with what Goldsmith calls the possible "insurance" of rumormongering about Belle being insane, silenced her.[19]

In a world that so tightly tied success to moral reputability, allegations of this sort often worked: they established a web of interlocking promises not to squeal. When the web was shattered, as in the Beecher-Tilton Scandal, the fireworks were a mass entertainment and a mass trauma. Middle-class Americans huddled by the hearth for solace: the rules of the game had failed to protect the players. In response, Beecher, the Tiltons, Woodhull, and many others, individually or in combination, singled each other out, and were singled out by the press, for severe flagellation. Everyone called somebody else a free lover. Elizabeth let on that there was a stream of insanity in Theodore's family, and

THE INSANITY QUESTION.
From the Cincinnati Commercial.
It is a circumstance curious enough to note that the Brooklyn *Eagle* undertook to prove Mr. Tilton's insanity because his brother died in a madhouse. It now labors to prove that Miss Isabella Hooker, who believes, or did at one time believe, in her brother's guilt, is also insane; but it does not draw the same inference as to the sanity of Mr. Beecher which it does in the other case, though the degree of consanguinity to the person it pronounces insane is the same in each instance. The *Eagle*, in its efforts to fix insanity upon Tilton and Mrs. Hooker, reverses its logic. Tilton is insane because his brother was, but Henry Ward is not the least tainted with lunacy, though his sister is. The *Eagle* should moderate its zeal in manufacturing candidates for the madhouse, lest the public come to suspect that its editor is not in the enjoyment of a sound mind in a sound body.

Isabella Beecher Hooker

Theodore threw back the hot potato: Elizabeth's mother was crazy, violent, and a born liar. He said Elizabeth slept with her pastor and others; she said Theodore slept with women on the road and even with aging housekeeper Ellen Dennis. Victoria Woodhull and her sister Tennessee Claflin were smeared as prostitutes (and poor white trash). And so on. If one or more of the principals in the Beecher-Tilton Scandal could be paraded about as certifiably at fault for the systemic disruption, the culture of character might be saved.[20]

III. Barbara Goldsmith's version of the Beecher-Tilton Scandal represented a new departure in subjecting Theodore Tilton to almost as much scorn as Henry Ward Beecher: Theodore pushed the abortion on Elizabeth, got an earlier abortion for a "girl" he'd slept with, and actually hit his wife ("then with a swift gesture he struck Lib full across the face"), among many other tawdry, hypocritical, or angry acts. Earlier twentieth-century writers, by contrast, had shielded Tilton from attack. They had to, since they were relying on Theodore to be their primary truth-teller. Goldsmith could not accord him that role, since he had turned on Woodhull in 1872. After that time his word could be trusted only some of the time—when he was not assailing Woodhull as a liar. Goldsmith gave the role of speaker-of-the-truth to Elizabeth Cady Stanton and Frank Moulton (along with Woodhull herself much of the time).[21]

The earlier writers were of course right that if Beecher was to be found guilty of adultery, Theodore had to be telling the truth about it. Theodore was in effect their secret commando, slipped back into the nineteenth century to explode the edifice of obfuscation erected to conceal Beecher's wrongdoing. Tilton's wholly sincere self-image as the man of utter honesty, the opponent of all corruption—"I lock my lips too close to speak a lie; I wash my hands too white to touch a bribe," he wrote in his "Faith-Confession" of the early 1860s—endeared him to secular modernist Paxton Hibben. "Tilton's candor," he wrote, "was in sharp contrast to [that of] Beecher's friends." Theodore was spare and straight-shooting. At the trial, said Hibben, "Theodore Tilton's case was presented simply and directly, without extraneous matter."[22]

Hibben was even fonder of Frank Moulton than he was of Tilton. Moulton was "by long odds the smartest figure that had ever graced Plymouth Church." He was not a church member, or a believer in God, and in Hibben's eyes that ensured his neutrality on matters relating to the scandal. "Frank Moulton represented a type in the life of America new to Henry Ward Beecher. Here was a young man whom the church had never touched"—not even Plymouth Church, tailor-made for "just such young men as Moulton and millions like him. This younger generation seemed to be moved neither by fear of future punishment nor hope of future reward, but to prefer integrity for its own sake." With opponents as upstanding as Moulton and Tilton, Beecher didn't stand a chance in the high-color drama of Hibben's text. Victory went to the generation of modernity heralded by Moulton. Henry stood for the old order, "the day of the vast nation-wide power of organized religion." Theodore and Elizabeth were caught in the middle, "striving desperately to reconcile conduct with creed and threshing themselves to pieces in the effort—doomed in any event." Theodore was a heroic martyr to the cause of secularity, Elizabeth a passive sacrificial victim, Moulton a wily standard-bearer who got to the mountaintop even if he died before reaching the modern promised land.[23]

Barbara Goldsmith and Paxton Hibben, writing a half century apart, gave Beecher an old-fashioned licking. But no twentieth-century writer did as subtle and interesting a dismantling of the Plymouth pastor as Ann Douglas, in her milestone book of 1977, *The Feminization of American Culture.* She had as little sympathy for Beecher's religion as Hibben or Goldsmith did. But Douglas's reason for disliking it was different than theirs. For them Beecher's preaching was sanctimony: it camouflaged the "real" goings-on, including adulterous affairs and the venal money-making of the Plymouth elite, who according to them collected big bucks from auctioned-off pews and Plymouth bonds. By contrast, Douglas faulted Beecher and his Plymouth followers (especially Elizabeth Tilton) for surrendering the tough, uncompromising Calvinism of their forefathers—a religion better equipped, in her view, to resist the cultural sentimentalism that accompanied, and helped cushion, the market capitalism of the nineteenth century. In Douglas's account Beecher and the Tiltons were still the exemplars of an insidious Victorianism, but their imputed offense was not hypocrisy about adultery or greedy pocket-lining. It was softhearted mushiness about religion. Douglas matched Hibben's sarcasm in bemoaning the Victorian preference for illusions over reality. But for her the reality they covered up was the general sinfulness of human nature, not particular venal acts. By blinding themselves to the power of sin, and hence to the full grandeur and tragedy of the human drama (as revealed in the work of Melville, one of her heroes, along with Margaret Fuller), Beecher and his ilk had set American culture up for a bland and complacent mediocrity.[24]

In Douglas's story, Henry and Elizabeth—both sentimental fictionists, one as author and the other as reader—became sappy characters in a lived-out fiction of their own. Douglas was so repelled by the Victorian worship of tender feeling—a sorry substitute for the no-nonsense stringency of the Puritan outlook, and a lamentable launching pad for the feel-good consumerism of the twentieth century—that she could not let Beecher or Mrs. Tilton be the authors of their own lives. Fifty years earlier they had been criticized for masking their wrongdoing. Now she saw them as masked to the core themselves: fictionists to the marrow, they could no longer distinguish reality from fantasy. Ultimately, as literal "reflections" of a flighty and deluded culture, they lost all substance, became nonentities. In the end there was no tragedy, only pathos, for Elizabeth Tilton—whom Douglas singled out as the chief victim of the scandal. "Finally abandoned by both husband and lover," Douglas wrote, "she died essentially of confusion, without a life, without a literary model to give her the illusion of life." [25]

Carrying the twentieth-century conceit to its logical endpoint—that if all the Victorian world's a stage then each must not only play their parts but be their parts—Douglas neglected to note that Beecher and both Tiltons used fiction to serve consciously chosen, deeply felt, and well–articulated ends. They used it to make money, they used it for escape from mental and emotional constraints, they used it to express truths they couldn't put any other way. Fiction for them was production and clarification and resolution, not just consumption and confusion. But for Douglas the sentimentalists had seceded from adulthood, become like children entranced in a make-believe world—a fate that made them oddly blameless since, for all their refinement, their capacities were so severely atrophied. Elizabeth Tilton the helpless victim could be seen, in Douglas's statement of her lot, as a stand-in for the larger culture: "attractive, charming, not particularly bright, emotionally unstable and immature. . . . This is not to condemn her. It is only to scrutinize at painfully close range the barrenness of her possibilities." In this paradigmatically twentieth-century move, the critic finds Victorianism guilty, but offers a last-minute reprieve because the defendant was without responsibility. [26]

Ann Douglas was far from the first to chastise Beecher for abandoning the tougher religion of his forbears. Her book resurrected a common complaint of his own day: Beecherism was sentimentalism. Where her work diverged from critics of a century earlier was in her firm knowledge that Beecher had committed adultery with Mrs. Tilton. A late-nineteenth-century observer such as E. L. Godkin was not so sure. He did not hold back from pronouncing Beecher guilty because of some desire to protect the Plymouth pastor from a costly fall. We know this because Godkin thought Beecher had already fallen. His poor judgment in friends—Theodore Tilton and Frank Moulton—was proof of a moral lapse so grave, according to Godkin, that Beecher's reputation was forever tarnished. But Beecher could not be pronounced guilty of adultery, since the witnesses against him were not credible. They were not credible because they were not honorable: Tilton because he did not discipline his wife and confront his pastor immediately upon her alleged confession of adultery (or else, if he wished to forgive them, keep an eternal silence about their sin); Moulton because he admitted to lying for years to protect a man he claimed to know was guilty of the vilest hypocrisy, and to hashing over the best means of lying as he sat in his parlor with his wife and her pastor. In Godkin's estimation, Beecher defense lawyer John Porter had destroyed Moulton's credibility in a single rapier exchange near the start of the cross-examination. Porter: "Did you lie for him?" Moulton: "I did." Porter: "We have your word. [Laughter.]"[27]

One of the mythic truths about the Beecher-Tilton Scandal passed on from one twentieth-century writer to another is that Beecher rebuilt his reputation when the jury let him off easy in 1875. After all, said the first generation of hagiographic biographers, the trial exonerated him and public opinion swung back to its default position: adoration of a great man. After all, said Beecher's twentieth-century detractors, beginning with Paxton Hibben, Beecher had some wealthy Plymouth Church investors behind him, and they would not permit their capital to plummet. *New Yorker* writer Robert Shaplen, who produced a bemused popular account of the scandal in 1954, suggested that Beecher regained his popularity not because of his virtue or his backers, but because of his adultery. His "new aura of sin now made him a stronger attraction than ever." But Godkin's verdict suggests that even if Beecher met success with a mass audience from the mid-1870s to the mid-1880s, he may have lost a substantial part of his earlier authority—the part that depended not upon fame alone, but a perception of moral excellence. One of the cultural shifts marked by Paxton Hibben's 1927 book is that Godkin's framework, according to which authentic renown depended on such excellence of character, was in tatters. From Hibben's vantage point, talk of a religiously based moral purity was one of those Victorian pretensions most in need of derisive treatment. Beecher had never had true integrity, so he could not have lost it. All he could have lost was his market value. Hibben did not see that Beecher's post-trial "name" was on a different cultural track than his earlier "good name."[28]

IV.   Each person's life is a kaleidoscope of stories, some chosen, others imposed, and even the chosen ones come from the limited range of tales available—psychologically, spiritually, socially—for the choosing. In the Beecher-Tilton Scandal all of the principals developed stories about themselves, about the others, and about the culture-at-large. The stories evolved as they were told and retold. New facts came along, and new convictions, but often the new departures—as in Mrs. Tilton's reading of *Griffith Gaunt*—were rediscoveries of old stories. Finding her way in the world meant placing herself inside that old story, and inside the even older one of the female Christian mystic seeking not to "imitate" Christ as in Thomas à Kempis, but to "marry" him as in Madame Guyon. Moving backwards from 1999—through the interpretations of the Beecher-Tilton Scandal offered by generations of writers, and through the lives of the principals, means peeling back the retellings of the story. But peeling them back does not deposit us at some original, uncontaminated "true" story of what happened. It leaves us at the start of the storytelling. And even that starting point, it turns out, offers us retellings of earlier stories, because people struggling to make sense of their lives or their times look for help in the tales they have already at hand.

The lawyers at the 1875 trial were storytellers like the rest. Attorneys for plaintiff and defendant alike agreed that the scandal disclosed deep truths about American society, that Beecher's and the Tiltons' lives could only be understood in relation to their historical conjuncture. Each side painted a portrait of a culture in crisis—a crisis from which the nation could be saved only by the appropriate verdict. A verdict for the defense, William Evarts held, would shield America from the insidious assault upon the family launched by renegades Tilton and Woodhull. A verdict for the plaintiff, William Beach countered, would save the family from clerical invaders who slipped into the boudoir under cover of the Bible. To show that an acclaimed pastor like Beecher could very easily lead a sordid double life, he read into the trial record the tales of fifteen formerly esteemed clergymen found to have practiced something naughtier than they preached.[29]

American jurymen and newspaper readers in 1875 knew without being told that men of the cloth had a checkered moral history. Nathaniel Hawthorne's *Scarlet Letter* did not break the news to them in 1850, but confirmed it and supplied a standard set of references for popular suspicions of wily holy men. The novel added the insight that a preacher's secret sin might ironically imbue his pulpit oratory with majestic force. William Beach did not hesitate to point out that parallel between Arthur Dimmesdale and Henry Ward Beecher, and to imply with clever reverse logic that Beecher's passionate preaching in the late 1860s might actually point to the spark of a hidden intimacy with Elizabeth Tilton. "It does seem as if, with the prophetic eye of genius,"

Beach said, "Hawthorne had described the actual experience of Henry Ward Beecher." In a real sense the original story of the Beecher-Tilton Scandal was told twenty-two years before Woodhull's public accusations. Hawthorne laid down a framework of clerical deception—public mastery upon a foundation of private dereliction—that would inform treatments of the case up to the present.[30]

As Elizabeth Tilton sat in the Brooklyn courthouse on Wednesday, June 16, 1875, and listened to William Beach read a lengthy passage from the forest encounter scene between Dimmesdale and Hester Prynne, she and everyone around her were putting two and two together. If Hawthorne had uncannily foreseen Henry's experience—in a refined act of precognition superior to Victoria Woodhull's seedier feats of prediction—he might be foretelling Elizabeth's too. A week earlier, near the start of his summation, Beach had primed his audience for that conclusion by imagining the scene at 174 Livingston Street in the days when Theodore was away and Henry came calling. "We find Mr. Beecher . . . secluded in the parlor of that house in dangerous proximity [to Mrs. Tilton], with confessed love, with free opportunity and the woman blushing, and scarlet and red as the woman described by Hawthorne." The lawyers were arguing that the Beecher-Tilton Scandal was not just a telling of new stories, but a retelling of old ones. Evarts had gone first with his summation: the story of Elizabeth and Henry was really the story of Catherine Gaunt and Brother Leonard (no adultery, just undue affection). Beach followed with his conclusion: Beecher and Mrs. Tilton were reincarnations of the prototype sinful couple of American fiction. Beach read from the forest scene: " 'Hester,' said he, 'hast thou found peace?' She smiled drearily, looking down upon her bosom. 'Hast thou?' she asked. 'None!—nothing but despair!' he answered. . . . 'Happy are you, Hester, that wear the scarlet letter openly upon your bosom! Mine burns in secret!' "[31]

Since the summer of 1874 the newspaper readers of America—including the lawyers, already planning their legal strategies for 1875— had been taught to see the scandal as a replay of the *Scarlet Letter*. "Observe, too, the skulking manner of Mr. Beecher in all this business, and the power of Mr. Tilton," wrote "Gath" in August 1874. "It is Arthur Dimmesdale and Roger Chillingworth over again." Mrs. Tilton might not have had a letter emblazoned to her chest, but the *New York Graphic* had published a facsimile copy of her retraction of her recantation: Americans could pin her signed confession of wrongdoing, in her own handwriting, to their wooden ice chests. *Frank Leslie's Illustrated Newspaper* offered full-page "pictures" (engravings) to go with its analysis of the novel in relation to the scandal: Hester Prynne at the start of the tale "emerging from Boston Jail on her way to the scaffold"; Arthur Dimmesdale at his "minister's vigil," standing "one black night, long before his death, without great peril of discovery, upon the platform on which Hester Prynne had suffered." In a long editorial on "'The Minister's Vigil,'" *Frank Leslie's* mentioned only the names of Prynne and Dimmesdale, a sign of how complete the identification was, in the minds of many, between the living and the fictional characters. "More than anything else," the paper said, "the strange, sad story . . . teaches the weakness of a good man and the shame of a gentle woman. For no doubt, Hester Prynne, shielding her pastor, had a noble soul."

> "Little accustomed," says Hawthorne, "in her long seclusion from society, to measure her ideas of right and wrong by any standard external to herself, Hester saw, or seemed to see, that there lay a responsibility upon her, in reference to this clergyman, which she owed to no other; nor to the whole world besides."

The full meaning of the scandal, for *Frank Leslie's*, emerged only when the case was put in relation to both *The Scarlet Letter* and *Griffith Gaunt*. But it surpassed both of those stories in the depths it sounded, and the wisdom it taught.

> The story is the most marvelous commentary in all history on human passion and selfishness, and whether or not there was sin in the relations of these people, all of them sinned grievously in this, that they have wronged themselves and wronged humanity by their folly.[32]

We can assume that Elizabeth, a passionate lover of fiction, had read *The Scarlet Letter*. We will never know, however, if in making sense of her life, she took a leaf from Hawthorne as she had from Charles Reade. *Griffith Gaunt* had given her a jolt of self-understanding. She was startled to find that Catherine's story was hers too. Did it occur to her as she heard William Beach read Dimmesdale's words—"Happy are you, Hester, that wear the scarlet letter openly upon your bosom! Mine burns in secret!"—that her continued concealment of what had truly happened between her and Henry was going to eat away at her no matter what the trial's outcome? Did she sense that peace would come to her finally only (as Theodore predicted) from a confession of adultery with her pastor? As she prepared for the confession that finally came in 1878, did she imagine that sewing the figurative "A" to her chest would bring the tranquility that it brought to Hester? Hester's community had come gradually to accept and love her. For, as Hawthorne's narrator explains, "human nature . . . loves more readily than it hates, . . . except where its selfishness is brought into play." Hester made it easy for them to accept her. "She never battled with the public, but submitted uncomplainingly to its worst usage; she made no claim upon it, in requital for what she suffered; she did not weigh upon its sympathies. Then, also, the blameless purity of her life, during all these years in which she had been set apart to infamy, was reckoned largely in her favor." Elizabeth confessed, she said, in order to find relief from "long months of mental anguish"; she would "leave the truth with God." Whether that truth was adultery of the flesh or the heart, she may well have looked at Hester Prynne with hopeful expectation. Certainly Elizabeth did come to be accepted among the Plymouth Brethren. Maybe the wider social world also took it easier on her after the confession—even if only by leaving her alone.[33]

The *Brooklyn Eagle* obituary writer who in 1897 told the story of her final years may well have had *The Scarlet Letter* sitting on his desk as he composed. Hawthorne had written that Hester "was self-ordained a Sister of Mercy," a comforter for those women buffeted by "the continually recurring trials of wounded, wasted, wronged, misplaced, or erring and sinful passion."

> Such helpfulness was found in [Hester]—so much power to do, and power to sympathize—that many people refused to interpret the scarlet A by its original signification. They said that it meant Able; so strong was Hester Prynne, with a woman's strength. . . . The scarlet letter ceased to be a stigma which attracted the world's scorn and bitterness, and became a type of something to be sorrowed over, and looked upon with awe, yet with reverence too. And, as Hester Prynne had no selfish ends, nor lived in any measure for her own profit and enjoyment, people brought all their sorrows and perplexities, and besought her counsel, as one who had herself gone through a mighty trouble.

The *Eagle* writer said that with Mrs. Tilton's death, there was taken away from her fellow Plymouth Brethren "a friend whose counsel and sympathy were to be had at all times, and were all the more valuable because she was one who knew the value of these intangible evidences of friendship, having herself stood in such sore need of them at one time in her life."[34]

Elizabeth Tilton prayed earnestly after 1875 to be let alone by the press, and she would probably have winced at the idea that a historian would write as much about her, a century after her death, as I have done. Her life was not significant, she might have said, only her faith.

But it was significant. She has as much to teach us about Victorian culture as her pastor and husband do. Theodore and Henry as orators, writers, and editors, Elizabeth as a reader, listener, and letter writer, did vital cultural work as builders of sentimentalism. Most twentieth-century observers—indebted to Woodhull's 1872 accusations, and even, indirectly, to Hawthorne's characters of 1850—have missed the particular vitality of sentimentalism by seeing it as a cover-up of wrong-doing, or of the deep truth of sin. The vigor of sentimentalism is well represented by Elizabeth Tilton curling up, after putting her four children to bed, with the novel *Griffith Gaunt*, and there discovering her sin.

Her reading experience put her into a community of readers with whom she achieved a long-sought personal autonomy, a vantage point from which she became a critic, at her best a sympathetic critic, of both the men she loved. Theodore had abused her, she thought, and Henry had misled her, but her religious conviction allowed her to contextualize and relativize her own harsh judgments, and to judge herself even more harshly than she judged them. She did not, as Ann Douglas suggested, die "essentially of confusion, without a life." She died in a gathering of religious intimates and a gathering of intimate stories that gave her a measure of support as well as autonomy, and the perspective with which, perhaps, to cultivate the virtues of gratitude and forgiveness.

V.　Hawthorne ended his story at "that burial ground beside which King's Chapel has since been built." Hester was laid to rest there beside Arthur Dimmesdale, "with a space between, as if the dust of the two sleepers had no right to mingle. Yet one tombstone served for both." And "on this simple slab of slate—as the curious investigator may still discern, and perplex himself with the purport—there appeared the semblance of an engraved escutcheon. It bore a device, a herald's wording of which might serve for a motto and brief description of our now concluded legend; so sombre is it, and relieved only by one ever-glowing point of light gloomier than the shadow:—
"ON A FIELD, SABLE, THE LETTER A, GULES."

The curious investigator on a sweltering August afternoon in 1998 finds Henry Ward Beecher's grave on Dawn Path at Greenwood Cemetery in Brooklyn, where he was laid in 1887. His grave also has an inscription in capital letters, chiseled into a simple block of granite. The unimposing rock monument is dwarfed by tall obelisks all around. It says, "HE THINKETH NO EVIL." The phrase comes from Paul's First Letter to the Corinthians 13:5, but in Paul's letter the subject of the sentence is not "he," not a person, but "charity," which "suffereth long, and is kind; charity envieth not; charity vaunteth not itself, is not puffed up, Doth not behave itself unseemly, seeketh not her own, is not easily provoked, thinketh no evil." First Corinthians 13 was Beecher's most cherished chapter in the entire Bible. He had urged Elizabeth to take comfort from it when she was distraught. William Evarts had tried in vain to enter Henry's recommendation of it into the trial record, and Judge Neilson had said there was no need to do so, everyone knew the verses.

Whoever inscribed the phrase on Beecher's tombstone knew he had identified himself, since the trial, with charity. His final story about himself concerned a long-suffering man who loved others. That was already how he wished to be remembered in July 1875, when he spoke to the summer residents of Peekskill. He could not help it if he trusted everyone, he said. He had done so his whole life, "and only once in forty years have I made a mistake. I shall love men; I shall not stop to think of their faults before I love them." Alongside Beecher is his wife Eunice, who died on March 8, 1897, a decade to the day after her husband.[35]

In April of that year, Elizabeth Tilton was buried in Greenwood too. She is a few hundred yards away from Henry and Eunice, across Ocean Hill, through the Sycamore Grove and the Grassy Dell, over the Hill of Graves, and up the Plateau, where she lies between the Altar of Liberty and the Monument to the New York Volunteers of the Civil War. Her hillside plot looks over to Manhattan, her birthplace. The World Trade Center towers are framed by lush sycamores of summer. She rests beside at least two of her children, Mattie and Paul, who died in infancy. Once when she and Theodore had fought, as she told the Church Committee in 1874, she had gone to that plot for solace. "I went there," she said,

> with my waterproof cloak on, and with the hood over my head, and lay down on the two graves, and felt peace; I had been there but a little while before the keeper of the grounds ordered me off; I paid no attention to him; I did not regard his order until he came again in a few moments and said, "I order you off these grounds; do you hear me?" I rose on my feet and said: "If there is one spot on earth that is mine, it is these two graves"; and he actually bowed down before me in apology; though he was a common workman, it was very hearty, and it was very grateful to me: he said, "I did not know that these were yours"; and he left me; I stayed there on the little graves the rest of the day.

That parable of self-assertion—so well-polished a monument to her self-awakening that it must have been told and retold by her on many previous occasions—is also "the story of her life," as we say ironically at the end of the twentieth century. Her self-empowerment amounts to the dubious freedom of being permitted to lie down, hunched in a shroud-like cloak, on a cemetery plot. Yet her grandest wish was to be reunited with her babies. Gripping their sod from above in the 1870s was the sweetest rest, a fond anticipation of lying alongside them for all eternity. Elizabeth's grave has no vertical tombstone, only a small rectangular nameplate in the ground, almost hidden in the grass. It says "Tilton." [36]

You cross "Atlantic Avenue" when you stroll overland from Henry's to Elizabeth's plots at Greenwood, but getting to Theodore Tilton's grave means crossing the real Atlantic, as he did when he went into exile in France. Like Hawthorne's Pearl, Arthur and Hester's daughter, he slipped away to the old world and was scarcely heard from again. He had loved France since at least 1870, when the Paris Commune arose to fight, in Theodore's eyes, for true republican equality. In 1871 he had firmly rejected the epithets "free lover" and "spiritualist" when they were thrown at him, but he gladly embraced "Communist." It was not "agrarianism, as many people ignorantly imagine," he wrote. "It is republicanism." The people of Paris had mounted "the noblest attempt at political liberty which Europe ever saw or crushed. But the Commune will yet arise and reign! God speed it!" Perhaps when Theodore departed for Paris he believed he could lend a hand in the battle for freedom. But a quarter century later, when he told his friend Kate Fuller where he wished to be buried, he did not mention the cemetery of his Communard hero Charles Delescluze, who had died on the barricades in 1871. He said he wanted to lie alongside Théodore Rousseau and Jean-François Millet, Barbizon School painters buried (in 1867 and 1875 respectively) at Chailly-en-Bière, near Fontainebleau. Tilton had always sought out great men as models for his rise toward purity, and these Romantic artists might have liked his poetry, so full of glistening gems of sentiment. Rousseau had made the Fontainebleau forest shimmer, and Millet had depicted simple farm folk, given them dignity and substance, bathed them in soft rays of light. Mass-produced copies of his "Angelus"—two farmers bowing their heads to the tilled earth—have hung over French and American hearths from the late nineteenth century to the late twentieth. [37]

That would have been how Tilton remembered his own New Jersey forebears, who were farmers near Middletown into his father's generation. Silas Tilton had left the countryside to make it as a shoemaker in Manhattan. His family lived above the shop on Greenwich Street, but

they spent a lot of time in New Jersey too, and Silas and his wife Eusebia, Theodore's mother, retired there. As a boy Theodore played with
Joseph and Elizabeth Richards in New York City, but he also loved the
New Jersey outback. The old editor of the Middletown paper, A. B.
Hallenbake, told a reporter in 1874 that the young Tilton "was fond
of strolling about the country all alone, apparently wrapped in study,
and the simple-minded residents deemed him unsociable, and so left
him alone."

> Later, as he matured, he had a way of contradicting his elders when
> he thought they were in error and a manner of arguing with them,
> too, that made the difference between himself and them more
> marked, although they grew to respect and even to be proud of him
> for his intelligence. "Many a time," said Mr. Hallenbake, "as I sat on
> the stoop of my father's store, have I seen Theodore coming down
> the road, a fishing-pole on his shoulder, his long hair flying in the
> breeze and his face flushed with excitement. He always stopped in
> the store, and if any of the loungers inside were talking he would join
> in. No matter what they were discussing, politics, religion, farming,
> be it what it might, he would take his part, and if he disagreed with
> anyone's views on any subject he would argue with them—with the
> schoolmaster or even the village dominie—and he always won his
> point." [38]

The perfect democrat: no group was too humble to be taken on in the
perpetual battle for truth and justice.

There is nothing bucolic about the Chailly-en-Bière *cimetière*. Theodore's untended grave is squeezed into a row of tombs in a walled-in,
almost treeless municipal compound. It looks much more like Hawthorne's King's Chapel burial ground in Boston, slate slabs akimbo, than
it does Henry and Elizabeth's spacious Greenwood, all rolling hills and
glens redolent of *Norwood*. Rousseau and Millet are only yards away, in
fancier shrines. Theodore lies beside his friend Kate Fuller under a
simple, six-foot-high stone. Fuller's apparently cheaper depression-era
monument lies in large chunks on the ground, and the foundation of
Theodore's is seriously eroded. No one has paid it any mind for a
very long time. French families bring abundant floral offerings to their
nearby dead. One of the French visitors must occasionally wonder,
reading the chiseled English words on the tombstone, by what circu-
itous route a "Theodore Tilton, Poet—Orator, 1835–1907" could
have come to rest in such an obscure corner of the Seine-et-Marne.

Henry Ward and Eunice Beecher's grave
(above); Theodore Tilton's grave,
Cimetière de Chailly-en-Bière (right).

Greenwood Cemetery. Elizabeth Tilton's plot in foreground, Manhattan in the distance.

Appendix

I . *Theodore Tilton to Henry Ward Beecher*

Brooklyn, June 17, 1863

H. W. B.

My Best of Friends,

It is Wednesday Evening, that is to say, *The Independent*'s Saturday night. I have just come into the house from watering my Wax Plant, which has been set in the garden since you saw it. I poured a cool drink over its leaves, and the leaf on which you scratched your initials held itself up to me as green as the memory in which I hold your Lordship. I received your first letter [from Europe] yesterday, and it is in the paper of today. The office looks as when you left it—only I find it already a little lonesome. I miss the walks up and down Broadway. I am beginning to know the saying, "Ye have not many fathers in Israel." Mr. Bowen has gone to Woodstock for three weeks. I have just received from him a letter in which he writes like a conquered man, whose sorrows have crushed him into the dust. He says that the world-life-fortune-ambition—all are almost as nothing to him, and he has never before felt so willing to die. Miss [Edna Dean] Proctor [the poet, and anthologizer of Beecher's sayings] is in New Hampshire, and has just written me a pleasant note mentioning her sister's marriage, and also making a remark which I copy for you: "I thank you," she says, "for your account of the Excursion. . . . I am very glad he has gone. It was time he breathed a new air, and saw life with new eyes. *God bless him,* and bring him safely back again with strength to be *true to himself,*

'And it doth follow, as the night the day,
He cannot then be false to any man.' "

I hope—and this letter helps my hope—that when you come home, you will find the former things passed away, and all things become new. The [Plymouth] Church grows thin, but not lean. Prof. Hitchcock satisfies most of the congregation, disappoints others, and puzzles some. Mr. Freeland says, "Theodore, that man's ideas are like dried fish, hung up in a cellar!" But Mr. Tappan is so delighted that every Sunday he asks, "Why can't that sermon be printed in *The Independent?*" to which I reply, "We have just now an itinerant minister [Beecher] preaching for us." The Sunday School were delighted with your letter, and with its gift. Tonight, the teachers go in a body on a North River barge to Mr. Beach's "Sunnybrook Farm," where he is to take charge of them for two days—quartering them upon the natives of that region—a grand pic-nic! Tonight is moonlight, and I suspect that at this very moment there is great business of music and dancing. Dr. Tyng has a contribution in the paper of today. I met him a few days ago on the cars, and he spoke of you so pleasantly and warmly that I shall always think the better of him for it. I have had a delightful letter from [John Greenleaf] Whittier: his very warm interest in what I do I can hardly account for. I send you *Vanity Fair* with an absurd picture, which will make you laugh. No: I will not burden the mail with so much trash, but cut out the picture and enclose it in this letter. If you should get into *Punch*, send yourself to me. Have you called on Robert Browning? Gilbert Haven has sent me some reminiscences of him. I hope you will not miss that visit. I would rather see him than a dozen Carlyles, or one Queen. Mrs. Beecher (I hear) has gone to Indianapolis, called by the sickness of her brother. Hattie Benedict [wife-to-be of Beecher's eldest son Henry], with father, mother, and sister, spent an evening last week at [ET's mother] Mama Morse's, at which I was present. I mention it as news concerning your prospective family. Fred Perkins [office assistant at the *Independent,* son of HWB's sister Mary Perkins, and father, in June 1863, of two-year-old Charlotte Perkins (later Gilman)] is turning out a prince in his behavior toward me. He is kind, generous, and helpful. He offers his services constantly when I am overpressed. If he were a brother, he could not do more. He has just written a splendid digest of Lyell's new book. Dr. [Joshua] Leavitt [a former *Independent* editor] is as cordial as I had any right to expect. I will not complain. But I think Fred is the better Christian of the two. Public affairs go slowly forward. I dined a day or two ago with Gov. Andrew. He said, "Things never have looked so well, on the whole, as now." I think the remark is true. The President's letter has given extraordinary satisfaction.* It has almost re-instated him among his friends. It is considered his best production. The editor of the *Cincinnati Commercial* (Mr. Potter) whom I met yesterday says that Vallandigham will be beaten in Ohio by 100,000 majority. My wife, who sits at the other end of my table (still waiting for her coming baby [Carroll]) sends this message: "Tell him (that is, *you,* not the baby) I love him dearly." So does her husband—now, henceforth, and forever. Amen.

T. T.

Beecher Family Papers, box 15, folder 615, Yale University Library Manuscripts and Archives.

*Judging by his repeated references to it in his summer correspondence with Beecher, Tilton is referring here to Lincoln's letter of June 12, 1863, on the Vallandigham affair. It is reprinted in *Abraham Lincoln: Speeches and Writings, 1859–1865* (New York: Library of America, 1989), pp. 454–63.

2.   *Henry Ward Beecher to Theodore Tilton*

London, October 18, 1863, Sunday

My Dear Theodore,

You know why I have not written you from England. I have been so full of work that I could not. God has been with me and prospered me. I have had health and strength and courage, and what is of unspeakably more importance, I have had the sweetest experience of Love to God and to man of all my life.

I have been enabled to love our enemies. All the needless ignorance, the party perversions, the wilful misrepresentations of many newspapers, the arrogance and obstinacy too often experienced—and yet more, the coolness of brethren of our faith and order, and the poisoned prejudices which have been arrayed against me, by the propagation of untruths or distorted reports—have not prevented my having a love for old England, an appreciation of the good that is here, and a hearty desire for her *whole* welfare. This I count a great blessing. God awakened in my heart a desire to be a full and true Christian towards England, the moment I put my foot on her shores—and he has answered the prayers which he inspired. I have spoken at Manchester, Glasgow, Edinburgh and Liverpool, and am now in London, preparing for Exeter Hall, Tuesday next. I have been buoyant and happy. The streets of Manchester and Liverpool have been filled with placards, in black and white letters, full of all lies and bitterness, but they have seemed to me only like the tracery of dreams. For hours I have striven to speak, amid interruptions of every kind: yellings, howlings, . . . every conceivable annoyance, save personal violence. But God kept me in perfect peace. I stood in Liverpool, and looked on the demoniac scene, almost without a thought that it was *me* that was meant. It seemed rather like a storm raging in the trees of the forest, that roared and impeded my progress, but yet, had nothing personal or wilful in it, against *me.*

You know, dear Theodore, how, when we are lifted by the inspiration of a great subject, and by the almost visible presence and vivid sympathy with Christ, the mind forgets the sediment and dregs of trouble, and sails serenely in an upper realm of peace, as untouched by the noise below as is a bird that flies across a battle-field. Just so, I had at Liverpool and Glasgow as sweet an inward peace, as ever I had in the loving meetings of dear old Plymouth Church.

And again and again, when the uproar raged, and I could not *speak,* my heart seemed to be taking of the infinite fulness of the Saviour's pity, and breathing it out upon those poor troubled men.

I never had so much the spirit of continuing and unconscious prayer, or rather, of communion with Christ. I have felt that I was his dear child, and that his arms were about me continually. And at times that "peace that passeth all understanding" has descended upon me, so that I could not keep tears of gratitude from falling, for so much tender goodness of my God. For what are outward prosperities compared with these interior intimacies of God? It is not the path to the temple, but the interior of the temple, that shows the glory and goodness of God. And I have been able to commit all to Him: myself, my family, my friends—and in an especial manner, the cause of my Country.

O Theodore, I have felt an inexpressible *wonder* that God should give it to *me*, to do something for the dear land. When, sometimes, [I have considered] the idea of my being clothed with power to stand up in this great kingdom against an inconceivable violence of prejudice and mistake, and clear the name of my dishonoured country, and let her brow shine forth crowned with Liberty, and glowing with love to man, I have seemed unable to live, almost. It almost took my soul's breath away!

I have not, in a single instance, gone to the speaking halls, without, all the way, breathing to God unutterable desires for inspiration, guidance, success—and I have had no disturbance of *personality*. I have been willing, yea, with eagerness, to be myself contemptible in men's sight, if only *my* disgrace might be to the honor of that cause, which is entrusted to our thrice dear Country. I have asked of God nothing but this: and this, with uninterrupted heart-flow of yearning request: *make me worthy to speak for God and man.*

I never felt my ignorance so painfully, nor the great want of moral purity and nobility of soul, as when approaching my tasks of defending Liberty, in her hour of trial. I have an ideal of what a man should be, who labours for such a cause—that constantly rebukes my real condition, and makes me feel painfully *how little I am.* Yet that is hardly painful. There passes before me a sense of God's glory, so pure, serene, uplifted, filling the ages, and more and more to be revealed—that I almost wish to lose my own identity—and to be like a drop of dew, that falls into the sea, and becomes a part of that sublime whole, that glows under every line of latitude, and sounds on every shore! *"That God may be all in all!"* That is not a prayer only, but a personal experience.

And in all this time, I have not had one unkind feeling toward a single human being. Even those who are oppressors, I have pitied with undying compassion. And enemies around me have seemed harmless, and objects of charity, rather than potent foes to be destroyed. "God be thanked, who giveth us the victory, through our Lord Jesus Christ!"

My dear Theodore, when I sat down to write, I did it under the impulse that I wanted somebody to know the secret of my life. I am in a noisy spectacle, and seem to thousands, as one employing merely worldly implements, and acting under secular motives. But should I die, on sea or land, I wanted to say to you, who have been so near and dear to me, that in God's own very truth, *"the life that I have lived in the flesh, I have lived by faith of the Son of God."* I wanted to leave it with some-one to say for me, that it was not in natural gifts, nor in great opportu-nities, nor in personal ambition, that I have been able to endure and labour. But that the secret spring of my outward life has been an in-ward, complete, and all-possessing faith of God's truth, and God's own self, *"working in me to will and to do, of His own good pleasure."*

MONDAY 19TH.

I do not know as you will understand the feeling, which led to the above outburst. I had spoken four times in seven days to immense au-diences, under great excitement, and with every effort of Southern sym-pathizers, through newspapers, street placards, and in every other way to prevent my being heard. I thought I had been through *furnaces* be-fore. But this ordeal surpassed all others. I was quite alone in England. I had no one to consult with. I felt the burden of having to stand for my country, in a half hostile land, and yet I never flinched for a moment, nor lost heart. But, after resting 20 weeks, to begin so suddenly such a tremendous strain upon my voice, has very much affected it. Today, I am somewhat fearful that I shall be unable to speak tomorrow night, in Exeter Hall. I want to speak there. If the Lord will only let me, I shall be willing to give up all the other openings in the Kingdom. I cannot stop to give you any sort of insight into affairs here. One more good victory, and England will be immovable. The best thinkers of England will be, at any rate.

I hope that my people will feel that I have done my duty. I know that I have *tried*. I should be glad to feel that my countrymen approved, but above all others, I should prise the knowledge that the people of Plym-outh Church were satisfied with me.

When this reaches you, I hope to be on the ocean.

I am, as ever, yours,

H. W. Beecher

Harriet Beecher Stowe Center, Hartford, Connecticut—copy of the origi-nal; reprinted in *Beecher-Tilton Investigation: The Scandal of the Age* (Philadelphia: Barclay & Co., 1874), pp. 61–63

3. *E. T., "Dying Deaths Daily"*

Into a sorrow-darkened soul,
A vision full of peace there stole.

An Angel stood beside her way,
As forth she went at dawn of day;

And said, "O weary and oppressed!
Know that at evening thou shalt rest.

"The cross of iron, the crown of thorn,
The weight of anguish thou hast borne,

"And e'en the sins thou hatest all
From off thy weary soul shall fall;

"To life and love and peace restored
Within the presence of thy Lord."

Then thankfulness and glad surprise
Flowed from the sorrow-laden eyes.

"With hope so near of rest," said she,
"No sorrow more shall dwell with me.

"No weight of care, no shade of gloom,
Can pass the portal of the tomb;

"And light as air I'll urge my way,
If burdens fall at close of day."

The Angel lingered, and a smile
Dawned o'er his pitying face, the while.

"O weak of heart and hope," he said,
"Deem'st thou all peace is with the dead?

"Or that thy Lord can dwell more near
To saints in bliss than toilers here?

"If but thou diest, day by day,
To sins that clog thy homeward way,

"Each night shall be a grave of care,
Each morn thy resurrection fair,

"And daily be thy strength restored
By the dear presence of thy Lord."

Independent, Jan. 5, 1865, p. 1. Although this poem is signed only "E. T.," there is every reason to think Elizabeth Tilton was the author. Ordinarily, the full names of the *Independent*'s non-staff contributors were published; the editor's wife would be a logical exception to this practice. The poem's sentiments certainly reflect Mrs. Tilton's, and the style bespeaks an admirer of Theodore Tilton's own verse, and that of his chief model, Elizabeth Barrett Browning. The poem's title may come from Hester Prynne's rebuke to her husband Roger Chillingworth (*Scarlet Letter*, ch. 14) for having caused her lover Arthur Dimmesdale "to die daily a living death."

4.   *Theodore Tilton to Henry Ward Beecher*

Midnight, Brooklyn, Nov. 30, 1865
Rev. Henry Ward Beecher
My Dear Friend:
Returning home late tonight, I cannot go to bed without writing you a letter. Twice I have been forced to appear as your antagonist before the public, the occasions five years apart. After the first I am sure our friendship, instead of being maimed, was strengthened; after this last, if I may guess your heart by knowing mine, I am sure the old love waxes instead of wanes. Two or three days ago, I know not how impelled, I took out of its hiding place your sweet and precious letter written to me from England, containing an affectionate message which you wished should live and testify after your death. Tonight I have been thinking that in case I should die first, which is equally probable, I ought to leave in your hand my last will and testament of reciprocated love. My friend, from my boyhood up you have been to me what no other man has been, what no other man can be. While I was a student the influence of your mind on mine was greater than all books and all teachers. The intimacy with which you honored me for twelve years has been, next to my wife and family, the chief affection of my life. By you I was baptized; by you married; you are my minister, teacher, father, brother, friend, companion. The debt I owe you I can never pay. My religious life, my intellectual development, my open door of opportunity for labor, my public reputation—all these, my dear friend, I owe in so great a degree to your own kindness that my gratitude cannot be written in words, but must be expressed only in love.

Then, what hours we have had together! What arm-in-arm wanderings about the streets! What hunts for pictures and books! What mutual revelations and communings! What interminglings of mirth, of tears, of prayers!

The more I think back upon this friendship, the more am I convinced that not your public position, not your fame, not your genius, but just your affection has been the secret of the bond between us. For, whether you had been high or low, great or common, I believe that my heart, knowing its mate, would have loved you exactly the same. Now, therefore, I want to say that if, either long ago or lately, any word of mine, whether spoken or printed, whether public or private, has given you pain, I beg you to blot it from your memory and to write your forgiveness in its place. Moreover, if I should die leaving you alive, I ask you to love my children for their father's sake, who has taught them to reverence you and to regard you as the man of men.

One thing more: my religious experiences have never been more refreshing than during the last year. Never before have I had such fair and winning thoughts of the other life. With these thoughts you stand connected in a strange and beautiful way. I believe human friendship outlasts human life. Our friendship is yet of the earth, earthy; but it shall one day stand uplifted above mortality, safe, without scar or flaw, without a breath to blot or a suspicion to endanger it.

Meanwhile, O, my friend, may our Father in heaven bless you on the earth, guide you, strengthen you, illumine you, and at last crown you with the everlasting crown. And, now, good night; and sweet be your dreams of your unworthy but eternal friend,

Theodore Tilton

TT v. HWB, 2: 738

5. *Excerpts from Theodore Tilton's "Toast" to New England Society Dinner, December 22, 1865*

> "*Woman*—The strong staff and beautiful rod which sustained and comforted our forefathers during every step of the Pilgrims' Progress"

Mr. Tilton being called upon to respond, spoke as follows:
Gentlemen: It is somewhat to a modest man's embarrassment, on rising to this toast, to know that it has already been twice partially spoken to this evening—first by my friend Senator Lane, from Indiana, and just now, most eloquently, by the mayor-elect of New York, who could not

utter a better word in his own praise, than to tell us that he married a Massachusetts wife. [Applause.] In choosing the most proper spot on this platform as the stand-point for such remarks as are appropriate to such a toast, my first impulse was to go to the other end of the table—for hereafter, Mr. Chairman, when you are in want of a man to speak for woman, remember that Hamlet said, "Bring me the *recorder!*" [Laughter.] But, on the other hand, here, at this end, a prior claim was put in from the State of Indiana, whose venerable Senator has expressed himself disappointed at finding no women present. So, as my toast introduces that sex, I feel bound to stand at the Senator's end of the room, not, however, too near the Senator's chair, for it may be dangerous to take woman too near that "good-looking man." [Laughter.] Therefore, gentlemen, I stand between these two chairs—the army on my right (General Hancock), the navy on my left (Admiral Farragut), and hold over their heads the name that conquered both—woman! [Applause.] The chairman has pictured a vice-admiral tied a little while to a *mast:* but it is the spirit of my sentiment to give you a vice-admiral tied life-long to a *master.* [Applause.] In the absence of woman, therefore, from this gilded feast, I summon her to your golden remembrance. You must not forget, Mr. President, in eulogizing the early *men* of New England, who are *your* clients tonight, that it was only through the help of the early *women* of New England, who are mine, that your boasted heroes could ever have earned their title of the Pilgrim Fathers [Great laughter.] A health, therefore, to the women in the cabin of the May-Flower! A cluster of may-flowers themselves, transplanted from summer in the old world to winter in the new! Counting over those matrons and maidens, they number, all told, just eighteen. Their names are now written among the heroines of history! For as over the ashes of Cornelia stood the epitaph, "The Mother of the Gracchi," so over these women of that Pilgrimage we write as proudly, "The Mothers of the Republic." [Applause.] There was good Mistress Bradford, whose feet were not allowed of God to kiss Plymouth Rock, and who, like Moses, came only near enough to see, but not to enter the promised land. She was washed overboard from the deck—and to this day the sea is her grave, and Cape Cod her monument! [Applause.] There was Mistress Carver, wife of the first governor, who, when her husband fell under the stroke of sudden death, followed him at first with heroic grief to the grave, and then, a fortnight after followed him with heroic joy up into heaven! [Applause.] There was Mistress White—the mother of the first child born to the New England Pilgrims on this continent. And it was a good omen, sir, that this historic babe was brought into the world on board the May-Flower, between the time of the casting of the anchor, and the landing of the passengers—a kind of amphibious prophecy that the new-born nation was to have a birthright inheritance over the sea and over the land. [Great applause.] There, also, was Rose Standish— whose name is a perpetual June fragrance, to mellow and sweeten those December winds. And there, too, was Mrs. Winslow, whose name is even more than a fragrance; it is a taste; for, as the advertisements say, "children cry for it"; it is a *soothing syrup*. [Great laughter.] Then, after the first vessel, with these women, came other vessels, with other women—loving hearts, drawn from the olden land by those silken threads which afterward harden into golden chains. For instance, Governor Bradford, a lonesome widower, went down to the sea-beach, and, facing the waves, tossed a love letter over the wide ocean into the lap of Alice Southworth in Old England, who caught it up, and read it, and said, "Yes, I will go." And she went! And it was said, that the governor at his second wedding married his first love! Which, according to the new theology, furnishes the providential reason why the first Mrs. Bradford fell overboard! [Great laughter.] Now, gentlemen, as you sit to-night in this elegant hall, think of the houses in which the May-Flower men and women lived in that first winter!

Think of a cabin in the wilderness—where winds whistled—where wolves howled—where Indians yelled! And yet within that log-house, burning like a lamp, was the pure flame of Christian faith, love, patience, fortitude, heroism! As the Star of the East rested over the rude manger where Christ lay, so—speaking not irreverently—there rested over the roofs of the pilgrims a Star of the West—the Star of Empire; and today, that Empire is the proudest in the world! [Applause.] And if we could summon up from their graves, and bring hither tonight that olden company of long-mouldered men, and they could sit with us at this feast, in their mortal flesh, and with their stately presence, the whole world would make a pilgrimage to see those pilgrims! [Applause.] How quaint their attire! How grotesque their names! How we treasure every relic of their day and generation! And of all the heirlooms of the earlier times in Yankee-land, what household memorial is clustered around about with more sacred and touching associations than the *spinning-wheel!* The industrious mother sat by it, doing her work while she instructed her children! The blushing daughter plied it diligently, while her sweetheart had a chair very close by! And you remember, too, another person who used it more than all the rest—that peculiar kind of maiden, well along in life, who, while she spun her yarn into one "blue stocking," spun herself into another. [Laughter.] But perhaps my toast forbids me to touch upon this well-known class of Yankee women—restricting me, rather, to such women as *"comforted"* the Pilgrims.

Linus Pierpont Brockett, *Men of Our Day* (Philadelphia: Zeigler, McCurdy, 1868), pp. 615–17.

6. *Theodore Tilton, "A Faith-Confession," c. 1865*

As other men have creeds, so I have mine;
I keep the holy faith in God, in man,
And in the angels ministrant between.

I hold to one true church of all true souls;
Whose churchly seal is neither bread nor wine,
Nor laying on of hands, nor holy oil,
But only the anointing of God's grace.

I hate all kings, and caste, and rank of birth,
For all the sons of men are sons of God;
Nor limps a beggar but is nobly born;
Nor wears a slave a yoke, nor czar a crown,
That makes him less or more than just a man.

I love my country and her righteous cause;
So dare I not keep silent of her sin;
And after Freedom, may her bells ring Peace!

I love one woman with a holy fire,
Whom I revere as priestess of my house;
I stand with wondering awe before my babes,
Till they rebuke me to a nobler life;
I keep a faithful friendship with my friend,

Whom loyally I serve before myself;
I lock my lips too close to speak a lie;
I wash my hands too white to touch a bribe;
I owe no man a debt I cannot pay—
Except the love that man should always owe.

Withal each day, before the blessed heaven,
I open wide the chambers of my soul,
And pray the Holy Ghost to enter in.

Thus reads the fair confession of my faith,
So crossed with contradictions by my life,
That now may God forgive the written lie.
Yet still, by help of Him who helpeth men,
I face two worlds, and fear not life nor death!
O Father! lead me by thy hand! Amen.

The Great Scandal: History of the Famous Beecher-Tilton Case (New York: American News Company, 1874), n.p. ("Letter-Press" section, no. 8).

7. *Excerpts of Theodore Tilton's and Henry Ward Beecher's Speeches at Woman's Rights Convention, May 10, 1866*

Susan B. Anthony, Elizabeth Cady Stanton, Lucretia Mott, and other women's movement leaders were joined at New York's Church of the Puritans by Tilton, Beecher, Wendell Phillips, O. B. Frothingham, and other supporters. Tilton's short speech introduced Beecher's featured one-hour address. At the conclusion of the address, Beecher and Tilton engaged in a spontaneous "colloquy" that displayed their joint talent for witty repartee and genial but still cutting one-upmanship. The National Woman Suffrage Association later published Beecher's speech in full in tract form.

THEODORE TILTON said: . . . Are women politically oppressed that they need the ballot for their protection? I leave that question to be answered by women themselves. I demand the ballot for woman, not for woman's sake, but for man's. *She* may demand it for her own sake; but today, *I* demand it for *my* sake. We shall never have a government thoroughly permeated with humanity . . . until both men and women shall unite in forming the public sentiment, and in administering that sentiment through the government. [Applause.] . . . But, shall we have a woman for President? I would thank God if today we had a *man* for President. [Laughter.] Shall women govern the country? Queens have ruled nations from the beginning of time, and woman has governed man from the foundation of the world! [Laughter.] I know that Plato didn't have a good opinion of women; but probably they were not as amiable in his day as in ours. They undoubtedly have wrought their full share of mischief in the world. The chief bone of contention among mankind, from the earliest ages down, has been that rib of Adam out of which God made Eve. [Laughter.] And I believe in

holding women to as great a moral accountability as men. [Laughter.]
I believe, also, in holding them to the same intellectual accountability. . . . Criticism nowadays never thinks of asking whether a book
be a woman's or a man's, as a preliminary to administering praise or
blame. . . . This is right. Would you have it otherwise? Not at all! We
are to stand upon a common level. . . . 'Learn to labor and to wait,'
saith the poet. There will be need of much laboring and of long waiting. . . . Salatri, the Italian, drew a design of Patience—a woman
chained to a rock by her ankles, while a fountain threw a thin stream
of water, drop by drop, upon the iron chain, until the link should be
worn away, and the wistful prisoner be set free. In like manner the
Christian women of this country are chained to the rock of Burmese
prejudice; but God is giving the morning and the evening dew, the early
and the latter rain, until the ancient fetters shall be worn away, and a
disfranchised sex shall leap at last into political liberty. [Applause.] And
now for Mr. Beecher.

MR. BEECHER . . . spoke for an hour, in a strain of great anima-
tion, as follows:

. . . Today this nation is exercising its conscience on the subject of
suffrage for the African. I have all the time favored that: not because he
was an African, but because he was a man; because this right of voting,
which is the symbol of everything else in civil power, inheres in every
human being. But I ask you, today, "Is it safe to bring in a million black
men to vote, and not safe to bring in your mother, your wife, and your
sister to vote?" [Applause.] This ought ye to have done, and to have
done quickly, and not to have left the other undone. [Renewed applause.] Today politicians of every party, especially on the eve of an
election, are in favor of the briefest and most expeditious citizenizing of
the Irishmen. I have great respect for Irishmen—when they do not
attempt to carry on war! [Laughter.] The Irish Fenian movement is a
ludicrous phenomenon past all laughing at. Bombarding England from
the shore of America! [Great laughter.] Paper pugnation! Oratorical
destroying! But when wind-work is the order of the day, commend me
to Irishmen! [Renewed laughter.] And yet I am in favor of Irishmen
voting. Just so soon as they give pledge that they come to America, in
good faith, to abide here as citizens, and forswear the old allegiance,
and take on the new, I am in favor of their voting. Why? Because they
have learned our Constitution? No; but because voting teaches. The
vote is a schoolmaster. They will learn our laws, and learn our Constitution, and learn our customs ten times quicker when the responsibility of knowing these things is laid upon them, than when they are

permitted to live in carelessness respecting them. And this nation is so strong that it can stand the incidental mischiefs of thus teaching the wild rabble that emigration throws on our shores for our good and upbuilding. We are wise enough, and we have educational force enough, to carry these ignorant foreigners along with us. . . . I ask, is an Irishman just landed, unwashed and uncombed, more fit to vote than a woman educated in our common schools? . . . Shall we take the fairest and best part of our society; those to whom we owe it that we ourselves are civilized; our teachers; our companions; those to whom we go for counsel in trouble more than to any others; those to whom we trust everything that is dear to ourselves—our children's welfare, our household, our property, our name and reputation, and that which is deeper, our inward life itself, that no man may mention to more than one—shall we take them and say, "they are not, after all, fit to vote where the Irishman votes, and where the African votes"? . . . *It is more important that woman should vote than that the black man should vote.* It is important that he should vote, that the principle may be vindicated, and that humanity may be defended; but . . . I claim that women should vote because society will never know its last estate and true glory until you accept God's edict and God's command . . . and read this one of God's Ten Commandments, written, if not on stone, yet in the very heart and structure of mankind, *Let those that God joined together not be put asunder.* . . .

What I am arguing, when I urge that woman should vote, is that she should do all things back of that which the vote means and enforces. She should be a nursing mother to human society. It is a plea that I make, that woman should feel herself called to be interested not alone in the household, not alone in the church, not alone in just that neighborhood in which she resides, but in the sum total of that society to which she belongs; and that she should feel that her duties are not discharged until they are commensurate with the definition which our Saviour gave in the parable of the Good Samaritan. I argue, not a woman's right to vote: I argue woman's *duty to discharge citizenship.* [Applause.] I say that more and more the great interests of human society in America are such as need the peculiar genius that God has given to woman. The questions that are to fill up our days are not forever to be mere money questions. Those will always constitute a large part of politics; but not so large a portion as hitherto. We are coming to a period when it is not merely to be a scramble of fierce and belluine passions in the strife for power and ambition. Human society is yet to discuss questions of work and the workman. Down below privilege lie the masses of men. More men, a thousand times, feel every night the ground, which is their mother, than feel the stars and the moon far up in the atmosphere of favor. As when Christ came the great mass carpeted the earth, instead of lifting themselves up like trees of Lebanon, so now and here the great mass of men are men that have nothing but their hands, their heads, and their good stalwart hearts, as their capital. . . . The great question of today is, How shall work find leisure, and in leisure knowledge and refinement? . . . And is there a man who does not know, that when questions of justice and humanity are blended, woman's instinct is better than man's judgment? From the moment a woman takes the child into her arms, God makes her the love-magistrate of the family; and her instincts and moral nature fit her to adjudicate questions of weakness and want. And when society is on the eve of adjudicating such questions as these, it is a monstrous fatuity to exclude from them the very ones that, by nature, and training, and instinct, are best fitted to legislate and to judge. . . . Questions of politics are to be more and more moral questions. And I invoke those whom God made to be peculiarly conservators of things moral and spiritual to come forward and help us in that work, in which we shall falter and fail without woman. . . . Woman can never become what she should be, and the nation can never become what it should be, until there is no distinction made between the sexes as regards the rights and duties of citizenship—until we come to the 28th verse of the third chapter of Galatians. What is it? [turning to Mr. Tilton, who said, "I don't know!"] Don't know? If it was Lucy Rushton, you would! [Great laughter.] "There is neither Jew nor Greek, there is neither bond nor free, there is neither male nor female; for ye are all one in Christ Jesus." . . . Hold that a minute, please [handing Mr. Tilton a pocket Testament from which he had read the foregoing passage of Scripture]. Theodore was a most excellent young man when he used to go to my church; but he has escaped from my care lately, and now I don't know what he does. [Laughter.] . . .

A Colloquy: When Mr. BEECHER took his seat, Mr. TILTON rose and said:

In the midst of the general hilarity produced throughout the house by my friend's speech, I myself have been greatly solemnized by being made (as you have witnessed) the public custodian of his New Testament. [Laughter.] At first I shared in your gratification at seeing that he carried so much of the Scripture with him. [Laughter.] But I found, on looking at the fly-leaf, that the book after all, was not his own, but the property of a lady—I will not mention her name. [Laughter.] I have, therefore, no right to accept my friend's gift of what is not his own. Now I remember that when he came home from England, he told me a story of a company of ten ministers who sat down to dine together. A dispute arose among them as to the meaning of a certain passage of Scripture—for aught I know the very passage in Galatians which he just now tried to quote, but couldn't. [Laughter.] Someone said, "Who has a New Testament?" It was found that no one had a copy. Pretty soon, however, when the dinner reached the point of champagne, someone exclaimed, "Who has a corkscrew?" And it was found that the whole ten had, every man, a corkscrew in his pocket! [Laughter.] Now, as there is no telling where a Brooklyn minister who made a temperance speech at Cooper Institute last night is likely to take his dinner today, I charitably return the New Testament into my friend's own hands. [Great merriment.]

Mr. BEECHER—Now I know enough about champagne to know that it don't need any corkscrew. [Laughter.]

Mr. TILTON—How is it that you know so much more about corkscrews than about Galatians? [Laughter.]

Mr. BEECHER, after making some playful allusions to the story of the ten ministers, remarked that he gave it as it was given to him, but that he could not vouch for its truthfulness, as he was not present on the occasion.

Elizabeth Cady Stanton, Susan B. Anthony, and Matilda Joslyn Gage, eds., *History of Woman Suffrage*, vol. 2 (Rochester, NY: Susan B. Anthony, 1881), pp. 155–67.

8. *Henry Ward Beecher to Theodore Tilton*

June 3, 1867
My Dear Theodore:
In thinking over our conversation respecting your position on religious matters, it occurs to me that you are liable to do yourself an unnecessary injustice by supposing or affirming that you have wandered from received opinions, whereas it seems to me that you have simply entered that stage of development in which every active mind explores the grounds and reasons of belief for himself. Now, it is impossible for one, unless cautious even to coldness, to pursue such investigations without great oscillations of belief, without seeming at one time averse to one view, and then again seeking it with greater

avidity than ever. It is a question so wide, so grave, that one ought not to commit himself upon the hasty result of a year or several years' reading. You seem to me to follow your *sympathies* largely in investigation. This has its advantages, and is one way of study; but it requires *far more time* and caution, inasmuch as it will surely lead you to accept things from poetic or emotive reasons, which are but *half true*, which need and will get by longer experience much modification. The formation of opinions upon religious questions in such a nature as yours is a matter of *growth* more than of logic. Under such a state of facts, therefore, I would submit whether you can wisely or even truly say you stand on this or on that ground, and whether you do not, in justice to your own final self, require all the privileges accorded to those who are *investigating*. In part I write from experience. I look back upon periods when, if I had expressed the then results of thought and reading, I should have committed myself to views which I have outlived or left behind. I find myself, slowly but surely, going toward those views of human nature and of divine government which have underlaid for a thousand years the Evangelical churches. It seems to me that I discern, arising from studies in natural science, a surer foothold of these views than they have ever had, in so far as theology is concerned. If I have one purpose or aim, it is to secure for the truths now developing in the spheres of natural science a religious spirit and a harmonization with all the great cardinal truths of religion which have thus far characterized the Christian system. I turn with more and more chill and dread from that bleak and fruitless desert of naturalism which so many are hailing as a second paradise. I regard the labors of naturalists as indispensable to the final adjustment of truth, and I would encourage such men as Spencer to say whatever is given them, not because they bare the full truth, but because they bring out the truth, and because the human mind must pass through that stage before it will come to the rest and glory of the final Christianity, the second coming of Christ—morally, not historically—in which He shall reign in heaven and on earth over faith and science, and untie and harmonize both. Believe me, Theodore, that I have great sympathy in your developments, and affection for you, and should be glad to help and sorry to hinder.

I have given up the idea of starting a newspaper. I am sure that I could not bear the strain and yet carry on my church. I am truly yours,

H. W. Beecher

TT v. HWB, 1 : 485.

9. *Elizabeth Tilton to Theodore Tilton and Mrs. Morse*

November, 1870

I feel my duty now and love to you, my dear mother, impels me to send to you a copy which I this morning have written to Theodore, which I insist that you destroy, and use not in conversation with him. This—because of my trust in you—*you will do, I'm sure.*

FRIDAY MORNING

Oh, Theodore, Theodore! what shall I say to you? My tongue and pen are dumb and powerless, but I must force my aching heart to protest against your cruelty. I do not willingly chide. *I* suffer most when I discover to you my feelings.

Do you not know that you are fulfilling your threat—that "I shall no longer be considered the saint"?

My life is before you. I have aspired to nothing save to do, through manifold infirmities, *my best*, and that not for human praise, but for the grateful love I feel towards Jesus Christ, my God.

Do you not know, also, that when in any circle you blacken Mr. B's name—and soon after couple mine with it—you blacken mine as well?

When, by your threats, my mother cried out in agony to me, "Why what have *you* done, Elizabeth, my child?" her worst suspicions were aroused, and I laid bare my heart then—that from *my* lips and not yours she might receive the dagger into her heart! Did not my dear child (Florence) learn enough by insinuations, that her sweet, pure soul agonized in secret, till she broke out with the *dreadful question?* I know not but it hath been her death blow!

When you say to my beloved brother—"Mr. B. preaches to forty of his m[istresse]s every Sunday," then follow with the remark that after *my* death you have a dreadful secret to reveal, need he be told any more ere the sword pass into *his* soul?

After this "you are my indignant champion," are you? It is now too late; you have blackened my character, and it is for my loved ones that I suffer; yea, for the agony which the revelation has caused *you*, my cries ascend to Heaven night and day that upon mine own head all the anguish may fall.

Believe you that I would thrust a like dart into your sister's or mother's heart were there occasion? No, no, I would not, indeed.

So after my death you will, to the bereaved hearts of those who love me, add the poisoned balm! In heathen lands the sins of our beloved are buried, and only their virtues are remembered!

Theodore, *your* past is safe with me, rolled up, put away never to be opened—though it is big with stains of various hue—unless you force me for the sake of my children and friends to discover it, in self-defence or their defence.

Would *you* suffer were I to cast a shadow on any lady whom you love? Certainly, if you have any manliness you would. Even so every word, look, or intimation against Mr. B., though I be in nowise brought in, is an agony beyond the piercing of myself a hundred times. His position and his good name are dear to me; and even thus do I agonize—yea, agony is the word—for *your* good name, and if you will only value it yourself to *keep it good,* I am and always will be your helper.

Once again I implore you for your children's sake, to whom you have a duty in this matter, that *my Past* be buried—left with me and my God. He is merciful. Will you, his son, be like him?

Do not be alarmed about mother; you are not responsible for *her* revelations. Do not think or say any more that my ill-health is on account of my sin and its discovery. It is not true, indeed. My sins and my life's record I have carried to my Saviour, and his delicacy and tenderness towards me passeth even a mother's love or "the love of woman." *I rest in him, I trust in him,* and though the way is darker than death, I do hear "the still small voice" which brings to me a peace life's experience has never before brought me. No, my prostration is owing to the suffering I have caused *you,* and will cause those I love in the future if the spirit of forgiveness does not exorcise the spirit of hate. And add to this the revelations you have made of your *fallen condition,* witness of which I am daily! This it is that breaks my heart. How can I but "linger at my praying" at the thought of you?

Oh, do avoid all stimulating drinks, my darling. *I know* many a heartache would have been saved, only you knew not what or how the cruel word was said! I have failed in my duty to you from lack of courage to speak of these things. Allow me to advise with you now, my dearly beloved, for surely I am your best friend, and for the sake of our precious born and unborn. I tell you that since I have *been conscious* of wronging you I needed only to *know* that, and always in everything I utterly forsake the wrong, repent before God alone, and strive to bring forth fruit worthy of repentance. Will you for the added reason of your soul's sake *do the same?*

I feel that you are not in the condition of mind to lead the "woman's suffrage" movement, and I implore you to break away from it and from your friends Susan [Anthony], Mrs. Stanton, and every one and everything that helps to make a conflict with your responsibilities as husband

and father. My life is still spared; my heart never yearned over you more in sorrowing love than now. But there must be a turning to God that will lead you to forsake forbidden ways, so that the sources and springs of your life be renewed, ere I shall feel it my duty to return.

I have gained a little, and with this small addition of strength my first impulse is to fly to you and comfort you in these new distractions which come to you through your business and its threatening changes. I have long felt, dear husband, you did not fill up your responsibilities towards the *Independent* as its religious chief and head. Oh, that you could be made to see and feel the amount of good you might do for Christ from that pulpit! Oh, my babe would leap in my womb for joy did your soul but awake to love God, and serve him with the fervor of the early days.

As I look out from my retirement here, these are my thoughts and desires.

I shall mourn if there seemeth to your aching heart a harsh word. I will pray God's spirit to follow the written line, and so it will not, cannot offend.

I do not hesitate to return to Brooklyn and renew my home-work. Far be it from me to shirk my duty; on the contrary, to have again the privilege of being with my entire family is the ambition I feel to gain in health here. Forgive the long letter. Good-night.

Your Dear Wife.

Postscript.

Dear Mother, I will now add a line to you. I should mourn greatly if my life was to be made yet known to father [ET's stepfather]: his head would be bowed indeed to the grave. I love him very much, and it would soothe my heart could you be restored to him. I was greatly touched by his saying to you that "you were still his wife."

Would not his sympathizing heart comfort you in your great sorrow?

Both your letter and Theodore's came together, concerning your interviews with Joseph.

You will see that by reading or showing this letter to any one you discover my secret. It is because I trust you, dear mother, that I send you this, that you may know my spirit completely toward you both.

I have been told, "Confide not in your mother"; but I reply, "To whom on earth can I confide?"

I think it pre-eminently wise for us to destroy our letters respecting this subject, lest Flory or some one should pick them up.

Darling

"Theodore Tilton's Sworn Statement" to the Plymouth Church Investigating Committee in 1874, in Charles F. Marshall, *The True History of the Brooklyn Scandal* (Philadelphia: National Publishing Co., 1874), pp. 535–37. The letter was sent from Marietta, Ohio, where Mrs. Tilton was staying with Bessie Turner and family friend Sarah Putnam. In her trial testimony Turner said she and Mrs. Tilton left Marietta for Brooklyn on November 9, 1870, which means the letter was written on November 4. Mrs. Tilton had been in Marietta between four and six weeks, according to Turner, so she had left her husband—after becoming pregnant with the child she would lose to miscarriage in late December—in late September or early October. This letter makes clear that she (and in all likelihood Theodore too) considered him— not Beecher, as Frank Moulton darkly insinuated in 1874—the father of the baby she was carrying. In her January 1871 letter to her "friend and sister" (see below) she refers to that fetus as her promised "love-babe."

I O. *Elizabeth Tilton's Recantation*

December 30, 1870

Wearied with importunity and weakened by sickness I gave a letter inculpating my friend Henry Ward Beecher under assurances that that would remove all difficulties between me and my husband. That letter I now revoke. I was persuaded to it—almost forced—when I was in a weakened state of mind. I regret it, and recall all its statements.

E. R. Tilton

I desire to say explicitly Mr. Beecher has never offered any improper solicitations, but has always treated me in a manner becoming a Christian and a gentleman.

Elizabeth R. Tilton

"Statement of Francis D. Moulton," in Marshall, *True History,* p. 317.

I I . *Elizabeth Tilton's Retraction of Her Recantation*

December 30, 1870, Midnight
My Dear Husband:

I desire to leave with you, before going to sleep, a statement that Mr. Henry Ward Beecher called upon me this evening, asked me if I would defend him against any accusation in a Council of

Ministers, and I replied solemnly that I would in case the accuser was any other person than my husband. He (H. W. B.) dictated a letter, which I copied as my own, to be used by him as against any other accuser except my husband. This letter was designed to vindicate Mr. Beecher against all other persons save only yourself. I was ready to give him this letter because he said with pain that my letter in your hands addressed to him, dated December 29, "had struck him dead, and ended his usefulness."

You and I both are pledged to do our best to avoid publicity. God grant a speedy end to all further anxieties. Affectionately,

Elizabeth

"Statement of Francis D. Moulton," in Marshall, *True History*, p. 318. Elizabeth's letter of December 29 was, according to Theodore's 1874 comment, "a statement by Mrs. Tilton of the substance of the confession which she had before made, and of her wish and prayer for reconciliation and peace between her pastor and her husband. This paper furnished to Mr. Beecher the first knowledge which he had as yet received that Mrs. Tilton had made such a confession." "Mr. Tilton's Sworn Statement," in Marshall, p. 117.

I 2. *Elizabeth Tilton, letter to "Friend and Sister" [probably Laura Curtis Bullard]*

174 Livingston Street, Brooklyn, January 13, 1871
My Dear Friend and Sister:
I was made very glad by your letter, for your love to me is most grateful, and for which I actually hunger. You, like me, have loved and been loved, and can say with Mrs. Browning,

> "Well enough I think we've fared,
> My heart and I."

But I find in you an element to which I respond; when or how, I am not philosopher enough of the human mind to understand. I cannot reason—only feel.

I wrote to you a reply on the morning of my sickness, and tinged with fears of approaching disaster, so that when mail day arrived I was safely over my sufferings, with a fair prospect of returning health. I destroyed it lest its morbid tone might shadow your spirit. I am now around my house again, doing very poorly what I want to do well. All these ambitions are failures, you know, darling, and when, in your last letter to Theodore—those good, true letters—you tell indirectly of

344

your life with your parents, I caught and felt the self-sacrifice, admired and sincerely appreciated your rare qualities of heart and mind. I am a more demonstrative and enthusiastic lover of *God* manifested in his children than you will believe, and my memories of you fill me with admiration and delight. I have caught up your card-picture, which we have, in such moments, and kissed it again and again, praying with tears for God's blessing to follow you, and to perfect in us three the beautiful promise of our nature. But, my sweet and dear ——, I realize in these months of our acquaintance how almost impossible it is to *bring out* these blossoms of our heart's growth—God's gifts to us—to human eyes. Our pearls and flowers are caught up literally by vulgar and base minds that surround us on every side, and so destroyed or abused that we know them no longer as our own, and thus God is made our only hope.

My dear, dear sister, do not let us disappoint each other. I expect much from you—you do of me. Not in the sense of draining or weariness to body or spirit, but trust and faith in human hearts. Does it not exist between us? I believe it! My husband has suffered much with me in a cruel conspiracy made by my poor suffering mother—with an energy worthy of a better cause—to divorce us by saying that *I* was seeking it because of Theodore's infidelity, making *her* feeling *mine*.

These slanders have been sown broadcast. I am quoted everywhere as the author of them. Coming in this form and way to Mr. Bowen, they caused his [Theodore's] immediate dismission from both the *Independent* and *Union*. Suffering thus both of us so unjustly—(I knew nothing of these plans)—anxiety night and day brought on my miscarriage: a disappointment I have never before known—a *love babe* it promised, you know. I have had sorrow almost beyond human capacity dear ——. It is my mother! That will explain volumes to your filial heart. Theodore has many secret enemies, I find, besides my mother, but with a faithfulness renewed and strengthened by experience *we* will, by silence, time, and patience, be victorious over them all. My faith and hope are very bright, now that I am off the sick-bed, and dear Frank Moulton is a friend indeed. (He is managing the case with Mr. Bowen.) We have weathered the storm, and, I believe, without harm to our *Best*. "Let not your heart be troubled," dear sweet—I love you. Be assured of it. I wish I could come to you. I would help you in the care of your loved ones, for *that* I can do. "My heart bounds towards all." Then your spirit would be free to write and think.

But hereunto I am not called. My spirit is willing. My dear children are all well. Flory, on her return at the holiday vacation, found me sick, and we concluded to keep her with us, and she has entered the Packer

[Institute]. Our household has indeed been sadly tossed about and the children suffer with the parents; but *the end has come,* and I write that you may have joy and not grief, for that has past! I am glad you love Alice. I have kissed her for you many times. I will teach all my darlings to love you and welcome your home-coming. Ralph is a fine, beautiful boy, and to be our only baby—very precious therefore. Carroll is visiting Theodore's parents at Keyport. I hope your mother is now better and that you have reached the sunshine. Our spirits cannot thrive in Nature's gloom. Give much love to your parents. I am yours, faithfully and fondly,

Sister Elizabeth

"Frank Moulton's First Statement" to the Plymouth Church Investigating Committee, in Marshall, *True History,* pp. 349–50. Moulton did not identify the recipient, but told the Committee she was the "lady" who was the subject of Henry Bowen's "accusations against Tilton" in 1870. Moulton presented the letter as evidence that Mrs. Tilton had not "desired a separation from her husband, as had been alleged, on account of his [alleged] infidelities with this lady." Marshall, p. 350.

I 3. *Henry Ward Beecher to Elizabeth Tilton, n.d. [March 1871 or 1872] (the "True Inwardness" letter)*

The blessing of God rest upon you! Every spark of light and warmth in your own house will be a star and a sun in my dwelling. Your note broke like Spring upon Winter, and gave me an inward rebound toward life. No one can ever know—none but God—through what a dreary wilderness I have wandered! There was Mount Sinai, there was the barren sand, there was the alternation of hope and despair that marked the pilgrimage of old. If only it might lead to the Promised Land!—or, like Moses, shall I die on the border? Your hope and courage are like medicine. Should God inspire you to restore and rebuild at home, and while doing it to cheer and sustain outside of it another who sorely needs help in heart and spirit, it will prove a life so noble as few are able to live! And, in another world, the emancipated soul may utter thanks!

If it would be a comfort to *you,* now and then, to send me a letter of true *inwardness*—the outcome of your inner life—it *would* be safe, for I am now at home here with my sister; and it is *permitted to you,* and it will be an exceeding refreshment to me, for your heart experiences are often like bread from heaven to the hungry. God has enriched your moral nature. May not others partake?

TT v. HWB, 1: 84, 2: 817. The version at 1: 84 has "spark of life," not "light," in sentence two.

I 4. *Elizabeth Tilton to Theodore Tilton (the "*Griffith Gaunt*" letter, or, the "*Catherine Gaunt*" letter)*

Schoharie, June 29, 1871

My Dear Theodore:

Today, through the ministry of Catharine Gaunt, a character of fiction, my eyes have been opened for the first time in my experience, so that I see clearly my sin. It was when I knew that I was loved, to suffer it to grow to a passion. A virtuous woman should check instantly an absorbing love. But it appeared to me in such false light. That the love I felt and received could harm no one, not even you, I have believed unfalteringly until four o'clock this afternoon, when the heavenly vision dawned upon me. I see now, as never before, the wrong I have done you, and hasten immediately to ask your pardon, with a penitence so sincere that henceforth (if reason remains) you may trust me implicitly. Oh! my dear Theodore, though your opinions are not restful or congenial to my soul, yet my own integrity and purity are a sacred and holy thing to me. Bless God, with me, for Catharine Gaunt, and for all the sure leadings of an all-wise and loving Providence. Yes; now I feel quite prepared to renew my marriage vow with you, to keep it as the Saviour requireth, who looketh at the eye and the heart. Never before could I say this. **I know not that you are yet able, or ever will be, to say this to me. Still, with what profound thankfulness that I am come to this sure foundation, and that my feet are planted on the rock of this great truth you cannot at all realize.** When you yearn toward me with **any** true feeling, be assured of the tried, purified, and restored love of

Elizabeth.

"Theodore Tilton's Sworn Statement" to the Plymouth Church Investigating Committee in 1874, in Marshall, *True History*, pp. 120–21. Bolded portions, omitted in Tilton's version, restored by William Evarts at the civil trial in 1875. *TT v. HWB* 1: 540, 544–45. Theodore not only deleted portions of the letter, but made other small changes too, as one discovers in comparing his published version to the facsimile copy reprinted on the last page of the "Prologue." In addition to some inconsequential alterations to punctuation, spelling (he put "Theodore" where she had "Theo.") and word order (he reversed "restful" and "congenial"), he improved and modernized his wife's grammar. He added "that" before "the love I felt and received," and had her saying "yet my own integrity and purity" rather than "mine own." He also changed his wife's "our all wise . . . Providence" to "an all-wise . . . Providence."

15. *Theodore Tilton, "Sir Marmaduke's Musings," November 1, 1871*

I won a noble fame,
    But, with a sudden frown,
    The people snatched my crown,
    And in the mire trod down
My lofty name.
I bore a bounteous purse,
    And beggars by the way
    Then blessed me day by day,
    But I, grown poor as they,
Have now their curse.
I gained what men call friends,
    But now their love is hate,
    And I have learned, too late,
    How mated minds unmate,
And friendship ends.
I clasped a woman's breast,
    As if her heart I knew
    Or fancied would be true.
    Who proved—alas! she too—
False like the rest.
I am now all bereft,
    As when some tower doth fall,
    With battlements and wall,
    And gate and bridge and all,
And nothing left.
But I account it worth
    All pangs of fair hopes crossed—
    All love and honors lost—
    To gain the heavens at cost

Of losing earth.
So, lest I be inclined
   To render ill for ill—
   Henceforth in me instil,
   O God, a sweet good-will
To all mankind.

Beecher-Tilton Investigation: The Scandal of the Age (Philadelphia: Barclay and Co., 1874), p. 43; *TT v. HWB*, 1: 84–85 (with minor changes); first published in TT's *The Golden Age*, November 1871.

16. *Henry Ward Beecher to Frank Moulton (the "Ragged Edge" letter)*

Monday, February 5, 1872
My Dear Friend:
   I leave town today, and expect to pass through from Philadelphia to New Haven; shall not be here until Friday.
   About three weeks ago I met T[heodore] in the cars going to B[oston]. He was kind. We talked much. At the end he told me to go on with my work without the least anxiety, in so far as his feelings and actions were the occasion of apprehension.
   On returning home from New Haven (where I am three days in the week delivering a course of lectures to the theological students), I found a note from E[lizabeth] saying that T[heodore] felt hard towards me, and was going to see or write me before leaving for the West. She kindly added: "Do not be cast down. I bear this almost always, but the God in whom we trust will *deliver us all safely*. I know you do and are willing abundantly to help him, and I also know your embarrassments."
   There were added words of warning, but also of consolation, for I believe E[lizabeth] is beloved of God, and that her prayers for me are sooner heard than mine for myself or for her. But it seems that a change has come to T[heodore] since I saw him in the cars. Indeed, even [ever?] since he felt more intensely the force of feeling in society, and the humiliations which environ his enterprise, he has growingly felt that I had a power to help which I did not develop, and I believe that you have participated in this feeling—it is natural you should. T[heodore] is dearer to you than I *can* be. He is with you. All his trials lie open to your eye daily. But I see you but seldom, and my personal relations, environments, necessities, limitations, dangers, and perplexities you

cannot see nor imagine. If I had not gone through this *great year of trouble*, I would not have believed that anyone could pass through my experience and be *alive* and *sane*.

I have been the centre of three distinct circles, each of which required clear-mindedness and peculiarly inventive, or originating power, viz.:

1. The *great church* [Plymouth].
2. The *newspaper* [the *Christian Union*].
3. The *book* [*The Life of Jesus, the Christ*].

The first I could neither get out of nor slight. The sensitiveness of so many of my people would have made any appearance of trouble or any remission of force an occasion of alarm and notice, and have excited where it was important that rumors should die and everything be quieted.

The newspaper I did roll off—doing but little except give general direction, and in so doing, I was continually spurred and exhorted by those in interest. It could not be helped.

"The Life of Christ," long delayed, had locked up the capital of the firm [J. B. Ford] and was likely to sink them—finished it *must* be. Was ever [a] book born of such sorrow as that was? The interior history of it will never be written.

During all this time you, literally, were all my *stay* and *comfort*. I should have fallen on the way but for the courage which you inspired and the hope which you breathed.

My vacation was profitable. I came back, hoping that the bitterness of death was passed. But T[heodore]'s trouble brought back the cloud, with even severer suffering. For, all this fall and winter, I have felt that you did not feel satisfied with me, and that I seemed both to you and Tilton as contenting myself with a cautious or sluggish policy—willing to save myself, but not willing to risk anything for Tilton. I have again and again probed my heart to see whether I was truly liable to such feeling, and the response is unequivocal that I am not.

No man can see the difficulties that environ me, unless he stands where I do. To *say* that I have a church on my hands is simple enough; but to have the hundreds and thousands of men pressing me, each one with his keen suspicion, or anxiety, or zeal; to see tendencies which if not stopped would break out into a ruinous defence of me; to stop them without seeming to do it; to prevent anyone questioning me; to meet and allay prejudices against T[heodore] which had their beginning years before this; to keep serene, as if I was not alarmed or disturbed; to be cheerful at home and among friends, when I was suffering the torments of the damned; to pass sleepless nights often, and yet to come up fresh and full for Sunday. All this may be talked about, but the real thing cannot be understood from the outside, nor its wearing and grinding on the nervous system.

God knows that I have put more thought, and judgment, and earnest desire into my efforts to prepare a way for T[heodore] and E[lizabeth] than ever I did for myself a hundred fold.

As to the outside public, I have never lost an opportunity to soften prejudices, to refute falsehoods, and to excite a kindly feeling among all whom I met. I am known among clergymen, public men, and generally, the makers of public opinion, and I have used every rational endeavor to restrain the evils which have been visited upon T[heodore], and with increasing success.

But the roots of this prejudice are long. The catastrophe which precipitated him from his place only disclosed feelings that had existed long. Neither he nor you can be aware of the feelings of classes in society on other grounds than late rumors. I mention this to explain why I *know* with *absolute* certainty that no mere statement, letter, testimony, or affirmation will reach the root of affairs and reinstate them. Time and work will. But chronic evil requires *chronic remedies.*

If my destruction will place him all right, that shall not stand in the way. I am willing to step down and out. No one can offer more than that; that I do offer. Sacrifice me without hesitation if you can clearly see your way to his happiness and safety thereby.

I do not think that anything would be gained by it. I should be destroyed but he would not be saved. Elizabeth and the children would have their future clouded.

In one point of view I could desire the sacrifice on my part. Nothing can possibly be so bad as the horror of great darkness, in which I spend much of my time. I look upon death as sweeter-faced than any friend I have in the world. Life would be pleasant if I could see that rebuilt which is shattered; but to live on the sharp and ragged edge of anxiety, remorse, fear, despair, and yet to put on all the appearances of serenity and happiness, cannot be endured much longer.

I am well-nigh discouraged. If you too cease to trust me, to love me, I am alone. I have not another person to whom I could go.

Well, to God I commit all—whatever it may be here, it shall be well there—with sincere gratitude for your heroic friendship, and with sincere affection, even though you love me not,

I am yours (though unknown to you),

H. W. B.

"Mr. Beecher's Defense," in Marshall, *True History*, pp. 275–77. A slightly different version of the "Ragged Edge" letter—produced by a different copyist—appears in Marshall, pp. 359–61. None of the differences are significant.

I 7 .   *Theodore Tilton to —— (letter to a "Complaining Friend")*

174 Livingston Street, Brooklyn, December 27, 1872

My Complaining Friend:

Thanks for your good letter of bad advice. You say, "How easy to give the lie to the wicked story [Woodhull's published accusation of November 2], and thus end it forever!" But stop and consider. The story is a whole library of statements—a hundred or more—and it would be strange if some of them were not correct, though I doubt if any are. To give a general denial to such an encyclopedia of assertions would be as vague and irrelevant as to take up the *Police Gazette*, with its twenty-four pages of illustrations, and say, "this is all a lie." So extensive a libel requires, if answered at all, a special denial of its several parts; and, furthermore, it requires, in this particular case, not only a denial of things misstated, but a truthful explanation of the things that remain unstated and in mystery. In other words, the false story, if met at all, should be confronted and confounded by the true one. Now, my friend, you urge me to speak; but when the truth is a sword, God's mercy sometimes commands it sheathed. If you think I do not burn to defend my wife and little ones, you know not the fiery spirit within me. *But my wife's heart is more a fountain of charity, and quenches all resentments. She says: "Let there be no suffering save to ourselves alone," and forbids a vindication to the injury of others. From the beginning she has stood with her hand on my lips, saying, "Hush!" So, when you prompt me to speak for her you countervail her more Christian mandate of silence.* Moreover, after all, the chief victim of the public displeasure is myself alone, and so long as this is happily the case, I shall try with patience to keep my answer within my own breast, lest it shoot forth like a thunderbolt through other hearts. Yours truly,

Theodore Tilton

"Theodore Tilton's Last Statement," in Marshall, *True History*, pp. 540–41.

I 8.   *Theodore Tilton to ——— (letter to a "friend in the west")*

174 Livingston Street, Brooklyn, December 31, 1872

My Dear Friend:

I owe you a long letter. I am unwell, and a prisoner in the house, leaning back in leather-cushioned idleness, and writing on my chair-board before the fire. Perhaps you wonder that I have a fire, or anything but a hearth-stone, broken and crumbled, since the world has been told that my household is in ruins. And yet it is more like your last letter—brimful of love and wit, and sparkling like a fountain in midwinter.

Nevertheless you are right. I am in trouble, and I hardly see a path out of it.

It is just two years ago today—this very day—the last of the year—that Mr. Bowen lifted his hammer, and with an unjust blow smote asunder my two contracts, one with *The Independent* and the other with *The Brooklyn Union*. The public little suspects that this act of his turned on his fear to meet the consequences of horrible charges which he made against Henry Ward Beecher. I have kept quiet on the subject for two years through an unwillingness to harm others even for the sake of righting myself before the public. But having trusted to time for my vindication, I find that time has only thickened my difficulties until these now buffet me like a storm.

You know that Bowen long ago paid to me the assessed pecuniary damages which grew out of his breaking of the contracts, and gave me a written vindication of *my* course, and something like an apology for *his*. This settlement, so far as I am concerned, is final.

But Bowen's assassinating dagger drawn against Beecher has proved as unable as Macbeth's to "trammel up the consequence." And the consequence is that the air of Brooklyn is rife with stories against its chief clergyman, not growing out of the Woodhull scandal merely, but exhaled with ever-fresh foulness, like Mephitic vapors, from Bowen's own charge against Beecher.

Verily, the tongue is a wild beast that no man can tame, and, like a wolf, it is now seeking to devour the chief shepherd of the flock, together, also, with my own pretty lambs.

For the last four or five weeks, or ever since I saw the Woodhull libel, I have hardly had a restful day, and I frequently dream the whole thing over at night, waking the next morning unfit for work.

Have you any conception of what it is to suffer the keenest possible injustice? If not, come and learn of me.

To say nothing of the wrong and insult to my wife, in whose sorrow I have greater sorrow, I have to bear the additional indignity of being misconstrued by half the public and by many friends.

For instance, it is supposed that I had a conspirator's hand in this unholy business, whereas I am as innocent of it as of the Nathan murder.

It is hinted that the libelous article was actually written by me; whereas (being in the north of New Hampshire), I did not know of its existence till a week after it had convulsed my own city and family. My wife never named it in her letters to me lest it should spoil my mood for public speaking. (You know I was then toiling day and night for Mr. Greeley's sake.)

Then, too, it is the sneer of the clubs that I have degenerated into an apostle of free-love; whereas the whole body of my writings stands like a monument against this execrable theory.

Moreover, it is charged that I am in financial and other relations with Mrs. Woodhull; whereas I have not spoken to, nor met, nor seen her for nearly a year.

The history of my acquaintance with her is this: In the Spring of 1871, a few months after Bowen charged Beecher with the most hideous crime known to human nature, and had slammed the door of *The Independent* in my face, and when I was toiling like Hercules to keep the scandal from the public, then it was that Mrs. Woodhull, hitherto a total stranger to me, suddenly sent for me and poured into my ears, not the Bowen scandal, but a new one of her own—namely, almost the same identical tale which she printed a few weeks ago. Think of it! When I was doing my best to suppress *one* earthquake, Mrs. Woodhull suddenly stood before me portentous with another. What was I to do? I resolved at all hazards to keep back the new avalanche until I could securely tie up the original storm. My fear was that she would *publish* what she told to me, and, to prevent this catastrophe, I resolved (and, as the result proves, like a fool, and yet with a fool's innocent and pure motive) to make her such a friend of mine that she would never think of doing me such a harm. So I rendered her some important services (including especially some labors of pen and ink), all with a view to put and hold her under an obligation to me and mine.

In so acting towards her I found, to my glad surprise and astonishment, that she rose almost as high in my estimation as she had done with Lucretia Mott, Mrs. H. B. Stanton, Isabella Beecher Hooker, and other excellent women. Nobody who has not met Mrs. Woodhull can have an adequate idea of the admirable impression which she is capable of producing on serious persons. Moreover, I felt that the current denunciations against her were outrageously unjust, and that, like myself, she had been put in a false position before the public, and I sympathized keenly with the aggravation of spirit which this produces. This fact lent a zeal to all I said in her defense.

Nor was it till after I had known her for a number of months, and when I discovered her purpose to libel a dozen representative women of the suffrage movement, that I suddenly opened my eyes to her real tendencies to mischief, and then it was that I indignantly repudiated her acquaintance, and have never seen her since.

Hence her late tirade.

Well, it is over, and *I* am left to be the chief sufferer in the public estimation.

What to do in the emergency (which is not clearing, but clouding itself daily) I have not decided. What I *could* do would be take from my writing-desk, and publish tomorrow morning, the prepared narrative and vindication, which with facts and documents, my legal advisers pronounce complete.

This would explain and clarify everything, both great and small (including the Woodhull episode, which is but a minor part of the whole case), but if I publish it, I must not only violate a kind of honorable obligation to be silent, which I had voluntarily imposed upon myself, but I must put my old friend Bowen to a serious risk of being smitten dead by Beecher's hand.

How far Bowen would deserve his fate I cannot say, but I know that all Plymouth Church would hunt him as a rat.

Well, perhaps the future will unravel my skein for me without my own hand; but whatever happens to my weather-beaten self, I wish to you, O prosperous comrade, a happy New Year.

Fraternally yours,

Theodore Tilton

P.S. Before sending this long letter (which pays my debt to you) I have read it to my wife, who desires to supplement it by sending her love and good will to the little white cottage and its little red cheeks.

"Frank Moulton's First Statement" to the Plymouth Church Investigating Committee in 1874, in Marshall, *True History*, pp. 373–74; also in *TT v. HWB*, 1: 156–57. In his trial testimony Moulton said he was unsure whether the letter was ever sent or who the "friend" might have been. If the letter had a real recipient, it may well have been the Mrs. Lovejoy mentioned in Tilton's letter to Elizabeth dated February 12, 1867 (see chapter 8).

He speaks there of an idyllic visit to Mrs. Lovejoy's "cottage" in Princeton, Illinois, and of his deep fondness for her. She was a surviving relative of abolitionist Owen Lovejoy, Republican congressman and Congregational minister from Princeton who had died in 1864. (He was the younger brother of abolitionist martyr Elijah Lovejoy, killed in 1837 at Alton, Illinois.)

19. *Henry Ward Beecher to Frank Moulton (the "Day of Judgment" letter)*

Sunday Morning, June 1, 1873

My Dear Frank:

The whole earth is tranquil and the heaven is serene, as befits one who has about finished his world-life. I could do nothing on Saturday. My head was confused. But a good sleep has made it like crystal. I have determined to make no more resistance. Theodore's temperament is such that the future, even if temporarily earned, would be absolutely worthless, filled with abrupt changes [charges?], and rendering me liable, at any hour or day, to be obliged to stultify all the devices by which we have saved ourselves. It is only fair that he should know that the publication of the card which he proposes would leave him far worse off than before.

The agreement [the Tripartite Covenant among Beecher, Bowen, and Tilton] was made after my letter, through you, was written. He had had it a year. He had condoned his wife's fault. He had enjoined upon me with the utmost earnestness and solemnity not to betray his wife, nor leave his children to a blight. I had honestly and earnestly joined in the purpose. Then, this settlement was made and signed by him. It was not my making. He revised his part so that it should wholly suit him, and signed it. It stood unquestioned and unblamed for more than a year. *Then it was published.* Nothing but that. That which he did in private, when made public, excited him to fury, and he charges me with *making him appear* as one *graciously pardoned by me!* It was his own deliberate act, with which he was perfectly content till others saw it, and then he charges a grievous wrong home on me!

My mind is clear. I am not in haste. I shall write for the public a statement that will bear the light of the judgment day. God will take care of me and mine. When I look on earth it is deep night. When I look to the heavens above I see the morning breaking. But oh! that I could put in golden letters my deep sense of your faithful, earnest, undying fidelity, your disinterested friendship. Your noble wife, too, has been to me one of God's comforters. It is such as she that renews a waning faith in womanhood. Now, Frank, I would not have you waste any more energy on a hopeless task. With such a man as T. T. there is no possible salvation for any that depend upon him. With a strong nature, he does not know how to govern it. With generous impulses, the undercurrent that rules him is self. With ardent affections, he cannot love long that which does not repay him with admiration and praise. With a strong, theatric nature, he is constantly imposed upon with the idea that a position, a great stroke, a *coup d'état,* is the way to success.

Besides these he has a hundred good things about him, but these named traits make him absolutely *unreliable.*

Therefore there is no use in further trying. I have a strong feeling upon me, and it brings great peace with it, that I am spending my *last Sunday* and preaching my last sermon.

Dear, good God, I thank thee I am indeed beginning to see rest and triumph. The pain of life is but a moment; the glory of everlasting emancipation is wordless, inconceivable, full of beckoning glory. Oh, my beloved Frank, I shall know you there, and forever hold fellowship with you, and look back and smile at the past. Your loving

HWB

"Mr. Beecher's Defense" at the Plymouth Church Investigating Committee in 1874, in Marshall, *True History,* pp. 280, 282. Frank Moulton also published the letter in his "First Statement" to the Committee, in Marshall, p. 365. There are several unimportant textual differences between the two; the only one of any significance is that Moulton's version has "abrupt charges" (probably a printer's error) where Beecher's has "abrupt changes" in the sixth sentence. The text of the Tripartite Covenant, together with Tilton's letter to Bowen of January 1, 1871 (summarizing Theodore's recollection of all the accusations Bowen had ever made against Beecher), came out in the mainstream press two days before Beecher wrote the "Day of Judgment" letter. For example, "Galvanizing a Filthy Scandal," *New York Times,* May 30, 1873, p. 5, with accompanying editorial, p. 4.

20.   *Eunice (Mrs. Henry Ward) Beecher to (her daughter) Harriet Beecher Scoville*

Brooklyn, August 9, 1874
My Darling Hattie,
    This has been a week of no rest. I have tried in vain to send you a word but could not. Today, Sunday, father [Henry] is at the farm hard at work and I here, where I have been from the first—

hunting, searching for papers, etc., and keeping watch and ward that no one gets access to father or *interviews* anyone. Aunt Hattie Stowe [Harriet Beecher Stowe] is here and makes my work much harder. She can't understand that till father has a chance to be heard we allow no talk to anyone that comes inside our door—for reporters to make lies over. But she has the greatest longing to talk with just the ones she must not. "Oh let me go, I'll soon settle it," she exclaims, when she hears me badgered by reporters as I stand in the door preventing their entrance. She'd make another *Byron muddle* if she could. I wish she'd go home, but she is father's sister. She loves him, but worries him just now.

If I ever see you again my dear son and daughter I will tell you many things that will then do to laugh over. Just now they are not so funny. But I must hasten. I wanted to write as soon as yours to father came, for dear children, I forget, in the din and whirl of *battle*—for it is just that—that you are not kept as fully informed as I am. Why, there is *now* no fear that father will not fight. His eyes are at last opened, and he sees both Tilton and Moulton in their naked depravity and baseness. It has been hard work to convince the dear guileless simple-hearted man that such baseness and treachery could exist save in the most sensational novels, and the process of opening his eyes was like dividing soul and body, as one by one the scales dropped from his eyes and he saw for whom he had been bearing burdens—for whom he had borne the blame in hopes of saving them from *mistakes,* he thought, but which now appear the vilest of deceit—for whom he seemed cold at times, lest I should refuse to see the *good* in them with which his kind unsuspicious heart had [?]. When he awoke to find how he had been blinded, for a week he suffered terribly, and sunk into a state of despondency that alarmed me. Yet under all—even while he trusted in Moulton's *friendship* but could no longer trust his *judgment*—he was hard at work getting together all the threads of this fearfully intricate web. But at last Moulton's insincerity and treachery stood confessed, and after one or two days of sharpest agony—equal to that which a young maiden ever felt when her idol lay shattered before her—the noble old *Lion* roused himself. He now shakes his mane *and paws,* restlessly chafing, while held back by the [Plymouth Church Investigating] Committee, till they can choke those letters out of Moulton's jaws. For don't you see, it is in vain for father to *answer* or *deny* letters that are kept from his sight, letters purporting to be those he has given to Moulton for *safekeeping!! Safekeeping,* as if he, the infernal villain, would be a safer repository than I, father's wife. Letters that have been always ready for *Tilton's inspection,* letters I say, that who knows if the letters father gave him are in existence. Who knows how many in Moulton's hands are *forgeries*. For three long weeks Moulton has been hunted for, far and near. Father has written him, first *asking* for, then *urging*, at last again *demanding* those letters but Moulton could not be found. At last he is unhoused and finds it will take *him a week* to collect those letters and bring forward a statement. Who wants a statement from him? No one.

It is the *letters — the letters*, only the letters. That is all they ask for. At last he promises them Saturday. The Committee, worn out, hard at work all the week, Sundays not excepted, urge him to let them have them Friday, so that they can hear him read the letters, and then call father for his examination Saturday p.m., and get off for rest Sunday. Moulton promises for Friday, but [?] will deign to appear on Saturday. Can you understand *why?* I guess not, for you have not been behind the scenes and do not understand this fiendish diplomacy, as we must who are under fire all the time. If he could delay so late Saturday that father could not be called for, don't you see, he could, as Tilton did, have someone *steal* his statement and publish it broadcast over the land in Sunday papers, giving him 24 hours advantage over father, for the community to try, judge, and execute your father before he could be heard and refute the lies.

But our Committee was too cute for them. They waited till last evening then sent word to Moulton that part of the Committee were compelled to be away and the rest needed the relaxation and therefore wished to defer his appearing till 3 Sunday p.m. It was bad in some respects to defer it, but better than to give him Sunday ahead. Don't you see that it is not any holding back on father's part, but the Committee into whose hands he has placed his care, and all the best lawyers from whom they have sought advice, refuse to hear father till they get all the others' testimony and know to the uttermost *whereof he is accused* — else were he to come before all this, they [Tilton and Moulton] could hatch up other crimes and keep him here all the year, or kill him.

Father is now roused to the fullest extent of indignation and holds back nothing. Many things that it is very hard for him to expose, as they show to what extent and how weakly he has trusted, how fearfully he has been Moulted, or blackmailed, not through *fear* but through *kindness and sympathy*. Now is explained his stern appeals to *me to be more careful*, to *economize*. He was on the verge of financial ruin and he was just finding out that his sympathies had carried him too far, and well nigh brought his family to poverty, without doubting these rascals. He yet began to see on the verge of what precipice he stood and then, finding their supplies cut off, Tilton began to threaten, bringing up all the old Bowen and Woodhull slanders. But mind you *to father* only claiming that father had ruined his (Tilton) family happiness by advising Mrs. Tilton to get *letters of separation,* when in truth they were, before that advice, he claimed, very happy together save when every few weeks she was a little unsettled in mind. Her statement will show *how very happy* they were. Moulton at this crisis all the time in the guise of an angel of light, coming in as peacemaker, but advising Henry on no account to allow Tilton to break out before the public.

There I can write no more and if this should be lost shall wish I had written nothing. But I couldn't bear you should feel that father was in any danger of compromising. He is full of fury, indignation, and full of hope. Friends rise up in every quarter and where unsuspected, and now any number are ready to testify to the blackings of Moulton's character. They say the only thing which has staggered them is the fact that father has been so thick with F. D. Moulton—and apparently so confidential. I have written so hurriedly that I fear you can't read it. If they carry this into court after this Investigation is over, as Tilton threatens, it can't come on before Sept. But now I fear there is no chance of our coming to you . . . [?]. . . . It is hard to lose this visit of which we have thought so much, but life seems very hard any how. Be sure that you either burn this or keep it under lock and key. In writing to father write hopefully, loving, full of faith, and with no fear of his not giving his life if need be to vindicate his good name and family honor.

With deepest love for you all, dear Samuel [Scoville, her son-in-law], my own Hattie, and the little ones, not forgetting Lilla.

Your loving mother EW Beecher.

I hope the Palmetto hats and trunk of linen have reached you safely. Have not heard from Turner, to whom I had to entrust the packing, and it is just possible that the linen is not all done. Nellie sent the hats . . . [?]

Beecher Family Papers, box 35, folder 1578, Yale University Library Manuscripts and Archives.

21. *Henry Ward Beecher, Prayers before and after the Sermon on "Christian Sympathy," Twin Mountain House, White Mountains, New Hampshire, August 30, 1874*

Prayer before the Sermon

We rejoice, our Father, that thou art leading our thoughts up to thee by all the associations of this sacred day; by the familiarities of friendship; by the rejoicing of love; by all the blessed memories which come to us in the calm and quiet of the Sabbath. We thank thee that the whole week doth not need to rush on with care and burden; and that we have a right to pause, and upon one whole day to rest in body and in soul, and to give our spirits, oppressed with labor and care, repose, or to give them incitement or instruction in the things that pertain to righteousness.

Wilt thou grant thy blessing to rest upon this day, and upon all that are present in this assembly, coming from a hundred experiences, bearing each his own thread of history, with sorrows not alike but in common, with joys also in common, and yet strangely different. O Lord, as thou dost look upon every heart here, and see that it is in weakness and sinfulness, and in everlasting need of God's help, grant that to every one may be given, this morning, that quickening Spirit which bears to the soul peace, and purity, and the sense of forgiveness and inspiration, so that courage, and hope, and joy may spring up from associations with thee. We need thy help, and thou art most helpful. We need thy forgiveness, and thou art most long-suffering, forgiving iniquity, transgression and sin. Thou art patient with those who are seeking, even in the least degree, to live aright; and assistance cometh to them from the divine offices of the Spirit. Not the sun, traveling in the greatness of his strength, sheds more light and life than thou, in the greater strength of thy nature, O Sun of righteousness, that dost come with healing in thy beams. Vouchsafe to every one in thy presence, this morning, we pray thee, the sanctifying influence of thy Spirit. We pray that thou wilt bless each one who puts forth the faintest endeavor to live better. May whatever is good in us ripen. May whatever is evil in us be more and more overruled. May we not refuse to go forward by sitting down in sinfulness and remorse, and forever looking backward and bemoaning our mistakes, or our want of improvement of privileges, or our sorrows in bereavement. May we forget what is behind. We are children not of the past, but of the future. We live by faith, and are filled with hope. May we look forward away from the mistakes and errors of the past. In the light of the hope that is in Christ Jesus, may we look forward and press forward toward the mark, for the prize of the high calling of God in Christ Jesus.

If there be those that are seeking to break down evil habits, give thou them, we beseech of thee, strength not only, but patience to persevere therein.

Be with those who are by every means endeavoring to build themselves up better, and more and more Christlike. Give them power to gain perfect dominion, at length, over every appetite, over every lust, over all selfishness, over pride, and envy, and jealousy, and every malign passion that is in the soul. And may all those that are seeking good help each other. Grant that there may be more pitifulness in our souls toward any whose purposes are good, but who are wafted hither and thither, not by their own will, but by that which is around about them.

We pray that we may be bound in sympathy even to those who are evil. May our hearts yearn for them as thy heart yearns for us. What should we have been but for the thought of God resting upon us, and for thy grace and patience with us? We should have been even as the poorest and most needy are. Let us, then, not be forgiven, and be the recipients every day of thy bounty, and consume it selfishly upon ourselves, turning censoriously upon those that are less favored than we, and condemn them, or pass them by with indifference. May we be joined in heart to those who are beneath and far away from us, even as we are joined in a blessed unity to thee and to thy Spirit.

Grant thy blessing to rest, we pray thee, today, upon this house, and all that dwell in it—upon those that direct and control it, and upon those that are recipients of their kindness. May thy blessing rest, also, upon all those who have gathered together here from neighboring places. Speak peace to every heart. Comfort the sorrowing. Strengthen the wavering. Inspire those who are discouraged. Give courage to men who are in places of peril, that they may resolutely, and with divine help, overcome their adversaries.

We pray that thou wilt follow our thoughts; for what Sabbath morning dawns upon the earth that our hearts do not search out whom we love everywhere? Some are in distant lands, some are upon the sea, some are in far remote places in our own land, and some sit sorrowful in their homes, waiting and watching. Wherever they are whom we love, love thou them this day, and bear to them some sense of our sympathy; and may our prayers fall as dews on flowers upon their heads.

Let thy blessing rest upon all the interest of this great land. Bless the President of these United States, and all those who are joined to him in authority. Bless the Governors of the different States, and the magistrates therein, and the citizens belonging thereto. Spread abroad the light of knowledge, we pray thee. May schools and seminaries of every kind flourish. May intelligence prevail throughout the whole land. And grant that this great nation may grow up in strength both outward and inward, not to tread down the poor, the weak, and the oppressed. May this nation not be filled with greed and avarice, but may it at last begin to shine abroad with the true light of Christian kindness, and become the defender of the helpless, and an example to those who are toiling in oppression. At last may that light come forth which shall emancipate the world. May men, touched with the divine Spirit, live again in their higher nature, and become too strong for manacles to hold them, and too wise for despots to oppress them. Thus may this whole world come to its liberty by coming to the Lord Jesus Christ, and receiving the new manhood that is in Christ Jesus.

And to thy name shall be the praise, Father, Son, and Spirit, evermore. *Amen.*

Prayer after the Sermon

Lord, grant thy blessing to rest upon us, to give us an understanding heart, not only, but to give us an applying disposition. Grant that the truth which we have heard may be as seed sown in good ground, springing up, and bringing forth a hundred fold. Pity those things which we blame in ourselves, and those things which we reprehend in others as their teachers. Have compassion upon us because we are sinners. Have compassion upon our motives. Have compassion upon all those faults which are full of weakness and selfishness. Thou that makest thy sun to rise on the good and bad alike, help us, because we need help. Thy goodness and our want join in one plea. Be merciful to us, and teach us to be merciful to each other. Spread abroad that large-mindedness and catholicity of feeling which shall unite us, with growing force, to thee and to our fellow-men, that at last we may understand thy law, that goes everywhere, disseminating liberty, being imperious, and yet full of freedom. May each one of us hear and obey the command, Thou shalt love the Lord thy God with all thy heart and thy neighbor as thyself. And to thy name shall be the praise, Father, Son, and Spirit, evermore. *Amen.*

HWB, *Plymouth Pulpit Sermons,* Library of Congress microfilm edition, vol. 1, pp. 562–64.

Acknowledgments

I wrote the bulk of this book at the École des Hautes Études en Sciences Sociales, where in 1997–1998 I held a post in American Civilization sponsored by the French-American Foundation. Linda Koike and her Foundation colleagues were generous with their support, as were Professor Jean Heffer and his fellow Americanists François Weil and Pap N'Dyaioue at the École. Jean Heffer gave me everything an American writer could possibly want: a quiet, spacious office in Paris. Caroline Béraud was gracious in offering secretarial help, not to mention many sharp insights into French and American cultures.

My first talks and essays on the scandal were written while I was a fellow at the Woodrow Wilson International Center for Scholars and the Oregon Humanities Institute. Those fellowships—and earlier ones from the Guggenheim Foundation and the American Council of Learned Societies that allowed me to do reading and archival research on nineteenth-century liberal Protestantism—are the material substratum of this book. Librarians at Boston University, the Brooklyn Historical Society, the Brooklyn Public Library (special thanks to Judith Walsh), the Harriet Beecher Stowe Center Library (special thanks to Margaret Mair, Diane Royce, and Suzanne Zack), Harvard University, the Library of Congress, the New York Historical Society, the New York Public Library, Radcliffe College's Schlesinger Library, Reed College (special thanks to Marilyn Kierstead), the Woodrow Wilson Center (special thanks to Zed David and several student interns), and Yale University's Manuscripts and Archives (special thanks to Judith Schiff) not only found me books, pamphlets, letters, and images, but often got interested in the topic themselves. The spontaneous communities of inquiry that form between scholars and librarians are one of the rewards of long days on the road and in the stacks. The archivist of the Mairie de Chailly-en-Bière is like many others I encountered. She spent an hour scanning folios of dusty cemetery records until she came upon the name of Theodore Tilton buried in his friend Kate Fuller's plot purchase agreement.

Hands-on editing is reportedly on the wane in American publishing, but if that's the trend, the University of Chicago Press is bucking it. Doug Mitchell guided this manuscript's journey through the editorial process with care and enthusiasm. Matthew Howard thankfully held out for the highest quality illustrations. Russell Harper elevated copyediting to a literary collaboration. I'm impressed, and very grateful.

The intellectual inspiration for this book comes from too many sources to list, but here are some of them. I see looking backward that Barton J. Bernstein, David Brion Davis, Carl N. Degler, and Christopher Lasch were my early guides in imagining history as a form of moral as well as factual inquiry. All of them encouraged me to follow my interests into the cultural history of religion. Lasch suggested I might want to explore the history of love, as he was doing at the time of his death in 1994. Degler always lit up at the idea of a new study of the Beecher-Tilton Scandal. Bernstein and Davis combined immersion in the details of the historical record with a broad vision of the intellectual life. I am grateful to all of them for pointing the way.

Certain books also influenced me by suggesting how to join the historical analysis of culture to the critical-sympathetic portrayal of individual lives. A. S. Byatt's *Possession*, Laurel Ulrich's *A Midwife's Tale*, Jack Miles's *God: A Biography*, Elaine Scarry's *The Body in Pain*, James Axtell's *The Invasion Within*, and David Hall's *Worlds of Wonder, Days of Judgment* were some of the most striking works I encountered as I was conceiving my own attempt to plumb what William James (in *Talks to Teachers*) calls the "reality" of other lives, indeed to "experience" that reality to the extent that our own chronic human "blindness" (and, for us historians, the limits of our documents) permits. James wishes we would strive to know and feel the reality of others as intensely as Whitman does, even those "others" in "Crossing Brooklyn Ferry" who will "cross from shore to shore . . . a hundred years hence, or ever so many hundred years hence." Like his novelist brother Henry, whose essay "The Art of Fiction" charges writers to become disciplined "historians" of real life, William is seeking out "the vast world of inner life beyond us, so different from that of outer seeming." The challenge for the writer, as Henry puts it, is to "try to be one of the people on whom nothing is lost."

Many colleagues, friends, and audience members have given me advice about this project, and responded to my earlier talks and papers on the scandal. I especially thank Joe Boskin, Ann Braude, Elizabeth Battelle Clark, Lizabeth Cohen, Nancy Cott, Jacqueline Dirks, Ellen DuBois, Phil Ethington, Eric Fassin, Jenny Franchot, Karin Gedge, Bryna Goodman, David Hall, Jacquelyn Dowd Hall, Karen Halttunen, Hendrik Hartog, Gerald Honigsblum, Daniel Horowitz, Helen Horowitz, James Johnson, Linda Kerber, James Kloppenberg, Jackson Lears, Christopher Lowe, Lisa Watt MacFarlane, Shitsuyo Masui, R. Laurence Moore, Jenni Ratner, Joan Shelley Rubin, Michael Smith, Altina L. Waller, and Robert Westbrook. Shirley Wajda gave me advice but she also kept sending old letters, books, and artifacts. For years she has been showing me that history may be in the words, but it's also in the stuff. Patricia Peknik, meanwhile, took on the words, catching mistakes in my writing and deciphering some hard-to-read nineteenth-century handwriting—Eunice Beecher's in particular.

For critiquing the final manuscript, Casey Blake, Jeanne Follansbee-Quinn, Karen Greenberg, Lori Kenschaft, Kathryn Kish Sklar, Adam Sticklor, Christopher P. Wilson, and fellow Beecher-Tilton *aficionados* Debbie Applegate and Laura Korobkin have my gratitude. Some of my father M. Bernard Fox's last writing was done in rickety scrawl on the margins of my chapter drafts; his critical enthusiasm for my work has been a sustaining gift from the beginning. Rachel, Laura, and Chris Fox, and Maia Davis, contributed to this book by offering their companionship while I was writing it. Laura and Chris took care of things in Boston during my expatriate year, and converted computer files into American-size hard copy. Rachel shared the *2ème étage droite* at 12 rue de la Roquette and *la table quatre* at *Au C'amelot*. Maia kept reminding me that the long view of the High Sierra puts historical time in its rightful place. As for Elizabeth, what can I say but thanks, my friend, for what Hannah Arendt would call the action of your speech. You knew how to tell this story well before I had a clue.

Notes

INTRODUCTION

1. Henry James, *Hawthorne* (1879; Ithaca: Cornell University Press, 1997), pp. 89, 91.

2. A well-known sourcebook on clerical moral transgressions, published just before the Beecher-Tilton Scandal broke, was W. F. Jamieson, *The Clergy a Source of Danger to the American Republic* (Chicago: W. F. Jamieson, 1872). The scandal was a major news story throughout the English-speaking Protestant world, and penetrated Western Europe as well. In his "Lettre des Etats-Unis," the New York correspondent of *Le Temps* reluctantly kept French readers informed. He explained in his first installment that "l'affaire Beecher-Tilton fait ici trop de tapage pour qu'il n'en soit pas arrivé quelque écho jusqu'à vous. . . . L'histoire a fait trop de sensation, et les personnages qui y jouent un rôle sont trop connus pour que je puisse m'en taire complètement. . . . Le New-York Tribune proclame [Beecher] le premier orateur chrétien après Saint Paul. C'est beaucoup dire." ("The Beecher-Tilton affair has made too much of an uproar here for an echo of it not to have reached you. . . . The story has caused too much of a sensation, and the figures in it are too well-known, for me to be able to remain completely silent about it. . . . The *New York Tribune* calls Beecher the greatest Christian orator since St. Paul. That's saying a lot.") Aug. 28, 1874, p. 2E. *Le Temps*' correspondent was not the only French writer to be provoked by the scandal. "It is said that George Sand intends to write a novel, the motive of which shall be the 'profound spiritual tragedy' exposed in the Beecher-Tilton affair." She "has written of many profound spiritual tragedies in her day, but never has found one in real life at all comparable for psychological effects with that with which she will deal in her new book." "Minor Topics," *New York Graphic*, Mar. 10, 1875, p. 72. Sand died in 1876, apparently before tackling the Beecher-Tilton affair.

3. E. L. Godkin, "Moulton's Story," *Nation*, Aug. 27, 1874, pp. 134–35; Godkin, "Chromo-Civilization," *Nation*, Sept. 24, 1874, p. 201. Godkin's editorials were unsigned, but Daniel C. Haskell, *The 'Nation': Indexes of Titles and Contributors* (New York: New York Public Library, 1951), establishes his authorship of the magazine's Beecher-Tilton editorials.

4. "Skeletons of the Ideal," *Frank Leslie's Illustrated Newspaper*, Aug. 8, 1874, p. 339. The most extensive comparison to *The Scarlet Letter* appeared in "The Minister's Vigil" [one of Hawthorne's chapter titles], *Frank Leslie's*, Aug. 22, 1874, pp. 370–71. Other literary parallels were offered in "Failure of the Ideal," *Frank Leslie's*, Sept. 5, 1874, pp. 402–3. At the adultery trial in 1875 Theodore Tilton's lawyer William Beach read several paragraphs of *The Scarlet Letter* into the record to demonstrate that Beecher was the spitting image of Arthur Dimmesdale. *Theodore Tilton vs. Henry Ward Beecher, Action for Crim[inal] Con[versation]* (New York: McDivitt, Campbell and Co., 1875) [hereafter *TT v. HWB*], vol. 3, p. 934 [hereafter in the form 3: 934]. Beecher and Tilton were not the only creative writers in their immediate families. In 1861 Henry's wife Eunice published the fictionalized but autobiographical *From Dawn to Daylight: The Simple Story of a Western Home*—an account of their early married years in Indiana—and Elizabeth Tilton appears to have published at least one poem, "Dying Deaths Daily" (text in Appendix). In later years Eunice also published books for young housekeepers such as *Motherly Talks* and *All Around the House*. J. C. Derby discusses her writing in *Fifty Years among Authors, Books and Publishers* (New York: G. W. Carlton, 1884).

5. Altina L. Waller, in her very useful *Reverend Beecher and Mrs. Tilton* (Amherst, MA: University of Massachusetts Press, 1982), p. 145, chooses Mrs. Tilton's confession of 1878 as the true statement of fact, claiming it was "a strong, nonambiguous statement of her own and Beecher's guilt in the affair." But Elizabeth's statements denying their guilt in 1874 and 1875 were equally strong and unambiguous. Like several other historians of the Great Scandal, Waller is convinced that adultery—physical sex—took place, but does not, to my mind, justify that judgment. I give further particulars on the historical literature in an earlier foray into the scandal, "Intimacy on Trial: Cultural Meanings of the Beecher-Tilton Affair," in Richard Wightman Fox and T. J. Jackson Lears, eds., *The Power of Culture: Critical Essays in American History* (Chicago: University of Chicago Press, 1993), p. 111–14, and in chapter 9 of this book.

6. Henry James, *The Bostonians* (1886; New York: Vintage / Library of America, 1991), p. 381 (chapter 39), p. 66 (chapter 10).

7. On the mutually supportive relationship between factual and moral inquiry, see the introduction to Richard Wightman Fox and Robert B. Westbrook, eds., *In Face of the Facts: Moral Inquiry in American Scholarship* (New York: Cambridge University Press, 1997).

CHAPTER ONE

1. "Theodore Tilton's Will Filed for Probate," *Brooklyn Eagle*, July 19, 1907, p. 1. Biographical information on the Tilton children is from the Tilton subject file of the *Eagle* morgue now at the Brooklyn Public Library.

2. "Mr. Theodore Tilton Pneumonia's Victim," *New York Herald* (European Edition), May 26, 1907, p. 1; "European Gossip," *New York Times*, Jan. 23, 1887, p. 6; Elizabeth Cady Stanton, *Eighty Years and More* (London: T. Fisher Unwin, 1898), p. 401; Kate Fuller to the Mayor of Chailly-en-Bière, Nov. 7, 1908, Archives of the Mairie.

3. "European Gossip," p. 6; John Joseph Conway, *Footprints of Famous Americans in Paris* (London: John Lane, 1912), p. 283; "Mr. Theodore Tilton Pneumonia's Vic-

tim," *New York Herald*, p. 1. Tilton's publications are listed in W. J. Burke and Will D. Howe, *American Authors and Books* (London: Nicholas Vane, 1963), p. 743; and Stanley Kunitz, ed., *American Authors, 1600–1900* (New York: H. W. Wilson, 1938), pp. 751–52. A copy of Tilton's *Complete Poetical Works* (Oxford: Clarendon Press, 1897), with the dedication to Elizabeth, is in his papers at the Library of Congress.

4. "Theodore Tilton's Funeral," "Theodore Tilton Dead," *Brooklyn Eagle*, May 26, 1907, clippings in the Tilton subject file, *Eagle* morgue, Brooklyn Public Library. I discuss Beecher in relation to "character" and "personality" in "The Culture of Liberal Protestant Progressivism, 1875–1925," *Journal of Interdisciplinary History* 23 (winter 1993): 639–60.

5. "Religion of Gush," *New York Herald* editorial quoted in the *Chicago Tribune*, Sept. 26, 1874, p. 5.

6. At the trial in 1875 Theodore said his wife was about 41, between a year and two years older than he was. His lawyer gave him a second chance to provide her exact age and he said again he didn't know exactly. No one else seems to have known either.

7. The *New York Times* made only a single mention of Elizabeth Tilton between her last confession in 1878 and her death in 1897. It reported on October 10, 1888 (p. 2), that with her mother Mrs. Nathaneal B. Morse she had attended the Brooklyn wedding of her son Carroll—an event restricted to near family. Mrs. Morse had separated from Judge Morse, her second husband, by the time of the scandal. Her first husband, named Richards (Elizabeth's father), died in the 1830s or 1840s.

8. "Elizabeth R. Tilton Dead," *Brooklyn Eagle*, n.d., n.p. [Apr. 14 or 15; Mrs. Tilton died April 13, 1897], in the Beecher-Tilton File at the Brooklyn Historical Society.

9. "Mrs. Tilton Buried," *New York Tribune*, Apr. 17, 1897, p. 7; "Elizabeth R. Tilton Dead," *Brooklyn Eagle*.

10. "Henry Ward Beecher. The Great Pastor's End," *Frank Leslie's Illustrated Weekly*, Mar. 19, 1887, p. 75.

11. HWB, *Plain and Pleasant Talk about Fruits, Flowers, and Farming* (New York: Derby and Jackson, 1859; rev. ed., New York: J. B. Ford, 1874).

12. *TT v. HWB*, 1: 623 (orange blossoms); 2: 687, 3: 671 (Beecher's gifts of flowers); "Theodore Tilton's Last Statement," in Charles F. Marshall, *The True History of the Brooklyn Scandal* (Philadelphia: National Publishing Co., 1874), p. 528 ("constantly supplied with flowers").

13. "Henry Ward Beecher. The Great Pastor's End," *Frank Leslie's*, p. 75.

14. "Henry Ward Beecher," *Andover Review* 7 (April 1887): 442.

15. "At Last," *Frank Leslie's*, Jan. 23, 1875, p. 325. Linus Pierpont Brockett's *Men of Our Day* (Philadelphia: Zeigler, McCurdy, 1868) gives six pages (pp. 612–18) to Tilton, and half of that space is an extended quotation from one of his after-dinner "toasts." By incorporating actual oratory into the biographical sketch, Brockett pays implicit as well as explicit homage to the power of eloquence in nineteenth-century American culture. I have included the toast in the Appendix.

16. "Henry Ward Beecher," *Andover Review*, pp. 419, 431, 441; "At Last," *Frank Leslie's*, p. 325 ("sinewy and stalwart").

17. "Henry Ward Beecher," *Andover Review*, pp. 429–31. On Lyman Beecher as

modernizer, see Richard Rabinowitz, *The Spiritual Self in Everyday Life: The Transformation of Personal Religious Experience in Nineteenth-Century New England* (Boston: Northeastern University Press, 1989), pp. 79–84. In the Appendix I have included Beecher's prayers before and after his sermon of August 30, 1874.

18. Lyman Abbott, *Henry Ward Beecher* (1903; New York: Chelsea House, 1980), p. 403.

19. "Gath" [George Alfred Townsend], "Pastoral Visits and Sentimental Religion," *Chicago Tribune*, Aug. 9, 1874, p. 8. "Gath" went on in the same *Tribune* piece to say Beecher's faith was "as pulpy as a banana or a clam." Likewise the *Tribune* editorial page, which early in the scandal was siding with Tilton, labeled Beecher the "Reverend Cream-Cheese" in a comment with that title, July 25, p. 6.

20. Paxton Hibben, *Henry Ward Beecher: An American Portrait* (New York: George H. Doran, 1927), p. 353.

CHAPTER TWO

1. David S. Reynolds, *Walt Whitman's America: A Cultural Biography* (New York: Knopf, 1995), pp. 172–73, 256, stresses the avid interest Whitman paid to Beecher, six years his senior. Whitman thought and wrote about him from the 1840s to the 1870s, and appropriated some of Beecher's oratorical strategies in his poetry. On Lincoln's and Thoreau's visits to Plymouth, Ralph Foster Weld, *Brooklyn Is America* (New York: Columbia University Press, 1950), p. 70; Justin Kaplan, *Walt Whitman: A Life* (New York: Simon and Schuster, 1980), p. 218. Not all visitors liked what they saw at Plymouth Church. British visitors were especially likely to complain about Beecher. "He is loud, denunciatory and arrogant," wrote Richard Cobden in 1859. "On the whole I was greatly disappointed by this celebrity." Lord Rosebery, fourteen years later, concurred. "I was greatly disappointed with him. . . . He is a buffoon without the merits of a buffoon." Elizabeth Hoon Cawley, ed., *The American Diaries of Richard Cobden* (1952; New York: Greenwood Press, 1969), pp. 194–95; A. R. C. Grant, ed., *Lord Rosebery's North American Journal—1873* (Hamden, CT: Archon Books, 1967), p. 91.

2. A good introduction to the nineteenth-century shift in focus from "liberty" to "society" can be found in several of the essays in Richard Wightman Fox and James T. Kloppenberg, eds., *A Companion to American Thought* (Cambridge: Blackwell, 1995): e.g., Daniel H. Borus, "Society," Dorothy Ross, "Social Science," Daniel T. Rodgers, "Republicanism" and "Freedom." On Washington Gladden as a key transitional figure in relation to Beecher and Social Gospeller Walter Rauschenbusch, see my essays "The Culture of Liberal Protestant Progressivism, 1875–1925," *Journal of Interdisciplinary History* 23 (winter 1993): 639–60; and "The Discipline of Amusement," in William R. Taylor, ed., *Inventing Times Square: Commerce and Culture at the Crossroads of the World* (New York: Russell Sage, 1991), pp. 83–98.

3. Walt Whitman quoted in Weld, *Brooklyn Is America*, p. 48; James E. Homans, "Brooklyn: An Historical Past, a Substantial Present, a Glorious Future," in Moses King, ed., *King's Views of New York, 1896–1915, and Brooklyn, 1905* ([1904] New York: Benjamin Blom, 1974), p. 2 of Brooklyn section.

4. "Theo. Tilton. Lecture on the Human Mind," undated newspaper clipping, Beecher-Tilton file, Brooklyn Public Library.

5. "Life—Theodore Tilton on the Problem It Presents," undated clipping from a Brooklyn newspaper, Beecher-Tilton file, Brooklyn Public Library; HWB quoted in William C. Beecher and Samuel Scoville, *A Biography of Rev. Henry Ward Beecher* (New York: Charles Webster, 1888), p. 553.

6. "Life—Theodore Tilton on the Problem It Presents."

7. Paxton Hibben, *Henry Ward Beecher: An American Portrait* (New York: George Doran, 1927), p. 331.

8. "Theodore Tilton's New Lecture," *New York Times*, Oct. 29, 1878, p. 8. Before moving to France Tilton not only lectured but published two books, *Thou and I* (1879) and *Swabian Stories* (1882). The *Times* gave them both short, mixed reviews, remarking of *Thou and I* that "he has a fine ear for the music of verse, and while too much given to short sentences, manages to make a pleasant impression. His unfortunate experiences in reality have left little trace on his verse, although from his proem it seems that he holds the opposite opinion" (Dec. 22, 1879, p. 3).

9. "Mr. Bowen's Reply to Mr. White," *Independent*, Feb. 10, 1876, p. 3.

10. HWB quoted in Beecher and Scoville, *A Biography of Rev. Henry Ward Beecher*, p. 553 ("focal point"), pp. 552–53 ("For so many years"), p. 546 ("I am questioned"), p. 545 ("Nothing that I say"). In "Henry Ward Beecher and the Advisory Council," *Frank Leslie's Illustrated Newspaper*, Mar. 4, 1876, pp. 410–11, the editor noted that for all its hype, the grand gathering of clergy—"the largest, beyond all question, ever brought together at the call of any one Church"—"has not brought to light the 'bottom facts'" about the scandal. It had therefore not "dispelled the cloud which rests upon the great Plymouth divine" (p. 410).

11. HWB quoted in Beecher and Scoville, *A Biography of Rev. Henry Ward Beecher*, pp. 553–54.

12. "Mrs. Tilton Pleads Guilty," *New York Times*, Apr. 16, 1878, p. 1; "Mrs. Tilton's Confession," *New York Times*, Apr. 19, 1878, p. 5.

13. "Beecher on Gilman's Crime," *New York Times*, Oct. 13, 1877, p. 8; editorial note, *Chicago Tribune*, Apr. 20, 1878, p. 4.

14. Lead editorial, *New York Times*, Apr. 16, 1878, p. 4; "Mrs. Tilton Pleads Guilty," *New York Times*, p. 1.

15. Editorial note, *Chicago Tribune*, Apr. 20, 1878, p. 4. Theodore was giving his lecture on "The Problem of Life" in Decatur, Iowa when he got word of his wife's confession. His only comment was that he had nothing to do with her change of story. His formal statement of noninvolvement was published around the country on April 19. "Tilton," *Chicago Tribune*, Apr. 19, 1878, p. 2. The *New York Times* reported "rumors of a reconciliation between Mr. and Mrs. Tilton" three weeks before Mrs. Tilton's confession. "Theodore Tilton's Wife," *New York Times*, Mar. 28, 1878, p. 5.

16. "Mrs. Tilton's Confession," *New York Times*, Apr. 19, 1878, p. 5.

17. "The Beecher-Tilton Scandal," *New York Times*, June 26, 1878, p. 8 [reprinting ET's letter of June 10]; "Reviving the Scandal," *New York Times*, June 22, 1878, p. 8.

18. "At Last," *Chicago Tribune*, Apr. 16, 1878, p. 1.

19. "Beecher," *Chicago Tribune*, Apr. 17, 1878, p. 1.

20. "Elizabeth R. Tilton Dead," *Brooklyn Eagle*, n.d. [Apr. 14 or 15, 1897], Beecher-Tilton File, Brooklyn Public Library.

21. "Mrs. Tilton's Confession," *New York Times*, Apr. 17, 1878, p. 2; HWB to Eunice Beecher, Dec. 16, 1878, Beecher Family Papers, Yale University. A page of this letter may be missing from the Yale collection, since Milton Rugoff, in his book *The Beechers: An American Family in the Nineteenth Century* (New York: Harper and Row, 1981), p. 503, quotes a sentence not contained in the four pages of the letter currently (in 1998) in box 8, folder 317 of the Beecher Papers. Rugoff cites Beecher's sentence "It shows how tenderly he cherishes my memory," drops the "although circumstances . . . an open friendship," and then adds the words "If only it were possible for us to be friends again," followed by an ellipsis. He concludes from those final words that Beecher truly wished to resurrect the friendship, since for him "amativeness was still all." But assuming the final sentence is indeed in the original letter, the context makes clear that Beecher was being drippingly ironic, not sincere, about desiring a restoration of fondness with Tilton and Moulton. In 1884 Frank Moulton died suddenly of an "inflammation of the stomach." "The Mutual Friend Dead," *New York Times*, Dec. 5, 1884, p. 8. Emma Moulton died on December 2, 1910.

22. Grover Cleveland to Mrs. HWB, May 22, 1887, in Allan Nevins, ed., *Letters of Grover Cleveland* (Cambridge: Houghton-Mifflin, 1933), p. 141.

23. Allan Nevins, *Grover Cleveland: A Study in Courage* (New York: Dodd, Mead, 1933), p. 26 (Beecher parable); Denis Tilden Lynch, *Grover Cleveland: A Man Four-Square* (New York: Horace Liveright, 1932), p. 517.

24. Cleveland's need for HWB's support is evident in his letter to Mrs. Beecher in late October, 1884, in which he expresses his wish, above all else, that HWB maintain a good opinion of him. Cleveland to Mrs. HWB, n.d. [about Oct. 20, 1884], in Nevins, *Letters of Grover Cleveland*, pp. 45–46.

25. Twining's report quoted in Lynch, *Grover Cleveland*, p. 228; details on the "Maria Halpin affair" are in Nevins, *Grover Cleveland*, pp. 164–69.

26. "Address of Henry Ward Beecher at the Brooklyn Rink, October 22, 1884," pamphlet issued by the National Committee of Republicans and Independents, New York City, copy in Harvard University's Widener Library, p. 8; Cleveland to Mrs. Beecher, n.d., in Nevins, *Letters of Grover Cleveland*, pp. 45–46.

27. Hibben, *Henry Ward Beecher*, p. 344; Rugoff, *The Beechers*, p. 509; Clifford E. Clark, *Henry Ward Beecher: Spokesman for a Middle-Class America* (Urbana: University of Illinois Press, 1978), p. 254.

28. I thank Jeanne Follansbee-Quinn for suggesting this interpretation of the Brooklyn Rink speech.

CHAPTER THREE

1. "Mr. Tilton's Reply to Dr. Bacon," in Charles F. Marshall, *The True History of the Brooklyn Scandal* (Philadelphia: National Publishing Co., 1874), p. 62.

2. All the kissing that took place among Beecher and Tiltons sparked much commentary, humorous and somber, throughout the scandal. For example, the writer Jane Grey Swisshelm, a well-known traditionalist critic of Beecher's liberal religion, provoked a long exchange of letters on the subject in the *Chicago Tribune*. See "Kissing," Apr. 5, 1875, p. 7. The *New York Graphic* divulged its revulsion against the bizarre kissing customs of the Brooklyn Romantics even as it tried to be lighthearted: "Mr. Beecher has testified that . . . he kissed Mr. Moulton, sat in Theodore Tilton's

lap and kissed him on the mouth, and, in fact, kissed pretty nearly everybody, whether male or female, with whom he had any intercourse. The public will begin to ask whether the alleged seduction of Mrs. Tilton, or the confessed kissing of Theodore's mouth, was the more unbecoming a Christian minister" (Apr. 7, 1875, p. 278).

3. "Tilton's Cross-Examination" and "Mrs. Tilton's Statement," in Marshall, *True History*, pp. 152, 158, 186; E. L. Godkin, "The Trial by Newspaper," *Nation*, July 30, 1874, pp. 70–71. Among the many other analyses of the crisis in middle-class marriage exposed by the scandal, "The Moral Estimate," *New York Graphic*, Oct. 3, 1874, p. 679, is especially interesting. It grasped that the basic issue confronting "the marriage relation" was whether men and women were to be considered equal in moral endowment and alike in moral temperament. Beecher and the Tiltons, along with their suffragist friends, favored equality and likeness; the writer did not. (See also the response "On Moral Lapsing," *New York Graphic*, Oct. 6, 1874, p. 693.)

4. Godkin, "The Trial by Newspaper," pp. 70–71. On the call for a trial, see for example, "A Judicial Verdict Demanded," *Chicago Tribune*, Aug. 16, 1874, p. 8.

5. Godkin, "The Trial by Newspaper," p. 71.

6. "Henry Ward Beecher," *Chicago Tribune*, June 14, 1874, p. 10. Lord Rosebery, visiting Plymouth seven months before "Most," described the same scene but included other details. "There is an enormous organ on each side of which are places for the choir. In front of the organ is a dais with a table, a desk, and a chair. On the table is a tall flower glass containing lilies and other flowers. A similar glass is on the dais." Beecher, "wearing a short opera cloak and holding a wideawake hat slipped into his chair, and sat for five minutes while the organ played a voluntary. The service began with an anthem which lasted about seven minutes, then came a prayer, then a hymn, then a short portion of the Bible, then a hymn, then the sermon, then a prayer and then a final hymn sung to the dear tune of the Russian national anthem. Beecher's sermon had two texts and five headings and lasted one hour. The five headings were written on a large sheet of paper, otherwise the sermon seemed extempore." A. R. C. Grant, ed., *Lord Rosebery's North American Journal—1873* (Hamden, CT: Archon Books, 1967), pp. 90–91. In 1859 Beecher's pulpit attire was "a surtout coat and black cravat." Elizabeth Hoon Cawley, ed., *The American Diaries of Richard Cobden* (1952; New York: Greenwood Press, 1969), p. 194.

7. "Henry Ward Beecher," *Chicago Tribune*, June 14, 1874, p. 10. Plymouth Church had a majority of female members—618 more women than men in January 1875 (*Frank Leslie's Illustrated Weekly*, Jan. 16, 1875, p. 307). The total membership in 1872 was 2,700, according to William C. Beecher and Samuel Scoville, *A Biography of Rev. Henry Ward Beecher* (New York: Charles L. Webster, 1888), p. 480. Of the 105 new members who joined during the trial in the winter and spring of 1875, 82 were women and 23 were men (*Mobile* [Alabama] *Register*, May 11, 1875, p. 3). If we assume that the 1875 membership was 3,000, and that there were 600 more women than men, the congregation was 60 percent female. That corresponds closely to the 58 percent figure (no year provided) computed by Altina Waller, based on an examination of the Register of Members at Plymouth Church, *Reverend Beecher and Mrs. Tilton* (Amherst, MA: University of Massachusetts Press, 1982), p. 54.

8. "Mr. Beecher's Defense," "Tilton's Cross-Examination," in Marshall, *True History*, pp. 256, 159.

9. "Mrs. Tilton's Statement," in Marshall, *True History*, p. 183 ("love to my friend and pastor").

10. "Mrs. Tilton's Statement" ("perfidy . . .") and "Mr. Tilton's Sworn Statement" ("*Griffith Gaunt*" letter), in Marshall, *True History*, pp. 183, 120–21. The text of the letter is in the Appendix. (The text Theodore published in 1874 omitted a passage highly critical of him; that passage is in boldface in the Appendix.) Charles Reade spelled his heroine's name "Catherine," but I have left it "Catharine," Elizabeth's spelling, when quoting her. Mrs. Tilton's "cross-examination" on July 31 was entirely friendly, like her secret session with the committee on July 8 (never published). She could answer any way she pleased, although her replies as released to the press may have been edited. The friendly committeemen asked questions designed to help Beecher in any future legal proceeding, and some of Elizabeth's formulations display the earmarks of lawyers' prose. But the preponderance of her remarks are without any doubt in her own words.

11. "Mrs. Tilton's Cross-Examination," in Marshall, *True History*, pp. 196–98.

12. "Mrs. Tilton's Statement" ("I rose quietly"), "Mrs. Tilton's Cross-Examination" ("mesmeric"), and "The Report of the Investigating Committee" ("medical testimony"), in Marshall, *True History*, pp. 188, 202, 427.

13. "Mrs. Tilton," *Boston Journal*, reprinted in *Chicago Tribune*, Oct. 3, 1874, p. 7; "Mr. Beecher's Defense," in Marshall, *True History*, p. 257.

14. "Mrs. Tilton's Cross-Examination," in Marshall, *True History*, p. 191.

15. "Tilton's Cross-Examination" ("born for war," "I loved that man," "penitence and anguish," "damnable"), "Mr. Tilton's Sworn Statement" ("this desperate man"), "Theodore Tilton's Last Statement" ("I know no words"), in Marshall, *True History*, pp. 176, 113, 153, 160, 162, 595–96.

16. "Theodore Tilton's Last Statement" ("I shall believe"), in Marshall, *True History*, pp. 525–26.

17. "Tilton's Cross-Examination," in Marshall, *True History*, p. 139.

18. "Tilton's Cross-Examination," in Marshall, *True History*, p. 150. The *New York Graphic* published lengthy extracts from "Mary Vail's" letters in Theodore Tilton's *Tempest-Tossed: A Romance* (New York: Sheldon and Co., 1874), on July 28, 1874, p. 188. "Vail" was one contemporary spelling for "veil."

19. "Theodore Tilton's Last Statement," in Marshall, *True History*, pp. 568–69.

20. Eunice Beecher to Anne B. Scoville, Aug. 9, 1874, Beecher Family Papers, Yale University (text of letter in Appendix).

21. Eunice Beecher to Anne B. Scoville, Aug. 9, 1874; "Cross-examination of Mr. Beecher," in Marshall, *True History*, p. 287. The press was virtually unanimous throughout the scandal in praising "the much-wronged and bravely-reticent Mrs. Beecher," as the *Philadelphia Sunday Republic* described her. Her stalwart defense of her husband drew praise even from that part of the press that took his infidelity for granted, as the *Philadelphia Sunday Republic* did. "Mr. Beecher's Wife," reprinted in the *Chicago Tribune*, Aug. 30, 1874, p. 16. Beecher's older sister Catharine, in the course of a ringing defense of her brother, gave some support to Tilton's notion of an emotional split between Henry and Eunice. Eunice "is liable to strong prejudices," she wrote in her "Appeal to the People," and sometimes gave Henry's siblings only a "civil" welcome, while Henry's was always "cordial." But Miss Beecher ridiculed the

notion that Henry was so alienated from Eunice that he would go to "such a scatter-brains" as Tilton and tell him he wanted a wife like his. *Chicago Tribune*, Sept. 25, 1874, p. 8. See also "Miss Beecher and Mrs. Beecher," *Chicago Tribune*, Sept. 26, 1874, p. 6.

22. "Tilton's Cross-Examination," in Marshall, *True History*, pp. 133, 147.

23. "Mr. Tilton's Sworn Statement" ("an intimate friendship"), "Theodore Tilton's Last Statement" ("near and dear"), in Marshall, *True History*, pp. 114, 516–17. The text of Beecher's 1863 letter to Tilton is in the Appendix.

24. "Theodore Tilton's Last Statement," "Mrs. Tilton's Cross-Examination," in Marshall, *True History*, pp. 521, 208.

25. "Gath," "Another Talk with Tilton," *Chicago Tribune*, Aug. 16, 1874, p. 1.

26. "Mr. Beecher's Defense" ("seemed like a son," "egotism," "blundering," "Woodhull," "disreputable people" and "wild views," "loose notions" and "free love"), "Cross-examination of Mr. Beecher" ("upper nature," "flattery"), in Marshall, *True History*, pp. 260, 289, 254, 288, 251, 258.

27. "Mrs. Tilton's Cross-Examination," "Theodore Tilton's Last Statement," in Marshall, *True History*, pp. 184, 560.

28. "Cross-examination of Mr. Beecher," in Marshall, *True History*, p. 297. "Gath" considered Henry and Eunice's idea that Elizabeth leave her husband in 1870 "a free love act more nearly than any of Tilton's antics amongst the free lovers." "Letter from 'Gath,'" *Chicago Tribune*, July 31, 1874, p. 1.

29. On Elizabeth's lack of "delicacy" in receiving "private visits from a gentleman against the repeated remonstrances of her husband," "Mrs. Tilton's Testimony," *Chicago Tribune*, Aug. 6, 1874, p. 4. Likewise, "Too Much Testimony," *St. Louis Globe*, reprinted in *Chicago Tribune*, Aug. 8, 1874, p. 7.

30. *TT v. HWB*, 1: 440–41; "Inquirer," *New York Graphic*, Aug. 7, 1874, p. 260. Asked whether he had given his wife permission to receive a letter from Beecher, Tilton made the same point. "My wife was a free agent, as I was. . . . I would not accord to her permission or denial. . . . She had a sovereign right to receive letters" (*TT v. HWB*, 1: 408). In her book *Other Powers: The Age of Suffrage, Spritualism, and the Scandalous Victoria Woodhull* (New York: Knopf, 1998), Barbara Goldsmith asserts that the "Inquirer" was Elizabeth Cady Stanton, who indeed claimed to have written anonymously for the *Graphic*. But the "Inquirer" was vocally antifeminist and anti-egalitarian. Stanton could not have written the columns unless she deliberately camouflaged her identity by stating views directly opposed to her own—and stating them with great rhetorical power. *Other Powers*, p. 489.

31. "Mr. Beecher's Defense," "Cross-examination of Mr. Beecher," in Marshall, *True History*, pp. 264, 266, 295.

32. "Mr. Beecher's Defense," in Marshall, *True History*, pp. 264–65, 256, 271.

33. "Cross-examination of Mr. Beecher," "Mr. Beecher's Defense," in Marshall, *True History*, pp. 292, 283, 285.

34. "Mr. Beecher's Defense," in Marshall, *True History*, pp. 265–66.

35. "Mr. Beecher's Defense," in Marshall, *True History*, pp. 294, 305; Isabella Hooker to Olympia Brown, Aug. 28, 1874, Olympia Brown collection, Schlesinger Library, Radcliffe College. My thanks to Ellen DuBois for alerting me to this letter.

36. "Tilton's Cross-Examination" (Mme. Guion), in Marshall, *True History*, p. 160;

ET to TT and Mrs. Morse, Nov. 1870, in Marshall, *True History*, pp. 535–36 (text in Appendix). Mme. Guyon, a seventeenth-century Catholic, was hailed by Protestants for her mystical piety. Tilton's reference to her is especially interesting in light of her intimate friendship with a clerical figure of high standing: the Abbé de Fénelon, the Archbishop of Cambrai. See Michael de la Bedoyere, *The Archbishop and the Lady: The Story of Fénelon and Madame Guyon* (London, 1956).

37. "Tilton's Sworn Statement," in Marshall, *True History*, pp. 127, 115.

38. TT to ET, Dec. 7, 1866 ("On the Cars, Northern Indiana"), *Chicago Tribune*, Aug. 13, 1874, p. 3, col. 5; *TT v. HWB*, 1: 495 (the text of the letter is included in chapter 8). Frank Luther Mott's *Golden Multitudes: The Story of Best Sellers in the United States* (New York: Macmillan, 1947), p. 309, puts *Griffith Gaunt* in the top rank of best-sellers (sales of at least 300,000) for 1866, along with *Alice's Adventures in Wonderland*. *Tempest-Tossed* did not make Mott's 1874 list, though the *St. Paul Pioneer* called it "the most successful book" of spring and summer in the view of New York's "best known publishers." "Tilton," *New York Graphic*, Oct. 30, 1874, p. 876.

39. TT to ET, Dec. 7, 1866; TT, *Tempest-Tossed*, p. 106 [Donne poem], p. 91 [photo of Mary]; John Donne, "Present in Absence," in Francis T. Palgrave, *The Golden Treasury*, 2 vols. in one (1861; New York: Macmillan, 1947), p. 8. Tilton quoted Donne's third (and last) stanza exactly except for the final line, which should be "And so enjoy her and none miss her."

40. TT to ET, Dec. 22, 1866, *Chicago Tribune*, Aug. 13, 1874, p. 4, cols. 1–2 (text of letter in chapter 8). Elizabeth, for her part, made a sharp distinction between Theodore's editorial writing—in which he was famous for rough-and-tumble, polemical name-calling—and his creative writing. "I have never had much pride in you as an editor," she wrote, "but I believe as a poet and essayist I might fall to worshiping." She wished him to "devote [himself] to reading, writing stories, poetry—in short, a literary life." ET to TT, Feb. 11, 1867, *Chicago Tribune*, Aug. 13, 1874, p. 1, col. 6.

41. "The Brooklyn Scandal," *New York Graphic*, Sept. 28, 1874, p. 633.

42. TT, *Tempest-Tossed*, pp. 126, 144; ET to TT, Feb. 7, 1869, *Chicago Tribune*, Aug. 13, 1874, p. 2, cols. 3–4 [*TT v. HWB*, 1: 491–92] (letter included in chapter 8). The real-life Elizabeth, besides writing of her "sin" rather than her "unworthiness," wrote of what her dead baby Paul—a Tilton infant who died in 1868—"will do for me" and not of the "blessing" that "God" might bestow (as Mary Vail had it).

CHAPTER FOUR

1. *TT v. HWB*, 1: 152 (ladies in gallery); 1: 756 ("brownkeetoes"); 2: 584 (James Woodley).

2. *TT v. HWB*, 1: 17. The three volumes of the official trial transcript contain the witnesses' testimony, the lawyers' lengthy arguments about evidence, their month-long closing summations, the judge's intricate instructions to the jury, and the stenographer's opinionated commentary on each day's proceedings. Court was in session for 112 days, and 107 witnesses were examined, some more than once. The transcript was sold to a mass audience in serial installments costing 50 cents each.

The three bound volumes of those installments, ranging in length from 800 to 1,000 pages, cost three dollars each. The courtroom layout is described in "The Brooklyn Scandal Court," *New York Graphic*, Feb. 6, 1875, p. 701.

3. *TT v. HWB*, 1: 98. When he testified in April, Beecher took a bouquet of flowers with him onto the stand each day and sniffed them whenever he could. The *New York Tribune* commentator asserted that Beecher was "entirely unconstrained" on the stand. He was so "perfectly at ease" during his testimony, according to the *Tribune* man, that "he sat most of the time with the two middle fingers of his right hand thrust in his vest." *TT v. HWB*, 2: 723.

4. *TT v. HWB*, 1: 34, 75. The jury was not sequestered during the trial. The judge pled with the jurors not to read the newspapers and to stop talking to people in the courtroom before or after the court session. He also asked the spectators standing right behind the jurors to please not comment so audibly on the evidence. The jurors (who were paid nine dollars a week) did read the papers, since the judge also begged the reporters to ask their editors not to analyze the evidence, thereby influencing the jurors. The papers energetically disregarded his instructions.

5. "Editorial Topics," *Frank Leslie's Illustrated Weekly*, Jan. 30, 1875, p. 339 [female journalist]; *Chicago Tribune* report quoted in "Weaving the Web," *St. Louis Dispatch*, Feb. 17, 1875, p. 1.

6. "The Brooklyn Legal Battle: The Ladies in and about the Courtroom during the Daily Sessions," *New York Graphic*, Feb. 4, 1875, p. 684.

7. "'Laertes' in New York," *New York Graphic*, Jan. 14, 1875, p. 532 [Townsend was "Laertes" in the *Graphic*, "Gath" in the *Chicago Tribune*]; "New York Notes," *Mobile* (Alabama) *Register*, Mar. 10, 1875, p. 2.

8. "Brooklyn," *Chicago Tribune*, Feb. 11, 1875, p. 1; "The Brooklyn Legal Battle," *New York Graphic*, p. 684; *TT v. HWB*, 2: 798 [Judge Neilson's barring women spectators]. Thirty women attended court on an especially crowded day in April, one on which "at least 3,000 people" were unable to get in. One who did gain admission was Congressman James A. Garfield of Ohio, by no means the most noteworthy of "many well-known gentlemen present." "On the Ragged Edge," *New York Graphic*, Apr. 5, 1875, p. 266. Judge Neilson could stanch the flow of women into his courtroom—there were only two "petticoated spectators" on Feb. 9, according to the *Chicago Tribune* report—but he was powerless to disperse what the *New York Graphic* called "the bevies" of up to two dozen "bright, merry-looking school-girls, with book satchels on their arms," who stood outside the courthouse from two to four in the afternoon waiting for a glimpse of the stars. This, to the *Graphic* reporter, was the "saddest . . . spectacle relating to this subject" ("The Brooklyn Legal Battle," p. 684).

9. "Mrs. Moulton's Testimony," *Chicago Tribune*, Feb. 21, 1875, p. 8; *TT v. HWB*, 3: 1032. The virtual awe in which the press held Mrs. Moulton did not earn her an exemption from the ogling notice that all the women in the court received. Her physical appearance, body language, and fashion choices were subjected to minute scrutiny.

10. *TT v. HWB*, 1: 735 ("treacherous").

11. Henry James, *The Bostonians* (1886; New York: Vintage / Library of America, 1991), p. 77 (chapter 11); *The Complete Notebooks of Henry James*, ed. Leon Edel and

Lyall H. Powers (New York: Oxford University Press, 1987), p. 20 ("the decline of the sentiment of sex").

12. *TT v. HWB*, 1: 371. Over the last generation an extraordinary scholarship has emerged on Victorian marriage in relation to the formation of the middle class and the development of ideas and experiences of love. Three works illustrate the range of treatments and the evolution of approaches: Carroll Smith-Rosenberg, *Disorderly Conduct: Visions of Gender in Victorian America* (New York: Oxford University Press, 1985), which includes her pathbreaking 1975 essay "The Female World of Love and Ritual"; Karen Lystra, *Searching the Heart: Women, Men, and Romantic Love in Nineteenth-Century America* (New York: Oxford University Press, 1989); and T. Walter Herbert, *Dearest Beloved: The Hawthornes and the Making of the Middle-Class Family* (Berkeley: University of California Press, 1993). The ongoing challenge for nineteenth- and twentieth-century cultural historians, in my view, is to give accounts of lived experience that rise to the standard set by Laurel Thatcher Ulrich's *A Midwife's Tale* (New York: Knopf, 1990), a richly textured narrative analysis of individual and communal life on the Maine frontier between 1785 and 1812.

13. *TT v. HWB*, 3: 323.

14. "Brooklyn," *Chicago Tribune*, Feb. 11, 1875, p. 1 ["little white sheets of paper"]; "Last Statement," *Chicago Tribune*, Feb. 17, 1875, p. 1 ["gold eyeglasses"]; "The Abrupt Close," *New York Graphic*, May 1, 1875, p. 466; *New York Sun* interview with Tilton cited in "Facts and Gossip," *Chicago Tribune*, May 13, 1875, p. 8.

15. "Mrs. Tilton," *Chicago Tribune*, May 9, 1875, p. 4 ; "The Injustice to Mrs. Tilton," *Chicago Tribune*, June 10, 1875, p. 4. The May 9 editorial is a plain statement of the mixed feelings observers expressed about her from the beginning of her public renown. This lengthy piece combines newfound compassion with the usual harsh judgment. It goes beyond the usual by noting that the press was partly responsible for her "pitiable condition," a state of such "affliction that mental oblivion seems to be the only possible relief or escape."

16. "Mrs. Tilton's Letter," *Chicago Tribune*, May 5, 1875, p. 1.

17. *TT v. HWB*, 3: 563–64 (Porter's closing statement for the defense); 3: 824–25 (Beach's summation for the plaintiff).

18. "Affidavit of Joseph Loader," *Chicago Tribune*, June 28, 1875, p. 2. The two upholsterers eventually admitted they had made up their story. "The Beecher Case," *Chicago Tribune*, July 1, 1875, p. 5. Into the fall there was talk of a lawsuit against Loader. "The Old Scoundrel," *Chicago Tribune*, Oct. 28, 1875, p. 3.

19. "Mrs. Tilton's Sworn Statement," *Chicago Tribune*, June 28, 1875, p. 2. Beecher himself repeatedly used the father-daughter trope in both 1874 and 1875 to define his relationship to Mrs. Tilton. In scribbled notes to himself prior to his trial testimony in 1875, he instructed himself to remember that with respect to Elizabeth "I did not come to a sudden acquaintance or *fall* into an enthusiasm—but like a child she had year by year unfolded into my esteem." Undated HWB memo, Beecher Family Papers, box 87, folder 210, Yale University Library Manuscripts and Archives.

20. For example, William Evarts tried unsuccessfully to persuade Judge Neilson to allow Beecher to recite a passage from 1 Corinthians 13 that Henry had urged Elizabeth to meditate upon in 1871. The judge said no, observing that in any case

everyone in the courtroom was quite familiar with the passage in question (*TT v. HWB*, 2: 810). The *Tribune* reporter did provide the whole citation—chapter 13, verses 4 to 8—in his daily commentary (2: 799).

21. *TT v. HWB*, 2: 754 (HWB's memory); 2: 751 (HWB's dramatizing); 1: 390 (TT's memory).

22. *TT v. HWB*, 2: 880. In legal terms, there was a difference in 1870s America between "criminal conversation" suits and "alienation of affections" inquiries. Criminal conversation suits—which arose in seventeenth-century England as an enlightened alternative to dueling, but had been abolished in 1857—were, despite the "criminal" name, civil suits about adultery. They were actions for damages: the plaintiff was seeking money, and the defendant stood no chance of imprisonment. Alienation of affections proceedings were American creations of the post–Civil War period. They could be brought by a spouse against anyone: a husband could sue a mother-in-law for stealing the affections of his wife. These were civil suits too, and the award of damages depended upon proving the defendant's *intent* to alienate. In criminal conversation, by contrast, intent was irrelevant; there it was about objective bodily penetration. Tilton's lawyers may initially have hoped the court would rule that the jury should find Beecher guilty if he had *either* committed adultery with Mrs. Tilton *or* intentionally alienated her affections. But Judge Neilson agreed with the defense that finding for the plaintiff would require a judgment of adultery. *TT v. HWB*, 3: 1035. I am indebted to my colleague Laura Korobkin for clarifying these issues. See her *Criminal Conversations: Sentimentality and Nineteenth-Century Legal Stories of Adultery* (New York: Columbia University Press, 1998), p. 128. She discusses aspects of the Beecher-Tilton Scandal in chapters 3 and 4. On the development of criminal conversation, see Lawrence Stone, *The Road to Divorce in England, 1530–1987* (Oxford: Oxford University Press, 1990), chapter 9.

23. *TT v. HWB*, 3: 72 ("improper advances" and "solicitations"); 2: 836 ("there was enough"); 2: 869 ("depression" and "hypochondria"). One of the most startling HWB letters of 1872 became known as the "ragged edge" letter (text in the Appendix).

24. *TT v. HWB*, 3: 1041 (jury foreman's comments); 1: 411 (TT on Ralph); 2: 797 (HWB on Ralph).

25. *TT v. HWB*, 1: 478.

26. *TT v. HWB*, 2: 735, 737–38 (HWB recollections), 1: 480 (TT recollections).

27. *TT v. HWB*, 1: 409.

28. *TT v. HWB*, 1: 480 (TT recollections), 2: 756 (HWB recollections).

29. *TT v. HWB*, 2: 756, 779; 3: 59.

30. "The Home of Mr. Beecher," and "Mr. Tilton's Home," *The Beecher-Tilton Investigation: The Scandal of the Age* (Philadelphia: Barclay and Co., 1874), p. 66; "P," "Reminiscences," *Brooklyn Eagle*, Aug. 22, 1874, p. 2 ("sofas and ottomans"); "Gath" [George Alfred Townsend], "The Tiltons," *Chicago Tribune*, July 17, 1874, p. 1 ("many beautiful pictures"); "The Tilton–Beecher Mystery," *Detroit Evening News*, July 10, 1874, p. 3 ("whoever in those years"). Gath befriended Tilton after Elizabeth left him in July 1874, and Theodore gave him a tour of the whole house. In the bedroom Gath noted pictures of "the three Horatii, swearing to avenge the injury to their kinswomen," and "Sixtus returning home from the wards to find his wife's body just breathless." "Everything," he concluded, "had its dread association. Neither

adultery nor murder will down." "Letter from Gath," *Chicago Tribune,* Aug. 24, 1874, p. 1. In the early 1870s Theodore gave the portrait of Beecher to Frank Moulton for safekeeping—along with all the sensitive letters and documents—and the painting was still hanging above the Moultons' second-floor mantlepiece at 49 Remsen Street in 1875. The Remsen Street house, to which they moved in the early 1870s, is still a private residence. The Tiltons' house is gone; P. S. (Public School) 78 stands on its lot. Beecher's brownstone has been replaced by a seven-story apartment building, the "Bethel Home" of the Watchtower Society (Jehovah's Witnesses). But other original brownstones on Columbia Heights, such as numbers 91, 140, and 142 (the last two from 1836), give a glimpse of how the street looked in Beecher's day.

31. *TT v. HWB,* 2: 757.

32. *TT v. HWB,* 2: 833 ("beloved of god"); 1: 602 ("as pure as . . .").

33. *TT v. HWB,* 1: 455–56; 1: 521.

34. *TT v. HWB,* 1: 619.

35. *TT v. HWB,* 1: 527.

36. *TT v. HWB,* 1: 629.

37. *TT v. HWB,* 2: 758 (HWB denials); 2: 882, 884, 886 (on Emma Moulton); 2: 765, 768 ("sexual intercourse"). According to Frank Moulton, Beecher not only used the phrase "sexual relation" to describe his tie to Elizabeth Tilton, but sometimes uttered "a worse term"—whatever that may have been. Defense attorney Benjamin Tracy cast doubt on Moulton's recollection of having heard Beecher say "sexual relation" by pointing out that "the word 'sexual,' to characterize that act out of wedlock," was "an unusual word to use." Judge Neilson concurred with Tracy's judgment about "the use of that word." *TT v. HWB,* 1: 215–16.

38. *TT v. HWB,* 2: 757 (affection "as a Christian woman"); 2: 893 (1874 statement).

39. *TT v. HWB,* 2: 893. Of course the veneration of female purity was a long-standing convention in the West, and Beecher and the Tiltons inhabited a middle-class Protestant world which had elevated that belief to the utter apex of cultural truth and ritual. In a sense, therefore, Henry and Theodore were programmed by their milieu to idolize a woman like Elizabeth. In their writing and public speaking they were esteemed cultural programmers, and in their trial testimony they kept up their work as ambassadors for this tribal religion of female blessedness. But culture is a resource as well as an imposed discipline, and envisioning Elizabeth as a saint permitted them to attain important ends of their own. Indeed, that may be how "culture"—not a discrete agent but a gathering of forces that amounts to a distinct power set over against individuals—most successfully exerts its "own" authority, by getting individuals to pursue their most passionately felt goals. Literary scholar T. Walter Herbert's *Dearly Beloved,* while too rigid, in my view, in its sexualization of the Hawthornes' impulses, nevertheless points the way to a fuller fusion of individual and cultural actions and scriptings than historians have typically attempted. He is unusually alive to the interpenetration of psychological, spiritual, and artistic promptings. Another model effort in probing the relation between individual experience and cultural "work"—a book even more attuned than Herbert to the intersections of the literary and spiritual—is Jenny Franchot's *Roads to Rome: The Antebellum Protestant Encounter with Catholicism* (Berkeley: University of California Press, 1994).

40. *TT v. HWB*, 2: 153 (Sarah Putnam testimony); 2:788 ("on his mouth"); 3: 72 ("I believe they kissed each other").

41. *TT v. HWB*, 3: 10.

42. *TT v. HWB*, 3: 20. Beecher knew ahead of time that kissing would come up in his cross-examination. In notes to himself prior to his testimony he made a long list of points to remember. Number 50 was "that my familiarity with ladies was never with them individually but always as *members of the whole family*, and it was extended *to all*—husband, children and inmates—and usually drew in the co-related circles, or families of brothers and sisters, and of children when married—that not always but usually it included in it such salutations as they were accustomed to interchange among themselves. Also, kissing men." Undated HWB memo, Beecher Family Papers, box 87, folder 210, Yale University Library Manuscripts and Archives.

43. *TT v. HWB*, 2: 818 (January 20, 1872, letter); 2: 817 ("true inwardness" letter, text in Appendix).

44. *TT v. HWB*, 2: 817.

45. *TT v. HWB*, 3: 79–80.

46. *TT v. HWB*, 2: 754.

47. *TT v. HWB*, 1: 551. (Text of "Sir Marmaduke's Musings" in the Appendix.)

48. *TT v. HWB*, 1: 415 (Tilton on Beecher and Woodhull); 2: 771 ("bereft of reason").

49. Perhaps Theodore felt more than a faint hope of victory. On June 6 the *Chicago Tribune* reported (apparently reprinting a story from the pro-Tilton *New York Sun* of June 4) that "a canvass of opinion among the 57 journalists employed in reporting the trial yesterday showed that 42 regarded Mr. Beecher as guilty, 11 were non-committal, and four were convinced of his innocence." "The Great Scandal," p. 13. But a week later the *Tribune* predicted either a Beecher victory or a hung jury, the latter being the most likely prospect. "The Verdict in the Beecher Case," June 13, 1875, p. 4.

50. *TT v. HWB*, 3: 12–15.

51. "Mr. Beecher's Defiance," *Chicago Tribune*, June 28, 1875, p. 2. Cf. the *Chicago Tribune*'s editorial of May 10, 1875, p. 4: "The Beecher trial has impressed upon the public mind the fact that the higher circles of Brooklyn are in a continual state of kissing and crying." Beecher and Tilton were "two long-haired men engaged in a frantic kissing-match, with a torrent of tears perambulating their respective noses."

52. "Beecher," *Chicago Tribune*, July 14, 1875, p. 8.

53. "Facts and Gossip," *Chicago Tribune*, May 19, 1875, p. 2 (reprinting a *New York Herald* story of May 15).

54. "Letter from Miss Catherine E. Beecher," *Chicago Tribune*, Sept. 25, 1874, p. 8: "at periods of child-bearing modest women who are sane in all other respects will accuse sometimes their husbands and sometimes themselves of adultery."

CHAPTER FIVE

1. *TT v. HWB*, 3: 72.

2. "Mr. Moulton's First Statement," in Charles F. Marshall, *The True History of the Brooklyn Scandal* (Philadelphia: National Publishing Co., 1874), p. 350.

3. ET to HWB, "Wednesday," in Marshall, *True History*, pp. 350–51.

4. HWB to EB, March 8 [1871 or 1872], *TT v. HWB*, 1: 84 (text in Appendix).

5. ET to HWB, May 3, 1871, in Marshall, *True History*, p. 351. (Marshall has her writing "large" untiring generosity; the trial transcript has "larger," *TT v. HWB*, 2: 812, 3: 982.)

6. *TT v. HWB*, 2: 812, 3: 74.

7. *TT v. HWB*, 3: 74–76. Henry was right when he claimed on the stand that Elizabeth was joyful in the spring of 1871 because of a reconciliation with Theodore. He was wrong to imply that reconciliation with Theodore ruled out a renewal of affection for him too.

8. "Mr. Moulton's First Statement," in Marshall, *True History*, p. 351.

9. HWB to Moulton, June 1, 1873, in Marshall, *True History*, p. 365; *TT v. HWB*, 2: 858.

10. *TT v. HWB*, 2: 858, 871, 879–80.

11. *TT v. HWB*, 2: 884, 837; 3: 949.

12. E. L. Godkin, "Tilton against Beecher," *Nation*, July 8, 1875, p. 23. See also Godkin's "The Great Scandal," *Nation*, Aug. 20, 1874, p. 118.

13. HWB to Moulton, Feb. 5, 1872, in Marshall, *True History*, p. 361.

14. HWB to Moulton, Feb. 5, 1872, in Marshall, *True History*, pp. 359–61 (text in Appendix).

15. HWB to Moulton, June 1, 1873, in Marshall, *True History*, p. 365 (text in Appendix).

16. Godkin, "The Great Scandal," *Nation*, Aug. 20, 1874, p. 119.

17. HWB to Henry Bowen, Jan. 2, 1871, in Marshall, *True History*, p. 317.

18. In his so-called "True Story," an unpublished narrative that Theodore prepared after Victoria Woodhull broke the scandal in November 1872, he wrote that "10 or 11 years ago [Bowen] ... told me one evening while crossing the Fulton Ferry that Henry Ward Beecher was guilty of adultery, a practice begun in Indianapolis and continued in Brooklyn. Between the years 1860 and 1870, Mr. Bowen repeated the accusation not less than a hundred times." *TT v. HWB*, 2: 716. Tilton's letter to Bowen of January 1, 1871, repeating to Bowen all that Theodore claimed to have heard from him about Beecher's supposed adulteries, was divulged to the press in 1873, along with the text of a secret accord signed by Beecher, Bowen, and Tilton in April 1872. "Galvanizing a Filthy Scandal," *New York Times*, May 30, 1873, p. 5. In its editorial (p. 4), the *Times* took for granted that Bowen's oft-repeated charges were unsubstantiated, and called the trio's secret pact "farcical."

19. *TT v. HWB*, 2: 717 (Tilton and Bowen's machinations regarding Beecher); TT to HWB, Dec. 26, 1870, in Marshall, *True History*, p. 312 ("quit the city of Brooklyn"). Bowen and Tilton were both clever judges of character: Bowen had good reason to think an appeal to "honor" would work with Tilton, and Tilton had good reason to believe a story about adultery would work with a man who was telling such tales not only about Beecher but about Tilton himself.

20. During a single week in December 1870, Bowen was spreading stories about Tilton's alleged adulteries, Tilton was spreading them about Beecher's, and Bowen was telling Tilton that he [Bowen] could not any longer spread stories about *Beecher's* since (according to Theodore's recollection of Bowen's words) his pastor had "made a confession to me and asked my pardon, which I granted, and I cannot reopen a

settled quarrel." Theodore, Bowen said, would have to confront Beecher with adultery charges on his own. (*TT v. HWB*, 2: 716.) In the April 1872 "tripartite covenant" that he wrote with Beecher and Tilton, Bowen wrote that "having given credit, perhaps without due consideration, to tales and innuendoes affecting Henry Ward Beecher, and being influenced by them, as was natural to a man who receives impressions suddenly, to the extent of repeating them (guardedly, however, and within limitations, and not for the purpose of injuring him, but strictly in the confidence of consultation), [I] now feel that therein I did him wrong. Therefore, I disavow all the charges and imputations that have been attributed to me as having been by me made against Henry Ward Beecher." (Marshall, *True History*, p. 101.)

21. *TT v. HWB*, 2: 734. Beecher's connection with the Bowens fit the pattern of his later bond with the Moultons—the wife as soulmate, the husband as "counterpart," a shrewd man of the world who took care of "business" while Henry took charge of all the sentiment. The difference between Moulton and Bowen was religious: Bowen was a believer.

22. "Mr. Bowen's Position," *New York Graphic*, Sept. 11, 1874, p. 510; E. L. Godkin, "Chromo-Civilization," *Nation*, Sept. 24, 1874, p. 202. Theatrical tropes turn up everywhere in the commentary on the Beecher-Tilton trial, as they do in discussions of Beecher's Plymouth pulpit. Both were "stages" mounting "performances" by accomplished or mediocre "players." This framing was a standard way of mocking Beecher, the Tiltons, their lawyers, and others, but it may also have been a means of making sense of some very disturbing events by taming them, conforming them to a conventional wisdom about the difference between spurious or deceitful appearances (theatre) and solid realities (the trusty practices of everyday life). Of course dramatists themselves had already long made a point of likening theatre to everyday life, especially to the behavior of the commercial marketplace. See Jean-Christophe Agnew, *Worlds Apart: The Market and the Theater in Anglo-American Thought, 1550–1750* (New York: Cambridge University Press, 1986). By the mid–nineteenth century, clerical performers like Beecher had explicitly embraced theatricality as a path to a more open-ended self. While his critics sternly dismissed him as a mere "actor," he was merrily dismantling their revered distinction between seeming and being, imagining and knowing. I treat the nineteenth-century Protestant shift on "amusements" in "The Discipline of Amusement," in William R. Taylor, ed., *Inventing Times Square: Commerce and Culture at the Crossroads of the World* (New York: Russell Sage, 1991), pp. 83–98.

23. Editorial, *New York Graphic*, May 6, 1875. A list of Bowen's (self-reported) Christian philanthropies appeared in the *Graphic* on May 14, 1875, p. 566. The paper published interviews with Bowen on Feb. 27 (p. 874) and May 8 (pp. 522–23), 1875.

24. "Mr. Tilton's Account of Mrs. Woodhull," *Golden Age Tracts*, number 3, 1871, pp. 19, 32, 35. At the trial Theodore claimed that he tried to talk Victoria out of the assertion that she had raised the dead, but she insisted that he include it.

25. Victoria Woodhull quoted in J. E. P. Doyle, ed., *The Romance of Plymouth Church* (Hartford: Park Publishing, 1874), p. 215. She also let the world know that Beecher's "private carriage could have been seen waiting before our door every afternoon for many months, to take us riding to Central Park" (p. 216).

26. *TT v. HWB*, 3: 227. On spiritualism in postbellum America, see Ann Braude, *Radical Spirits: Spiritualism and Women's Rights in Nineteeth-Century America* (Boston: Beacon Press, 1989), and R. Laurence Moore, *In Search of White Crows: Spiritualism, Parapsychology, and American Culture* (New York: Oxford University Press, 1977). See also Bret E. Carroll, *Spiritualism in Antebellum America* (Bloomington: Indiana University Press, 1997).

27. Victoria Woodhull's card to the *New York Times* (see p. 132 in this book) and *New York World*, May 22, 1871, in Marshall, *True History*, p. 121 (and in *TT v. HWB*, 1: 88); Woodhull to HWB, Nov. 19, 1871, in Marshall, *True History*, p. 358.

28. Victoria Woodhull to HWB, June 3, 1872, in Marshall, *True History*, p. 363.

29. "Vic. Woodhull on the Rampage—Scurrilous Attacks upon Public Men," *Boston Herald*, Sept. 11, 1872, p. 4. The reporter added that one portion of the audience "deprecated her remarks" but "were so astounded that they did not think to hiss her down or drive her from the stage." Another group applauded her "vociferously," evidence of "depravity beyond the comprehension of respectable minds." He concluded by noting that "the language used in this report is mild in comparison with her own words, which are too obscene to place before our readers." Woodhull gave another speech the following night, but the *Herald* gave no details. "A short abstract would do injustice to this harangue, which was loudly applauded. Whatever may be her faults and errors she is evidently a popular speaker before the American Association of Spirtualists." "Convention of the American Spiritualists," Sept. 12, 1872, p. 2. Several later writers on Beecher and on Woodhull have asserted that no Boston paper dared to repeat even the gist of what the free-wheeling Victoria had said in her September 10 blast at Henry. The *Herald* report shows that Boston was not in this instance a uniformly repressive fortress of silence. On Woodhull's arrest and indictment, "The Claflin Family," *New York Times*, Nov. 3, 1872, p. 1, and "Woodhull and Claflin," Nov. 5, 1872, p. 2. The *Times* heaped scorn on Greeley's Presidential campaign by devoting three columns to citations from his high-profile supporter Theodore Tilton's biography of Woodhull, followed by a few choice comments of Victoria's on free love. A vote for Greeley, in the *Times* partisan calculus, was a vote for Woodhull. "A Greeley Reformer," Sept. 14, 1872, p. 11.

30. "The Woodhull and Claflin Trial—Discharge of Defendants," *New York Times*, June 28, 1873, p. 2 ("secret agent of the post office"). I give further attention to Woodhull's charges, including the juicy stories, in my discussion of the history of interpretation of the scandal in chapter 9.

31. "Victoria C. Woodhull's Complete and Detailed Version of the Beecher-Tilton Affair" [1872], in Madeleine B. Stern, ed., *The Victoria Woodhull Reader* (Weston, MA: M & S Press, 1974), pp. 4, 9–10.

32. No historian has yet produced a full account of Stanton's complex connection to Woodhull, but a good initial foray is provided by Elisabeth Griffith, *In Her Own Right: The Life of Elizabeth Cady Stanton* (New York: Oxford University Press, 1984), pp. 147–59. See also Lois Banner, *Elizabeth Cady Stanton* (Boston: Little Brown, 1980), pp. 134–35, Alma Lutz, *Created Equal: A Biography of Elizabeth Cady Stanton* (New York: John Day, 1940), p. 222, and William Leach, *True Love and Perfect Union: The Feminist Reform of Sex and Society* (New York: Basic Books, 1980), which provides much important context. Samuel Wilkeson, who published the Beecher-Tilton-

Bowen "tripartite covenant" in 1873, was Stanton's brother-in-law. She roundly denounced Wilkeson and Beecher alike during the scandal. She (like Theodore Tilton) alleged that Wilkeson and other well-placed supporters of Plymouth Church were disposed to discredit Bowen and Tilton because of a big financial stake in Beecher's career. Wilkeson, a journalist for most of his career, and (since 1870) a publicity man for Jay Cooke, was also a copartner in the J. B. Ford Company, which published Beecher's works. Although Stanton defended Theodore against Henry, she also criticized Tilton for having turned on Victoria Woodhull. "Mrs. Stanton's Story," *Chicago Tribune*, July 23, 1874, p. 1.

33. "Theodore Tilton's Last Statement," in Marshall, *True History*, p. 565; *TT v. HWB*, 3: 807 (Evarts's comment on "criminal intimacy"). Frank Moulton said in 1874 that *he* accused Beecher of "criminal intercourse" on the evening of December 30, 1870, and that Beecher "confessed and denied not, but confessed." Here again the alleged confession was apparently no more than a non-denial, since Moulton goes on to say, "As he did not deny this charge so explicitly made by me, whatever inferences I may have made from his words at other times, he certainly could not have mistaken mine at this time. When speaking of the relations of a man and a woman, 'criminal intercourse' has but one 'legal or literary meaning,' even to a clergyman." "Mr. Moulton's Last Statement," in Marshall, *True History*, pp. 478–79. Moulton may have realized in 1874 how ambiguous Tilton's phrase "criminal intimacy" was and therefore "remembered" using the much more pointed "criminal intercourse" in 1870.

34. TT's "Complaining Friend" card, *Brooklyn Eagle*, Dec. 27, 1872 (text in Appendix), and ET to TT, Dec. 28, 1872, in Marshall, *True History*, pp. 540–41. The denials by Henry, Elizabeth, Paulina Wright Davis, and Elizabeth Cady Stanton were entered into the trial transcript in 1875. *TT v. HWB*, 1: 600–601.

35. HWB to ET, n.d. [spring, 1873], *TT v. HWB*, 1: 566–67.

36. ET comment on Woodhull charges, November, 1872, *TT v. HWB*, 1: 601.

37. Barbara Goldsmith thinks Tilton "carried on a long-term love affair" with Laura Bullard, but does not provide evidence for her view. (*Other Powers: The Age of Suffrage, Spiritualism, and the Scandalous Victoria Woodhull* [New York: Knopf, 1998], p. 218.) The supposed affair with Bullard is part of the sexually open marriage that Goldsmith believes the Tiltons embraced for a time in the late 1860s. Her evidence for that claim is flimsy at best. (I discuss Goldsmith's book in chapter 9.) Altina L. Waller rightly observes that "whether Tilton and Bullard ever had an affair is impossible to determine, but there were many rumors to that effect. In January 1871 the *Brooklyn Eagle* reported that the two had 'eloped' to Europe." (*Reverend Beecher and Mrs. Tilton: Sex and Class in Victorian America* [Amherst: University of Massachusetts Press, 1982], p. 121.) Those appear to be the particular rumors that Henry Bowen used to get Beecher's support for Tilton's ouster from the *Independent* and *Brooklyn Union*. After Beecher assured himself the rumors were false and apologized to Tilton, Theodore was able to make light of the story in a letter to Anna Dickinson in February, 1871. He told her that Elizabeth was "sitting in the next room, writing a sisterly letter to the lady with whom I was supposed to have run away to Europe." (Feb. 23, 1871, Anna Dickinson Papers, Library of Congress.)

38. "Beecher's Trial," *Chicago Tribune*, July 28, 1874, p. 1. The *Tribune* reported

on July 29 (p. 4) that Mrs. Tilton denied the truth of Mrs. Stanton's interview. Stanton gave the *Brooklyn Argus* a further interview on August 1, in which she acknowledged that in 1872 Theodore had denied the truth of her recollection of the encounter in 1870. The August 1 interview was reprinted in "Beecher's Trial," *Chicago Tribune,* Aug. 2, 1874, p. 1.

39. "Mrs. Tilton's Cross-Examination," in Marshall, *True History,* pp. 207–8. Theodore's brother "died in a madhouse," according to a report in the *Brooklyn Eagle.* "The Insanity Question," *Chicago Tribune,* Aug. 13, 1874, p. 10 (see p. 306 in this book).

40. "Mrs. Tilton's Cross-Examination," in Marshall, *True History,* p. 208.

41. "A Hard Case," *Chicago Tribune,* Aug. 1, 1874, p. 1 (Anthony's quip). Anthony's August 1, 1874, interview with the *Utica Herald* was reprinted in the *Tribune* in "Beecher-Tilton," Aug. 4, 1874, p. 1. She offered an analysis of gossip, sensationalism, and the responsibilities of friendship that closely accorded with E. L. Godkin's views expressed that summer in the *Nation.* "I will not of my free will minister to mere public gossip," she said. "Gossip lives as well by denial as by affirmation. . . . What I know [about Beecher and the Tiltons] I learned in a way that forbids my repeating it for the public gratification. I should consider myself unworthy of friendship or confidence did I fail to be silent at this time." The *Tribune* editorialized the following day (August 5) that Anthony was "one of the most accomplished masters of diplomacy the world has ever known" ("Miss Anthony Interviewed," p. 4).

42. Susan B. Anthony to Mrs. Hooker, Nov. 16, 1872, in "Theodore Tilton's Last Statement," in Marshall, *True History,* p. 524. (Hooker leaned toward Stanton's and Woodhull's views of Henry's guilt, and published the letter from Anthony without Anthony's permission in 1874.)

43. ET to TT and Mrs. Morse, Nov., 1870, in "Theodore Tilton's Last Statement," in Marshall, *True History,* pp. 535–37 (text of letter in Appendix).

44. "Mr. Beecher's Defense," in Marshall, *True History,* p. 262 ("the winds were out"); ET to HWB, Dec. 30, 1870, *TT v. HWB,* 2: 762–64 (text in Appendix). Beecher repeated his story, in somewhat different language, during cross-examination. One page of the transcript of the cross-examination (*TT v. HWB,* 3: 31) is reprinted on p. 172 of this book. One hundred and thirty years later, the Moultons' residence at 143 Clinton Street is still a private dwelling.

45. ET to TT, Dec. 30, 1870, in Marshall, *True History,* p. 118 (text in Appendix).

46. Frank Moulton's account of Elizabeth's responsibility for the December 30 encounter between Theodore and Henry is especially cogent. Marshall, *True History,* p. 315.

47. ET to ——, Jan. 13, 1871, in Marshall, *True History,* pp. 349–50 (text in Appendix). In 1874 Frank Moulton said that it was very odd for a mother of four to use the expression "love babe," unless it referred to the fruit of a secret liaison. But, contrary to Moulton's insinuation, it was not unusual for a mother of four to use the phrase if the newborn was to be a foundation for the rebirth of love in her marriage.

48. "Tilton's Cross-Examination," in Marshall, *True History,* p. 143–44.

49. TT to ET, Dec. 6 and Dec. 7, 1866, *Chicago Tribune,* Aug. 13, 1874, p. 3. (Theodore's reading of *Griffith Gaunt,* letters reprinted in chapter 8.) Of course if his

wife *did* confess adultery to him in the summer of 1870, that would explain his erroneous belief that the sin of Catherine Gaunt, to whom Elizabeth likened herself, was also adultery. See the "Prologue" and Appendix for the June 29, 1871, "*Griffith Gaunt*" letter from ET to TT (also called the "Catherine Gaunt" letter).

50. ET to TT, July 4, 1871, *TT v. HWB*, 1: 682.

51. ET to ——, Jan. 13, 1871, in Marshall, *True History*, pp. 349–50 (text in Appendix).

CHAPTER SIX

1. "Theodore Tilton," in Linus Pierpont Brockett, ed., *Men of Our Day* (Philadelphia: Ziegler, McCurdy, 1868), pp. 612–14, 618 (published excerpts from the toast in the Appendix).

2. TT to HWB, Sept. 18, 1863 ("furnished for a substitute"), Aug. 9, 1863 ("my chief aim"); Thurlow Weed letter to the *Albany Evening Journal*, n.d., n.p., enclosed in TT to HWB, Sept. 24, 1863, Beecher Family Papers, Yale University.

3. On "domesticity" and "virtue," see the excellent essays on those topics by Nancy Cott and Joan Williams in Richard Wightman Fox and James T. Kloppenberg, eds., *A Companion to American Thought* (Cambridge: Blackwell, 1995).

4. HWB sermon, *Independent*, Dec. 27, 1866, p. 2. A common leap made by twentieth-century interpreters of Beecher is to infer adultery with Elizabeth Tilton and other women on the basis of this sermon's endorsement of "elective affinity." Paxton Hibben, *Henry Ward Beecher: An American Portrait* (New York: George H. Doran, 1927), p. 212, and Barbara Goldsmith, *Other Powers: The Age of Suffrage, Spiritualism, and the Scandalous Victoria Woodhull* (New York: Knopf, 1998), p. 224. I discuss the Hibben-to-Goldsmith interpretive line in Chapter 9.

5. HWB, "A Letter to the Office Editors," *Independent*, Apr. 21, 1859, p. 1. Romantic male friendships of the sort Tilton and Beecher cultivated may have been especially common among antebellum Protestants. See Karen V. Hansen, "'Our Eyes Behold Each Other': Masculinity and Intimate Friendship in Antebellum New England," in Peter M. Nardi, ed., *Men's Friendships* (Newbury Park: Sage, 1993), pp. 35–58. George Chauncey offers a wise discussion of the growing literature on romantic male friendship in *Gay New York: Gender, Urban Culture, and the Making of the Gay Male World, 1890–1940* (Chicago: University of Chicago Press, 1994), esp. p. 403, n. 50. He suggests that intense male friendship may have been even more widespread than we have thought, and cautions against judging romantic friendship as "heterosexual" on the sole grounds that it was not "homosexual." In the nineteenth century, he argues, *neither* category existed. David S. Reynolds's able discussion of the same subject in his *Walt Whitman's America: A Cultural Biography* (New York: Knopf, 1995), pp. 392–94, surveys cases of nineteenth-century male romantic friendship that were decidedly more sexual in expression than we have any reason to think Beecher and Tilton's was. Theirs was physical in its sitting on laps and kissing on cheeks, and emotional-spiritual in its rhapsodies of soul-bonding.

6. TT to HWB, June 17, July 3, Aug. 7, Sept. 18 and 24, 1863, Beecher Family Papers, Yale University.

7. TT to HWB, June 17, "Wednesday, 30th" (misdated by TT; it was either

Tuesday, June 30, or Wednesday, July 1), Sept. 18 ("the little lady had a long sickness"), Sept. 24, 1863 ("the little lady is overwhelmed by your kind remembrance. . . . I am hungry to look into your eyes").

8. "Mr. Tilton's Sworn Statement," in Charles F. Marshall, *The True History of the Brooklyn Scandal* (Philadelphia: National Publishing Co., 1874), p. 114; HWB to TT, Oct. 18, 1863, Harriet Beecher Stowe Center (copy of the original; text in Appendix).

9. Hibben, *Henry Ward Beecher*, pp. 188–90. The story of Beecher's heroic and influential exploits in England was so uncontested in the 1870s that attorneys on both sides at the civil trial accepted it. William Evarts used it as character-building material for Beecher, while Tilton's attorney William Beach, in his summation, denied that the preacher's undoubted patriotic achievements were relevant to the issue of personal virtue. *TT v. HWB*, 3: 869.

10. HWB to TT, Oct. 18, 1863, Stowe Center; HWB to TT, Oct. 21, 1863, Tilton Papers, New York Historical Society.

11. Report of Beecher's address cited in Carl Sandburg, *Abraham Lincoln: The War Years*, vol. 2 (New York: Harcourt, Brace, 1939), p. 517. Sandburg writes that "no citizen of the United States had ever before so dramatized himself as an American David combating the British Goliath on British soil. Yet . . . his results were slight" (p. 516). The letter from Tilton read by Beecher to the Liverpool crowd is TT to HWB, Sept. 18, 1863, in the Beecher Family Papers, Yale University. The excerpt reproduced by Sandburg diverges from the original in several ways (the differences in the original are italicized): "revealed to me a great growth of wisdom *in his ugly head*"; "the gradual *system* of emancipation"; "desirous that the *conquered* states shall form free constitutions"; "will be made feasible by calling *the loyal men 'the state,' and giving disloyalists no vote.*"

12. "Mr. Tilton's Sworn Statement," in Marshall, *True History*, p. 114. Fifteen years was also the exact duration of Tilton's career at the *Independent* (1855–1870).

13. "Mrs. Tilton's Cross-Examination," in Marshall, *True History*, p. 192 ("his attention to the ladies"), p. 197 ("sensual influence"). We have it only on Theodore's authority that Elizabeth used the term "counterpart," but she very likely did since he says so in one of his letters to her. He does not claim that she used the term with reference to Beecher, but it seems quite possible, judging by her rhapsodic comments about Henry to the Plymouth Church Investigating Committee in 1874. "The number of people who mate each other—who fit one another exactly—who are (to use your word) 'counterparts,' is very small." TT to ET, Feb. 12, 1867, *TT v. HWB*, 1: 496–97. Note that Beecher appears to have used the term "counterpart" in the opposite sense: Frank Moulton was his counterpart because they were so different, yet for that reason magnetically attractive to one another. And yet the divergence in usage may be minimal: perhaps both Beecher and Mrs. Tilton meant to signal that perfect mating was the product of complementarity rather than likeness.

14. TT to HWB, n.d., Beecher Family Papers, Yale University.

15. The *Independent* published a note on Jan. 31, 1861, p. 4, entitled "Circulation Nearly 70,000." Frank Luther Mott noted that the circulation dipped at the start of the war but rebounded to around 75,000 before Appomattox. *A History of American Magazines, 1850–1865* (Cambridge: Harvard University Press, 1957), p. 372.

16. TT, "Memorial," *Last Poems of Elizabeth Barrett Browning with a Memorial by Theodore Tilton* (New York: James Miller, 1863), pp. 14–15, first printed as TT, "Elizabeth Barrett Browning: In Memorium," *Independent,* July 25, 1861, p. 1. The letters the Tiltons wrote each other in the late 1860s were compared in the press to the love letters of Elizabeth Barrett and Robert Browning, and one of Elizabeth's surviving letters to a woman friend quotes the last ten words of Mrs. Browning's "My Heart and I," published in *Last Poems,* pp. 121–23. See ET to "Friend and Sister," Jan. 13, 1871 (text in Appendix; ET's "Dying Deaths Daily" is also in the Appendix).

17. *Vanity Fair* and *Round Table* quoted in Mott, *A History of American Magazines,* p. 373; Henry Bowen, "Our History and Our Plans for the Future," *Independent,* Dec. 29, 1870, p. 4. In the late 1860s E. L. Godkin took up the critique of Tilton's editorial style. He sent him a private letter complaining about a "personal" attack against him that the *Independent* had printed. In a private response Theodore disclaimed responsibility for the attack, which he regretted, but he defended "Personal Journalism" in an editorial published a week after receiving Godkin's letter. *Independent,* Sept. 17, 1868, p. 4. At the same time he sent Godkin a letter of condolence on the loss of his two-month-old son. Godkin was touched, and referred in a grateful letter to Tilton's gesture. "You, who have, I believe, lost older children, have, perhaps, touched lower depths of this great sorrow than we [Godkin and his wife] have as yet reached." Godkin to TT, Sept. 7 and Sept. 15, 1868, in William M. Armstrong, ed., *The Gilded Age Letters of E. L. Godkin* (Albany: State University of New York Press, 1974), pp. 122–23.

18. Lyman Abbott, *Henry Ward Beecher* (1903; New York: Chelsea House, 1980), p. 79–80 ("meeting house"), p. 83 ("pure democracy").

19. "The American Board and American Slavery," *Speech of Theodore Tilton in Plymouth Church, Brooklyn, January 28, 1860,* reported by Wm. Henry Burr (pamphlet in author's possession), p. 38 ("total depravity"), p. 41 (Sharpe's rifle), p. 42 ("testimony"); *TT v. HWB,* 1 : 458.

20. *TT v. HWB,* 1 : 458; "The American Board and American Slavery," pp. 3–4.

21. Anonymous letter to *Pittsburgh Commercial,* reprinted in J. E. P. Doyle, ed., *The Romance of Plymouth Church* (title on binding), *Plymouth Church and Its Pastor, or Henry Ward Beecher and His Accusers* (title on title page) (Hartford: Park Publishing Co., 1874), p. 203. The letter was sent from Brooklyn Heights on July 21, 1874, and reprinted in other newspapers, including the *Chicago Tribune,* the de facto organ of record for the scandal in 1874–1875. One can follow the progress of the tale from unattributed story to established "fact" in Hibben, *Henry Ward Beecher,* p. 185, and Sandburg, *Abraham Lincoln: The War Years,* vol. 2, pp. 577–78.

22. *TT v. HWB,* 1 : 481 (TT's recollection), 2 : 737 (HWB's recollection). As an important voice in the Radical Republican circles that Lincoln had a political interest in cultivating, Tilton saw Lincoln on other occasions, so it is entirely plausible that he saw him about Beecher's son, and that Lincoln would have wished to do him a favor.

23. TT to HWB, Nov. 30, 1865, *TT v. HWB,* 2 : 738; *TT v. HWB,* 2 : 737 ("loose conduct with women"), 2 : 323, 3 : 671 ("lost my faith in man"), 2 : 738 ("either's friends"). Theodore's letter to Henry is in the Appendix.

24. ET to TT, Dec. 28, 1866, *Chicago Tribune,* Aug. 13, 1874, p. 1, col. 4 (*TT v.*

HWB, 1: 493, text of letter in chapter 8); TT to Henry Bowen, Jan. 1, 1871, in "Statement of Francis D. Moulton," in Marshall, *True History*, p. 313. Moulton correctly noted that Tilton's letter also claimed Bowen had earlier charged Beecher not just with debauching Lucy Bowen, but with "a rape, or something very nearly like ravishment" of another unidentified woman. In his summation for the defense, William Evarts tried to use Tilton's 1871 letter against him. Having apparently heard in the early 1860s about Beecher's alleged sexual assaults and adulteries (going back to his Indiana days) from Bowen, Tilton would have been vigilant about allowing Henry near his wife. Yet Theodore begged Henry to come around more and more often, and to see his wife while Theodore himself was away lecturing. Tilton did not seem to have taken Bowen's charges very seriously—nor, by implication, should the jury credit Tilton's. (*TT v. HWB*, 3: 676.)

25. TT to HWB, June 17, 1863, Beecher Family Papers, Yale University (text in Appendix).

26. *TT v. HWB*, 2: 738 ("lovers' quarrel").

27. HWB, "Shall We Compromise?" *Independent*, Feb. 21, 1850, p. 30.

28. HWB speeches quoted in Abbott, *Henry Ward Beecher*, pp. 185–86 (fugitive slaves), p. 202 (Kansas-Nebraska bill), pp. 211–12 (Beecher's Bibles).

29. *TT v. HWB*, 1: 457 ("extreme Abolitionist"). In an 1863 speech Tilton claimed he had first sworn "eternal hostility to American slavery" while visiting Virginia. He had walked into a slave market in Richmond and "under the red flag of a slave auctioneer . . . heard a voice crying, 'This woman's name is MARY—how much am I bid for her?'—and there . . . was a woman holding a babe at her breast, a boy standing at one side, and a girl at the other!" "My soul," he said, "flushed into my face like fire." *Proceedings of the American Anti-Slavery Society at Its Third Decade* [Philadelphia, Dec. 3–4, 1863] (1864; New York: Negro Universities Press, 1969), pp. 96–97.

30. TT to ET, Oct. 25, 1865, reprinted in *Chicago Tribune*, Aug. 13, 1874, p. 3, col. 1; HWB, "Conditions of a Restored Union," Oct. 29, 1865, quoted in Abbott, *Henry Ward Beecher*, pp. 274, 278.

31. HWB to Charles G. Halpine, et al., Aug. 30, 1866, *TT v. HWB*, 1: 476–77; HWB quoted in Abbott, *Henry Ward Beecher*, p. 278.

32. [TT,] "Mr. Beecher," *Independent*, Sept. 6, 1866, p. 4, (reprinted in *TT v. HWB*, 1: 620, as part of Tilton's testimony on the Cleveland letter).

33. TT, "The Negro," speech to the 1863 convention of the American Antislavery Society, quoted in James M. McPherson, "A Brief for Equality: The Abolitionist Reply to the Racist Myth, 1860–1865," in Martin Duberman, ed., *The Antislavery Vanguard: New Essays on the Abolitionists* (Princeton: Princeton University Press, 1965), pp. 166, 170.

34. *TT v. HWB*, 2: 735 ("a paper that I had helped fashion"), 1: 479 ("very sore"); HWB to TT, June 3, 1867, *TT v. HWB*, 1: 485 (text in Appendix). Family friend Sarah Putnam testified at the trial that after the Cleveland letter flap Theodore and Elizabeth turned a plaster bust of Beecher—which they kept "on a little bracket right at her sitting-room door on the second story"—so that its face was to the wall. Putnam asked Elizabeth why and she replied, "Theodore says that our pastor has

proved himself a traitor to the Republican Party." (*TT v. HWB*, 2: 163.) In an *Independent* editorial saluting the new *Christian Union* in 1870, Theodore mixed praise of the new editor with poisonous potshots.

We wish [Beecher] joy in his task. Yes, and we half envy the pleasure of his young confreres and companions in toil. They will find him the easiest of masters and pleasantest of friends. True, they will need to carry a gentle goad in their hands, and to ply it upon him day and night, in order to procure his "copy" in season. And then too, his manuscript, when ready, will look as if purposely redeemed from what Hamlet called the baseness of writing fair. But, when once worried out of him, and got fairly in type, it will always show itself full of sense, spice, originality, and Christian charity. The opening number (in which he has written more than we ever knew him to write in any one number of *The Independent*) is excellent both in matter and spirit. We are sorry, however, to detect in it a certain languor of style quite foreign to the author's habitual freshness, showing a somewhat overworked and weary pen. His salutatory is a shade more orthodox and conservative than he would have written ten years go, when his temper was more defiant and aggressive than it has grown to be during these later and older years. ("Editorial Notes," Jan. 6, 1870, p. 6)

In 1893 the *Christian Union* became the outwardly secular *Outlook*, and in 1928 it merged with its former antagonist to form the *Outlook and Independent*.

35. *TT v. HWB*, 1: 479.

36. [TT,] "The Soilure of a Fair Name," *Independent*, May 7, 1868, p. 4, also quoted in "Evarts and Tilton," *New York Graphic*, Feb. 2, 1875, p. 669, which cites Tilton's later *Independent* editorial on Evarts becoming Attorney-General. It gives the date for that editorial as September 8, 1868, but the *Independent* was not published on that date. Since the *Graphic* also got the date of the May editorial wrong, while quoting it correctly, it stands to reason that the later quotation is also accurate. It matches other comments Theodore made about Evarts at the time. In the *Independent* of July 23, 1868 ("Editorial Notes," p. 4), for example, he observed that "the renegade Republican" Evarts's acceptance of President Johnson's offer called to his [Tilton's] mind a Bible verse: "Verily I say unto you, they have their reward."

37. HWB, *Norwood, or Village Life in New England* (New York: Charles Scribner, 1868), p. 204.

38. TT to ET, Nov. 12, 1866, *Chicago Tribune*, Aug. 13, 1874, p. 3, col. 3.

39. During the trial in 1875 the popular press generated a raft of rumors and stories about the "mystery" of Bessie Turner's origins. Some thought she was an orphan, others believed her father "Captain" Turner and her mother, now married to a well-to-do gentleman on "Park Avenue," had each tried during her childhood to get her back from the Tiltons.

40. *TT v. HWB*, 2: 529 (Bessie Turner testimony).

41. "Mrs. X" letter to the *New York Graphic*, reprinted in the *Chicago Tribune*, May 31, 1875, p. 8; "Mrs. Tilton's Cross-Examination," in Marshall, *True History*, p. 190.

42. Lucy Stone quoted in "A Kind Word for Mrs. Tilton," *Brooklyn Daily Eagle*, Aug. 31, 1874, p. 2; ET to TT, Jan. 13, 1867, *Chicago Tribune*, Aug. 13, 1874, p. 1, cols. 3–4 (letter reprinted in chapter 8).

43. *TT v. HWB*, 2: 500 ("a mother to me always"), 2: 569 ("Because I loved Mrs. Tilton"); Bessie Turner to ET, May 24, 1869, *TT v. HWB*, 2: 492.

44. Editorial Note, *New York Graphic*, Apr. 27, 1875, p. 426.

45. "Bessie Turner's Testimony," *New York Sun*, Mar. 20, 1875, reprinted in the *Chicago Tribune*, Mar. 22, 1875, p. 2; Neil Harris, *Humbug: The Art of P. T. Barnum* (Chicago: University of Chicago Press, 1973). "A complicated hoax," writes Harris, was "competition between victim and hoaxer, each seeking to outmaneuver the other" (p. 77).

46. "Mrs. X" letter, *Chicago Tribune*, May 31, 1875, p. 8; TT to ET, Aug. 21, 1865, *Chicago Tribune*, Aug. 13, 1874, p. 3, col. 1. (The letter is misdated Aug. 20 in the *Tribune*; it was written on the "Monday" following Sunday, Aug. 20.)

47. *The Beecher-Tilton Investigation: The Scandal of the Age* (Philadelphia: Barclay and Co., 1874), pp. 101–2. The letters from Chase, Child, and Curtis were addressed to Theodore; that from Gerrit Smith and Wife to Mr. and Mrs. Tilton. "Many other letters," according to the compiler, "were sent to this festival."

48. TT, "The Excursion to Fort Sumter," *Independent*, Apr. 27, 1865, p. 4; "C," "A Novel Sabbath in Charleston," *Independent*, Apr. 27, 1865, p. 3; HWB, "Narrative of His Trip to South Carolina," *Independent*, May 11, 1865, p. 2. Beecher's Fort Sumter address was printed in toto in the Apr. 27 issue: "The Old Flag at Sumter," p. 2.

49. TT to ET, Jan. 13, 1865, *Chicago Tribune*, Aug. 13, 1874, p. 2, col. 7 (*TT v. HWB*, 1: 498–99); TT to ET, Aug. 5, 1865, *Chicago Tribune*, Aug. 13, 1874, p. 3, col. 1.

50. *TT v. HWB*, 2: 756.

CHAPTER SEVEN

1. David Brion Davis's document collection *Antebellum American Culture: An Interpretive Anthology* (1979; University Park: Pennsylvania State University Press, 1997) exhibits the extraordinary range of institutions and rituals that cemented the internalization of social control as a pillar of middle-class life.

2. It is because lived experience is always interpreted experience that we, looking back at Beecher and the Tiltons from our distance, can claim some very partial access to their lived experience. Their fumbling or wise articulations of it, transmitted to us in documents, were part of their experience from the beginning.

3. ET to TT, Jan. 7, 1867, *Chicago Tribune*, Aug. 13, 1874, p. 1. col. 4 (*TT v. HWB*, 1: 448, text in chapter 8). All of the *Tribune* letters are from the Aug. 13 issue.

4. TT to ET, Mar. 18, 1867, *Tribune*, p. 9, col. 1 (*TT v. HWB*, 1: 497).

5. TT to ET, Jan. 26, 1868, *Tribune*, p. 9, col. 2 (*TT v. HWB*, 1: 617–18); TT to ET, Feb. 9, 1868, *Tribune*, p. 9, col. 2 (*TT v. HWB*, 1: 451, text in chapter 8).

6. ET to TT, Jan. 29, 1867, *Tribune*, p. 1, col. 5; ET to TT, Jan. 31, 1868, *Tribune*, p. 1, cols. 6–7 (*TT v. HWB*, 1: 503, text in chapter 8).

7. ET to TT, Feb. 3, 1868, *Tribune*, p. 1, col. 7 (*TT v. HWB*, 1: 487–88, in ch. 8).

8. ET to TT, Feb. 18, 1868, *Tribune*, p. 2, col. 1 (*TT v. HWB*, 1: 494).

9. Barbara Goldsmith's *Other Powers: The Age of Suffrage, Spiritualism, and the Scan-*

dalous Victoria Woodhull (New York: Knopf, 1998) claims (p. 91) that "the sexual act itself was for Lib, as she was later to explain, one of dutiful submission." Goldsmith provides no evidence for this statement. I suspect that Elizabeth's supposed "later explanation" was actually an insinuation made by some third party, probably Frank Moulton, whom Goldsmith takes as an unproblematic truth-teller. Elizabeth never made direct reference, so far as we know, to "the sexual act." ("Lib" was Elizabeth's familial nickname, but she signed all her letters to her husband "Elizabeth." It is unclear why Goldsmith, along with some other historians, calls her "Lib" but does not then call Theodore "Dory," his familial nickname. The effect of such usage is to make Elizabeth his immature subordinate, "docile and domestic," as Goldsmith inaccurately describes her, p. 89.)

10. TT to ET, Dec. 7, 1866, *Tribune*, p. 3, col. 5 (*TT v. HWB*, 1: 495, text in chapter 8).

11. TT to ET, Dec. 27, 1866, *Tribune*, p. 4, col. 2 (*TT v. HWB*, 1: 495–96); ET to TT, Jan. 24, 1867, *Tribune*, p. 1, col. 5; ET to TT, Feb. 13, 1867, *Tribune*, p. 1, col. 6 (*TT v. HWB*, 1: 449 [the trial transcript, based on what the stenographer "heard," has "sole lover," but the context makes clear it should be "soul lover"]); ET to TT, Feb. 18, 1868, *Tribune*, p. 2, col. 1.

12. ET to TT, Dec. 28, 1866, *Tribune*, p. 1, col. 4 (*TT v. HWB*, 1: 493, text in chapter 8); TT to ET, Dec. 27, 1866, *Tribune*, p. 4, col. 2 (*TT v. HWB*, 1: 495–96); TT to ET, Feb. 21, 1867, *Tribune*, p. 4, col. 7 (*TT v. HWB*, 1: 498).

13. ET to TT, Jan. 28, 1867, *Tribune*, p. 1, col. 5 (*TT v. HWB*, 1: 488, text in chapter 8).

14. ET to TT, Jan. 25, 1867, *Tribune*, p. 1, col. 5 (*TT v. HWB*, 1: 499, text in chapter 8).

15. ET to TT, Feb. 4, 1869, *Tribune*, p. 2, col. 3 (text in chapter 8).

16. ET to TT, Feb. 18, 1868, *Tribune*, p. 2, col. 1 (*TT v. HWB*, 1: 494); ET to TT, Feb. 10, 1869, *Tribune*, p. 2, col. 4 (text in chapter 8).

17. ET to TT, Feb. 1, 1868, *Tribune*, p. 1, col. 7 (*TT v. HWB*, 1: 489–90, text in chapter 8).

18. ET to TT, Jan. 25, 1867, *Tribune*, p. 1, col. 5 (*TT v. HWB*, 1: 499, text in chapter 8); ET to TT, Feb. 29, 1868, *Tribune*, p. 2, col. 2; ET to TT, Jan. 28, 1868, *Tribune*, p. 1, col. 6 (*TT v. HWB*, 1: 449).

19. Ida Husted Harper, *The Life and Work of Susan B. Anthony*, vol. 1 (Indianapolis: Hollenbeck Press, 1898), p. 308.

20. *TT v. HWB*, 1: 629–31.

21. TT to ET, Dec. 12, 1866, *Tribune*, p. 3, col. 6 (*TT v. HWB*, 1: 495); TT to ET, Dec. 18, 1866, *Tribune*, p. 3, col. 7.

22. TT to ET, Jan. 3, 1867, *Tribune*, p. 4, cols. 3–4; TT to ET, Jan. 21, 1867, *Tribune*, p. 4, col. 5; TT to ET, Mar. 15, 1868, *Tribune*, p. 9, col. 4.

23. TT to ET, Feb. 1, 1867, *Tribune*, p. 4, cols. 5–6.

24. ET to TT, Dec. 28, 1866, *Tribune*, p. 1, col. 4 (*TT v. HWB*, 1: 493, text in chapter 8).

25. ET to TT, Feb. 3, 1867, *Tribune*, p. 1, col. 6 (*TT v. HWB*, 1: 489); ET to TT, Aug. 3, 1869, *Tribune*, p. 2, col. 5 (*TT v. HWB*, 1: 492). Elizabeth's weight-gaining regime had gotten her up to 108¹/₂ pounds as of August 3 (she was just under five

feet tall), but as she told Theodore, "I hope to reward your loving care by an increase of ten or twelve pounds when next you see me."

26. TT to ET, Aug. 28, 1869, *Tribune,* p. 9, col. 6 (*TT v. HWB,* 1: 504, in ch. 8).

27. TT to ET, Nov. 3, 1868, *Tribune,* p. 9, cols. 4–5 (*TT v. HWB,* 1: 500, text in chapter 8). This was the only published letter in the correspondence written between March 1868 and January 1869.

28. ET to TT, Jan. 26, 1869, *Tribune,* p. 2, col. 3 (*TT v. HWB,* 1: 450); ET to TT, Feb. 5, 1869, *Tribune,* p. 2, col. 3.

29. ET to TT, Feb. 4, 1869, *Tribune,* p. 2, col. 3 (text in chapter 8); TT to ET, Jan. 15, 1869, *Tribune,* p. 9, cols. 5–6 (text in chapter 8); ET to TT, Feb. 7, 1869, *Tribune,* p. 2, cols. 3–4 (*TT v. HWB,* 1: 491–92, text in chapter 8); "Mrs. X" letter, *Chicago Tribune,* May 31, 1875, p. 8.

30. "Mrs. X" letter, p. 8; *TT v. HWB,* 1: 462.

31. "Mrs. Tilton as a Reformer," *New York Graphic,* Aug. 11, 1874, p. 288.

32. ET to TT, Mar. 13, 1869, *Tribune,* p. 2, col. 5.

33. *New York Sun* story quoted in "Theodore Tilton's Last Statement," in Charles F. Marshall, *The True History of the Brooklyn Scandal* (Philadelphia: National Publishing Co., 1874), p. 561. Charles Dana's *Sun* frequently exposed the alleged moral failings of the New York elite. It was one of the few New York papers to come to Theodore Tilton's defense in 1874 and 1875.

34. "The Richardson Case—Card from Mr. Beecher," *Hartford Courant,* Dec. 8, 1869, p. 2. An excellent recent treatment of the case is Hendrik Hartog's "Lawyering, Husbands' Rights, and 'the Unwritten Law' in Nineteenth-Century America," *Journal of American History* 84 (June, 1997): 67–96.

35. Elizabeth Cady Stanton, "Speech to the McFarland-Richardson Protest Meeting," in Ellen Carol DuBois, *Elizabeth Cady Stanton and Susan B. Anthony: Correspondence, Writings, Speeches* (New York: Schocken Books, 1981), p. 129; TT, "Love, Marriage, and Divorce," *The Independent,* Dec. 1, 1870, reprinted in *TT v. HWB,* 1: 464.

36. TT, "Reply to the Editor of *The Hearth and Home,*" n.d. [fall 1871], reprinted in *TT v. HWB,* 1: 466–67. The *Hearth and Home* editor also accused Tilton of being a Woodhullian, a spiritualist, and a Communist. Theodore defended Woodhull as "altogether a Christian," denied he was a spiritualist, and agreed he was a Communist, that is, a supporter of the "republicanism" of the Paris Commune.

37. "Beecher-Tilton," *Chicago Tribune,* Aug. 31, 1874, p. 1 ("courting each other by mutual piety").

38. *TT v. HWB,* 2: 742. *Norwood* fell short of the 300,000 in sales attained by Louisa Alcott's *Little Women* and Wilkie Collins's *The Moonstone,* the two best-selling novels of 1868. Frank Luther Mott does list it as a runner-up "better seller," along with *The Gates Ajar* by Elizabeth Stuart Phelps and *The Black Sheep* by Edmund Yates. *Golden Multitudes: The Story of Best Sellers in the United States* (New York: Macmillan, 1947), p. 321.

39. ET to TT, Mar. 8, 1868, *Tribune,* p. 2, col. 2 (*TT v. HWB* 1: 490); "Theodore Tilton's Last Statement," in Marshall, *True History,* p. 517 (*Norwood* inscription and recollection). Theodore's memory of good cheer with Beecher, and harmony all

around regarding *Norwood*, was important to his developing legal case in 1874: it helped show that until the alleged adultery beginning in October 1868, there was nothing amiss, either in his family or between him and Henry.

40. ET to TT, Feb. 10, 1869, *Tribune*, p. 2, col. 4 (text in chapter 8); HWB, *The Life of Jesus, the Christ* (1871; New York: Bromfield & Co., 2 vols., 1891), p. 33.

41. HWB, *Norwood, or, Village Life in New England* (New York: Charles Scribner, 1868), p. 304 (Barton and Tom), p. 204 ("fanaticism").

42. HWB, *Norwood*, p. 119 ("one soul in two bodies").

43. William G. McLoughlin, *The Meaning of Henry Ward Beecher: An Essay on the Shifting Values of Mid-Victorian America, 1840–1870* (New York: Knopf, 1970). Henry Nash Smith, "A Textbook of the Genteel Tradition: Henry Ward Beecher's *Norwood*," *Prospects* 3 (1977): 135–53, surveys the by-now-conventional literary case against the novel. Also in Smith, *Democracy and the Novel* (New York: Oxford University Press, 1978).

44. HWB, *Norwood*, p. 531.

45. HWB, *The Life of Jesus, the Christ*, p. 36–37. Cf. Beecher's lengthy oral statement of his personal faith to the New York and Brooklyn Association of Congregational Ministers in 1882: "I believe miracles are possible now; they not only were possible, but were real in the times gone by, especially the two great miracles that began and ended the Christian dispensation—the miraculous conception of Christ and His resurrection from the dead." HWB, "Theological Statement," in Lyman Abbott, *Henry Ward Beecher*, pp. 436–37.

46. HWB, *The Life of Jesus, the Christ*, p. 52 ("Man's nature and God's nature"); p. 341 ("disinterested benevolence"); *Norwood*, p. 316 ("a deep and true love"), p. 161 ("buoyant, joyous"). Rose Wentworth never made it to college—"women don't go to college," she said as a teenager, although "if I were a man I should certainly go" (p. 142)—but the narrator adds that "she studied with profound sympathy the writings of Jonathan Edwards and Madam Guion" (p. 294). Henry's *Norwood* must be put in relation to his sister Harriet's *The Minister's Wooing* (1857), a work that surely influenced his. Stowe's heroine Mary Scudder has much in common with Rose Wentworth—they are both Romantic Protestant saints who elevate affective instincts over rational doctrines—but Mary, like Little Eva, is directly chosen of God, marked from the start for sainthood. Rose is also chosen by God, but in the way anyone might be who had gotten the natural and Christian nurture provided by the woods and by her human father's love and wisdom. For all her own interest in liberalizing the Calvinist worldview, Harriet's vision preserves a tension between the natural and supernatural that tends to evaporate in Henry's.

47. HWB, *Norwood*, ch. 11 ("rose-culture" is the chapter title), p. 186 ("sentimental girl"), p. 241 ("fall in love," a phrase Beecher puts in quotation marks, "gradual unfolding . . . ordained of God")

48. HWB, *Norwood*, p. 167.

49. HWB, *Norwood*, p. 163 ("every part of her nature"), p. 437–38 ("plaintive call").

50. HWB, *Norwood*, p. 82. In the novel the nest-hiding relationship is between Reuben Wentworth and his wife, with whom he does not share the immediate "sympathy" that he does with his daughter Rose. He and his wife have "unlike natures":

he is forthright, she is oblique. Their love is deep and lasting, but she chooses to "hide the precious secret by flinging over it vines and flowers, by mirth and raillery, as a bird hides its nest under tufts of grass, and behind leaves and vines, as a fence against prying eyes."

51. HWB, *Norwood,* p. 186 ("real" and "ideal"), p. 234 ("awaked the mother in me"), p. 278 ("reputation for health"), p. 188 ("a place of favorite resort"), p. 60 ("all the world").

52. Ann Douglas's *The Feminization of American Culture* (New York : Knopf, 1977) is the primary text in the recent interpretation of Beecher as a feminizer, sentimentalist, and ground-clearer for therapeutic consumerism. I discuss her argument in chapter 9.

53. *New York Graphic,* Aug. 1, 1874, p. 221; HWB, *Norwood,* p. 209. The liberalism of John Locke, Adam Smith, or Henry George was never purely self-interested. It was cushioned by one or another form of "sympathy" that shored up communal solidarity in the face of unleashed individualism. Yet many Christians as well as "republicans" considered liberal practice a threat to the commonweal. The whole subject of moneymaking in relation to nineteenth-century Protestantism deserves new study. Beecher was not the only one who took it up after the Civil War. See, e.g., abolitionist merchant Lewis Tappan's pamphlet *Is It Right to Be Rich?* (New York: Anson D. F. Randolph & Co., 1869).

54. Gladden's "social" stance threw out the baby of Romantic selfhood along with the bathwater of individualist excess. His "liberalism" was implicitly allied with traditionalist criticism of Beecher's quest for novel experience.

55. TT to ET, Aug. 23, 1866, *Chicago Tribune,* Aug. 13, 1874, p. 3, col. 1. This letter is misdated. Internal evidence suggests it was written on August 27.

56. HWB, "Cross-examination of Mr. Beecher," in Marshall, *True History,* p. 305. The statue of Beecher remains on display in Brooklyn, but in the 1950s it was moved several blocks north. It now faces the old Post Office building at Cadman Plaza.

57. ET to TT, Jan. 31, 1868, *Chicago Tribune,* Aug. 13, 1874, p. 1, cols. 6–7 (*TT v. HWB,* 1: 503, text in chapter 8); HWB, "Prayer before the Sermon," Aug. 30, 1874, in HWB, *Plymouth Pulpit Sermons,* vol. 1, p. 562 (text in Appendix). (The *Plymouth Pulpit Sermons* were published in several editions. The Library of Congress microfilm edition puts the "Christian Sympathy" sermon of August 30, 1874, in vol. 1, p. 562, but Halford R. Ryan, *Henry Ward Beecher: Peripatetic Preacher* [New York: Greenwood, 1990], which provides a complete chronology of Beecher's speeches and sermons, puts it in vol. 2.) On Elizabeth's Plymouth Brethren, see Paul Boyer, *When Time Shall Be No More: Prophecy Belief in Modern American Culture* (Cambridge: Harvard University Press, 1992), pp. 87–88.

58. "Facts and Folks," *New York Graphic,* Mar. 9, 1875, p. 64.

CHAPTER NINE

1. Lyman Abbott, *Henry Ward Beecher* (1903; New York: Chelsea House, 1980), p. 299; Janna Malamud Smith, "Our Celebrities, Ourselves," *New York Times,* Sept. 8, 1997, p. A11. On the alleged Wesley "scandal," see "Facts and Gossip," *Chicago Tribune,* Mar. 20, 1875, p. 6.

2. Victoria Woodhull, "Victoria C. Woodhull's Complete and Detailed Version of the Beecher-Tilton Affair" [1872], in Madeleine B. Stern, ed., *The Victoria Woodhull Reader* (Weston, MA: M & S Press, 1974), p. 2 ("ventilate"), p. 3 ("bomb-shell"), p. 4 ("conniving"), p. 13 ("duty," "prophetess," "exposé"). Paxton Hibben, *Henry Ward Beecher: An American Portrait* (New York: George H. Doran, 1927); Ann Douglas, *The Feminization of American Culture* (New York: Knopf, 1977); Barbara Goldsmith, *Other Powers: The Age of Suffrage, Spiritualism, and the Scandalous Victoria Woodhull* (New York: Knopf, 1998).

3. Rheta Childe Dorr, *Susan B. Anthony: The Woman Who Changed the Mind of a Nation* (New York: Frederick A. Stokes, 1928), p. 271. Twentieth-century commentators' fondness for the term "Gilded Age"—taken from Charles Dudley Warner and Mark Twain's 1873 novel by that name—stems from their often covert contrastive judgment that while the late nineteenth century is Baroque, frilly, and obfuscating, the twentieth-century is spare, unadorned, and direct. Twentieth-century history textbooks, which in the interest of objectivity avoid undue excoriation of Gilded Age "excess," have usually assumed Beecher's guilt on the adultery charge. When they have not, they exploit him for laughs. After recounting the sober story of Reconstruction, they often pause for light relief with Beecher and the Tiltons before getting back to business with the robber barons. Claude G. Bowers's *The Tragic Era: The Revolution after Lincoln* (Boston: Houghton-Mifflin, 1929) set the tone: "Even so, the year [1874] had its light and amusing side. All through the summer, men and women were thrilling to the exotic story of Henry Ward Beecher and Theodore Tilton running in the press" (p. 418). The survey textbook by Stephen Brier, et al., *Who Built America?* vol. 2, *From the Gilded Age to the Present* (New York: Pantheon, 1992), p. 96, writes assuredly of Henry Ward Beecher's "extramarital affairs," and runs the satirical cartoon "Discord among the Angels" (see p. 52 in this book).

4. Woodhull, "The Beecher-Tilton Affair," p. 7 ("embroglio"), p. 8 ("whole history").

5. Woodhull, "The Beecher-Tilton Affair," p. 8 ("gusts of inspiration"), p. 9 ("effete"), p. 17 ("moral coward"), p. 18 ("representative"). The "effete" phenomenon for Woodhull was "the marriage institution," (p. 9) but that superannuated practice was the cornerstone of the entire "social system" (p. 13). Like "slavery and monarchy," marriage had been "good or necessary" at one time, but it was now a brake on liberty—that of individuals to "adjust their love relations precisely as they do their religious affairs in this country, in complete personal freedom." Her view of personal autonomy in the love relation was absolute: "I hold that Mr. Tilton himself, that Mrs. Beecher herself, have no more right to inquire, or to know, or to spy over with a view to knowing, what has transpired between Mr. Beecher and Mrs. Tilton than they have to know what I ate for breakfast" (p. 19).

6. Goldsmith occasionally second-guessed a claim of Woodhull's. She conceded, for example, that Woodhull's reported statement that she had "slept every night for three months" in Theodore Tilton's "arms" could not be taken at face value. It might have been invented by the *Chicago Times*, which reported it, or it might have been said "by a Victoria possessed by the spirits, who was another woman altogether." Goldsmith did not hesitate to trust such newspaper reports when they spread other

gossip about Beecher and the Tiltons, and to rely on other statements by Woodhull as straightforward truth-telling. Goldsmith, *Other Powers*, p. 290.

7. "Scandal," *Oxford English Dictionary*, 2nd ed. (Oxford: Clarendon Press, 1989), vol. 14, pp. 573–74.

8. HWB, *Yale Lectures on Preaching* (1873; New York: Fords, Howard, and Hulbert, 1889), vol. 2, pp. 216, 218, 279. I discuss Beecher's "spiritual engineering" in "The Culture of Liberal Protestant Progressivism, 1875–1925," *Journal of Interdisciplinary History* 23 (winter 1993): 639–60.

9. *TT v. HWB*, 3: 742–43. On the "narrativity" of the Beecher-Tilton trial of 1875, and Evarts's analysis of *Griffith Gaunt*, see also Laura Korobkin, *Criminal Conversations: Sentimentality and Nineteenth-Century Legal Stories of Adultery* (New York: Columbia University Press, 1999), chs. 3 and 4.

10. *TT v. HWB*, 3: 664.

11. Woodhull, "The Beecher-Tilton Affair," p. 10 ("poltroon"), p. 15 ("true sense of honor"). Woodhull understood that her "bomb-shell" was an act of cruelty toward Beecher. In her statement she asked his forgiveness, perhaps sincerely. But in her view his well-being (along with that of Elizabeth Tilton, to whom she did not apologize) had to be sacrificed to the higher cause of social advance.

12. William Evarts to HWB, July 1875 [day unreadable], Beecher Family Papers, Yale University.

13. Francine du Plessix Gray, "Sex, Scandals, and Suffrage," *New Yorker*, Apr. 20, 1998, p. 96 ("consummate showman"), p. 97 ("skillfully devious"), p. 98 ("corrupt," "unctuous smile").

14. Gray, "Sex, Scandals, and Suffrage," p. 97; Millicent Bell, "Victoria's Secrets," *New York Review of Books*, May 14, 1998, p. 30; Goldsmith, *Other Powers*, pp. 223–24. Bell goes beyond Goldsmith a second time. "In private," Bell writes, "Beecher justified his own affair with Elizabeth Tilton as an expression of free love." She has him telling Frank Moulton that "the red lounge on which we consummated our love was to me an almost sacred object" (Bell, p. 32). But Goldsmith wrote: "Beecher denied that he had also justified his behavior by saying to Moulton, 'The red lounge on which we consummated our love was to me an almost sacred object'" (Goldsmith, p. 244).

15. Goldsmith, *Other Powers*, p. 224; Woodhull, "The Beecher-Tilton Affair," p. 12. Goldsmith also did not report to her readers that Woodhull has Tilton telling Stanton (p. 13) that Henry and Elizabeth conducted "terrible orgies" with "boldness" in "the presence of his children." Besides peppering her account with such reconfigured or invented third-party imaginings, Woodhull claimed that Beecher, in direct conversation with her, had said, "I am a moral coward" (to explain why he didn't introduce her at one of her speeches). She also stated he had agreed with her scheme for the "scientific" breeding of people: "We shall never have a better state," she has him telling her, "until children are begotten and bred on the scientific plan. Stirpiculture is what we need." The chance that he ever said these things to her is near or at zero. Woodhull's creative license is so evident in these direct conversations with Beecher that we have even more reason to doubt the reliability of her third-party information about the alleged adultery (p. 16, "stirpiculture," p. 17, "moral coward"). Paxton Hibben, a firm believer in Beecher's guilt, and hence in the truth

of Woodhull's basic adultery charge, was right when he noted that Victoria engaged in "high fantasy. She could not resist adding sensational incidents lacking even the vaguest verisimilitude." Hibben, *Henry Ward Beecher*, p. 285.

16. Woodhull, "The Beecher-Tilton Affair," pp. 11, 13; "Mrs. Tilton's Cross-Examination," in Charles F. Marshall, *The True History of the Brooklyn Scandal* (Philadelphia: National Publishing Co., 1874), p. 208.

17. The only evidence that Mrs. Tilton was pregnant at any time in July comes from another third party's supposed remark to Woodhull. Paulina Wright Davis allegedly informed Woodhull that Elizabeth had told her that the lost fetus was six months old. In that case, Elizabeth would have conceived it around June 24, quite likely too late for her to have known she was pregnant by July 3. But there is no reason to believe Woodhull's story about a six-month-old fetus, even if Davis did tell her that. Elizabeth's own nurse Lucy Mitchell said at the trial in 1875 that the lost fetus was three months old. We cannot put any special trust in Lucy Mitchell's story, but we cannot assume the truth of Woodhull's either. After Woodhull's bombshell, Elizabeth Tilton denied ever having spoken to Paulina Wright Davis about her personal life, and Davis denied having spoken to Elizabeth about it. Theodore and Elizabeth Cady Stanton took a different tack. Each produced contradictory statements distancing themselves from Woodhull's allegations while agreeing that there was some unspecified truth to them (see Theodore's "Letter to a Complaining Friend" in the Appendix). Stanton did not "corroborate" Woodhull's allegations when she called them "substantially true," as Goldsmith claimed (*Other Powers*, p. 475). It all depends on what she meant by "substance." To judge by another comment of Stanton's cited by Goldsmith (p. 358), the wheat in Woodhull's story was, in Stanton's view, mixed with chaff: "Victoria's story is exaggerated, rather higher-colored than I heard it." And in a statement of November 5, 1872, quoted at the trial in 1875, and unreported by Goldsmith, Stanton went much further. She said that Woodhull's charges brought to mind the "good old Latin motto," "False in one point, false in all." Stanton definitely believed Beecher and Mrs. Tilton had slept together, but there is no evidence she thought he had gotten her pregnant. (*TT v. HWB*, 1: 601.)

18. Goldsmith, *Other Powers*, pp. 225, 235. Goldsmith thinks Elizabeth was so distressed in December 1870 at "all this torture, embarrassment and humiliation" that she was ready for an abortion (p. 230). Leave aside the fact that, according to Marshall's *True History of the Brooklyn Scandal*, p. 212, Elizabeth's actual words were "all this trouble, and embarrassment, and humiliation." None of the alleged troubles to which Goldsmith refers us—carrying Beecher's baby, no coal for a fire, no food in the house—are mentioned by Elizabeth herself. The coal and food problem developed in 1871 after her husband left the *Independent*, and hence after the miscarriage (or fancied abortion) of December 1870. Nor did the trouble Elizabeth referred to have anything to do with her being pregnant. We know from her November 1870 and January 1871 letters (included in the Appendix) that her pregnancy with the "love babe" fathered by Theodore was the one bright spot on her horizon. The trouble she spoke of in the source cited by Goldsmith was Theodore's putting a new housekeeper, middle-aged Miss Ellen Dennis, at the head of the household while Elizabeth was in Ohio, and keeping her there after his wife's return. Goldsmith's

story that Theodore once got an abortion for "some girl he'd gotten pregnant" (*Other Powers*, p. 225) seems to have originated in a *New York Tribune* report of an interview with Susan B. Anthony's brother in Kansas. He claimed his sister had told him of hearing Elizabeth Tilton say that Theodore "had procured an abortion for a young lady of Brooklyn whom he had seduced." "Inquirer," "The Great Social Scandal," *New York Graphic*, July 30, 1874, p. 205.

19. Goldsmith, *Other Powers*, p. 358. Goldsmith drew this account of Tilton threatening to accuse Isabella Hooker of adultery from "the testimony of Frank Moulton," for her (as for Paxton Hibben) a reliable truth-teller. Whether or not Tilton actually delivered the threat, Moulton's story that he did is perfectly in keeping with the practice of hurling intimidating allegations in which Beecher, Tilton, Woodhull, Moulton, Bowen, and many others of their acquaintance excelled.

20. Theodore's parents addressed the insanity-in-the-family rumor in a press interview, the reliability of which, given the reporter's jauntily satirical tone, seems questionable. "Mrs. [Eusebia] Tilton expressed considerable indignation at the false reports of hereditary insanity in the family. She said they were untrue in almost every particular. She should not be surprised if there had been some queer people in the family. 'We may all be peculiar. I don't know. But we are not crazy.'" *Beecher-Tilton Investigation: The Scandal of the Age* (Philadelphia: Barclay and Co., 1874), p. 101.

21. Goldsmith, *Other Powers*, p. 225 ("he struck Lib"). Goldsmith provided no evidence that Theodore ever hit Elizabeth. The closest Elizabeth ever came to asserting that he did was in her Church Committee statement in 1874, when she spoke of having been afraid he was going to hit her—on the evening Susan Anthony protected her against Theodore's wrath (Stanton's version) or tried to prevent her from going to assuage him (Mrs. Tilton's).

22. TT, "A Faith-Confession," in *The Great Scandal: History of the Famous Beecher-Tilton Case* (New York: American Magazine Co., 1874), n.p. ("Letter-Press" section, no. 8; text in the Appendix); Hibben, *Henry Ward Beecher*, pp. 311–12. The other main works in the Tilton-as-truth-bearer school of interpretation are Robert Shaplen, *Free Love and Heavenly Sinners* (New York: Knopf, 1954), which beginning with the first sentence of page one uses Theodore's story as the true one, and Altina L. Waller, *Reverend Beecher and Mrs. Tilton* (Amherst: University of Massachusetts Press, 1982), which praises Shaplen's book as an "accurate portrayal of the people and events of the scandal" (p. 13). Waller bridges Shaplen and Goldsmith, for she trusts Tilton when he is cataloguing Beecher's sins, but does not trust him when he is denying his own. She actively pursued the rumors of Theodore's infidelities—a subject artfully avoided by Hibben—and judged Tilton an adulterer. But unlike Goldsmith, Waller found the evidence for an affair between him and Laura Curtis Bullard inconclusive. See chapter 5, footnote 37.

23. Hibben, *Henry Ward Beecher*, pp. 223–24, 308 ("by long odds the smartest"). The third main witness against Beecher at his trial, Emma Moulton, was Hibben's third truth-teller. "Over and over this story the cleverest lawyer of his generation [Evarts] took this shy little woman, so patently truthful, so obviously sincere in her sorrow over Beecher's fall. He could not shake her testimony. . . . When Emma Moulton stepped down from the witness stand, it did not matter a particle what the jury might decide. The judgment of history was recorded" (p. 318).

24. The "pew rent" phenomenon has drawn the scorn of anti-Beecher writers for almost a century and a half. It is more complicated than Hibben or Goldsmith allow it to be. All churches raise money one way or another. According to Lyman Abbott, who granted that objections to the practice could easily be made, Plymouth chose the method of selling "subscriptions to stock" and auctioning off pews to the highest bidder, and had a hearty good time doing it (*Henry Ward Beecher*, pp. 80–81). A report in the *Independent* in 1861 asserted that demand for pews was so great that two hundred families in the membership could not get their own places (they had to come early to be sure of getting an unreserved folding seat along the aisle). Much as the pastor and members hated to distribute pews according to the ease of a family's circumstances, the article said, no alternative to the system seemed workable. Perhaps the auction system was preserved because it had the salutary effect of making the wealthy pay a higher share of the church's expenses. Pew rents brought in $30,000 in 1860. The interest on stock purchases, meanwhile, was paid out only in pew rents; the so-called "Plymouth bonds," or "scrip," which twentieth-century critics have pointed to as evidence of the corruption of Beecher and his cronies, were apparently not convertible investments. "Annual Pew Renting at Mr. Beecher's Church," Jan. 10, 1861, p. 5. The pew rent receipts had doubled to $60,000 by 1874, when the highest bidders were Edward Ovington ($400) and Henry Bowen ($385). "Plymouth Church Sale of Pews Last Evening," *New York Times*, Jan. 7, 1874, p. 5.

Plymouth thumbed its nose at critics who charged that the pew-rents or church bonds amounted to money-changing in the temple, just as Beecher scoffed at detractors who admonished him for loving the things of this world and the high salary that made them possible. We may well wish to criticize Beecher for failing to live the simple life, but we need to separate that judgment from the question of church finance *per se*.

25. Ann Douglas, *The Feminization of American Culture* (1977; New York: Avon Books, 1978), p. 292.

26. Douglas, *Feminization of American Culture*, pp. 290–91. See also Elizabeth White, "Sentimental Heresies: Rethinking *The Feminization of American Culture*," *Intellectual History Newsletter* 15 (1993): 23–31.

27. *TT v. HWB*, 1: 145. Godkin finds Beecher guilty of moral inadequacy, but not of adultery, in "Some Plain Truths about the Scandal," *Nation*, June 3, 1875, pp. 372–73, and "Tilton Against Beecher," July 8, 1875, pp. 22–23.

28. Shaplen, *Free Love and Heavenly Sinners*, p. 265. Altina Waller rightly observes that "although he remained popular" after the trial, Beecher "was no longer taken quite as seriously." *Reverend Beecher and Mrs. Tilton*, p. 146. Shaplen's book fits into the Hibben-Goldsmith line of interpretation, but maintains an ironic distance from the actors. That distance, to my mind, is the appropriate starting point for the kind of critically sympathetic history that I wish to write, one that lets the Victorians remain "other" while enriching our own sense of what it means to be human. Although he uncritically takes Theodore Tilton's vantage point as true, Shaplen wisely refrains from refighting nineteenth-century battles.

29. *TT v. HWB*, 3: 844–46.

30. *TT v. HWB*, 3: 935.

31. *TT v. HWB*, 3: 851 ("scarlet and red"); 3: 934 (forest scene). Beach read

from Hawthorne's chapter 11 (all but the last three sentences of the paragraph beginning "While thus suffering . . .") and chapter 17 (from "Hester, hast though found peace?" to, several paragraphs later, "But, now, it is all falsehood!—all emptiness!—all death!").

32. *New York Graphic*, Aug. 1, 1874, p. 221; *Frank Leslie's*, Aug. 22, 1874, p. 370; "Skeletons of the Ideal," *Frank Leslie's*, Aug. 8, 1874, p. 339.

33. Nathaniel Hawthorne, *The Scarlet Letter* (1850; New York: St. Martin's, 1991), p. 130 (chapter 13, paragraph 2); "Mrs. Tilton Pleads Guilty," *New York Times*, Apr. 16, 1878, p. 1. If Elizabeth in fact wrote the poem "Dying Deaths Daily," as seems likely, that is further evidence of her having read *The Scarlet Letter*. The poem's title would appear to come from Hawthorne's phrase "dying daily a living death," itself derived perhaps from Paul's comment in 1 Cor. 15: 31, "I die daily." (See poem in Appendix.)

34. Hawthorne, *The Scarlet Letter*, p. 131 ("she was self-ordained" [chapter 13, paragraph 3]), pp. 200–201 ("continually recurring trials," "the scarlet letter ceased," [penultimate paragraph of concluding chapter]); "Elizabeth R. Tilton Dead," *Brooklyn Eagle* undated clipping (Apr. 14 or 15, 1897), Beecher-Tilton File, Brooklyn Historical Society.

35. "Beecher," *Chicago Tribune*, July 14, 1875, p. 8.

36. "Mrs. Tilton's Cross-Examination," in Marshall, *True History*, pp. 212–13.

37. TT reply to editor of *Hearth and Home*, n.d. [fall 1871], reprinted in *TT v. HWB*, 1: 467.

38. Jessie Grundy, "Theodore Tilton's Early Life," *New York Graphic*, July 31, 1874, p. 212.

Bibliography

The essential primary source for the Beecher-Tilton Scandal is the "official" transcript of the civil trial of 1875: *Theodore Tilton vs. Henry Ward Beecher, Action for Crim. Con. Tried in the City Court of Brooklyn*, 3 vols. (New York: McDivitt, Campbell, and Co., 1875). This same transcript was published day-by-day as the trial progressed in the *New York Tribune*, whose stenographer had been selected by Judge Joseph Neilson to serve as the court's scribe. (If the *Tribune*'s man left the courtroom momentarily, another newspaper's stenographer took his place.) The official transcript is full of small errors—the stenographer heard "Harold," for example, when Theodore Tilton, listing his children's names, said "Carroll"—and the trial transcripts published elsewhere sometimes diverge from the *Tribune*'s report. On March 3, 1875, for example, the *Tribune* had defense witness Maria Ovington reporting an 1874 conversation with Theodore in which he said that Elizabeth had made "a fine impression" testifying to the Plymouth Church Investigating Committee (*TT v. HWB*, 2: 123). The Associated Press report had him saying "a fine confession" (*Chicago Tribune*, Mar. 3, 1875, p. 1).

For a late-twentieth-century reader the most curious thing about the "official" court transcript is that it includes the *Tribune* writer's very tendentious daily observations, which, in keeping with the *Tribune*'s editorial line, were decidedly pro-Beecher. But that jaundiced commentary is a valuable historical document in its own right. And the transcript itself—2,702 densely packed, double-columned pages—is a unique treasure for historians of the 1870s. It is an archive of Victorian American culture and society. There is a bounty here for historians of religion, politics, business, labor, law, journalism, and gender. There is excellent material for studies of utopianism, spiritualism, radicalism, oratory, humor, and for the social history of the city, including race and class relations. And the transcript opens up the most delicate kinds of cultural and moral inquiry: the history of gestures, of honor and deference, of linguistic status markers, of the meaning of a kiss. The witnesses thought they were testifying about Beecher and the Tiltons, but they were also attesting to an entire way of life. Because they were unconscious of speaking to us—although one suspects that William Evarts, in his closing eight-day speech, had an inkling his oratory would outlive him—they are especially valuable as historical voices. The transcript is available in several public and private libraries, and is also on microfiche.

A second published "transcript" of the trial, assembled by defense attorney Austin Abbott (brother of Lyman Abbott, Beecher's biographer and successor as Plymouth Church pastor), is the *Official Report of the Trial of Henry Ward Beecher*, 2 vols. (New York, G. W. Smith, 1875). Beecher detractor Paxton Hibben (*Henry Ward Beecher*, p. 366) judges Abbott's edition "neither official nor complete." He does not specify how it is incomplete, but he is right that it is not official. Whichever transcript one uses, it is critical to start one's study of the scandal with the trial proceedings, rather than with the secondary literature or with Theodore's, Henry's, or Elizabeth's published statements of 1874. The trial transcript forces one to confront the basic truth of the entire affair: conflicting stories were told by the principals, and there is no nonarbitrary way of deciding who was telling the truth. Certainly Theodore Tilton's and Frank Moulton's 1874 statements, taken by many writers as factual foundation, must be viewed with great skepticism even if one wishes to conclude, as the *New York Times* did after mulling over Beecher's own fevered statements, that the preponderance of the evidence pointed to adultery.

For the 1874 statements of Beecher, the Tiltons, and Frank Moulton, Charles F. Marshall, *The True History of the Brooklyn Scandal* (Philadelphia: National Publishing Co., 1874) has become the most often cited source. Moulton's and Theodore Tilton's statements contain some of the letters exchanged among the four of them and among many of their friends and associates, but the versions printed in 1874 often differ from those entered into the 1875 trial record. Theodore's 1874 printing of his wife's "*Griffith Gaunt*" letter, for example, omitted a crucial passage that William Evarts gleefully restored in 1875 (see Appendix). Historians are at the mercy of the stenographers (including Theodore himself), who copied and recopied all of the "original" documents many times. With the best of intentions, they made many small mistakes. Hence a particular letter was sometimes published in different places with slightly altered language. The trial transcript is the best arbiter in such cases, since the lawyers worked over the documents to establish their correctness—and to imply the chicanery of one or another copier.

Three other useful collections of the 1874 documentary fireworks are *The Beecher-Tilton Investigation: The Scandal of the Age* (Philadelphia: Barclay and Co., 1874); *The Great Scandal: History of the Famous Beecher-Tilton Case* (New York: American News Company, 1874); and J. E. P. Doyle, ed., *The Romance of Plymouth Church* (title on binding), *Plymouth Church and Its Pastor, or Henry Ward Beecher and His Accusers* (title on title page) (Hartford: Park Publishing Co., 1874). Where Marshall stuck by and large to the documents issued by the principals (accented by his own pro-Beecher comments along the way), the other three volumes gave additional attention to Tilton or even (in the case of Doyle) to Victoria Woodhull. In the process they retrieved many out-of-the-way, sensational items ignored by the august Marshall.

The Beecher-Tilton Investigation, for example, included previously published interviews with Theodore, with his parents, and with Elizabeth Cady Stanton. The volume illustrates how hot the story was in 1874: as new material became available, the volume was reset to incorporate it, in the manner of a newspaper issuing "late" editions. (This practice plays havoc with later historians' desire to pin down page numbers.) *The Great Scandal* gave Theodore's voice more weight than Marshall did by printing Theodore's "Letter to a Complaining Friend" (included in the Appendix), and one of his *Golden Age* pieces on the scandal. *The Romance of Plymouth Church* presented Woodhull and her family as central to the scandal's cast of characters, and gathered a wide sampling of the scandal's outcroppings, including an enviable spoof of Theodore's poem "Sir Marmaduke's Musings."

These three volumes, all skeptical of Beecher, are a good barometer of 1874 opinion in the heartland, where Tilton stood for many as a populist David slinging stones at the eastern and especially New York establishment. As the trial moved into the spring of 1875 and Beecher took the stand for the defense, press (and apparently the public's) opinion shifted markedly in his favor, even in the "west." The *Chicago Tribune* typified the cooling-on-Tilton current: in the summer of 1874 its reporter "Gath" (George Alfred Townsend) became a personal friend of Theodore's, telegraphed glowing interviews to the paper, and obtained the Tiltons' marital correspondence for the *Tribune*. The editorial columns followed suit in bashing Beecher. But by early 1875 their tone was shifting to one of detachment, and by spring the paper was writing of the tragic tangle in which no one could be sure who had done precisely what to whom.

The other major 1874 collections are Robert L. Orr, *The Beecher-Tilton Controversy: A Graphic Record of the Most Remarkable Social Sensation in the World's History* (Chicago: Empire, 1874); *The Beecher-Tilton Scandal: A Complete History of the Case* (Brooklyn: n.p., 1874); *The Great Brooklyn Romance: All the Documents in the Famous Beecher-Tilton Case, Unabridged* (New York: J. H. Paxon, 1874); Francis P. Williamson, *Beecher and His Accusers: A Complete History of the Great Controversy* (Philadelphia: Flint & Co., 1874); *The Veil Removed; or, Henry Ward Beecher's Trial and Acquittal Investigated* (New York: n.p., 1874). These 1874 anthologies borrowed liberally from publications that appeared in the wake of Victoria Woodhull's 1872 charges. The 1874 compilers relied particularly upon Leon Oliver, *The Great Sensation: A Full, Complete and Reliable History of the Beecher-Tilton-Woodhull Scandal with Biographical Sketches of the Principal Characters* (Chicago: The Beverly Co., 1873) for their biographical information, not all of it "reliable." Their compilations undoubtedly affected the testimony witnesses gave at the trial in 1875. The plaintiff's attorneys tried, for example, to scuttle Bessie Turner's credibility by suggesting she had learned her lines from reading *The Great Brooklyn Romance*. She granted that the defense team had given her a copy to peruse, but said she hadn't read it.

Many of the 1874 anthologies include samples of the Tiltons' intimate correspondence published first in the *Chicago Tribune* on August 13, 1874, but there is no substitute for the *Tribune*'s own five-page spread (thirty-two long columns) of selections from 201 of the letters. The *Tribune*'s excerpting must be compared to the fuller versions of many letters entered into the trial record in 1875 (see chapter 8). The news and editorial columns of the *Tribune* are also an indispensable source on the scandal, since the paper avidly pursued rumors and stories from all over the country—including those from the Brooklyn and Manhattan press. In New York City, the *Daily Graphic* was without peer in its interviewing, satirizing, and innovating, especially in its "fac-simile" reproduction of the major letters that figured in the scandal. One can get a quick sense of how truly national the scandal was by consulting the microfilm edition of the countless small-city newspapers collected at the Library of Congress. Beecher-Tilton was page-one news everywhere for a solid year, July 1874 to July 1875, and small regional papers had their own correspondents filing exclusive copy from Brooklyn. One of the most insightful and entertaining was "Seymour" of the *Mobile* (Alabama) *Register,* whose "New York Notes" were a regular feature. On March 10, 1875, he called Henry Bowen the "Bowen of contention" since in Seymour's view he knew too much for the liking of either defense or plaintiff.

LIBRARY COLLECTIONS

Several manuscript collections have papers relevant to the scandal, but privately held material touching on the adultery question was probably shredded long before friends, relatives, or descendents made manuscript donations to libraries. As a result, the published record from the 1870s is much more significant for the student of the scandal than archival documents. The library collections I found most useful are listed alphabetically:

The **Brooklyn Historical Society** has a Beecher-Tilton Scrapbook of cartoons and portraits. Most are from the *New York Daily Graphic* and *Frank Leslie's Illustrated Newspaper,* but a few are from hard-to-find sources such as *The Jolly Joker* and *The Arcadian* (its May 29, 1875, cartoon features Elizabeth floating in the air, hands clasped and a halo over her head, saying, "Let me tell my little story." Henry and Theodore flail at her with axes from below.)

The **Brooklyn Public Library** has the "official phonographic report" of the Congregational Council of 1874 that looked into the rumors about Beecher's behavior and provoked Theodore to issue his first self-exculpatory "statement." It also has the old "morgue" of the *Brooklyn Daily Eagle* (an important source of Tilton family obituaries), and a scrapbook of Brooklyn newspaper clippings that includes reports of Beecher sermons and Tilton lectures. A scrapbook on the scandal, with clippings mostly from the *New York Herald,* was missing when I tried to consult it.

The **Harriet Beecher Stowe Center Library** has scrapbooks of clippings on the scandal, but more significantly it possesses the voluminous Isabella Beecher Hooker collection. "Belle" must have written letters several hours a day year after year. There are significant ones exchanged with Susan B. Anthony and Elizabeth Cady Stanton, as well as her prodigious correspondence with her husband John Hooker. They wrote each other at length about the scandal. The collection also contains originals or copies of letters to and from important third parties such as Paulina Wright Davis, one of Victoria Woodhull's alleged sources of information for her public accusation. The Hooker collection is available on microfiche.

The **Library of Congress** collection of Henry Ward Beecher papers has a few interesting letters regarding Henry Bowen's business arrangements with both Beecher and Tilton, including a touching letter from Theodore (Jan. 5, 1860) listing all the Beecher sermons he had copied for the *Independent* and computing how much Bowen owed him. The collection has the manuscript of *The Life of Jesus, the Christ,* written during the scandal cover-up, and an extensive series of sermon drafts composed over the half century from 1837 to 1886. The Library also has collections of papers of Susan B. Anthony, Anna Dickinson, and Theodore Tilton, although there is little in any of them of importance to the scandal (pages of Susan B. Anthony's notebooks that might have addressed it were ripped out long ago).

The **New York Historical Society** has a Tilton collection that includes a few letters about the scandal, one of them from Anna Dickinson, and a letter Henry sent to Theodore from England in 1863. It is one of several to the young editor from such writers as Frederick Douglass, Susan B. Anthony, and William Lloyd Garrison.

The **New York Public Library** has a set of eight scrapbooks of newspaper clippings on the scandal assembled in the office of the *Independent* (in 1874–1875 under the editorial control of Henry Bowen—perhaps the only other person in the early 1870s besides Victoria Woodhull to have had both Henry and Theodore on his hit list). Paxton Hibben said the scrapbooks were donated to the library by Bowen's grandson Hamilton Holt.

The **Schlesinger Library** at Radcliffe College has a Beecher collection with a few important letters on the scandal written by Harriet Beecher Stowe, Victoria Woodhull, and George Bell, a Plymouth parishioner who testified at the civil trial. The Olympia Brown Papers also has material. The women's movement of the 1870s was so deeply embroiled in (and threatened by) Beecher's and the Tiltons' troubles that comments on them turn up in the papers of Brown and many other reformers of the time.

Yale University Library's Manuscript and Archives Division has the major collection of Henry Ward Beecher papers (part of its Beecher Family Papers). The "Tilton Scandal" folder in box 45 has forty-eight items, mostly letters from one clergyman to another, or one church committee to another. But it also contains an alleged copy of an undated letter Elizabeth wrote to "I. K. P." and an alleged diary fragment of Elizabeth's marked Saturday, May 20 [hence 1871], both of which describe supposed encounters with Henry and Theodore. Neither encounter is at all unique or revealing, and the handwriting in the diary item is not Elizabeth's. For that reason I chose not to use them. Box 87 has three folders (210–212) with sixty-six pages of Beecher's "memos regarding the Tilton scandal" jotted down in 1874 or 1875. He made a list of the dates of his various encounters with the Tiltons going back to the 1850s, and he outlined answers to questions he was likely to get during "cross-examination." He referred (in the memo book in folder 211) to Elizabeth Tilton's May 20, 1871, diary fragment: "At this date Mrs. Tilton records in her diary 'Reconciliations. Dory's [Theodore's] better nature victorious. A pleasant visit with Mr. Beecher.'" (The fragment in his possession may have been copied out of her diary by someone else, and given to him to help him prepare his testimony.) One memo book in folder 212 includes the pencilled notes he took down during Theodore Tilton's trial testimony in February 1875. Among all the memos there are occasionally interesting reflections on the Tiltons, but nothing surprising. And they are difficult to attribute in all cases to Beecher, since they are written in several different hands; it appears that anonymous scribes tried to organize Beecher's often illegible and always disorganized ruminations—evidence, perhaps, of his frazzled state of mind in 1874 and 1875. Yale also has eight letters (in box 15) exchanged between Theodore and Henry in 1863, when Henry was off battling pro-Confederate sentiment in Britain, and some letters from William Evarts (box 10), including his congratulatory telegram at the end of the trial in 1875.

BIOGRAPHIES

Of the biographies that appeared in the aftermath of Beecher's death, only Lyman Abbott, *Henry Ward Beecher* (Boston: Houghton Mifflin, 1903; reprint edition, New York: Chelsea House, 1980)—which came out sixteen years after his burial—approaches scholarly standards by placing Beecher in the context of his times and abstaining from overt idolization. Abbott's chapter 12, "Under Accusation," pp. 288–99, while asserting Beecher's innocence of adultery, tries to minimize the importance of the scandal—in keeping with the author's ill-starred prediction that "future history" would forget about it. The earlier biographies, all of them hagiographic, put more emphasis on the scandal in a continuing effort to exculpate and heroize the Plymouth pastor: John Henry Barrows, *Henry Ward Beecher: The Shakespeare of the Pulpit* (NY: Funk and Wagnalls, 1893) (chapters 37 and 38 on the scandal); William C. Beecher and Samuel Scoville, *A Biography of Rev. Henry Ward Beecher* (New York: Charles L. Webster, 1888) (chapters 24 and 25); Joseph Howard, Jr., *Life of Henry Ward Beecher* (Philadelphia: Hubbard Bros., 1887) (Chapter 9); and Thomas W. Knox, *Life and Work of Henry Ward Beecher* (Philadelphia: International Publishing Co., 1887) (chapters 19 and 20). Among the many fascinating discussions of Beecher's oratory in the wake of his death, Lewis O. Brastow's chapter on him in *Representative American Preachers* (New York: Macmillan, 1904) stands out.

SECONDARY LITERATURE

The secondary literature I consulted on the Beecher-Tilton Scandal is listed alphabetically. I include some works that touch only tangentially on it, but which offer intriguing ideas or analysis.

Kenneth R. Andrews, *Nook Farm: Mark Twain's Hartford Circle* (Cambridge: Harvard University Press, 1950).

Deborah Mari Applegate, "The Culture of the Novel and the Consolidation of Middle-Class Consciousness: Henry Ward Beecher and the Uses of Sympathy, 1830–1880," Ph.D. dissertation, Yale University, 1997.

Chester L. Barrows, *William Maxwell Evarts* (Chapel Hill: University of North Carolina Press, 1941).

Kathleen Barry, *Susan B. Anthony: A Biography of a Singular Feminist* (New York: New York University Press, 1988).

Nicola Beisel, *Imperiled Innocents: Anthony Comstock and Family Reproduction in Victorian America* (Princeton: Princeton University Press, 1997).

Jeanne Boydston, et al., *The Limits of Sisterhood: The Beecher Sisters on Women's Rights and Woman's Sphere* (Chapel Hill: University of North Carolina Press, 1988).

Ann Braude, *Radical Spirits: Spiritualism and Women's Rights in Nineteenth-Century America* (Boston: Beacon Press, 1989).

Daniel Calhoun, *The Intelligence of a People* (Princeton: Princeton University Press, 1973).

A. Cheree Carlson, "The Role of Character in Public Moral Argument: Henry Ward Beecher and the Brooklyn Scandal," *Quarterly Journal of Speech* 77 (Feb. 1991): 38–52.

Paul Carter, *The Spiritual Crisis of the Gilded Age* (DeKalb: Northern Illinois, 1971).

Marie Caskey, *Chariot of Fire: Religion and the Beecher Family* (New Haven: Yale University Press, 1978).

Clifford E. Clark, *Henry Ward Beecher: Spokesman for a Middle-Class America* (Urbana: University of Illinois Press, 1978).

Kenneth Cmiel, *Democratic Eloquence: The Fight over Popular Speech in Nineteenth-Century America* (New York: William Morrow, 1990).

Lionel Crocker, *Henry Ward Beecher's Speaking Art* (New York: Fleming H. Revell Co., 1937).

Ann Douglas, *The Feminization of American Culture* (New York: Knopf, 1977; reprinted 1987 and 1998 with new prefaces).

Brainerd Dyer, *The Public Career of William Maxwell Evarts* (Berkeley: University of California Press, 1933).

Jane Shaffer Elsmere, *Henry Ward Beecher: The Indiana Years, 1837–1847* (Indianapolis: Indiana Historical Society, 1973).

Mary Gabriel, *Notorious Victoria: The Life of Victoria Woodhull, Uncensored* (Chapel Hill, NC: Algonquin Books, 1998).

Barbara Goldsmith, *Other Powers: The Age of Suffrage, Spiritualism, and the Scandalous Victoria Woodhull* (New York: Knopf, 1998).

John Harvey Gossard, "The New York City Congregational Cluster, 1848–1871: Congregationalism and Antislavery in the Careers of Henry Ward Beecher, George B. Cheever, Richard S. Storrs, and Joseph P. Thompson," Ph.D. dissertation, Bowling Green University, 1986.

Elisabeth Griffith, *In Her Own Right: The Life of Elizabeth Cady Stanton* (New York: Oxford University Press, 1984).

Joan D. Hedrick, *Harriet Beecher Stowe: A Life* (New York: Oxford University Press, 1994).

Paxton Hibben, *Henry Ward Beecher: An American Portrait* (New York: George H. Doran, 1927).

Thomas E. Jenkins, *The Character of God: Recovering the Lost Literary Power of American Protestantism* (New York: Oxford University Press, 1997).

Laura Korobkin, *Criminal Conversations: Sentimentality and Nineteenth-Century Legal Stories of Adultery* (New York: Columbia University Press, 1998).

William Leach, *True Love and Perfect Union: The Feminist Reform of Sexual Society* (New York: Basic Books, 1980).

Karen Lystra, *Searching the Heart: Women, Men, and Romantic Love in Nineteenth-Century America* (New York: Oxford University Press, 1989).

Dan McCall, *Beecher: A Novel* (New York: E. P. Dutton, 1979).

David McCullough, *The Great Bridge: The Epic Story of the Building of the Brooklyn Bridge* (New York: Simon and Schuster, 1972).

William G. McLoughlin, *The Meaning of Henry Ward Beecher: An Essay on the Shifting Values of Mid-Victorian America* (New York: Knopf, 1970).

Constance Rourke, *Trumpets of Jubilee* (New York: Harcourt Brace, 1927, reprinted 1963).

Milton Rugoff, *The Beechers: An American Family in the Nineteenth Century* (New York: Harper and Row, 1981).

Halford R. Ryan, *Henry Ward Beecher: Peripatetic Preacher* (New York: Greenwood Press, 1990).

Hal D. Sears, *The Sex Radicals: Free Love in High Victorian America* (Lawrence: Regents Press of Kansas, 1977).

Robert Shaplen, *Free Love and Heavenly Sinners: The Great Henry Ward Beecher Scandal* (New York: Knopf, 1954).

Kathryn Kish Sklar, *Catharine Beecher: A Study in American Domesticity* (New Haven: Yale University Press, 1973).

John C. Spurlock, *Marriage and Middle-Class Radicals in America, 1825–1860* (New York: New York University Press, 1988).

Stephen H. Snyder, *Lyman Beecher and His Children: The Transformation of a Religious Tradition* (Brooklyn: Carlson, 1991).

Taylor Stoehr, *Free Love in America: A Documentary History* (New York: AMS Press, 1979).

Lawrence Stone, *The Road to Divorce in England, 1530–1987* (Oxford: Oxford University Press, 1990).

Lyman B. Stowe, *Saints, Sinners and Beechers* (Indianapolis: Bobbs-Merrill, 1934).

David Tatham, "Keppler vs. Beecher: Prints of the Great Brooklyn Scandal," *Imprint* 23 (Spring 1998): 2–8.

Edwin Terry, "Theodore Tilton as Social Reformer, Radical Republican, Newspaper Editor, 1863–1872," Ph.D. dissertation, St. John's University, 1971.

Edward Wagenknecht, *Ambassadors for Christ: Seven American Preachers* (New York: Oxford University Press, 1972).

Altina L. Waller, *Reverend Beecher and Mrs. Tilton: Sex and Class in Victorian America* (Amherst: University of Massachusetts Press, 1982).

Index